BY THE EDITORS OF CONSUMER GUIDE®

RATING THE MOVIE STARS FOR HOME VIDEO · TV · CABLE

BY JOEL HIRSCHHORN

BEEKMAN HOUSE
New York

Louis Weber, President
Publications International, Ltd.
3841 West Oakton Street
Skokie, Illinois 60076

Manufactured in the United States of America
10 9 8 7 6 5 4 3 2 1

Library of Congress Catalog Card Number: 83-62120

ISBN: 0-517-41444-9

This edition published by:
Beekman House
Distributed by Crown Publishers, Inc.
One Park Avenue
New York, New York 10016

Cover Design: Jeff Hapner
Photo Tinting: Katherine Stetson

Written by Joel Hirschhorn, with contributions by Richard Bozanich, Randy Dolnick, Scott Levine, Darrell Moore, Harvey Nosowitz, Richard Peña, Rich Peterson, Rob Pinsel, Barbara Scharres, and Ron Thompson.

The photographs in this book are courtesy of the following studios and organizations: Universal City Studios; Columbia Pictures; United Artists; Metro-Goldwyn-Mayer; Warner Brothers, Inc.; 20th Century Fox; Avco-Embassy Pictures; RKO Radio Pictures; Favorite Films Corporation; British Lion Films, Ltd.; Dominant Pictures Corp.; Paramount Pictures; Universal-International; MGM/UA; ABC Television Network; National General Pictures; Fox Films; Mack Sennett Productions; Hal Roach Productions; Young & Rubicam Publicity; Screen Gems; CBS Television; American Communications Industries; Allied Artists; Cinema Center Films; American International Pictures; Cinema 5; The Ladd Company; Classic Pictures; Simon Film Productions; Claridge Pictures; Walter Disney Productions; Associated Film Distribution; Republic Pictures; International Classics; English Films Inc.; Janus Films; Filmways Pictures, Inc.; Wilderness/Filmhaus Productions.

CONTENTS

The Power of Performance 6
A Word about the Ratings 9
Abbott & Costello 12
Alan Alda 12
Jane Alexander 13
Woody Allen 13
June Allyson 15
Judith Anderson 16
Dana Andrews 16
Julie Andrews 17
Ann-Margret 18
Eve Arden 19
Alan Arkin 20
Jean Arthur 21
Ed Asner 22
Fred Astaire 23
Mary Astor 24
Richard Attenborough 25
Gene Autry 26
Frankie Avalon 27
Lew Ayres 27
Lauren Bacall 28
Lucille Ball 29
Martin Balsam 31
Anne Bancroft 31
Tallulah Bankhead 32
Brigitte Bardot 33
Ethel Barrymore 34
John Barrymore 34
Lionel Barrymore 35
Alan Bates 36
Anne Baxter 37
The Beatles 38
Warren Beatty 39
Barbara Bel Geddes 40
Ralph Bellamy 40
Jean-Paul Belmondo 41
William Bendix 42
Richard Benjamin 43
Joan Bennett 43
Jack Benny 44
Robby Benson 45
Candice Bergen 45
Ingrid Bergman 46
Charles Bickford 47
Jacqueline Bisset 48
Karen Black 49
Dirk Bogarde 50
Humphrey Bogart 51
Pat Boone 52
Ernest Borgnine 53
David Bowie 54
Charles Boyer 55
Peter Boyle 56
Marlon Brando 57
Eileen Brennan 58

Walter Brennan 58
Jeff Bridges 60
Lloyd Bridges 60
Charles Bronson 61
Mel Brooks 63
Yul Brynner 63
Genevieve Bujold 64
Carol Burnett 65
George Burns 65
Raymond Burr 66
Ellen Burstyn 67
Richard Burton 68
Gary Busey 69
Red Buttons 69
James Caan 70
James Cagney 71
Michael Caine 72
Dyan Cannon 73
Art Carney 73
Leslie Caron 74
David Carradine 75
John Carradine 76
Leo G. Carroll 78
Madeleine Carroll 78
John Cassavetes 79
Richard Chamberlain 80
Jeff Chandler 80
Charlie Chaplin 81
Cyd Charisse 82
Chevy Chase 83
Julie Christie 83
Jill Clayburgh 84
Montgomery Clift 85
Colin Clive 85
James Coburn 86
Claudette Colbert 87
Ronald Colman 88
Sean Connery 90
Eddie Constantine 91
Elisha Cook, Jr. 92
Gary Cooper 92
Joseph Cotten 94
Broderick Crawford 95
Joan Crawford 96
Richard Crenna 98
Donald Crisp 99
Bing Crosby 100
Robert Cummings 101
Jamie Lee Curtis 102
Tony Curtis 102
Dan Dailey 104
Linda Darnell 104
Bette Davis 105
Doris Day 107
James Dean 108
Yvonne De Carlo 109
Sandra Dee 110
Olivia De Havilland 110
Alain Delon 112
William Demarest 113
Catherine Deneuve 114
Robert De Niro 114
Sandy Dennis 115
Gerard Depardieu 116
Bruce Dern 117
Angie Dickinson 117
Marlene Dietrich 118
Matt Dillon 119
Troy Donahue 120
Robert Donat 121
Kirk Douglas 121
Melvyn Douglas 122
Michael Douglas 123

Richard Dreyfuss 124
Faye Dunaway 125
Irene Dunne 125
Dan Duryea 126
Robert Duvall 127
Shelley Duvall 128
Clint Eastwood 129
Nelson Eddy 130
Douglas Fairbanks, Jr. 130
Frances Farmer 131
Mia Farrow 132
Alice Faye 132
Jose Férrer 133
Mel Ferrer 134
Sally Field 134
W. C. Fields 135
Peter Finch 136
Albert Finney 137
Carrie Fisher 137
Barry Fitzgerald 138
Errol Flynn 139
Henry Fonda 140
Jane Fonda 142
Peter Fonda 143
Joan Fontaine 143
Glenn Ford 144
Harrison Ford 145
Jodie Foster 146
Annette Funicello 147
Clark Gable 147
Eva Gabor 149
Greta Garbo 149
Ava Gardner 151
John Garfield 152
Judy Garland 153
James Garner 154
Teri Garr 155
Betty Garrett 156
Greer Garson 156
Janet Gaynor 157
Ben Gazzara 157
Richard Gere 158
Mel Gibson 159
John Gielgud 159
Paulette Goddard 160
Ruth Gordon 161
Lou Gossett, Jr. 161
Elliott Gould 162
Betty Grable 162
Gloria Grahame 164
Farley Granger 165
Cary Grant 166
Kathryn Grayson 167
Sidney Greenstreet 168
Alec Guinness 169
Gene Hackman 170
Jean Harlow 171
Richard Harris 172
Rex Harrison 172
Laurence Harvey 173
Goldie Hawn 174
Sterling Hayden 175
Helen Hayes 176
Susan Hayward 177
Rita Hayworth 178
Audrey Hepburn 179
Katharine Hepburn 181
Charlton Heston 182
Wendy Hiller 183
Dustin Hoffman 184
William Holden 185
Judy Holliday 186
Bob Hope 187
Anthony Hopkins 188
Dennis Hopper 189
John Houseman 190
Leslie Howard 190
Trevor Howard 191
Rock Hudson 192
Jeffrey Hunter 193
Tab Hunter 194
John Hurt 195
Walter Huston 195
Betty Hutton 196
Timothy Hutton 197
Burl Ives 197
Glenda Jackson 198
Dean Jagger 199
Ben Johnson 200
Van Johnson 201
James Earl Jones 202
Jennifer Jones 202
Shirley Jones 203
Louis Jourdan 204
Boris Karloff 204
Danny Kaye 206
Diane Keaton 207
Howard Keel 208
Gene Kelly 209
Grace Kelly 210
Deborah Kerr 211
Margot Kidder 212
Ben Kingsley 212
Nastassia Kinski 213
Kris Kristofferson 213
Alan Ladd 214
Veronica Lake 215
Hedy Lamarr 216
Dorothy Lamour 217
Burt Lancaster 218
Elsa Lanchester 219
Jessica Lange 220
Angela Lansbury 221
Charles Laughton 222
Laurel and Hardy 223
Peter Lawford 224
Cloris Leachman 225
Janet Leigh 225
Vivien Leigh 226
Jack Lemmon 227
Oscar Levant 228
Jerry Lewis 229
Gina Lollobrigida 230
Carole Lombard 231
Sophia Loren 232

Peter Lorre 234
Myrna Loy 235
Bela Lugosi 236
Ida Lupino 237
Mercedes McCambridge 238
Joel McCrea 239
Jeanette MacDonald 240
Roddy McDowall 241
Malcolm McDowell 242
Ali MacGraw 243
Dorothy McGuire 243
Shirley MacLaine 244
Fred MacMurray 245
Kristy McNichol 247
Steve McQueen 247
Anna Magnani 248
Dorothy Malone 249

Jayne Mansfield 250
Fredric March 250
Herbert Marshall 252
Dean Martin 253
Steve Martin 254
Lee Marvin 254
The Marx Brothers 255
James Mason 256
Marsha Mason 258
Walter Matthau 259
Victor Mature 260
Burgess Meredith 261
Ethel Merman 262
Bette Midler 262
Ray Milland 263
Ann Miller 264
John Mills 265
Sal Mineo 267
Liza Minnelli 267
Robert Mitchum 268
Marilyn Monroe 270
Maria Montez 271
Robert Montgomery 272
Monty Python 273
Dudley Moore 274
Mary Tyler Moore 274
Roger Moore 275
Agnes Moorehead 276
Robert Morley 276
Vic Morrow 277
Zero Mostel 278
Paul Muni 278
Eddie Murphy 279
Patricia Neal 279
Paul Newman 280
Jack Nicholson 281
David Niven 282
Nick Nolte 284
Kim Novak 284
Warren Oates 285
Merle Oberon 286
Edmond O'Brien 286
Maureen O'Hara 287
Laurence Olivier 288
Ryan O'Neal 290
Tatum O'Neal 291
Peter O'Toole 291
Al Pacino 292
Gregory Peck 293
Sean Penn 295
George Peppard 295
Anthony Perkins 296
Walter Pidgeon 297
Christopher Plummer 298
Sidney Poitier 298
Dick Powell 300
William Powell 300
Tyrone Power 302
Elvis Presley 303
Robert Preston 304

Vincent Price 305
Richard Pryor 306
Anthony Quinn 307
George Raft 309
Claude Rains 310
Tony Randall 312
Basil Rathbone 312
Aldo Ray 313
Ronald Reagan 314
Robert Redford 315
Michael Redgrave 316
Vanessa Redgrave 317
Donna Reed 318
Oliver Reed 319
Christopher Reeve 319
Burt Reynolds 320
Debbie Reynolds 321
Ralph Richardson 322
Thelma Ritter 323
Jason Robards, Jr. 324
Cliff Robertson 325
Edward G. Robinson 325
Ginger Rogers 327
Mickey Rooney 329
Katharine Ross 330
Gena Rowlands 331
Jane Russell 331
Rosalind Russell 332
Robert Ryan 333
Eva Marie Saint 334
George Sanders 334
Susan Sarandon 336
Roy Scheider 336
George C. Scott 337
Randolph Scott 338
Jean Seberg 339
George Segal 340
Peter Sellers 341
Robert Shaw 342
Norma Shearer 343
Martin Sheen 343
Ann Sheridan 344
Jean Simmons 345
Frank Sinatra 346
Everett Sloane 347
Carrie Snodgress 348
Sissy Spacek 348
Robert Stack 349
Sylvester Stallone 350
Barbara Stanwyck 351
Rod Steiger 352
James Stewart 353
Meryl Streep 355
Barbra Streisand 355
Margaret Sullavan 356
Donald Sutherland 357
Elizabeth Taylor 358
Robert Taylor 359
Shirley Temple 360
Gene Tierney 361
Franchot Tone 362
Rip Torn 363
Spencer Tracy 364
John Travolta 365
Claire Trevor 366
Lana Turner 367
Jon Voight 368
Robert Wagner 369
Robert Walker 370

John Wayne 370
Clifton Webb 372
Johnny Weissmuller 373
Raquel Welch 374
Tuesday Weld 374
Orson Welles 375
Mae West 376
Billy Dee Williams 377
Shelley Winters 378
Natalie Wood 379
Joanne Woodward 380
Jane Wyman 381
Loretta Young 382
Robert Young 383

THE POWER OF PERFORMANCE

BY JOEL HIRSCHHORN

When critics review a motion picture today, they tend to dwell on the direction, the camera work, or the special effects. Audiences are given their choice of a George Lucas film, a Steven Spielberg film, or an Ingmar Bergman film. Stars are important, but the media projects an attitude that actors are expensive instruments to serve director and script—useful, glittering tools, window dressing. Only after combing through movie history do you begin to recognize what an indispensable part *performances* played in turning mediocre pictures into memorable ones.

As a two-time Oscar-winning songwriter, I've had the privilege of meeting many stars personally, often during the making of films that featured my music. I was invariably amazed when I watched the rushes (unedited footage). Ordinary, at times excruciatingly bad lines suddenly sounded human, infused with the individuality and magnetism of the performer. An unexpected pause, a halting smile, a burst of emotion—seemingly minor things—turned banal scenes into mesmerizing experiences.

Star quality is difficult to define, but my personal definition was formed after a lunch with Bette Davis. At the time (1972), Davis was to appear in the musical "Copperfield," which I had co-written with Al Kasha. Al and I went to the Bel Air Hotel to play the score for her. She was a petite, almost delicate woman, but there was nothing timid about her direct gaze and authoritative speaking voice. We needed a piano and the empty dining room didn't have one, so she told a workman, "We *must* have a piano *immediately.*" She wasn't rude, but her firmness brooked no argument. The piano materialized in seconds. She applauded after we performed the songs, and I modestly ventured that "We had a lot of help from Dickens." She responded, "Yes, but look what you *did* with him!" Her conviction made me feel we were on par with Dickens, that he was lucky to have *us* as collaborators!

Over lunch, Davis talked about her films—*The Catered Affair* and *All About Eve.* As in her film work, the power of the Davis personality obliterated everything and everyone around her. She had wit, intelligence, force, charm, vulnerability—but most of all, a highly charged *belief* in herself, in her ability to dominate.

The performer who has this belief and this assured, takeover quality can make film vehicles timeless. An early Academy Award winner, *Grand Hotel,* looks creaky and ancient today, but remains fascinating because of Joan Crawford, John Barrymore, Wallace Beery, Lionel Barrymore, and Greta Garbo. I've read reviews that called *It Happened One Night* "actor proof," owing to its story, solid structure, and sparkling wit. Although stars Clark Gable and Claudette Colbert both won Oscars for their roles, they were considered fortunate to have such fine material. Then the movie was redone in 1956 as *You Can't Run Away From It* (featuring Jack Lemmon and June Allyson) and died a quick commercial death. Vivien Leigh once commented to columnist Radie Harris, "Scarlett is such a fabulous role that I'm sure *any* actress who played her would have won an Oscar." Radie's reply: "Fiddle-dee-dee! A good role remains good in the performance of a competent actress, but in the hands of a great actress it becomes transcendental."

Imagine *Casablanca* with the two leads who almost played it—Ronald Reagan and Ann Sheridan—and the crucial nature of performance becomes clear. Think of Robert Taylor's manly authority in *Waterloo Bridge,* and switch to the remake *Gaby,* with the sincere but unspectacular John Kerr in the lead. Cable television recently cast Jacqueline Bisset in an updated version of *The Spiral Staircase*—playing Dorothy McGuire's old role as an endangered mute servant. Bisset's inability to convey the terror and confusion of the character with her *eyes* (as McGuire did) canceled out all suspense. John Garfield and Lana Turner created unforgettable chemistry as the two murderers in *The Postman Always Rings Twice;* after that the picture was updated and redone—disastrously—with Jack Nicholson and Jessica Lange.

These were all sturdy, even classic, vehicles that flourished with inspired casting and collapsed when the performers were inappropriate. The power of performance is more tellingly exemplified by films that lack good scripts and directors. Film critic Leonard Maltin gazed indifferently at the soggy 1948 trifle, *Mr. Peabody and the Mermaid* (starring William Powell) but had to conclude that "Powell makes anything look good." *Rebel Without a Cause* could have been just another juvenile delinquency drama—it was overly melodramatic, weakly motivated, the parents were all caricatures—yet, after nearly 30 years, James Dean still speaks for the lost, searching teenager in all of us. A more modern success, *An Officer and a Gentleman,* is little more than a reworking of old 1930s and 1940s service dramas. The anger, fear and desperation projected by Richard Gere gave surprising energy to a succession of well-done but basically clichéd sequences.

I had the opportunity in 1970 to write a song for Henry Fonda and James Stewart in *The Cheyenne Social Club.* Neither, to put it mildly, could sing—but both gave odd, comedic readings of the lyrics. Their rendition of "Rollin' Stone" brought magic to a slender screenplay, and was so well received that the company released it as a successful single. The same thing happened when I co-wrote the score for a Disney musical, *Pete's Dragon,* and had to create material for Mickey Rooney. Rooney was impatient, overflowing with ideas and anecdotes. It was impossible to teach him the exact words and melody. After our meeting I drove home depressed, sure that my work was about to be butchered. True, he didn't do it exactly as Al and I had specified, he did it *better!* Shelley Winters was equally effective with another of our tunes from the film. The story was slight, the movie was overlong, and these two pros had to compete with an animated dragon (a more formidable competitor than a dog or a child), yet they made their magnetism felt. They stole the picture, making it a world wide smash.

Pauline Kael once praised Jeff Bridges for pulling off a similar feat in a plodding, tedious thriller, *Somebody Killed Her Husband:* "His (Bridges') way of giving a line a slight de-emphasis that makes it *his* and funny helps to lend the film some semblance of contemporaneity. If you say his lines over to yourself, you can't understand how he did it."

A more debatable judgment of Kael's concerns Jill Clayburgh's appearance in *An Unmarried Woman:* "The camera isn't in love with her." The fact remains, when the camera *is* in love with a performer, that performer can compensate for any defect in the material. Greta Garbo's close-up at the end of *Queen Christina* is remembered by fans who have scant recollection of the movie as a whole. Doris Day said of Judy Garland: "Right, left, up, down, it didn't matter. Judy and the camera were always harmonious." Day herself—though freckled, with less-than-classic features—lit up the screen in a way predecessors June Haver and Janis Paige never did. Yet neither Garland or Day appeared regularly in classics. For every *A Star Is Born,* there was *Till the Clouds Roll By, Presenting Lily Mars,* and *The Pirate* (now revered by buffs, but failures in their time). Day had a great role in *Love Me or Leave Me,* but she also had a way of turning trivial material into box-office success *(On Moonlight Bay, April in Paris, Lullaby of Broadway).* The camera loved Kim Novak when she danced in *Picnic.* The camera today loves Meryl Streep in anything.

Motion pictures of the 1980s tend to slight actors in favor of technology, but the current superstars—Meryl Streep, John Travolta, Sylvester Stallone—dominate their vehicles. *Sophie's Choice, Saturday Night Fever* and *Rocky* would be unthinkable without their three leads. Matt Dillon's gutsy performance made *Little Darlings* worth watching. *Gandhi* would have joined all the over-produced boring spectacles of the 1960s if not for Ben Kingsley's quiet intensity, his shading, his total immersion in the role. And *48 Hours* rode to success on the talented shoulders of Eddie Murphy.

There have been a multitude of books rating *films,* but none have rated the individual performances of the stars who often transformed these films. It's my belief that actors—the great stars and the colorful, irreplaceable character people—merit individual ratings for all their contributions to the art of motion pictures. This book is a way of awarding them specific credit that is long overdue.

A WORD ABOUT THE RATINGS...

As a 3.00 rated star, Steve Martin, might say, "Well, excuuuse me!" We realize that everyone takes his or her favorite movie stars personally and doesn't want them graded like a side of beef. *Rating the Movie Stars* simply wants to compare the *careers* of various stars and find a new and novel way to judge their achievements. To do that, we had to set up a system for rating every movie star and apply it unblinkingly to all.

To wit: we rated the actor's *performance* in every film that he or she was in (not the quality of the film itself), added them up, and derived the cumulative ratings that appear in each entry below the star's name. We left out early roles in which the performance was too short to rate (bit) or later guest appearances that could not be fairly judged (cameo). Documentaries were not rated because one is presumably not acting in them. Narrations were also not rated, and short films (less than feature length) were omitted.

The individual rating for each film can be seen in the filmography that follows each essay. These filmographies are as complete and as accurate as our information would allow. There are often variances and discrepancies in the year of a film's release and in its title. A film title often changes several times in search of an audience. In the case of foreign films, we used the American release title or the original language title if the film was never released in this country.

The ratings for each performance were based upon the authors' viewing and evaluation. They are necessarily subjective. We chose authors who would be able to evaluate a wide range of films from the entire span of film history. We ultimately chose to eliminate silent film stars because of the authors' inability to see and evaluate the films involved. In those cases where no author had seen the film (and performances), we used reviews to determine the rating.

We believe that our rating system offers an interesting and fun way to look at the careers of these movie stars. However, we should point out two ways in which these ratings are inevitably skewed. Great stars—who made many, many movies and had fallow periods, whether at the beginning where they learned their craft or in their twilight when they worked on in spite of failing abilities—will suffer lowered averages. And rising young stars of today (whom we made a special effort to include) will inevitably have inflated scores. They've started out hot, and haven't had time to make any of those "filler films" that plague all but the greatest superstars.

The ranking below, therefore, should be taken with a grain of salt. We hope you'll take the list in the spirit of fun in which it was intended.

MOVIE STARS RATING CHART

Four stars were given for an excellent performance, three stars for a good performance, two stars for a fair performance, and one star for a poor performance. The ratings listed below represent the average for a performer's entire filmography.

James Dean	4.00
Ben Kingsley	4.00
Eddie Murphy	4.00
Walter Huston	3.85
Leslie Howard	3.76
Wendy Hiller	3.71
Thelma Ritter	3.68
Donald Crisp	3.67
Robert Donat	3.67
Greta Garbo	3.67
Timothy Hutton	3.67
Charles Laughton	3.66
Claude Rains	3.66
Fred Astaire	3.62
Peter Lorre	3.62
Charlie Chaplin	3.60
Sissy Spacek	3.56
Sydney Greenstreet	3.55
W. C. Fields	3.53
Trevor Howard	3.52
James Cagney	3.51
Ronald Colman	3.51
Spencer Tracy	3.51
Jane Alexander	3.50
Robert Duvall	3.50
Margaret Sullavan	3.50
Agnes Moorehead	3.48
Judy Holliday	3.45
Grace Kelly	3.45
Judith Anderson	3.44
Alan Bates	3.44
Robert De Niro	3.44
John Garfield	3.44
The Marx Brothers	3.43
George C. Scott	3.43
John Gielgud	3.42
Anna Magnani	3.42
Mercedes McCambridge	3.41
Basil Rathbone	3.40

Star	Rating
Jean Simmons	3.40
Billy Dee Williams	3.40
Dirk Bogarde	3.39
Elsa Lanchester	3.39
Edward G. Robinson	3.39
Barbara Stanwyck	3.39
Melvyn Douglas	3.38
Dorothy McGuire	3.38
Bing Crosby	3.37
Barry Fitzgerald	3.37
Fredric March	3.36
Humphrey Bogart	3.35
Charles Boyer	3.35
John Mills	3.35
Vanessa Redgrave	3.35
Ralph Richardson	3.35
Angela Lansbury	3.34
Claudette Colbert	3.33
Matt Dillon	3.33
Carole Lombard	3.33
Malcolm McDowell	3.33
Sean Penn	3.33
Everett Sloane	3.33
James Stewart	3.33
Judy Garland	3.31
Cary Grant	3.31
Ethel Barrymore	3.30
Alec Guiness	3.30
William Powell	3.30
Gary Busey	3.29
Betty Garrett	3.29
George Sanders	3.29
Ralph Bellamy	3.28
Herbert Marshall	3.28
Lee Marvin	3.28
Michael Redgrave	3.28
Robert Ryan	3.28
Claire Trevor	3.28
Ingrid Bergman	3.27
Harrison Ford	3.27
Jodie Foster	3.27
Deborah Kerr	3.27
Joel McCrea	3.27
Robert Montgomery	3.27
Ann Sheridan	3.27
Bruce Dern	3.26
Dan Duryea	3.26
John Hurt	3.26
Burt Lancaster	3.26
John Barrymore	3.25
David Bowie	3.25
Sally Field	3.25
Lou Gossett, Jr.	3.25
Robert Shaw	3.25
Dustin Hoffman	3.24
Warren Oates	3.24
Martin Sheen	3.24
Colin Clive	3.22
Jean Harlow	3.22
Clifton Webb	3.22
Joanne Woodward	3.22
Joan Bennett	3.21
Jeff Bridges	3.21
Peter Finch	3.21
Rex Harrison	3.21
William Holden	3.21
Vivien Leigh	3.21
Edmond O'Brien	3.21
Mary Astor	3.20
Genevieve Bujold	3.20
Madeleine Carroll	3.20
Marlene Dietrich	3.20
Charles Bickford	3.19
Laurence Olivier	3.19
Jane Wyman	3.19
Eve Arden	3.18
Ben Johnson	3.18
Gene Kelly	3.18
Myrna Loy	3.18
James Mason	3.18
Loretta Young	3.18
Barbara Bel Geddes	3.17
Eileen Brennan	3.17
Art Carney	3.17
Eddie Constantine	3.17
Mel Gibson	3.17
Boris Karloff	3.17
Kristy McNichol	3.17
Burgess Meredith	3.17
Rip Torn	3.17
Mae West	3.17
Ruth Gordon	3.16
Robert Walker	3.16
Irene Dunne	3.15
Henry Fonda	3.15
Janet Leigh	3.15
Walter Matthau	3.15
Gena Rowlands	3.15
Jamie Lee Curtis	3.14
Ben Gazzara	3.14
Audrey Hepburn	3.14
Katharine Hepburn	3.14
Patricia Neal	3.14
Eva Marie Saint	3.14
Woody Allen	3.13
Dyan Cannon	3.13
Olivia De Havilland	3.13
Gerard Depardieu	3.13
Anthony Hopkins	3.13
Dorothy Malone	3.13
Ray Milland	3.13
Sidney Poitier	3.13
Robert Young	3.13
Martin Balsam	3.12
Clark Gable	3.12
Helen Hayes	3.12
Burl Ives	3.12
William Bendix	3.11
Janet Gaynor	3.11
Betty Hutton	3.11
Dean Jagger	3.11
Ida Lupino	3.11
Robert Mitchum	3.11
Meryl Streep	3.11
Lew Ayres	3.10
Jack Benny	3.10
Vincent Price	3.10
Lloyd Bridges	3.09
Paul Muni	3.09
Cliff Robertson	3.09
Richard Dreyfuss	3.08
José Ferrer	3.08
Dudley Moore	3.08
Walter Pidgeon	3.08
Richard Attenborough	3.07
Ellen Burstyn	3.07
Leslie Caron	3.07
Gary Cooper	3.07
Douglas Fairbanks, Jr.	3.07
Goldie Hawn	3.07
Diane Keaton	3.07
Jeanette MacDonald	3.07
Richard Pryor	3.07
Teri Garr	3.06
Fred MacMurray	3.06
Robert Morley	3.06
Susan Sarandon	3.06
Roy Scheider	3.06
Lionel Barrymore	3.05
George Burns	3.05
Raymond Burr	3.05
Kirk Douglas	3.05
Shirley Jones	3.05
Sal Mineo	3.05
Paul Newman	3.05
Steve McQueen	3.04
Peter O'Toole	3.04
Gregory Peck	3.04
Rosalind Russell	3.04
Norma Shearer	3.04
Lucille Ball	3.03
Alice Faye	3.03
James Garner	3.03
Jack Lemmon	3.03
Donald Sutherland	3.03
Gene Tierney	3.03
Alain Delon	3.02
Bob Hope	3.02
Dick Powell	3.02
Rod Steiger	3.02
Orson Welles	3.02
Roddy McDowall	3.01
Ginger Rogers	3.01
Edward Asner	3.00
The Beatles	3.00
Julie Christie	3.00
Sean Connery	3.00
Shelley Duvall	3.00
Frances Farmer	3.00
Richard Gere	3.00
Rita Hayworth	3.00
Jessica Lange	3.00
Oscar Levant	3.00
Steve Martin	3.00
Bette Midler	3.00
Monty Python	3.00

Vic Morrow	3.00
Nick Nolte	3.00
Tatum O'Neal	3.00
Carrie Snodgress	3.00
Dana Andrews	2.99
Jean Arthur	2.99
Anne Baxter	2.98
Susan Hayward	2.98
Tyrone Power	2.98
Gloria Grahame	2.97
Louis Jourdan	2.97
Jack Nicholson	2.97
Michael Caine	2.96
Brigitte Bardot	2.95
John Cassavetes	2.95
Glenda Jackson	2.95
Cloris Leachman	2.95
Tony Randall	2.95
Ernest Borgnine	2.94
Leo G. Carroll	2.94
Montgomery Clift	2.94
Bette Davis	2.94
Clint Eastwood	2.94
Gene Hackman	2.94
Danny Kaye	2.94
Christopher Plummer	2.94
Jill Clayburgh	2.93
Joan Fontaine	2.93
Sterling Hayden	2.93
James Earl Jones	2.93
David Niven	2.93
Mickey Rooney	2.93
Frank Sinatra	2.93
Franchot Tone	2.93
Julie Andrews	2.92
Howard Keel	2.92
Shelley Winters	2.92
Dan Dailey	2.91
Jason Robards, Jr.	2.91
Tuesday Weld	2.91
James Coburn	2.90
Glenn Ford	2.90
Van Johnson	2.90
Shirley MacLaine	2.90
Marsha Mason	2.90
Michael Douglas	2.89
Carrie Fisher	2.89
Peter Fonda	2.89
Richard Harris	2.89
Walter Brennan	2.88
Carol Burnett	2.88
John Carradine	2.88
Richard Crenna	2.88
Albert Finney	2.88
Greer Garson	2.88
Farley Granger	2.88
Liza Minnelli	2.88
George Peppard	2.88
Robert Preston	2.88
Peter Sellers	2.88
Robert Stack	2.88
Doris Day	2.87
Maureen O'Hara	2.87
Peter Boyle	2.86
Red Buttons	2.86
James Caan	2.86
Elisha Cook, Jr.	2.86
Joan Crawford	2.86
Betty Grable	2.86
Katharine Ross	2.84
Joseph Cotten	2.83
Linda Darnell	2.83
Laurel and Hardy	2.83
Zero Mostel	2.83
Al Pacino	2.83
Barbra Streisand	2.83
John Houseman	2.82
Robert Redford	2.82
Warren Beatty	2.81
Paulette Goddard	2.81
Dorothy Lamour	2.81
Gina Lollobrigida	2.81
Marilyn Monroe	2.81
Ryan O'Neal	2.80
Jon Voight	2.80
David Carradine	2.79
Angie Dickinson	2.79
Anthony Quinn	2.79
June Allyson	2.78
Anne Bancroft	2.78
Yul Brynner	2.78
Richard Chamberlain	2.78
Errol Flynn	2.77
Charlton Heston	2.77
Sylvester Stallone	2.77
Eva Gabor	2.76
Margot Kidder	2.76
Burt Reynolds	2.76
George Segal	2.76
Natalie Wood	2.75
Alan Alda	2.73
Sophia Loren	2.73
Lana Turner	2.73
Mel Ferrer	2.72
Cyd Charisse	2.71
Chevy Chase	2.71
Rock Hudson	2.71
Charles Bronson	2.70
Merle Oberon	2.70
Robert Taylor	2.69
Robert Cummings	2.68
Alan Ladd	2.68
Donna Reed	2.68
Jane Fonda	2.67
Ava Gardner	2.67
Kris Kristofferson	2.67
Aldo Ray	2.67
Elizabeth Taylor	2.66
Shirley Temple	2.66
Jeff Chandler	2.65
Kathryn Grayson	2.65
Debbie Reynolds	2.65
Lauren Bacall	2.64
Anthony Perkins	2.64
Laurence Harvey	2.62
Jeffrey Hunter	2.62
Peter Lawford	2.62
Jean Seberg	2.62
Jennifer Jones	2.58
Randolph Scott	2.58
Mary Tyler Moore	2.57
John Travolta	2.57
Marlon Brando	2.55
Faye Dunaway	2.54
Dennis Hopper	2.54
Ethel Merman	2.54
Richard Burton	2.53
Veronica Lake	2.52
Alan Arkin	2.50
Karen Black	2.50
Mel Brooks	2.50
Sandra Dee	2.50
Christopher Reeve	2.50
Oliver Reed	2.49
Mia Farrow	2.47
Hedy Lamarr	2.45
John Wayne	2.45
Richard Benjamin	2.44
Broderick Crawford	2.44
Roger Moore	2.44
Jane Russell	2.43
Dean Martin	2.42
Jean-Paul Belmondo	2.41
Ronald Reagan	2.40
Jacqueline Bisset	2.39
Tony Curtis	2.38
Nastassia Kinski	2.38
Victor Mature	2.38
Ann Miller	2.38
William Demarest	2.35
Tab Hunter	2.32
Elliott Gould	2.31
Candice Bergen	2.30
Gene Autry	2.29
Yvonne De Carlo	2.29
Tallulah Bankhead	2.27
George Raft	2.27
Ann-Margret	2.25
Sandy Dennis	2.20
Robert Wagner	2.19
Abbott & Costello	2.17
Johnny Weissmuller	2.17
Troy Donahue	2.16
Raquel Welch	2.14
Catherine Deneuve	2.13
Kim Novak	2.08
Nelson Eddy	2.06
Jerry Lewis	2.02
Bela Lugosi	1.90
Pat Boone	1.79
Frankie Avalon	1.77
Ali MacGraw	1.67
Elvis Presley	1.65
Jayne Mansfield	1.63
Annette Funicello	1.62
Maria Montez	1.58

ABBOTT AND COSTELLO
★★ 2.17 STARS

Abbott and Costello are mainly remembered today for their classic "Who's on First?" routine. Other than that, it is hard to figure out what was so funny about their slapstick and patter, which was hugely successful in its day. Youngsters still cluster around the TV set whenever their movies are programmed, but tastes have certainly veered from the time when Abbott and Costello were box-office champs.

Abbott was born in Asbury Park, New Jersey, in 1895; Costello in Paterson, New Jersey, in 1906. They banded together in 1931 and scored on radio and in vaudeville. In 1940, they broke into movies in a minor and unsuccessful musical, *One Night in the Tropics.* However, their first real starring vehicle, *Buck Privates,* was a smash. The tall, lean Abbott played straight man to the short, chubby Costello, who always got the laugh. This film, and most of their subsequent films, was a continuation of their vaudeville sketches with thinly disguised plots. In short order they wreaked havoc on all the armed forces: the army *(Buck Privates),* the navy *(In the Navy),* and the air force *(Keep 'em Flying).* Kathryn Grayson added some semi-operatic interludes to *Rio Rita,* but it was basically more slapstick, this time on a ranch invaded by Nazis. *The Time of Their Lives* relied less on sight gags and more on plot. The lapse into dramatics was temporary however, soon they were reviving old ideas *(Buck Privates Come Home).* When their box-office potency began to run down, they tried a new formula with *Abbott and Costello Meet Frankenstein.* Kids loved it, so they followed with *Abbott and Costello Meet the Invisible Man* and *Abbott and Costello Meet the Killer Boris Karloff.* In the years following, Abbott and Costello went to Mars and met the mummy, Dr. Jekyll and Mr. Hyde, and the Keystone Kops. Personal friction exploded into hostility and the team split. Costello was thought to be the key to their success, so he was offered the lead in *The 30 Foot Bride of Candy Rock.* It didn't please their fans and Costello died shortly afterward of a heart attack at age fifty-three. Abbott died in 1974. Their private lives were apparently filled with bitterness and competition (as was later the case with Dean Martin and Jerry Lewis). However, Abbott and Costello movies still offer mindless fun, the kind of pie-in-the-face humor Mel Brooks now specializes in.

Bud Abbott (left) and Lou Costello.

FILMOGRAPHY

1940

One Night in the Tropics ★★

1941

Buck Privates ★★★
In the Navy ★★
Hold That Ghost ★★
Keep 'em Flying ★★★

1942

Ride 'em Cowboy ★★
Rio Rita ★★
Pardon My Sarong ★★
Who Done It? ★★★

1943

It Ain't Hay ★★
Hit the Ice ★★

1944

In Society ★★
Lost in a Harem ★★

1945

Here Come the Co-Eds ★★
The Naughty Nineties ★★
Abbott and Costello in Hollywood ★★

1946

Little Giant ★★
The Time of Their Lives ★★★

1947

Buck Privates Come Home ★★★
The Wistful Widow of Wagon Gap ★★★

1948

The Noose Hangs High ★★★
Abbott and Costello Meet Frankenstein ★★★
Mexican Hayride ★★

1949

Africa Screams ★
Abbott and Costello Meet the Killer Boris Karloff ★★

1950

Abbott and Costello in the Foreign Legion ★★

1951

Abbott and Costello Meet the Invisible Man ★★
Comin' Round the Mountain ★★

1952

Jack and the Beanstalk ★★
Lost in Alaska ★
Abbott and Costello Meet Captain Kidd ★★

1953

Abbott and Costello Go to Mars ★★
Abbott and Costello Meet Dr. Jekyll and Mr. Hyde ★★

1955

Abbott and Costello Meet the Keystone Kops ★★
Abbott and Costello Meet the Mummy ★★

1956

Dance with Me Henry ★★

LOU COSTELLO ONLY

1959

The 30 Foot Bride of Candy Rock ★

ALAN ALDA
★★½ 2.73 STARS

Alan Alda's screen presence has grown with age and experience. When he began, Alda was a gangling, rather sexless type of leading man, and his physique and voice lacked power. But he has developed a mature style that has resulted in a loyal new following.

Alda was born on January 28, 1936, in New York City. He decided to follow in his father's, Robert Alda's, footsteps and made his screen debut at twenty-seven in

Gone Are the Days (a remake of *Purlie Victorious)* playing a preacher. Five years later, he had the lead in *Paper Lion*, an amusing comedy about a writer who becomes an honorary member of a football team. Unfortunately, the momentum was lost with *The Extraordinary Seaman* and *The Moonshine War.* Alda wasn't very good in the moderately engrossing occult thriller *The Mephisto Waltz* since the chemistry with co-star Jacqueline Bisset was missing and the script fell apart before the fadeout. His movie career took a backseat for a few years to what has become his greatest role: Hawkeye Pierce in the television series, "M*A*S*H."

When he returned to films in *Same Time Next Year* as Ellen Burstyn's once-a-year lover, the sparkle of the Broadway original disappeared, and Alda lacked the goofy sexuality of predecessor Charles Grodin. *California Suite* pitted him against a tart and aggressive Jane Fonda; both tossed off Neil Simon's dialogue like champions. He grew more confident in *The Seduction of Joe Tynan*, but he still wasn't a box-

Alan Alda with Meryl Streep in *The Seduction of Joe Tynan.*

office draw until *The Four Seasons* which he also wrote and directed. The film was a huge moneymaker (a complete surprise to the studio), and it hilariously explored all the petty conflicts and traumas of married life. Alda held the center, but costars Carol Burnett and Len Cariou (in particular) were invaluable to the success of the enterprise. Alda continues to test himself in feature films, and his fans have the seemingly endless pleasure of "M*A*S*H" reruns on TV.

FILMOGRAPHY

1963

Gone Are the Days ★★★

1968

Paper Lion ★★★

1969

The Extraordinary Seaman ★★

1970

The Moonshine War ★★
Jenny ★★

1971

The Mephisto Waltz ★★

1972

To Kill a Clown ★★★

1978

Same Time Next Year ★★
California Suite ★★★

1979

The Seduction of Joe Tynan ★★★★

1981

The Four Seasons ★★★★

JANE ALEXANDER
★★★½ 3.50 STARS

Rarely has Jane Alexander had movie parts worthy of her abilities, but whenever she speaks a line it contains a ring of truth that upstages all the other performers around her.

Born Jane Quigley in 1939, her first big break came at the age of thirty-one. Her performance on Broadway in "The Great White Hope" drew critical superlatives, and she repeated the part on film with equal success. She marked time in *A Gunfight* and *The New Centurions*, a mangled version of Joseph Wambaugh's best-seller. A brief scene in *All the President's Men* brought her an Oscar nomination, and she gave badly needed class to *The Betsy.* On television, in *Playing for Time*, Alexander's performance took a backseat to the publicity surrounding lead Vanessa Redgrave's political views. However, Alexander's portrayal had more shading, more poignancy than Redgrave's. *Kramer Vs. Kramer* benefited from her warmth as Dustin Hoffman's friend, and there was another TV triumph when she played Eleanor Roosevelt in the well-done *Eleanor and Franklin.* One hopes fame will someday catch up with her talent.

Jane Alexander in *Kramer Vs. Kramer.*

FILMOGRAPHY

1970

The Great White Hope ★★★★

1971

A Gunfight ★★★

1972

The New Centurions ★★★

1976

All the President's Men ★★★★

1978

The Betsy ★★★

1979

Kramer Vs. Kramer ★★★★

1980

Brubaker ★★★★

1981

Night Crossing ★★★

WOODY ALLEN
★★★ 3.13 STARS

Woody Allen's comedy has a true center—the neuroses and failures associated with modern relationships. The ordinary guy, struggling to belong, identifies with all of Woody's fears and fantasies. When Allen won multiple Oscars for *Annie Hall*, Neil Simon said he felt happy that

Woody Allen in *Stardust Memories.*

Woody was proclaimed a "genius," but felt slightly dejected that his own work didn't merit similar acclaim. Trouble is, Simon is only out for a laugh, and Allen's work is rooted in humanity.

Born Allen Stuart Konigsberg in 1935 in Brooklyn, Woody Allen's early break came as one of the writers on Sid Caesar's "Your Show of Shows." He attracted a following in Greenwich Village and on TV as a stand-up comic before succeeding in movies with *What's New, Pussycat?* It was popular, though panned by critics. Allen's klutzy loser in *Take the Money and Run* won over reviewers, though this time audiences were smaller. It took *Bananas* to catch the fancy of both. Allen threw out gag after gag and most of them were caught by the audiences, particularly in the scenes with co-star Louise Lasser. *Play It Again, Sam* was a screen adaption of his Broadway hit about a guy who dreamt of being Bogart, and Allen had a new and irresistible partner in Diane Keaton. Keaton was just as funny as Lasser, and her presence added sex appeal to the Allen image. *Everything You Always Wanted to Know About Sex (But Were Afraid to Ask)* borrowed only the title from David Reuben's best-seller and was inspired lunacy (Allen played a sperm, and Gene Wilder fell in love with a sheep named Daisy). *Sleeper* was calm by comparison, a clever satire that found him in a police state in the year 2173 with Diane Keaton on hand again. The pairing was successfully repeated in *Love and Death.*

But Keaton wasn't around to help *The Front*, a serious but sluggish study of blacklist victims in the 1950s. The sight of Zero Mostel—himself a victim of blacklisting—gave the picture moments of grim authenticity. The film didn't appeal to most of Allen's fans, but *Annie Hall* appealed to everyone. Allen's pre-Annie Hall movies were not automatic box-office smashes—nor were they commercial dynamite overseas. The romance between Allen and Keaton was bittersweet, touching, and uproariously funny, and was deservedly rewarded with Oscars for Best Picture, Best Director and Best Screenplay.

Annie Hall, despite its humor, heralded a move toward more dramatic territory. Allen conceived *Interiors,* a stark close-up of a troubled family. Allen directed the film, but did not act in it. Orson Welles publicly bemoaned the fact that comic masters had to punish us with boring tragedies, but the movie *had* moments of power.

It was a relief to return to *Manhattan*, possibly his funniest picture. Diane Keaton, Meryl Streep, Michael Murphy, and the refreshing Mariel Hemingway all contributed to the nonstop hilarity. Allen got pretentious again in *Stardust Memories,* an ego trip that alienated and puzzled his fans. But the digression was temporary. *A Midsummer Night's Sex Comedy* was light and enjoyable, if not brilliant in the manner of *Annie Hall* and *Manhattan. Zelig,* however, was both comically inventive and stretched Allen's range as an actor to new heights. Woody Allen is one of the most original and brilliant men of the century, and we can safely depend on him for years for imaginative, deeply felt entertainment.

FILMOGRAPHY

1965

What's New, Pussycat? (screenplay) ★★★

1966

What's Up, Tiger Lily? (co-screenplay, narrator) ★★★

1967

Casino Royale ★★

1969

Take the Money and Run (direction, co-screenplay) ★★★

1971

Bananas (direction, co-screenplay) ★★★★

1972

Play It Again, Sam (screenplay) ★★★
Everything You Always Wanted to Know About Sex (But Were Afraid to Ask) (direction, screenplay) ★★★

1973

Sleeper (direction, screenplay) ★★★

1975

Love and Death (direction, screenplay) ★★★

1976

The Front ★★★

Woody Allen in *Love and Death.*

1977

Annie Hall (direction, co-screenplay) ★★★★

1979

Manhattan (direction, screenplay) ★★★★

1980

Stardust Memories (direction, screenplay) ★★

1982

A Midsummer Night's Sex Comedy (direction, screenplay) ★★★

1983

Zelig (direction, screenplay) ★★★★

JUNE ALLYSON
★★★ 2.78 STARS

In his book, The Great Movie Stars, David Shipman says, "The niceness of June Allyson has gone out of fashion. Watching an Allyson movie on TV is like drowning in sugar."

It's a brutal indictment and on closer look an unfair one. A great many of Allyson's films *were* saccharine, but others demonstrated a strong, individual talent. Born in 1917, she was Broadway-trained in "Sing Out the News," "Panama Hattie," and "Best Foot Forward," and she showed charm and star quality in the movie *Two Girls and a Sailor,* stealing the show from another MGM hopeful Gloria De Haven.

It was *The Secret Heart,* which cast her as Claudette Colbert's jealous stepdaughter, that revealed the neurotic potential behind the smile. She gave an effervescent performance in *Good News* and was convincing as the nice Constance in *The Three Musketeers.*

Little Women elicited cries of negative criticism from those who loved the Katharine Hepburn version, but Allyson's ingratiating, tomboyish Jo gave the movie its chief energy. Her series of "perfect wife" roles began with *The Stratton Story* and reached its height with the schmaltzy but tuneful *The Glenn Miller Story.* She stayed the "perfect wife" through *Executive Suite, Woman's World, Strategic Air Command,* and *The McConnell Story.* However, *The Shrike* exploited the dark side suggested by *The Secret Heart,* and she was convincing as Jose Ferrer's domineering wife.

Now that her long personal battle with alcoholism has been won, Allyson could tackle rather involved character parts and use the talents so long ignored by Hollywood.

FILMOGRAPHY

1943

Best Foot Forward ★★★
Thousands Cheer ★★★
Girl Crazy ★★★

1944

Two Girls and a Sailor ★★★
Meet the People ★★★

1945

Music for Millions ★★
Her Highness and the Bellboy ★★★

1946

The Sailor Takes a Wife ★★★
Two Sisters from Boston ★★★
Till the Clouds Roll By ★★★
The Secret Heart ★★★★

1947

High Barabee ★★
Good News ★★★★

1948

The Bride Goes Wild ★★
The Three Musketeers ★★★
Words and Music ★★★★

1949

Little Women ★★★★
The Stratton Story ★★★★

1950

The Reformer and the Redhead ★★
Right Cross ★★★

1951

Too Young to Kiss ★★

1952

The Girl in White ★★★

1953

Battle Circus ★★
Remains to be Seen ★★

1954

The Glenn Miller Story ★★★
Executive Suite ★★★
Woman's World ★★★

1955

Strategic Air Command ★★
The Shrike ★★★
The McConnell Story ★★

1956

The Opposite Sex ★★★
You Can't Run Away from It ★★

1957

Interlude ★★★
My Man Godfrey ★★

1959

Stranger in My Arms ★★

1972

They Only Kill Their Masters ★★★

1978

Blackout ★★

June Allyson in *The Girl in White.*

JUDITH ANDERSON
★★★½ 3.44 STARS

As Mrs. Danvers in *Rebecca*, Judith Anderson epitomized female villainy. Regal in the role of the bloodless housekeeper, she played ruthless psychological games on the frightfully naive Mrs. de Winter. "You look overwrought, Madam. I've opened a window for you," Mrs. Danvers said with chilling tones as waves crashed below. "You've nothing to live for, really, have you? Look down there. It's easy, isn't it? Why don't you? Why don't you?"

Born in 1898 in Australia, she was performing on a stage by the age of 17. While her work on film was occasional and limited to unsympathetic roles, Dame Judith Anderson scored major triumphs in "Mourning Becomes Electra" (1932), "Hamlet" (1936), "Macbeth" (1937 and 1941), and "Medea" (1947 and 1949). She was named Dame in 1960.

In film, she was at her best when orchestrating the fates of others. Judith Anderson was keenly dominant as Big Mama in *Cat on a Hot Tin Roof* and as Lady Macbeth (opposite Maurice Evans) in George Schaefer's *Macbeth* in 1960.

While she was a "Great Lady" in the theatre, Judith Anderson limited her film career to small character roles. It was as if, after sizing up the possibilities, she found the meaty character roles more in keeping with her great talents.

FILMOGRAPHY

1933

Blood Money ★★★★

1940

Rebecca ★★★★
Forty Little Mothers ★★★

1941

Free and Easy ★★★
Lady Scarface ★★★

1942

All Through the Night ★★★
King's Row ★★★★

1943

Edge of Darkness ★★★
Stage Door Canteen (cameo)

1944

Laura ★★★★

1945

And Then There Were None ★★★★

1946

The Strange Love of Martha Ivers ★★★★
The Diary of a Chambermaid ★★★★
Specter of the Rose ★★★

1947

Pursued ★★★
The Red House ★★★★
Tycoon ★★★

1950

The Furies ★★★★

1953

Salome ★★★

1956

The Ten Commandments ★★★

1958

Cat on a Hot Tin Roof ★★★★

1960

Cinderfella ★★★

1961

Don't Bother to Knock ★★★

1963

Macbeth ★★★★

1970

A Man Called Horse ★★★

1974

Inn of the Damned ★★★

DANA ANDREWS
★★★ 2.99 STARS

Dana Andrews fitted the parts he played like a glove. He never dominated, hammed it up, or built a career on notoriety (despite a personal battle with alcoholism). He is simply an actor who has brought conviction and authority to a wide variety of roles.

He was born Carver Dana Andrews in 1909 in Mississippi. He was first cast in unexceptional films including: *Lucky Cisco Kid* with Caesar Romero, *Kit Carson*, and *Tobacco Road*. *Belle Starr* with Gene Tierney was a step forward, and he co-starred with Tyrone Power in the ordinary *Crash Dive*. *The Ox-Bow Incident* showed him to be a superbly sensitive actor with high-grade material. The film, a painfully realistic study of unjust lynching, was too downbeat for mass acceptance. After two undistinguished war dramas, *The North Star* and *The Purple Heart*, Andrews wound up in the classic *Laura*, again opposite Tierney, as a detective who fell in love with a dead woman. *Fallen Angel* with Linda Darnell was moderately gripping, and then he received the role of his life, as a disillusioned soldier in director William Wyler's memorable *The Best Years of Our Lives*. He was quite convincing as Susan Hayward's doomed boyfriend in one of the best tearjerkers, *My Foolish Heart*. Andrews was reunited a third time with Tierney for the brutal *Where the Sidewalk Ends* and trapped in the somber *Edge of Doom* as a priest. After that, the quality of his parts took a nose dive, and he was little more than background as Elizabeth Taylor's foreman in *Elephant Walk*. In *Brainstorm* his sadistic portrayal of a tycoon revealed another dimension to a versatile talent. In an age where performers zigzag erratically from brilliance to mediocrity, one has to applaud Andrews' consistent professionalism.

Dana Andrews in *The Ox-Bow Incident*.

FILMOGRAPHY

1940

Lucky Cisco Kid ★★★
The Westerner ★★★
Sailor's Lady ★★★
Kit Carson ★★★

1941

Tobacco Road ★★★
Belle Starr ★★★
Swamp Water ★★★
Ball of Fire ★★★

1942

Berlin Correspondent ★★★

1943

The Ox-Bow Incident ★★★★
Crash Dive ★★★
The North Star ★★★

1944

Up in Arms ★★★
The Purple Heart ★★★
Wing and a Prayer ★★★
Laura ★★★★

1945

State Fair ★★★
Fallen Angel ★★★★

1946

A Walk in the Sun ★★★★
Canyon Passage ★★★
The Best Years of Our Lives ★★★★

1947

Boomerang ★★★★
Night Song ★★
Daisy Kenyon ★★★★

1948

No Minor Vices ★★
Deep Waters ★★★
The Iron Curtain ★★★

1949

The Forbidden Street ★★★
Sword in the Desert ★★★

1950

My Foolish Heart ★★★★
Where the Sidewalk Ends ★★★
Edge of Doom ★★★

1951

The Frogmen ★★★
I Want You ★★★
Sealed Cargo ★★★

Dana Andrews in *The Frozen Dead.*

1952

Assignment—Paris ★★★

1954

Elephant Walk ★★★
Duel in the Jungle ★★★
Three Hours to Kill ★★★

1955

Smoke Signal ★★★
Strange Lady in Town ★★★

1956

Comanche ★★★
While the City Sleeps ★★★
Beyond a Reasonable Doubt ★★★

1957

Night of the Demon ★★★
Spring Reunion ★★★
Zero Hour ★★★

1958

Enchanted Island ★
The Fearmakers ★★★

1960

The Crowded Sky ★★★

1962

Madison Avenue ★★

1965

The Satan Bug ★★★
In Harm's Way ★★★
Crack in the World ★★★
Brainstorm ★★★★
Town Tamer ★★★
The Loved One ★★★
Battle of the Bulge ★★★
Spy in Your Eye ★★★

1966

Johnny Reno ★★★

1967

The Cobra ★★
Hot Rods to Hell ★★
The Frozen Dead ★★

1968

The Devil's Brigade ★★★
I Diamanti che Nessuno Voleva Rubare (cameo)

1972

Innocent Bystanders ★★★

1974

Airport 1975 ★★

1975

Take a Hard Ride (cameo)

1976

The Last Tycoon ★★★

1978

Good Guys Wear Black ★★★
Born Again ★★★

1979

The Pilot ★★★

JULIE ANDREWS
★★★ 2.92 STARS

Unlike Doris Day, who claimed to hate her sunny image yet only did films that promoted it, Julie Andrews has made definite—even startling—efforts to scrape the sugar from her movie identity. It's not an easy job because her fundamental class and impeccable diction are always in evidence.

These sophisticated qualities worked exquisitely well for her in the first phase of her career. She was born in 1935 to music hall parents who groomed her for stage success. On stage her meticulous acting and

Julie Andrews with Robert Preston in *Victor Victoria.*

crystal-clear soprano voice enchanted audiences in "The Boy Friend," "Camelot," and "My Fair Lady." She was disappointed when Jack Warner engaged Audrey Hepburn to be his "Fair Lady" in the film version. When she received an Oscar for *Mary Poppins* (against nominees that did not include Miss Hepburn), she said, "I want to thank Jack Warner, who made this possible." *My Fair Lady* suffered because of Warner's decision, and *Mary Poppins* gained immeasurably. She had "the sexiness of ironed sheets" in *The Americanization of Emily,* writer Paddy Chayefsky's witty antiwar tract. She also had an ideal co-star in James Garner.

The Sound of Music was attacked by critics, but audiences made it the most popular picture in history for a time. It was, in fact, much less maudlin than the Rodgers and Hammerstein stage original, and Andrews was superb as the governess who falls in love with a widower and his army of children. She gave the part more of an edge than predecessor Mary Martin despite Christopher Plummer's remark that "working with her is like being hit over the head with a Valentine's card."

She soared to number one at the box office, and not even the tedious Hitchcock potboiler, *Torn Curtain*, could wrench her out again. Hitchcock later admitted that she was miscast. *Hawaii*, a meandering spectacle based on James Michener's novel, and *Thoroughly Modern Millie* also coasted to success on the good will built up by her name.

It took *Star!*, an overwrought biography of Gertrude Lawrence, to bring her down. The score was filled with favorite old standards, but all the numbers were stiffly staged and Andrews' acerbic, hostile characterization looked like playacting. The descent continued with *Darling Lili*, a lumbering spectacle that also trapped Rock Hudson.

While searching for the right role, she did an expertly produced but low-rated TV series, "The Julie Andrews Hour." *The Tamarind Seed*, her second thriller, was mildly suspenseful, but she and Omar Shariff struck no sparks together.

Julie Andrews in *The Sound of Music*.

After nearly riding out the 1970s, the tide turned when she made *10* with Dudley Moore. Bo Derek's beauty was visually distracting, and Andrews seemed a mature choice as Moore's patient girlfriend, but the movie was hilarious. The imaginary sweetheart was gone and she came across as gutsy and real. *S.O.B.* was another story—an incoherent, tasteless satire of Hollywood. She did a scene topless, but it wasn't the turn-on expected. *Victor Victoria* brought better luck. It was expertly directed by her husband, Blake Edwards, (who had also directed *Darling Lili*, *10*, and *S.O.B.*). Old co-star James Garner was on hand to provide the needed chemistry and Andrews gave a delightful comedy performance and was nominated for an Oscar.

One can certainly understand her desire to escape the *Mary Poppins* image as she grows older. But the blatant sexuality of *S.O.B.* is equally unsuitable. As long as she walks the middle ground, her comeback will continue because her all-around talent is as strong as ever.

FILMOGRAPHY

1964

Mary Poppins ★★★
The Americanization of Emily ★★★★

1965

The Sound of Music ★★★★

1966

Torn Curtain ★★
Hawaii ★★★

1967

Thoroughly Modern Millie ★★★

1968

Star! ★★

1970

Darling Lili ★★

1974

The Tamarind Seed ★★★

1979

10 ★★★

1981

S.O.B. ★

1982

Victor Victoria ★★★★

ANN-MARGRET
★★ 2.25 STARS

Sex symbols rarely turn into respected dramatic actresses. An exception is Ann-Margret, who projected sensuality through a series of mediocre, money-losing films, and then suddenly emerged in *Carnal Knowledge* as a sensitive and capable performer.

She was born in 1941 in Valsjobyn, Sweden. At sixteen she shone on "Ted Mack's Amateur Hour," and then worked in nightclubs. Her appearances in *Pocketful of Miracles*

Ann-Margret.

and *State Fair* meant little, since both movies failed, but *Bye Bye Birdie* (plus a sizzling, in-person performance at the Oscar ceremonies) made people take notice. Her impact was due to her magnetic presence and audience rapport, rather than to her limited vocal ability. *Viva Las Vegas* was her second success—and "provides Elvis Presley with his ideal co-star—his female equivalent," said Douglas McVay in his book The Musical Film. Both Presley and Ann-Margret had the animal magnetism to surmount the usual assembly-line Presley script. At this point, her

Ann-Margret with Walter Matthau in *I Ought to Be in Pictures.*

movie career tumbled downhill, and she was oddly matched with John Forsythe in the ludicrous *Kitten with a Whip. The Pleasure Seekers* was a routine remake of *Three Coins in the Fountain,* with routine co-stars (Pamela Tiffin and Carol Lynley). *Bus Riley's Back in Town* featured a catatonic Michael Parks and was so bad that writer William Inge had his name removed from the credits.

Ann-Margret seemed out of place in *Once a Thief* with Alain Delon, but then her luck temporarily turned. *The Cincinnati Kid* had a strong script and cast (Steve McQueen, Edward G. Robinson, and Tuesday Weld), and she played her vampish part well. However, it was another stereotyped sex role, the least original aspect of the movie. *Stagecoach* was a misguided attempt to redo the John Wayne classic, and *The Swinger* had the dubious distinction of being director George Sidney's worst film.

She needed help desperately, and after *The Tiger and The Pussycat* and *C.C. and Company* (a horrendous Joe Namath biker movie), she got it when director Mike Nichols requested her for *Carnal Knowledge.* She knew it was her big chance and worked painstakingly, living the character after hours. She claimed that the over-the-hill model had painful parallels with her own life. Her successful performance led to more opportunities, and she later starred in Ken Russell's deafening version of the Who's rock opera *Tommy.* "There's a surprisingly good performance by Ann-Margret," said critic Stephen H. Scheuer, and the "surprisingly" was still a grudging tag that she would have to overcome. *Joseph Andrews* brought fine personal reviews, but no audiences. Her flair for comedy was effectively utilized in Marty Feldman's zany *The Last Remake of Beau Geste,* a spoof of the foreign legion. She also graced *The Cheap Detective,* a take-off of an old property, *Casablanca,* and she was the most human element of *Magic,* an uninspired adaptation of William Goldman's best-seller.

Ambition to improve is an admirable thing, especially when (as in Ann-Margret's case) the obstacles presented by bad material are so great. She still knocks herself out in Las Vegas and delivers good entertainment. Whether on TV, stage, or film, she is that increasingly rare bird—a pro.

FILMOGRAPHY

1961

Pocketful of Miracles ★★

1962

State Fair ★★

1963

Bye Bye Birdie ★★★

1964

Viva Las Vegas ★★★
Kitten with a Whip ★
The Pleasure Seekers ★★

1965

Bus Riley's Back in Town ★
Once a Thief ★★
The Cincinnati Kid ★★★

1966

Made in Paris ★★
Stagecoach ★★
The Swinger ★
Murderers' Row ★★

Ann-Margret in *The Tiger and the Pussycat.*

1967

Criminal Affair ★★
The Tiger and the Pussycat ★★

1970

C.C. and Company ★
R.P.M. ★★

1971

Carnal Knowledge ★★★★

1972

The Train Robbers ★★
The Outside Man ★★

1975

Tommy ★★★

1976

The Prophet ★★
Follies Bourgeoises ★★

1977

Joseph Andrews ★★★
The Last Remake of Beau Geste ★★★

1978

The Cheap Detective ★★★
Magic ★★★★

1979

The Villain ★★

1980

Middle Age Crazy ★★

1982

Looking to Get Out ★★
The Return of the Soldier ★★
I Ought to Be in Pictures ★★★

EVE ARDEN
★★★ 3.18 STARS

Eve Arden is one of the screen's great comediennes, like Lucille Ball. Most people remember her today as "Our Miss Brooks," but she has also made dozens of films, and some of them are classics.

Arden was born Eunice Quedens in Mill Valley, California, in 1912. Her movie career began inauspiciously in 1937 at the age of twenty-five with *Oh Doctor!* opposite Edward Everett Horton. But *Stage Door* which followed was a sparkling study of aspiring actresses (Ginger Rogers and Katharine Hepburn were two of the others), and Arden was hilariously hard-boiled in a mediocre Clark Gable comedy, *Comrade X.* She stole scenes from Gene Kelly and Rita Hayworth in

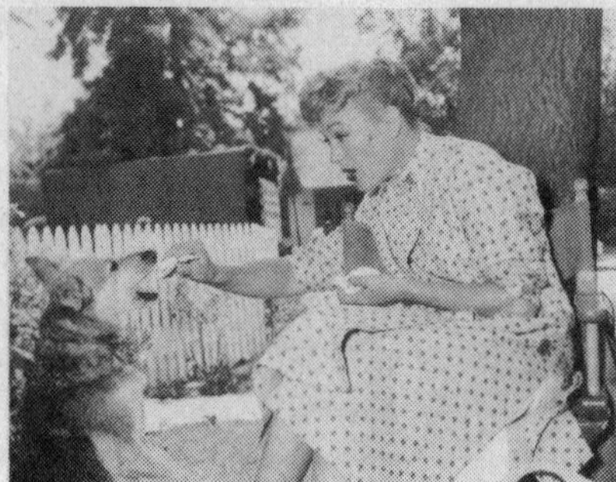

Eve Arden.

Cover Girl and had her finest performance as Joan Crawford's friend in *Mildred Pierce.* Arden was nominated for an Oscar for that, and she went on brightening pictures like *My Dream Is Yours* and the ebullient *Tea for Two.* She and Crawford made good chemistry again in the underrated *Goodbye My Fancy.* Her best dramatic part was in *The Dark at the Top of the Stairs,* as Dorothy McGuire's sexually neglected sister.

Eve Arden's most typical screen roll is the bitingly witty sidekick of the heroine. Her repartee still sparkles, even in awful films like *Grease 2.*

FILMOGRAPHY

(billed as Eunice Quedens)

1929

The Song of Love ★★★

1933

Dancing Lady (bit)

(billed as Eve Arden)

1937

Oh Doctor! ★★★
Stage Door ★★★

1938

Having Wonderful Time ★★★
Letter of Introduction ★★★

1939

Eternally Yours ★★★
At the Circus ★★★

1940

A Child Is Born ★★★
Slightly Honorable ★★★
No No Nanette ★★★
Comrade X ★★★★

1941

Ziegfeld Girl ★★★
That Uncertain Feeling ★★★
Manpower ★★★
Whistling in the Dark ★★★
She Couldn't Say No ★★★

1942

Bedtime Story ★★★★

1943

Let's Face It ★★★

1944

Cover Girl ★★★★
The Doughgirls ★★★★

1945

Pan-Americana ★★★
Earl Carroll Vanities ★★★
Patrick the Great ★★★
Mildred Pierce ★★★★

1946

My Reputation ★★★
The Kid from Brooklyn ★★★
Night and Day ★★★

1947

Song of Scheherazade ★★★
The Arnelo Affair ★★★
The Unfaithful ★★★
The Voice of the Turtle ★★★★

1948

One Touch of Venus ★★★
Whiplash ★★★

1949

My Dream Is Yours ★★★★
The Lady Takes a Sailor ★★★

1950

Tea for Two ★★★★
Curtain Call at Cactus Creek ★★★
Paid in Full ★★★

1951

Goodbye My Fancy ★★★★
Three Husbands ★★★

1952

We're Not Married ★★★

1953

The Lady Wants Mink ★★★

1956

Our Miss Brooks ★★★

1959

Anatomy of a Murder ★★★

1960

The Dark at the Top of the Stairs ★★★★

1965

Sergeant Deadhead ★★★

1975

The Strongest Man in the World ★★★

1978

Grease ★★★

1981

Under the Rainbow ★★★

1982

Grease 2 ★★

ALAN ARKIN
★★½ 2.50 STARS

Critics have always been in Alan Arkin's corner, from his first Broadway appearance in "Enter Laughing" through a succession of varied films. Yet Arkin lacks the star quality and charisma to build a consistent movie following despite the fact that he is equally adept at comedy and drama.

Arkin was born in New York City, in 1934. His strong performance in his first feature, *The Russians Are Coming, the Russians Are Coming,* and his spine-chilling acting in *Wait Until Dark* with Audrey Hepburn established his position as an actor. However, he compared unfavorably to Peter Sellers as *Inspector Clouseau.* But disaster was averted by *The Heart Is a Lonely Hunter.* Arkin's portrait of a deaf mute won him the New York Film Critics Award. After the uneven *Catch-22,* his popularity plummeted as he appeared in a number of second-rate films. *Freebie and the Bean* was total trivia, and in *Rafferty and the Gold Dust Twins* he was cast as a dim-witted driving instructor. Yet he was quite compelling as Sigmund Freud opposite Sherlock Holmes in *The Seven-Per-Cent Solution,* and he pushed his personal charm to the limit in the title role of *Simon.* No matter how inconsistent his acting career has been, he deserves credit for taking risks, and his versatility is bound to yield other worthwhile films in the future.

FILMOGRAPHY

1966

The Russians Are Coming, the Russians Are Coming ★★★

1967

Woman Times Seven ★★
Wait Until Dark ★★★★

1968

Inspector Clouseau ★★
The Heart Is a Lonely Hunter ★★★★

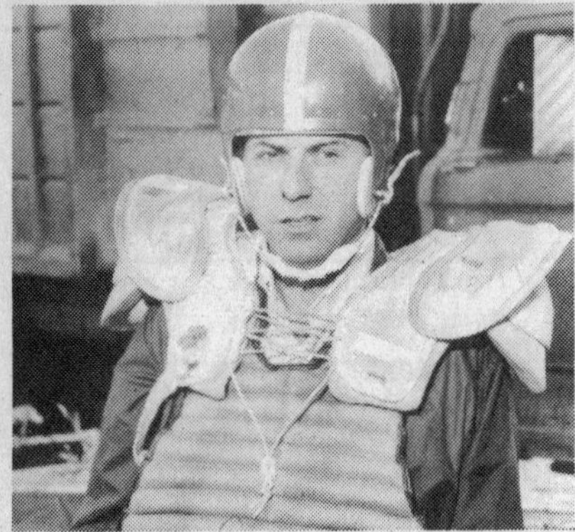

Alan Arkin in *Fire Sale.*

1969

The Monitors ★ ★
Popi ★ ★ ★

1970

Catch-22 ★ ★ ★

1971

Little Murders ★ ★ ★

1972

Deadhead Miles ★ ★
Last of the Red Hot Lovers ★ ★

1974

Freebie and the Bean ★ ★

1975

Rafferty and the Gold Dust Twins ★ ★
Hearts of the West ★ ★ ★

1976

The Seven-Per-Cent Solution ★ ★ ★

1977

Fire Sale ★

1979

The Magician of Lublin ★ ★
The In-Laws ★ ★ ★
Simon ★ ★ ★

1981

Chu Chu and the Philly Flash ★

1982

The Last Unicorn (voice only)

JEAN ARTHUR
★ ★ ★ 2.99 STARS

In the 1930s, there were a host of lovely, talented comediennes including Claudette Colbert, Rosalind Russell, Carole Lombard, and Myrna Loy. Jean Arthur fit well into this select group of what film critic Pauline Kael called, "clever funny girls. . . wisecracking heroines who could be counted on to be sassy and sane." During her movie career, Arthur spoke to men on equal terms without dissolving into helpless tears, and her strength of character is the main reason why her performances seem so modern when viewed today.

Arthur was born in New York in 1905, and she began a long apprenticeship in silent films with *Cameo Kirby* in 1923 at the age of eighteen. Most of her early films were westerns and slapstick comedies, with an occasional horror movie thrown in (*The Mysterious Dr. Fu Manchu,* with Warner Oland). After these, Arthur went to New York to concentrate on theatre work. She appeared in "Foreign Affairs" and "The Man Who Reclaimed His Head" with Claude Rains. Upon her return to Hollywood, she signed with Columbia, and after an uneventful tearjerker, *The Most Precious Thing in Life,* her motion picture career finally gained momentum with *The Whole Town's Talking,* blossoming under John Ford's direction. *Mr. Deeds Goes to Town* was her first comedy classic, and Arthur was ideally cast as a reporter who fell in love with wealthy do-gooder Gary Cooper. *The Ex-Mrs. Bradford* blended humor and mystery in the same vein as *The Thin Man.* She returned to westerns, playing a rambunctious Calamity Jane opposite Gary Copper in Cecil B. DeMille's *The Plainsman.*

In her funniest film, *Easy Living* by screenwriter Preston Sturges, Arthur played a secretary mistaken for a millionaire's mistress. Her performance was nonstop hilarity, with audiences barely able to catch their breaths, especially in the automat scene. Her flair for comedy also made her quite a refreshing romantic lead opposite Charles Boyer in the ultra-romantic *History Is Made at Night.*

After a quarrel with her studio, she came back to do another classic. *You Can't Take It With You* won a Best Picture Oscar, but Arthur was overlooked in the nominations for her performance. She was a tough show girl involved with pilot Cary Grant in *Only Angels Have Wings,* and continued her remarkable run with *Mr. Smith Goes to Washington,* director Capra's companion piece to *Mr. Deeds* and every bit as good. James Stewart was the lovable bumbler this time.

A Foreign Affair was fast-moving, with Arthur as a smart-aleck American Congresswoman in Berlin. In her last film, *Shane,* Arthur's unexpressed feeling for Alan Ladd was one of the picture's most haunting ingredients. Her premature retirement at age forty-eight deprived viewers of any more great performances. Among the films she made, however, there exist as many classics as any star has made before or since.

FILMOGRAPHY

1923

Cameo Kirby ★ ★
The Temple of Venus (bit)

1924

Biff Bang Buddy ★ ★
Fast and Fearless ★ ★
Bringin' Home the Bacon ★ ★
Travelin' Fast ★ ★
Thundering Romance ★ ★

1925

Seven Chances (bit)
Drug Store Cowboy ★ ★
The Fighting Smile ★ ★
A Man of Nerve ★ ★
Tearin' Loose ★ ★
Hurricane Horseman ★ ★
Thundering Through ★ ★

1926

Under Fire ★ ★
Born to Battle ★ ★ ★
The Fighting Cheat ★ ★ ★
Double Daring ★ ★ ★
Lightning Bill ★ ★ ★
The Cowboy Cop ★ ★ ★
Twisted Triggers ★ ★ ★
The College Boob ★ ★ ★
The Block Signal ★ ★ ★

1927

The Masked Menace (serial) ★ ★ ★
Husband Hunters ★ ★ ★
The Broken Gate ★ ★ ★
Horse Shoes ★ ★ ★
The Poor Nut ★ ★ ★
Flying Luck ★ ★ ★

1928

Wallflowers ★ ★ ★
Warming Up ★ ★ ★
Brotherly Love ★ ★ ★
Sins of the Fathers ★ ★ ★

Jean Arthur.

1929

The Canary Murder Case ★ ★ ★
Stairs of Sand ★ ★ ★
The Greene Murder Case ★ ★ ★
The Mysterious Dr. Fu Manchu ★ ★ ★
The Saturday Night Kid ★ ★ ★
Half-Way to Heaven ★ ★ ★

1930

Return of Dr. Fu Manchu ★ ★ ★
Danger Lights ★ ★ ★
The Silver Horde ★ ★
Street of Chance ★ ★
Young Eagles ★ ★
Paramount on Parade ★ ★

1931

The Gang Busters ★ ★ ★
Virtuous Husband ★ ★ ★
The Lawyer's Secret ★ ★ ★
Ex-Bad Boy ★ ★ ★

1933

Get That Venus ★ ★ ★
The Past of Mary Holmes ★ ★ ★

1934

Whirlpool ★ ★ ★
The Defense Rests ★ ★ ★
The Most Precious Thing in Life ★ ★ ★

1935

The Whole Town's Talking ★ ★ ★ ★
Public Hero #1 ★ ★ ★ ★
Party Wire ★ ★ ★
Diamond Jim ★ ★ ★
The Public Menace ★ ★ ★
If You Could Only Cook ★ ★ ★

1936

The Ex-Mrs. Bradford ★ ★ ★ ★
Mr. Deeds Goes to Town ★ ★ ★ ★
Adventures in Manhattan ★ ★ ★
More Than a Secretary ★ ★ ★

1937

The Plainsman ★ ★ ★
History Is Made at Night ★ ★ ★ ★
Easy Living ★ ★ ★ ★

1938

You Can't Take It With You ★ ★ ★ ★

1939

Only Angels Have Wings ★ ★ ★ ★
Mr. Smith Goes to Washington ★ ★ ★ ★

1940

Too Many Husbands ★ ★ ★ ★
Arizona ★ ★ ★ ★

1941

The Devil and Miss Jones ★ ★ ★ ★

1942

The Talk of the Town ★ ★ ★ ★

1943

The More the Merrier ★ ★ ★ ★
A Lady Takes a Chance ★ ★ ★

1944

The Impatient Years ★ ★ ★

1948

A Foreign Affair ★ ★ ★ ★

1953

Shane ★ ★ ★ ★

EDWARD ASNER
★ ★ ★ 3.09 STARS

Bald, stocky Edward Asner has accomplished the remarkable feat of playing romantic leads on television opposite beautiful young actresses. On the TV screen he has the strength and charisma to make it plausible. Perhaps he could have done the same in feature films if he had been given challenging roles.

Asner was born in Kansas City in 1929 and began acting during his college years. His early career included Shakespearean roles as well as modern parts in stock and off-Broadway theatres. His big break came with "The Mary Tyler Moore Show" as the crusty Lou Grant. However, the comedic sense displayed there was only used in Disney's *Gus*, (where he played second fiddle to a mule) and *Skin Game*. Both *Change of Habit* and *The Satan Bug* were second rate films

Ed Asner with Meredith Baxter Birney in the TV Movie, *A Happy Family*.

which limited Asner's performing abilities. His performance in the television drama *Roots* was remarkable, and he won an Emmy in 1977 for his portrayal of Captain Davies, a "Christian" involved in the slave trade. He was an excellent albeit minor part of Paul Newman's police drama *Fort Apache, The Bronx.*

Now that Asner has shown such brilliance on television, hopefully motion picture producers will use him for the roles he's capable of playing.

FILMOGRAPHY

1965

The Satan Bug ★★★
The Slender Thread ★★★

1967

The Venetian Affair ★★★
El Dorado ★★★
Gunn ★★★

1969

Change of Habit ★★★

1970

They Call Me Mister Tibbs ★★★

1971

Skin Game ★★★

1974

The Wrestler ★★★

1976

Gus ★★★

1981

Fort Apache, The Bronx ★★★

1983

Daniel ★★★

FRED ASTAIRE
★★★½ 3.62 STARS

"Fred Astaire can give an audience pleasure just by walking across the floor," Gene Kelly once commented. No one who loves dancing can deny it. He seems to have no bones, no flesh. Nothing seemed to get in the way of his skillfully executed movements. Astaire made every one of his partners appear more graceful than they would look without him.

Fred Astaire was born Frederick

Fred Astaire in *Three Little Words.*

Austerlitz in 1899, in Omaha, Nebraska. When he was seven years old, he and his sister Adele toured the vaudeville circuit as a dance team. Later, on Broadway, they had a series of hits including "Lady Be Good," "Funny Face," and "The Band Wagon," until Adele married royalty and retired.

Movie audiences first saw him in *Dancing Lady* with Joan Crawford. Stardom came when RKO paired him with Ginger Rogers in *Flying Down to Rio.* They started a nationwide craze with their dance, the Carioca, and the studio teamed them again in *The Gay Divorcee, Roberta,* and *Top Hat,* firmly entrenching them in the box-office top 10. Their success meant that they had to tolerate each other's personalities. Apparently it was difficult, judging from Astaire's later reference to Rogers as "Miss Wasp," and her comment that "I have a dentist who dances better than he does." But they were incredibly intimate and at ease with each other on the screen and sustained their winning pattern throughout the 1930s. However, their final pairing in the series, *The Story of Vernon & Irene Castle,* played to a lukewarm reaction.

Audiences saw only the warmth and harmony and regretted the team's breakup, but Astaire held his public with *Broadway Melody of 1940,* which included a fabulous tap dance with partner Eleanor Powell. He had Cole Porter songs and Rita Hayworth in *You'll Never Get Rich,* and according to choreographer Onna White, Hayworth was Fred's favorite partner. *You Were Never Lovelier* again teamed him with Hayworth, and *Holiday Inn* scored big with his new partner Bing Crosby. But *Yolanda and the Thief* was overproduced and overwrought. ("My first interesting failure," according to director Vincente Minnelli.) Astaire retired from show business after the popular *Blue Skies* but came back to do *Easter Parade* when Gene Kelly broke his ankle. It was one of the best musicals of his career; "A Couple of Swells" with Judy Garland is regarded as a classic number by fans. Garland was forced to withdraw from a proposed follow-up, *The Barkleys of Broadway,* because of illness. She was replaced by Ginger Rogers and more backstage dissension. The movie itself (their first in color) was witty and tuneful. *Three Little Words* paired him effectively with Red Skelton, and he was delightful opposite Jane Powell in *Royal Wedding.*

After giving highly acclaimed performances in *The Band Wagon, Silk Stockings,* and *Funny Face,* he gave up musicals for straight dramatic parts. His acting was always professional—he even received an Oscar nomination for *The Towering Inferno*—but his range was rather limited. One performance was relatively the same as next. Not that it matters, Astaire has spread enough magic across the screen in his musicals for two careers.

FILMOGRAPHY

1933

Dancing Lady ★★★
Flying Down to Rio ★★★★

1934

The Gay Divorcee ★★★★

1935

Roberta ★★★★
Top Hat ★★★★

1936

Follow the Fleet ★★★★
Swing Time ★★★★

1937

Shall We Dance ★★★★
A Damsel in Distress ★★★★

1938

Carefree ★★★★

1939

The Story of Vernon & Irene Castle ★★★★

1940

Second Chorus ★★★
Broadway Melody of 1940 ★★★★

1941

You'll Never Get Rich ★★★★

1942

You Were Never Lovelier ★★★★
Holiday Inn ★★★★

1943

The Sky's the Limit ★★★

1945

Yolanda and the Thief ★★★

1946

Ziegfeld Follies ★★★★
Blue Skies ★★★★

1948

Easter Parade ★★★★

1949

The Barkleys of Broadway ★★★★

1950

Three Little Words ★★★★
Let's Dance ★★★

1951

Royal Wedding ★★★★

1952

The Belle of New York ★★★

1953

The Band Wagon ★★★★

1955

Daddy Long Legs ★★★★

1957

Funny Face ★★★★
Silk Stockings ★★★

1959

On the Beach ★★★

Fred Astaire with Ginger Rogers in *The Gay Divorcee.*

1961

The Pleasure of His Company ★★★

1962

The Notorious Landlady ★★★

1968

Finian's Rainbow ★★★

1969

Midas Run ★★★

1974

That's Entertainment (narration)
The Towering Inferno ★★★★

1976

That's Entertainment II (narration)

1977

The Amazing Dobermans ★★★
The Purple Taxi ★★★

1981

Ghost Story ★★★

MARY ASTOR
★★★ 3.21 STARS

Many of the performers who become over-the-title stars wind up forgotten. Others, like Mary Astor, spend a lifetime in minor roles and by virtue of sheer talent end up with brighter reputations than the "names" they've supported.

Mary Astor's career, from shorts and two-reelers in the early 1920s to stardom, scandal, and character parts in the 1960s, reads like a history of Hollywood.

She was born Lucille Vasconcellos Langhanke in 1906 in Quincy, Illinois, and was driven and exploited by a tyrannical father who put her in films at age fifteen. She was a leading lady by 1924, but her greatest successes came in talkies. *Red Dust* was her first classic; she was the married woman who couldn't resist Clark Gable. Her autobiography, My Story, reveals that "sexually, I was out of control . . . spoiled, sick, and selfish," a fact that was confirmed when her diary, full of intimate details, was quoted in the press. Her adulterous affair with playwright George S. Kaufman became front page news. Despite the scandal, audiences applauded her warm, sensitive portrayal in *Dodsworth.* She was spectacularly bitchy as Bette Davis's rival in *The Great Lie,* winning an Oscar for Best Supporting Actress. In *The Maltese Falcon* with Humphrey Bogart, Sydney Greenstreet, and Peter Lorre—Mary Astor more than held her own as the seemingly sweet but deadly Brigid O'Shaughnessy. Then, in her words, "the lights went out," and she was saddled with motherly roles. Some of these roles were memorable, and she performed well as Judy Garland's mother in *Meet Me in St. Louis* and June Allyson's mother in *Little Women.* Later, Astor was brilliant as a middle-aged whore in the gripping *Act of Violence.*

Along the way she conquered a drinking problem, and a heart condition has restricted her activity in recent years. Astor has written several novels and two autobiographies. Her work has undergone a critical reappraisal that has resulted in a recent Life magazine story.

FILMOGRAPHY

1922

The Man Who Played God ★★★
John Smith ★★★

1923

Second Fiddle ★★★
Success ★★★
The Bright Shawl ★★★
Hollywood (cameo)
The Marriage Maker ★★★
Puritan Passions ★★★
The Rapids ★★★
Woman-Proof ★★★
The Scarecrow ★★★

1924

The Fighting Coward ★★★
Beau Brummel ★★★★
The Fighting American ★★★
Unguarded Women ★★★
The Price of a Party ★★★
Inez From Hollywood ★★★

1925

Oh Doctor! ★★★
Enticement ★★★
Playing With Souls ★★★
Don Q Son of Zorro ★★★
The Pace That Thrills ★★★
Scarlet Saint ★★★

1926

High Steppers ★★★
The Wise Guy ★★★
Don Juan ★★★★
Forever After ★★★

Mary Astor in *Turnabout.*

1927

The Sea Tiger ★★★
The Rough Riders ★★★
The Sunset Derby ★★★
Rose of the Golden West ★★★
No Place to Go ★★★
Two Arabian Nights ★★★★

1928

Sailors' Wives ★★★
Dressed to Kill ★★★★
Three-Ring Marriage ★★★
Heart to Heart ★★★
Dry Martini ★★★★
Romance of the Underworld ★★★

1929

The Woman From Hell ★★★
New Year's Eve ★★★

1930

Ladies Love Brutes ★★★
The Runaway Bride ★★★
Holiday ★★★★
The Lash ★★★
Misbehaving Ladies ★★★

1931

The Royal Bed ★★★★
Behind Office Doors ★★★
The Sin Ship ★★★
Other Men's Women ★★★
White Shoulders ★★★
Smart Woman ★★★

1932

Men of Chance ★★★
The Lost Squadron ★★★★
A Successful Calamity ★★★
Those We Love ★★★
Red Dust ★★★★

1933

The Little Giant ★★★
Jennie Gerhardt ★★★
The World Changes ★★★
The Kennel Murder Case ★★★
Convention City ★★★

1934

Easy to Love ★★★
Upper World ★★★
Return of the Terror ★★★
The Man With Two Faces ★★★
The Case of the Howling Dog ★★★

1935

I Am a Thief ★★★
Red Hot Tires ★★★
Straight From the Heart ★★★
Dinky ★★★★
Page Miss Glory ★★★
Man of Iron ★★★

1936

The Murder of Dr. Harrigan ★★★
And So They Were Married ★★★
Trapped by Television ★★★
Dodsworth ★★★★
Lady From Nowhere ★★★

1937

The Prisoner of Zenda ★★★★
The Hurricane ★★★★

1938

Paradise for Three ★★★
No Time to Marry ★★★
There's Always a Woman ★★★
Woman Against Woman ★★★
Listen Darling ★★★

1939

Midnight ★★★★

1940

Turnabout ★★★
Brigham Young ★★★

1941

The Great Lie ★★★★
The Maltese Falcon ★★★★

1942

In This Our Life (cameo)
Across the Pacific ★★★★
The Palm Beach Story ★★★★

1943

Thousands Cheer ★★★
Young Ideas ★★★

1944

Blonde Fever ★★★
Meet Me in St. Louis ★★★★

1946

Claudia and David ★★★

1947

Fiesta ★★★
Cynthia ★★★
Desert Fury ★★★★
Cass Timberlane ★★★

Mary Astor with Bogart, Lorre and Greenstreet in *The Maltese Falcon.*

1949

Act of Violence ★★★★
Little Women ★★★★
Any Number Can Play ★★★

1953

So This Is Love ★★★

1956

A Kiss Before Dying ★★★
The Power and the Prize ★★★

1957

The Devil's Hairpin ★★★

1958

This Happy Feeling ★★★

1959

Stranger in My Arms ★★★

1961

Return to Peyton Place ★★★★

1964

Youngblood Hawke ★★★

1965

Hush...Hush, Sweet Charlotte ★★★

RICHARD ATTENBOROUGH
★★★ 3.07 STARS

After a lifetime of acting, Richard Attenborough took home an Oscar for Best Director in 1982 for *Gandhi.* The award is richly deserved, but Attenborough's directorial achievement does not obscure his excellent contributions as a performer.

Richard Attenborough was born in 1923, in Cambridge, England. He began acting during the Second World War. Attenborough's acting range is enormous—he was vicious in *Brighton Rock* as a gangleader, but more sympathetic in *Eight O'Clock Walk* as a taxi driver falsely accused of murder. Two amiable service comedies *(Private's Progress* and *The Baby and the Battleship)* demonstrated his lighter side, and he added a spiritual depth in his portrayal of the shady dealings of a medium in *Seance on a Wet Afternoon.* He played the psychologically distraught navigator in *The Flight of the Phoenix* and brightened the dreary *Doctor Dolittle* before turning back to murder in *Ten Rillington Place.* He was believable in The *Hu-*

man Factor, although the movie directed by Otto Preminger was a poor adaptation of Graham Greene's superb spy novel.

FILMOGRAPHY

1942

In Which We Serve ★★★

1943

Schweik's New Adventures ★★★

1944

The Hundred Pound Window ★★★

1945

Journey Together ★★★

1946

Stairway to Heaven ★★★
School for Secrets ★★★

1947

The Smugglers ★★★
Dancing With Crime ★★★
Brighton Rock ★★★★

1948

Dulcimer Street ★★★

1949

The Guinea Pig ★★★
The Lost People ★★★

1950

Operation Disaster ★★★★
Boys in Brown ★★★

1951

Hell Is Sold Out ★★★
The Magic Box ★★★★

1952

The Gift Horse ★★★
Father's Doing Fine ★★★

1954

Eight O'Clock Walk ★★★★

1955

The Ship That Died of Shame ★★★

1956

Private's Progress ★★★
The Baby and the Battleship ★★★

1957

Brothers in Law ★★★
The Scamp ★★★

1958

Dunkirk ★★★
The Man Upstairs ★★★
Desert Patrol ★★★

1959

Breakout ★★★
Jet Storm ★★★
I'm All Right Jack ★★★
S.O.S. Pacific ★★★

Richard Attenborough in *The Man Upstairs.*

1960

The Angry Silence ★★★★
The League of Gentlemen ★★★

1962

Only Two Can Play ★★★
All Night Long ★★★
Trial and Error ★★★

1963

The Great Escape ★★★★

1964

The Third Secret ★★★
Seance on a Wet Afternoon ★★★★
Guns at Batasi ★★★

1965

The Flight of the Phoenix ★★★★

1966

The Sand Pebbles ★★★

1967

Doctor Dolittle ★★★

1968

The Bliss of Mrs. Blossom ★★★
Only When I Larf ★★★

1969

The Magic Christian ★★

1970

The Last Grenade ★★★
David Copperfield ★★

1971

A Severed Head ★★★
Loot ★★★
Ten Rillington Place ★★★★

1974

Ten Little Indians ★★

1975

Brannigan ★★
Rosebud ★★
Conduct Unbecoming ★★★

1977

The Chess Players ★★★

1980

The Human Factor ★★★

GENE AUTRY
★★½ 2.29 STARS

Like Roy Rogers and the Lone Ranger, Gene Autry personifies the good guy in the white cowboy hat. Discovered by Will Rogers, Gene Autry began his career singing cowboy and country and western songs. Born in 1907, near Tioga, Texas, he started singing on a local radio station at the age of twenty-one. After succeeding with his own radio show and several recordings, Autry landed his first movie appearance in the 1934 film *In Old Santa Fe*. Next, "the singing cowboy" had the lead in the thirteen chapter adventure serial, *Phantom Empire*.

Gene Autry, along with his horse Champion, made dozens of westerns for Republic. He became the most popular of the western stars and his films were big moneymakers. He was a prolific songwriter and his hit song, "Here Comes Santa Claus," continues to be a Christmas favorite. After serving in World War II, Autry returned to westerns, this time for Columbia Pictures. An astute businessman, Gene Autry is the California Angel's number one fan and owner.

Gene Autry.

FILMOGRAPHY

1934

In Old Santa Fe ★★

1935

Phantom Empire (serial) ★★
Tumblin' Tumbleweeds ★★
The Singing Vagabond ★★

1937

The Singing Cowboy ★ ★ ★
Oh Susannah! ★ ★
Boots and Saddles ★ ★
Manhattan Merry-Go-Round ★ ★
Springtime in the Rockies ★ ★

1938

Rhythm of the Saddle ★ ★

1939

In Old Monterey ★ ★
South of the Border ★ ★ ★

1940

Shooting High ★ ★
Melody Ranch ★ ★ ★
Rancho Grande ★ ★ ★

1941

Down Mexico Way ★ ★ ★

1942

Cowboy Serenade ★ ★ ★

1947

Sioux City Sue ★ ★
Robin Hood of Texas ★ ★

1949

Loaded Pistols ★ ★

1950

Mule Train ★ ★

1951

Texans Never Cry ★ ★

1952

Apache Country ★ ★

1953

On Top of Old Smoky ★ ★ ★

FRANKIE AVALON
★ ★ 1.77 STARS

In terms of his singing, Frankie Avalon is a little better than Fabian; in films, he's a cut above Annette Funicello. These are questionable virtues, but it's difficult to assess a man's ability on the basis of Avalon's second-rate filmography.

He was born in September 1939 in Philadelphia. He played the trumpet well at the age of nine, and started singing during his teen years. His records, particularly "Venus," hit the top 10 regularly, and he had a boy-next-door look that made him perfect for teen-oriented movies. Avalon began in one of John Wayne's worst westerns, *The Alamo*, but gave a creditable performance in the compelling *Panic in the Year Zero!* Instead of challenges, he settled for drive-in fare such as: *Beach Party, Operation Bikini,* and *Beach Blanket Bingo*. The beach party movies showed him off poorly—his acting was as stiff as a surfboard. There was temporary rescue in a Bob Hope comedy, *I'll Take Sweden*, but then it was back to *How to Stuff a Wild Bikini*. In 1978 he had a humorous scene in *Grease*.

Most actors have more memorable highlights in their careers than looking out at the waves and yelling "Kowabunga!"

Frankie Avalon in *The Alamo*.

FILMOGRAPHY

1957

Jamboree ★ ★

1960

Guns of the Timberland ★ ★
The Alamo ★ ★

1961

Voyage to the Bottom of the Sea ★ ★

1962

Panic in the Year Zero! ★ ★ ★

1963

Beach Party ★
The Castilian ★ ★
Drums of Africa ★ ★
Operation Bikini ★ ★

1964

Bikini Beach ★
Muscle Beach Party ★

1965

Beach Blanket Bingo ★
I'll Take Sweden ★ ★ ★
Sergeant Deadhead ★ ★
How to Stuff a Wild Bikini ★
Mr. Goldfoot and the Bikini Machine ★

1966

Fireball 500 ★

1967

The Million Eyes of Su-Muru ★

1968

Skidoo ★ ★

1970

Horror House ★

1974

The Take ★ ★ ★

1978

Grease ★ ★ ★

LEW AYRES
★ ★ ★ 3.10 STARS

Sometimes a performer gets the role of a lifetime early in his career, and everything after it is anticlimatic. This happened to Lew Ayres, a highly capable and sincere actor. The film was *All Quiet on the Western Front*, with Ayres brilliantly playing a soldier who loses his idealistic notions of war during combat.

Born in 1908, in Minneapolis, Minnesota, he gained international acclaim at the age of twenty-two. As the disillusioned soldier in *All Quiet on the Western Front* his performance summed up the way many felt after the First World War. His next movies were letdowns to those who had lauded him a great actor: *East Is West* with Lupe Velez, *Up for Murder*, and *The Impatient Maiden*, one of his first doctor roles. *State Fair*, with Will Rogers, though inferior to the musical remake, had a warm, folksy feeling. He slid into a group of films too minor for even late-night TV: *Cross Country Cruise, Let's be Ritzy,* and *The Leathernecks Have Landed*.

Ayres came back in *Holiday* as Katharine Hepburn's wastrel brother. This led to other strong co-stars: Lana Turner in *These Glamour*

Lew Ayres with Jane Wyman in *Johnny Belinda.*

Girls, Jeanette MacDonald in *Broadway Serenade,* and Greer Garson in *Remember?* (A film she refers to as "Forgive and Forget").

In 1938, Ayres began his best phase (commercially) as Doctor Kildare. He made nine Kildare films, and Laraine Day was his partner until she died on *Dr. Kildare's Wedding Day.* His career died shortly after when he registered as a conscientious objector during the war and stirred up the contempt of Hollywood. But his beliefs were apparently sincere; he became a chaplain, and then an orderly on the front lines.

His two best performances came at the war's end: as the sympathetic doctor who rescues mute Jane Wyman in *Johnny Belinda,* and as a psychiatrist who has to decide which of two twins (played by Olivia De Havilland) is an insane murderess in *The Dark Mirror.*

Ayres, like Joel McCrea, who starred in the first Kildare film, is underrated today because his work lacks flash, but his acting is a quiet demonstration of a master at work.

FILMOGRAPHY

1929

The Sophomore (bit)
The Kiss ★★★

1930

All Quiet on the Western Front ★★★★
The Doorway to Hell ★★★
Common Clay ★★★
East Is West ★★

1931

Many a Slip ★★★
Iron Man ★★
Up for Murder ★★
The Spirit of Notre Dame ★★★
Heaven on Earth ★★★

1932

The Impatient Maiden ★★★
Night World ★★★
Okay America ★★

1933

State Fair ★★★
Don't Bet on Love ★★
My Weakness ★★

1934

Cross Country Cruise ★★★
Let's Be Ritzy ★★★
She Learned About Sailors ★★★
Servants' Entrance ★★★

1935

The Lottery Lover ★★★
Silk Hat Kid ★★★
Spring Tonic ★★★

1936

The Leathernecks Have Landed ★★★
Panic on the Air ★★★
Shakedown ★★★
Lady Be Careful ★★★
Murder With Pictures ★★★
Hearts in Bondage ★★★

1937

The Crime Nobody Saw ★★★
The Last Train From Madrid ★★★
Hold 'Em Navy ★★★

1938

Scandal Street ★★★
King of the Newsboys ★★★
Holiday ★★★★
Rich Man, Poor Girl ★★★
Young Dr. Kildare ★★★★
Spring Madness ★★★

1939

Ice Follies of 1939 ★★
Broadway Serenade ★★★
These Glamour Girls ★★★
The Secret of Dr. Kildare ★★★★
Remember? ★★
Calling Dr. Kildare ★★★

1940

Dr. Kildare's Strange Case ★★★★
Dr. Kildare Goes Home ★★★★
The Golden Fleecing ★★★
Dr. Kildare's Crisis ★★★★

Lew Ayres in *Holiday.*

1941

Maisie Was a Lady ★★★
The People vs. Dr. Kildare ★★★★
Dr. Kildare's Wedding Day ★★★★

1942

Dr. Kildare's Victory ★★★★
Fingers at the Window ★★★

1946

The Dark Mirror ★★★★

1947

The Unfaithful ★★★★

1948

Johnny Belinda ★★★★

1950

The Capture ★★★

1951

New Mexico ★★★

1953

No Escape ★★★
Donovan's Brain ★★★

1962

Advise and Consent ★★★★

1964

The Carpetbaggers ★★★★

1972

The Biscuit Eater ★★★
The Man ★★★

LAUREN BACALL
★★½ 2.64 STARS

A Broadway producer recently remarked, "If it wasn't for Bogart, Bacall would have been washed up years ago." In light of her many accomplishments since his death in 1957, this seems dubious. On stage and screen she has demonstrated a flair for comedy, for the musical (though she candidly asks, "Why wasn't I born with a voice?") and for serious drama. Stardom is one thing—but her marriage to Bogart has made her, by association, a legend.

Before the legend began, Bacall (born Betty Perske in the Bronx, 1924) modeled for magazine covers. Director Howard Hawks developed her cool, cynical sexuality and paired her with Bogart in *To Have and Have Not.* It was an electric combination that worked offscreen as well, and they were married shortly afterwards. Reaction to the film was enthusiastic, and they scored again in the enjoyable though incomprehensible *The Big Sleep*. In *Confidential Agent*, Bacall felt the director, Herman Shumlin, gave her no help and claimed it took her years to climb back up to the "Goddamn ladder." *Dark Passage* and *Key Largo* were follow-ups with Bogart, but in the former she was overshadowed by Agnes Moorehead, and in the latter by Claire Trevor. In *Young Man with a Horn*,

Lauren Bacall with Humphrey Bogart in *The Big Sleep*.

she was cast as a neurotic dilettante who destroyed trumpet player Kirk Douglas. Claire Gaucher wrote in Movie Story, "Fans will like everything about it except the wooden performance of 'Baby' Bacall." She was better in *Bright Leaf* as the madam who waits patiently for Gary Cooper.

Movie roles dried up, and she jumped at the chance to play in *How to Marry a Millionaire* ("My best part in years.") It showcased her as a light comedienne, and her barrel voice was ideal for witty dialogue. *Woman's World* was just as good; Bacall was the wife of an executive (Fred MacMurray) who urged him to get out of the corporate rat race. *The Cobweb* was much less entertaining, a wildly overwrought study of mental patients. Bacall was one of the few sane members of the cast. There wasn't much to do in John Wayne's *Blood Alley*, though she was surprised to find him "warm, likeable and helpful." *Written on the Wind* was a shameless melodrama, but the combined acting contributions of Bacall, Robert Stack, and Dorothy Malone (who won an Oscar) made it hypnotically watchable.

Returning to comedy, she carried *Designing Woman*, since co-star Gregory Peck had "no sense of humor" (Sheilah Graham). *The Gift of Love* was a remake of *Sentimental Journey* and even sudsier. *Sex and the Single Girl* and *Shock Treatment* were, respectively, frantic comedy and poor melodrama.

Broadway handed her a new lease on life when the quality of her pictures declined. "Goodbye Charlie" drew theatre audiences on her name, despite a labored script, and she got more love letters from critics for "Cactus Flower," "Applause," and "Woman of the Year."

The differences between her work with Bogart and without him have nothing to do with her star quality. Today Bacall has glamour, authority, indestructibility, and a commanding charm. But the suggestion of softness, the vulnerability behind the poised exterior is gone.

FILMOGRAPHY

1944

To Have and Have Not ★★★★

1945

Confidential Agent ★★

1946

Two Guys from Milwaukee (cameo)
The Big Sleep ★★★★

1947

Dark Passage ★★★

1948

Key Largo ★★★

1950

Young Man With a Horn ★★
Bright Leaf ★★★

1953

How to Marry a Millionaire ★★★

1954

Woman's World ★★★

1955

The Cobweb ★★
Blood Alley ★★

Lauren Bacall in *The Fan*.

1957

Written on the Wind ★★★
Designing Woman ★★★

1958

The Gift of Love ★★

1959

North West Frontier ★★★

1964

Shock Treatment ★★

1965

Sex and the Single Girl ★★

1966

Harper ★★★

1974

Murder on the Orient Express ★★★

1976

The Shootist ★★★

1979

Health ★

1981

The Fan ★★

LUCILLE BALL
★★★ 3.03 STARS

Lucille Ball once told columnist Rex Reed, "I made loads of films, but I never really made it the easy way. TV made me what I am today." Looking back over her movies, one has to conclude that Lucy was right. She was energetic and appealing in all of her films, but they rarely matched her talent.

She was born in 1911, in Jamestown, New York. After a brief period as a Hattie Carnegie model, she had bit parts in *Nana*, *Broadway Bill*, and *Roberta*. Hollywood was indifferent, so she went to Broadway in "Hi Diddle Diddle." Her first

Lucille Ball.

"class" film was *Stage Door,* and she had star billing in *Too Many Girls* with Desi Arnaz ("A prophetic title," Hedda Hopper said later, referring to their marital troubles). It wasn't until *The Big Street,* in which she played a crippled actress, that she got strong critical acclaim. She outshone Tracy and Hepburn in the dreary *Without Love* and did the same to stars Esther Williams and Van Johnson in *Easy to Wed.* She gave an underrated dramatic performance in *Lured,* as the target of murderous Cedric Hardwicke and made good chemistry with William Holden in the clever *Miss Grant Takes Richmond.*

Her best movies pre-"I Love Lucy" were Bob Hope comedies, *Fancy Pants* and *Sorrowful Jones.* As a result of her TV success, she was offered *The Long, Long Trailer,* a comedy triumph with Arnaz. *Forever Darling* was outdated fluff about a guardian angel (James Mason), but *The Facts of Life* with Hope was a delight. Lucy overreached herself when she tried a musical; in her own words, "I never could sing, though I tried in *Mame.*"

Despite the up-and-down quality of her pictures, Ball's talent is undeniable. She's one of our great comediennes, and when the material is right, a fine dramatic actress too.

FILMOGRAPHY

1933

Broadway Thru a Keyhole (bit)
Blood Money (bit)
Roman Scandals (bit)

1934

Moulin Rouge (bit)
Nana (bit)
Bottoms Up (bit)
Hold That Girl (bit)
Bulldog Drummond Strikes Back (bit)
The Affairs of Cellini (bit)
Kid Millions (bit)
Broadway Bill (bit)
Jealousy (bit)
The Fugitive Lady (bit)
Men of the Night (bit)

1935

Carnival ★★★
Roberta (bit)
Old Man Rhythm (bit)
Top Hat ★★★
I Dream Too Much ★★★

1936

Chatterbox ★★★
Follow the Fleet ★★★
Bunker Bean ★★★
The Farmer in the Dell ★★★

1937

Stage Door ★★★★
That Girl from Paris ★★★
Winterset (bit)
Don't Tell the Wife ★★★

1938

Go Chase Yourself ★★★
Having Wonderful Time ★★★
Joy of Living ★★★
The Affairs of Annabel ★★★
Room Service ★★★
Next Time I Marry ★★★
Annabel Takes a Tour ★★★

1939

Beauty for the Asking ★★★
Twelve Crowded Hours ★★★
Panama Lady ★★★
Five Came Back ★★★
That's Right—You're Wrong ★★★

1940

The Marines Fly High ★★★
You Can't Fool Your Wife ★★★★
Dance Girl Dance ★★★
Too Many Girls ★★★

1941

A Girl, a Guy and a Gob ★★★
Look Who's Laughing ★★★

1942

Valley of the Sun ★★★
The Big Street ★★★★
Seven Days' Leave ★★★

1943

Du Barry Was a Lady ★★★
Best Foot Forward ★★★
Thousands Cheer (cameo)

1944

Meet the People ★★

1945

Without Love ★★★
Abbott and Costello in Hollywood (cameo)

1946

Ziegfeld Follies (cameo)
The Dark Corner ★★★
Lover Come Back ★★★
Easy to Wed ★★★★
Two Smart People ★★★

1947

Her Husband's Affairs ★★★
Lured ★★★★

1949

Sorrowful Jones ★★★★
Miss Grant Takes Richmond ★★★★
Easy Living ★★★

1950

A Woman of Distinction (cameo)
Fancy Pants ★★★★
The Fuller Brush Girl ★★★

1951

The Magic Carpet ★ ★

1954

The Long, Long Trailer ★ ★ ★ ★

1956

Forever Darling ★ ★

1960

The Facts of Life ★ ★ ★

1963

Critic's Choice ★ ★

1967

A Guide for the Married Man (cameo)

1968

Yours, Mine and Ours ★ ★ ★

1974

Mame ★

MARTIN BALSAM
★ ★ ★ 3.12 STARS

Some actors have a personality that imposes itself on every role. Others disappear totally into whatever part they play. Martin Balsam falls into the latter category. His man-on-the-street face and physique are ideally suited for heroes, weaklings, and villains—anything the script requires.

He was born in New York, in 1919. Balsam also got his training in New York at the Actor's Studio. His first film was the prize winning *On the Waterfront*, and he was impressive in his second, Sidney Lumet's masterful *12 Angry Men. Time Limit* gave him a good role as a cynical officer's aide, and he was convincing as Natalie Wood's suitor in the otherwise disappointing *Marjorie Morningstar.* He increased his range playing a detective in *Psycho* and did some other fine pictures: *Breakfast at Tiffany's, Seven Days in May,* and *Summer Wishes, Winter Dreams.* In 1965, he won an Oscar for Best Supporting Actor for *A Thousand Clowns.* Always reliable but rarely recognized, Martin Balsam is the type of actor that Hollywood needs more of.

Martin Balsam in *The Sentinel.*

FILMOGRAPHY

1954

On the Waterfront ★ ★ ★

1957

12 Angry Men ★ ★ ★ ★
Time Limit ★ ★ ★ ★

1958

Marjorie Morningstar ★ ★ ★

1959

Al Capone ★ ★ ★
Middle of the Night ★ ★ ★

1960

Psycho ★ ★ ★ ★
Everybody Go Home! ★ ★ ★

1961

Ada ★ ★ ★
Breakfast at Tiffany's ★ ★ ★

1962

Cape Fear ★ ★ ★
Conquered City ★ ★ ★

1963

Who's Been Sleeping in My Bed? ★ ★ ★

1964

The Carpetbaggers ★ ★ ★
Seven Days in May ★ ★ ★

1965

A Thousand Clowns ★ ★ ★ ★
Harlow ★ ★ ★
The Bedford Incident ★ ★ ★

1966

After the Fox ★ ★ ★

1967

Hombre ★ ★ ★

1969

Me Natalie ★ ★ ★ ★
Trilogy ★ ★ ★
The Good Guys and the Bad Guys ★ ★ ★

1970

Catch-22 ★ ★ ★
Tora! Tora! Tora! ★ ★
Little Big Man ★ ★ ★

1971

The Anderson Tapes ★ ★ ★
Confessione di un Commissario di Polizia al Procuratore della Repubblica ★ ★ ★

1972

The Man ★ ★ ★

1973

The Stone Killer ★ ★ ★
Summer Wishes, Winter Dreams ★ ★ ★ ★
I Consiglieri ★ ★ ★

1974

The Taking of Pelham One Two Three ★ ★ ★
Murder on the Orient Express ★ ★ ★
Counselor at Crime ★ ★ ★

1975

Il Tempo degli Assassini ★ ★ ★
Mitchell ★ ★ ★

1976

All the President's Men ★ ★ ★
Two-Minute Warning ★ ★ ★

1977

The Sentinel ★ ★ ★
Silver Bears ★ ★ ★

1979

Cuba ★ ★ ★

1980

Cry Onion ★ ★ ★

ANNE BANCROFT
★ ★ ★ 2.78 STARS

For a performer who once claimed, "the man I marry must accept the fact that I am a totally involved actress," Anne Bancroft's series of 'B' picture roles in the early 1950s must have been frustrating. Fortunately for her (and for us), she went back to New York and acted so brilliantly on Broadway that Hollywood was forced to take a second look.

Bronx born, in 1931, she changed her real name, Anna Maria Louise Italiano, to Anne Marno before Bancroft. She started out in television and went to 20th Century Fox for *Don't Bother to Knock.* Her portrayal of a nightclub singer was more believable than Marilyn Monroe's performance as a deranged babysitter. But no one noticed, and she got trapped in mediocre films like *Gorilla at Large* and *Demetrius and the Gladiators.* Lessons with Herbert Berghof were "the beginning of

Anne Bancroft in *Seven Women.*

a whole new approach to acting, a deeper, more fulfilling and more thinking approach." The training showed when she got raves on Broadway as Gittel in "Two for the Seesaw" and a Tony award for her portrayal of Anne Sullivan in "The Miracle Worker." Later, Bancroft received an Oscar for her performance in *The Miracle Worker* when it was transferred to film.

Of all her fine parts, the one best remembered and most treasured is still Mrs. Robinson in *The Graduate.* Cunning, provocative, and vaguely evil, she contributed immeasurably to some of the funniest scenes in movie history. She was also superb as an aging ballerina in *The Turning Point.* Her versatility has recently been displayed in other fields as well—she wrote and directed *Fatso.*

Bancroft has an unusual aptitude; she can be funky or classy, whatever the occasion demands. This intriguing mixture makes her a human being audiences feel they can identify with—and appreciate.

FILMOGRAPHY

1952

Don't Bother to Knock ★★★

1953

Tonight We Sing ★★
Treasure of the Golden Condor ★★
The Kid from Left Field ★★

1954

Gorilla at Large ★★
Demetrius and the Gladiators ★★
The Raid ★★

1955

New York Confidential ★★★
A Life in the Balance ★★★
The Naked Street ★★★
The Last Frontier ★★★

1956

Walk the Proud Land ★★★

1957

Nightfall ★★★
The Restless Breed ★★★
The Girl in Black Stockings ★★★

1962

The Miracle Worker ★★★★

1964

The Pumpkin Eater ★★★★

1965

The Slender Thread ★★★

1966

Seven Women ★★

1967

The Graduate ★★★★

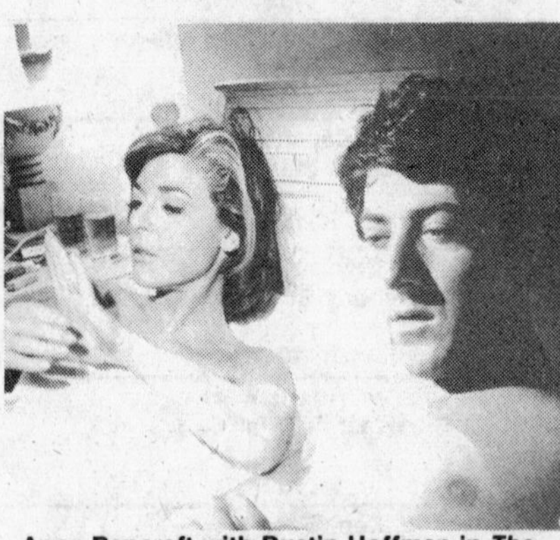
Anne Bancroft with Dustin Hoffman in *The Graduate.*

1972

Young Winston ★★★

1975

The Prisoner of Second Avenue ★★
The Hindenburg ★★

1976

Lipstick ★★★
Silent Movie (cameo)

1977

The Turning Point ★★★★

1979

Fatso (direction, screenplay) ★★

1980

The Elephant Man ★★★

TALLULAH BANKHEAD
★★½ 2.27 STARS

Tallulah Bankhead's name sets a specific image in the minds of movie buffs—deep voice, sophistication, and unconventional sexual behavior. Yet it's unlikely that even devoted fans remember her films, with the exception of Hitchcock's *Lifeboat.*

Always controversial, she seemed more adept at generating publicity than movie parts. She was born in Huntsville, Alabama, in 1903, the daughter of a Congressional Speaker of the House. At age fifteen, she left her convent school to work on the New York stage. Shortly afterwards, she moved to London where she was the star of the theatre scene. Her striking good looks, raspy voice, "Noel Coward-esque" wit and much publicized promiscuity assured her the limelight. When she tried her touch on Hollywood, though, her star never shone quite as bright.

Tarnished Lady and *My Sin* were two of her early melodramas, and she was as artificial as the unimaginative plots. Gary Cooper costarred in *Devil and the Deep,* but Bankhead's career was sinking until *Lifeboat* pulled it ashore. She won the New York Film Critics Award for that and made people sit up, especially since it followed her legendary Regina in "The Little Foxes" on Broadway. Bankhead also hosted a radio program, "The Big Show," and later did TV. But good movie scripts were hard to find, and her

Tallulah Bankhead in *Lifeboat.*

swan song was *Die! Die! My Darling!* as the madwoman who imprisoned Stephanie Powers (of "Hart to Hart"). It was a sad farewell to a vivid and original personality.

FILMOGRAPHY

1918

When Men Betray ★★
30 a Week ★★

1928

His House in Order ★★
A Woman's Law ★★

1931

Tarnished Lady ★★
My Sin ★★
The Cheat ★★

1932

Devil and the Deep ★★
Thunder Below ★★
Make Me a Star (cameo)
Faithless ★★★

1943

Stage Door Canteen ★★

1944

Lifeboat ★★★★

1945

A Royal Scandal ★★★

1953

Main Street to Broadway ★★

1965

Die! Die! My Darling! ★★

1966

The Daydreamer (voice only)

BRIGITTE BARDOT
★★★ 2.95 STARS

Many glamour stars who pout or play at being a sex kitten seem too knowing, too narcissistic. But Brigitte Bardot really *seemed* like a naughty child enjoying the fuss she was creating.

Born in 1934, in Paris, Bardot was a magazine cover girl at the age of fifteen when director Roger Vadim detected her potential, He married her and created her sex-kitten image in *And God Created Woman*. Suddenly, French movies were not only "art" films but also mainstream commercial cinema. Forgotten were her minor parts in such films as

Brigitte Bardot.

Doctor at Sea, one of a popular series with Dirk Bogarde. A series of hits, *Les Bijoutiers du Claire de Lune, En Cas de Malheur,* and *La Femme et le Pantin*, established her as the leading sex symbol of the late 1950s and 1960s. In 1957, Bardot divorced Vadim and married the costar of *Babette s'en va-t-en Guerre*, Jacques Charrier. A suicide attempt in 1960 created further notoriety. Some of her English-speaking ventures proved she couldn't "translate" the way Sophia Loren and others had. *Shalako* was a tedious western with Sean Connery, and *Dear Brigitte*, a comedy with James Stewart, was one of his few box-office flops. *Viva Maria* with Jeanne Moreau did well in its native country but was ignored in the U.S.

She hosted a TV special that garnered low ratings, and then announced her retirement. Bardot had announced it several times before, but this time (in 1973) she kept her word. Journalists now take her more than seriously as an actress than they did in her heyday, and her work in *La Vérité* seems to justify their enthusiasm.

FILMOGRAPHY

1952

Le Trou normand ★★★
Manina La Fille sans Voiles ★★★

1953

Les Dents longues ★★★
Le Portrait de son Père ★★★

1954

Si Versailles m'était conte ★★★
Act of Love ★★★
Tradita ★★★

1955

Le Fils de Caroline Chérie ★★★
Futures Vedettes ★★★
Doctor at Sea ★★★
Frou-Frou ★★★
Les Grandes Manoeuvres ★★★

1956

Helen of Troy ★★★
La Lumière d'en Face ★★★
Cette Sacrée Gamine ★★★
Mio Figlio Nerone ★★★
En effeuillant la Marguerite ★★★
And God Created Woman ★★★★
La Mariée est trop Belle ★★★

1957

Une Parisienne ★★

1958

Les Bijoutiers du Claire de Lune ★★★
En Cas de Malheur ★★★

1959

La Femme et le Pantin ★★
Babette s'en va-t-en Guerre ★★★
Voulez-vous danser avec moi? ★★★

1960

Le Testament d'Orphee ★★★
La Vérité ★★★★

1961

La Bride sur le Cou ★★★
Les Amours célèbres ★★★

1962

La Vie privée ★★★
Le Repos du Guerrier ★★★

1963

Le Mépris ★★★

1964

Une Ravissante Idiote ★★★

1965

Viva Maria ★★
Dear Brigitte (cameo)

1966

Masculine Feminine (cameo)

1967

A coeur joie ★★★

1968

Shalako ★★
Histoires extraordinaires ★★★
Spirits of the Dead (cameo)

1969

Les Femmes ★★★

1970

L'Ours et la Poupée ★★★

1971

Boulevard du Rhum ★★★
Les Pétroleuses ★★★

1973

Don Juan 1973 ou Si Don Juan était une Femme ★★★
Colinot Trousse-Chemise ★★★

ETHEL BARRYMORE
★ ★ ★ ½ 3.30 STARS

All great stars have instantly recognizable voices, and Ethel Barrymore's voice was one of the most distinctive. It gave a touch of class to every film she appeared in.

Born in 1879, she first appeared on stage with her uncle, John Drew, at the age of fifteen and then had a starring part in "Captain Jinks of the Horse Marines" in 1900 on Broadway. After winning recognition as the First Lady of the American Theatre, Barrymore turned to films. There were several silents—*The Nightingale, Life's Whirlpool,* and *The Eternal Mother*—and a notable sound feature, *Rasputin and the Empress* in 1933, with brothers John and Lionel. *None But the Lonely Heart* brought her an Oscar, and she dominated her scenes in *The Spiral Staircase* as the bedridden mother of a psychopath. Her warmth brought magic to *The Farmer's Daughter,* and she was the only saving grace of *Night Song.* There were other films, some worthy of her—*Pinky, Portrait of Jennie,* and *Young at Heart* but others were overblown trash that desperately needed her authority—*The Paradine Case* and *The Red Danube.* Barrymore died in 1959, leaving a legacy of glowing supporting portrayals behind her.

Ethel Barrymore in *The Red Danube.*

FILMOGRAPHY
(features only)

1918

Our Mrs. McChesney ★ ★ ★

1919

The Divorcee ★ ★ ★

1933

Rasputin and the Empress ★ ★ ★

1944

None But the Lonely Heart ★ ★ ★ ★

1946

The Spiral Staircase ★ ★ ★ ★

1947

The Farmer's Daughter ★ ★ ★ ★
Moss Rose ★ ★ ★ ★
Night Song ★ ★ ★

1948

The Paradine Case ★ ★ ★
Moonrise ★ ★ ★

1949

Portrait of Jennie ★ ★ ★
The Great Sinner ★ ★ ★
That Midnight Kiss ★ ★ ★
The Red Danube ★ ★ ★
Pinky ★ ★ ★ ★

1951

Kind Lady ★ ★ ★ ★
The Secret of Convict Lake ★ ★ ★

1952

It's a Big Country ★ ★ ★
Deadline U.S.A. ★ ★ ★
Just For You ★ ★ ★

1953

The Story of Three Loves ★ ★ ★
Main Street to Broadway (cameo)

1955

Young at Heart ★ ★ ★ ★

1957

Johnny Trouble ★ ★ ★

JOHN BARRYMORE
★ ★ ★ 3.25 STARS

The sight of young Drew Barrymore in *E.T.* is a new and touching reminder of her glittering heritage. Lionel, Ethel, and John were all literally worshipped for their talents by their contemporaries, and Mary Astor referred to John Barrymore as "one of the few greats of our time." He was a romantic hero, known as The Great Profile, a modern dramatic actor and a master of Shakespeare. He was also a heavy drinker by age twenty-five but continued in the limelight for another 35 years.

John Barrymore.

Born in 1882, Barrymore was receiving rave reviews on the stage by 1907 and made his first silent *An American Citizen* in 1913. *Dr. Jekyll and Mr. Hyde* was a huge success on the screen, and Barrymore's performance was held up as definitive 20 years later by critics reviewing Spencer Tracy's interpretation. He did a play, "Claire de Lune," written by his second wife, Michael Strange (mother of Diana) and then played Sherlock Holmes in 1922. Barrymore's rebellious streak became apparent during the shooting of *Beau Brummel* with his then-lover Mary Astor. He made bawdy remarks instead of following the script (the film was silent), and hundreds of deaf people read his lips and wrote in to express their shock. *Don Juan,* again with Astor, made a fortune, and was the first silent released with Vitaphone music and sound effects.

One of his early talkies was *Moby Dick,* again a performance remembered favorably when Gregory Peck remade it. *Svengali* was more enjoyable, though, and Barrymore hammed it up exuberantly as the coach who hypnotized singer Marion Marsh into stardom.

Grand Hotel won an Oscar for Best Picture, and though it seems antiquated today, Barrymore had Garbo and Crawford to help put it over at the box office. *A Bill of Divorcement* held up better, although the debuting Katharine Hepburn reportedly said she would never act with him again (to which Barrymore answered, "Have you?"). *Dinner at Eight* featured both the Barrymore brothers, but crusty Marie Dressler stole the film. By this time his drinking was interfering with his ability to remember lines. *Twentieth Century* was considered by many buffs to be his finest hour, a lunatic comedy aboard a train with Carole Lombard. It spawned a Broadway musical hit but now appears noisy and strained.

He brought his Shakespearean training to the screen in *Romeo and Juliet*, and as Jeanette MacDonald's husband in *Maytime*, he supplied relief from some of the ear-splitting operetta. Except for the hilarious *Midnight*, there wasn't much to be said for Barrymore's later pictures: *Bulldog Drummond Comes Back* and *Night Club Scandal*. *Marie Antoinette* was more prestigious but boring, and *The Great Profile* parodied the drunk old actor he had become.

It's important for today's film lovers to look beyond the self-destruction and deterioration of once-great performers like Barrymore and study them at their height. Too much can be lost if gossip and headlines are allowed to obscure the kind of brilliance Barrymore displayed in *Dr. Jekyll and Mr. Hyde* or *A Bill of Divorcement*.

FILMOGRAPHY
(features only)

1918

The Test of Honor ★★★
On the Quiet ★★★

1919

Here Comes the Bride ★★★

1920

Dr. Jekyll and Mr. Hyde ★★★★

1921

The Lotus Eater ★★★

1922

Sherlock Holmes ★★★★

1924

Beau Brummel ★★★

1926

Don Juan ★★★
The Sea Beast ★★★★

1927

When a Man Loves ★★★
The Beloved Rogue ★★★

1928

Tempest ★★★

1929

Eternal Love ★★★
The Show of Shows ★★★

1930

General Crack ★★★
The Man from Blankley's ★★★
Moby Dick ★★★★

1931

Svengali ★★★★
The Mad Genius ★★★★

1932

Arsène Lupin ★★★
Grand Hotel ★★★
State's Attorney ★★★
A Bill of Divorcement ★★★★

John Barrymore with Greta Garbo in *Grand Hotel*.

1933

Counselor at Law ★★★★
Rasputin and the Empress ★★★
Topaze ★★★★
Reunion in Vienna ★★★
Dinner at Eight ★★★★
Night Flight ★★★

1934

Twentieth Century ★★★
Long Lost Father ★★★

1936

Romeo and Juliet ★★★

1937

Maytime ★★★
Bulldog Drummond Comes Back ★★★
Night Club Scandal ★★★
True Confession ★★★
Bulldog Drummond's Revenge ★★★

1938

Bulldog Drummond's Peril ★★★
Romance in the Dark ★★★
Marie Antoinette ★★★★
Spawn of the North ★★★
Hold That Co-Ed ★★★★

1939

The Great Man Votes ★★★★
Midnight ★★★★

1940

The Great Profile ★★★

1941

The Invisible Woman ★★
World Premiere ★★★
Playmates ★★

LIONEL BARRYMORE
★★★ 3.05 STARS

Modern opinion is divided on Lionel Barrymore. Some, like critic David Shipman, call him an old bore; others, like Joan Crawford, testify to his greatness. While he made far more films than either of his siblings, he seemed to have less effect. Whatever the truth, he was one of a kind—a distinct individual, a true Barrymore like Ethel and John.

Philadelphia-born in 1878, Lionel made his mark on the stage and started his movie career in 1911 with *Fighting Blood*. His first talkie featured some effective courtroom fireworks in *A Free Soul* with Clark Gable, and he appeared with brother John in the Oscar-winning *Grand Hotel*. He overdid things in *Rasputin and the Empress*, and the critics were not kind about *Camille*. His portrayal of Dan Peggotty in *David Copperfield* was much more controlled, and he made an effective Andrew Jackson in *The Gorgeous Hussy*. There were other classic films—*Captains Courageous* and *You Can't Take It With You*—until Barrymore reached the peak of his popularity in the *Dr. Kildare* series. He was a sympathetic psychiatrist in *The Secret Heart* and gave a superb performance as the gruff sea captain who trained his nephew to be a good sailor in *Down to the Sea in Ships*.

He was partially paralyzed in 1938 and continued to act from a wheelchair for the last fifteen years of his life.

FILMOGRAPHY

(features only)

1917

His Father's Son ★★★
The Millionaire's Double ★★★
Life's Whirlpool ★★★

1920

The Copperhead ★★★
The Devil's Garden ★★★
The Master Mind ★★★

1921

The Great Adventure ★★★
Jim the Penman ★★★

1922

Boomerang Bill ★★★
The Face in the Fog ★★★

1923

The Enemies of Women ★★★
Unseeing Eyes ★★★
The Eternal City ★★★

1924

Decameron Nights ★★★
America ★★★
Meddling Women ★★★
I Am the Man ★★★

1925

The Iron Man ★★★
Children of the Whirlwind ★★★
The Wrongdoers ★★★
The Splendid Road ★★★

1926

The Barrier ★★★
Brooding Eyes ★★★
The Lucky Lady ★★★
Paris at Midnight ★★★
The Bells ★★★
The Temptress ★★★

1927

The Show ★★★
Women Love Diamonds ★★★
Body and Soul ★★★
The Thirteenth Hour ★★★

1928

Sadie Thompson ★★★
Drums of Love ★★★
The Lion and the Mouse ★★★
West of Zanzibar ★★★
The River Woman ★★★

1929

Alias Jimmy Valentine ★★★
The Mysterious Island ★★★

1931

A Free Soul ★★★★
Guilty Hands ★★★
Yellow Ticket ★★★
Mata Hari ★★★

1932

Grand Hotel ★★★★
Broken Lullaby ★★★
Arsène Lupin ★★★
The Washington Masquerade ★★★

Lionel Barrymore with Elissa Landi in *Yellow Ticket.*

1933

Rasputin and the Empress ★★
Sweepings ★★★
Looking Forward ★★★
The Stranger's Return ★★★
Dinner at Eight ★★★★
One Man's Journey ★★★
Night Flight ★★★
Christopher Bean ★★★
Should Ladies Behave? ★★★

1934

This Side of Heaven ★★★
Carolina ★★★
The Girl from Missouri ★★★
Treasure Island ★★★★

1935

David Copperfield ★★★★
The Little Colonel ★★★
Mark of the Vampire ★★★
Public Hero No. 1 ★★★
The Return of Peter Grimm ★★★
Ah, Wilderness ★★★★

1936

The Voice of Bugle Ann ★★★
The Road to Glory ★★★
The Devil-Doll ★★★
The Gorgeous Hussy ★★

1937

Camille ★★
A Family Affair ★★★
Captains Courageous ★★★
Saratoga ★★★
Navy Blue and Gold ★★★

1940

A Yank at Oxford ★★★
Test Pilot ★★★
You Can't Take It With You ★★★
Young Dr. Kildare ★★★
(15 Kildare films, with Barrymore as Dr. Gillespie)
Let Freedom Ring ★★★
On Borrowed Time ★★★

1941

The Penalty ★★★
Lady Be Good ★★★

1942

Calling Dr. Gillespie ★★★
Tennessee Johnson ★★★

1943

A Guy Named Joe ★★★

1944

Three Men in White ★★★
Since You Went Away ★★★

1945

The Valley of Decision ★★★

1946

Three Wise Fools ★★★
The Secret Heart ★★★
It's a Wonderful Life ★★★

1947

Dark Delusion ★★★
Duel in the Sun ★★★★

1948

Key Largo ★★★

1949

Down to the Sea in Ships ★★★★

1950

Malaya ★★★
Right Cross ★★★

1951

Bannerline ★★★

1952

Lone Star ★★★

1953

Main Street to Broadway (cameo)

ALAN BATES
★★★½ 3.44 STARS

English actors sometimes seem distant and formal to American audiences. Even Dirk Bogarde, brilliant as he is, draws a thin line between himself and the viewer. Alan Bates makes direct contact. He's warm and approachable, even in unsympathetic roles.

He was born in Allestree, Derbyshire, England, in 1934. A number of stage successes, "Look Back In Anger," and "The Caretaker," preceded his film debut in *The Entertainer.* He was convincing as a

Alan Bates in *The Rose.*

runaway criminal in *Whistle Down the Wind* with Hayley Mills and outstanding in *A Kind of Loving* as a young man forced to marry his pregnant girlfriend. His sincerity was the sole asset of *The Running Man,* a thriller without suspense. He had better material in *Nothing But the Best* as a charming climber who resorted to murder. *Zorba the Greek* presented him as an uptight Englishman humanized by Anthony Quinn, and he was quietly effective against Quinn's excesses. *Georgy Girl* yielded an offbeat role as Lynn Redgrave's manic, free-spirited lover. Bates all but stole *Far from the Madding Crowd* an unjustly dismissed version of the Hardy novel, and he received an Oscar nomination for *The Fixer,* as a victim of anti-Semitism.

Recent parts, with the exception of *Women in Love,* have been less challenging, but he held together *An Unmarried Woman* with his warmth, making it impossible to believe Jill Clayburgh's rejection of him at the end. He went slightly overboard in *The Rose,* possibly infected by Bette Midler's hysteria, but his authority shone through the wreckage of *Nijinsky.* It is Bates's *authority* as an actor that is his greatest asset. He exudes a trustworthiness that makes him a sort of British Alan Alda.

1960

The Entertainer ★★★

1961

Whistle Down the Wind ★★★★

1962

A Kind of Loving ★★★

1963

The Running Man ★★★

1964

The Guest ★★★★
Nothing But the Best ★★★

1965

Zorba the Greek ★★★★

1966

Georgy Girl ★★★★
King of Hearts ★★★★

1967

Far from the Madding Crowd ★★★★

1968

The Fixer ★★★★

1970

Women in Love ★★★★
Three Sisters ★★★★

1971

The Go-Between ★★★★

1972

A Day in the Life of Joe Egg ★★★

1973

Impossible Object ★★★

1974

Butley ★★★★

1975

In Celebration ★★★
Royal Flash ★★★

1978

An Unmarried Woman ★★★★
The Shout ★★★
The Rose ★★

1979

Nijinsky ★★★

1981

Quartet ★★★
Return of the Soldier ★★★

ANNE BAXTER
★★★ 2.98 STARS

Journalist John Gold once commented, "In Hollywood, Miss Baxter is known for three things—driving ambition, unlimited energy and a completely honest, if occasionally withering tongue." This provides an excellent example of how real-life personality can be different from screen image.

Born in 1923, in Michigan City, Indiana, Baxter is the granddaughter of architect Frank Lloyd Wright. In films, Baxter is remembered today chiefly as the ever-loyal wife or the woman waiting on the sidelines for her man. Such sentimental films as *The Pied Piper* and *Crash Dive* reinforced her image of selfless devotion. *Sunday Dinner for a Soldier* (opposite husband John Hodiak) was the most successful of these harmless romances. She was brilliant on the two occasions when she was not typecast. The first, as the drunk and suicidal Sophie in *The Razor's Edge,* won her an Oscar for Best Supporting Actress. The second, *All About Eve,* gave her an exciting opponent in Bette Davis. With more opportunities like these, Baxter might have become a high-voltage presence on the screen, like Susan Hayward or even Bette Davis herself.

Anne Baxter in *Bedevilled.*

FILMOGRAPHY

1940

20 Mule Team ★★★
The Great Profile ★★★

1941

Charley's Aunt ★★★
Swamp Water ★★★

1942

The Magnificent Ambersons ★★★
The Pied Piper ★★★

1943

Crash Dive ★★★
Five Graves to Cairo ★★★★
The North Star ★★★

1944

The Sullivans ★★★
The Eve of St. Mark ★★★
Sunday Dinner for a Soldier ★★★
Guest in the House ★★★

1945

A Royal Scandal ★★★

1946

Smoky ★★★
Angel on My Shoulder ★★★
The Razor's Edge ★★★★

1947

Mother Wore Tights (narration)
Blaze of Noon ★★★

1948

Homecoming ★★★
The Walls of Jericho ★★★
The Luck of the Irish ★★★

1949

Yellow Sky ★★★
You're My Everything ★★★

1950

A Ticket to Tomahawk ★★★
All About Eve ★★★★

1951

Follow the Sun ★★★

1952

The Outcasts of Poker Flat ★★★
O. Henry's Full House ★★★★
My Wife's Best Friend ★★★

1953

I Confess ★★★★
The Blue Gardenia ★★★

1954

Carnival Story ★★★

1955

Bedevilled ★★
One Desire ★★★

1956

The Spoilers ★★★
The Come-On ★★
The Ten Commandments ★★★

1957

Three Violent People ★★★

1958

Chase a Crooked Shadow ★★★

1959

Summer of the Seventeenth Doll ★★★

1960

Cimarron ★★★

1962

A Walk on the Wild Side ★★

1963

Mix Me a Person ★★★

1965

The Family Jewels (cameo)

1966

The Tall Women ★★

1967

The Busy Body ★★

1971

Fool's Parade ★★★

1972

The Late Liz ★★★
Lapin 360 ★★

1980

Jane Austen in Manhattan ★★★

THE BEATLES
★★★ 3.00 STARS

Together and separately, the Beatles made legendary contributions to pop music. All of them had charm, wit, and individuality, but little of this ever came through on film.

John Lennon (born 1940, died 1980), Paul McCartney (born 1942), Ringo Starr (born Richard Starkey, 1940), and George Harrison (born 1943) were all raised in the slums of Liverpool. Brian Epstein, owner of a successful record store, discovered them and promoted the group into an unparalleled phenomenon. Their popularity led to their first film appearance in *A Hard Day's Night*, Richard Lester's goofy, freewheeling glimpse of their daily existence. It was the only first-rate movie they made. *Help!* had a few funny sight gags, but no coherence, and they contributed only vocals to *Yellow Submarine*, a lively animated feature mixing surrealism with fairytale plotting. They also appeared in a number of documentaries: *Pop Gear, What's Happening, Let It Be*, and *The Day the Music Died*.

The Beatles in *A Hard Day's Night*.

Lennon tried a solo acting career in the overlong but imaginative *Oh! What a Lovely War* (Richard Attenborough's first directing effort). Lennon was just one of several names, for his co-stars included Laurence Olivier, John Mills, John Gielgud, Michael Redgrave, and Dirk Bogarde. He also played a dying soldier in Richard Lester's black comedy *How I Won the War*.

Ringo showed more camera presence and an affable, unpretentious flair for comedy. Some of his films were horrifyingly bad *(Candy, The Magic Christian* and *Caveman)*, but he was relaxed in *That'll Be the Day* co-starring David Essex. It was a well-done tale about a youth searching for a niche in the rock world. Ringo appeared with George Harrison in the much-publicized *Concert for Bangladesh* and was also a participant in one of Ken Russell's hatchet jobs on classical composers, *Lisztomania*. George Harrison has recently entered films via producing and scoring in collaboration with the Monty Python gang. He produced *Time Bandits, The Life of Brain*, and *The Meaning of Life*.

Overall, it's strange that a foursome so witty and charismatic translated so uninterestingly to the screen.

FILMOGRAPHY

1964

A Hard Day's Night ★★★★

1965

Help! ★★
Pop Gear (documentary)

1968

Yellow Submarine (vocals only)

1970

What's Happening (documentary)
Let It Be (documentary)

1977

The Day the Music Died (documentary)

1982

The Compleat Beatles (documentary)

JOHN LENNON ONLY

1967

How I Won the War ★★★
Diaries, Notes, and Sketches (documentary)

John Lennon in *How I Won the War*.

1969

Oh! What a Lovely War ★ ★ ★

1971

Superstars in Film Concert (documentary)

RINGO STARR ONLY

1968

Candy ★ ★

1970

The Magic Christian ★ ★

1971

200 Motels ★ ★

1972

Concert For Bangladesh (documentary)
Blindman ★ ★

1974

That'll Be the Day ★ ★ ★
Son of Dracula ★ ★

1975

Lisztomania ★ ★

1978

Sextette ★ ★
The Last Waltz (documentary)

1981

Caveman ★ ★ ★

GEORGE HARRISON ONLY

1972

Concert for Bangladesh (documentary)

PAUL McCARTNEY ONLY

1981

Wings Over America (documentary)

WARREN BEATTY
★ ★ ★ 2.81 STARS

Warren Beatty's looks and his reputation for being a ladies' man (former lover Joan Collins called him "insatiable") are enough to sustain his career. But Beatty, who was once tagged "affected and oddly amateurish" by the New York Times, has matured into a fine actor and light comedian.

He was born in Richmond, Virginia, in 1937 and began acting in college. A Broadway role in William Inge's "A Loss of Roses" ended quickly, but he attracted attention on television's "The Affairs of Dobie Gillis." Beatty then made a much-publicized debut in *Splendor in the Grass*. He was called a "Brando and Dean copier," but his performance effectively projected the agonies of adolescent sexuality. He and co-star Natalie Wood made beautiful chemistry on *and off* the screen, but the scandalous publicity (Wood was married to Robert Wagner) didn't boost box-office receipts for Beatty's next film *The Roman Spring of Mrs. Stone*. Beatty was physically perfect as the gigolo who pursued Vivien Leigh, but his accent was unconvincing. He was outstanding in *All Fall Down*, but his character's name (Berri Berri) was distractingly silly and hurt the movie's overall impact. *Lilith* was a downbeat drama about life in a mental institution, and *Mickey One* was "an art film in the worst sense of that term," according to Pauline Kael. There were more failures: *Promise Her Anything*, a so-called comedy, and *Kaleidoscope*.

Up to this point, Beatty's slow, self-conscious delivery was his principal weakness as an actor. In *Bonnie and Clyde* (which he produced), the delivery was speeded up, and the results were gratifying for the film and his career. Beatty was nominated for an Oscar, but he chose a weak film for his next venture—*The Only Game in Town*, a dated and actionless love story with Elizabeth Taylor. *McCabe and Mrs. Miller*, with real-life love Julie Christie, had pretensions to art. Critics praised it, but audiences were wise enough to keep away.

Warren Beatty with Faye Dunaway in *Bonnie and Clyde.*

The film *$* borrowed from a hundred other heist thrillers, but *The Parallax View* was much better, an exciting thriller about political killings. Beatty finally found consistent footing when he produced and starred in *Shampoo*. The script teased his playboy image by casting him as a sexually active hairdresser. *The Fortune* wasn't nearly so fortunate at the box office, and film critic John Simon called him "disappointing," but *Heaven Can Wait* was as gigantically popular as *Shampoo*. A remake of *Here Comes Mr. Jordan*, it was lighthearted, irresistible entertainment. Beatty was endearing as the prizefighter who returned to earth after being sent to heaven before his time. The film also enjoyed terrific supporting performances by Charles Grodin, Dyan Cannon and Jack Warden. Beatty also wrote, directed, produced and starred in *Reds* with Diane Keaton (another in his long list of girlfriends). Although there were good moments in his overlong saga, Beatty failed to suggest the strength and commitment of communist hell-raiser John Reed.

Beatty's sharp intelligence in real life creeps into his performances. This shrewdness, blended with sex appeal and a continuing effort to stretch his talent bodes well for his continued prominence.

FILMOGRAPHY

1961

Splendor in the Grass ★ ★ ★ ★
The Roman Spring of Mrs. Stone ★ ★

1962

All Fall Down ★ ★ ★

1964

Lilith ★ ★ ★

1965

Mickey One ★ ★

1966

Promise Her Anything ★ ★
Kaleidoscope ★ ★

1967

Bonnie and Clyde ★ ★ ★ ★

Warren Beatty in *McCabe and Mrs. Miller.*

1970

The Only Game in Town ★ ★

1971

McCabe and Mrs. Miller ★ ★ ★
$ ★ ★ ★

1973

Year of the Woman (documentary)

1974

The Parallax View ★ ★ ★ ★

1975

The Fortune ★ ★
Shampoo ★ ★ ★

1978

Heaven Can Wait (direction) ★ ★ ★

1982

Reds (direction) ★ ★

BARBARA BEL GEDDES
★ ★ ★ 3.17 STARS

As J.R.'s mother on Dallas, Barbara Bel Geddes is known to millions. She has always been a powerful box-office name on Broadway, but somehow, her film career never took definite shape. She is unquestionably gifted but has failed to develop a specific image.

Born in 1922, in New York, she made her stage debut at the age of nineteen on Broadway in "Out of the Frying Pan." Her first film was *The Long Night* with Henry Fonda, a bleak, depressing drama that audiences shunned. However, critics were impressed when she played thirteen-year-old Katrin in the popular *I Remember Mama.* She received an Oscar nomination for successfully acting half her age. Although Bel Geddes lacked sex appeal and her vocal tendency to shoot upward at the end of every line made her sound pretentious, she showed sincerity and warmth. Her best early picture was *Caught,* as the bewildered bride of a maniacal, Howard Hughes-like millionaire. She appeared with Richard Widmark in an excellent Elia Kazan-directed thriller, *Panic in the Streets,* and she brought urgency to the role of Richard Basehart's worried girlfriend in *Fourteen Hours.* None of these registered with the public, so Bel Geddes returned to Broadway for "The Moon Is Blue" and "Cat on a Hot Tin Roof."

Her best opportunity came with Hitchcock's *Vertigo,* offering plain-faced normalcy as an interesting contrast to Kim Novak's enigmatic blonde beauty. The movie achieved classic status with a plot that "makes no sense whatsoever,"—Stephen H. Scheuer. Bel Geddes' mastery of the role of Midge in *Vertigo* seemed to offer an analogy of her professional situation: she offered warmth, sanity, and wit but still got passed over for sexier types.

Bel Geddes is not fundamentally a movie star, and the camera isn't in love with her. She does demonstrate great acting talent and by doing so proves again that acting ability has little to do with being a star.

Barbara Bel Geddes in *I Remember Mama.*

FILMOGRAPHY

1947

The Long Night ★ ★ ★

1948

I Remember Mama ★ ★ ★ ★
Blood on the Moon ★ ★ ★

1949

Caught ★ ★ ★ ★

1950

Panic in the Streets ★ ★ ★

1951

Fourteen Hours ★ ★ ★ ★

1958

Vertigo ★ ★ ★ ★

1959

The Five Pennies ★ ★ ★
Five Branded Women ★ ★

1961

By Love Possessed ★ ★ ★

1971

Summertree ★ ★ ★
The Todd Killings ★ ★

RALPH BELLAMY
★ ★ ★ ½ 3.28 STARS

Since his Broadway triumph in "Sunrise at Campobello," Ralph Bellamy has come to be linked in people's minds with President Roosevelt. He also played Roosevelt in the endless TV mini-series *The Winds of War.* But before his inauguration, there were dozens of varied parts in comedy and drama that showcased Bellamy's immense versatility.

Born in 1904, in Chicago, Illinois, he began his stage career in his teens, and at the age of twenty-three formed The Ralph Bellamy Players. His early film roles were in forgettable low-budget films. Bellamy's first great movie was *The Awful Truth,* which netted him a Best Supporting Actor Oscar nomination. Another classic comedy *His Girl Friday* followed.

Some of Bellamy's roles were routine—the *Ellery Queen* series, *The Wolf Man, The Ghost of Frankenstein*—but he brought power to *The Professionals.* He repeated his Roosevelt part in the

Ralph Bellamy in *His Girl Friday.*

screen adaptation of *Sunrise at Campobello* and coped bravely under the depressing circumstances with *Doctor's Wives*. His most recent appearance in *Trading Places*, as a cantankerous and mischievous magnate, shows that he still has some enjoyable performances left in him.

FILMOGRAPHY

1931

The Secret Six ★★★
The Magnificent Lie ★★★
Surrender ★★★

1932

Forbidden ★★★
Rebecca of Sunnybrook Farm ★★★★
Air Mail ★★★

1933

Second Hand Wife ★★★
Destination Unknown ★★★
The Picture Snatcher ★★★
Flying Devils ★★★
Ace of Aces ★★★

1934

Spitfire ★★★
This Man Is Mine ★★★

1935

Helldorado ★★★
Gigolette ★★★
Hands Across the Table ★★★★

1936

Dangerous Intrigue ★★★
The Man Who Lived Twice ★★★★

1937

Let's Get Married ★★★
The Awful Truth ★★★★

1938

Fools for Scandal ★★★
Boy Meets Girl ★★★★
Carefree ★★★

1939

Trade Winds ★★★
Let Us Live ★★★
Blind Alley ★★★

1940

His Girl Friday ★★★★
Brother Orchid ★★★
Dance Girl Dance ★★★

1940-41

The Ellery Queen series ★★★

1941

Footsteps in the Dark ★★★
Affectionately Yours ★★★
Dive Bomber ★★★
The Wolf Man ★★★★

1942

The Ghost of Frankenstein ★★★
Lady in a Jam ★★★

1944

Guest in the House ★★★★

1945

Delightfully Dangerous ★★★
Lady on a Train ★★★★

1955

The Court Martial of Billy Mitchell ★★★★

1960

Sunrise at Campobello ★★★★

1966

The Professionals ★★★★

1968

Rosemary's Baby ★★★★

1971

Doctor's Wives ★★★

1972

Cancel My Reservation ★★★

1977

Oh God! ★★★

1983

Trading Places ★★★

JEAN-PAUL BELMONDO
★★½ 2.41 STARS

Often typecast as a likable rogue, Jean-Paul Belmondo has made numerous bad films along with the good. He sometimes tends to let his image do the work for him, but he is always competent and, at his best, seems to portray his characters effortlessly.

Born outside of Paris in 1933, Belmondo studied at the Paris Conservatory and worked in the Paris theatre. He made his film debut in 1958, appearing in Marcel Carne's *The Cheaters* and in Marc Allegret's *Be Beautiful But Shut Up*. His performance in Jean-Luc Godard's first feature film, *Breathless*, established a relationship between actor and director that continued through *A Woman Is a Woman* and culminated in *Pierrot le Fou*. In *Breathless*, Belmondo portrayed a sympathetic but self-involved antihero, emanating a charming fatalism that made him a favorite of French audiences and an international star. Since his work with Godard, the highlights of his career have included *Leon Morin—Pretre*, *Mississippi Mermaid*, *Stavisky*, and *The Thief of Paris*.

Jean-Paul Belmondo with Jean Seberg in *Breathless.*

Jean-Paul Belmondo remains one of the dominant figures of French cinema. In addition to Marcel Carne and Jean-Luc Godard, he has worked with nearly all the major French directors of his generation including Francois Truffaut, Alain Resnais, Jean-Pierre Melville and Louis Malle.

FILMOGRAPHY

1958

Be Beautiful But Shut Up ★★
Drôle de Dimanche ★★

1959

Web of Passion ★★
Ein Engel auf Erden ★★★

1960

The Big Risk ★★
Breathless ★★★★
Moderato Cantabile ★★★
Love and the Frenchwoman ★★
Two Women ★★
Rita ★★

1961

The Love Makers ★★
Leon Morin—Pretre ★★★
A Woman Is a Woman ★★★
Un nomée La Rocca ★★

1962

A Monkey in Winter ★★

1963

Doulos—The Finger Man ★★
L'Aine de Ferchaux ★★
Sweet and Sour ★★★

1964

That Man From Rio ★★
Greed in the Sun ★★
Weekend at Dunkirk ★★
Banana Peel ★
Backfire ★
Male Hunt ★★

1965

Pierrot le Fou ★★★
Up to His Ears ★★

1966

Is Paris Burning? ★★★
Tender Scoundrel ★★

1967

Casino Royale (cameo)
The Thief of Paris ★★★

1968

Ho! ★★

1969

The Brain ★★
Mississippi Mermaid ★★★
Love Is a Funny Thing ★★

1970

Borsalino ★★

1971

Les Mariés de l'An Deux ★★★
The Burglars ★★★

1972

The Inheritor ★★★
Docteur Popaul ★★

1974

Le Magnifique ★★★
Stavisky ★★★★

1975

L'Incorrigible ★★
Night Caller ★

1976

L'Alpageur ★★★
Le Corps de mon Ennemi ★★★

1977

L'Animal ★★★

1979

Flic ou Voyou ★★★

1980

Le guignolo ★★★

1981

Le Professionel ★★★

WILLIAM BENDIX
★★★ 3.11 STARS

William Bendix was equally comfortable as a lovable family man or a homicidal maniac. He looked and talked like the Brooklyn-born man he was, but—in common with Walter Matthau—his ordinary mug disguised a complete mastery of characterization.

Born in 1906, he entered movies at the age of thirty-six. Bendix supported Spencer Tracy in *Woman of the Year* and shortly after had a brutal, showy role in *The Glass Key.* As a wisecracking marine, he added humor to the hard-hitting *Guadalcanal Diary.* In Hitchcock's *Lifeboat,* he played a superb role as a seaman who had his leg amputated, for which he received a Best Supporting Actor Oscar nomination. Praise was heaped on his performances in *The Hairy Ape, The Blue Dahlia,* and *The Dark Corner.* His one notable misfire was the sticky and superficial, *The Babe Ruth Story,* despite the fact that he had once actually played baseball in the minor leagues. But his low-key portrayals in *A Bell for Adano, The Big Steal,* and *Detective Story* made clear to any viewer why Bendix ranks among the top character actors of all time.

William Bendix in *China.*

FILMOGRAPHY

1942

Woman of the Year ★★★
Brooklyn Orchid ★★★
Wake Island ★★★
The Glass Key ★★★★
Who Done It? ★★★

1943

Taxi Mister ★★★
China ★★★
Hostages ★★★
Guadalcanal Diary ★★★★
Crystal Ball ★★★
Star Spangled Rhythm ★★★

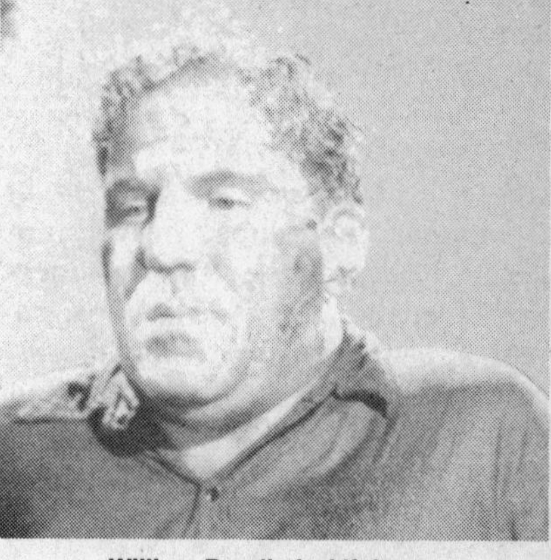

William Bendix in *Lifeboat.*

1944

Lifeboat ★★★★
The Hairy Ape ★★★★
Greenwich Village ★★★
Abroad With Two Yanks ★★★

1945

It's in the Bag ★★★
A Bell for Adano ★★★★
Don Juan Quilligan ★★★

1946

Sentimental Journey ★★★
The Dark Corner ★★★★
The Blue Dahlia ★★★★
Two Years Before the Mast ★★★★
White Tie and Tails ★★★

1947

Blaze of Noon ★★★
Calcutta ★★★
The Web ★★★
Where There's Life ★★★

1948

The Time of Your Life ★★★
The Babe Ruth Story ★★

1949

A Connecticut Yankee in King Arthur's Court ★★★
The Life of Riley ★★★
Streets of Laredo ★★★
The Big Steal ★★★★
Johnny Holiday ★★★
Cover Up ★★★

1950

Kill the Umpire ★★★
Gambling House ★★★

1951

Detective Story ★★★★
Submarine Command ★★★

1952

A Girl in Every Port ★★★★
Macao ★★★
Blackbeard the Pirate ★★

1954

Dangerous Mission ★★★

1955

Crashout ★★★
Battle Stations ★★★

1958

The Deep Six ★★★

1959

The Rough and the Smooth ★★★
Idle on Parade ★★

1961

Johnny Nobody ★★★

1962

Toller Hecht auf Krummer Tour ★★★

1963

Boy's Night Out ★★★
The Young and the Brave ★★★
For Love or Money ★★★

1964

Law of the Lawless ★★

1965

Young Fury ★★

RICHARD BENJAMIN
★★½ 2.44 STARS

Like Dustin Hoffman, Richard Benjamin's looks fall into the likably-average category, but he lacks the sex appeal Hoffman has in romantic leading roles. He can be excellent in light, comedic roles, though.

New York born in 1938, Benjamin studied drama at the High School of Performing Arts. He made two unimportant films as a teenager: *Crime Wave,* with the then-unknown Charles Bronson, and *Thunder Over the Plains.* Broadway stardom came with "The Star Spangled Girl," and he returned to films in a popular, well-done adaptation of author Philip Roth's *Goodbye Columbus.* It may still be his most effective performance. He was prissy and fastidious—but not very appealing—in *Diary of a Mad Housewife. The Marriage of a Young Stockbroker* was based on a novel by Charles Webb, author of *The Graduate,* but it lacked that film's sprightly pace and direction.

Richard Benjamin in *Westworld.*

Portnoy's Complaint was defeated by a heavy-handed treatment, but he was comfortable with the breezy dialogue in *The Last of Sheila,* and excellent in *Westworld.* He had a good, though subsidiary, role in *The Sunshine Boys* and provided amusing support for Walter Matthau in *House Calls. Love at First Bite* showed him off at his best as the doctor out to expose George Hamilton's Count Dracula. There was no saving *The Last Married Couple in America,* Natalie Wood's last film, but Benjamin then directed Peter O'Toole to a magnificent performance (which was Oscar nominated) in *My Favorite Year.* It looks as though he's opened a door to a bright new future on the other side of the camera.

FILMOGRAPHY

1953

Thunder Over the Plains ★★

1954

Crime Wave ★★

1969

Goodbye Columbus ★★★★

1970

Diary of a Mad Housewife ★★★
Catch-22 ★★★

1971

The Marriage of a Young Stockbroker ★★

1972

Portnoy's Complaint ★

1973

The Last of Sheila ★★★
Westworld ★★★

1975

The Sunshine Boys ★★

1978

House Calls ★★★

1979

Love at First Bite ★★★
The Last Married Couple in America ★★

1980

How to Beat the High Cost of Living ★★
First Family ★★

1981

Saturday the 14th ★★

JOAN BENNETT
★★★ 3.21 STARS

When she claimed, "I made more than 70 movies. . .six were worthwhile," Joan Bennett underrated herself. Although she didn't get the coveted Scarlett O'Hara role, commenting, "I wish Vivien Leigh had stayed in England," she did do a number of enjoyable pictures.

She was born into a theatrical family in 1910, in Palisades, New Jersey; her sister, Constance, father, Richard, and mother, Adrienne Morrison were all involved in acting. Joan Bennett's film career actually began with her portrayal of the witty heroine in one of the first good talkies, *Bulldog Drummond.* She was in the classic rendering of *Little Women* with Katharine Hepburn, and she joined Claudette Colbert and Charles Boyer in *Private Worlds,* a study of life in a mental institution, with excellent results. Her most famous phase—as a lethal femme fatale—began with *The Woman in the Window.*

Comedy also proved to be her forte when she played the mother in *Father of the Bride* opposite Spencer Tracy. A number of minor films including *Highway Dragnet* and *Desire in the Dust* marked a decline, but she made frequent guest appearances on TV.

Joan Bennett with Spencer Tracy in *Father of the Bride.*

FILMOGRAPHY

1916

The Valley of Decision (bit)

1923

The Eternal City (bit)

1928

Power ★★

1929

Bulldog Drummond ★★★
Three Live Ghosts ★★
Disraeli ★★★
Mississippi Gambler ★★★

1930

Puttin' on the Ritz ★★★
Crazy That Way ★★★
Moby Dick ★★★
Maybe It's Love ★★★
Scotland Yard ★★★

1931

Doctors' Wives ★★★
Many a Slip ★★★
Hush Money ★★★

1932

She Wanted a Millionaire ★★★★
Careless Lady ★★★
The Trial of Vivienne Ware ★★★★
Week-Ends Only ★★★
Wild Girl ★★★
Me and My Gal ★★★★

1933

Arizona to Broadway ★★★
Little Women ★★★★

1934

The Pursuit of Happiness ★★★

1935

The Man Who Reclaimed His Head ★★★
Private Worlds ★★★★
Mississippi ★★★
She Couldn't Take It ★★★★
The Man Who Broke the Bank at Monte Carlo ★★★
Two for Tonight ★★★

1936

13 Hours by Air ★★★
Big Brown Eyes ★★★
Two in a Crowd ★★★
Wedding Present ★★★

1938

I Met My Love Again ★★★
The Texans ★★★
Artists and Models Abroad ★★★
Vogues of 1938 ★★★

1939

Trade Winds ★★★★
The Man in the Iron Mask ★★★
The Housekeeper's Daughter ★★★

1940

Green Hell ★★★
The House Across the Bay ★★★★
The Man I Married ★★★★
The Son of Monte Cristo ★★★

1941

Man Hunt ★★★★
She Knew All the Answers ★★★
Wild Geese Calling ★★★
Confirm or Deny ★★★

1942

Twin Beds ★★★
The Wife Takes a Flyer ★★★
Girl Trouble ★★★

1943

Margin for Error ★★★

1944

The Woman in the Window ★★★★

1945

Nob Hill ★★★

1946

Colonel Effingham's Raid ★★★
Scarlet Street ★★★★

1947

The Macomber Affair ★★★★
The Woman on the Beach ★★★★

1948

Secret Beyond the Door ★★★
The Scar ★★★★

1949

The Reckless Moment ★★★★

1950

For Heaven's Sake ★★★
Father of the Bride ★★★★

1951

Father's Little Dividend ★★★★
The Guy Who Came Back ★★★

1954

Highway Dragnet ★★★

1956

There's Always Tomorrow ★★★
Navy Wife ★★★

1960

Desire in the Dust ★★★

1970

House of Dark Shadows ★★★

1977

Suspiria ★★★

JACK BENNY
★★★ 3.10 STARS

Jack Benny used vanity and stinginess to his supreme advantage in his comedy routines. What made it all so palatable was the warmth he exuded even at his most egocentric comedic moments. He had a gift for timing that made him one of the greatest stand-up comics of his day.

Benny was born Benny Kubelsky in 1894, in Waukegan, Illinois. He was a huge success on radio, but somewhat less so in films. His first film performance was a sketch in *Hollywood Revue of 1929,* and after playing in *Bright Moments* (a short), he did some amiable farces, *Transatlantic Merry-Go-Round, It's in the Air,* and *Artists and Models. Charley's Aunt* was a breakthrough—Benny played a man masquerading as an old lady and extracted the most from the visual incongruities. *To Be or Not To Be* gave him his only meaty part—an actor fleeing from the Nazis. He had a superb co-star in Carole Lombard, but the public preferred *George Washington Slept Here* with Ann Sheridan. Benny frequently referred to *The Horn Blows at Midnight* as his worst film, but in fact there were some hilarious sequences, particularly the finale when he was tossed around in a huge coffee cup. He almost had Spencer Tracy's role in *Father of the Bride,* but director Vincente Minnelli felt he was a comedian rather than an actor. It may have been true, but as a comedian he was unrivalled.

Jack Benny in *To Be or Not To Be.*

FILMOGRAPHY

1929

Hollywood Revue of 1929 ★★★

1930

Chasing Rainbows ★★★
The Medicine Man ★★★

1935

Transatlantic Merry-Go-Round ★★★
It's in the Air ★★★
Broadway Melody of 1936 ★★★

1936

The Big Broadcast of 1937 ★★★

1937

College Holiday ★★★
Artists and Models ★★★

1938

Artists and Models Abroad ★★★

1939

Man About Town ★★★

1940

Love Thy Neighbor ★★★
Buck Benny Rides Again ★★★

1941

Charley's Aunt ★★★★

1942

To Be or Not To Be ★★★★
George Washington Slept Here ★★★

1943

The Meanest Man in the World ★★★

1944

Hollywood Canteen (cameo)

1945

The Horn Blows at Midnight ★★★
It's in the Bag ★★★

1967

A Guide for the Married Man ★★★

ROBBY BENSON
★★ 2.10 STARS

Robby Benson is sometimes too boyish and gangling for his own good. In his early films, he had a tendency to collar the audience and say "love me!" If he can overcome it, his career will be on firmer ground because he does have some acting ability.

Born in Dallas, Texas in 1956, Benson wallowed in his self-conscious charm in the early *Jeremy*, as the cellist who fell in love with

Robby Benson in *The Chosen.*

Glynnis O'Connor. *Lucky Lady* was so bad that nobody could have improved it, and Benson was mannered and cloying in the contrived screen version of *Ode to Billy Joe.* The solution to what happened on the Tallahachee Bridge made one wish the question had gone unanswered. *One on One* was a hit, but Benson's sincerity wasn't enough to convince audiences he could be a star basketball player. He finally found his niche as the focal point of *The Chosen*—a superb, deeply felt portrayal of a young, religious Jew who wanted to break with his father's iron-clad traditions.

FILMOGRAPHY

1973

Jory ★★
Jeremy ★★

1975

Lucky Lady ★★

1976

Ode to Bille Joe ★

1977

One on One ★★

1978

The End ★★

1979

Ice Castles ★★

1980

Tribute ★★★
Die Laughing ★

1982

The Chosen ★★★★

CANDICE BERGEN
★★½ 2.30 STARS

Candice Bergen has been, in her own words, "creamed by the critics." She admits she used to choose her movies for the locations or because the money was too tempting to turn down, and it showed. Occasionally, though, a glimpse of warmth and talent came through her ice-maiden facade, and lately it's coming through more often.

She was born in 1946, in Beverly Hills, California, the daughter of ventriloquist/comic Edgar Bergen. She started out strongly in films in *The Group*, but her performances in *The Day the Fish Came Out*, *The Magus*, and *The Adventurers* were nearly the death knell of a promising career. She improved in *Getting Straight*, opposite Elliott Gould, and in *Carnal Knowledge*, as Art Garfunkel's girlfriend. *T. R. Baskin*, *11 Harrowhouse*, and *Oliver's Story* were more dire mistakes, but her neat comedic performance in *Starting Over* won a surprise Oscar nomination. *Rich and Famous* also gave her a fine role as a flighty novelist, and she dug into the part with likable abandon. She was credible as Margaret Bourke-White in *Gandhi* but looked bad in comparison to Ben Kingsley's amazing performance.

Candice Bergen in *Rich and Famous.*

Candice Bergen's dominant screen image is one of lackadaisical casualness, somewhat akin to James Garner. Unfortunately, whereas this trait works to Garner's advantage it seems to undermine the authority of Bergen's performances.

FILMOGRAPHY

1966

The Group ★★★
The Sand Pebbles ★★

1967

Live for Life ★★★
The Day the Fish Came Out ★

1968

The Magus ★

1970

The Adventurers ★
Getting Straight ★★★
Soldier Blue ★★★

1971

Carnal Knowledge ★★★
The Hunting Party ★★
T. R. Baskin ★

1974

11 Harrowhouse ★★

1975

The Wind and the Lion ★★★
Bite the Bullet ★★

1977

The Domino Principle ★★
A Night Full of Rain ★★★

1978

Oliver's Story ★★

1979

Starting Over ★★★★

1981

Rich and Famous ★★★

1982

Gandhi ★★

INGRID BERGMAN
★★★½ 3.27 STARS

Colleen Dewhurst once said of Ingrid Bergman: "She has her scotches, she stays up late, she tells jokes, but she looks glorious. Nothing that she is, is the result of any massage parlor or any face makeup." Bergman's naturalness and unaffected charm were the qualities that made her unique in the 1940s when she first began. She was unique in one other respect too—unlike Davis, Hepburn, and Crawford, her acting remained simple and unmannered throughout her career.

Ingrid Bergman with Cary Grant in *Notorious.*

Bergman was born in Stockholm, Sweden, in 1915. Her first husband, Peter Lindstrom, encouraged her acting ambitions, and she attained stardom in a series of Swedish films including *Dollar* and *Intermezzo.*

Producer David O. Selznick signed Bergman to do the English version, *Intermezzo: A Love Story,* and she made an immediate impact on Hollywood. Her combination of sincerity and strength were the main assets of *Adam Had Four Sons* and *Rage in Heaven.*

She stole the notices from Spencer Tracy in *Dr. Jekyll and Mr. Hyde* and shared the famous sleeping bag with Gary Cooper in *For Whom the Bell Tolls.* Ann Sheridan and Ronald Reagan were the first choices for *Casablanca,* but fortunately, she and Bogart were recruited at the last minute. Her wholesome sexuality furnished a classic contrast to Bogart's affectionate cynicism. Shortly before she died, Bergman ran the movie for a college class and exclaimed in surprise at the end, "My, what a good *picture!*" echoing the sentiments that have persisted until today. *Gaslight* won her an Oscar, and she was a scheming adventuress in *Saratoga Trunk. Spellbound* gave her a battery of psychological platitudes to speak. The film's dialogue, with its on-the-spot cures, seems ludicrous today, but Bergman's delivery is still believable. There were more hits with *The Bells of St. Mary's* and *Notorious,* her best role (and possibly Hitchcock's best film). It had a superb script, Cary Grant, and one of the most breathtaking climaxes in any suspense movie.

The quality of her pictures dipped with *Arch of Triumph* and *Under Capricorn.* But the serious damage to her career was done when she became pregnant by Italian director Roberto Rossellini and unleashed the Hollywood scandal of the century. A Senator denounced her ("Perhaps out of Ingrid Bergman's ashes will come a better Hollywood"), and her movies with Rossellini were repudiated by press and public. It took *Anastasia* in 1956 to restore her to the front ranks. A second Oscar solidified her gains, and final forgiveness came when she and Rossellini divorced. Most subsequent films were weak, rescued only by her participation: *The Inn of the Sixth Happiness,* an overlong and corny tale of a Chinese missionary; *Goodbye Again,* an ill-match with Tony Perkins; and *The Visit,* her first totally unlikable part.

She was already seriously ill with cancer when she made *Autumn Sonata,* a lumbering psychological piece by Ingmar Bergman. Her own performance was superb, and she excelled again as Golda in a notable TV mini-series. Her death in 1982 was one of the greatest losses ever experienced by the film world. Ingrid Bergman was that elusive presence that the camera is always longing for but so rarely finds.

Ingrid Bergman with Humphrey Bogart in *Casablanca.*

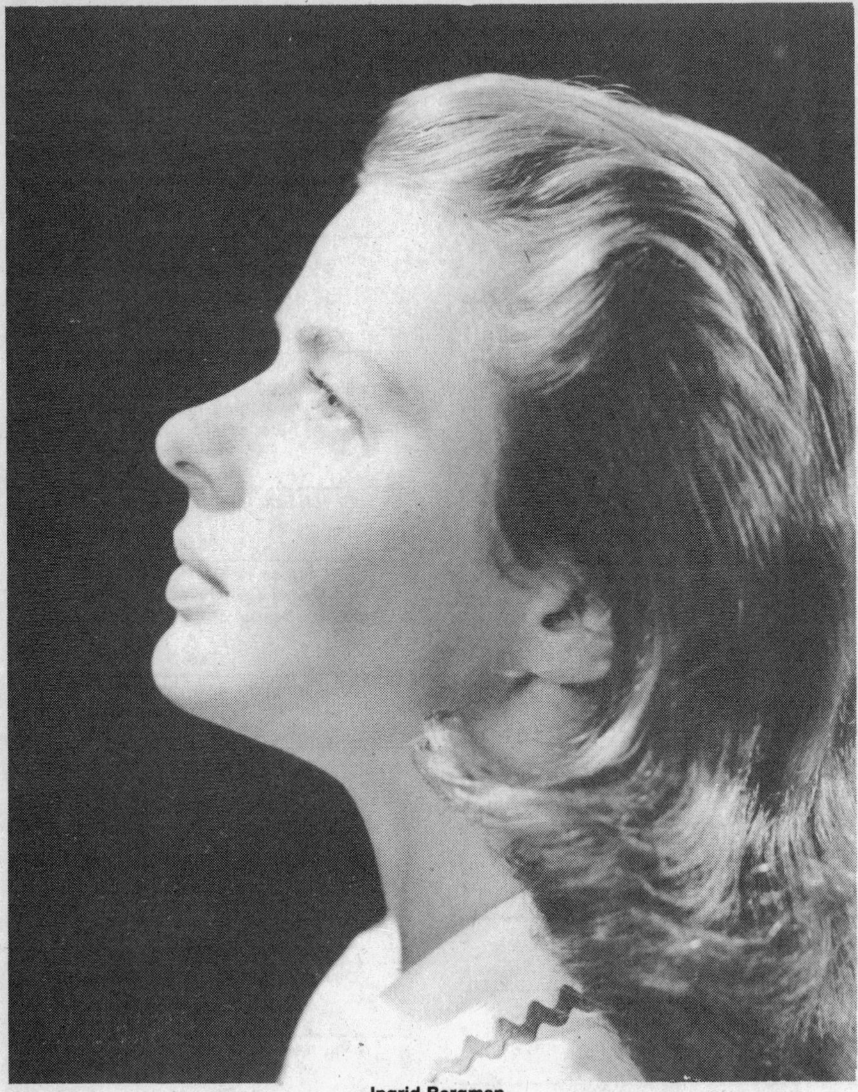

Ingrid Bergman.

FILMOGRAPHY

1934

The Count From the Monk's Bridge ★ ★ ★

1935

The Surf ★ ★ ★
Swedenhielms ★ ★ ★
Walpurgis Night ★ ★ ★

1936

On the Sunny Side ★ ★ ★
Intermezzo ★ ★ ★ ★

1938

Die Vier Gesellen ★ ★ ★
Dollar ★ ★ ★
A Woman's Face ★ ★ ★ ★
One Single Night ★ ★ ★

1939

Intermezzo: A Love Story ★ ★ ★ ★

1940

A Night in June ★ ★ ★

1941

Adam Had Four Sons ★ ★ ★
Rage in Heaven ★ ★ ★
Dr. Jekyll and Mr. Hyde ★ ★ ★ ★

1943

Casablanca ★ ★ ★ ★
Swedes in America (documentary)
For Whom the Bell Tolls ★ ★ ★ ★

1944

Gaslight ★ ★ ★ ★

1945

Spellbound ★ ★ ★ ★
Saratoga Trunk ★ ★ ★ ★
The Bells of St. Mary's ★ ★ ★ ★

1946

Notorious ★ ★ ★ ★

1948

Arch of Triumph ★ ★ ★
Joan of Arc ★ ★ ★

1949

Under Capricorn ★ ★ ★
Stromboli ★ ★

1952

The Greatest Love ★ ★ ★

1953

We the Women ★ ★ ★
The Lonely Woman ★ ★ ★

1954

Joan at the Stake ★ ★ ★
Fear ★ ★ ★

1956

Paris Does Strange Things ★ ★ ★
Anastasia ★ ★ ★ ★

1958

Indiscreet ★ ★ ★ ★
The Inn of the Sixth Happiness ★ ★ ★

1961

Goodbye Again ★ ★

1964

The Visit ★ ★ ★
The Yellow Rolls Royce ★ ★ ★

1967

Stimulantia ★ ★ ★

1969

Cactus Flower ★ ★ ★

1970

A Walk in the Spring Rain ★ ★

1973

From the Mixed-Up Files of Mrs. Basil E. Frankweiler ★ ★ ★

1974

Murder on the Orient Express ★ ★ ★ ★

1976

A Matter of Time ★ ★ ★

1978

Autumn Sonata ★ ★ ★ ★

CHARLES BICKFORD
★ ★ ★ 3.19 STARS

Charles Bickford had a powerful, commanding presence that could suggest brute force or tenderness, and a total mastery of comedy and drama. One of the glaring injustices of Hollywood history is the Academy's failure to vote him an Oscar.

He was born in 1889, in Cambridge, Massachusetts. After early training on the stage, Bickford had a hit in *Anna Christie* as the sailor who loved Garbo. He dominated his sequences in *The Farmer's Daughter* as Joseph Cotten's loyal butler and was equally effective playing Linda Darnell's killer in *Fallen Angel.* Bickford was Jane Wyman's stern but caring father in *Johnny Belinda,* and his death three quarters through was a loss viewers never quite recovered from. Perhaps most poignant of all was the moment in *Days of Wine and Roses* when he broke down at the realization that daughter Lee Remick was a hopeless alcoholic. Bickford was nominated for a Best Supporting Actor award three times *(The Song of Bernadette, The Farmer's Daughter,* and *Johnny Belinda),* but he never won. We can be grateful to television for reminding us, over and over, of his unforgettable contributions to the art of motion picture acting.

FILMOGRAPHY

1929

South Sea Rose ★★★
Dynamite ★★★

1930

Hell's Heroes ★★★
Anna Christie ★★★★
The Sea Bat ★★★
River's End ★★★
Passion Flower ★★★

1931

The Squaw Man ★★★
Pagan Lady ★★★
East of Borneo ★★★
Men in Her Life ★★★

1932

Panama Flo ★★★
Scandal for Sale ★★★
Thunder Below ★★★
The Last Man ★★★
Vanity Street ★★★

1933

No Other Woman ★★★
Song of the Eagle ★★★
This Day and Age ★★★
White Woman ★★★

1934

Little Miss Marker ★★★
A Wicked Woman ★★★

1935

Under Pressure ★★★
A Notorious Gentleman ★★★
The Farmer Takes a Wife ★★★
East of Java ★★★

1936

Rose of the Rancho ★★★
Pride of the Marines ★★★
Red Wagon ★★★

1937

The Plainsman ★★★★
High, Wide, and Handsome ★★★★
Thunder Trail ★★★
Night Club Scandal ★★★
Daughter of Shanghai ★★★

1938

Gangs of New York ★★★
Valley of the Giants ★★★
The Storm ★★★

1939

Stand Up and Fight ★★★
Romance of the Redwoods ★★★
Street of Missing Men ★★★
Our Leading Citizen ★★★
One Hour to Live ★★★
Mutiny in the Big House ★★★
Thou Shalt Not Kill ★★★

1940

Of Mice and Men ★★★★
Girl from God's Country ★★★
South to Karanga ★★★
Queen of the Yukon ★★★

1941

Burma Convoy ★★★
Riders of Death Valley (serial) ★★★

1942

Reap the Wild Wind ★★★
Tarzan's New York Adventure ★★★

1943

Mr. Lucky ★★★
The Song of Bernadette ★★★★

1944

Wing and a Prayer ★★★

1945

Captain Eddie ★★★
Fallen Angel ★★★★

1947

The Farmer's Daughter ★★★★
Duel in the Sun ★★★★
The Woman on the Beach ★★★★
Brute Force ★★★★

Charles Bickford in *A Star Is Born.*

1948

The Babe Ruth Story ★★★
Four Faces West ★★★
Johnny Belinda ★★★★

1949

Command Decision ★★★
Roseanna McCoy ★★★

1950

Whirlpool ★★★
Guilty of Treason ★★★
Riding High ★★★

1951

Branded ★★★★
Jim Thorpe—All American ★★★
The Raging Tide ★★★
Elopement ★★★

1954

A Star Is Born ★★★★

1955

Prince of Players ★★★
Not as a Stranger ★★★★
The Court-Martial of Billy Mitchell ★★★

1956

You Can't Run Away from It ★★★

1957

Mister Cory ★★★

1958

The Big Country ★★★★

1960

The Unforgiven ★★★

1962

Days of Wine and Roses ★★★★

1966

A Big Hand for the Little Lady ★★★

JACQUELINE BISSET
★★½ 2.39 STARS

Jacqueline Bisset has all the qualifications for stardom—a hauntingly beautiful face, a lovely, cultured voice, and a curvaceous figure. She isn't a *bad* actress either, but there's something tightly reserved about her performances. She has no exuberance or fire, yet one always feels that the fire is there, waiting to explode in the right role.

She was born in 1944, in England, and began her professional career as a model. Curiously, in a shoddy motorcycle picture, *The Sweet Ride,* she projected more heat than she ever would again. Her first

Jacqueline Bisset with Nick Nolte in *The Deep.*

strong starring part was in *Airport*, as Dean Martin's stewardess girlfriend. But Bisset has a reputation for "taking on any movie if it has six good lines in it," and that's part of the problem. For every moderately entertaining film like *Murder on the Orient Express*, there were a slew of mediocre ones like *The Greek Tycoon, End of the Game, St. Ives,* and *The Day the World Ended.* Bisset is probably beautiful enough to keep going, but one hopes she'll find that special part—like Julie Christie had in *Darling*—to give her the elusive acting triumph she keeps searching for.

FILMOGRAPHY

1965

The Knack (bit)

1966

Cul-de-Sac ★★★

1967

Casino Royale ★★
Two for the Road ★★★

1968

The Detective ★★★
The Sweet Ride ★★★
Bullitt ★★★

1969

The First Time ★★
Secret World ★★

1970

Airport ★★★
The Grasshopper ★★

1971

The Mephisto Waltz ★★★
Believe in Me ★★

1972

Stand Up and Be Counted ★
The Life and Times of Judge Roy Bean ★★

1974

The Thief Who Came to Dinner ★★★
Day for Night ★★★
Le Magnifique ★★
Murder on the Orient Express ★★★

1975

End of the Game ★★★

1976

The Sunday Woman ★★★
St. Ives ★★

1977

The Deep ★★★

1978

Secrets ★★
Who is Killing the Great Chefs of Europe? ★★★
The Greek Tycoon ★

1979

The Day the World Ended ★★

1980

Inchon ★★

1983

Class ★

KAREN BLACK
★★½ 2.50 STARS

It's hard to decide if Karen Black is a character actress or a star. Every now and again she gets a role that wins acclaim and awards, but the lustre dims after more bad films, putting her back at the starting gate again.

Black was born Karen Ziegler in 1942, in Park Ridge, Illinois. She made her debut in Francis Ford Coppola's *You're a Big Boy Now*, a zany farce that critics liked better than audiences did. She was impressive in the hugely successful but now dated *Easy Rider* and delivered a magnificent performance—her best—as Jack Nicholson's waitress-girlfriend in *Five Easy Pieces.* An Oscar nomination for that seemed to indicate stardom, but follow-up roles in *Cisco Pike* and the unbearable *Portnoy's Complaint* were a letdown. *Airport 1975* gave her a few dramatic moments as a stewardess who had to pilot a crippled airplane. She was wonderfully bitchy in Robert Altman's *Nashville* and even wrote her own country songs. Black was also lively in Hitchcock's *Family Plot*, but the master of suspense no longer had his old flair. She was excellent on both stage and screen in *Come Back to the 5 and Dime, Jimmy Dean, Jimmy Dean*, reminding everyone of what a terrific actress she can be.

Her latest roles reveal a more conscious and careful selection of material, a factor that may yet guarantee her stardom.

Karen Black with Dennis Hopper in *Easy Rider.*

FILMOGRAPHY

1967

You're a Big Boy Now ★★★

1969

Hard Contract ★★
Easy Rider ★★★

1970

Five Easy Pieces ★★★★

1971

Drive, He Said ★★★
A Gunfight ★★
Born to Win ★★★

1972

Cisco Pike ★★★
Portnoy's Complaint ★

1973

Little Laura and Big John ★★
The Pyx ★★
The Outfit ★★★

1974

The Great Gatsby ★★★
Rhinoceros ★★
Airport 1975 ★★★
Law and Disorder ★★★

1975

Nashville ★★★
The Day of the Locust ★★★
An Ace Up My Sleeve ★★★

1976

Crime and Passion ★★
Family Plot ★★★
Burnt Offerings ★★

1978

The Rip-Off ★★
Capricorn One ★★★
In Praise of Older Women ★★

1979

The Number ★★
The Naked Sun ★★

1980

Danny Travis ★★

1981

Chanel Solitaire ★★
Separate Ways ★★

1982

Greed ★★
Come Back to the 5 and Dime, Jimmy Dean, Jimmy Dean ★★★

DIRK BOGARDE
★★★½ 3.39 STARS

Dirk Bogarde has elegance, style, looks, and extraordinary talent. It can truthfully be said of him that he never gave a bad performance. Yet the British press was indifferent to his work until *Victim* (1961). Perhaps some of the lightweight material he did delayed proper recognition. But there are few, if any, who would deny his ability today.

Bogarde was born Derek Van Den Bogaerde in London, in 1920. He worked briefly as a commercial artist (his father was an art editor for the Times), and then turned to theatre work and films. He was excellent in an episode of author Somerset Maugham's popular *Quartet* and played a fine romantic lead opposite Jean Simmons. *Doctor in the House* made him a top box-office star in Britain and resulted in a series, but fans ignored one of his best performances in Joseph Losey's neglected *The Sleeping Tiger. Victim* made everyone take notice because, in his words, "it was a thriller hung on a serious theme"—the exposure of a respected lawyer as a homosexual.

Dirk Bogarde in *The Gentle Gunman.*

Most of Bogarde's pictures—*The Spanish Gardener, Cast a Dark Shadow, A Tale of Two Cities, The Password Is Courage*—were entertaining, but few were classics until *The Servant,* a weird, decadent tale about a valet who takes over his master's life and soul. He was much more sympathetic as Julie Christie's betrayed lover in *Darling* and magnificent in *The Fixer.* He was cast as Liszt in the endless *Song Without End,* but his portrait of a haunted composer (based on Mahler) in *Death in Venice* finally supplied the artistic appreciation he had been waiting for. His excellent diction and precise delivery were one of the highlights of Alain Resnais' complex *Providence.* Dirk Bogarde remains one of the greatest examples of intelligent acting.

FILMOGRAPHY

1939

Come On George (bit)

1947

Dancing With Crime (bit)

1948

Esther Waters ★★★
Quartet ★★★★
Once a Jolly Swagman ★★★

1949

Dear Mr. Prohack ★★★
Boys in Brown ★★★

1950

The Blue Lamp ★★★★
So Long at the Fair ★★★★
The Woman in Question ★★★

1951

Blackmailed ★★★

1952

Hunted ★★★
Penny Princess ★★
The Gentle Gunman ★★★

1953

Appointment in London ★★★
Desperate Moment ★★★★
They Who Dare ★★★

1954

Doctor in the House ★★★★
The Sleeping Tiger ★★★★
For Better For Worse ★★★
The Sea Shall Not Have Them ★★★

Dirk Bogarde in *A Bridge Too Far.*

1955

Simba ★★★★
Doctor at Sea ★★★★
Cast a Dark Shadow ★★★

1956

The Spanish Gardener ★★★★

1957

Night Ambush ★★★★
Doctor at Large ★★★
Campbell's Kingdom ★★★★

1958

The Wind Cannot Read ★★★★
A Tale of Two Cities ★★★★

1959

The Doctor's Dilemma ★★★★
Libel ★★★★

1960

Song Without End ★★★
The Angel Wore Red ★★

1961

The Singer Not the Song ★★★
Victim ★★★★

1962

Damn the Defiant! ★★★
The Password Is Courage ★★★★
We Joined the Navy (cameo)

1963

The Mind Benders ★★★
I Could Go on Singing ★★★★
Doctor in Distress ★★★
The Servant ★★★★

1964

Hot Enough for June ★★★
King and Country ★★★

1965

The High Bright Sun ★★★
Darling ★★★★

1966

Modesty Blaise ★★★

1967

Accident ★★★★
Our Mother's House ★★★★

1968

Sebastian ★★★
The Fixer ★★★★

1969

Oh! What a Lovely War ★★★
Justine ★★★
The Damned ★★★★

1971

Death in Venice ★★★★

1973

The Serpent ★★★

1974

The Night Porter ★★★

1975

Permission to Kill ★★★

1977

Providence ★★★★
A Bridge Too Far ★★★

1978

Despair ★★★

Humphrey Bogart.

HUMPHREY BOGART
★★★½ 3.33 STARS

Some stars such as Gary Cooper and Spencer Tracy are affectionately remembered; others like Clark Gable are legends in their lifetimes. Bogart was among the few who acquired more relevance and power with each succeeding generation. Like Cooper, Tracy, and Gable, Bogart was a fine actor, but unlike them, he epitomized nonconformity, a man who faced life on his own terms. Whether criminal or hero, he had his own, unshakeable code of honor, a characteristic that has made him timeless.

Bogart was born in New York, in 1899. His early stage work consisted of foppish tennis-playing juveniles, until he played a vicious gangster in "The Petrified Forest" with Leslie Howard. He repeated his role on film at Howard's insistence and became one of the three resident gangsters on the Warner Brothers lot (Edward G. Robinson and James Cagney were the others). The pictures including *Bullets or Ballots*, *The Great O'Malley*, and *San Quentin* survived only because he was in them. *Marked Woman* and *Kid Galahad* were better (they co-starred Bette Davis), but his rise really began with *Dead End*, a gripping drama of life in New York tenements. *Angels With Dirty Faces* was outstanding, but he was thoroughly miscast in *Dark Victory*.

High Sierra showed his depth—he was the gentle Mad Dog Earle, who helps lame Joan Leslie back to health. It was *The Maltese Falcon* that began the Bogart legend; he was shrewd, worldly, and cynically humorous as Sam Spade, falling in love with the treacherous Mary Astor while fully understanding her evil motives. *Across the Pacific* reunited them, though the script was weaker.

He played Rick in *Casablanca*, and to gauge his effectiveness one only has to look at the legions who still line up at the theatre marquees to see it. *Casablanca* and the Bogart legend are inseparable. *To Have and Have Not* paired him with Lauren Bacall. The movie, seen today, lacks the structure and freshness of *Casablanca*, but he and Bacall still struck sparks. She became his fourth wife (after three notably turbulent marriages), and they teamed up in *The Big Sleep*, *Key Largo*, and *Dark Passage* as well.

In a Lonely Place cast Bogart as a hot-tempered and possibly murderous Hollywood screenwriter. He was superlative, brilliantly blending vulnerability with rage. *The Treasure of the Sierra Madre* gave him an opportunity to project greed and growing madness. Critics were enthusiastic; the public wasn't.

Bogart's portrayal of the whiskey-soaked boatman in *The African Queen* won him an Oscar and according to Lauren Bacall's autobiography, the "rebel" expressed genuine pleasure before and after the Academy Award ceremonies. He was breathtaking as the neurotic, fearful Captain Queeg in *The Caine Mutiny* (although Bogart claimed, "I didn't think it was so hot. They crapped it up with an unnecessary love story"). *Beat the Devil* was a spoof that Bogart-followers loved, and *Sabrina* handed him a Cary Grant-type role (Grant was actually signed at one point) as a middle-aged millionaire in love with youthful Audrey Hepburn.

Bogart was clearly all the things his enemies called him: a cruel prankster and a heavy drinker who was abusive and then "drew a blank" the next morning. But he was also courageous (especially in the face of death), unwavering in his beliefs, and most of all, more individual than any other actor in Hollywood history.

Humphrey Bogart in *The Caine Mutiny*.

FILMOGRAPHY

1930

A Devil With Women ★★★
Up the River ★★★

1931

Body and Soul ★★★
Bad Sister ★★★
Women of All Nations ★★★
A Holy Terror ★★★

1932

Love Affair ★★★
Big City Blues ★★★
Three on a Match ★★★

1934

Midnight ★★★

1936

The Petrified Forest ★★★★
Bullets or Ballots ★★★
Two Against the World ★★★
China Clipper ★★★
Isle of Fury ★★★

1937

Black Legion ★★★
The Great O'Malley ★★★
Marked Woman ★★★★
Kid Galahad ★★★★
San Quentin ★★★★
Dead End ★★★★
Stand In ★★★

1938

Swing Your Lady ★★★
Crime School ★★★
Men Are Such Fools ★★★
The Amazing Dr. Clitterhouse ★★★
Racket Busters ★★★
Angels With Dirty Faces ★★★★

1939

King of the Underworld ★★★
The Oklahoma Kid ★★
Dark Victory ★★
You Can't Get Away With Murder ★★★
The Roaring Twenties ★★★
The Return of Doctor X ★★★
Invisible Stripes ★★★

1940

Virginia City ★★★
It All Came True ★★★
Brother Orchid ★★★
They Drive by Night ★★★★

1941

High Sierra ★★★★
The Wagons Roll at Night ★★★
The Maltese Falcon ★★★★

1942

All Through the Night ★★★
The Big Shot ★★★
In This Our Life (cameo)
Across the Pacific ★★★★

1943

Casablanca ★★★★
Action in the North Atlantic ★★★
Thank Your Lucky Stars ★★★
Sahara ★★★★

1944

Passage to Marseilles ★★★

1945

To Have and Have Not ★★★★
Conflict ★★★

1946

Two Guys from Milwaukee (cameo)
The Big Sleep ★★★★

1947

Dead Reckoning ★★★★
The Two Mrs. Carrolls ★★★★
Dark Passage ★★★

1948

Always Together (cameo)
The Treasure of the Sierra Madre ★★★★
Key Largo ★★★★

1949

It's a Great Feeling (cameo)
Knock on Any Door ★★★★
Tokyo Joe ★★★

1950

Chain Lightning ★★★
In a Lonely Place ★★★★

1951

The Enforcer ★★★
Sirocco ★★★

1952

The African Queen ★★★★
Road to Bali (cameo)
Deadline U.S.A. ★★★

1953

Love Lottery (cameo)
Battle Circus ★★★

1954

Beat the Devil ★★★★
The Caine Mutiny ★★★★
The Barefoot Contessa ★★★★
Sabrina ★★★★

1955

We're No Angels ★★★
The Left Hand of God ★★★
The Desperate Hours ★★★★

1956

The Harder They Fall ★★★★

PAT BOONE
★★ 1.79 STARS

At the peak of his success as a pop singer, Pat Boone offered a clean-living alternative to the "bad" Elvis Presley. He was religious, a good husband, and a good family man. He wasn't, however, a good actor. Even his singing triumphs owe more to "cover" records of Rhythm and Blues material than to any great vocal gift.

Born in 1934, early recognition came on "The Ted Mack Amateur Hour" and Arthur Godfrey's "Talent Scouts." But when Boone made his film debut in *Bernadine*, he was as sexless as a milkshake on the screen. *April Love* was probably his best performance, opposite another wholesome star (but one with real dramatic ability), Shirley Jones. A further disadvantage was his vehicles, none of which had any merit. *State Fair* was José Ferrer's leaden remake of a 1940's favorite, and Boone's co-stars (Bobby Darin, Alice Faye, Tom Ewell) gave him no help. *Goodbye Charlie* offered a thankless part, and *The Perils of Pauline* began as a pilot for a TV series.

Pat Boone in *Yellow Canary.*

FILMOGRAPHY

1957

Bernadine ★★
April Love ★★★

1958

Mardi Gras ★★

1959

Journey to the Center of the Earth ★★

1961

All Hands on Deck ★

1962

State Fair ★
The Main Attraction ★★

1963

Yellow Canary ★★★

1964

Never Put It in Writing ★★
The Horror of It All ★
Goodbye Charlie ★

1965

The Greatest Story Ever Told ★

1967

The Perils of Pauline ★★

1970

The Cross and the Switchblade ★★

1978

Matilda (voice only)

ERNEST BORGNINE
★★★ 2.94 STARS

Ernest Borgnine was one of the screen's most convincing villains, and after that, one of its best sympathetic actors. Even when he overplayed, he was able to project a believable, everyday honesty.

Borgnine was born in Hamden, Connecticut, in 1917. He began in small parts (*The Whistle at Eaton Falls, The Mob*, and even had a Broadway appearance in "Mrs. McThing" with Helen Hayes). But he found his niche as the terrifying Fatso in *From Here to Eternity.* After murdering Frank Sinatra in the stockade, he was typecast: *The Stranger Wore a Gun, Johnny Guitar, Demetrius and the Gladiators, Vera Cruz*, and *Run for Cover* all made use of his villainy. *Marty* turned the tide; Borgnine was a lonely butcher who meets "dog" Betsy Blair at a dance, then has to cope with his mother's objections to the romance. It won him an Oscar and showed his ability to be warm as well as vicious.

He was sympathetic again in another Paddy Chayefsky piece (*The Catered Affair*). It wasn't as good, due to Bette Davis's overacting, but he was likable in a musical *The Best Things in Life Are Free* (a supposed life story of songwriters Brown, De Sylva, and Henderson). He was hateful again in *The Vikings.* A successful TV series in the mid-1960s "McHale's Navy" gave further impetus to his career, sparking a movie version and starring roles in *The Flight of the Phoenix* and *The Wild Bunch.* There was script trouble when he was paired again with Bette Davis in *Bunny O'Hare.* Director Ronald Neame allowed him to shout too much in the record-breaking *The Poseidon Adventure,* though acting was incidental to the exciting details of escaping from an upside-down ocean liner. Most of his subsequent pictures have been fairly routine (though he made a superb Lucifer in *The Devil's Rain*), but he was excellent in a TV movie *Jesus of Nazareth.*

FILMOGRAPHY

1951

China Corsair ★★★
The Whistle at Eaton Falls ★★★
The Mob ★★★

1953

The Stranger Wore a Gun ★★★
From Here to Eternity ★★★★

1954

Johnny Guitar ★★★
Demetrius and the Gladiators ★★
The Bounty Hunter ★★★
Vera Cruz ★★★★

1955

Marty ★★★★
Bad Day at Black Rock ★★★★
Run for Cover ★★★
Violent Saturday ★★★
The Last Command ★★★

1956

The Square Jungle ★★★
Jubal ★★★★
The Catered Affair ★★★
The Best Things in Life Are Free ★★★

1957

Three Brave Men ★★★

1958

The Vikings ★★★★
The Badlanders ★★★
Torpedo Run ★★★

1959

The Rabbit Trap ★★★
Summer of the Seventeenth Doll ★★★

1960

Man on a String ★★★
Pay or Die ★★★★

1961

Go Naked in the World ★★★
Il Re di Poggioreale ★★★
Il Giudizio Universale ★★★
Barabbas ★★

1962

I Briganti Italiani ★★★

1964

McHale's Navy ★★★

1965

The Flight of the Phoenix ★★★★

1966

The Oscar ★★★

1968

Chuka ★★★
The Dirty Dozen ★★★★

1968

The Legend of Lylah Clare ★★★
The Split ★★
Ice Station Zebra ★★★

Ernest Borgnine in *Torpedo Run.*

1969

The Wild Bunch ★★★★

1970

A Bullet For Sandoval ★★
The Adventurers ★★
Suppose They Gave a War and Nobody Came ★★

1971

Willard ★★★★
Bunny O'Hare ★★
Rain for a Dusty Summer ★★
Hannie Caulder ★★

1972

The Revengers ★★★
Ripped-Off ★★★
The Poseidon Adventure ★★★

1973

The Neptune Factor ★★★
Emperor of the North Pole ★★★★

1974

Law and Disorder ★★★

1975

Sunday in the Country ★★
The Devil's Rain ★★★★
Hustle ★★

1976

Natale in Casa di Appuntamento ★★★
Won Ton Ton-The Dog That Saved Hollywood (cameo)
Shoot ★★★

1977

The Greatest ★★★
The Prince and the Pauper ★★★

1978

Convoy ★★★

1979

The Double McGuffin ★★★
The Black Hole ★★
Six Against the Rock ★★★
Ravagers ★★★
Holiday Hookers ★★

1980

When Time Ran Out ★★

1981

Escape From New York ★★★
High Risk ★★
Deadly Blessing ★★★
Super Fuzz ★★

DAVID BOWIE
★★★ 3.25 STARS

Except for Elvis Presley, no rock star has yet been able to translate his popularity into a movie career. However, David Bowie seems likely to change that record. He has a magnetism and image that few of today's movie stars can match, and he has the sort of intelligence, style, and creativity that can be worked into any medium.

He was born David Jones in London, England in 1947. Growing up through the Mod era, he began a musical career in the late 1960s after changing his name to Bowie. In an effort to succeed, he adopted a spaceman image and had a hit with the song, "Space Oddity." Developing his image to a sort of illogical conclusion he created the persona of Ziggy Stardust for the album "The Rise and Fall of Ziggy Stardust and the Spiders from Mars." Bowie discovered that his image—his bizarre makeups and weird clothes—were almost more popular than his music. He began to change his looks and styles with every subsequent album, gaining the title of the rock 'n' roll chameleon.

Bowie's elusiveness and mystery were tailor-made for director Nicholas Roeg, who needed someone to play an alien from outer-space in *The Man Who Fell to Earth*. Bowie was superb in the role, but almost *too* good. His first film role served to typecast him as the "weirdo" and gave no indication of his range as an actor. Meanwhile, his musical career led him into the pioneering development of rock videos. His videotape for the song, "Ashes to Ashes," remains a classic of that young medium.

He was acting again in *Just a Gigolo,* a convoluted tale of a young Prussian officer after World War I. The film featured Kim Novak and Marlene Dietrich and proved that Bowie was capable of adapting to roles. However, the film itself was a mess and received only spotty distribution. His next film role required him to play a vampire and to age 300 years in one scene. *The Hunger* was a glossy and sophisticated horror tale that often looked more like a rock video than a film. But, once again, David Bowie displayed more promise than the film. He brought a warmth and desperation to his role that was nowhere in evidence in his co-star, Catherine Deneuve.

Bowie's cinematic breakthrough came in *Merry Christmas, Mr. Lawrence*—his first good film since *The Man Who Fell to Earth* and the only one that hasn't relied on his rock-star strangeness for characterization. Bowie played a British POW in a Japanese prison camp during World War II.

David Bowie seems to be at the very peak of his career in rock music. With a demonstrated ability to act, and a worldwide popular audience that idolizes him, he should be able to take his movie career anywhere he chooses.

David Bowie with Catherine Deneuve in *The Hunger.*

FILMOGRAPHY

1976

The Man Who Fell to Earth ★★★★

1980

Just a Gigolo ★★

1983

The Hunger ★★★
Merry Christmas, Mr. Lawrence ★★★★

CHARLES BOYER
★★★½ 3.34 STARS

Charles Boyer never really said, "Come with me to the Casbah," any more than Ingrid Bergman said, "Play it again, Sam." But the line typified him: exotic, romantic, and exciting. Boyer was—and still is—the best continental lover the American screen ever had.

He was born on August 28, 1897, in Figeac, France. His theatre career began when he was twenty-three, and there were several French films (*L'Homme du Large, L'Esclave,* and *Revolte dans la Prison*) before he achieved international fame. *Private Worlds* with Claudette Colbert drew critical and public attention to him, and he was effective opposite Katharine Hepburn in *Break of Hearts,* though the movie itself stimulated little interest. He and Greta Garbo compensated for a sluggish script as Napoleon and Maria Walewska in *Conquest.* He sailed through the ultimate romance in *History Is Made at Night* with Jean Arthur, and his lover image acquired further credence as Pepe Le Moko in *Algiers. Love Affair* was a touching romantic comedy with Boyer at his most sincere (Cary Grant played the lead in the 1957 remake, *An Affair to Remember*). Boyer had other hits with *All This and Heaven Too, Hold Back the Dawn,* and *The Constant Nymph. Gaslight* contained his best performance; he was suavely villainous as the husband who tried to drive Ingrid Bergman insane. His assurance disguised the inadequacies of Lauren Bacall in *Confidential Agent,* and he committed murder again in Preminger's absorbing *The Thirteenth Letter.* Some of his later pictures (*The Cobweb, Adorable Julia,* and *Love Is a Ball*) were unworthy of him, but he contributed style and elegance to all of them until his suicide in 1978.

FILMOGRAPHY

1920

L'Homme du Large ★★★

1921

Chantelouve ★★★

1922

Le Grillon du Foyer ★★★

1923

L'Esclave ★★★

1927

La Ronde Infernale ★★★★

1929

Le Capitaine Fracasse ★★★★
Le Procès du Mary Dugan ★★★★

1930

Revolte dans la Prison ★★★
La Barcarolle d'Amour ★★★

1931

Tumultes ★★★
The Magnificent Lie ★★★

1932

The Man from Yesterday ★★★
Red-Headed Woman ★★★
F.P. I ne répond plus ★★★

1933

Moi et l'Imperatrice ★★★
The Only Girl ★★★
Les Amoureux ★★★

1934

The Battle ★★★
Liliom ★★★
Caravan ★★

1935

Le Bonheur ★★★
Private Worlds ★★★★
Break of Hearts ★★★
Shanghai ★★★★

1936

Mayerling ★★★★
The Garden of Allah ★★★

1937

History Is Made at Night ★★★★
Conquest ★★★★
Tovarich ★★★★

1938

Algiers ★★★★
Orage ★★★

1939

Love Affair ★★★★
When Tomorrow Comes ★★★★

1940

All This and Heaven Too ★★★★

1941

Back Street ★★★★
Hold Back the Dawn ★★★★
Appointment for Love ★★★★

1942

Tales of Manhattan ★★★★

1943

The Heart of a Nation (narration)
Flesh and Fantasy ★★★★
The Constant Nymph ★★★

1944

Gaslight ★★★★
Together Again ★★★

1945

Confidential Agent ★★★★

1946

Cluny Brown ★★★★

Charles Boyer with Claudette Colbert in *Tovarich.*

1948

A Woman's Vengeance ★★★★
Arch of Triumph ★★★

1951

The Thirteenth Letter ★★★★
The First Legion ★★★

1952

The Happy Time ★★★

1953

Thunder in the East ★★★
The Earrings of Madame de ★★★

1955

Nana ★★★
The Cobweb ★★★★

1956

Lucky to Be a Woman ★★★
Paris Hotel ★★★
Around the World in 80 Days (cameo)

1957

Une Parisienne ★★★

1958

Maxime ★★★
The Buccaneer ★★★

1961

Fanny ★★★★

1962

The Four Horsemen of the Apocalypse ★★★
Les Demons de Minuit ★★★
Adorable Julia ★★★

1963

Love Is a Ball ★★★

1965

A Very Special Favor ★★★

1966

Is Paris Burning? ★★★
How to Steal a Million ★★★

1967

Casino Royale ★★★
Barefoot in the Park ★★★★

1968

The Day the Hot Line Got Hot ★★★

1969

The April Fools ★★
The Madwoman of Chaillot ★★

1972

Lost Horizon ★★

1974

Stavisky ★★★

1976

A Matter of Time ★★★

PETER BOYLE
★★★ 2.86 STARS

Peter Boyle is an actor of wide range. His films have emphasized a flair for both comedy and drama, but few have been notable except for his performances.

He was born in 1933, in Philadelphia. Amusingly, in the light of his later villainous roles, he was a Christian monk before appearing in off-Broadway productions. His first films—*The Virgin President* and *Medium Cool*—caused little reaction. However, his portrayal of a psychopathic bigot in *Joe* was so powerful that Boyle labored under the shadow of it in many subsequent movies. His role was small in *Diary of a Mad Housewife*, and *T. R. Baskin* was so sluggish and depressing that his good acting went for naught. Boyle was hilarious as the monster in Mel Brooks' best film, *Young Frankenstein*, but ludicrous in a silly costume comedy, *Swashbuckler.*

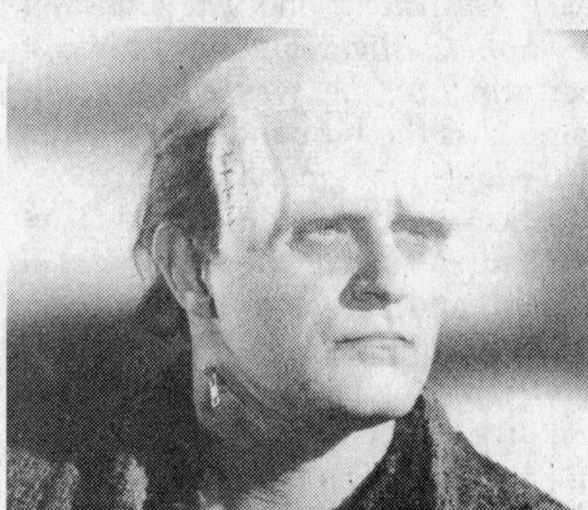

Peter Boyle in *Young Frankenstein.*

In Crazy Joe he was cast as racketeer Joe Gallo, but the film was fairly routine. He was perfectly cast in *Taxi Driver* as the not-very-sage Wizard. His mastery of low-life characters continued when he played a sleazy private eye in *Hardcore.* Another gangland film, *The Brinks Job*, was more entertaining, helped by co-stars Peter Falk and Gena Rowlands. Boyle had his meatiest part in years as the hipster lawyer in the out-of-control *Where the Buffalo Roam.* Peter Boyle continues to add broad dimension to the characters he plays, if only he could get parts worthy of his talent.

FILMOGRAPHY

1968

The Virgin President ★★★

1969

Medium Cool ★★★

1970

Joe ★★★★
Diary of a Mad Housewife ★★★

1971

T. R. Baskin ★★

1972

The Candidate ★★★

1973

Steelyard Blues ★★★
Slither ★★★
Kid Blue ★★★
The Friends of Eddie Coyle ★★★

1974

Crazy Joe ★★★
Young Frankenstein ★★★★

1976

Taxi Driver ★★★★
Swashbuckler ★

1978

F.I.S.T. ★★★
The Brinks Job ★★★

1979

Beyond the Poseidon Adventure ★★
Hardcore ★★★

1981

Where the Buffalo Roam ★★★
In God We Trust ★★

1982

Outland ★★★
Hammett ★★

MARLON BRANDO
★★½ 2.55 STARS

Brando! The name inspires awe in other actors, and respect from most critics. When he performs badly (as he did in *Bedtime Story* and *Mutiny on the Bounty*), his champions apologize by criticizing the director, the film, or unsympathetic studio executives. However, an overall view of this actor's career indicates that he can veer wildly from brilliance to staggering mediocrity, and outside factors aren't always to blame.

Nebraska-born in 1924, Brando gravitated toward theatre under the influence of his mother, who was an acting coach. A Broadway role in "Truckline Cafe" started the furor, and it intensified with "A Streetcar Named Desire." He was already being difficult, upstaging co-star Jessica Tandy, and his rebellious nature incurred the permanent wrath of gossip columnists Louella Parsons, Hedda Hopper, and Sheilah Graham when he came to Hollywood. He debuted in *The Men* as a crippled war vet; it was one of his best, most natural performances. He was predictably superb as Stanley Kowalski in the film adaptation of *A Streetcar Named Desire* (though all the other leads—Vivien Leigh, Karl Malden, and Kim Hunter—won Oscars, and he didn't).

Marlon Brando with Vivien Leigh in *A Streetcar Named Desire.*

In *Viva Zapata!* he was cast effectively as a Mexican peasant, and he showed his versatility as Mark Anthony in *Julius Caesar.* It was back to defiance in *The Wild One.* To the question, "What are you rebelling against?" he replied, "What have you got?" *On the Waterfront* brought him the Oscar he should have won for *Streetcar.* Even Brando detractors agreed that these two portrayals were beyond praise.

From this point on, however, opinions became more divided on the merit of Brando's work. Nobody cared for *Desiree* or Brando's portrayal of Napoleon, and he was a liability to the over-produced *Guys and Dolls.* He couldn't sing or dance, and Frank Sinatra was justified in referring to him derisively as "mumbles." *The Teahouse of the August Moon* was another mistake. He was better in *Sayonara*, playing a pilot in love with a Japanese girl. In *The Young Lions*, he took the hardened Nazi of Irwin Shaw's bestseller and made the part more likable; an artistic move that infuriated many observers, including co-star Montgomery Clift.

The mumbling continued in *The Fugitive Kind*, one of author Tennessee Williams' lesser plays. *One-Eyed Jacks* was a creative but ultimately unsatisfying western, and Brando's interpretation of Fletcher Christian in *Mutiny on the Bounty* provoked film author Leonard Maltin into writing, "Where are you, Clark Gable?"

His worst performance came in *Bedtime Story,* a disastrous stab at comedy with David Niven. He took another unfunny pratfall in Chaplin's *The Countess From Hong Kong.* The scripts were partly to blame, and the same remained true of *Reflections in a Golden Eye*, John Huston's version of the Carson McCullers novel. Brando's role of the repressed homosexual officer was realized with depth, despite a somewhat actorish approach to the part.

The Godfather restored him to favor. He won a second Oscar and rave reviews. He played the aging Don Vito Corleone with such zest and control that the entire film rested on his performance. *Last Tango in Paris* was both vilified (as mere pornography) and worshipped (as having the impact of Stravinsky's Rites of Spring), but Brando was praised for taking the role as far as it would go. There was only criticism for his maniacal cowboy in *The Missouri Breaks*, and his bit in *Superman* added nothing to the picture (except a three and a half million dollar salary to the budget). In *Apocalypse Now* he played the mad Commander Kurtz—the only jarring element in an otherwise powerful film about Vietnam. All of Brando's noted mannerisms still could not create the necessary mystique.

Marlon Brando appears to have retired after enduring a barrage of criticism in the last decade. Either the Great Method Actor has run out of method, or he's made enough money.

FILMOGRAPHY

1950

The Men ★★★★

1951

A Streetcar Named Desire ★★★★

1952

Viva Zapata! ★★★★

1953

Julius Caesar ★★★

1954

The Wild One ★★★★
On the Waterfront ★★★★
Desiree ★★

1955

Guys and Dolls ★★

1956

The Teahouse of the August Moon ★★★

1957

Sayonara ★★★

1958

The Young Lions ★★

1960

The Fugitive Kind ★★

1961

One-Eyed Jacks ★★★

1962

Mutiny on the Bounty ★★

1963

The Ugly American ★★★

Marlon Brando in *The Missouri Breaks.*

1964

Bedtime Story ★

1965

Morituri ★★

1966

The Chase ★★
The Appaloosa ★★

1967

A Countess From Hong Kong ★
Reflections in a Golden Eye ★★★

1968

Candy ★

1969

The Night of the Following Day ★★
Burn! ★★

1971

The Nightcomers ★★★

1972

The Godfather ★★★★
Last Tango in Paris ★★★★

1976

The Missouri Breaks ★

1978

Superman ★★

1979

Apocalypse Now ★★

1980

The Formula ★★

EILEEN BRENNAN
★★½ 2.42 STARS

Eileen Brennan is a diamond in the rough; a square-jawed actress who always gives more complexity to a role than the role usually demands. Brennan softens the hard edges of her characters—beaten and weary, maybe, but somehow tender.

Her stage work included some outstanding Broadway and off-Broadway productions as diversified as "The Miracle Worker," "Hello Dolly!" "Bells Are Ringing," and even a one-woman show called "An Evening with Eileen Brennan." Her big break came with the lead in the off-Broadway musical "Little Mary Sunshine."

She had a small part in Bud Yorkin's *Divorce, American Style* before landing a role as the waitress Genevieve in *The Last Picture Show*, an excellent movie based on Larry McMurtry's chronicle of life in a small town in Texas. She was Paul Newman's girlfriend in *The Sting* and managed some good scenes in Robert Aldrich's *Hustle.* She caught the public eye in *Private Benjamin* as Captain Doreen Lewis, a caricature that continues on television and grows more audacious under her command.

Eileen Brennan in *The Cheap Detective.*

FILMOGRAPHY

1967

Divorce, American Style ★★★

1971

The Last Picture Show ★★★

1973

Scarecrow ★★★
The Sting ★★★★

1974

Daisy Miller ★★★★

1975

At Long Last Love ★★
Hustle ★★★

1976

Murder by Death ★★★

1977

The Last of the Cowboys ★★★

1978

FM ★★
The Cheap Detective ★★

1980

Private Benjamin ★★★★

WALTER BRENNAN
★★★ 2.88 STARS

One of Hollywood's greatest sidekicks, Walter Brennan was rarely placed center-stage though he often stole the show. He had a knack for lending his ease and naturalness to the films he appeared in. He most often played the seemingly dim-witted partner to romantic action heroes, but his warmth and humor assured that he didn't have to be the butt of the jokes.

Walter Brennan was born on July 25, 1894, in Swampscott, Massachusetts. He studied to be an engineer but soon drifted into vaudeville, also supporting himself as a lumberjack, a bank clerk, and a doughboy. His first film work was as an extra and a stunt man. He was the first actor to win three Oscars—for *Come and Get It* in 1936, for *Kentucky* in 1938, and for his role as Judge Roy Bean in *The Westerner.*

Though versatile—he appeared in the Astaire-Rogers film *The Story of Vernon & Irene Castle* and in the Bogart-Bacall film *To Have and Have Not*—Brennan is best remembered as a western actor. He worked with an extraordinary variety of directors on a number of great films: Fritz Lang's *Fury,* King Vidor's *Northwest Passage,* Frank Capra's *Meet John Doe,* Jean Renoir's *Swampwater,* Howard Hawks' *Red River* and *Rio Bravo,* and John Ford's *My Darling Clementine* lead a long list. Brennan's quintessential role was the faithful, deceptively wily sidekick, a man who preferred to stand in the background and have a good laugh at the world—but he could always be counted on to be there when he was needed. His occasional villain roles, as in *My Darling Clementine*, were all the more effective for playing against type.

Ironically, despite his countless great film performances, a whole generation will think of him as the hobbling grandfather of television's "The Real McCoys." A more appropriate moment to remember him might be the end of *Rio Bravo*, where he gleefully lobbed sticks of dynamite at the bad guys in the company of John Wayne, Dean Martin, and Ricky Nelson. Brennan died of emphysema on September 21, 1974, in Oxnard, California.

FILMOGRAPHY

1927

The Riding Rowdy ★★
Tearin' Into Trouble ★★

1928

The Ballyhoo Buster ★★

1929

The Lariat Kid ★★
The Long, Long Trail ★★★
Shannons of Broadway ★★★
Smilin' Guns ★★★
One Hysterical Night ★★★

1930

The King of Jazz ★★

1931

Dancing Dynamite ★★★
Neck and Neck ★★★

1932

The Airmail Mystery (serial) ★★★
Law and Order ★★★
Texas Cyclone ★★★
Two-Fisted Law ★★★
All American ★★★

1933

One Year Later ★★★
Parachute Jumper ★★★
Man of Action ★★★
Fighting for Justice ★★★
Sing, Sinner, Sing ★★★
Strange People ★★★
The Phantom of the Air (serial) ★★★
Silent Men ★★★

1934

Good Dame ★★★
Half a Sinner ★★★

1935

The Wedding Night ★★
Northern Frontier ★★★
Laddy Tubbs ★★
Man on the Flying Trapeze ★★★
Barbary Coast ★★★
Seven Keys to Baldpate ★★
Law Beyond the Range ★★
Bride of Frankenstein ★★★★
Metropolitan ★★★

1936

Three Godfathers ★★★
These Three ★★★
Come and Get It ★★★★
Banjo on My Knee ★★★
The Moon's Our Home ★★★
The Prescott Kid ★★★
Fury ★★★★

1937

When Love Is Young ★★★★
The Affairs of Cappy Ricks ★★★
Wild and Wooly ★★★
She's Dangerous ★★★

1938

The Adventures of Tom Sawyer ★★★★
The Buccaneer ★★★
Kentucky ★★★★
The Texans ★★★
Mother Carey's Chickens ★★
The Cowboy and the Lady ★★

1939

Stanley and Livingstone ★★★
The Story of Vernon & Irene Castle ★★★
They Shall Have Music ★★★
Joe and Ethel Turp Call on the President ★★★

1940

The Westerner ★★★★
Northwest Passage ★★★★
Maryland ★★★★

1941

Sergeant York ★★★★
Meet John Doe ★★★★
Swampwater ★★★
This Woman Is Mine ★★★
Nice Girl? ★★★
Rise and Shine ★★★

1942

Pride of the Yankees ★★★★
Stand by for Action ★★★

1943

The North Star ★★★
Slightly Dangerous ★★★
Hangmen Also Die ★★★

1944

The Princess and the Pirate ★★★
To Have and Have Not ★★★
Home in Indiana ★★★

1945

Dakota ★★★

1946

My Darling Clementine ★★★★
Centennial Summer ★★★
A Stolen Life ★★★
Nobody Lives Forever ★★★

Walter Brennan in *Joe and Ethel Turp Call on the President.*

1947

Driftwood ★★★

1948

Scudda Hoo! Scudda Hay! ★★★
Red River ★★★★
Blood on the Moon ★★★★

1949

Brimstone ★★★
The Green Promise ★★★
Task Force ★★★
The Great Dan Patch ★★★

1950

Curtain Call at Cactus Creek ★★★
A Ticket to Tomahawk ★★★
Singing Guns ★★★
Surrender ★★★
The Showdown ★★★

1951

Best of the Badmen ★★★
The Wild Blue Yonder ★★★
Along the Great Divide ★★★

1952

Lure of the Wilderness ★★★
Return of the Texan ★★★

1953

Sea of Lost Ships ★★

1954

Drums Across the River ★★
Four Guns to the Border ★★
Bad Day at Black Rock ★★

1955

The Far Country ★★
At Gunpoint ★★

1956

Glory ★★★
Come Next Spring ★★★
Goodbye My Lady ★★★
The Proud Ones ★★★

1957

Tammy and the Bachelor ★★★★
The Way to the Gold ★★★
God Is My Partner ★★★

1959

Rio Bravo ★★★

1962

How the West Was Won ★★★
Shoot Out at Big Sag ★★

1964

Those Calloways ★★★

1966

The Oscar ★★

1967

The Gnome-Mobile ★★★
Who's Minding the Mint? ★★

1968

The One and Only, Genuine, Original Family Band ★★

1969

Support Your Local Sheriff! ★★★

1973

The Love Bug Rides Again ★★★

JEFF BRIDGES
★★★3.21 STARS

Like his father Lloyd and brother Beau, Jeff Bridges is a totally natural, unaffected performer. His performances have an almost documentary authenticity, as well as a direct, virile charm.

Bridges was born in 1949, in Los Angeles. He made an unnoticed acting debut in a tale of teenage crime, *Halls of Anger* but blossomed in Peter Bogdanovich's *The Last Picture Show*. Among a group of sensitive juvenile performers (Timothy Bottoms, Randy Quaid, and Cybill Shepherd), Bridges stood out and even received a Best Supporting Actor nomination.

In *The Last American Hero* he played a determined race-car driver. He successfully met the challenge of a Eugene O'Neill drama, *The Iceman Cometh*, stealing the reviews from lead Lee Marvin. He overshadowed Clint Eastwood in an engaging crime story, *Thunderbolt and Lightfoot*, and received his second Oscar nomination.

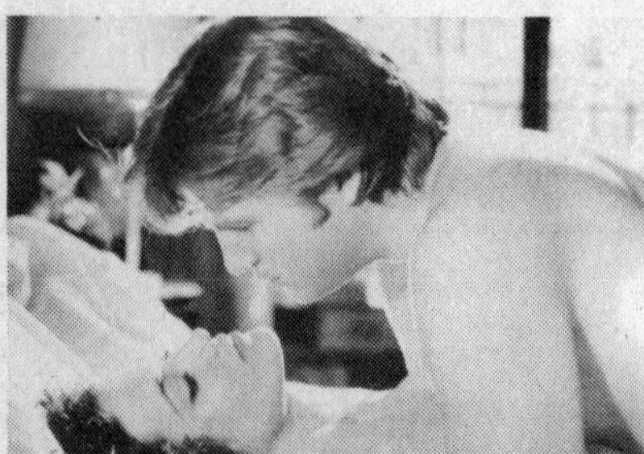

Jeff Bridges with Belinda Bauer in *Winter Kills.*

His easy-going charm was perfected in *Hearts of the West*, a witty homage to moviemaking directed by Howard Zieff. *Stay Hungry* was an equally enjoyable close-up of the weight-lifting world with Sally Field, and the remake of *King Kong* had him playing straight man to a gorilla.

Jeff Bridges with Blythe Danner in *Hearts of the West.*

Somebody Killed Her Husband (with Farrah Fawcett) was a puzzlingly old-fashioned, unexciting thriller. He also played the lead in two dizzily entertaining box-office bombs directed by William Richert, *Winter Kills* and *The American Success Company.* Few young actors have been so talented and so unlucky in box-office terms.

FILMOGRAPHY

1970

Halls of Anger ★★★

1971

The Last Picture Show ★★★★

1972

Fat City ★★★★
Bad Company ★★★

1973

The Last American Hero ★★★★
The Iceman Cometh ★★★★
Lolly Madonna XXX ★★★

1974

Thunderbolt and Lightfoot ★★★★

1975

Rancho Deluxe ★★★
Hearts of the West ★★★★

1976

Stay Hungry ★★★★
King Kong ★★

1978

Somebody Killed Her Husband ★★

1979

Winter Kills ★★★

1980

The American Success Company ★★★
Heaven's Gate ★★

1981

Cutter's Way ★★★★

1982

Tron ★★★
Kiss Me Goodbye ★★

LLOYD BRIDGES
★★★ 3.09 STARS

Some actors are perennial second leads, offering firm backup to leading men generally less talented than they are. Lloyd Bridges held up the rear in dozens of minor films, achieving lead status only on television.

Born in San Leandro, California, in 1913, Bridges appeared on the screen at age twenty-eight after Broadway and stock experience. *The Lone Wolf Takes a Chance* was part of a popular series, and Bridges appeared briefly in a famous fantasy, *Here Comes Mr. Jordan* (remade as *Heaven Can Wait*).

He made some good pictures—*Sahara* and *A Walk in the Sun*—but no lasting impression until *Home of the Brave.* As the sympathetic white friend of black soldier James Edwards, Bridges projected a simple humanity that held the picture together. He was a likably dependable action hero in one of the early science-fiction dramas, *Rocket Ship X-M*, and he stood out as the deputy sheriff in *High Noon.* He also mimicked a superb Joe DiMaggio opposite Kim Stanley's Marilyn Monroe in *The Goddess.* This admirable performance didn't improve his

Lloyd Bridges.

material—*Attack on the Iron Coast*, *Daring Game*, and *Lost Flight*.

TV gave him a hit series, "Sea Hunt," and a string of successful made-for-television movies that brought him deserved and overdue popularity. His hilarious performance in *Airplane!* was marked as a sort of triumphant return.

FILMOGRAPHY

1941

The Lone Wolf Takes a Chance ★★★
Here Comes Mr. Jordan ★★★
Two Latins from Manhattan ★★★

1942

Alias Boston Blackie ★★★
Shut My Big Mouth ★★★
Talk of the Town ★★★

1943

Sahara ★★★
Passport to Suez ★★★

1944

Louisiana Hayride ★★★
The Master Race ★★★

1945

A Walk in the Sun ★★★
Miss Susie Slagle's ★★★

1946

Abilene Town ★★★
Canyon Passage ★★★

1947

Ramrod ★★★

1948

16 Fathoms Deep ★★★

1949

Home of the Brave ★★★★
Red Canyon ★★★
Calamity Jane and Sam Bass ★★★

1950

Colt 45 ★★★
Rocket Ship X-M ★★★
The White Tower ★★★★
The Sound of Fury ★★★★

1951

Three Steps North ★★★
Whistle at Eaton Falls ★★★★

1952

High Noon ★★★★
Plymouth Adventure ★★★

1953

The Kid from Left Field ★★★

1954

Pride of the Blue Grass ★★★

1955

Wichita ★★★

1956

The Rainmaker ★★★★

1957

Ride Out for Revenge ★★★

1958

The Goddess ★★★★

1966

Around the World Under the Sea ★★★

1968

Attack on the Iron Coast ★★★
Daring Game ★★★

1969

The Happy Ending ★★★

1971

Lost Flight ★★★

1972

To Find a Man ★★★

1975

Deliver Us From Evil ★★★

1979

The Fifth Musketeer ★★★

1981

Airplane! ★★★
Bear Island ★★★

1982

Airplane II—The Sequel ★★★

CHARLES BRONSON
★★½ 2.70 STARS

Charles Bronson proves conclusively that magnetism and leading man authority have nothing to do with conventional good looks. His craggy features and wrestler's body suggest power, and he is a capable actor when the script is right (a not-too-frequent occurrence).

Bronson (Charles Buchinsky) was born in Pennsylvania in 1921, the ninth of fifteen children. His father was a coal miner, but Bronson rejected life in the mines for acting. As Charles Buchinsky, he did minor parts in a number of films, including *The People Against O'Hara* and *The Mob*. His appearance as a fighter in *Pat and Mike* attracted attention, and there were supporting stints in more well-known films like *Vera Cruz* with Gary Cooper.

As newly christened Charles Bronson, he showed up in the violent *Big House, USA* and a good John Ford western, *Jubal*. But he remained only a convincing supporting actor until *The Magnificent Seven*—a classic western which cast him as a paid gunslinger. He stood out in a talented cast that included Steve McQueen, Eli Wallach, James Coburn, and Robert Vaughn.

He was still a supporting player—although an increasingly popular one—and *Master of the World* with Vincent Price did nothing to change that status. He did lend some authenticity to Elvis Presley's plastic *Kid Galahad*. His most outstanding film, *The Great Escape*, was based on fact and dynamically directed by John Sturges. It was the story of a large-scale escape from a German prison camp, and Bronson had enough powerful moments to make him, at last, a name to reckon with at the box office. *The Sandpiper* was successful but ludicrous, and he was a refreshing sight beside the pretentious affected performances of Richard Burton and Elizabeth Taylor. *The Dirty Dozen* with Lee Marvin was his next high blockbuster.

Bronson was forty-six and just hitting his peak as a leading man. Like Clint Eastwood, he garnered a fanatical European following and kept his hold by making pictures like *Rider on the Rain*, an appealing thriller with Marlene Jobert and his wife Jill Ireland. It was one of the few films to utilize his sly charm. He was back with Ireland again as a professional killer in *The Mechanic*.

Mr. Majestyk was a cinematic bloodbath, and he went somewhat overboard on violence in the popular *Death Wish,* as a man who hunted down criminals after his wife had been raped and murdered. Critics were too busy questioning the film's take-the-law-into-your-own-hands philosophy to credit the gripping screenplay, tight direction, and strong central performance. Walter Hill's *Hard Times* contained his best acting; he was a street fighter promoted by small-time hustler James Coburn.

St. Ives couldn't recover from the inadequacies of Jacqueline Bisset, but he was back into the *Death Wish* theme with *From Ten to Midnight.* The script again insisted that if the law is wrong, a man must resort to unethical means to protect citizens. And again, excellent acting by Bronson and Andrew Stevens couldn't keep the L.A. Times from calling the picture "inflammatory and dangerous." Bronson himself should probably take the blame for being continually cast into such hard-nose material, but he likewise deserves more credit as an actor.

Bronson needs to try lightening his image a la Clint Eastwood by playing against his tough guy looks. Nothing could be more disarming than a Charles Bronson comedy.

FILMOGRAPHY

(billed as Charles Buchinsky)

1951

You're in the Navy Now ★★★
The People Against O'Hara ★★★
The Mob ★★★

1952

Red Skies of Montana ★★
My Six Convicts ★★★
The Marrying Kind (bit)
Pat and Mike ★★★
Diplomatic Courier (bit)
Bloodhounds of Broadway ★★

1953

House of Wax ★★

1954

Miss Sadie Thompson ★★
Crime Wave ★★
Tennessee Champ ★★★
Riding Shotgun ★★★
Apache ★★★
Vera Cruz ★★★

Charles Bronson.

(billed as Charles Bronson)

1955

Drum Beat ★★
Big House, USA ★★★
Target Zero ★★★

1956

Jubal ★★★★

1957

Run of the Arrow ★★★

1958

Gang War ★★★
Showdown at Boot Hill ★★
Machine Gun Kelly ★★★
When Hell Broke Loose ★★★

1959

Never So Few ★★

1960

The Magnificent Seven ★★★★

1961

Master of the World ★★
A Thunder of Drums ★★

1962

X-15 ★★★
Kid Galahad ★★★

1963

The Great Escape ★★★★
Four for Texas ★★★

1965

The Sandpiper ★★★
Battle of the Bulge ★★★

1966

This Property Is Condemned ★★★

1967

The Dirty Dozen ★★★★

1968

Guns for San Sebastian ★★
Villa Rides ★★★
Adieu l'Ami ★★★

Once Upon a Time in the West ★★★
Rider on the Rain ★★★★

1970

You Can't Win 'Em All ★★
The Family ★★★
Cold Sweat ★★
twinky ★★

1971

Someone Behind the Door ★★★
Soleil rouge ★★

1972

The Valachi Papers ★★★
Chato's Land ★★
The Mechanic ★★★

1973

Valdez the Halfbreed ★★
The Stone Killer ★★★

1974

Mr. Majestyk ★★★
Death Wish ★★★★

Charles Bronson in *Hard Times.*

1975

Hard Times ★★★★
Breakout ★★

1976

Breakheart Pass ★★
St. Ives ★★
From Noon Till Three ★★

1977

The White Buffalo ★
Telefon ★★★

1979

Love and Bullets ★★
Cabo Blanco ★★

1980

Borderline ★★

1981

Death Hunt ★★★

1982

From Ten to Midnight ★★★
Death Wish II ★★

MEL BROOKS
★★½ 2.50 STARS

In a world that demands too much thinking, Mel Brooks provides the perfect escape. You don't have to work hard to comprehend his humor as you sometimes do at a Woody Allen movie. Every child can "get" a Mel Brooks joke because most of his jokes are aimed at a ten-year-old mentality. His magic is that he appeals to the child in all of us.

Brooks was born Melvin Kaminsky in Brooklyn in 1926. He made his first impact on TV, as one of Sid Caesar's script writers, a stable of talent that also included Neil Simon and Woody Allen. He went on to do stand-up comedy (his two-thousand-year-old-man routine was a classic), play in Broadway musicals ("All America"), and create his own television series ("Get Smart") which he wrote with Buck Henry.

Brooks wrote and directed his first film, *The Producers.* The film, starring Zero Mostel and Gene Wilder, dealt with an investor (Mostel) who deliberately set out to sabotage a show and wound up with a hit. The concept was funnier than the movie (except for the unforgettably brilliant "Springtime for Hitler" number), but that was partly the fault of labored direction. Brooks won an Oscar for his screenplay.

His second movie *The Twelve Chairs* was, like the first, a commercial letdown. It was a farce about the search for one of twelve chairs with jewels sewn into it. Dom DeLuise gave the picture its only charm, and Brooks gave himself only a small part in it. *Blazing Saddles* was a western spoof, directed with the subtlety of a sledgehammer, totally incoherent and tasteless. Veteran comics like Madeleine Kahn, Gene Wilder, Harvey Korman, and Brooks himself squeezed laughter from slapstick.

Young Frankenstein marked a leap forward. It was more controlled, more skillfully directed, and less prone to do anything for a laugh. Brooks concentrated on directing and had no role in the film.

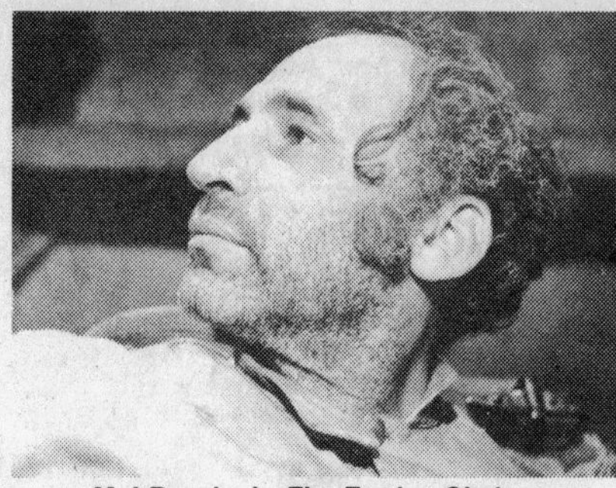

Mel Brooks in *The Twelve Chairs.*

The upward curve continued, both artistically and commercially, with *Silent Movie.* Brooks played a film producer trying for a comeback, and there was a marvelous cameo by Burt Reynolds spoofing his self-love and egotism. The cast again included the Brooks' "regulars" Dom DeLuise, Gene Wilder, and Bernadette Peters (as an enduring substitute for Madeleine Kahn).

In *High Anxiety,* Brooks played a psychiatrist who headed a sanitarium for the very, very nervous. The movie was a spoof of Hitchcock thrillers—generally amusing (especially the *Psycho* shower sequence) but not the comedy classic it could have been.

Brooks is undeniably a great comedic talent, but in common with most creators who try to write, direct, star, and produce, he overreaches himself. He never seems to have grown out of the sketch format of Sid Caesar's TV show. His acting seems to run out of steam at the end of every scene. Brooks has given many people pleasure; someday, when he tightens his storylines, he may give them comic art as well.

FILMOGRAPHY

1970

The Twelve Chairs ★★ (screenplay, direction)

1974

Blazing Saddles ★★ (screenplay, direction)

1976

Silent Movie ★★★ (screenplay, direction)

1977

High Anxiety ★★★ (screenplay, direction)

1979

The Muppet Movie (cameo)

1981

History of the World—Part I ★★ (screenplay, direction)

1983

To Be or Not To Be ★★★ (screenplay, direction)

YUL BRYNNER
★★★ 2.78 STARS

After an unimpressive beginning with hair, Yul Brynner shaved his head and shot to stardom. Baldness seemed to emphasize his intense, burning eyes and even add a rich, sexual timbre to his voice.

Brynner was born in 1915, on Sakhalin, an island east of Siberia, and his family tree included gypsies. After a stint as a trapeze artist in Paris, he concentrated on acting. His first movie *Port of New York* was a tale of drug trafficking that held little entertainment value.

Success in a Broadway musical "The King and I" made the difference, and he repeated his part in the successful, though stodgy, film version. A Best Actor Oscar resulted, insuring good roles such as the fortune hunter of *Anastasia.* Brynner trained Ingrid Bergman to impersonate one of the Czar's daughters and then found that she might be the real thing. The Brynner-Bergman chemistry was magical.

He had the required authority as Ramses V in *The Ten Commandments* and as a communist officer in *The Journey,* a heavy drama about the Hungarian revolution. Brynner was convincing and even touching as Joanne Woodward's harsh guardian in *The Sound and the Fury.* He replaced Tyrone Power in *Solomon and Sheba* after the latter's untimely death, and then Brynner tried a couple of comedies—*Once More With Feeling and Surprise Package*—without success.

The Magnificent Seven was a classic western, and Brynner dominated in a cast of colorful names including Steve McQueen, James Coburn, and Charles Bronson.

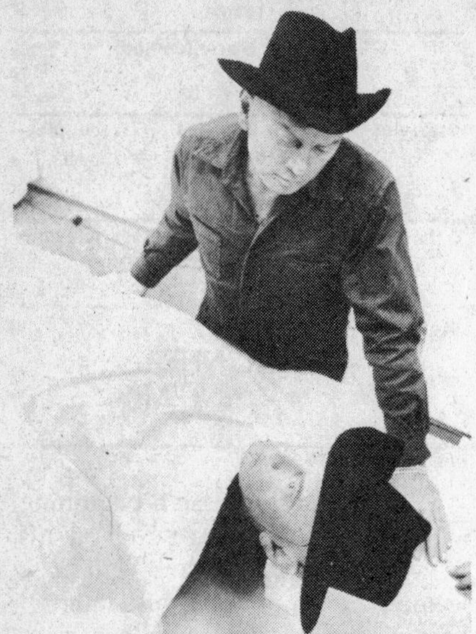

Yul Brynner in *Westworld.*

Taras Bulba was a synthetic spectacle, and the public yawned at *Cast a Giant Shadow, Morituri* (with Marlon Brando), and *Triple Cross. Return of the Seven* was Brynner's best part until he played the potentially murderous robot in *Westworld.* His screen power is still potent, but he won't recover his former glory until he gets a few films with the caliber of those that first made him a star.

FILMOGRAPHY

1949

Port of New York ★★

1956

The King and I ★★★★
Anastasia ★★★★
The Ten Commandments ★★★

1958

The Brothers Karamazov ★★★
The Buccaneer ★★★

1959

The Journey ★★
The Sound and the Fury ★★★
Solomon and Sheba ★★★

1960

The Testament of Orpheus (cameo)
Once More With Feeling ★★
Surprise Package ★★
The Magnificent Seven ★★★★

1962

Escape from Zahrain ★★★
Taras Bulba ★★

1963

Kings of the Sun ★★

1964

Flight from Ashiya ★★
Invitation to a Gunfighter ★★★

1965

Morituri ★★★

1966

The Poppy Is Also a Flower (cameo)
Cast a Giant Shadow ★★★
Return of the Seven ★★★
Triple Cross ★★★

1967

The Double Man ★★★
The Long Duel ★★★

1968

Villa Rides ★★★

1969

The File of the Golden Goose ★★
The Madwoman of Chaillot ★★

1970

Battle of Neretva ★★
The Magic Christian (cameo)

1971

Adios Sabata ★★
Catlow ★★★
The Light at the Edge of the World ★★★
Romance of a Horsethief ★★

1972

Fuzz ★★★

1973

The Serpent ★★★
Westworld ★★★★

1976

The Ultimate Warrior ★★★
Futureworld ★★★
Gli Indesiderabili ★★★

GENEVIÈVE BUJOLD
★★★ 3.20 STARS

Elizabeth Taylor once visited the set of *Anne of the Thousand Days,* a movie featuring husband Richard Burton and Geneviève Bujold, and indicated her jealousy. Bujold's response was, "I'm going to give that bitch an acting lesson she'll never forget," and her superb performance as Anne Boleyn did exactly that.

The spunky Bujold was born in 1942, in Montreal, Canada. She worked her way through drama school and appeared on stage in "The Barber of Seville." *The Adolescents* was her first movie role. She had a well-remembered part as one of the inmates of an insane asylum in *King of Hearts.* Louis Malle cast her opposite Jean-Paul Belmondo in an entertaining comedy-drama, *The Thief of Paris.*

Then, she made three pictures (*Isabel, Act of the Heart,* and *Journey*) with Paul Almond, who became her husband. Almond commented, "It was with the camera itself that she had her really powerful attraction... even though I might be crouching right next to the lens during a take, I confess I never really knew just what was going on between her and that camera." Audiences knew, however, and responded warmly to her Oscar-nominated performance in *Anne of the Thousand Days.*

Genevieve Bujold in *Coma.*

Swashbuckler was a cardboard derivation of the old Errol Flynn spectacular, but she was luminous in Brian De Palma's *Obsession*—a take-off on Alfred Hitchcock thrillers. *Coma* also showed her off to advantage—she played a doctor who suspected that patients were being murdered and having their organs sold.

Bujold was too old and too mannered for the distressingly phony *Monsignor* with Christopher Reeve. Still, she generated the only moments of tension in that misconceived fiasco, a feat she always accomplished no matter what the quality of the script.

FILMOGRAPHY

1964

The Adolescents ★★★

1966

The War Is Over ★★★
King of Hearts ★★★★

1967

The Thief of Paris ★★★

1968

Isabel ★★★

1969

Anne of the Thousand Days ★★★★

1970

Act of the Heart ★★★

1971

The Trojan Women ★★★★

1972

Journey ★★★

1974

Earthquake ★★★★
Kamouraska ★★★

1976

Obsession ★★★★
Alex and the Gypsy ★★★
Swashbuckler ★★

1977

Another Man Another Chance ★★★

1978

Coma ★★★★

1979

Murder by Decree ★★★

1980

The Last Flight of Noah's Ark ★★★

1981

The Incorrigible ★★★

1982

Monsignor ★★

CAROL BURNETT
★★★2.88 STARS

Carol Burnett is much more popular on TV than in films but—like Mary Tyler Moore—she has the range, charm, and appeal to be equally successful on the big screen.

Burnett was born in 1933, in San Antonio, Texas. She conquered Broadway as a singer, comic, and actress and then went on to do the same with her long-running "The Carol Burnett Show" on TV. In her first movie, *Who's Been Sleeping in My Bed?*, she stole the notices.

Pete 'n' Tillie offered her a powerful dramatic role as the mother of a dying son, and she had a shattering emotional scene. She tried too hard in Billy Wilder's funny update of *The Front Page*, but her sequences in Robert Altman's *A Wedding* were the only bright spots in that disjointed farce. Her fine performance in *The Four Seasons* cancelled out the disastrous *Chu Chu and the Philly Flash*. *Annie* suffered from miscasting, awkward choreography, and bad direction, but Burnett managed to make her scenes sparkle.

Burnett's broad overplaying generally fares worse on the screen than on television, but as she gets older her performances seem to get more precise and cinematic.

Carol Burnett in *Pete 'n' Tillie.*

FILMOGRAPHY

1963

Who's Been Sleeping in My Bed? ★★★

1972

Pete 'n' Tillie ★★★★

1974

The Front Page ★★

1978

A Wedding ★★★

1979

Health ★★

1981

The Four Seasons ★★★★
Chu Chu and the Philly Flash ★★

1982

Annie ★★★

GEORGE BURNS
★★★ 3.10 STARS

George Burns is warm, honest, and likable in real life, and these qualities come through on the screen. It only makes one regret the gap of over thirty years between *Two Girls and a Sailor* (1944) and his comeback film, *The Sunshine Boys*.

Burns was born Nathan Birnbaum in 1896, in New York City. He started out in vaudeville, and then tried a roller-skating act before finding his niche in comedy. His partnership with Gracie Allen charmed radio audiences and proved equally irresistible on television. They were the only outstanding feature of the pictures they made together, such as *College Holiday, Here Comes Cookie,* and *College Swing.* Burns was widowed in 1964.

He returned to films to win a 1975 Oscar for *The Sunshine Boys.* It was slow-moving and mushy, except for his performance, and he performed similar miracles in *Oh, God!* with John Denver. The sequel, *Oh God! Book II,* proved an obstacle even Burns couldn't overcome, but he did brighten *Just You and Me, Kid* singlehandedly.

George Burns retains the same sharp qualities in his octogenarian career as he possessed in his younger days: a slow-burn wit and disarmingly precise delivery.

FILMOGRAPHY

1932

The Big Broadcast ★★★

1933

College Humor ★★★
International House ★★★

1934

Six of a Kind ★★★
We're Not Dressing ★★★
Many Happy Returns ★★★

1935

Love in Bloom ★★★
Big Broadcast of 1936 ★★★
Here Comes Cookie ★★★

1936

College Holiday ★★★

George Burns in *Oh, God!*

1937

A Damsel in Distress ★ ★ ★

1938

College Swing ★ ★ ★

1939

Honolulu ★ ★ ★

1944

Two Girls and a Sailor ★ ★ ★

1975

The Sunshine Boys ★ ★ ★ ★

1977

Oh, God! ★ ★ ★ ★

1978

Sgt. Pepper's Lonely Hearts Club Band ★ ★ ★

1979

Just You and Me, Kid ★ ★ ★
Going in Style ★ ★ ★ ★

1980

Oh God! Book II ★ ★ ★

RAYMOND BURR
★ ★ ★ 3.05 STARS

It took television to make a sympathetic actor out of Raymond Burr. In movies he was always menacing, usually murderous. Hitchcock's *Rear Window* presented him at his loathsome best, as the man across the courtyard who hacked up his wife and stuffed her in a suitcase.

Born in 1917, in New Westminster, Canada, he came to film after extensive work in radio. Burr's mellifluous voice continued to serve him well, and his stout frame and burning eyes made him ideal for villainous roles. In *The Pitfall* you could understand why Lizabeth Scott ran to Dick Powell for protection against Burr's attentions.

Routine fare like *His Kind of Woman* would perk up when Burr came in as a maniacal mobster. Even when he stayed on the right side of the law, as a D.A. in *A Place in the Sun,* he incurred the audience's ire by fighting to place Montgomery Clift in the electric chair. He mixed menace with madness as Natalie Wood's kidnapper in *A Cry in the Night.*

Please Murder Me gave Burr his one starring part and billing as a crooked attorney in love with Angela Lansbury. Dieting made the difference, and he found long-overdue stardom as "Perry Mason" and "Ironside." But along the way, the screen lost possibly its best villain.

Raymond Burr in *The Blue Gardenia.*

FILMOGRAPHY

1946

San Quentin ★ ★ ★

1947

Desperate ★ ★ ★

1948

Ruthless ★ ★ ★
Sleep My Love ★ ★ ★
Raw Deal ★ ★ ★ ★
The Pitfall ★ ★ ★ ★
Walk a Crooked Mile ★ ★ ★
Adventures of Don Juan ★ ★ ★

1949

Bride of Vengeance ★ ★
Black Magic ★ ★ ★
Red Light ★ ★ ★
Abandoned ★ ★ ★

1950

Key to the City ★ ★ ★
Love Happy ★ ★ ★
Borderline ★ ★ ★

1951

M ★ ★ ★
His Kind of Woman ★ ★ ★ ★
The Magic Carpet ★ ★ ★
New Mexico ★ ★ ★
A Place in the Sun ★ ★ ★

Raymond Burr in the TV movie, *Portrait: A Man Whose Name was John.*

1952

Mara Maru ★ ★ ★
Horizons West ★ ★ ★
Meet Danny Wilson ★ ★ ★

1953

The Blue Gardenia ★ ★ ★
Tarzan and the She-Devil ★ ★ ★
Fort Algiers ★ ★ ★

1954

Gorilla at Large ★ ★ ★
Casanova's Big Night ★ ★ ★
Rear Window ★ ★ ★ ★
Passion ★ ★ ★

1955

You're Never Too Young ★ ★ ★
A Man Alone ★ ★ ★

1956

Godzilla (narration)
Please Murder Me ★ ★ ★
Ride the High Iron ★ ★ ★
Great Day in the Morning ★ ★ ★
A Cry in the Night ★ ★ ★ ★

1957

Crime of Passion ★ ★ ★
Affair in Havana ★ ★ ★

1960

Desire in the Dust ★ ★

1968

P.J. ★ ★ ★

1978

Tomorrow Never Comes ★ ★ ★

ELLEN BURSTYN
★★★3.07 STARS

Ellen Burstyn's chief strength—her versatility—may also be her worst failing in terms of stardom. She can be a waitress, an anxious mother, or a faith healer with equal conviction, but she hasn't, as writer Robert Osborne once put it, found "a public image in keeping with her new stature as a film world first lady."

Burstyn was born in Detroit as Edna Rae Gillooly in 1932. She was poor and received no encouragement for her aspirations, but her perserverance led to modeling jobs (by then her name was shortened to just Edna Rae). She changed her name again to Keri Flynn and tested at 20th Century Fox as Erica Dean. There was a Broadway role, in "Fair Game," which inspired her to perfect her craft with acting coach Stella Adler and later the Actors Studio.

An early movie, *Pit Stop* (as Ellen McRae) indicated that success was still a while away. She appeared next in a forgettable comedy *For Those Who Think Young* with Pamela Tiffin and Tina Louise, and kept in the background for *Goodbye Charlie*—a wise move, considering the material involved.

Her next movies were closer to the public eye though still uneven and not commercially accepted. In *Tropic of Cancer* she played Henry Miller's wife (an engaging performance). *Alex in Wonderland* was boring and self-indulgent, but Burstyn stood out amidst the weak material.

Ellen Burstyn with Tom Skerritt in *Silence of the North*.

Director Peter Bogdanovich spotted the full extent of her range and cast her in *The Last Picture Show*. She was Cybill Shepherd's promiscuous mother and won a deserved Best Supporting Actress Award from the New York Film Critics. The movie was touching and memorable, and its tremendous success finally brought Burstyn to the attention of wider audiences.

She lost *Five Easy Pieces* to Karen Black but surfaced in the tedious *The King of Marvin Gardens*. Burstyn was livelier than co-stars Jack Nicholson and Bruce Dern, but audiences were uninterested. Her next movie was her biggest in box-office terms, the horrifying *The Exorcist*. In "the film that everybody is throwing up about," Burstyn's underplaying brought humanity to the sordid contrivances. She had a much smaller role in *Harry and Tonto*, as Art Carney's daughter, and her brittle defensiveness contrasted nicely with Carney's warmth.

The peak of her career came with *Alice Doesn't Live Here Anymore*, a bright, penetrating and vibrant comedy about a waitress with hopeless dreams of becoming a singing star. The script had been rejected as a soap opera by studio executives, but Burstyn fought to get it made. Her portrayal was a rich blend of anger, pathos, lost ambition, and motherly devotion, and the Academy named her its Best Actress in 1974.

Always ready to take on a challenge, Burstyn blundered. *Providence* was an obscure, stream-of-consciousness drama about a writer (John Gielgud) trying to complete his last novel. *A Dream of Passion* was updated Greek tragedy and a tragedy at the box office. She repeated her Broadway role in *Same Time Next Year*, but her characterization on film lacked the bite it had on the stage. The winds shifted again when she did *Resurrection*, an excellent drama about faith healing, immeasurably helped by her sincere and thoughtful performance. Ellen Burstyn is an intelligent actress willing to take risks.

Ellen Burstyn in *The Exorcist*.

FILMOGRAPHY

(billed as Ellen McRae)

1964

For Those Who Think Young ★★★
Goodbye Charlie ★★

1969

Pit Stop ★★

(billed as Ellen Burstyn)

1970

Tropic of Cancer ★★★
Alex in Wonderland ★★★

1971

The Last Picture Show ★★★★

1972

The King of Marvin Gardens ★★★

1973

The Exorcist ★★★★

1974

Harry and Tonto ★★★

1975

Alice Doesn't Live Here Anymore ★★★★

1977

Providence ★★★

1978

A Dream of Passion ★★★
Same Time Next Year ★★★

1979

Resurrection ★★★★

1981

Silence of the North ★★★

RICHARD BURTON
★★½ 2.53 STARS

Richard Burton is continually referred to by journalists as a man of great magnetism, sexuality, and charm in private life. Unfortunately, as columnist Sheilah Graham put it, "the warmth still does not come through (on film)." He can occasionally achieve greatness in the right role, but his box office, at its height, owed more to viewer imagination (fueled by lurid headlines) than to his acting.

Burton, the son of a miner, was born Richard Walter Jenkins, Jr. in South Wales in 1925. He made his initial mark on the stage in "The Lady's Not For Burning" with John Gielgud. His first films (*The Last Days of Dolwyn* and *Now Barabbas Was a Robber*) were unmemorable though Burton gained worldwide attention in *My Cousin Rachel* as a young man who fell for possible murderess Olivia De Havilland. The movie's unsatisfying and unresolved ending hurt it at the box office, but Burton won critical praise. *The Robe* continued him on his winning course, but *Prince of Players* was a boring biography of 19th century actor Edwin Booth. He had a better opportunity in *The Rains of Ranchipur,* an adequate remake of *The Rain Came* and he played *Alexander the Great* with authority.

Burton was shipwrecked with nun Joan Collins in *Sea Wife*, a waterlogged version of *Heaven Knows Mr. Allison* and not nearly as popular. He was also artistically impaled by *The Bramble Bush,* a Peyton Place-type soap opera which brought out all the rigid, overly-theatrical aspects of his acting style.

Richard Burton in *Massacre in Rome.*

He was, however, superb as King Arthur in the hit musical "Camelot," and shortly after that became Mark Anthony to Elizabeth Taylor's *Cleopatra.* Their love affair made him a household name, and the film drew crowds of curious and unlucky viewers. He was too remote and Shakespearean in *The V.I.P.S.* (Maggie Smith stole every scene), and *The Sandpiper* reached a new height in cinematic silliness—Burton was a married minister in love with beatnik Taylor.

During this period, all Burton's pictures without Taylor had more merit than the ones they made together. Two "without Taylor" were the absorbing *The Spy Who Came in from the Cold* and *The Night of the Iguana* in which Ava Gardner's sensuality humanized his aloofness in a way that Taylor never did.

The Burtons had one fine moment together in *Who's Afraid of Virginia Woolf?* Mike Nichols had predicted beforehand that "everybody is going to be surprised" and we were. *The Taming of the Shrew* and *Dr. Faustus* pounded more nails in the coffin of their creative partnership, and the final disasters were *Boom* and *Hammersmith Is Out.*

Burton's first wife Sybil had once predicted, "If Elizabeth and Richard ever break up, it will be Richard who drives her to it." Her predictions proved accurate when Taylor divorced Burton because of his drinking. He managed to get on the wagon and do a Tony-award winning performance in "Equus," but poor films continued to plague him—*Bluebeard, Massacre in Rome,* and the unbelievably bad sequel, *Exorcist II: The Heretic.* In 1983 he and Taylor co-starred in "Private Lives" to small praise and big ticket sales.

Burton's problem, despite his talent, may be that he's a stage actor who managed by tenacity and timing to achieve success in films. But the theatre is clearly where he belongs, the medium that best accommodates his expansive, larger-than-life voice and style.

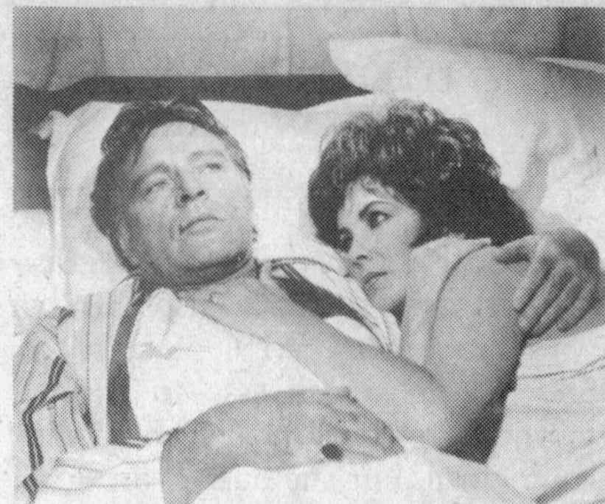
Richard Burton with Elizabeth Taylor in *The Comedians.*

FILMOGRAPHY

1949
The Last Days of Dolwyn ★★★
Now Barabbas Was a Robber ★★★

1950
Waterfront ★★★
The Woman With No Name ★★★

1951
Green Grow the Rushes ★★★

1952
My Cousin Rachel ★★★★

1953
The Desert Rats ★★★
The Robe ★★★

1955
Prince of Players ★★★
The Rains of Ranchipur ★★

1956
Alexander the Great ★★★★

1957
Sea Wife ★★
Bitter Victory ★★★

1959
Look Back in Anger ★★★★

1960
The Bramble Bush ★
Ice Palace ★★

1962
The Longest Day ★★★

1963
Cleopatra ★★
The V.I.P.S. ★★

1964
Becket ★★★★
The Night of the Iguana ★★★★
Hamlet ★★★★

1965
What's New, Pussycat? (cameo)
The Sandpiper ★★
The Spy Who Came in from the Cold ★★★★

1966
Who's Afraid of Virginia Woolf? ★★★★

1967

The Taming of the Shrew ★★★
Dr. Faustus ★
The Comedians ★★

1968

Boom ★
Candy ★

1969

Where Eagles Dare ★★★
Staircase ★★
Anne of the Thousand Days ★★★★

1971

Raid on Rommel ★★
Villain ★★

1972

Hammersmith Is Out ★★
Sutjeska ★★
Bluebeard ★★
The Assassination of Trotsky ★★

1973

Massacre in Rome ★★
Under Milk Wood ★★

1974

The Voyage ★★
The Klansman ★★

1977

Exorcist II: The Heretic ★
Equus ★★★★

1978

The Medusa Touch ★★
The Wild Geese ★★

1979

Sergeant Steiner ★★

1981

Absolution ★

GARY BUSEY
★★★½ 3.29 STARS

Hefty good ol' boy Gary Busey was born in Texas, the son of a foot-loose construction worker and grew up in Tulsa, Oklahoma. He played football at Oklahoma State University but didn't graduate. In the early 1970s he worked in television, appearing on "Bonanza," "Baretta," and "Gunsmoke" and had a featured role on the short-lived "Texas Wheelers."

A musician as well as an actor, Busey toured as a drummer with Leon Russell's band under the pseudonym "Teddy Jack Eddy," the name of a character Busey originated on a Los Angeles cable TV show. His musical training stood him in good stead in his most demanding role to date, that of Buddy Holly in *The Buddy Holly Story.* A natural actor, Busey seemed to alter even his husky physique to fit Holly's lanky frame.

Other roles of note include Masochist in John Milius' surf epic *Big Wednesday* and a clumsy farm boy turned outlaw in Fred Schepisi's overlooked western *Barbarosa,* in which Busey held his own opposite the commanding presence of Willie Nelson.

Gary Busey does not project a single image. Rather he sinks into his roles with chameleon-like abandon. Like Robert De Niro, his intensity is the connecting link between his performances.

Gary Busey with Maria Richwine in *The Buddy Holly Story.*

FILMOGRAPHY

1973

The Last American Hero ★★★
Lolly Madonna XXX (bit)

1976

A Star Is Born ★★★

1978

The Buddy Holly Story ★★★★
Big Wednesday ★★★

1980

Carny ★★★★
Foolin' Around ★★★

1982

Barbarosa ★★★

RED BUTTONS
★★★ 2.86 STARS

Red Buttons is a fine comedian, but he also rates consideration as a serious actor. His name is a handicap, and so is his carrot-colored hair which looks as though it was dipped in paint.

Buttons was born Aaron Chwatt in New York, in 1919. He refined his comic skill in Catskill Mountain hotels and starred in a TV series before making his best-remembered movie, *Sayonara.* It won him a Best Supporting Actor Oscar but there were no worthy follow-ups. *Imitation General, Five Weeks in a Balloon* and *The Big Circus* were trivial entertainment, and he couldn't do much with the garish, fictionalized film version of *Harlow.*

Another juicy role finally came his way in *They Shoot Horses, Don't They?* and he played it superbly. His honest, unaffected "little man" characterization was an asset to *The Poseidon Adventure. Gable and Lombard* had one of the worst scripts of the decade, but *Pete's Dragon* gave Buttons a good role as Jim Dale's bumbling sidekick. *Movie Movie* was a witty collection of Hollywood skits, brightened by his participation, and then he did another Irwin Allen directed disaster movie, *When Time Ran Out...,* a disaster in every sense of the word.

Red Buttons never seems to have taken up acting as his central career. Though it was an adjunct to his stand-up comedy, he has the talent to become a great actor.

FILMOGRAPHY

1944

Winged Victory ★★★

1957

Sayonara ★★★★

1958

Imitation General ★★

1959

The Big Circus ★★★

Red Buttons in *Imitation General.*

1961

One, Two, Three ★★★

1962

Five Weeks in a Balloon ★★★
Hatari! ★★★
The Longest Day ★★★
Gay Purr-ee (voice only)

1963

A Ticklish Affair ★★

1965

Your Cheatin' Heart ★★★
Up from the Beach ★★★
Harlow ★★

1966

Stagecoach ★★★

1969

They Shoot Horses, Don't They? ★★★★

1971

Who Killed What's 'er Name? ★★★

1972

The Poseidon Adventure ★★★★

1976

Gable and Lombard ★★

1977

Viva Knievel! ★★
Pete's Dragon ★★★★

1978

Movie Movie ★★★

1979

C.H.O.M.P.S. ★★

1980

When Time Ran Out... ★★

JAMES CAAN
★★★ 2.86 STARS

After his violent, sexually riveting performance in *The Godfather,* James Caan was touted as Hollywood's brightest new star. The talent still exists, but none of his later scripts matched the quality of the earlier ones.

Caan was born in 1939, in New York City. He was a lifeguard, camp counselor, and bouncer before making his off-Broadway stage debut in "La Ronde." Caan was villainous in *Lady in a Cage* and then had a strong role with John Wayne in *El Dorado. Brian's Song,* a TV movie about the dying Brian Piccolo, accomplished what his films couldn't—it made him a household name. *T.R. Baskin* was a glum and pathetic piece that, fortunately for Caan's career, disappeared quickly.

Then, Francis Ford Coppola hired him for *The Godfather,* and his open, high-spirited amorality was one of the high points of a great film. He teamed beautifully with Marsha Mason in the touching but unpopular *Cinderella Liberty.* His finest moment came when he played *The Gambler,* a shocking (though inconclusively resolved) close-up of gambling addiction. Caan captured all the compulsiveness of the main character in *The Gambler,* and he softened Barbra Streisand's harshness in *Funny Lady.*

James Caan.

Co-star Marsha Mason received all the plaudits and the Oscar nomination for their second movie together, *Chapter Two,* and Caan hated the whole experience. He directed and starred in *Hide in Plain Sight*—a true-life tale of a father searching for his missing child. His direction was a bit too muted but indicated his ability to stretch out in other directions.

James Caan seems to have lost the fiery intensity of his earlier performances, but he remains a competent actor in search of an image.

FILMOGRAPHY

1963

Irma la Douce (bit)

1964

Lady in a Cage ★★

1965

The Glory Guys ★★★
Red Line 7000 ★★★

1967

Games ★★
El Dorado ★★★

1968

Countdown ★★★
Journey to Shiloh ★★★
Submarine X-1 ★★★

1969

The Rain People ★★★★

1970

Rabbit Run ★★

1971

T.R. Baskin ★★

1972

The Godfather ★★★★

1973

Cinderella Liberty ★★★★
Slither ★★

1974

The Gambler ★★★★
Freebie and the Bean ★★
The Godfather Part II (cameo)

1975

Funny Lady ★★★
Rollerball ★★★
Gone With the West ★★
The Killer Elite ★★

1976

Harry and Walter Go to New York ★★
Silent Movie (cameo)

1977

A Bridge Too Far ★★
Another Man, Another Chance ★★★

1978

Comes a Horseman ★ ★ ★ ★

1979

Hide in Plain Sight (direction) ★ ★ ★ ★
Chapter Two ★ ★ ★

1981

Thief ★ ★ ★ ★

1982

Kiss Me Goodbye ★ ★

JAMES CAGNEY
★ ★ ★ ½ 3.51 STARS

On screen, James Cagney is *alive*, as few actors have ever been. He has, in his own words, "a touch of the gutter." He's a fighter and frequently a victim, whose dimension was clearly revealed as The Gimp, Doris Day's gangster lover in *Love Me or Leave Me.* Cagney played an insensitive, hostile villain who was also confused, rejected, and pathetic. Consequently, the viewer sympathized with his most despicable actions.

Unlike the screen's other legendary gangster Humphrey Bogart, who was born to wealth, Cagney began life on New York's Lower East Side in 1899. He said later that he *knew* the hard-bitten, aggressive little guys he played. They came from his own tough neighborhood, and this familiarity made all his portrayals authentic. He was memorable in *The Public Enemy,* an enjoyable con man in *Blonde Crazy,* and a prizefighter in the lively *Winner Take All.*

He abandoned the underworld temporarily for *Hard to Handle,* as a promoter who organized a marathon dance, and helped reform school kids in *The Mayor of Hell.* In *Lady Killer,* he was cast as a gangster turned movie star. He was back to crime in *Frisco Kid,* a chilling performance, and there were unintentional echoes of biography in his line from *G-Men,* "I seen too many back alleys as a kid to want to go back to them."

A Midsummer Night's Dream marked a complete change of pace; his performance as Bottom compen-

James Cagney with Doris Day in *Love Me or Leave Me.*

sated for Mickey Rooney's overacting. *Boy Meets Girl* was a comedy, popular at the time, but rather strained now. Cagney was a hood in *Angels With Dirty Faces,* and Pat O'Brien was his boyhood pal turned priest. The oft-used plot received new life via superb acting.

He alternated between the right and wrong side of the law for his next few films, *The Oklahoma Kid, Each Dawn I Die,* and *The Roaring Twenties.* In *City for Conquest,* he was a boxer devoted to his younger brother, Arthur Kennedy. *The Strawberry Blonde* provided another change of pace: Cagney played a small-town dreamer too in love with the shallow Rita Hayworth to recognize the sincerity of the sweet Olivia De Havilland.

His greatest hit at the time, *Yankee Doodle Dandy,* won him an Oscar and had the world applauding his dancing. It seems *too* sentimental and patriotic now and revives badly compared to his other pictures. However, there were more great performances—in *White Heat* (as a particularly vicious ganster), *Come Fill the Cup* (as an alcoholic), and *13 Rue Madeleine.*

After a few undistinguished films (*A Lion Is in the Streets* and *What Price Glory*), Cagney played hood Marty Snyder in *Love Me or Leave Me,* a film he personally rates as "one of the top five of the sixty-two pictures I made." His cantankerous captain in *Mister Roberts* added spice to that popular film, and he was at his comic best in *One, Two, Three* (he played a Coca-Cola executive fighting the cold war). After a 20-year retirement, Cagney came back in *Ragtime* with his power undiminished.

James Cagney defines acting this way: "What all the good ones have is the ability to project the simple, direct statement of a simple, direct idea without cluttering it. . . . Just plant yourself, look the other actor in the eye and tell him the truth." Cagney is a living example of his own definition.

FILMOGRAPHY

1930

Sinner's Holiday ★ ★ ★
Doorway to Hell ★ ★ ★ ★

1931

Other Men's Women ★ ★ ★
The Millionaire ★ ★ ★
The Public Enemy ★ ★ ★ ★
Smart Money ★ ★ ★
Blonde Crazy ★ ★ ★

1932

Taxi ★ ★ ★ ★
The Crowd Roars ★ ★ ★ ★
Winner Take All ★ ★ ★ ★

James Cagney in *White Heat.*

1933

Hard to Handle ★ ★ ★ ★
Picture Snatcher ★ ★ ★ ★
The Mayor of Hell ★ ★ ★ ★
Footlight Parade ★ ★ ★ ★
Lady Killer ★ ★ ★ ★

1934

Jimmy the Gent ★ ★ ★ ★
He Was Her Man ★ ★ ★ ★
Here Comes the Navy ★ ★ ★ ★
The St. Louis Kid ★ ★ ★ ★

1935

Devil Dogs of the Air ★ ★ ★ ★
G-Men ★ ★ ★ ★
The Irish in Us ★ ★ ★ ★
Frisco Kid ★ ★ ★ ★
A Midsummer Night's Dream ★ ★ ★

1936

Ceiling Zero ★ ★ ★
Great Guy ★ ★ ★

1937

Something to Sing About ★ ★ ★

1938

Boy Meets Girl ★ ★ ★
Angels With Dirty Faces ★ ★ ★ ★

1939

The Oklahoma Kid ★ ★ ★
The Roaring Twenties ★ ★ ★
Each Dawn I Die ★ ★ ★ ★

1940

The Fighting 69th ★ ★ ★
Torrid Zone ★ ★ ★
City for Conquest ★ ★ ★ ★

1941

The Strawberry Blonde ★ ★ ★ ★
The Bride Came C.O.D. ★ ★ ★

1942

Captains of the Clouds ★ ★ ★
Yankee Doodle Dandy ★ ★ ★ ★

1943

Johnny Come Lately ★ ★ ★

1945

Blood on the Sun ★ ★ ★ ★

1947

13 Rue Madeleine ★ ★ ★ ★

1948

The Time of Your Life ★ ★ ★

1949

White Heat ★ ★ ★ ★

1950

Kiss Tomorrow Goodbye ★ ★ ★
The West Point Story ★ ★ ★

1951

Starlift (cameo)
Come Fill the Cup ★ ★ ★ ★

1952

What Price Glory ★ ★ ★

1953

A Lion Is in the Streets ★ ★ ★

1955

Run for Cover ★ ★ ★
Love Me or Leave Me ★ ★ ★ ★
Mister Roberts ★ ★ ★ ★
The Seven Little Foys ★ ★ ★

1956

Tribute to a Bad Man ★ ★ ★
These Wilder Years ★ ★ ★

James Cagney with Priscilla Lane and Gladys George in *The Roaring Twenties.*

1957

Man of a Thousand Faces ★ ★ ★ ★

1959

Never Steal Anything Small ★ ★ ★
Shake Hands with the Devil ★ ★ ★

1960

The Gallant Hours ★ ★ ★

1961

One, Two, Three ★ ★ ★ ★

1981

Ragtime ★ ★ ★

MICHAEL CAINE
★ ★ ★ 2.96 STARS

Michael Caine's amiable reserve and wit make him soothing and easy for audiences to take. He rarely creates sparks, but all his characterizations are believable.

Caine (Maurice Micklewhite) was born in 1933, in London. He worked as a laborer before devoting his full time to acting and appeared in a few now-forgotten movies (*A Hill in Korea* and *How to Murder a Rich Uncle*) before hitting his stride in *Alfie* in 1966. His portrayal of a womanizer without conscience in *Alfie* drew critical raves even from normally crusty critics like John Simon. An Oscar nomination insured good roles, and Caine found a niche as secret agent Harry Palmer in the absorbing *The Ipcress File. Hurry Sundown* proved that he wasn't exactly the right actor to appear bare chested, nor could he surmount the brainlessness of the script. He was on firmer ground with *Billion Dollar Brain,* another Harry Palmer thriller.

He waded bravely through the confusing vagaries of *The Magus,* a poor adaptation of author John Fowles' best-seller. In *X, Y and Zee,* he was cast as Elizabeth Taylor's philandering husband, a good performance in an underrated movie. *Sleuth* gave him the prestige and audience that *Woman Times Seven, The Italian Job,* and *The Last Valley* had taken away. He was the sole virtue of a dull suspense tale, *The Black Windmill,* and his low-key honesty was particularly helpful in John Huston's entertaining *The Man Who Would Be King.* Caine had his best part in years as Maggie Smith's homosexual husband in *California Suite.* When Smith won her Best Supporting Oscar, she paid tribute to Caine, subsequently telling interviewers he should have won too.

He also contributed an Oscar-worthy portrayal in the fiendishly clever *Deathtrap.* A moment to be savored occurred when he faced murderous Christopher Reeve and asked slowly, "Do you know the term. . .sociopath?"

Michael Caine in *A Bridge Too Far.*

FILMOGRAPHY

1956

A Hill in Korea ★ ★ ★

1957

How to Murder a Rich Uncle ★ ★ ★

1958

The Key ★ ★ ★
Blind Spot ★ ★ ★

1959

The Two-Headed Spy ★ ★ ★

1960

Foxhole in Cairo ★ ★ ★
The Bulldog Breed ★ ★ ★

1961

The Day the Earth Caught Fire ★ ★ ★

1962

Solo for Sparrow ★ ★ ★

1963

The Wrong Arm of the Law ★ ★ ★

1964

Zulu ★ ★ ★

1965

The Ipcress File ★★★★

1966

Alfie ★★★★
The Wrong Box ★★★
Gambit ★★★★
Funeral in Berlin ★★★

1967

Hurry Sundown ★
Billion Dollar Brain ★★★
Woman Times Seven ★★

1968

Tonight Let's All Make Love in London (documentary)
Deadfall ★★★
The Magus ★★

1969

Play Dirty ★★★
The Italian Job ★★★
The Battle of Britain ★★★

1970

Too Late the Hero ★★★

1971

The Last Valley ★★★
Get Carter ★★★
Kidnapped ★★★

1972

X, Y and Zee ★★★
Pulp ★★
Sleuth ★★★★

1974

The Black Windmill ★★★
The Wilby Conspiracy ★★★
The Destructors ★★★

1975

The Romantic Englishwoman ★★★★
The Man Who Would Be King ★★★★

1976

Peeper ★★
Harry and Walter Go to New York ★★
The Eagle Has Landed ★★★

1977

A Bridge Too Far ★★
Silver Bears ★★★

1978

The Swarm ★★
California Suite ★★★★

1979

Ashanti ★★★
Beyond the Poseidon Adventure ★★

1980

The Island ★★★
Dressed to Kill ★★★

1981

The Hand ★★★
Victory ★★★

1982

Deathtrap ★★★★

DYAN CANNON
★★★ 3.13 STARS

"If I help her, she can be the biggest star in pictures but now, poor baby, it's hit and miss." These were ex-husband Cary Grant's thoughts on Dyan Cannon, but he underestimated her talent and tenacity. Cannon has sex appeal and comic style, qualities that have been consistently evident since her first big success in 1969.

Cannon (Samille Diane Friesen) was born in 1939, in Tacoma, Washington. She first sang at a Seattle Reform synagogue and then worked as a model. She appeared on Broadway in a series of unsuccessful shows, married Cary Grant, and gave him a daughter. Two early pictures *(The Rise and Fall of Legs Diamond* and *This Rebel Breed)* did nothing for her career.

She was superb in *Bob & Carol & Ted & Alice,* as Elliott Gould's sexually discontented wife, and her Oscar nomination led to an exciting role in Sidney Lumet's thriller, *The Anderson Tapes.* She sparkled briefly in *Doctors' Wives,* the only good ingredient in that film (though the producers mistakenly killed her off in the first half hour). *The Love Machine* was the *worst* of three adaptations of Jacqueline Susann novels—an incredible feat—so Cannon's competence went unnoticed. She had a juicy starring part in the sometimes hokey, sometimes witty *Such Good Friends.* She played a wife who learned that her dying husband had been unfaithful.

Cannon's presence energized *The Last of Sheila.* She was the best part of *Heaven Can Wait,* for which she received another Oscar nomination. A third Oscar nomination was merited when she wrote, produced, directed, and co-edited a 42-minute film *Number One* sponsored by the American Film Institute.

Dyan Cannon seems to be in her prime. Her most recent performance is among her very best: as the conniving (and connived upon) wife of Michael Caine in *Deathtrap.*

Dyan Cannon with Charles Grodin in *Heaven Can Wait.*

FILMOGRAPHY

1960

The Rise and Fall of Legs Diamond ★★
This Rebel Breed ★★★

1969

Bob & Carol & Ted & Alice ★★★★

1971

The Burglars ★★★
The Anderson Tapes ★★★
Doctors' Wives ★★★
The Love Machine ★★★
Such Good Friends ★★★★

1973

Shamus ★★★
The Last of Sheila ★★★

1974

Child Under a Leaf ★★

1978

Heaven Can Wait ★★★★
Revenge of the Pink Panther ★★★

1981

Honeysuckle Rose ★★★
Coast to Coast ★★★

1982

Deathtrap ★★★★

ART CARNEY
★★★ 3.17 STARS

Although Art Carney was TV's best second banana for eight years on "The Honeymooners," it took the big screen to project his greatness.

Carney (Arthur William Mathew Carney) was born in 1918, in Mount Vernon, New York. He started his career with a dance band by imitating celebrities and then switched to radio ("Gang Busters," and "Aunt Jenny's Kitchen"), but his movie career was, and remains, less than prolific. In *Pot O' Gold* he had only a bit part, and his participation in *The Yellow Rolls Royce* was irrelevant.

Paul Mazursky persuaded him, against his will, to do *Harry and Tonto*. As the fifty-five-year-old man who traveled cross-country with his cat, Tonto, Carney's performance was nothing less than a tour de force. Every possible emotion—curiosity, hope, lost illusions, sexual awakening, anger—was contained in his portrayal. He won an Oscar over such formidable competition as Al Pacino *(The Godfather)* and Jack Nicholson *(Chinatown)*. His tremendous success led only to a dim-witted but likable Burt Reynolds comedy, *W.W. and the Dixie Dance Kings*.

Won Ton Ton-The Dog Who Saved Hollywood was, unfortunately, a dog of a film, but Lily Tomlin proved a lively teammate in the eccentric and pleasant *The Late Show*. There were more excellent parts in good pictures *(House Calls* and *Movie Movie)* and bad ones *(Sunburn)*. We can only hope that Carney continues to act and to get parts worthy of his talent.

Art Carney with Jackie Gleason and Jayne Meadows on "The Honeymooners."

FILMOGRAPHY

1941

Pot O' Gold (bit)

1964

The Yellow Rolls-Royce ★ ★ ★

Art Carney with Lily Tomlin in *The Late Show*.

1967

A Guide for the Married Man ★ ★ ★

1974

Harry and Tonto ★ ★ ★ ★

1975

W. W. and the Dixie Dance Kings ★ ★ ★ ★

1976

Won Ton Ton - the Dog Who Saved Hollywood ★ ★ ★

1977

The Late Show ★ ★ ★ ★
Scott Joplin ★ ★ ★

1978

House Calls ★ ★ ★ ★
Movie Movie ★ ★ ★ ★

1979

Steel ★ ★ ★
Sunburn ★ ★ ★
Ravagers ★ ★ ★
Going in Style ★ ★ ★

1980

Defiance ★ ★ ★
Roadie ★ ★
Steel ★ ★ ★

1982

Take This Job and Shove It ★ ★
St. Helens ★ ★ ★

LESLIE CARON
★ ★ ★ 3.07 STARS

When Leslie Caron first appeared on film, she had an irresistible gamine appeal and wide saucer eyes that glowed with innocence. This innocence was exquisitely utilized in her early musicals. Maturity added sophistication and an expanded acting range, but it also subtracted some of her individuality.

Caron was born near Paris in 1931. She was a successful ballerina when Gene Kelly discovered her and cast her in *An American in Paris*. The film won a Best Picture Oscar and a special Oscar for Gene Kelly, but Caron's bewitching charm was the unexpected plus factor that made the picture legendary. MGM wasted her fabulous debut by following up with three ordinary dramas—*The Man With a Cloak*, *Glory Alley*, and *The Story of Three Loves*.

Then Charles Walters directed her in *Lili*—she played an orphan in love with puppeteer Mel Ferrer. The acclaim was so great that the studio ordered another grown-up fairytale, *The Glass Slipper*. It was talkier and less magical than its predecessor, but Caron and leading man Michael Wilding brought it off.

Now fully established, she was paired with Fred Astaire in *Daddy Long Legs*. They had a fine score (including Johnny Mercer's jubilant "Something's Gotta Give") and a chemistry equal to the Caron-Kelly teaming. *Gaby* wasn't as successful (a melodramatic remake of *Waterloo Bridge*), but Caron's sincere, luminous portrait of an unhappy dancer had a beauty not sufficiently appreciated at the time.

Gigi was the high point of her career—a perfect musical, with a witty score, engaging performances (by Caron, Maurice Chevalier, Louis Jourdan, and Hermione Gingold), and an eye-filling production design. Difficulty arose, according to lyricist Alan Jay Lerner, when Caron insisted on singing the songs herself—apparently her singing voice is harsh, not in keeping with the gamine image. However, she finally acquiesced to having her voice dubbed.

She voiced her resentment of these waif-like roles, but when she departed from the stereotype, the results were mixed. *The Doctor's Dilemma* was too talky, although she did well as Mrs. Dubedat. Neither *The Man Who Understood Women* or *The Subterraneans* pleased her fans.

Fanny presented a more mature version of her Gigi/Lili/Gaby image. It had Maurice Chevalier and Charles Boyer and worked well as a play (the original had been a Broadway musical). She gave her best dramatic performance in the touching *The L-Shaped Room* as a pregnant girl in a London boardinghouse.

Father Goose was thin material, propped up by Cary Grant's ageless charm, and Caron seemed out of place in two forced comedies: *Promise Her Anything* (with real-life lover Warren Beatty) and *A Very Special Favor.*

Caron's attitude about her roles makes an interesting point. She apparently railed against all the musical parts that made her famous, although they were clearly the best examples of her talent. It makes one realize that studios did know best. Performers aren't necessarily the best judges of material for themselves.

Leslie Caron with Avis Bunnage in *The L-Shaped Room.*

FILMOGRAPHY

1951

An American in Paris ★★★★
The Man With a Cloak ★★★

1952

Glory Alley ★★★

1953

The Story of Three Loves ★★★
Lili ★★★★

1955

The Glass Slipper ★★★
Daddy Long Legs ★★★★

1956

Gaby ★★★★

1958

Gigi ★★★★
The Doctor's Dilemma ★★★

1959

The Man Who Understood Women ★★★

1960

Austerlitz ★★★
The Subterraneans ★★★

1961

Fanny ★★★★

1962

Guns of Darkness ★★★
The L-Shaped Room ★★★★
Three Fables of Love ★★★

1964

Father Goose ★★★

1965

A Very Special Favor ★★

1966

Promise Her Anything ★★
Is Paris Burning? ★★★

1968

The Head of the Family ★★★

1970

Madron ★★

1971

Chandler ★★

1976

Serail ★★★

1977

The Man Who Loved Women ★★★
Valentino ★★

1979

Golden Girl ★★★

1982

Contract ★★★

DAVID CARRADINE
★★★ 2.79 STARS

Combining the rebelliousness of a Jack Nicholson with silent-loner image of a Charles Bronson, David Carradine makes an ideal action hero. His failure to become a big box-office success has made him something of a cult actor, however.

He was born in 1936, the son of prolific actor John Carradine. He seems to have acquired his father's commanding presence, though none of his loquaciousness. He was able to use his connections to get bit parts in films, but struck no sparks of his own until he played the lead in the television series, "Kung Fu." That show's combination of karate and mysticism was a huge hit and set his image in action films.

His first starring role was in Martin Scorsese's directorial debut, *Boxcar Bertha*, a seedy tale of young hobos in love. It featured steamy sex scenes with co-star Barbara Hershey that generated an off-camera romance. Cars and sex seemed to be his forte and he co-starred with Mary Woronov in *Death Race 2000*, with Kate Jackson in *Thunder and Lightning*, and with Claudia Jennings in *Deathsport*.

David Carradine in *Bound for Glory.*

Carradine's big chance to move out of the drive-in circuit came when he portrayed folksinger Woody Guthrie in *Bound for Glory.* He brilliantly captured both the mannerisms and attitude of that Depression-era hero, but the film garnered him little except for rave reviews. Another box-office failure in a lousy art film by Ingmar Bergman, *The Serpent's Egg*, signaled the end of his attempt at stardom.

After that he was content to play in more kung fu epics like *Lone Wolf McQuade* or drive-in fare like *Q*, a horror film about a winged monster. His role in *Q* cleverly cast him against type as an authority figure. Though his roles in these films are written with little depth, David Carradine always invests them with more wit and intelligence than they deserve.

FILMOGRAPHY

1964

Taggart ★★

1965

Bus Riley's Back in Town (cameo)

1967

The Violent Ones ★★

1969

Heaven with a Gun ★★
Young Billy Young ★★★
The Good Guys and the Bad Guys ★★★

1970

The McMasters ★★★
Macho Callahan ★★★

1972

Boxcar Bertha ★★★

1973

Mean Streets (bit)

1975

You and Me (direction) ★★★
Death Race 2000 ★★★

1976

Cannonball ★★
Bound for Glory ★★★★

1977

Gray Lady Down ★★
The Serpent's Egg ★★★
Thunder and Lightning ★★★

1978

Deathsport ★★

1979

Cloud Danger ★★★
The Mandate of Heaven ★★★
Circle of Iron ★★★

1980

Roger Corman, Hollywood's Wild Angel (documentary)
The Long Riders ★★★★

1981

Americana (direction) ★★★

1982

Q ★★★
Tricks or Treats ★★★

1983

Lone Wolf McQuade ★★

JOHN CARRADINE
★★★ 2.88 STARS

Tall, gaunt and given to melodramatic readings, John Carradine has been a fixture in films for over five decades. He has acted leads, supporting roles, character and bit parts in over 180 films. Although mostly closely associated with horror films, his work spans all genres. His ghostly appearance and Shakespearean delivery make him appear overpowering and hammy on screen, but he always enlivens his roles with his great energy.

He was born Richmond Reed Carradine in 1906, in New York City. He tramped about the country as an itinerant artist and theatrical trouper before settling in Hollywood and taking bit parts. His first films included several classics like *Sign of the Cross, The Invisible Man, The Black Cat, Les Miserables,* and *Bride of Frankenstein.* Though his parts were little more than walk-ons, his distinctive features make him recognizable in those films when seen today.

He first attracted attention for his role as the villainous sergeant in John Ford's *The Prisoner of Shark Island*. He subsequently appeared in seven more John Ford films. He had a few other memorable roles in the 1930s—*Winter, Kidnapped* and *Of Human Hearts* among them—along with his host of filler parts. His role as Casey in John Ford's 1940 dustbowl drama, *The Grapes of Wrath* helped boost him up to lead status.

Carradine moved up to lead roles, alright, but inevitably in low-budget trash like *Hitler's Madman* or *Voodoo Man*. He typically gave every role his best and even managed to create some effectively moody dramas like *Bluebeard* when given the chance. When he played Dracula in *House of Frankenstein,* he was typecast in horror films for the rest of the 1940s.

In the 1950s, Carradine moved back into supporting roles in mainstream films. He delivered memorable bits to *Johnny Guitar, The Court Jester, The Ten Commandments,* and *Around the World in 80 Days*. In the late 1960s, he moved into another horror cycle and his films were worse than ever: *Billy the Kid Vs. Dracula, The Astro-Zombies, Blood of Dracula's Castle, Vampire Men of the Lost Planet,* ad nauseum. He played with his son, David Carradine, in *Boxcar Bertha* and even popped up in Woody Allen's sex comedy, *Everything You Always Wanted to Know About Sex*.

John Carradine continues to act bit parts in films as he nears eighty. He has recently made memorable contributions to *The Howling* and *The Secret of Nimh*. Carradine has been known to overact at times, but it is probably a reflex reaction to having to compensate for the many bad films that this fine actor has unfortunately been saddled with.

FILMOGRAPHY

1930

Tol'able David ★★★

1931

Bright Lights ★★★

1932

Sign of the Cross ★★★

1933

The Invisible Man ★★★★

1934

The Black Cat ★★★★
Of Human Bondage ★★★
Cleopatra ★★★

1935

The Man Who Broke the Bank at Monte Carlo ★★★
Alias Mary Dow ★★★
Les Miserables ★★★★
The Crusades ★★★
Bride of Frankenstein ★★★★
Clive of India ★★★

1936

Transient Lady ★★★
Cardinal Richelieu ★★★
Captain January ★★★
The Prisoner of Shark Island ★★★
Under Two Flags ★★★
White Fang ★★★
Ramona ★★★
Dimples ★★★
Mary of Scotland ★★★
Daniel Boone ★★★
Winterset ★★★★
The Garden of Allah ★★★
Message to Garcia ★★★
Anything Goes ★★★

1937

Nancy Steele is Missing ★★★
Danger...Love at Work! ★★★
This Is My Affair ★★★
Love Under Fire ★★★
Thank You, Mr. Moto ★★★
Captains Courageous ★★★★
The Last Gangster ★★★★
The Hurricane ★★★★
Laughing at Trouble ★★★
Ali Baba Goes to Town ★★

1938

International Settlement ★★★
Four Men and a Prayer ★★★
I'll Give a Million ★★★
Kentucky Moonshine ★★★
Kidnapped ★★★
Alexander's Ragtime Band ★★★
Gateway ★★★
Submarine Patrol ★★★
Of Human Hearts ★★★

1939

Jesse James ★★★
The Hound of the Baskervilles ★★★★
Frontier Marshal ★★★
Drums Along the Mohawk ★★★
The Three Musketeers ★★★
Stagecoach ★★★★
Captain Fury ★★★
Five Came Back ★★★
Mr. Moto's Last Warning ★★★

John Carradine with Woody Allen in *Everything You Always Wanted to Know About Sex (But Were Afraid to Ask.)*

1940

The Grapes of Wrath ★★★★
The Return of Frank James ★★★
Brigham Young-Frontiersman ★★★
Chad Hanna ★★★

1941

Western Union ★★★
King of the Zombies ★★★
Blood and Sand ★★★
Man Hunt ★★★
Swamp Water ★★★

1942

Whispering Ghosts ★★★
The Black Swan ★★★
Son of Fury ★★★
Northwest Rangers ★★★
Reunion in France ★★

1943

Silver Spurs ★★★
Gangway for Tomorrow ★★★
I Escaped the Gestapo ★★★
The Isle of Forgotten Sins ★★
Hitler's Madman ★★★★

1944

Bluebeard ★★★★
Barbary Coast Gent ★★★
The Mummy's Ghost ★★★
The Adventures of Mark Twain ★★★
Black Parachute ★★★
The Invisible Man's Revenge ★★★
Return of the Ape Man ★★★
Voodoo Man ★★★
Waterfront ★★★
Revenge of the Zombies ★★★
Captive Wild Woman ★★★

1945

Alaska ★★★
House of Dracula ★★★★
House of Frankenstein ★★★★
It's in the Bag ★★★
Captain Kidd ★★

1946

G-Men ★★★
Down Missouri Way ★★★
Face of Marble ★★★

1947

The Private Affairs of Bel-Ami ★★★

1949

C-Man ★★★

1953

No Escape ★★★

1954

Thunder Pass ★★★
Casanova's Big Night ★★★
Johnny Guitar ★★★★
The Egyptian ★★

1955

Stranger on Horseback ★★★
Desert Sands ★★
The Kentuckian ★★★
Dark Venture ★★★

1956

Female Jungle ★★
The Black Sheep ★★
The Ten Commandments ★★★
Around the World in 80 Days ★★★
Hidden Guns ★★★
The Court Jester ★★★

1957

The Unearthly ★★★
Half Human ★★★
Hellship Mutiny ★★★
The True Story of Jesse James ★★★
The Story of Mankind ★★

1958

The Proud Rebel ★★★★
The Last Hurrah ★★★★
Showdown at Boot Hill ★★★

1959

The Oregon Trail ★★★
The Cosmic Man ★★★
Invisible Invaders ★★★

1960

Invasion of the Animal People ★★
The Adventures of Huckleberry Finn ★★★
Tarzan the Magnificent ★★
Sex Kittens Go to College ★★
Incredible Petrified World ★★

1962

The Man Who Shot Liberty Valance ★★★

1964

The Patsy ★★
Cheyenne Autumn ★★★
Curse of the Stone Hand ★★
The Wizard of Mars ★★

1965

Billy the Kid Vs. Dracula ★★

1966

Night of the Beast ★★★
Night Train to Mundo Fine ★★
Dr. Terror's Gallery of Horrors ★★★
Munster, Go Home ★★★
Broken Sabre ★★★

1967

Hillbillies in the Haunted House ★★
The Astro-Zombies ★★
Operation M ★★
Blood of Dracula's Castle ★★
The Hostage ★★★

1968

They Ran for Their Lives ★★★

1969

Is This Trip Really Necessary? ★★
Trip to Terror ★★★
The Good Guys and the Bad Guys ★★★
The Trouble With Girls ★★
Archy and Mehitabel (voice only)
King Gun ★★
Bigfoot ★★
Las Vampiras ★★

1970

Myra Breckinridge ★★
Hell's Bloody Devils ★★
Vampire Men of the Lost Planet ★★
The McMasters ★★★

1971

Shinbone Alley ★★
Five Bloody Graves ★★
The Seven Minutes ★★

1972

Boxcar Bertha ★★★
Everything You Always Wanted to Know About Sex but Were Afraid to Ask ★★★

1973

The Gatling Gun ★★★
Terror in the Wax Museum ★★★
Bad Charleston Charlie ★★★
Hex ★★

1974

The House of Seven Corpses ★★
Silent Night, Bloody Night ★★
Moon Child ★★

1975

Mary, Mary, Bloody Mary ★★

1976

The Shootist ★★★
The Last Tycoon ★★★
The Killer Inside Me ★★★

1977

The Sentinel ★★★
The White Buffalo ★★★
Crash ★★★
Satan's Cheerleaders ★★
Journey into the World ★★★
Shock Waves ★★★

1978

Sunset Cove ★★
Vampire Hookers ★★
The Bees ★★

1979

Nocturna ★★★
Americathon ★★★

1980

The Bogey Man ★★★

1981

The Nesting ★★★
The Howling ★★★

1982

The Secret of Nimh (voice only)

LEO G. CARROLL
★★★ 2.94 STARS

With his imposing diction, crumbled face, and stately frame, Leo G. Carroll was the ideal Englishman. Whether playing the heavy, the eccentric uncle, or the bemused bureaucrat, he was a consistently good character actor.

Born in England, in 1892, Leo G. Carroll had a distinguished career in the theatre, commuting from London to New York and successful on both sides of the Atlantic. In 1934, his film career began with parts in such reputable productions as *The Barretts of Wimpole Street* and *A Christmas Carol,* in which he played the ghost of Marley. His long association with Alfred Hitchcock began with the director's first American film, *Rebecca,* and continued through *Suspicion, Spellbound,* and *Strangers on a Train* to one of Carroll's most memorable roles, as the Secret Service chief who allowed Cary Grant to be mistaken for a nonexistent agent in *North by Northwest.* Carroll also turned in fine performances for other great directors such as: Douglas Sirk (*The First Legion*) and Vincente Minnelli (*Father of the Bride* and *The Bad and the Beautiful*).

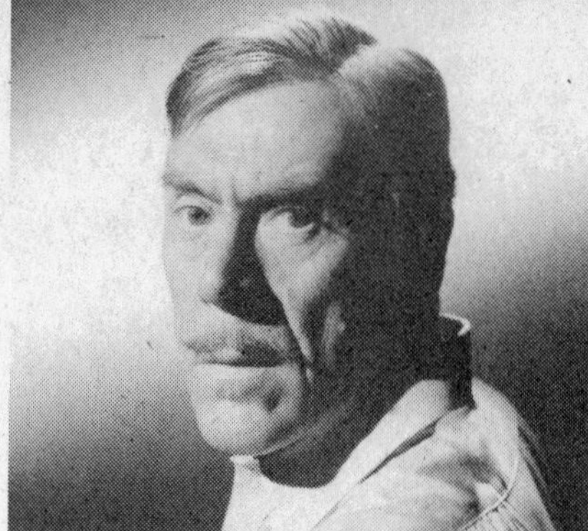

Leo G. Carroll in *Bahama Passage.*

Toward the end of his career, his film persona began to shift from distinguished reserve to comic befuddlement. His television roles included Cosmo Topper in "Topper" and Mr. Waverly in "The Man from U.N.C.L.E." Carroll died on October 16, 1972, in Hollywood.

FILMOGRAPHY

1934

Sadie McKee (bit)
The Barretts of Wimpole Street ★★★
Outcast Lady ★★

1935

Clive of India ★★★

1937

London by Night ★★★

1938

A Christmas Carol ★★★★

1939

The Private Lives of Elizabeth and Essex ★★★
Wuthering Heights ★★★
Tower of London ★★★

1940

Rebecca ★★★
Waterloo Bridge ★★★

1941

Suspicion ★★★
Scotland Yard ★★★
Bahama Passage ★★★

1945

Spellbound ★★★★
The House on 92nd Street ★★★★

1947

Song of Love ★★★
Forever Amber ★★
The Paradine Case ★★

1948

So Evil My Love ★★★

1950

The Happy Years ★★★
Father of the Bride ★★★★

1951

The First Legion ★★★★
Strangers on a Train ★★★
The Desert Fox ★★★★

1952

The Snows of Kilimanjaro ★★★

1953

Young Bess ★★
The Bad and the Beautiful ★★★

1955

We're No Angels ★★★
Tarantula ★★

1956

The Swan ★

1959

North by Northwest ★★★★

1963

The Prize ★★★

1966

The Spy with My Face ★★★

1969

From Nashville with Music ★

MADELEINE CARROLL
★★★ 3.20 STARS

Madeleine Carroll was a beautiful and talented actress. She was never less than professional in any of her pictures, but somehow her personality lacked the glue to stick in the memory. When one thinks about *The 39 Steps,* for example, the story is much more vivid than the heroine.

She was born in England, in 1906, and appeared in several West End plays before her film career gained impetus. Movies like *Atlantic, Young Woodley,* and *School for Scandal* made her a number one attraction in Britain. Hitchcock selected her for *The 39 Steps* and *Secret Agent,* and the success of these projects stirred Hollywood's interest.

Some of her films, *The Prisoner of Zenda* with Ronald Colman, and *The General Died at Dawn* with Gary Cooper, are now classics. She made a few enjoyable comedies *(Honeymoon in Bali* and *Cafe Society)* and then shifted to heavily emotional acting in *My Son, My Son.* Carroll made an ideal foil for Bob Hope in *My Favorite Blonde,* but her films after that *(The Fan* and *Don't Trust Your Husband)* were uninteresting. She scored a big hit on Broadway with "Goodbye, My Fancy" and then retired from the screen.

Madeleine Carroll in *The World Moves On.*

FILMOGRAPHY

1928

The Guns of Loos ★★★
The First Born ★★★
What Money Can Buy ★★★

1929

The Crooked Billet ★★★
L'Instinct ★★★
The American Prisoner ★★★
Atlantic ★★★

1930

Young Woodley ★★★
The W Plan ★★★
French Leave ★★★
Escape ★★★
School for Scandal ★★★
Madame Guillotine ★★★

1931

The Kissing Cup Race ★★★
Fascination ★★★
The Written Law ★★★

1933

Sleeping Car ★★★
I Was a Spy ★★★

1934

The World Moves On ★★★

1935

The Dictator ★★★
The 39 Steps ★★★★

1936

Secret Agent ★★★★
The Case Against Mrs. Ames ★★★
The General Died at Dawn ★★★★
Lloyds of London ★★★★

1937

On the Avenue ★★★★
The Prisoner of Zenda ★★★★
It's All Yours ★★★

1938

Blockade ★★★

1939

Cafe Society ★★★★
Honeymoon in Bali ★★★★

1940

My Son, My Son ★★★★
Safari ★★★
Northwest Mounted Police ★★★

1941

Virginia ★★★
One Night in Lisbon ★★★

1942

Bahama Passage ★★
My Favorite Blonde ★★★★

1946

White Cradle Inn ★★★

1948

Don't Trust Your Husband ★★

1949

The Fan ★★★

JOHN CASSAVETES
★★★ 2.95 STARS

John Cassavetes has become known in recent years as the director of strange and controversial films. Opinions on the merit of his directing work are sharply divided and tend to obscure his much greater gifts as an actor.

Born in 1929, in New York, his gritty, street-flavored style was first

John Cassavetes in *The Dirty Dozen.*

seen in low-budget melodramas like *The Night Holds Terror* and *Crime in the Streets.* He teamed with Sidney Poitier in the shatteringly powerful *Edge of the City,* Cassavetes' finest performance. He was also impressive as Robert Taylor's lawless brother in *Saddle the Wind.* Cassavetes stood out in the popular *The Dirty Dozen* and added conviction to *Rosemary's Baby.*

As a director, he won a critic's award in Venice for *Shadows.* The films that he directed usually featured his talented wife Gena Rowlands and an inordinate amount of improvisation. John Cassavetes continues to act, being seen most recently in the tempestuous *Tempest.*

FILMOGRAPHY

1951

14 hours (bit)

1953

Taxi ★★

1955

The Night Holds Terror ★★★

1956

Crime in the Streets ★★★

1957

Edge of the City ★★★★
Affair in Havana ★★

1958

Saddle the Wind ★★★★
Virgin Island ★★★

1962

The Webster Boy ★★★

1964

The Killers ★★★

1967

The Dirty Dozen ★★★★
Devil's Angels ★★

John Cassavetes with Gena Rowlands in *Tempest.*

1968

Rosemary's Baby ★★★★
Machine Gun McCain ★★★

1969

If It's Tuesday, This Must Be Belgium (cameo)
Bandits in Rome ★★

1976

Two-Minute Warning ★★★
Mikey and Nicky ★★★

1978

The Fury ★★★
Brass Target ★★★

1981

Whose Life Is It Anyway? ★★★

1982

The Tempest ★★★
The Incubus ★★

RICHARD CHAMBERLAIN
★★★ 2.78 STARS

Richard Chamberlain was an ideal Dr. Kildare on television—so ideal, in fact, that many people still question his ability to portray anything else. Despite a number of varied, challenging roles, Chamberlain's image still conjures up the good doctor.

He was born in Beverly Hills, California, in 1935. Initial parts, like *Joy in the Morning* with Yvette Mimieux capitalized on his glossy physical perfection. *Petulia* widened his range and *Julius Caesar* was a radical attempt to shed his pretty-boy image.

He played Tchaikovsky in *The Music Lovers,* Ken Russell's completely fictionalized biography of the composer's life. From then on he made mostly disaster films *(The Towering Inferno* and *The Swarm)* or costume dramas *(Lady Caroline Lamb, The Slipper and the Rose, The Count of Monte Cristo,* and *The Three Musketeers).* He had a meaty role as an Australian lawyer defending an aborigine accused of murder in *The Last Wave.* However, Chamberlain's two biggest triumphs were in TV mini-series—*Shogun* and *The Thorn Birds.*

FILMOGRAPHY

1960

Secret of the Purple Reef ★★

1961

A Thunder of Drums ★★★

1963

Twilight of Honor ★★★

Richard Chamberlain in *Twilight of Honor.*

1965

Joy in the Morning ★★★

1968

Petulia ★★★★

1969

The Madwoman of Chaillot ★★

1970

Julius Caesar ★★

1971

The Music Lovers ★★

1972

Lady Caroline Lamb ★★★

1974

The Three Musketeers ★★★★
The Towering Inferno ★★★

1975

The Four Musketeers ★★★

1976

The Slipper and the Rose ★★
The Count of Monte Cristo ★★★

1978

The Swarm ★★

1979

The Last Wave ★★★

1981

Shogun ★★★

1983

Murder by Phone ★★★

JEFF CHANDLER
★★½ 2.65 STARS

Jeff Chandler was a strikingly handsome, talented actor who got lost in second-rate films. Contemporaries Rock Hudson and Tony Curtis survived to play that one role that made them more than fan magazine material (Hudson in *Giant* and Tony Curtis in *The Defiant Ones)*—but Chandler died of blood poisoning at age forty-two.

He was born Ira Grossel in New York, in 1918. His radio work ("Michael Shayne, Detective" and "Our Miss Brooks") brought a movie offer, but the mediocre parts began immediately with *Johnny O'Clock* and *The Invisible Wall.* There was a brief moment of glory—as Cochise in *Broken Arrow*—but it vanished with the *Flame of Araby* and *The Battle at Apache Pass.*

He played Joan Crawford's gigolo lover in *Female on the Beach,* but the film was one of her corniest melodramas. Chandler supplied the one believable element in *Jeanne Eagels* as Kim Novak's faithful boyfriend, but critics were too busy lambasting his co-star to notice.

Jeff Chandler with Laraine Day in *Toy Tiger.*

FILMOGRAPHY

1942

Johnny O'Clock ★ ★
The Invisible Wall ★ ★
Roses Are Red ★ ★

1949

Mr. Belvedere Goes to College ★ ★
Sword in the Desert ★ ★ ★
Abandoned ★ ★ ★

1950

Broken Arrow ★ ★ ★ ★
Two Flags West ★ ★ ★
Deported ★ ★ ★

1951

Bird of Paradise ★ ★
Smuggler's Island ★ ★
Iron Man ★ ★ ★
Flame of Araby ★ ★

1952

The Battle at Apache Pass ★ ★
Red Ball Express ★ ★
Yankee Buccaneer ★ ★
Because of You ★ ★ ★

1953

The Great Sioux Uprising ★ ★
East of Sumatra ★ ★

1954

War Arrow ★ ★
Yankee Pasha ★ ★
Sign of the Pagan ★ ★
Taza, Son of Cochise ★ ★

1955

Firefox ★ ★ ★
Female on the Beach ★ ★ ★
The Spoilers ★ ★ ★

1956

Toy Tiger ★ ★
Away All Boats ★ ★ ★
Pillars of the Sky ★ ★ ★

1957

The Tattered Dress ★ ★ ★
Jeanne Eagels ★ ★ ★
Drango ★ ★ ★

1958

Man in the Shadow ★ ★ ★
The Lady Takes a Flyer ★ ★
Raw Wind in Eden ★ ★ ★

1959

Stranger in My Arms ★ ★ ★
Thunder in the Sun ★ ★ ★
The Jayhawkers ★ ★ ★ ★
Ten Seconds to Hell ★ ★ ★

1960

The Plunderers ★ ★ ★

1961

Return to Peyton Place ★ ★ ★

1962

Merrill's Marauders ★ ★ ★
A Story of David ★ ★ ★ ★

CHARLIE CHAPLIN
★ ★ ★ ½ 3.60 STARS

It was not surprising, given his background of bitter poverty, that Charlie Chaplin once commented, "I went into this business for the money and the art grew out of it." But great art—as opposed to journeyman competence—grows from an individual, almost unconscious vision. Chaplin perceived life in a unique light and was able to give his vision tangible shape so that millions of viewers could see it as well.

His childhood resembled a chapter from a Dickens novel. He was born in London, England in 1889, and sent to a poorhouse after his mother died from malnutrition. He made his first stage appearance at five and worked in shows until 1913, when the Keystone Co. hired him to do a one-reeler, *Making a Living.* He followed it with other one- and two-reelers, some of which were completed in a single afternoon. *The Tramp* was his breakthrough, and in it he created a character that all the downtrodden took to their hearts. With increased popularity, he accepted an offer from Mutual Studios for $10,000 a week.

Charlie Chaplin with Edna Purviance.

Charlie Chaplin.

His next films—*The Floorwalker, The Count, The Pawnshop, The Rink,* and *Easy Street*—met with universal public and critical applause. The character of the tramp appeared in *The Kid, The Idle Class,* and *Pay Day,* and audiences continued to identify with this pathetic, resilient underdog. Chaplin now had the time to perfect his work and the budgets to do films as he saw fit. *The Gold Rush* took two years, and it was another box-office success. He joined a traveling circus and fell in love with a bareback rider in *The Circus,* a film that won him a Special Oscar for "versatility and genius in writing, acting, directing, and producing."

Many Chaplin lovers consider *City Lights* his masterpiece. It was a touching tale of a tramp's love for a blind girl and his most sentimental picture up to that time. He made one more silent picture, *Modern Times,* a penetrating attack on the machine age. Paulette Goddard was the star and also his wife. She was with him again in *The Great Dictator,* in which he played a dual role as a Jewish barber and dictator Adenoid Hynkel (suggesting Hitler). After that, storm clouds of bad publicity built up—a paternity suit that offended Hollywood columnists (though he was cleared); words of approval for the Russian cause (during the war, when the U.S. and Russia were allies); and general criticism of his private life (in the course of his life, Chaplin married three women when they were sixteen).

Monsieur Verdoux, a comedy about a mass murderer, proved that language was not his strongest point. Katharine Hepburn, for instance, disliked it until she ran it without sound and recognized its visual genius. *Limelight,* which was touching but slow, centered on an over-the-hill clown who helped ballerina Claire Bloom. Chaplin was denied a re-entry visa when he went abroad and stayed permanently in Switzerland, an injustice the Academy tried to correct in 1972 with a Special Oscar. Despite the abysmal failure of his last picture *A Countess From Hong Kong*, he retained his spirit to the end. He told a newspaper man after receiving the award, "My pictures were much better than the insufferable mediocrities they make today." Millions of moviegoers the world over would agree with him.

Charlie Chaplin with Claire Bloom in *Limelight*.

FILMOGRAPHY

(features only)

1914

Tillie's Punctured Romance ★★★★

1921

The Kid (direction) ★★★★

1923

A Woman of Paris (cameo, direction)

1925

The Gold Rush (direction) ★★★★

1928

The Circus (direction) ★★★★

1931

City Lights (direction) ★★★★

1935

Modern Times (direction) ★★★★

1940

The Great Dictator (direction) ★★★★

1947

Monsieur Verdoux (direction) ★★★

1952

Limelight (direction) ★★★

1957

A King in New York (direction) ★★

1967

A Countess From Hong Kong (cameo, direction)

CYD CHARISSE
★★½ 2.71 STARS

Dance critic Arlene Croce stated: "The sexiest of (Astaire's) other partners, Cyd Charisse and Rita Hayworth, did very little for him." Most people viewing a number like "Dancing in the Dark" from *The Band Wagon* would disagree. Charisse and Astaire moved with a sensual grace that matched anything in the Astaire and Rogers films.

Born Tula Ellice Finklea in 1921, in Amarillo, Texas, she joined the Ballet Russe at age thirteen. After extensive touring with dance troups, she went to Hollywood. She used the stage name Lily Norwood from 1943 to 1946, and then changed her name to Cyd Charisse.

In dramatic roles, such as *Tension*, she was a convincing heroine, but dancing transformed her into a magical creature. The high point of *Singin' in the Rain* is her ballet with Gene Kelly. She also enlivened the boring *Brigadoon* and the overplotted *It's Always Fair Weather*.

Unfortunately, the musicals that starred Charisse *(The Band Wagon, It's Always Fair Weather,* and *Silk Stockings)* were commercial disappointments. Perhaps if she had not broken her leg and lost the female lead in *Easter Parade* or bowed out of *An American in Paris* due to pregnancy, she would be regarded today as a musical legend, rather than just one of the screen's notable dancers.

FILMOGRAPHY

(billed as Lily Norwood)

1943

Mission to Moscow ★★
Something to Shout About ★★

(billed as Cyd Charisse)

1946

The Harvey Girls ★★★
Ziegfeld Follies ★★★
Three Wise Fools ★★★
Till the Clouds Roll By ★★★

1947

Fiesta ★★★
The Unfinished Dance ★★★

Cyd Charisse with Fred Astaire in *The Band Wagon*.

1948

On an Island With You ★★★
Words and Music ★★★

1949

The Kissing Bandit ★★
East Side, West Side ★★★
Tension ★★★

1951

Mark of the Renegade ★★

1952

Singin' in the Rain ★★★★
The Wild North ★★

1953

Sombrero ★★
The Band Wagon ★★★★
Easy to Love (cameo)

1954

Brigadoon ★★★
Deep in My Heart ★★★

1955

It's Always Fair Weather ★★★

1956

Meet Me in Las Vegas ★★★

1957

Invitation to the Dance ★★★
Silk Stockings ★★★

1958

Twilight for the Gods ★★
Party Girl ★★

1960

Black Tights ★★★

1961

Five Golden Hours ★★

1962

Two Weeks in Another Town ★ ★ ★

1963

Assassination in Rome ★ ★

1966

The Silencers ★ ★ ★

1967

Maroc 7 ★ ★ ★

1976

Won Ton Ton - the Dog Who Saved Hollywood ★ ★

1978

Warlords of Atlantis ★ ★

CHEVY CHASE
★ ★ ½ 2.71 STARS

Woody Allen is a parody of the Jewish fumbler; Chevy Chase (in his Brooks Brothers shirts, corduroy pants, and canvas sneakers) satirizes the WASP equally well. His deadpan delivery and put-on wit sparkled on television and has enlivened his films as well—a blessing, considering the material involved.

Chase was born in New York City, in 1943. His father was an editor at G.P. Putnam's; his mother (Cathalene Crane Chase) was a plumbing heiress. He didn't inherit any money, however, because his grandfather married a Zen Buddhist and left his fortune to the Buddhist temple. A class cutup, Chase formed Channel One, an *off* off-Broadway production company in a storefront theatre. The company lampooned commercials, newscasts, kiddie shows, and documentaries. He also played with a rock group and worked as a truck driver, bartender, and tennis pro before his huge success on "Saturday Night Live" (He won two Emmys).

Chevy Chase in *Foul Play.*

Movies beckoned with an excellent part opposite Goldie Hawn in *Foul Play*—an uneven but hilarious comedy-thriller. Richard Schickel of Time Magazine commented, "He should thank his genes for the natural ease and charm he has to fall back on." After *Foul Play, Oh Heavenly Dog* was a disappointment and so was a Neil Simon farce, *Seems Like Old Times.*

He seemed to be sleep-walking through his latest films, *Modern Problems* and *National Lampoon's Vacation*, but he does so better than most comic actors who idle through weak material. Chase is a welcome face in any vehicle and his movies, inevitably, have to improve.

FILMOGRAPHY

1978

Foul Play ★ ★ ★ ★

1980

Oh Heavenly Dog ★ ★ ★
Seems Like Old Times ★ ★ ★
Caddyshack ★ ★ ★

1981

Under the Rainbow ★ ★
Modern Problems ★ ★

1983

National Lampoon's Vacation ★ ★

JULIE CHRISTIE
★ ★ ★ 3.00 STARS

Julie Christie was expected to be one of the great, enduring superstars. In *Darling*, her husky voice and magnetically sexual personality set fire to the screen, and she represented the carefree, independent mood of the 1960s. However, she made few films, and one can only conclude that her lack of personal ambition prevented her from reaching that legendary status that she was capable of.

She was born in 1941, in Chukua, Assam, India but studied drama in London. *Darling* was only her fourth movie, but it won her a Best Actress Oscar. Director David Lean thought she was perfect for *Doctor Zhivago*, but the reviews of the film were mixed—a mystery, since Christie's portrayal of Lara had warmth and beauty and almost single-handedly held the sprawling storyline together. *Fahrenheit 451* provided a dual role, but Truffaut's version of a Ray Bradbury short story was colorless. *Far from the Madding Crowd* improved things, a sweepingly romantic and faithful adaptation of the Thomas Hardy novel. Christie was pursued by three men (Terence Stamp, Peter Finch, and Alan Bates) and one could easily understand their enthusiasm. Her free-spirited *Petulia* was as fascinating to viewers as to co-star George C. Scott, but the script was choppy and unsatisfying.

Julie Christie with Warren Beatty in *Shampoo.*

One of Christie's lesser portrayals—the Madam in Robert Altman's boring *McCabe and Mrs. Miller*—ironically drew critic's raves. It was easy to ignore *Don't Look Now*, an over-stylized, complicated occult thriller. She appeared in two enormous hits—*Shampoo*

Julie Christie with Tom Courtenay in *Dr. Zhivago.*

and *Heaven Can Wait*—with boyfriend Warren Beatty, but the roles were merely supporting parts with star billing. Christie's radiance is too dominant, too magical to be given such short shrift, and we can only hope someone will again fashion a film for her that lets her occupy center-stage.

Julie Christie in *Demon Seed*.

FILMOGRAPHY

1962
Crooks Anonymous ★★

1963
The Fast Lady ★★
Billy Liar ★★★★

1965
Darling ★★★★
Doctor Zhivago ★★★★
Young Cassidy ★★★

1966
Fahrenheit 451 ★★

1967
Far from the Madding Crowd ★★★★

1968
Petulia ★★★

1970
In Search of Gregory ★★

1971
The Go-Between ★★★
McCabe and Mrs. Miller ★★★

1973
Don't Look Now ★★★

1975
Shampoo ★★★★
Nashville (cameo)

1977
Demon Seed ★★

1978
Heaven Can Wait ★★★★

1982
The Memoirs of a Survivor ★★★
The Animal's Film (narration)

1983
Heat and Dust ★★★

JILL CLAYBURGH
★★★ 2.93 STARS

In *An Unmarried Woman,* Jill Clayburgh found a strong, modern image—the liberated (or yearning-to-be-liberated) woman. Her talent for drama and comedy is one of the keys to her success, but her physical appearance is even more significant. Clayburgh is pretty enough to be an attractive housewife, to invite female identification, and yet not pretty enough to be a threat.

Clayburgh was born in New York, in 1944 into a wealthy family. She attended Sarah Lawrence College. Broadway stardom came with "Pippin" and "The Rothschilds." After an innocuous beginning on film *(The Wedding Party* and *The Telephone Book),* she appeared in a major movie (with minor virtues), *Portnoy's Complaint.* In *Gable and Lombard* she had a starring role, but the script used both main title characters to create a meaningless, completely fictionalized hodgepodge. Although Clayburgh fought to make Lombard credible, viewers were too busy yawning to notice.

She was appealing in a small role as Ryan O'Neal's ex-wife in *The Thief Who Came to Dinner,* and she really proved herself an outstanding comedienne in *Silver Streak.* A notable performance in a TV movie *(Griffin and Phoenix)* with Peter Falk increased her popularity.

Jill Clayburgh in *Silver Streak*.

Semi-Tough was a Burt Reynolds film that blended romance, football, and pop psychology in an uneasy mixture. Clayburgh was not only adequate, but brilliant in *An Unmarried Woman.* She played a similar part in the less entertaining *It's My Turn* and co-starred with Burt Reynolds again in the distortion of Dan Wakefield's fine book, *Starting Over.* A sameness began to creep into her work, so she opted for a change of pace in *I'm Dancing as Fast as I Can.* It reminded critics of her versatility, though the public was less interested.

Jill Clayburgh with Nicol Williamson in *I'm Dancing as Fast as I Can*.

FILMOGRAPHY

1969
The Wedding Party ★★

1971
The Telephone Book ★★

1972
Portnoy's Complaint ★★

1973
The Thief Who Came to Dinner ★★★

1974
The Terminal Man ★★★

1976
Gable and Lombard ★★
Silver Streak ★★★★

1977
Semi-Tough ★★★

1978
An Unmarried Woman ★★★★

1979
Luna ★★★
Starting Over ★★★

1980
It's My Turn ★★★

1981
First Monday in October ★★★

1982
I'm Dancing as Fast as I Can ★★★★

MONTGOMERY CLIFT
★ ★ ★ 2.94 STARS

An actor must die at the right time to become a legend. James Dean's dramatic demise at age twenty-four made him a romantic idol. Montgomery Clift began with the same potential, but he deteriorated slowly and made inferior movies that dimmed the memory of his early promise.

Born in 1920, in Omaha, Nebraska, Clift's formative years as an actor were spent on the stage, most notably in "There Shall Be No Night" and Lillian Hellman's "The Searching Wind." His first film, *Red River,* was quite successful, and Clift's three-dimensional cowboy exposed John Wayne's one-note acting style. *The Search* was equally memorable, a heartbreaking study of a GI and the displaced European child he protected.

The Heiress pointed up his principal weakness—a tendency to make unlikable characters too sympathetic. His portrayal of a scheming fortune hunter was so charming that one could't believe he would desert the trusting Olivia De Havilland. *A Place in the Sun* garnered Clift his greatest acclaim. He was, again, a shade too sensitive as murderer George Eastman, but Shelley Winters' abrasive nagging put the audience firmly on his side.

His sensitive performance in *I Confess* made the farfetched premise that a priest would not reveal the identity of a killer he discovered in confession seem almost plausible. In *From Here to Eternity,* he finally combined his sensitivity with the strength he showed in *Red River,* and as Prewitt, a dedicated army man, he gave his finest performance.

Clift's drinking was out of control by this time, and he had a near-fatal car accident that permanently damaged his face. It seemed to damage some of his portrayals, in *Lonelyhearts* and *Raintree County,* but his ability was unimpaired in *The Young Lions* and particularly in *Judgment at Nuremberg,* in which he played a Nazi victim. He was wooden in *Freud,* but no actor could have triumphed over a script that made such a travesty of psychoanalysis. In *The Misfits* he appeared vague and out of place, and Marilyn Monroe commented, "He's the only person I know who's worse off than I am."

Clift died at forty-five, a classic case of greatness unrealized.

Montgomery Clift.

Montgomery Clift with Frank Sinatra in *From Here to Eternity.*

FILMOGRAPHY

1948

Red River ★ ★ ★ ★
The Search ★ ★ ★ ★

1949

The Heiress ★ ★ ★

1950

The Big Lift ★ ★ ★

1951

A Place in the Sun ★ ★ ★

1953

I Confess ★ ★ ★
From Here to Eternity ★ ★ ★ ★
Indiscretion of an American Wife ★ ★ ★

1957

Raintree County ★ ★

1958

The Young Lions ★ ★ ★

1959

Lonelyhearts ★ ★
Suddenly Last Summer ★ ★ ★

1960

Wild River ★ ★ ★

1961

The Misfits ★ ★
Judgment at Nuremberg ★ ★ ★ ★

1962

Freud ★ ★

1966

The Defector ★ ★

COLIN CLIVE
★ ★ ★ 3.22 STARS

With his arch-sounding voice, gaunt features, and intense gaze, Colin Clive was cinema's greatest sado-masochist. Besmocked and determined, he was the finest Dr. Frankenstein, playing the role in *Frankenstein* and the *Bride of Frankenstein,* and suffering intensely as the forlorn creator. The incredulity he registered as monster Boris Karloff began to wreak havoc on his noble efforts was gleefully palpable.

Born Clive Greig in 1898, in St. Malo, France, he abandoned an early career in the British army to take up acting. He began in British films and stage plays, and his career was closely associated with director James Whale's. In 1930 he accompanied Whale to Hollywood to recreate his acclaimed stage role as the alcoholic hero in the all-male war drama *Journey's End.*

In *History Is Made at Night,* director Frank Borzage presented Clive as the inverse of his masochistic portrayal of Dr. Frankenstein. As an aristocratic businessman, he was obsessed with maintaining a loveless marriage to Jean Arthur. He murdered a chauffeur in order to frame his wife's lover Charles Boyer and even shipwrecked his own ocean liner because his wife was aboard.

Clive died young, in 1937, leaving behind a short but striking film portrait of fanatic determination, humiliation, and hate.

Colin Clive with Elsa Lanchester in *Bride of Frankenstein.*

FILMOGRAPHY

1930

Journey's End ★★★

1931

The Stronger Sex ★★★
Frankenstein ★★★★

1932

Lily Christine ★★★

1933

Christopher Strong ★★★
Looking Forward ★★★

1934

Jane Eyre ★★★
The Key ★★★
One More River ★★★

1935

Bride of Frankenstein ★★★★
Clive of India ★★★
The Right to Live ★★★
The Widow from Monte Carlo ★★★
The Girl from 10th Avenue ★★★
Mad Love ★★★★
The Man Who Broke the Bank at Monte Carlo ★★★

1937

History Is Made at Night ★★★★
The Woman I Love ★★★

JAMES COBURN
★★★ 2.90 STARS

James Coburn is a convincing presence in action films with his interestingly rangy, weatherbeaten look and a distinctive voice. What he lacks is a sympathetic leading-man charm. His grin is sinister, more appropriate to villians than heroes.

Nebraska-born in 1928, Coburn studied with Stella Adler and appeared on "Studio One" and other TV shows. He started out strongly in motion pictures—his third picture was *The Magnificent Seven,* a classic western. After *Hell Is for Heroes,* he had another blockbuster, *The Great Escape,* and his murderous villain stood out in *Charade.* Coburn's womanizing officer in *The Americanization of Emily* could not be faulted though the focus was on James Garner. Stardom came with *Our Man Flint,* a pseudo-James Bond thriller-spoof.

Its sequel *In Like Flint* gave Coburn a starring role but not much room to move. Small parts in dismal films like *Candy* and *The Loved One* did nothing to further his career. *The President's Analyst* gave him a featured comedy role somewhat more demanding than the "Flint" films. Since then he has veered back to more tough-guy roles.

Coburn is prone to overacting. Perhaps for this reason, one of his best roles was in a film directed by Sergio Leone, whose excesses matched Coburn's own. *Duck You Sucker!* featured Coburn as an Irish revolutionary in Mexico, dispensing liberal quantities of explosives all over the Mexican countryside. Coburn managed to give the part a certain wacky charm, although his Irish accent was almost as bad as co-star Rod Steiger's attempt at a Mexican accent.

James Coburn in *The Last Hard Man.*

Coburn's most recent roles have tended to show him in a more dignified light. Unfortunately, his authority figures have also been less interesting than his rogues.

FILMOGRAPHY

1959

Ride Lonesome ★★
Face of a Fugitive ★★

1960

The Magnificent Seven ★★★★

1962

Hell Is for Heroes ★★★

1963

The Great Escape ★★★★
Charade ★★★★

1964

The Man from Galveston ★★★
The Americanization of Emily ★★★★

1965

Major Dundee ★★★
A High Wind in Jamaica ★★★
The Loved One (cameo)

1966

Our Man Flint ★★★
What Did You Do in the War, Daddy? ★★
Dead Heat on a Merry-Go-Round ★★★

1967

In Like Flint ★★★
Waterhole No. 3 ★★★
The President's Analyst ★★

1968

Duffy ★★
Candy ★★

1969

Hard Contract ★★★

1970

The Last of the Mobile Hot-Shots ★★★

1972

Duck You Sucker! ★★★
The Honkers ★★★
The Carey Treatment ★★★

1973

Pat Garrett and Billy the Kid ★★★
The Last of Sheila ★★★
Harry in Your Pocket ★★★

1974

A Reason to Live, a Reason to Die ★★
The Internecine Project ★★★

1975

Jackpot ★★
Bite the Bullet ★★★
Hard Times ★★★★

James Coburn in *The President's Analyst.*

1976

Sky Riders ★ ★ ★
The Last Hard Man ★ ★ ★
Midway ★ ★ ★

1977

White Rock (narration)
Cross of Iron ★ ★ ★

1979

Golden Girl ★ ★ ★
The Dain Curse ★ ★
Crimes Obscurs en Extreme Occident ★ ★ ★
The Muppet Movie (cameo)
The Baltimore Bullet ★ ★

1980

Firepower ★ ★ ★

1981

Looker ★ ★ ★
High Risk ★ ★ ★

CLAUDETTE COLBERT
★ ★ ★ ½ 3.33 STARS

Today, more attention is given to Claudette Colbert's peculiar quirk (she would only be photographed on one side of her face) than her talent, which does her a disservice. Even if, in Doris Day's words, "God wasted half a face on Claudette," Colbert was a consummate comedienne and dramatic actress. Wit, worldliness, and warm femininity marked all her film performances.

Colbert was born Claudette Lily Chauchoin in Paris in 1905 and raised in New York. Her Broadway career began in 1923, and four years later she made her first movie, *For the Love of Mike.* Although she concentrated on comedy later in her career, her early films were very stark. She kidnapped a child in *The Hole in the Wall* and was convicted in *Manslaughter.* Her big advance was *The Sign of the Cross,* a lavish Cecil B. De Mille spectacle in which her Poppaea was appropriately evil and sexy. She played a fisherman's daughter in the grimly realistic *I Cover the Waterfront* and she also did De Mille's *Four Frightened People,* a drab and atypical film about four people stranded in the jungle.

It's now well known that Colbert and Clark Gable fought bitterly against doing *It Happened One Night.* Director Frank Capra remembered, "Colbert fretted, pouted and argued about her part . . . she was a tartar, but a cute one." However, the effort resulted in Oscars for both stars.

She was *Cleopatra* in 1934 and more convincing than Elizabeth Taylor in the later version, and Colbert was honest and moving in the tearful *Imitation of Life.* The soap opera was notable because it was one of the first Hollywood pictures to deal with racism.

There were several hit comedies—*The Gilded Lily* and *The Bride Comes Home,* both with Fred MacMurray, and *She Married Her Boss* with Melvyn Douglas. *Midnight* was one of her very best comedies, and she made a surprisingly authentic western heroine in *Drums Along the Mohawk.*

Colbert had a knack for selecting appropriate films stating, "I do work hard, sacrifice everything to get ahead." She was shrewd enough

Claudette Colbert.

to forgo top billing to appear in a hit, *Boom Town*, with Spencer Tracy and Clark Gable in which Colbert's chic, feminine charm outmatched the more obvious sexual posturing of Hedy Lamarr. She did some of her finest work in the two memorable dramas—*Tomorrow Is Forever*, as a wife still haunted by the death of her husband Orson Welles and *The Secret Heart*, as a guilty widow who must cope with the hatred of her stepdaughter June Allyson.

Her last outstanding comedy was *The Egg and I*, again with comic partner Fred MacMurray. She was miscast in the western *Texas Lady* but charmingly sincere as Troy Donahue's mother in the heavy-breathing tobacco saga, *Parrish*.

Colbert's elegance and chic will be remembered. She never made the mistake of playing an axe murderess, or, as Myrna Loy once put it, the "psychotic old bags offered to the older actresses." She knew when to get off the stage and how to keep her lovely image permanently intact.

FILMOGRAPHY

1927

For the Love of Mike ★★★

1929

The Hole in the Wall ★★★
The Lady Lies ★★★

1930

L'Enigmatique M. Parkes ★★★
The Big Pond ★★★
Young Man of Manhattan ★★★
Manslaughter ★★★

1931

Honor Among Lovers ★★★
The Smiling Lieutenant ★★★
Secrets of a Secretary ★★★
His Woman ★★★

1932

The Wiser Sex ★★★
The Misleading Lady ★★★
The Man from Yesterday ★★★
The Phantom President ★★★
The Sign of the Cross ★★★

1933

Tonight Is Ours ★★★
I Cover the Waterfront ★★★
Three Cornered Moon ★★★
Torch Singer ★★★

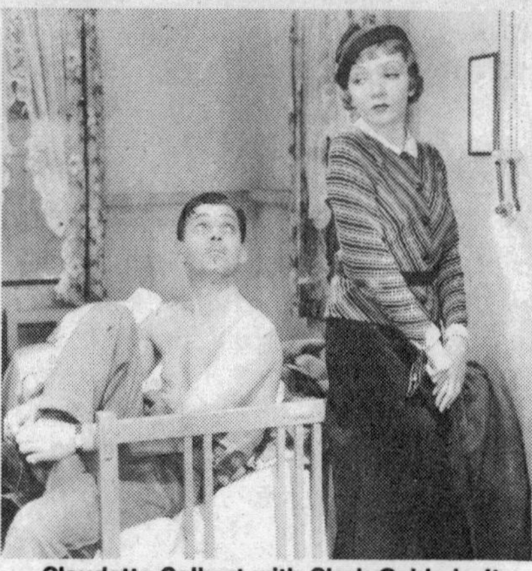

Claudette Colbert with Clark Gable in *It Happened One Night.*

1934

Four Frightened People ★★★
It Happened One Night ★★★★
Cleopatra ★★★★
Imitation of Life ★★★★

1935

The Gilded Lily ★★★
Private Worlds ★★★★
She Married Her Boss ★★★★
The Bride Comes Home ★★★★

1936

Under Two Flags ★★★

1937

Maid of Salem ★★★
I Met Him in Paris ★★★★
Tovarich ★★★★

1938

Bluebeard's Eighth Wife ★★★★

1939

Zaza ★★★
Midnight ★★★★
It's a Wonderful World ★★★★
Drums Along the Mohawk ★★★★

1940

Boom Town ★★★★
Arise My Love ★★★

1941

Skylark ★★★★

1942

Remember the Day ★★★★
The Palm Beach Story ★★★★

1943

So Proudly We Hail ★★★
No Time for Love ★★★

1944

Since You Went Away ★★★★

1945

Practically Yours ★★★
Guest Wife ★★★

1946

Tomorrow Is Forever ★★★★
Without Reservations ★★★
The Secret Heart ★★★★

1947

The Egg and I ★★★★

1948

Sleep My Love ★★★★

1949

Family Honeymoon ★★★
Bride for Sale ★★★

1950

Three Came Home ★★★★
The Secret Fury ★★★

1951

Thunder on the Hill ★★★
Let's Make It Legal ★★★

1952

The Planter's Wife ★★★

1953

Daughters of Destiny ★★★

1955

Texas Lady ★★

1957

Royal Affairs in Versailles ★★★

1961

Parrish ★★★

RONALD COLMAN
★★★½ 3.51 STARS

Like Cary Grant, Ronald Colman demonstrated that sophistication can be achieved without sacrificing the common touch. Mary Astor said of him, "As an actor Ronnie was always excellent—easy, skillful, always in touch of warmth."

Ronald Colman was born in England, in 1891. After a stage success in the 1918 production of "Damaged Goods," Colman made some undistinguished silents—*The Toilers, A Son of David, Snow in The Desert*, and *The Black Spider.* The film that made the big difference was *The White Sister* with Lillian Gish, and he worked his way up into two major hits, *The Dark Angel* and *Stella Dallas*.

The 1926 version of *Beau Geste* showed Colman at his most dashing, and he was equally at home in a western, *The Winning of Barbara Worth*. From there he moved to swashbucklers with *The Night of Love.*

Talkies arrived, destroying the careers of high-voiced leads like John Gilbert and many others, but Colman's magically silky voice was tailor made for the new medium. He instinctively knew—rare for silent performers—how to tone down, use his eyes, and when not to indulge in over-explicit mugging. His transitional movie was *Bulldog Drummond.* Although John Howard, Ron Randell, Tom Conway, John Lodge, and Ray Milland all played Drummond in later films, Colman's portrayal is still the definitive interpretation. He made the second of three versions of *Raffles* and a comedy with Loretta Young, *The Devil to Pay.* He was outstanding in John Ford's classic adaptation of the Sinclair Lewis novel, *Arrowsmith.* Colman played his first double role—a journalist pretending to be a member of Parliament in *The Masquerader.*

Ronald Colman in *A Tale of Two Cities*.

After another Drummond film, *Bulldog Drummond Strikes Back,* Colman defeated Indian rebels in *Clive of India.* He then created the definitive Sidney Carton in a brilliant production of *A Tale of Two Cities.* When Frank Capra wanted to direct *Lost Horizon,* Ronald Colman was the only possible choice and as a man seeking peace in Shangri-La, he brought honesty and thoughtfulness to the part. It might have been a travesty in less capable hands, but his performance was inexplicably ignored by Academy voters. The next performance, equally masterful, was also neglected; in *The Prisoner of Zenda,* Colman played in another dual role as a commoner forced to impersonate his royal look-alike.

His finest romantic role and the one modern audiences cherish most came with *Random Harvest.* If his part in *Lost Horizon* was difficult, this one was nearly impossible—an amnesiac who regained only part of his memory and worked with a loyal secretary (Greer Garson) whom he didn't remember marrying. Garson's unwillingness to reveal her identity strained credibility, but the deft teamwork of the two stars made everything seem believable. He finally won an Oscar for *A Double Life,* another of his by now legendary dual roles. He played an actor unduly affected by the roles he played on stage.

In this age of warts-and-all realism, Ronald Colman remains a refreshing alternative. His style and charisma make one wonder if the Hoffmans and Pacinos are a viable substitute for star magnetism after all.

FILMOGRAPHY

1918

Sheba ★★★

1919

The Toilers ★★★
A Son of David ★★★
Snow in The Desert ★★★

1920

The Black Spider ★★★
Anna the Adventuress ★★★

1921

Handcuffs or Kisses ★★★

1923

The Eternal City ★★★
The White Sister ★★★★

1924

$20 a Week ★★★
Tarnish ★★★
Her Night of Romance ★★★
Romola ★★★

1925

A Thief in Paradise ★★★
His Supreme Moment ★★★
The Sporting Venus ★★★
Her Sister from Paris ★★★
The Dark Angel ★★★★
Stella Dallas ★★★★
Lady Windermere's Fan ★★★★

Ronald Colman.

1926

Kiki ★★★
Beau Geste ★★★★
The Winning of Barbara Worth ★★★★

1927

The Night of Love ★★★
The Magic Flame ★★★

1928

Two Lovers ★★★

1929

The Rescue ★★★
Bulldog Drummond ★★★★
Condemned ★★★★

1930

Raffles ★★★★

1931

The Devil to Pay ★★★★
The Unholy Garden ★★★★
Arrowsmith ★★★★

1932

Cynara ★★★★

1933

The Masquerader ★★★

1934

Bulldog Drummond Strikes Back ★★★★

1935

Clive of India ★★★★
The Man Who Broke the Bank at Monte Carlo ★★★★
A Tale of Two Cities ★★★★

1936

Under Two Flags ★★★★

1937

Lost Horizon ★★★★
The Prisoner of Zenda ★★★★

1938

If I Were King ★★★★

1940

The Light That Failed ★★★★
Lucky Partners ★★★

1941

My Life With Caroline ★★★

1942

The Talk of the Town ★★★★
Random Harvest ★★★★

1944

Kismet ★★★★

1947

The Late George Apley ★★★★

1948

A Double Life ★★★★

1950

Champagne for Caesar ★★★★

1956

Around the World in 80 Days (cameo)

1957

The Story of Mankind ★★★

SEAN CONNERY
★★★ 3.00 STARS

It's ironic that Sean Connery is still the definitive James Bond. The present Bond, Roger Moore, is much closer to author Ian Fleming's sophisticated hero, but Connery has the character's earthiness and passion—and a virility that has been missing since he left the series. His Bond characterization was so strong, in fact, that the public has refused to accept him in several other worthwhile films.

Connery was born Thomas Connery in 1930, in Edinburgh, Scotland. He concentrated on body building as a youth, and that led to modeling jobs, and a part in the chorus of the English "South Pacific." There was nothing particularly interesting about his early films—*No Road Back, Hell Drivers,* and *Action of the Tiger*—or his performances in them. On television, he remade "Anna Christie" (and married his leading lady, Diane Cilento).

A role in *Another Time, Another Place* brought him some attention, particularly since he was rumored to be involved with Lana Turner while she was embroiled with the death of former lover Johnny Stompanato.

Dr. No launched the Bond phenomenon. It was exciting and fast-paced, and Connery had a luscious co-star in Ursula Andress. *From Russia with Love* was equally gripping, and his name became synonymous with a reliable box-office audience. However, *Woman of Straw* with Gina Lollobrigida had no commercial impact even though it was a fine thriller. Even Alfred Hitchcock's name didn't help *Marnie,* an underrated drama of a kleptomaniac and the man (Connery) who saved her. Leading lady Tippi Hedren was probably to blame.

Two more Bond pictures equaled the success of the first pair—*Goldfinger* and *Thunderball. The Hill* was a relentlessly grim study of a prison camp, and the public avoided it despite critical approval. Connery then tried an odd part—a radical poet—in the strange, sometimes creative *A Fine Madness. You Only Live Twice* (Bond again) was another unstoppable hit.

The expected chemistry between Connery and Brigitte Bardot didn't materialize in the western *Shalako,* and he was brilliant but unseen as a miner in *The Molly Maguires.* Finally, a non-Bond thriller *The Anderson Tapes,* rang a bell with audiences, and Connery broke his jinx.

He continued to be both engaging and believable in a number of wide-ranging films that were good but less than box-office smashes, including: *Murder on the Orient Express, The Wind and the Lion, The Man Who Would Be King, A Bridge Too Far, Robin and Marian,* and *Outland.* He also tackled some weird material (a futuristic Spartacus in *Zardoz* and King Agamemnon in *Time Bandits*) and some truly awful films. *The Next Man* was one of the ten worst thrillers of all time, and *Meteor* was an unsuspenseful end-of-the-world drama.

Sean Connery with Claudine Auger in *Thunderball.*

Connery combines the looks and masculine force of past years with the funky man-on-the-street naturalism of today. This image insures that James Bond will be only a small part of a steadily accelerating future success.

Sean Connery in *Wrong Is Right.*

FILMOGRAPHY

1956

No Road Back ★★

1957

Hell Drivers ★★
Time Lock ★★
Action of the Tiger ★★

1958

Another Time, Another Place ★★

1959

Darby O'Gill and the Little People ★★★
Tarzan's Greatest Adventure ★★★

1961

The Frightened City ★★★
On the Fiddle ★★

1962

The Longest Day ★★★
Dr. No ★★★★

1963

From Russia with Love ★★★★

1964

Marnie ★★★★
Woman of Straw ★★★
Goldfinger ★★★★

1965

The Hill ★★★★
Thunderball ★★★

1966

A Fine Madness ★★★

1967

You Only Live Twice ★★★★

1968

Shalako ★★★

1970

The Molly Maguires ★★★★

1971

The Red Tent ★★★
The Anderson Tapes ★★★★
Diamonds Are Forever ★★★★

1973

The Offense ★★★

1974

Zardoz ★★
Murder on the Orient Express ★★★

1975

Ransom ★★★
The Wind and the Lion ★★★
The Man Who Would Be King ★★★★

1976

Robin and Marian ★★
The Next Man ★★

1977

A Bridge Too Far ★★

1978

Meteor ★★

1979

The Great Train Robbery ★★★
Cuba ★★★

1981

Time Bandits ★★★★
Outland ★★★

1982

Wrong Is Right ★★★
Five Days One Summer ★★★

1983

Never Say Never Again ★★★

EDDIE CONSTANTINE
★★★ 3.17 STARS

Just as one could say that French directors like Jean-Luc Godard and Claude Chabrol took the *essence* of American movies and translated it into Gallic terms, Eddie Constantine—an American-turned-French-actor born in Los Angeles—is the French "distillation" of Hollywood tough guys from Cagney to Bogart. This distance between Constantine and the characters he plays—he's always acting "like someone else"—introduces a note of gentle self-mockery into his performances.

Eddie Constantine in *SOS Pacific.*

Born in 1917, he was a stage and cabaret star by the early 1950s. Constantine naturally gravitated into the movies, where his rough, earthy good looks and cool manner made him ideal for the French taste in detectives. The mere title of many of his popular thrillers gives a sense of their pulpy origin: *Passport to Shame*, *Riff Raff Girls*, *Hot Money Girl*, or *Hail Mafia!*

The best films of his early period center almost obsessively on his physical presence; few American films, for example, would place more weight on the detective than on his case.

Jean-Luc Godard extracted Constantine's greatest performance as detective Lemmy Caution in *Alphaville*, and in recent years Constantine has acted in nondetective roles for a variety of international directors, notably Rainer Werner Fassbinder in *Beware of a Holy Whore* and *The Third Generation.*

FILMOGRAPHY

1953

La Môme Vert de Gris ★★★
Oet Homme est dangereux ★★★★

1954

Les Femmes s'en balancent ★★★★
Avanzi di Galera ★★

1955

Ca va barder ★★★
Je suis un Sentimental ★★★

1956

Les Truands ★★★

1957

Folies-Bergère ★★★
L'Homme et 1'Enfant ★★★
Le Grand Bluff ★★★

1958

Incognito ★★★★
Ces Dames préfèrent le Mambo ★★★

1959

Passport to Shame ★★★
Room 43 ★★★
Riff Raff Girls ★★★★
SOS Pacific ★★★★
The Treasure of San Teresa ★★
Hot Money Girl ★★

1960

Bomben auf Monte Carlo ★★

1961

Le Chien de Pique ★★★
Mani in Alto ★★★
Lemmy pour les Dames ★★★

1962

Les Sept Péchés capitaux ★★★★
Cléo de 5 à 7 ★★★
Lé Empire de la Nuit ★★★

1964

Lucky Jo ★★★

1965

Alphaville ★★★★
Hail Mafia! ★★★

1969

Lions Love ★★★

1970

Malatesta ★★★

1971

Beware of a Holy Whore ★★★★

1975

Souvenir de Gibraltar ★★★

1977

Le Couple témoin ★★★

1978

It Lives Again ★★★

1979

The Third Generation ★★★★

1982

The Long Good Friday ★★★★

ELISHA COOK, JR.
★★★ 2.86 STARS

Elisha Cook, Jr. always projected a sense of being in over his head, of not being big enough or good enough to fill the shoes he was given. This wonderful little character actor has played the inadequate sycophant or the inept weasel in scores of great films.

Perhaps the key to his effectiveness in his typecast roles lies in the "Jr.". He was born in 1906, in San Francisco, California, the son of a famous stage actor. The decision to become an actor was thrust upon him at an early age, and he appeared in vaudeville and on Broadway before settling into character roles in film. His first great role was in *The Maltese Falcon* as Sydney Greenstreet's bumbling muscleman, Wilmer. In the film Humphrey Bogart's cool professionalism made a perfect foil to Cook's ineptitude. The scenes where Bogey minced Cook with a few choice words or gestures are classic.

Cook was teamed with Bogart again in *The Big Sleep* for his greatest performance as Jonesy, a mousy little man with a ridiculous and finally fatal love. He had other memorable roles in *Phantom Lady, I, the Jury, Shane,* and *The Killing*. Elisha Cook, Jr. has continued to work up to the present day and was most recently seen in *Hammett*.

FILMOGRAPHY

1929
Her Unborn Child ★★

1936
Two in a Crowd ★★

Elisha Cook, Jr. in *Carny*.

1937
Love Is News ★★
They Won't Forget ★★★

1938
Submarine Patrol ★★
Newsboy's Home ★★★

1939
Grand Jury Secrets ★★

1940
The Stranger on the Third Floor ★★★
Tin Pan Alley ★★

1941
Love Crazy ★★★
The Maltese Falcon ★★★★
I Wake Up Screaming ★★★★

1942
A Haunting We Will Go ★★★

1944
Phantom Lady ★★★★
Up in Arms ★★★
Dark Waters ★★★

1945
Dillinger ★★★

1946
Cinderella Jones ★★★
The Falcon's Alibi ★★★
The Big Sleep ★★★★

1947
Fall Guy ★★★
Born to Kill ★★★
The Long Night ★★★
The Gangster ★★★

1949
Flaxy Martin ★★★
The Great Gatsby ★★★

1951
Behave Yourself ★★★

1952
Don't Bother to Knock ★★★

1953
Shane ★★★★
I, the Jury ★★★★

1954
Drum Beat ★★★

1956
The Killing ★★★★

1957
Chicago Confidential ★★★
Voodoo Island ★★★
Baby Face Nelson ★★★★

1959
House on Haunted Hill ★★

1960
Platinum High School ★★
College Confidential ★★

1961
One-Eyed Jacks ★★★★

1963
Black Zoo ★★
The Haunted Palace ★★
Johnny Cool ★★

1964
Blood on the Arrow ★★★

1967
Welcome to Hard Times ★★

1968
Rosemary's Baby ★★★

1969
The Great Bank Robbery ★★

1970
El Condor ★★

1972
The Great Northfield Minnesota Raid ★★★
Blacula ★★

1973
Emperor of the North Pole ★★
Electra Glide in Blue ★★

1974
The Outfit ★★★

1975
Messiah of Evil ★★★
Winter Hawk ★★★
The Black Bird ★★★

1976
St. Ives ★★★

1979
The Champ ★★★

1980
Carny ★★★★

1982
Hammett (cameo)

GARY COOPER
★★★ 3.07 STARS

Irene Dunne expressed a minority opinion when she said that Gary Cooper never learned to act. More prevalent is D.W. Griffith's view that Cooper was able—unlike almost anyone else—to be perfectly natural.

Cooper was born Frank James Cooper in Helena, Montana, in 1901. Despite his "aw shucks" image, he was raised in a sophisticated environment. His father was a judge, and he was taught to appreciate the best clothes and cars. Cooper began as a cartoonist but succumbed to the allure of acting after some work as an extra gave him a taste for it. *The Winning of Barbara Worth* launched him, and he costarred with Clara Bow in *Children of Divorce*. Bow resented his inability to act but later changed her tune.

He made a number of silents—*Nevada, The Last Outlaw, The Legion of the Condemned*, and *The Shopworn Angel*—before his first talkie, *The Virginian*. The success of that picture at that crucial moment in filmmaking history established his career in talkies. He made seven pictures in 1930, the most notable being *Morocco* with Marlene Dietrich.

Devil and the Deep with Tallulah Bankhead slowed his progress momentarily, and he looked uncomfortable in the Joan Crawford war drama *Today We Live*. However, *A Farewell to Arms* hit the mark. It was touching and popular, and Cooper's natural warmth seemed to melt the staginess from co-star Helen Hayes.

He was cast against type for a drawing room comedy, *Design for Living* and floundered in a peculiar version of *Alice in Wonderland*. *Lives of a Bengal Lancer* was a different story; it was a rousing yarn of soldiers on the Indian frontier, and Cooper had strong co-stars in Franchot Tone and Richard Cromwell. He softened his stiff mannerisms for the nearly hallucinatory romanticism of *Peter Ibbetson*. Appealingly reteamed with Marlene Dietrich in *Desire*, he made a romantic comedy about a jewel thief and her victim.

Frank Capra offered him his first classic picture and his permanent image with *Mr. Deeds Goes to Town*. Cooper was the hick who stumbled into corruption and learned to deal with it. Jean Arthur was his love interest, and she appeared with him again in an exciting De Mille epic, *The Plainsman*.

Beau Geste, The Westerner, and *Northwest Mounted Police* were action-packed adventures, his home turf. Cooper returned to the Mr. Deeds characterization for *Meet John Doe*. It was just as powerful as its predecessor, but the public expressed less enthusiasm. *Sergeant York* brought Cooper his first Oscar. He starred in the true story (the Hollywood version of true) of a Tennessee farm boy who registered as a conscientious objector in World War I, and then went on to become its greatest hero. Displaying his great versatility, he went straight into another comedy, the hilarious *Ball of Fire*. He was Lou Gehrig in the memorable *Pride of the Yankees*, still the best baseball picture ever made.

Gary Cooper with Grace Kelly in *High Noon*.

A spell of bad luck marked his roles in the late 1940s. He was too old and staid for *The Fountainhead*, and *Dallas* was a ho-hum western. *High Noon* restored his momentum—miraculously—since Stanley Kramer had originally pronounced it a bomb, and director Fred Zinnemann had shot acres of footage focusing on Grace Kelly which were later scrapped.

From that point on, most of Cooper's films were worthy of him. *Friendly Persuasion* was a glowing story of Quakers trying to reconcile war and pacifism. *Love in the Afternoon* also had charm, but the age difference between Cooper and Audrey Hepburn was slightly jarring. The May-December combination seemed to function more effectively with Suzy Parker in *Ten North Frederick*. Cooper's last picture was a thriller with Deborah Kerr, *The Naked Edge*.

Shortly before Gary Cooper died in 1961, Jimmy Stewart appeared on the Academy Awards show and broke into tears at the mention of Cooper's name, inadvertently revealing the seriousness of his physical condition. It was a touching example of the high esteem he elicited from the film industry.

FILMOGRAPHY

1926

The Winning of Barbara Worth ★★

1927

Children of Divorce ★★
It ★★
Arizona Bound ★★
Wings ★★★
Nevada ★★★
The Last Outlaw ★★★

1928

Beau Sabreur ★★
The Legion of the Condemned ★★★
Doomsday ★★★
Half a Bride ★★★
Lilac Time ★★★
The First Kiss ★★★
The Shopworn Angel ★★★

1929

Wolf Song ★★★
Betrayal ★★★
The Virginian ★★★

1930

Only the Brave ★★★
Paramount on Parade ★★★
The Texan ★★★
Seven Days Leave ★★★
A Man from Wyoming ★★★
The Spoilers ★★★
Morocco ★★★★

1931

Fighting Caravans ★★★
City Streets ★★★
I Take This Woman ★★★
His Woman ★★★

1932

Make Me a Star (cameo)
Devil and the Deep ★★
If I Had a Million ★★
A Farewell to Arms ★★★★

1933

Today We Live ★★
One Sunday Afternoon ★★★★
Design for Living ★★★
Alice in Wonderland ★★

1934

Operator 13 ★★★
Now and Forever ★★

1935

The Wedding Night ★★
Lives of a Bengal Lancer ★★★★
Peter Ibbetson ★★★★

1936

Desire ★★★
Mr. Deeds Goes to Town ★★★★
Hollywood Boulevard (cameo)
The General Died at Dawn ★★★★

1937

The Plainsman ★★★★
Souls at Sea ★★★

1938

The Adventures of Marco Polo ★★★
Bluebeard's Eighth Wife ★★★★
The Cowboy and the Lady ★★★

1939

Beau Geste ★★★★
The Real Glory ★★★

1940

The Westerner ★★★★
Northwest Mounted Police ★★★

1941

Meet John Doe ★★★★
Sergeant York ★★★★

1942

Ball of Fire ★★★★
Pride of the Yankees ★★★★

1943

For Whom the Bell Tolls ★★★★

1944

The Story of Dr. Wassell ★★★
Casanova Brown ★★★

1945

Along Came Jones ★★★
Saratoga Trunk ★★★

1946

Cloak and Dagger ★★★

1947

Unconquered ★★★
Variety Girl (cameo)

1948

Good Sam ★★

1949

The Fountainhead ★★
It's a Great Feeling (cameo)
Task Force ★★★

1950

Bright Leaf ★★★
Dallas ★★★

1951

You're in the Navy Now ★★★
Starlift (cameo)
Distant Drums ★★★
It's a Big Country ★★★

1952

High Noon ★★★★
Springfield Rifle ★★★

1953

Return to Paradise ★★★
Blowing Wild ★★★

Gary Cooper.

1954

Garden of Evil ★★★
Vera Cruz ★★★★

1955

The Court-Martial of Billy Mitchell ★★★

1956

Friendly Persuasion ★★★★

1957

Love in the Afternoon ★★

1958

Ten North Frederick ★★★★
Man of the West ★★★

1959

The Hanging Tree ★★★
Alias Jesse James (cameo)
They Came to Cordura ★★★
The Wreck of the Mary Deare ★★★

1961

The Naked Edge ★★★

JOSEPH COTTEN
★★★ 2.83 STARS

Joseph Cotten's sophisticated good looks and romantic voice made him the perfect actor for sentimental dramas. When he had a meaty character part, (such as his role as the pulp writer in *The Third Man)*, he always rose to the occasion and played with subtlety and conviction.

Cotten was born in 1905, in Petersburgh, Virginia. He was a drama critic for the Miami Herald and a member of Orson Welles' Mercury Theater. After a Broadway hit "The Philadelphia Story," opposite Katharine Hepburn, Cotten made a superb film debut in *Citizen Kane*. *The Magnificent Ambersons*, again directed by Welles, increased his stature as a dramatic actor.

Shadow of a Doubt by Alfred Hitchcock offered him his best part ever—as smiling Uncle Charlie, worshipped by niece Teresa Wright before she began to discover his murderous tendencies. He offered solace to the mentally disintegrating Ingrid Bergman in *Gaslight* although Charles Boyer had the big scenes. Cotten was genuinely touching as a shell-shocked war veteran who met convict Ginger Rogers in *I'll Be Seeing You.*

Love Letters cast him melodramatically as a man who sent letters to Jennifer Jones and accidentally triggered her breakdown. Cotten's best part since *Shadow of a Doubt* came with *The Steel Trap* again opposite Teresa Wright—he played a man who stole his firm's money and then regretted it.

Throughout the late 1940s, Cotten was cast in a series of melodramas and too-sweet love stories including: *Duel in the Sun*, *September Affair*, and *Portrait of Jennie*. In the midst of this rut, however, he had one of his most complex roles in *The Third Man*, as an American pulp novelist in post-war Vienna looking for his old buddy, now in the black market.

Most of his movies since *(The Bottom of the Bottle*, *The Last Sunset*, *The Oscar*, and *Airport '77)* haven't been on par with his earlier

Joseph Cotten with Alida Valli in *The Third Man.*

work, but along the way he did a nice cameo in Welles' *Touch of Evil* and had good moments with Olivia De Havilland in the gruesome *Hush...Hush, Sweet Charlotte.* Cotten made acting look easy—possibly the reason he was never nominated for an Oscar.

Joseph Cotten in *Soylent Green.*

FILMOGRAPHY

1941

Citizen Kane ★★★★
Lydia ★★★

1942

The Magnificent Ambersons ★★★★
Journey Into Fear ★★★

1943

Shadow of a Doubt ★★★★
Hers to Hold ★★★

1944

Gaslight ★★★★
Since You Went Away ★★★★

1945

I'll Be Seeing You ★★★★
Love Letters ★★★★

1946

Duel in the Sun ★★★

1947

The Farmer's Daughter ★★★★

1948

Portrait of Jennie ★★★

1949

Under Capricorn ★★★
Beyond the Forest ★★★
The Third Man ★★★★

1950

Two Flags West ★★★
Walk Softly Stranger ★★★

1951

September Affair ★★★
Half Angel ★★★
Peking Express ★★★
The Man With a Cloak ★★★

1952

Untamed Frontier ★★★
The Steel Trap ★★★★

1953

Niagara ★★★
A Blueprint for Murder ★★★

1955

Special Delivery ★★★

1956

The Bottom of the Bottle ★★★
The Killer Is Loose ★★★

1957

The Halliday Brand ★★★

1958

Touch of Evil (cameo)
From the Earth to the Moon ★★★

1960

The Angel Wore Red ★★

1961

The Last Sunset ★★

1965

Hush...Hush, Sweet Charlotte ★★★
The Great Sioux Massacre ★★★

1966

The Oscar ★★
The Money Trap ★★★
The Tramplers ★★

1967

The Hell Benders ★★
Brighty of the Grand Canyon ★★
Jack of Diamonds ★★
Some May Live ★★

1968

Petulia ★★★★
Days of Fire ★★
White Comanche ★★

1969

Latitude Zero ★★★
Hour of Vengeance ★★

1970

The Grasshopper ★★★
Tora! Tora! Tora! ★★

1971

The Abominable Dr. Phibes ★★★
Lady Frankenstein ★★

Joseph Cotten in *Shadow of a Doubt.*

1972

Baron Blood ★★★
Doomsday Voyage ★★★

1973

A Delicate Balance ★★★
Soylent Green ★★★

1974

F for Fake ★★

1975

Timber Tramps ★★

1977

Twilight's Last Gleaming ★★★
Airport '77 ★★★

1978

The Wild Geese ★★★
L'Ordre et la Securite du Monde ★★
Caravans ★★

1979

The Fish Men ★★
L'Affaire Concorde ★★
Guyana: Cult of the Damned ★★

1980

The Hearse ★★★
Heaven's Gate ★★

1981

Delusion ★★
Screamers ★★

BRODERICK CRAWFORD
★★½ 2.44 STARS

Broderick Crawford has usually been tough, abrasive, and unsympathetic on the screen. These are qualities that usually limit an actor to supporting roles, but Crawford was lucky. His best parts in *Born Yesterday* and *All the King's Men* called for thuggish nastiness.

He was born William Broderick Crawford in Philadelphia, in 1911, the son of vaudeville performers. He had an auspicious start, climbing up from vaudeville to a lead role on Broadway. His first movies were mostly westerns, such as *When the Daltons Rode*, *Trail of the Vigilantes*, and *Texas Rangers Ride Again*. He graduated to modern police work in *The Time of Your Life* with James Cagney and took a strident stab at comedy in the forgettable farce *A Kiss in the Dark* with Jane Wyman.

All the King's Men cut through all the mediocrity and brought

Crawford an Oscar. As power-mad demagogue Willie Stark, he was superb, and he held his own perfectly with Judy Holliday in *Born Yesterday*. He had one other good role in *Not as a Stranger*, but he was relegated back to supporting roles and villains for the remaining bulk of his career. The public probably remembers Crawford best for his hit TV series, "Highway Patrol."

FILMOGRAPHY

1937

Woman Chases Man ★★★
Submarine D-I ★★★

1938

Start Cheering ★★★

1939

Sudden Money ★★
Undercover Doctor ★★
Beau Geste ★★★
The Real Glory ★★★
Eternally Yours ★★★

1940

Slightly Honorable ★★★
When the Daltons Rode ★★
Seven Sinners ★★★
Trail of the Vigilantes ★★
Texas Rangers Ride Again ★★

1941

The Black Cat ★★★
Tight Shoes ★★
South of Tahiti ★★
Badlands of Dakota ★★

1942

North to the Klondike ★★
Larceny Inc. ★★★
Butch Minds the Baby ★★★
Broadway ★★
Sin Town ★★
Men of Texas ★★

1946

The Runaround ★★★
Black Angel ★★

1947

Slave Girl ★★
The Flame ★★

1948

The Time of Your Life ★★★
Sealed Verdict ★★★
Bad Men of Tombstone ★★

1949

Night Unto Night ★★
Anna Lucasta ★★★
All the King's Men ★★★★
A Kiss in the Dark ★★

1950

Cargo to Capetown ★★
Born Yesterday ★★★★
Convicted ★★★

1951

The Mob ★★

1952

Scandal Sheet ★★
Stop You're Killing Me ★★
Lone Star ★★★
The Last of the Comanches ★★

1953

The Last Posse ★★

1954

Night People ★★★
Human Desire ★★★
Down Three Dark Streets ★★★

1955

The Swindle ★★
New York Confidential ★★★
Big House U.S.A. ★★★
Not as a Stranger ★★★

1956

Between Heaven and Hell ★★★
The Fastest Gun Alive ★★★

Broderick Crawford in *All the King's Men*.

1958

The Decks Ran Red ★★★

1960

Goliath and the Dragon ★★

1961

Square of Violence ★★

1962

Convicts Four ★★★

1963

The Castilian ★

1964

A House Is Not a Home ★★

1965

Up from the Beach ★★
The Vulture ★

1966

The Oscar ★★
Texican ★★
Kid Rodello ★★

1967

Per Un Dollaro di Gloria ★★
Smashing the Crime Syndicate ★★

1970

Hell's Bloody Devils ★★

1971

Ransom Money ★★

1972

Embassy ★★★

1973

Terror in the Wax Museum ★★★

1976

Won Ton Ton-the Dog Who Saved Hollywood ★★

1977

Proof of the Man ★★
The Private Files of J. Edgar Hoover ★★

1979

A Little Romance ★★★
There Goes The Bride (cameo)

JOAN CRAWFORD
★★★ 2.87 STARS

In her final interview, Joan Crawford expressed resentment that while she was a mere movie star, Bette Davis was considered an *actress*. In her good pictures, *Mildred Pierce* and *Sudden Fear*, Crawford was the equal of Davis. The problem was, few of her good films were that good.

Born Lucille Fay Le Sueur in 1904, in San Antonio, Texas, she began as a dancer and made her film debut in *Lady of the Night* in 1925. There were a whole rush of now-forgotten films like *Old Clothes* with Jackie Coogan and *Tramp, Tramp, Tramp* with Harry Langdon. Her portrait of a flapper in *Our Dancing Daughters* gave her a public image and widespread popularity, however, she wanted approval as an actress and fought for a dramatic part in *Paid*. Her fans increased, but critics were still cautious until *Grand Hotel*.

Viewed now, Crawford seems more natural and contemporary than either Greta Garbo or John Barrymore. After playing an overblown Sadie Thompson in *Rain*, she teamed with Clark Gable in *Dancing Lady* and solidified her success. They fell in love off screen, drawn together by common roots and mutual insecurity. "We knew we couldn't act and we wanted to learn," she said later.

Joan Crawford.

All her films during this time hit the mark, except *The Gorgeous Hussy,* an unfortunate venture into historical drama. She followed that with a series of failures—*The Bride Wore Red, Ice Follies of 1939,* and *Mannequin* with Spencer Tracy. They had an affair in real life, but no chemistry together on the screen.

A Woman's Face supplied a temporary upswing, and Crawford, carefully drilled by director George Cukor, was superb as the potential killer reformed by her plastic surgeon. Then the unsuccessful movies resumed, and she left MGM "by the back gate."

Mildred Pierce at Warner Brothers again showed what she could accomplish as an actress under a talented director, in this case Michael Curtiz. A Best Actress Oscar re-energized her, leading to the extravagantly enjoyable corn of *Humoresque* and the mesmerizing melodrama of *Possessed*. She was totally convincing as *Daisy Kenyon*, the girl who loved the married Dana Andrews, and her performance deserved more credit than it received. Her charming Congresswoman in *Goodbye, My Fancy* was also overlooked, but everybody raved about *Sudden Fear,* a classic woman-on-the-run thriller with Jack Palance.

"There's no excuse for a picture as bad as this one," Crawford said of *Johnny Guitar,* but it was in fact a marvelously nonsensical western, pitting her against Mercedes McCambridge, an arch enemy off-screen. She loved *Autumn Leaves,* asking, "Why can't they make more pictures like this?" and the sobbing women in the audience agreed. Crawford played a middle-aged typist in love with the younger, psychotic Cliff Robertson.

What Ever Happened to Baby Jane? was a grotesque but entertaining horror movie. Crawford, as Bette Davis's crippled sister, wisely subdued her acting excesses in the face of Davis's flashiness and came off believably. There was more horror with *I Saw What You Did* and *Strait-Jacket* in which she was cast as an axe murderess.

Her amazing intensity and dedication as an actress hinted at a stormy private life, but she was able to keep it hidden throughout her lifetime. She was married four times, including to the actors Douglas Fairbanks, Jr. and Franchot Tone. But after her death in 1977, her behind-the-screen veneer was stripped off in a sensationalized biography, Mommie Dearest, written by her adopted daughter, Christina.

Crawford *smouldered* on screen—there's no other word for it. She *demanded* audience involvement. People were impressed by her rags-to-riches story and the ambition that took her from nothing to an awesomely long career, and they felt that drive and conviction in her screen roles.

FILMOGRAPHY

1925

Lady of the Night ★★
Pretty Ladies ★★
The Only Thing (bit)
Old Clothes ★★
Sally, Irene and Mary ★★★

1926

The Boob ★★★
Tramp, Tramp, Tramp ★★★
Paris ★★★

1927

The Taxi Dancer ★★
Winners of the Wilderness ★★★
The Understanding Heart ★★★
The Unknown ★★★
Twelve Miles Out ★★★
Spring Fever ★★★

1928

West Point ★★★
Rose Marie ★★★
Across to Singapore ★★★
The Law of the Range ★★★
Four Walls ★★★
Our Dancing Daughters ★★★★
Dream of Love ★★★

1929

The Duke Steps Out ★★★
Hollywood Revue of 1929 ★★★
Our Modern Maidens ★★★
Untamed ★★★

1930

Montana Moon ★★★
Our Blushing Brides ★★★
Paid ★★★

1931

Dance Fools Dance ★★★
Laughing Sinners ★★★
This Modern Age ★★★
Possessed ★★★★

1932

Letty Lynton ★★★
Grand Hotel ★★★★
Rain ★★

1933

Today We Live ★★
Dancing Lady ★★★★

1934

Sadie McKee ★★
Chained ★★★
Forsaking All Others ★★★

1935

No More Ladies ★★★
I Live My Life ★★★

1936

The Gorgeous Hussy ★★
Love on the Run ★★★

1937

The Last of Mrs. Cheyney ★★★
The Bride Wore Red ★★

1938

Mannequin ★★
The Shining Hour ★★

1939

Ice Follies of 1939 ★★
The Women ★★★★

1940

Strange Cargo ★★★★
Susan and God ★★

1941

A Woman's Face ★★★★
When Ladies Meet ★★

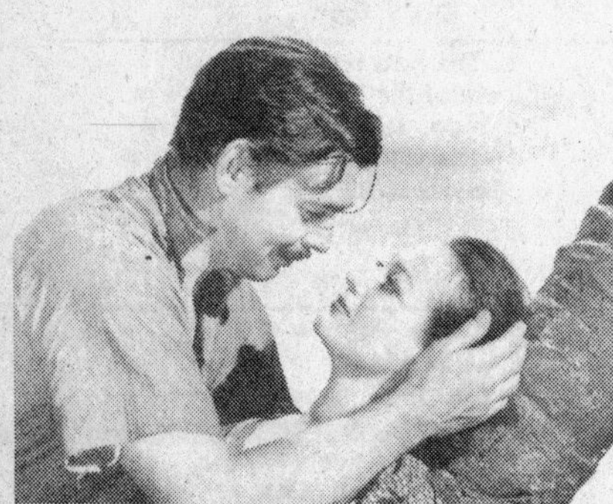

Joan Crawford with Clark Gable in *Strange Cargo.*

1942

They All Kissed the Bride ★★★
Reunion in France ★★

1943

Above Suspicion ★★

1944

Hollywood Canteen ★★

1945

Mildred Pierce ★★★★

Joan Crawford.

1946

Humoresque ★★★★

1947

Possessed ★★★★
Daisy Kenyon ★★★★

1949

Flamingo Road ★★★★
It's A Great Feeling (cameo)

1950

The Damned Don't Cry ★★★
Harriet Craig ★★★

1951

Goodbye, My Fancy ★★★★
This Woman Is Dangerous ★★

1952

Sudden Fear ★★★★

1953

Torch Song ★★

1954

Johnny Guitar ★★★

1955

Female on the Beach ★★
Queen Bee ★★★

1956

Autumn Leaves ★★★★

1957

The Story of Esther Costello ★★★

1959

The Best of Everything ★★★

1962

What Ever Happened to Baby Jane? ★★★★

1963

The Caretakers ★★

1964

Strait-Jacket ★★

1965

I Saw What You Did ★★

1967

Berserk ★★

1970

Trog ★★

RICHARD CRENNA
★★★ 2.88 STARS

Richard Crenna has made steady and impressive strides as an actor. He was a gawky, gangling juvenile, but his latest features show a firm, masculine authority which may bring him long overdue stardom in theatrical films.

He was born in 1926 in Los Angeles, and performed on radio serials as a youngster. His comic skill was an asset to a trio of popular TV shows, "Our Miss Brooks," "The Real McCoys," and "Slattery's People." He repeated his characterization of Walter Denton in the screen version of *Our Miss Brooks* and did a couple of undistinguished comedies, *It Grows on Trees* which prompted Irene Dunne to retire and *John Goldfarb, Please Come Home*.

Crenna's first authentic acting opportunity came in a Steve McQueen film, *The Sand Pebbles*. He also had a powerful part as Alan Arkin's accomplice in *Wait Until Dark*. He was cast in *Marooned*, a dreary drama about astronauts, and *Doctors' Wives* did not utilize his talents properly. However, Crenna's portrait of an unsuspecting husband murdered by William Hurt in *Body Heat* suggested dynamic reserves of talent, and points to a career in the 1980s that may surpass his former work.

Richard Crenna with Micheline Lerner in *Made in Paris.*

FILMOGRAPHY

1952

Red Skies of Montana ★★★
The Pride of St. Louis ★★★
It Grows on Trees ★★★

1956

Our Miss Brooks ★★★
Over-Exposed ★★★

1964

John Goldfarb, Please Come Home ★★

1966

Made in Paris ★★
The Sand Pebbles ★★★

1967

Wait Until Dark ★★★★

1968

Star! ★★★

1969

Midas Run ★★
Marooned ★★

1971

The Deserter ★★★
Catlow ★★★
Red Sky at Morning ★★★
Doctors' Wives ★★

1972

Un Flic ★★★

1973

The Man Called Noon ★★★

1976

Breakheart Pass ★★★

1978

The Evil ★★★

1979

Hard Ride to Rantan ★★★
Stone Cold Dead ★★★

1980

Death Ship ★★★

1981

Body Heat ★★★★

1982

First Blood ★★★

1983

Table for Five ★★★

DONALD CRISP
★★★½ 3.67 STARS

Half the classic films made since 1914 featured Donald Crisp. He acted well into his eighties and every movie benefited from his authoritative, dominating presence.

Crisp was born in 1880, in Aberfeldy, Scotland. He became D. W. Griffith's assistant on *The Birth of a Nation* and also directed before concentrating exclusively on acting. His versatile acting ability becomes clear with a partial listing of his films—*The Return of Sherlock Holmes, Svengali, Red Dust, Mutiny on the Bounty,* and *The Charge of the Light Brigade.*

He won an Oscar for a beautiful portrayal of Mr. Morgan in *How Green Was My Valley* and was convincingly unlikable as the tycoon who tried to destroy Gary Cooper in *Bright Leaf.* He was also effective in three Lassie films: *Lassie Come Home, Son of Lassie,* and *Hills of Home.*

A switch to horses proved worthwhile in the memorable *National Velvet.* Whether out west (*Whispering Smith*), in the England of the Middle Ages (*Prince Valiant*), or at West Point (*The Long Gray Line*), Crisp was equally at home. He is the very prototype of the professional film actor, slipping into every role and infusing it with its own life.

FILMOGRAPHY
(features only)

1915

The Birth of a Nation ★★★★

1919

Broken Blossoms ★★★★

1926

The Black Pirate ★★★

1928

The River Pirate ★★★
The Viking ★★★

1929

The Pagan ★★★
Trent's Last Case ★★★★
The Return of Sherlock Holmes ★★★★

1930

Scotland Yard ★★★★

1931

Svengali ★★★★
Kick In ★★★

1932

Red Dust ★★★★

1934

The Key ★★★
The Crime Doctor ★★★
What Every Woman Knows ★★★
The Little Minister ★★★★

1935

Vanessa: Her Love Story ★★★
Laddie ★★★
Oil for the Lamps of China ★★★
Mutiny on the Bounty ★★★★

1936

The White Angel ★★★
Mary of Scotland ★★★
The Charge of the Light Brigade ★★★★
Beloved Enemy ★★★★

1937

Parnell ★★★
The Life of Emile Zola ★★★★

1938

Jezebel ★★★★
Beloved Brat ★★★★
Dawn Patrol ★★★★
Valley of the Giants ★★★★
The Amazing Dr. Clitterhouse ★★★★
The Sisters ★★★★

1939

Juarez ★★★★
Daughters Courageous ★★★★
Wuthering Heights ★★★★
The Oklahoma Kid ★★★★
The Old Maid ★★★★
The Private Lives of Elizabeth and Essex ★★★★

1940

Dr. Ehrlich's Magic Bullet ★★★★
Brother Orchid ★★★★
The Sea Hawk ★★★★
City for Conquest ★★★★

Donald Crisp in *The Last Hurrah.*

1941

Shining Victory ★★★
Dr. Jekyll and Mr. Hyde ★★★★
How Green Was My Valley ★★★★

1943

The Gay Sisters ★★★
Forever and a Day ★★★
Lassie Come Home ★★★★

1944

The Uninvited ★★★★
The Adventures of Mark Twain ★★★★
National Velvet ★★★★

1945

Son of Lassie ★★★★
The Valley of Decision ★★★★

1948

Hills of Home ★★★★

1949

Whispering Smith ★★★

1950

Bright Leaf ★★★★

1954

Prince Valiant ★★★

1955

The Long Gray Line ★★★★
The Man from Laramie ★★★★

1958

The Last Hurrah ★★★★

1960

A Dog of Flanders ★★★
Pollyanna ★★★★

1961

Greyfriars Bobby ★★★

1963

Spencer's Mountain ★★★

BING CROSBY
★★★½ 3.37 STARS

Bing Crosby is the latest actor to be massacred in print as an unfit parent by his son Garry Crosby in Going My Own Way. The revelations, like Christina Crawford's horror stories in Mommie Dearest, are probably somewhat true. This makes Crosby's ability to project warmth, sincerity, and casual charm all the more remarkable.

Crosby was born Harry Lillis Crosby in 1904. At age nineteen, he began singing professionally. His vocal popularity led to the film *King of Jazz*, but he became nationally famous initially via radio. *The Big Broadcast* demonstrated his physical ease, and within a few years he was one of the top box-office attractions.

Most of his early films have been forgotten, although *Anything Goes* with Ethel Merman still figures prominently in revival houses. He teamed up with Bob Hope in 1940 for the still-popular "Road" pictures. *Road to Singapore*, a zany tale of two playboys who swore off women in Singapore, established the tone, and *Road to Zanzibar* was a satire on jungle pictures and the best of the series. Crosby had a huge hit with Fred Astaire in *Holiday Inn* and then played in the *Road to Morocco*.

Going My Way drew attention to his acting. The film is dated and sentimental now, but at the time it won him an Oscar. Co-star Barry Fitzgerald also won as Best Supporting Actor. *The Bells of St. Mary's*, a sequel, has maintained more of its freshness due to Ingrid Bergman's radiant portrait of a nun. However, the strong image of Bing Crosby as an Irish Catholic priest lingered from both films.

Road to Utopia had Hope and Crosby searching for a gold mine in Alaska, and Crosby had another enjoyable reunion in *Blue Skies* with Astaire. *The Emperor Waltz* with Joan Fontaine was an overblown fairytale, but Crosby's nonchalance made it work. He couldn't do much with *Top O' the Morning* despite the presence of Barry Fitzgerald again, and *A Connecticut Yankee in King Arthur's Court* was paper-thin, with average songs.

Here Comes the Groom was much closer to the high standard set by his best pictures, and he showed strong dramatic talent in *Little Boy Lost*. *White Christmas* was a remake of *Holiday Inn*, and it had Irving Berlin songs, Danny Kaye, and an appealing performance by Rosemary Clooney.

In any other year, Crosby would have won another Oscar for *The Country Girl*, but Marlon Brando was his competition in *On the Waterfront*. Crosby played an alcoholic singer attempting a comeback, a man who milked people for sympathy by making his wife appear domineering. His portrait of a compulsive nice guy made one wonder if there *were* dark sides behind his congenial exterior.

Bing Crosby.

High Society was a musical update of *The Philadelphia Story*, an even more entertaining film than its predecessor and populated with charming performers like Frank Sinatra, Grace Kelly, and Celeste Holm.

After *High Society*, his film career died with *Say One for Me* in which he played another priest, and *High Time*, a juvenile comedy with Fabian and Tuesday Weld. Oddly enough, Crosby's unparalleled singing success ("White Christmas" is still the number one record-seller in history) and consistent box-office power haven't led to legendary status. While Sinatra is still of interest to new generations, Crosby has dated. Maybe he was just too casual, too lazy, too unassuming for the fast-moving, highly charged viewers of today.

FILMOGRAPHY

1930

King of Jazz ★★★

1932

The Big Broadcast ★★★

1933

College Humor ★★★
Too Much Harmony ★★★
Going Hollywood ★★★

1934

We're Not Dressing ★★★
She Loves Me Not ★★★
Here Is My Heart ★★★

1935

Mississippi ★★★
The Big Broadcast of 1936 ★★★
Two for Tonight ★★★

1936

Anything Goes ★★★★
Rhythm on the Range ★★★★
Pennies from Heaven ★★★★

1937

Waikiki Wedding ★★★
Double or Nothing ★★★

1938

Dr. Rhythm ★★★
Sing You Sinners ★★★

1939

Paris Honeymoon ★★★★
East Side of Heaven ★★★
The Star Maker ★★★

1940

Road to Singapore ★★★★
If I Had My Way ★★★
Rhythm on the River ★★★

1941

Road to Zanzibar ★★★★
Birth of the Blues ★★★★

1942

Holiday Inn ★★★★
Road to Morocco ★★★★
Star Spangled Rhythm ★★★★

1943

Dixie ★★★★

1944

Going My Way ★★★★
Here Come the Waves ★★★

Bing Crosby with Barry Fitzgerald in *Going My Way.*

1945

Duffy's Tavern ★★★
The Bells of St. Mary's ★★★★

1946

Road to Utopia ★★★★
Blue Skies ★★★★

1947

Variety Girl ★★★
Welcome Stranger ★★★★
Road to Rio ★★★★

1948

The Emperor Waltz ★★★

1949

A Connecticut Yankee in King Arthur's Court ★★★
Top O' the Morning ★★★

1950

Riding High ★★★★
Mr. Music ★★★

1951

Here Comes the Groom ★★★

1952

Just for You ★★★
Road to Bali ★★★

1953

Little Boy Lost ★★★★

1954

White Christmas ★★★★
The Country Girl ★★★★

1956

Anything Goes ★★★
High Society ★★★★

1957

Man on Fire ★★★★

1959

Say One for Me ★★★

1960

Let's Make Love ★★★
High Time ★★★
Pepe ★★★

1962

Road to Hong Kong ★★

1964

Robin and the Seven Hoods ★★★

1966

Stagecoach ★★★

1974

That's Entertainment (narration)

ROBERT CUMMINGS
★★½ 2.68 STARS

Robert Cummings was a pleasing light comedian and a moderately effective dramatic actor. Although he lacked the charisma of the superstars, directors could always depend on him to do a competent job.

He was born Clarence Robert Orville Cummings, in 1908 in Missouri, and got his first Broadway job by faking a required English accent. He also pretended to be a Texan named Brice Hutchens to get his role in *The Virginia Judge*. Such zeal and dedication brought him steady work in films such as *So Red the Rose* and *Millions in the Air.* In 1936 alone he made seven films.

A Deanna Durbin film, *Three Smart Girls Grow Up*, displayed his flair for comedy. His comedic touch was honed sharper in *The Devil and Miss Jones* in which he played a union organizer opposite the delightful Jean Arthur.

In *Kings Row*, he was cast as a small-town doctor who befriended rakish Ronald Reagan, a triumph for both of them. *Saboteur* was exciting though second-class Hitchcock. Cummings was believable in *The Lost Moment* as a publisher whose search for a poet's love letters involved him with the mysterious Susan Hayward.

Later, he proved an asset to *Sleep My Love, The Accused* (as murderess Loretta Young's boyfriend), *Dial M for Murder* (rescuing Grace Kelly), and *The Carpetbaggers* (double-crossing George Peppard). Robert Cummings always seemed to be delivering his lines satirically—even in straight roles—and therefore worked best in comedy.

FILMOGRAPHY

1935

The Virginia Judge ★★
So Red the Rose ★★
Millions in the Air ★★

1936

Desert Gold ★★
Arizona Mahoney ★★
Border Flight ★★
Forgotten Faces ★★
Three Cheers for Love ★★★
Hollywood Boulevard ★★★
The Accusing Finger ★★★

1937

Hideaway Girl ★★★
The Last Train from Madrid ★★
Souls at Sea ★★★
Sophie Lang Goes West ★★★
Wells Fargo ★★★

1938

College Swing ★★★
You and Me ★★★
The Texan ★★★
Touchdown Army ★★★
I Stand Accused ★★★

Robert Cummings in *Kings Row.*

1939

Three Smart Girls Grow Up ★★★★
The Under-Pup ★★★
Rio ★★
Everything Happens at Night ★★★
Charlie McCarthy Detective ★★

1940

And One Was Beautiful ★★
Private Affairs ★★★
Spring Parade ★★★
One Night in the Tropics ★★

1941

Free and Easy ★★
The Devil and Miss Jones ★★★
Moon Over Miami ★★★
It Started with Eve ★★★★

1942

Kings Row ★★★★
Saboteur ★★★★
Between Us Girls ★★★

1943

Forever and a Day ★★★
Princess O'Rourke ★★★
Flesh and Fantasy ★★★

1945

You Came Along ★★

1946

The Bride Wore Boots ★★
The Chase ★★

1947

The Lost Moment ★★★
Heaven Only Knows ★★★

1948

Sleep My Love ★★★★
Let's Live a Little ★★

1949

The Accused ★★★★
Free for All ★★
Tell It to the Judge ★★
The Black Book ★★

1950

Paid in Full ★★★
The Petty Girl ★★★
For Heaven's Sake ★★

1951

The Barefoot Mailman ★★

1952

The First Time ★★★

1953

Marry Me Again ★★★

1954

Lucky Me ★★
Dial M for Murder ★★★★

1955

How to Be Very, Very Popular ★★

1962

My Geisha ★★

1963

Beach Party ★★

1964

What a Way to Go! ★★
The Carpetbaggers ★★★

1966

Promise Her Anything ★★★
Stagecoach ★★★

1967

Five Golden Dragons ★★

JAMIE LEE CURTIS
★★★ 3.14 STARS

Call it biting the hand that feeds you, but Jamie Lee Curtis, who made her name shrieking her way to the bank in the creep-shows *Halloween* and *Halloween II* says she hates horror films. "They are very low-budget, quickly made, slipshod productions. I mean, how many different ways can you find somebody dead?"

She was born in 1959 to the famous actors Tony Curtis and Janet Leigh. Screaming seems to run in the family. Jamie's mom, Janet Leigh, received a bloodbath in the shower scene of Hitchcock's *Psycho*.

Jamie Lee Curtis in *Halloween II.*

Whether or not her films were shoddy (schlock for schlock's sake), Curtis, the current queen of the B's, always portrayed strong women. Her role in a number of movies—*Road Games, The Fog, Terror Train,* and *Prom Night*—was that of a survivor fighting off assailants.

After stretching her range on television in *Death of a Centerfold: The Dorothy Stratten Story,* she tried her hand at comedy in *Trading Places* with Dan Aykroyd and Eddie Murphy. If she's able to maintain her strong woman type and transfer it effectively to other genres, Jamie Lee Curtis could become one of the big stars of the 1980s.

FILMOGRAPHY

1978

Halloween ★★★

1980

The Fog ★★★
Prom Night ★★★
Terror Train ★★★

1981

Road Games ★★★
Halloween II ★★★

1983

Trading Places ★★★★

TONY CURTIS
★★½ 2.38 STARS

Tony Curtis brought a Bronx accent to ancient Rome, the old west, and modern Paris. Eventually, he acquired enough acting skill to make some viewers forget that they were watching the former Bernie Schwartz.

Curtis was born in 1925, in New York. After a financially deprived Bronx childhood, he took acting classes at New York's Dramatic Workshop and pushed his way through the gates of Universal. His pretty boy looks ("but unmistakable masculinity" according to columnist Sheilah Graham) brought mass approval from female fans, and he appeared in *Criss Cross, City Across the River,* and *Francis*.

The Prince Who Was a Thief increased his popularity, and as *Houdini*, the famed magician, he suggested some acting ability beneath the fan-magazine facade. A much publicized marriage to Janet Leigh also kept him in the limelight, and she was his love interest in *The Black Shield of Falworth, The Vikings, The Perfect Furlough,* and *Who Was That Lady?*

Trapeze was an absorbing circus drama bolstered by Burt Lancaster, and Curtis won over more critics. Artistic respectability was totally achieved with Lancaster again in the sordid *Sweet Smell of Success*. This Clifford Odets tale of a Walter Winchell-type columnist and his oily press agent was too bitter a pill for Curtis fans, but they flocked to *Some Like It Hot*.

Curtis looked comfortable in drag clothing though he complained that kissing Marilyn Monroe was like "kissing Hitler," and he was believably shallow in *Kings Go Forth*. *The Defiant Ones* garnered him an Oscar nomination though the ending (when Sidney Poitier sacrificed himself for Curtis's benefit) is disturbingly unconvincing today.

He was a ludicrous Roman in *Spartacus*, and there were a series of disastrous comedies including *Sex and the Single Girl, Boeing Boeing,* and *Not With My Wife You Don't*. He had one more notable characterization in *The Boston Strangler*.

Tony Curtis's bad parts seem to have outlasted his good, and he is remembered today as a cross between a cheesecake and a ham.

FILMOGRAPHY

1949

Criss Cross ★★
City Across the River ★★
The Lady Gambles ★★
Johnny Stool Pigeon ★★

1950

Francis ★★
I Was a Shoplifter ★★
Winchester '73 (bit)
Sierra ★★
Kansas Raiders ★★

1951

The Prince Who Was a Thief ★★

1952

Flesh and Fury ★★★
No Room for the Groom ★★
Son of Ali Baba ★★

1953

Houdini ★★★
The All-American ★★

1954

Forbidden ★★
Beachhead ★★
Johnny Dark ★★
The Black Shield of Falworth ★

Tony Curtis in *Forbidden*.

1955

So This Is Paris ★★★
The Purple Mask ★★
Six Bridges to Cross ★★★

1956

The Square Jungle ★★
Trapeze ★★★★
The Rawhide Years ★★★

1957

Mister Cory ★★★
Sweet Smell of Success ★★★★
The Midnight Story ★★★

1958

The Vikings ★★★
Kings Go Forth ★★★
The Defiant Ones ★★★★

1959

The Perfect Furlough ★★★
Some Like It Hot ★★★★
Operation Petticoat ★★★

1960

Pepe (cameo)
Who Was That Lady? ★★
The Rat Race ★★★
Spartacus ★★

1961

The Great Impostor ★★★★

1962

The Outsider ★★★
Taras Bulba ★

1963

Forty Pounds of Trouble ★★
The List of Adrian Messenger ★★★

1964

Captain Newman M.D. ★★★★
Wild and Wonderful ★★
Goodbye Charlie ★
Paris When It Sizzles ★★

1965

Sex and the Single Girl ★★
The Great Race ★
Boeing Boeing ★

1966

Not With My Wife You Don't! ★★
Chamber of Horrors (cameo)
Arrivederci, Baby! ★

1967

Don't Make Waves ★★

1968

The Boston Strangler ★★★★
The Chastity Belt ★★

1969

Those Daring Young Men in Their Jaunty Jalopies ★★

1970

Suppose They Gave a War and Nobody Came ★★
You Can't Win 'Em All ★★

1975

Capone ★★★
Lepke ★★★

1976

The Last Tycoon ★★★★
The Count of Monte Cristo ★★

1977

Casanova ★★

1978

The Manitou ★★
Sextette ★
The Bad News Bears Go to Japan ★★

1978

It Rained All Night the Day I Left ★★
Title Shot ★★

1980

Little Miss Marker ★★
The Mirror Crack'd ★★★

DAN DAILEY
★ ★ ★ 2.91 STARS

If Gene Kelly was acrobatic and Fred Astaire ballroom-elegant, then Dan Dailey was the epitome of a vaudeville hoofer. He and Betty Grable were never *great* dancers, but they knew how to give energy and zest to a number.

Born in 1914, in New York, Dailey worked in vaudeville and had a strong part in "Stars in Your Eyes" on Broadway. His first film, *The Mortal Storm*, was a starkly serious exposé of Nazi cruelty, but *Ziegfeld Girl* and *Lady Be Good* set the tone for his later work. He first teamed with Grable in a light but pleasing and enormously popular musical, *Mother Wore Tights*. Public reaction necessitated another teaming, and they were paired in *When My Baby Smiles at Me* which netted Dailey an Oscar nomination.

Jeanne Crain was his partner in *You Were Meant for Me*, a modest musical filmed in black-and-white, and he was Celeste Holm's daydreaming husband in the drab *Chicken Every Sunday.* Anne Baxter was his love interest in the lifeless *You're My Everything*.

He reteamed with Betty Grable in *My Blue Heaven* which was, unfortunately, a sloshy tale of two radio performers who struggled to adopt a child. *Call Me Mister* was their last pairing, a featherweight story casting Dailey as a soldier who went AWOL to win back his ex-wife.

Dan Dailey in *It's Always Fair Weather.*

A baseball biography of Dizzy Dean, *The Pride of St. Louis*, showed Dailey at his most breezily likable. There was one more successful if mediocre musical comedy, *There's No Business Like Show Business*, and one unpopular but excellent film, *It's Always Fair Weather*, which gave him his best role.

None of his other pictures—*Meet Me in Las Vegas, The Best Things in Life Are Free*, or *The Wayward Bus*—made headway with audiences. Dailey died in 1978, and as of this writing, he has no cult status like his contemporary song and dance rivals Gene Kelly and Fred Astaire.

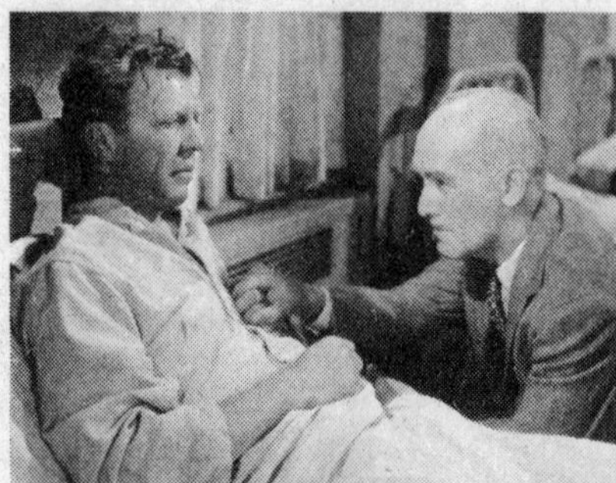
Dan Dailey with James Gleason in *When My Baby Smiles at Me.*

FILMOGRAPHY

1940

The Mortal Storm ★ ★ ★
Dulcy ★ ★ ★
Susan and God ★ ★ ★
Hullabaloo ★ ★ ★

1941

Ziegfeld Girl ★ ★ ★
Lady Be Good ★ ★
Washington Melodrama ★ ★
The Wild Man of Borneo ★ ★

1942

Panama Hattie ★ ★ ★

1948

You Were Meant for Me ★ ★ ★
Mother Wore Tights ★ ★ ★ ★
Give My Regards to Broadway ★ ★ ★
When My Baby Smiles at Me ★ ★ ★ ★

1949

Chicken Every Sunday ★ ★
You're My Everything ★ ★ ★

1950

When Willie Comes Marching Home ★ ★ ★
My Blue Heaven ★ ★ ★
I'll Get By (cameo)
A Ticket to Tomahawk ★ ★ ★

1951

Call Me Mister ★ ★ ★
I Can Get It for You Wholesale ★ ★ ★ ★

1952

The Pride of St. Louis ★ ★ ★
What Price Glory ★ ★
Meet Me at the Fair ★ ★

1953

Taxi ★ ★ ★
The Girl Next Door ★ ★ ★
The Kid from Left Field ★ ★ ★

1954

There's No Business Like Show Business ★ ★ ★

1955

It's Always Fair Weather ★ ★ ★ ★

1956

Meet Me in Las Vegas ★ ★
The Best Things in Life Are Free ★ ★ ★

1957

The Wings of Eagles ★ ★ ★
Oh Men! Oh Women! ★ ★
The Wayward Bus ★ ★ ★

1960

Pepe ★ ★ ★

1962

Hemingway's Adventures of a Young Man ★ ★ ★

LINDA DARNELL
★ ★ ★ 2.83 STARS

Certain roles, like Scarlett O'Hara (Vivien Leigh) and Rebecca (Joan Fontaine) inspired extensive Hollywood searches for just the right actress. Amber, in author Kathleen Windsor's *Forever Amber*, also fell into that category. However, Linda Darnell, who was awarded the part, wasn't as lucky as Leigh and Fontaine. The movie was ponderous, and her performance lacked the sex appeal that would have made it sizzle.

It was a shame because Darnell had beauty and talent and showed it in other, less-publicized films. Born Monetta Eloyse Darnell in 1921 in Dallas, Texas to ambitious parents, she received childhood training that led her straight into films. She made a strong impression in some early films, *The Mark of Zorro* and *Blood and Sand*, and was a convincing tramp in *Fallen Angel*.

Her finest hour came in *A Letter to Three Wives*, as the grasping wife of Paul Douglas. She nearly stole the film, and should have been nom-

Linda Darnell.

inated for an Oscar. Most of her movies after that were mediocre, like *Island of Desire* and *Blackbeard the Pirate*. She died at forty-four after falling asleep with a lighted cigarette that set fire to her room.

FILMOGRAPHY

1939

Hotel for Women ★★
Daytime Wife ★★

1940

Star Dust ★★★
Brigham Young ★★★
The Mark of Zorro ★★★★
Chad Hanna ★★★

1941

Blood and Sand ★★★
Rise and Shine ★★

1942

The Loves of Edgar Allan Poe ★★★

1943

City Without Men ★★
The Song of Bernadette (cameo)

1944

It Happened Tomorrow ★★★
Buffalo Bill ★★★
Summer Storm ★★★★
Sweet and Lowdown ★★

1945

Hangover Square ★★★★
The Great John L ★★★
Fallen Angel ★★★

1946

My Darling Clementine ★★★
Anna and the King of Siam ★★★
Centennial Summer ★★★

1947

Forever Amber ★★

1948

The Walls of Jericho ★★★
Unfaithfully Yours ★★★

1949

Slattery's Hurricane ★★
A Letter to Three Wives ★★★★
Everybody Does It ★★★★

1950

No Way Out ★★★★
Two Flags West ★★★

1951

The Thirteenth Letter ★★★
The Guy Who Came Back ★★★
The Lady Pays Off ★★

1952

Island of Desire ★★
Night Without Sleep ★★★
Blackbeard the Pirate ★★

1953

Angels of Darkness ★★
Second Chance ★★★

1954

This Is My Love ★★★

1955

Gli Ultimi Cinque Minuti ★★★

1956

Dakota Incident ★★

1957

Zero Hour ★★★

1963

The Castilian ★★★

1965

Black Spurs ★★

BETTE DAVIS
★★★ 2.94 STARS

There are some who claim that Bette Davis is a personality rather than an actress. Katharine Hepburn contradicted that theory best when she said, "Show me a woman who isn't a personality and I'll show you a woman who isn't a star." Bette Davis fuses the two elements—personality and acting—more forcefully than any other person on the screen. She keeps a hypnotic hold on the viewer's attention even when she is working with poor material.

Her 1962 autobiography, The Lonely Life, makes it clear that the only true love of her life was her career. She fought for it like a tiger, aided by her ambitious mother. She was born Ruth Elizabeth Davis in 1908 in Lowell, Massachusetts. Her first Broadway performance was on the stage in "Broken Dishes," and then Universal took her on despite their concern about her lack of sex appeal.

Early roles in *Bad Sister, Way Back Home*, and *The Menace* are now forgotten, but late night movie watchers can still see Davis in the movie that made her famous, *The Man Who Played God* opposite George Arliss. After that performance she worked with bigger stars, including Barbara Stanwyck in *So Big* and Spencer Tracy in *20,000 Years in Sing Sing*.

She disappointed critics in *Ex-Lady* but stunned them in *Of Human Bondage* as the self-involved, manipulative Mildred. Twenty-eight years later in her autobiography, she still expressed rage that the Academy overlooked her performance in *Bondage* and gave the Best Actress award to Claudette Colbert for *It Happened One Night*. She received her first Oscar, a consolation statuette, the following year for *Dangerous*.

After the rather stagy *The Petrified Forest*, Davis sued Warners for saddling her with unsuitable roles. The court ruled against her, but her parts improved starting with *Marked Woman*. *Jezebel* was a Southern saga designed to compete with *Gone With the Wind*. Today, it comes in a poor second, but Davis' portrait of a convention-defying Southern belle stands the test of time. *Dark Victory* presented her as an heiress dying of a brain tumor after finding true love, and *The Letter* featured one of her finest performances as a murderess.

Variety called her performance in *The Great Lie* "a most persuasive portrayal" even though Mary Astor stole the film. She quarreled with director William Wyler about her interpretation of *The Little Foxes*. Seen today, Wyler was right—her

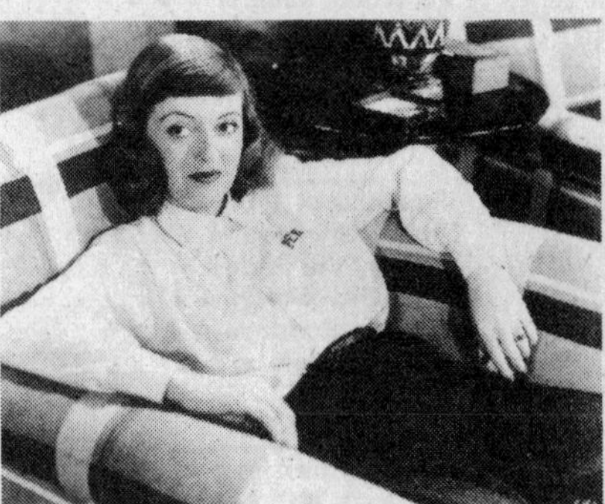
Bette Davis.

Regina was too heavy-handed and too mannered. *Now, Voyager* was a superb soap opera, prompting The National Board of Review Magazine to say, "she makes the film worthwhile and gives it a dignity not fully warranted by the script."

Beyond the Forest was a low point, a hysterical hodgepodge about a small-town wife who wanted to move to Chicago. However, *All About Eve* came along just in time to confirm Davis' talent. Her Margo Channing is still on everyone's list of favorite performances.

Nothing afterward matched *All About Eve*, but *What Ever Happened to Baby Jane?* is still a classic to horror buffs, and *Hush...Hush, Sweet Charlotte* has genuinely frightening moments. Davis continues to be active on television, and some of her portrayals such as the poor widow in *White Mama* equalled the standard set by her best screen work. She received the American Film Institute's Life Achievement Award in 1977, the most deserving recipient since that award began.

Bette Davis.

FILMOGRAPHY

1931

Bad Sister ★★
Waterloo Bridge ★★
Seed ★★

1932

Way Back Home ★★★
The Menace ★★★
Hell's House ★★★
The Man Who Played God ★★★
So Big ★★★
The Rich Are Always With Us ★★★
The Dark Horse ★★★
Cabin in the Cotton ★★★
Three on a Match ★★★

1933

20,000 Years in Sing Sing ★★★
Parachute Jumper ★★★
The Working Man ★★★
Ex-Lady ★★
Bureau of Missing Persons ★★★

1934

Fashions of 1934 ★★★
The Big Shakedown ★★★
Jimmy the Gent ★★★
Fog Over Frisco ★★★
Of Human Bondage ★★★★
Housewife ★★★

1935

Bordertown ★★★★
The Girl from 10th Avenue ★★★
Front Page Woman ★★★
Special Agent ★★★
Dangerous ★★★★

1936

The Petrified Forest ★★★
The Golden Arrow ★★★
Satan Met a Lady ★★★

1937

Marked Woman ★★★
Kid Galahad ★★★
That Certain Woman ★★★
It's Love I'm After ★★★

1938

Jezebel ★★★★
The Sisters ★★★

1939

Dark Victory ★★★
Juarez ★★★
The Old Maid ★★★★
The Private Lives of Elizabeth and Essex ★★★

1940

The Letter ★★★★
All This and Heaven Too ★★★

1942

The Great Lie ★★★
The Bride Came C.O.D. ★★★
The Little Foxes ★★
The Man Who Came to Dinner ★★★
In This Our Life ★★★
Now, Voyager ★★★★

1943

Watch on the Rhine ★★★
Thank Your Lucky Stars ★★★
Old Acquaintance ★★★

1944

Mr. Skeffington ★★★
Hollywood Canteen ★★★

1945

The Corn Is Green ★★★

1946

A Stolen Life ★★★
Deception ★★★

1948

Winter Meeting ★★
June Bride ★★★

1949

Beyond the Forest ★

1950

All About Eve ★★★★

1951

Another Man's Poison ★★
Payment on Demand ★★★

1952

Phone Call from a Stranger ★★★
The Star ★★★

1955

The Virgin Queen ★★★

1956

Storm Center ★★
The Catered Affair ★★

1959

John Paul Jones (cameo)
The Scapegoat ★★★

1961

A Pocketful of Miracles ★★★

Bette Davis in *What Ever Happened to Baby Jane?*

1962

What Ever Happened to Baby Jane? ★★★★

1964

The Empty Canvas ★★
Dead Ringer ★★★
Where Love Has Gone ★★★

1965

Hush . . . Hush, Sweet Charlotte ★★★★
The Nanny ★★★

1967

The Anniversary ★★

1970

Connecting Rooms ★★

1971

Bunny O'Hare ★

1976

Burnt Offerings ★★★

1978

Return from Witch Mountain ★★★
Death on the Nile ★★★★

1980

The Watcher in the Woods ★★★

DORIS DAY
★★★ 2.87 STARS

"I knew Doris Day before she was a virgin," commented Oscar Levant about the series of comedies (starting with *Pillow Talk*) that required Day to worry and fret about saving her honor. The public laughed, but her loyal fans saw the sad irony. In capitalizing on a Goody Two-Shoes image, Day abandoned her musical career, made her weakest movies, and lost the critical respect she had built up in the 1950s.

The Pollyanna image had no connection with her actual background. Born Doris von Kappelhoff in 1924 in Cincinnati, Ohio, Day escaped the stress of her parents' unhappy marriage by dancing. A serious auto accident destroyed her dream of being the next Ginger Rogers, and she switched to singing. While with Les Brown's band she experienced a hit record "Sentimental Journey" and two painful divorces.

Her first film, *Romance on the High Seas*, gave her a great song, "It's Magic," and *Young Man With a Horn* offered her strong dramatic scenes in which she seemed warmly natural against the artificial posturing of Lauren Bacall.

By the Light of the Silvery Moon and *On Moonlight Bay* threatened to give audiences a sugar overdose, but *I'll See You in My Dreams* compensated—a surprisingly compelling account of songwriter Gus Kahn and his devoted wife who pushed him too hard. As Grace Kahn, Day abandoned her sweetness and light to play a not altogether likable character.

Doris Day.

She suffered a nervous breakdown during the making of *Lucky Me*, a film poor enough to endanger anyone's peace of mind. But the mid-1950s featured her best work. She was superb as *Calamity Jane*, intense and fiery and in top vocal form. An outstanding score by Sammy Fain and Paul Francis Webster, including the Oscar-winning "Secret Love," guaranteed first-rate entertainment. *Love Me or Leave Me* was even better, a hard-hitting biography of songstress Ruth Etting. It was the first film to showcase her sexuality. Hitchcock's *The Man Who Knew Too Much* provided her with a startlingly effective hysteria scene.

Day's box office sagged with *The Tunnel of Love* and *It Happened to Jane*, and she bolstered it with comedy. *Pillow Talk* was the first of her Good Girl films co-starring Rock Hudson. Others included *Please Don't Eat the Daisies* (based on Jean Kerr's book), *Lover Come Back*, *Move Over, Darling* (a pathetically unfunny remake of the classic *My Favorite Wife*), and *Send Me No Flowers*. *That Touch of Mink* also focused on her virtue, but Cary Grant lent it an air of class.

Day's awesome box-office achievement (number one for four years) preceded a sudden, unexpected decline. Among the films responsible were *Caprice*, *The Glass*

Bottom Boat, and *Where Were You When the Lights Went Out?*

In Doris Day's case, the lights went out because she ignored the talent that had originally made her great—her singing. She was a competent comedienne and a capable dramatic actress, but when she sang she was incandescent. Nothing in her movies from 1959 to 1966 can touch the beauty and sincerity of her vocals on "It's Magic" and "Secret Love."

FILMOGRAPHY

1948

Romance on the High Seas ★★★★

1949

My Dream Is Yours ★★★
It's a Great Feeling ★★

1950

Young Man With a Horn ★★★
Tea for Two ★★★★
The West Point Story ★★★

1951

Storm Warning ★★
Lullaby of Broadway ★★★
On Moonlight Bay ★★
I'll See You in My Dreams ★★★★
Starlift (cameo)

1952

The Winning Team ★★
April in Paris ★★★

1953

By the Light of the Silvery Moon ★★★
Calamity Jane ★★★★

1954

Lucky Me ★★

1955

Young at Heart ★★★★
Love Me or Leave Me ★★★★

1956

The Man Who Knew Too Much ★★★★
Julie ★★

1957

The Pajama Game ★★★★

1958

Teacher's Pet ★★★★
The Tunnel of Love ★★

1959

It Happened to Jane ★★
Pillow Talk ★★★

1960

Please Don't Eat the Daisies ★★★
Midnight Lace ★★★

1962

Lover Come Back ★★★
That Touch of Mink ★★★
Jumbo ★★★★

1963

The Thrill Of It All ★★★★
Move Over, Darling ★★

1964

Send Me No Flowers ★★

1965

Do Not Disturb ★★★

1966

The Glass Bottom Boat ★★★

1967

Caprice ★★

1968

The Ballad of Josie ★★★
Where Were You When the Lights Went Out? ★★
With Six You Get Eggroll ★★★

JAMES DEAN
★★★★ 4.00 STARS

When James Dean first appeared on the screen in *East of Eden*, Bosley Crowther of the New York Times scolded director Elia Kazan for allowing his star to imitate Marlon Brando. He dismissed Dean as a "mass of histrionic gingerbread."

This is a classic example of a contemporary critic's inability to forecast a trend. Dean's shuffling and mumbling was ideally suited to portray a lonely, misunderstood teenager. The tentative movements and vulnerable, wounded looks made a direct and lasting impression with youthful audiences.

His own background gave him a personal understanding of the "lost quality" he projected. Dean was born on a farm in Marion, Indiana, in 1931. His mother died when he was nine, and he had little rapport with his father who wanted him to study law. His decision to become an actor resulted in bit parts in *Fixed Bayonets* and *Sailor Beware* as well as TV work, and he later scored on Broadway in two plays, "See the Jaguar" and "The Immoralist."

His first major film, *East of Eden* received a huge publicity buildup, and Dean fueled the press fires by dressing sloppily and conducting a turbulent romance with Pier Angeli. When released in 1955, the movie caused a sensation. Hollywood rewarded him with an Oscar nomination although he lost, unfairly, to Ernest Borgnine's *Marty.* The scene where Dean pleaded with his unloving father (Raymond Massey) to accept a gift of money is still unbearably poignant.

James Dean.

Rebel Without a Cause turned him from a star into a legend. Dean's brooding intensity brought out acting depth in co-star Natalie Wood that she had never shown previously. His third and last picture, *Giant,* was big box office, and Dean was believable though miscast as a cowboy with a lifelong yen for Elizabeth Taylor.

Death came on September 30, 1955, provoking an international mourning that has never subsided. The film *September 30, 1955* and a Broadway play "Come Back to the 5 & Dime, Jimmy Dean, Jimmy Dean" still focus on his personality and career. The way he died was an important key. Dean who was nearsighted had allegedly been racing his new Porsche without glasses. This final, foolish tempting of the fates was consistent with the rebel image that still reverberates nearly 30 years later.

James Dean in *Giant.*

FILMOGRAPHY

1951

Sailor Beware (bit)
Fixed Bayonets (bit)

1952

Has Anybody Seen My Gal (bit)

1953

Trouble Along the Way (bit)

1955

East of Eden ★★★★
Rebel Without a Cause ★★★★

1956

Giant ★★★★

YVONNE DE CARLO
★★½ 2.29 STARS

Some stars like Claire Trevor make a name for themselves in action films and then *graduate* to more dramatically fulfilling roles. Yvonne De Carlo played in westerns *or* in costume dramas, adding flashy B-movie decorations to her forgettable adventure films.

She was born Peggy Yvonne Middleton in 1922, in Canada. Her training as a dancer proved useful in the kind of exotic roles that shaped her image, in films such as *Song of Scheherazade* and *Salome, Where She Danced* (cast as a sultry spy). She had strong co-stars in *Slave Girl* (Broderick Crawford and George Brent), but the material hardly varied in *Calamity Jane and Sam Bass, Black Bart, Buccaneer's Girl,* and *The Desert Hawk.*

Occasionally, there was a part that required some characterization, and she was competent. One of these was *The Captain's Paradise* with Alec Guinness; *Casbah* was more standard fare, but the time-tested story was stronger than her usual scripts. *The Ten Commandments* and *Band of Angels* were elaborate "A" pictures that offered more prestige without better dramatic opportunities.

De Carlo showed a comic flair on her TV series, "The Munsters," that the movies had totally neglected.

FILMOGRAPHY

1942

Harvard Here I Come! ★★
This Gun for Hire ★★★
Road to Morocco ★★★
Lucky Jordan ★★★
Youth on Parade ★★

1943

Rhythm Parade ★★
The Crystal Ball ★★
Salute for Three ★★
For Whom the Bell Tolls ★★★
So Proudly We Hail! ★★★
Let's Face It ★★
True to Life ★★
The Deerslayer ★★★

1944

Standing Room Only ★★
The Story of Dr. Wassell ★★★

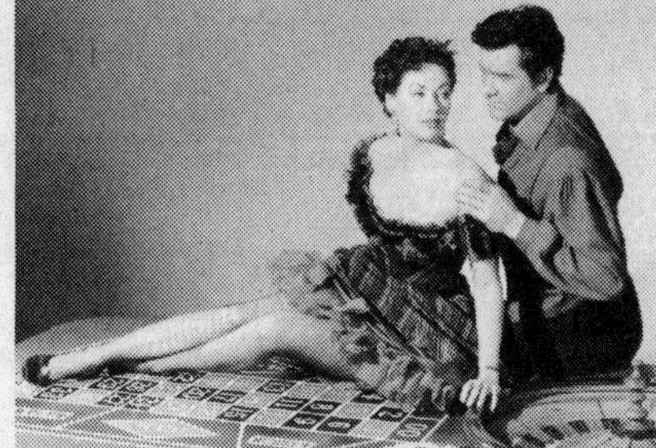

Yvonne De Carlo with Rock Hudson in *Scarlet Angel.*

Rainbow Island ★★
Kismet ★★
Practically Yours ★★★
Here Come the Waves ★★★

1945

Bring on the Girls ★★
Salome, Where She Danced ★★
Frontier Gal ★★

1947

Song of Scheherazade ★★
Brute Force ★★★
Slave Girl ★★

1948

Black Bart ★★
Casbah ★★★
River Lady ★★

1949

Criss Cross ★★★
Calamity Jane and Sam Bass ★★
The Gal Who Took the West ★★

1950

Buccaneer's Girl ★★
The Desert Hawk ★★

1951

Tomahawk ★★
Hotel Sahara ★★
Silver City ★★

1952

The San Francisco Story ★★
Scarlet Angel ★★
Hurricane Smith ★★

1953

Sombrero ★★
She Devils ★★
Fort Algiers ★★
The Captain's Paradise ★★★

1954

La Castiglione ★★
Border River ★★
Happy Ever After ★★
Passion ★★

1955

Shotgun ★★

1956

Flame of the Islands ★★
Magic Fire ★★★
Raw Edge ★★★
Death of a Scoundrel ★★★
The Ten Commandments ★★★

1957

Band of Angels ★★★

1958

Mary Magdalene ★★

1959

Timbuktu ★★

1963

McLintock! ★★★

1964

A Global Affair ★★
Law of the Lawless ★★

1965

Tentazioni proibite (documentary)

1966

Munster, Go Home ★★★

1967

Hostile Guns ★★

1968

The Power ★★
Arizona Bushwhackers ★★

1970

The Delta Factor ★★

1971

The Seven Minutes ★★

1975

It Seemed Like a Good Idea at the Time ★★

1977

Satan's Cheerleaders ★★

1979

Nocturna ★★

1980

Sam Marlow Private Eye ★★
Guyana: Cult of the Damned ★★

SANDRA DEE
★★½ 2.50 STARS

Sandra Dee was the Brooke Shields of the early 1960s—a successful model at twelve and a fresh-faced heroine in lightweight romances. But there is a difference. Dee, though caught in fluffy material, had some acting ability.

Born Alexandra Zuck in 1942 in New Jersey, she had little to do in her first film, *Until They Sail*. However, she made more of an impression in *The Reluctant Debutante* with John Saxon. The mother and daughter confrontation scenes with Lana Turner in *Imitation of Life* showed undeniable talent, and she was appealing in the *The Restless Years*.

Sandra Dee with Bobby Darin in *If a Man Answers*.

Gidget launched a brief superstar period, and Dee played the title role energetically, resisting its saccharine pitfalls. *A Summer Place* also showed her to advantage despite a corny scene when she confessed to daddy Richard Egan about her "naughty thoughts."

Her box-office appeal held when she and husband Bobby Darin teamed in *Come September*, but the scripts, *Take Her, She's Mine*, *I'd Rather Be Rich*, and *A Man Could Get Killed*, grew steadily worse. One gets the feeling that her film career ended before she had a chance to really develop.

FILMOGRAPHY

1957

Until They Sail ★★★

1958

The Reluctant Debutante ★★★
The Restless Years ★★★

1959

Imitation of Life ★★★
Gidget ★★★
A Summer Place ★★★
Stranger in My Arms ★★★
The Wild and the Innocent ★★★

1960

A Portrait in Black ★★★

1961

Romanoff and Juliet ★★
Tammy Tell Me True ★★
Come September ★★

1962

If a Man Answers ★★

1963

Tammy and the Doctor ★★
Take Her, She's Mine ★★

1964

I'd Rather Be Rich ★★★

1965

That Funny Feeling ★★

1966

A Man Could Get Killed ★★

1967

Doctor, You've Got to Be Kidding ★★

1968

Rosie! ★★

1970

The Dunwich Horror ★★★

1971

Ad est di Marsa Matruh ★★

OLIVIA DE HAVILLAND
★★★ 3.13 STARS

In 1955, Newsweek called Olivia De Havilland the "mistress of sentimental overstatement." This tendency, however, surfaced only occasionally at the peak of her career. Today, violins can be heard in every line she speaks, and one has to look back at *The Heiress* and *The Snake Pit* to remember how accomplished she was.

De Havilland was born in Tokyo, in 1916. She became involved with college dramatics and began her career at Warner Brothers with *Alibi Ike*. However, the action films she made with Errol Flynn actually launched her career. *Captain Blood* was the first, followed by the equally exciting *The Charge of the Light Brigade*.

Her films without Flynn, *Call It a Day* with Ian Hunter and *Gold Is Where You Find It* with George Brent, were less interesting. *The Adventures of Robin Hood* capped the height of her "adventurer's lady" period, a swashbuckler that remains the best example of its genre. She was forceful in *Dodge City* but bland in *The Private Lives of Elizabeth and Essex*.

Her performance as Melanie in *Gone With the Wind* remains luminous 43 years later. Director George Cukor (in private coaching not revealed until years later) controlled her saccharine excesses, and her performance contrasted vividly with the driving ambition projected by Vivien Leigh's Scarlett. She was Oscar-nominated but lost to Hattie McDaniel who played in the same picture.

Strawberry Blonde presented her as the girl James Cagney turned to after Rita Hayworth rejected him. One could understand why he found solace in her company.

Hold Back the Dawn was another Oscar-nominated performance, but she lost to her sister Joan Fontaine. By then their feud had become common knowledge. Fontaine once called it "a problem of temperament. In fact, bigger than Hiroshima." When De Havilland won the Oscar in 1949 (for *The Heiress*), Fontaine stretched out her hand in congratulations and De Havilland walked by, ignoring the gesture.

They Died with Their Boots On, *The Male Animal*, and *In This Our Life* were all strong diversions, but *Devotion* presented De Havilland as Charlotte Bronte in a biography that distorted the Bronte family beyond recognition. She had a better script and a chance to play good and evil twins in *The Dark Mirror*, and

Olivia De Havilland in *The Dark Mirror*.

she won an Oscar for her role as an unwed mother in *To Each His Own*.

Her two best portrayals followed in *The Snake Pit*, an absorbing and for the time extremely honest close-up of mental illness, and *The Heiress*. Her ugly duckling portrayal in *The Heiress* was painfully touching, and she brought pathos and fire to her brilliant exit line, "I can be cruel. I have been taught by masters." The movie was a box-office disappointment, however, as Selznick had predicted. He felt the downbeat ending would keep audiences away.

De Havilland was fascinating but too enigmatic in *My Cousin Rachel* and somewhat sugary as a princess in *That Lady*. Her last great performance was in *Not as a Stranger*; De Havilland was the Swedish nurse who loved a medical student, Robert Mitchum. *The Ambassador's Daughter* was a juiceless comedy, and she hammed it up with a vengeance in *Lady in a Cage*.

De Havilland's appeal was in her ladylike demeanor, but one sensed the willfulness, the strength behind her sweetness. This contradiction, combined with her loveliness, made her one of the most appealing heroines of the 1930s and 1940s.

FILMOGRAPHY

1935

A Midsummer Night's Dream ★★★
Alibi Ike ★★★
The Irish in Us ★★★
Captain Blood ★★★

1936

Anthony Adverse ★★
The Charge of the Light Brigade ★★★

1937

Call It a Day ★★★
The Great Garrick ★★★
It's Love I'm After ★★★

1938

Gold Is Where You Find It ★★★
The Adventures of Robin Hood ★★★★
Four's a Crowd ★★★
Hard to Get ★★★

1939

Wings of the Navy ★★★
Dodge City ★★★
The Private Lives of Elizabeth and Essex ★★★
Gone With the Wind ★★★★

1940

Raffles ★★★
My Love Came Back ★★★
Santa Fe Trail ★★★

1941

Strawberry Blonde ★★★★
Hold Back the Dawn ★★★★
They Died with Their Boots On ★★★★

1942

The Male Animal ★★★
In This Our Life ★★★

Olivia De Havilland in *The Heiress*.

1943

Thank Your Lucky Stars (cameo)
Princess O'Rourke ★★★★
Government Girl ★★★

1946

Devotion ★★★
The Well-Groomed Bride ★★★
To Each His Own ★★★★
The Dark Mirror ★★★★

1948

The Snake Pit ★★★★

1949

The Heiress ★★★★

1953

My Cousin Rachel ★★★★

1955

That Lady ★★
Not as a Stranger ★★★★

1956

The Ambassador's Daughter ★★★

1958

The Proud Rebel ★★★

1959

Libel ★★★

1962

The Light in the Piazza ★★★

1964

Lady in a Cage ★★

1965

Hush . . . Hush, Sweet Charlotte ★★★

1970

The Adventurers ★★★

1972

Pope Joan ★★★

1977

Airport '77 ★★

1978

The Swarm ★

1979

The Fifth Musketeer ★★★

ALAIN DELON
★★★ 3.02 STARS

His forceful personality and dashing good looks are the main reasons Alain Delon has remained an international star. The epitome of suave French male sensuality, Delon typically played in French and Italian reworkings of suspense dramas in the Bogart style.

Delon was born in 1935, in Sceaux, France. Not content to work in his stepfather's pork butcher store and bored by a series of other jobs, Delon attended the 1957 Cannes Film Festival. Spotted by an agent of producer David O. Selznick, Delon was offered a screen test provided that he learned English. Instead, he appeared in small roles in French films and then gained international acclaim in *Purple Noon* and *Rocco and His Brothers.*

Rocco, directed by Luchino Visconti, dealt with a good brother (Delon) who had to forsake the girl he loved and save his family from squalor by working as a prizefighter. Critics said the believability of the film rested on Delon's performance.

Frustrated at the reaction of critics to his films following his first two hits, Delon formed his own production company. Although he did make the film market sizzle with *Borsalino*, Delon has never been quite able to cross over into the American market. He made a forgettable western, *Texas Across the River* with Dean Martin and an all-star soap opera, *The Yellow Rolls-Royce.*

Alain Delon with Marianne Faithfull in *Naked Under Leather.*

In an interview with Film International, Delon said, "Only through Hollywood can there be world-wide recognition for an actor. France is too small for me. I don't see why there should be barriers in the movies. I want to make films with Albert Finney or Paul Newman."

FILMOGRAPHY

1958
Quand la Femme s'en Mèle ★★★
Sois Belle et Tais-toi ★★★

1959
Christine ★★★
Faibles Femmes ★★★
Le Chemin des Ecoliers ★★★

1960
Purple Noon ★★★★
Rocco and His Brothers ★★★

1961
Che Gioia Vivere ★★★
Lés Amours Célèbres ★★★

1962
L'Eclisse ★★★★
Le Diable et les Dix Commandements ★★★

1963
Mélodie en Sous-Sol ★★★
The Leopard ★★★

1964
La Tulipe Noire ★★★
Joy House ★★★★
L'Insoumis ★★★

1965
The Yellow Rolls-Royce ★★★
Once a Thief ★★

1966
The Lost Command ★★★
Is Paris Burning? ★★★
Texas Across the River ★★

1967
Les Aventuriers ★★★
Le Samourai ★★★★

1968
Diaboliquement Vôtre ★★★
Histoires Extraordinaires ★★★
Naked Under Leather ★★★
Adieu l'Ami ★★★

1969
La Piscine ★★★
Jeff ★★★
Le Clan des Siciliens ★★★

1970
Borsalino ★★★★
Le Cercle Rouge ★★★

1971
Madly ★★★
Doucement les Basses ★★★
Red Sun ★★★
La Veuve Couderc ★★★

1972
The Assassination of Trotsky ★★
La Prima Notte di Quiete ★★★
Un Flic ★★★

1973
Traitement de Choc ★★★
Scorpio ★★
Les Granges Brûlees ★★★
Tony Arzenta è Big Guns ★★★
Deux Hommes dans la Ville ★★★

1974
Les Seins de Glace ★★★
La Race des Seigneurs ★★★
Borsalino et Cie ★★★

1975
Zorro ★★★
Flic Story ★★★
Le Gitan ★★★
No Way Out ★★★

1976
Mr. Klein ★★★★
Comme un Boomerang ★★★

1977
Le Gang ★★★
Armaguedon ★★★
L'Homme Pressé ★★★
Mort d'un Pourri ★★★

1978
Attention les Enfants Regardent ★★★
Opium ★★★

1979
Airport 79 Concorde ★★
Harmonie ★★★

1980
Trois hommes à abattre ★★★

1981
For a Cop's Hide ★★★

1982
The Shock ★★★

1983
The Cache ★★★

WILLIAM DEMAREST
★★½ 2.35 STARS

A salty, engaging character actor, William Demarest is most closely identified with his role as Al Jolson's manager in *The Jolson Story.*

Demarest was born in 1892, in Minnesota, and he performed in vaudeville before debuting in his first film *Fingerprints.* His second film was the now-legendary *The Jazz Singer* and he had good parts in *Fog Over Frisco, Diamond Jim,* and *Rebecca of Sunnybrook Farm.*

Two political comedies, *Mr. Smith Goes to Washington* and *The Farmer's Daughter* moved his career into high gear. He stayed in good parts through *Tin Pan Alley, The Great McGinty,* and a couple of classics—*The Lady Eve* and *Sullivan's Travels* (both written by Preston Sturges). He was a natural for the world of Damon Runyon in *Sorrowful Jones,* as well as *Jolson Sings Again,* which was even bigger box office than *The Jolson Story.*

Demarest added spice to a good chiller, *Night Has a Thousand Eyes,* and Stanley Kramer's zany comedy, *Its a Mad Mad Mad Mad World.* Younger generations may remember him as Uncle Charlie on the "My Three Sons" television series.

FILMOGRAPHY

1927

Fingerprints (bit)
The Jazz Singer (bit)
Don't Tell the Wife (bit)
Matinee Ladies (bit)
A Million Bid (bit)
Old San Francisco (bit)
The First Auto (bit)

1928

A Girl in Every Port (bit)
The Escape (bit)
Sharp Shooters (bit)
The Butter and Eggs Man (bit)

1929

Broadway Melody (bit)

1932

The Crash (bit)

1934

Fog Over Frisco ★★
Many Happy Returns ★★

1935

Diamond Jim ★★
Bright Lights ★★
Hands Across the Table ★★

1936

Wedding Present ★★
Love on the Run ★★
Charlie Chan at the Opera ★★★

1937

Easy Living ★★★★
Big City ★★
Don't Tell the Wife ★★
Time Out For Romance ★★
The Hit Parade ★★
Oh, Doctor ★★
The Great Gambini ★★
The Great Hospital Mystery ★★
Blonde Trouble ★★

1938

Rebecca of Sunnybrook Farm ★★
One Wild Night ★★
Josette ★★
While New York Sleeps ★★
Peck's Bad Boy With the Circus ★★
The Great Man Votes ★★★
King of the Turf ★★
The Gracie Allen Murder Case ★★
Miracles for Sale ★★

1939

Mr. Smith Goes to Washington ★★★★

1940

The Farmer's Daughter ★★★★
Tin Pan Alley ★★★★
The Great McGinty ★★★★
Comin' Round the Mountain ★★
Christmas in July ★★★
The Golden Fleecing ★★
Little Men ★★

1941

The Lady Eve ★★★★
Sullivan's Travels ★★★★
The Devil and Miss Jones ★★★
Ride on Vaquero ★★
Rookies on Parade ★★
Dressed to Kill ★★
All Through the Night ★★★

1942

My Favorite Spy ★★
Pardon My Sarong ★★
True to the Army ★★
Life Begins at 8:30 ★★
The Palm Beach Story ★★★

1943

Johnny Doughboy ★★
Stage Door Canteen (cameo)
True to Life ★★

1944

Hail the Conquering Hero ★★★★
The Miracle of Morgan's Creek ★★★★
Once Upon a Time ★★
The Great Moment ★★★★

1945

Along Came Jones ★★★
Salty O'Rourke ★★★
Duffy's Tavern (cameo)

William Demarest in *That Darn Cat.*

1946

The Jolson Story ★★★★
Pardon My Past ★★★
Our Hearts Were Growing Up ★★

1947

The Perils of Pauline ★★
Variety Girl (cameo)

1948

Night Has a Thousand Eyes ★★★
A Miracle Can Happen ★★
The Sainted Sisters ★★

1949

Sorrowful Jones ★★★
Jolson Sings Again ★★★
Whispering Smith ★★
Red Hot and Blue ★★

1950

Riding High ★★★
When Willie Comes Marching Home ★★★
He's a Cockeyed Wonder ★★
Never a Dull Moment ★★
Tea for Two (cameo)

1951

The First Legion ★★★★
Excuse My Dust ★★
Behave Yourself ★★

1952

What Price Glory ★★

1953

Escape From Fort Bravo ★★
The Lady Wants Mink ★★
Dangerous When Wet ★★
Here Come the Girls ★★

1955

The Far Horizons ★★
Jupiter's Darling ★
The Private War of Major Benson ★★
Lucy Gallant ★★
Sincerely Yours ★

1956

Hell On Frisco Bay ★★
The Rawhide Years ★★★
The Mountain ★★

1960

Pepe (cameo)

1961

King of the Roaring Twenties ★★

1963

It's a Mad Mad Mad Mad World (cameo)
Son of Flubber ★★

1965

That Darn Cat ★★

1975

The Wild McCullochs ★

CATHERINE DENEUVE
★★ 2.13 STARS

Catherine Deneuve is undeniably beautiful. One has the feeling she could run in the wind and not one hair would fall out of place. This makes her a movie "Goddess" but also something less than human.

She was born Catherine Dorléac in Paris, in 1943, and achieved world prominence in *The Umbrellas of Cherbourg,* a haunting love story set entirely to music. Roman Polanski's *Repulsion* was a shockingly effective change of pace, and her icy, unreadable beauty was perfect for the part.

In *Belle de Jour* she was cast as a housewife who secretly worked as a prostitute in the afternoon, possibly her most intriguing performance. Then Deneuve stumbled with *Mayerling,* a sluggish saga about Austrian royalty, and *The April Fools* as a curiously rigid "free spirit" who lured Jack Lemmon away from his executive prison.

She was a completely sexless whore in *Hustle* with Burt Reynolds, a film that exposed her acting limitations more sharply than any other. Her latest major role, that of a chic vampire in *The Hunger,* continued to prey upon her image of a sterile, icy beauty.

FILMOGRAPHY

1956

Les Collégiennes (bit)

1959

Wild Roots of Love (bit)

1960

Les Portes claquent ★★

1962

Tales of Paris ★

1963

Vice and Virtue ★
Vacances Portugaises ★

1964

The Umbrellas of Cherbourg ★★★
Male Hunt ★★★
Male Companion ★★

1965

Repulsion ★★★
Le Chant du Monde ★★

1966

La Vie de Château ★★
Les Créatures ★★

1967

The Young Girls of Rochefort ★★
Belle de Jour ★★★★

1968

Benjamin ★★★★
Manon 70 ★
Mayerling ★
La Chamade ★★★

Catherine Deneuve in *Benjamin.*

1969

The April Fools ★
Mississippi Mermaid ★★★

1970

Tristana ★★★★

1971

Donkey Skin ★★
It Only Happens to Others ★

1972

Dirty Money ★★★

1973

A Slightly Pregnant Man ★★

1974

Touchez pas la Femme blanche ★★
The Woman With Red Boots ★★
La Grande Bourgeoise ★★

1975

Act of Agression ★★
The Savage ★★
Zig Zag ★★
Hustle ★★★

1976

Si c'était a refaire ★★

1977

Anima Persa ★★
March or Die ★★

1978

L'Argent des Autres ★★
Ecoute Voir . . . ★★

1979

Si je suis comme ca c'est le Faute à Papa ★★
An Adventure for Two ★★
Ils sont grand ces Petits ★★

1980

The Last Metro ★★★

1981

I Love You ★★
Choice of Weapons ★★

1982

Hotel of the Americas ★★
The Shock ★★

1983

The African ★★
The Hunger ★★★

ROBERT DE NIRO
★★★½ 3.44 STARS

Robert De Niro suggests power, a sense of violence simmering just below the surface. He makes no attempt to sweeten the neurotic, unlikable characters he plays, an act of dramatic bravery that has taken its toll in commercial terms.

New York-born in 1943, De Niro studied acting with Stella Adler. His first movie was a low-budget, underground film, *The Wedding Party,* and he followed it with Brian De Palma's self-indulgent but entertaining *Greetings,* a lopsided look at the culture of the 1960s. In his third film, the sordid *Bloody Mama* with Shelley Winters, De Niro was effective as one of her psychotic sons.

Hi, Mom! was another satire of the 1960s and did nothing for his career, nor did *Born to Win*, a George Segal comedy about drug addiction. He also co-starred with Jerry Orbach and Leigh Taylor-Young in *The Gang That Couldn't Shoot Straight*, a chaotic comedy about crooks.

In all his mediocre earlier films, De Niro demonstrated an ability to bring humanity to cardboard characters. He finally found a character to play with some humanity built into the script in *Bang the Drum Slowly*. As the dim-witted, mortally ill baseball player who found friendship with Michael Moriarty in his last days, De Niro was superb. Nobody promoted the picture despite excellent reviews. He was back to violence and life in the gutter in *Mean Streets*, a formless Mafia melodrama. De Niro's portrayal was garish and operatic, but there were no protagonists a viewer could care about.

People cared more about his devastatingly brilliant portrait of a young Godfather in *The Godfather, Part II*. He won a Best Supporting Oscar, richly deserved, and the film itself won Best Picture and Best Director. His next part was even less appetizing, the psychotic cabbie in *Taxi Driver*. The character was pathetic but puzzling, and his explosion of violence seemed illogical. De Niro's performance, however, had enough intensity to keep onlookers involved.

The Last Tycoon was the latest attempt to transfer F. Scott Fitzgerald's work to film. De Niro played the Irving Thalberg-like tycoon with absolute authenticity, but the screenplay was totally devoid of action or suspense. The same charge was applicable in connection with *New York, New York*, an overlong saga of a saxophonist and the band singer (Liza Minnelli) he married. The musical interludes had electricity, but De Niro gave his first really grating performance. His conception of the part was so abrasive and irritating that viewer patience ran out before the picture was half-way through.

Robert De Niro with Cybill Shepherd in *Taxi Driver.*

He atoned with an Oscar-winning portrayal of Jake La Motta in director Martin Scorsese's *Raging Bull*. Again, De Niro fearlessly exposed the viciousness and brutality of the main character in a performance too raw for the squeamish. It was possibly too raw for the masses, because the movie—artistically admirable as it was—lost money at the box office.

De Niro once again proved his artistic brillance and commercial naivete in *The King of Comedy*. His portrayal of pathetic, would-be comic Rupert Pupkin was uncanny genius, but the character whom he played to perfection was so embarrassingly out of sorts that audiences decided not to suffer through his life story.

De Niro may be our greatest contemporary actor, but something stands between him and the national following a star needs. Perhaps he has a problem that Hollywood rarely encounters—an overdeveloped sense of artistic integrity.

FILMOGRAPHY

1968

The Wedding Party ★★★

1969

Greetings ★★★
Sam's Song ★★★

1970

Hi Mom! ★★★
Bloody Mama ★★★

1971

Born to Win ★★★
The Gang That Couldn't Shoot Straight ★★★

1974

Bang the Drum Slowly ★★★★
Mean Streets ★★★★
The Godfather, Part II ★★★★

Robert De Niro in *Raging Bull.*

1976

Taxi Driver ★★★★
The Last Tycoon ★★★★
1900 ★★★★

1977

New York, New York ★★

1978

The Deer Hunter ★★★★

1980

Raging Bull ★★★★

1981

True Confessions ★★★

1983

The King of Comedy ★★★★

SANDY DENNIS
★★ 2.20 STARS

A quality of stillness is one of the prerequisites of great screen acting. A performer must let the camera do the work, not compete with it. Sandy Dennis never learned this lesson. The neurotic tics that brought her success on Broadway have overwhelmed most of her screen performances.

Born in 1937, in Hastings, Nebraska, she was trained at the Actor's Studio and later made her film debut in *Splendor in the Grass*. Her next part, as the simpering, naive girl in *Who's Afraid of Virginia Woolf?* garnered an inexplicable Best Supporting Oscar. John Simon, after crucifying Elizabeth Taylor's performance in the same film, said that Dennis achieved the well-nigh impossible feat of being even worse.

She gained some control of her blinking and gulping in *The Fox* and was warmly human for the first time in *Up the Down Staircase*. However, *Sweet November* brought the mannerisms back with a vengeance. Alan Alda managed to tone her down for *The Four Seasons*, but she was outclassed by Carol Burnett.

Her overly mannered style was put to its most effective use in Robert Altman's filmed stage play, *Come Back to the 5 & Dime, Jimmy Dean, Jimmy Dean*, but she remains a clear example of the failure of stage acting translated to film.

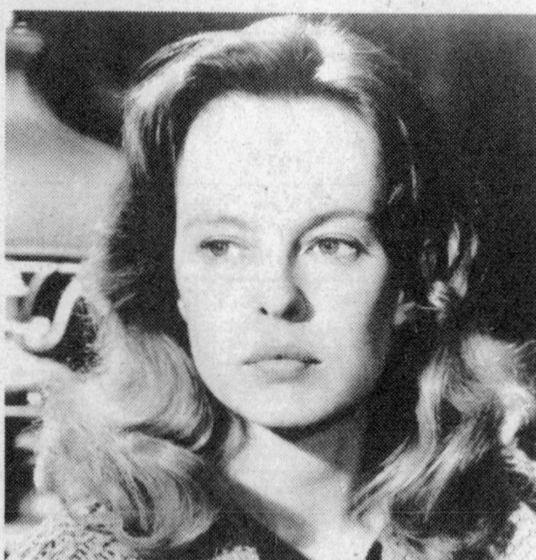

Sandy Dennis in *Up the Down Staircase*.

FILMOGRAPHY

1961

Splendor in the Grass ★★

1966

Who's Afraid of Virginia Woolf? ★★

1967

Up the Down Staircase ★★★

1968

The Fox ★★★
Sweet November ★★

1969

That Cold Day in the Park ★★
A Touch of Love ★★

1970

The Out-of-Towners ★★

1971

The Only Way Out Is Dead ★★

1975

Mr. Sycamore ★

1976

Nasty Habits ★★★
God Told Me To ★★

1977

The Three Sisters ★★

1981

The Four Seasons ★★★

1982

Come Back to the 5 & Dime, Jimmy Dean, Jimmy Dean ★★

GERARD DEPARDIEU
★★★ 3.13 STARS

Husky, strong-willed, and innocent, Gerard Depardieu is, more or less, a French equivalent of Gary Busey. Even in a weak part he gives a strong performance, and he seems to be able to find the complexities and subtleties of even the most straightforward characters.

Born in France, in 1948, Depardieu began his film career in the early 1970s and quickly became a leading figure in contemporary French films. He made a stunning appearance as a traveling salesman undergoing a crisis in Marguerite Duras' *Nathalie Granger* and later played in Duras' controversial *Le Camion*.

His performance in *The Last Woman* provoked one critic to call him "the thinking man's lug." He played other roles in films such as: Bernardo Bertolucci's *1900*, Bertrand Blier's *Get Out Your Handkerchiefs*, Francois Truffaut's *The Last Metro*, and a small role in German novelist Peter Handke's *The Left-Handed Woman*.

He gave a tour-de-force performance as Isabelle Huppert's wildly irresponsible lover in *Lou Lou*, and another as a young executive caught in the rat race in Alain Resnais' *Mon Oncle d'Amerique*. Depardieu seems to grow stronger with each part he plays; he is probably the best young actor in Europe today.

FILMOGRAPHY

1970

Le Cri du Cormoran le Soir au-dessus des Jonques (bit)

1971

Le Tueur ★★★

Gerard Depardieu with Catherine Deneuve in *The Last Metro*.

1972

Nathalie Granger ★★★★
L'Affaire Dominici ★★★

1973

Deux Hommes dans la Ville ★★★
Rude Journée pour la Ville ★★★
The Holes ★★

1974

Going Places ★★★
Stavisky ★★★

1975

Vincent, Francois, Paul and the Others ★★
7 Morts sur Ordonnance ★★★
The Wonderful Crook ★★★
Maitresse ★★★★

1976

1900 ★★★★
The Last Woman ★★★
Barocco ★★★

1977

Baxter—Vera Baxter ★★★★
Le Camion ★★★
René la Canne ★★★
Violanta ★★★★
La Nuit tous les Chats sont gris ★★★

1978

Get Out Your Handkerchiefs ★★★
Bye Bye Monkey ★★★
Le Sucre ★★★

1979

Lou Lou ★★★★
The Left-Handed Woman (cameo)

1980

Mon Oncle d'Amerique ★★★★
The Last Metro ★★★
Inspecteur la Bavure ★★

1981

La Chèvre ★★★
La femme d'a'côté ★★★

1983

The Return of Martin Guerre ★★★★
The Moon in the Gutter ★★

BRUCE DERN
★★★½ 3.26 STARS

Bruce Dern once complained to the L.A. Times that his films were consistent failures at the box office. The bitterness was understandable. Dern is a commanding and polished actor, and his best performances have gone largely unnoticed.

The grandson of a former Utah Governor, Dern was born in Chicago, in 1936. He pursued acting in New York and his Broadway appearances led to a part in Kazan's *Wild River.* His peculiar mixture of good/bad luck surfaced immediately with Hitchcock's *Marnie*... great director, good script, and little audience response. *Hush...Hush, Sweet Charlotte* proved he could do horror films, and he fit nicely into several of the Peter Fonda "trip" movies, *The Wild Angels, Psych-Out,* and *The Trip.*

The skill—and disappointing commercial results—continued through *The War Wagon, Will Penny,* and *The King of Marvin Gardens.* Dern was superb in the under-attended *They Shoot Horses, Don't They?* His luck finally turned with an Oscar nomination and respectable box office when he did *Coming Home* with Jane Fonda.

Tatoo showed that he is still being typecast into neurotic and psychotic roles. Bruce Dern has the talent to be more than "a poor man's Robert De Niro."

Bruce Dern in *The Driver.*

FILMOGRAPHY

1960
Wild River ★★★

1964
Marnie ★★★

1965
Hush... Hush, Sweet Charlotte ★★★

1966
The Wild Angels ★★★

1967
The St. Valentine's Day Massacre ★★★
Waterhole #3 ★★★
The Trip ★★★
The War Wagon ★★★

1968
Psych-Out ★★★
Will Penny ★★★★
Hang 'em High ★★★

1969
Support Your Local Sheriff! ★★★
Castle Keep ★★★
Number One ★★★
They Shoot Horses, Don't They? ★★★★

1970
Cycle Savages ★★★
Bloody Mama ★★★

1971
Drive, He Said ★★★★
The Incredible Two-Headed Transplant ★★★

1972
The Cowboys ★★★★
Silent Running ★★★
The King of Marvin Gardens ★★★★

1973
The Laughing Policeman ★★★

1974
The Great Gatsby ★★★★

1975
Smile ★★★★
Posse ★★★

1976
Family Plot ★★★★
Won Ton Ton - the Dog Who Saved Hollywood ★★★
Folies Bourgeoises ★★★

1977
Black Sunday ★★★★

1978
Coming Home ★★★★
The Driver ★★★

1980
Middle Age Crazy ★★★

1981
Tattoo ★★

1982
That Championship Season ★★★

ANGIE DICKINSON
★★★ 2.79 STARS

Angie Dickinson was always sexy and likable on the screen, yet she dangled on the fringes of stardom for years. It took TV's "Police Woman" to show her earthy dimension.

Dickinson (Angeline Brown) was born in 1931, in Kulm, North Dakota. She appeared briefly in one of Doris Day's worst musicals, *Lucky Me,* and had a better role in a gripping thriller, *Cry Terror. Rio Bravo* with John Wayne established her as a believable heroine in action films.

She was fine in *The Bramble Bush,* especially in scenes with the hollow and grandiose Richard Burton. She also played in *Oceans Eleven,* one of the more popular of the "rat pack" sagas (the "rat pack" included Frank Sinatra, Dean Martin, Sammy Davis Jr., and Peter Lawford).

Dickinson portrayed a missionary nurse in *The Sins of Rachel Cade.* She was credible even when the script lapsed into melodrama, and she had a strong co-star in Peter Finch.

The camera focused on Troy Donahue and Suzanne Pleshette in *Rome Adventure,* but Dickinson's portrayal of a bitchy, liberated artist supplied a tart flavor to the general sweetness. Her feminine naturalness was particularly appropriate against Gregory Peck's upstanding sincerity in *Captain Newman M.D.*

The Killers is only remembered because Ronald Reagan played a vicious gangster (a role he regretted doing). Subsequent pictures such as *The Art of Love, Sam Whiskey,*

Some Kind of a Nut, and *Big Bad Mama* were also disappointing.

Fortunately, Dickinson made a big hit in the TV series "Police Woman," and with her newfound sensuality and assurance, she gave a vivid performance in Brian De Palma's *Dressed to Kill*.

FILMOGRAPHY

1954

Lucky Me ★★

1955

Man with the Gun ★★
The Trouble Shooter ★★
The Return of Jack Slade ★★

1956

Tennessee's Partner ★★
Hidden Guns ★★
Gun the Man Down ★★
Tension at Table Rock ★★★

1957

The Black Whip ★★
Shoot Out at Medicine Bend ★★★
Calypso Joe ★★
China Gate ★★

1958

I Married a Woman ★★
Cry Terror ★★★★

1959

Rio Bravo ★★★★

1960

The Bramble Bush ★★★
Ocean's Eleven ★★★

1961

The Sins of Rachel Cade ★★★★
A Fever in the Blood ★★★
I'll Give My Life ★★★

1962

Jessica ★★
Rome Adventure ★★★★

1963

Captain Newman M.D. ★★★★

1964

The Killers ★★★★

1965

The Art of Love ★★

1966

The Chase ★★★
Cast a Giant Shadow ★★★

1967

The Last Challenge ★★★
Point Blank ★★★★
The Pistolero of Red River ★★★

Angie Dickinson in *A Fever in the Blood.*

1969

Sam Whiskey ★★★
Young Billy Young ★★★
The One with the Fuzz ★★★
Some Kind of a Nut ★

1971

Pretty Maids All in a Row ★★★
The Resurrection of Zachary Wheeler ★★★

1973

The Outside Man ★★★

1974

Big Bad Mama ★★★

1980

Dressed to Kill ★★★★
Klondike Fever ★★

1981

Charlie Chan and the Curse of the Dragon Queen ★★
Death Hunt ★★★

MARLENE DIETRICH
★★★ 3.20 STARS

Marlene Dietrich reportedly hoped the Academy would single her out for her fine performance in *Witness for the Prosecution*. She wasn't even nominated though she should have been. Her portrayal of a murderess offered a fascinating mixture of desire and vulnerability, but there were too many outlandish costume dramas in her past for voters to take her seriously.

Dietrich was born Maria Magdalene Dietrich in 1901, in Berlin. She made several silent German films (*Manon Lescaut*, *Eine Dubarry von heute*, *Sein grösster Bluff*) before director Josef Von Sternberg cast her in the role that made her a legend in *The Blue Angel*. Her enchanting song from that film, "Falling in Love Again," has become her trademark. She played the same part, a temptress who enslaved men, in many future films. Her follow-up was *Morocco*, in which she portrayed a nightclub singer in love with French legionnaire Gary Cooper. There was a third hit, *Dishonored*, but her movies after that, *Song of Songs* and *The Scarlet Empress*, were indifferently received.

All her parts were in pretentious escapist adventures, and *Desire*, a comedy with Gary Cooper, came along just in time. She and Charles Boyer fell in love in *The Garden of Allah*, a movie notable only for its lavish production values.

Dietrich had been overglamorized into something decorative and inhuman. She needed to make direct contact with viewers (a 1937 Exhibitor's poll named her box-office poison), and *Destry Rides Again* gave her that opportunity. Her characterization was lusty and sexual, and she maintained the fire in *Seven Sinners*. She had to choose between Roland Young and Bruce Cabot in *The Flame of New Orleans*, another sultry drama, and she even allowed herself to be painted gold for *Kismet*.

Marlene Dietrich.

A Foreign Affair was her best role in years, and she nearly stole the film as a singer with eyes for John Lund. She made a seductive gypsy in *Golden Earrings* and then appeared in Hitchcock's *Stage Fright*.

Hitchcock said, "Marlene Dietrich is a *professional*—a professional actress, a professional dress designer, a professional cameraman." The implied friction between director and star didn't reduce her effectiveness in this unsuspenseful thriller in which she sang "The Laziest Gal in Town."

No Highway in the Sky was an absorbing tale of passengers traveling on a defective airplane, and Dietrich, possibly influenced by co-star James Stewart's naturalness, gave a completely unmannered performance. However, there was trouble on the set of *The Monte Carlo Story* when she clashed with Natalie Trundy, a young actress in the cast. The conflict made one recall her announcement in 1941, "I'm going to quit working. A film star's career must necessarily be brief. It can last only as long as one's youth lasts."

She failed to heed her own words and fought to maintain the youth and glamour of her early years, but along the way there were a few notable characterizations. In *Witness for the Prosecution*, she played Tyrone Power's loyal girlfriend, and in *Judgment at Nuremberg*, she was excellent as the widow of a Nazi war criminal.

Dietrich is a legend, not for any single achievement, but for a kind of European sultriness and glamour that seems to have vanished from the screen.

FILMOGRAPHY

1923

Der Kleine Napoleon ★★★
Tragedy of Love ★★★
Der Mensch am Wege ★★★

1924

Der Sprung ins Leben ★★★

1925

The Street of Sorrow (bit)

1926

Manon Lescaut ★★★
Eine Dubarry von heute ★★★
Kopf Hoch Charly! ★★★
Madame Wants No Children ★★★

1927

Der Juxbaron ★★★
Sein grösster Bluff ★★★
Cafe Electric ★★★

1928

The Art of Love ★★★

1929

I Kiss Your Hand, Madame ★★★
Three Loves ★★★
The Ship of Lost Men ★★★
Gefahren der Brautzeit ★★★

1930

The Blue Angel ★★★★
Morocco ★★★★

Marlene Dietrich with Gary Cooper in *Morocco*.

1931

Dishonored ★★★

1932

Shanghai Express ★★★★
Blonde Venus ★★★★

1933

Song of Songs ★★★

1934

The Scarlet Empress ★★★

1935

The Devil is a Woman ★★★

1936

Desire ★★★★
The Garden of Allah ★★

1937

Knight Without Armor ★★★
Angel ★★★★

1939

Destry Rides Again ★★★★

1940

Seven Sinners ★★★

1941

The Flame of New Orleans ★★★
Manpower ★★★

1942

The Lady Is Willing ★★★
The Spoilers ★★★
Pittsburgh ★★★

1944

Follow the Boys (cameo)
Kismet ★★★

1946

The Room Upstairs ★★★

Marlene Dietrich in *Rancho Notorious*.

1947

Golden Earrings ★★★

1948

A Foreign Affair ★★★★

1949

Jigsaw (cameo)

1950

Stage Fright ★★★★

1951

No Highway in the Sky ★★★★

1952

Rancho Notorious ★★★★

1956

Around the World in 80 Days (cameo)

1957

The Monte Carlo Story ★★

1958

Witness for the Prosecution ★★★★
Touch of Evil (cameo)

1961

Judgment at Nuremberg ★★★

1962

Black Fox (narration, documentary)
Paris When It Sizzles (cameo)

1978

Just a Gigolo ★★

MATT DILLON
★★★½ 3.33 STARS

Matt Dillon has many attributes that make him star material. He was nominated "Super Hunk of the Month" by the fan magazines. His eyes and mouth look sensitive and frequently hurt, yet he comes on cocky ("I like playing bad guys").

Matt Dillon in *The Outsiders.*

He's naive ("Would you believe I'd never been on a plane before I made my first movie?"), yet confident. Best of all, he has natural acting ability.

Dillon was born in New York, in 1964. Talent scout Victor Ramos discovered him one day while he was playing hookey and cast him in *Over the Edge*. The film made Vincent Canby's alternate Ten Best List, and director Ronald F. Maxwell gave him the juvenile lead opposite Kristy McNichol in *Little Darlings.* He was charismatic, the best thing about the picture, and he had another striking part again as a tough kid in *My Bodyguard.* Disney Studios got the message and gave him the lead in *Tex*, a touching story of two brothers forced to make it without parental help. His work in Francis Ford Coppola's film versions of S. E. Hinton's stories, *The Outsiders* and *Rumblefish*, continued to display the combination of vulnerability and strength that guarantees him a permanent place on the screen.

FILMOGRAPHY

1979

Over the Edge ★★★

1980

Little Darlings ★★★★
My Bodyguard ★★★

1982

Tex ★★★★

1983

The Outsiders ★★★
Rumblefish ★★★

TROY DONAHUE
★★ 2.16 STARS

Troy Donahue was Tab Hunter's replacement. Tall and blond, with choir-boy features, he usually substituted sincerity for dramatic ability. Even in bad films, he had the aura of a star.

Donahue (Merle Johnson, Jr.) was born in 1936 in New York City. He appeared in stock productions before achieving TV popularity in the series "Surfside 6" and "Hawaiian Eye." Donahue had small roles in the films, *Man Afraid* and *This Happy Feeling*, but *A Summer Place* was the beginning of his brief box-office reign. He glowered intensely as Sandra Dee's boyfriend in this enjoyable overwrought version of Sloan Wilson's best-seller.

An airplane got all the best lines in *The Crowded Sky,* a watered-down rehash of *The High and the Mighty,* but *Parrish* focused in on Donahue. It was a hard-breathing tale of a tobacco man and his various entanglements with Connie Stevens, Sharon Hugueny, and Diane McBain. In *Susan Slade,* Donahue wore one determined expression but showed a hint of variety as a novelist who loved Connie Stevens in spite of her illegitimate baby. *Palm Springs Weekend* was trivial even by the standards of beach movies.

Rome Adventure gave Donahue his one fine moment. Opposite a luminous Suzanne Pleshette (who became his wife for a while) and set against breathtaking Italian locations, Donahue unbent and projected the depth of young love. He was with Pleshette again in *A Distant Trumpet*, but the chemistry had already vanished.

Troy Donahue with Suzanne Pleshette in *Rome Adventure.*

Popularity vanished overnight as well with *My Blood Runs Cold, Come Spy With Me*, and *Sweet Savior.* Director Francis Ford Coppola used him for a minor part in *The Godfather, Part II*, and he showed up again doing virtually a walk-on in a TV film, *Malibu*.

FILMOGRAPHY

1957

Man Afraid ★★

1958

This Happy Feeling ★★
Voice in the Mirror ★★

1959

The Perfect Furlough ★★
Imitation of Life ★★
A Summer Place ★★★

1960

The Crowded Sky ★★

1961

Parrish ★★
Susan Slade ★★★

1962

Rome Adventure ★★★

1963

Palm Springs Weekend ★

1964

A Distant Trumpet ★★★

1965

My Blood Runs Cold ★★

1967

Come Spy With Me ★★
Rocket to the Moon ★★

1971

Sweet Saviour ★

1974

Cockfighter ★★★
The Godfather, Part II ★★★

1977

The Legend of Frank Woods ★

ROBERT DONAT
★★★½ 3.67 STARS

Some stars make 100 films and leave virtually no imprint. Robert Donat made only 18 and yet achieved respect and popularity on both sides of the Atlantic.

He was born in Manchester, England, in 1905, and became an actor at sixteen. After proving mastery in Shakespeare and other classical roles, he played in the films *Men of Tomorrow* and *That Night in London*, securing fame in *The Private Life of Henry VIII.* One fine picture followed the next starting with *The Count of Monte Cristo*, the first of four versions and easily the best.

Donat's "wonderful voice" (Mark Robson) and graceful acting style brought class to a brilliant Hitchcock thriller, *The 39 Steps*, and he showed his comic expertise in Robert Sherwood's amusing fantasy, *The Ghost Goes West.* He was perfect as A.J. Cronin's doctor hero in *The Citadel* and incomparable playing author James Hilton's starchy schoolmaster in *Goodbye, Mr. Chips.* For *Mr. Chips*, Donat won an Oscar against Clark Gable's Rhett Butler.

Donat did a few other fine films including *Vacation from Marriage*, *The Winslow Boy*, and *The Inn of the Sixth Happiness* with Ingrid Bergman. He died of asthma in 1958.

FILMOGRAPHY

1932

Men of Tomorrow ★★★

1933

That Night in London ★★★
For Love or Money ★★★
The Private Life of Henry VIII ★★★★

1934

The Count of Monte Cristo ★★★★

1935

The 39 Steps ★★★★
The Ghost Goes West ★★★★

1937

Knight Without Armor ★★★★

Robert Donat in *The Magic Box.*

1938

The Citadel ★★★★

1939

Goodbye, Mr. Chips ★★★★

1942

The Young Mr. Pitt ★★★

1943

The Adventures of Tartu ★★★

1945

Vacation from Marriage ★★★★

1947

Captain Boycott (cameo)

1948

The Winslow Boy ★★★★

1949

The Cure for Love ★★★

1951

The Magic Box ★★★★

1954

Lease of Life ★★★★

1958

The Inn of the Sixth Happiness ★★★★

KIRK DOUGLAS
★★★ 3.05 STARS

Some actors have unlimited range; they can play comedy and drama with equal finesse. Others—like Kirk Douglas—excel in only one key. Douglas has been harshly, savagely convincing in films like *Lust for Life* and *Ace in the Hole*, but he's too intense and serious for the fluff of *My Dear Secretary* and *For Love or Money.*

Douglas was born Issur Danielovitch in New York, in 1916. After some small parts in Broadway shows "Spring Again," "Trio," and "The Wind is Ninety," he was signed by Hal Willis for a gripping Barbara Stanwyck film, *The Strange Love of Martha Ivers.* He also had the good fortune to appear as a gangster in one of the classic Hollywood thrillers, *Out of the Past. I Walk Alone* was less interesting, and *The Walls of Jericho* was a rambling story of political ambition. However, *Champion*, a gutsy boxing drama with Douglas at his most aggressive, made him a star.

Critics downgraded Douglas' performance in *Young Man With a Horn*, but he projected the right mixture of drive and sincerity. He was also perfect as the gentleman caller in Tennessee Williams' *The Glass Menagerie* and almost too real as a calculating reporter in Billy Wilder's blistering *Ace in the Hole.*

Douglas was reportedly and justifiably bitter about the lack of Academy recognition for his portrayal in *Detective Story.* Two duds followed, *The Big Trees* and *The Big Sky*, but he was again outstanding in Minnelli's sharp insider's account of Hollywood, *The Bad and the Beautiful.*

After *The Juggler*, a touching story of a man's readjustment to life after years in a concentration camp, Douglas had one of his most popular roles in *20,000 Leagues Under the Sea.* Viewed today, it's livelier and more entertaining than *Lust for Life*, the meticulously mounted biography of painter Vincent Van Gogh. The acting by Douglas and co-star Anthony Quinn in *Lust for Life* compensated for a heavy, depressing screenplay. *Paths of Glory* was also too downbeat for wide public endorsement, yet it was poignant—a tale of three innocent men sacrificed to save the good face of the military. He underplayed admirably as the idealistic lawyer who tried to save them and deserved credit for his part in getting the picture produced.

The Vikings was a rousing adventure and *Last Train from Gun Hill* was a well-written western. He was lucky to walk unscathed through *Spartacus;* co-star Tony Curtis sounded more Lower East Side than Roman. *Strangers When We Meet* paired him awkwardly with Kim Novak, and only co-star Barbara Rush rose above the suds.

Despite a string of box-office failures (*The War Wagon, The Hook, The List of Adrian Messenger,* and *The Arrangement*), Douglas kept working. The same bad streak hit his frequent co-star Burt Lancaster, and Lancaster finally emerged with his finest performance ever in *Atlantic City.* It's only a matter of time until Douglas gets *his* once-in-a-lifetime part and surprises audiences and critics again.

Kirk Douglas.

FILMOGRAPHY

1946

The Strange Love of Martha Ivers ★★★★

1947

Mourning Becomes Electra ★★
Out of the Past ★★★★

1948

I Walk Alone ★★★
The Walls of Jericho ★★★
My Dear Secretary ★

1949

A Letter to Three Wives ★★★★
Champion ★★★★

1950

Young Man With a Horn ★★★★
The Glass Menagerie ★★★★

1951

Along the Great Divide ★★★
Ace in the Hole ★★★★
Detective Story ★★★★

1952

The Big Trees ★★★
The Big Sky ★★★
The Bad and the Beautiful ★★★★
The Story of Three Loves ★★★
The Juggler ★★★

1954

Act of Love ★★★
20,000 Leagues Under the Sea ★★★★

1955

The Racers ★★★
Ulysses ★★
Man Without a Star ★★★
Indian Fighter ★★★

1956

Lust for Life ★★★★

1957

Top Secret Affair ★
Gunfight at the O.K. Corral ★★★★

1958

Paths of Glory ★★★★
The Vikings ★★★★

1959

Last Train from Gun Hill ★★★★
Devil's Disciple ★★

1960

Strangers When We Meet ★★
Spartacus ★★★★

1961

The Last Sunset ★★
Town Without Pity ★★★

1962

Lonely Are the Brave ★★★★
Two Weeks in Another Town ★★★

1963

The Hook ★★★
The List of Adrian Messenger ★★★★
For Love or Money ★

1964

Seven Days in May ★★★★

1965

In Harm's Way ★★
The Heroes of Telemark ★★

1966

Cast a Giant Shadow ★★
Is Paris Burning? ★★★

1967

The Way West ★★★
The War Wagon ★★★

Kirk Douglas with Farrah Fawcett in *Saturn 3.*

1968

A Lovely Way to Die ★★★
The Brotherhood ★★★

1969

The Arrangement ★★

1970

There Was a Crooked Man ★★★★

1971

The Light at the Edge of the World ★★★
A Gunfight ★★★
Catch Me a Spy ★★★

1972

Hearts and Minds ★★★

1973

Scalawag ★★★

1975

Once Is Not Enough ★★★
Posse ★★★

1977

Holocaust 2000 ★★★

1978

The Fury ★★★★
The Villian ★★★

1979

Saturn 3 ★★★
The Final Countdown ★★★

1980

The Villain ★★

1981

Home Movies ★★

1983

The Man from Snowy River ★★

MELVYN DOUGLAS
★★★½ 3.38 STARS

"All acting, if it's any good, is character acting," said Melvyn Douglas. Nobody demonstrated the validity of this better than Douglas himself. Even in lightweight romantic leads, he suggested colors and complexities not specifically indicated by the script.

Born Melvyn Edouard Hesselberg in 1901, in Macon, Georgia, Douglas's Broadway hits included "Tonight or Never" and "A Free Soul." He repeated his *Tonight or Never* on film, and co-starred with Greta Garbo in *As You Desire Me.* He played the husband she didn't remember.

Counsellor-at-Law was a gripping William Wyler-directed drama, and Douglas held up his end opposite a colorful John Barrymore. He proved himself a master at comedy in *She Married Her Boss* with Claudette Colbert and thoroughly comfortable in a sagebrush setting in *Annie Oakley,* with Barbara Stanwyck.

Douglas appeared with all the great female stars of the 1930s and the 1940s including: Joan Crawford (*The Gorgeous Hussy, A Woman's Face*); Irene Dunne (*Theodora Goes Wild*); Myrna Loy (*Third Finger Left Hand*). *Ninotchka,* with Greta Garbo, was probably his most popular picture of the 1930s.

He won an Oscar for *Hud* as Paul Newman's disapproving dad and had one of his finest roles as James Garner's mentally disturbed superior officer in *The Americanization of Emily.* But all previous performances paled against Douglas's magnificant portrayal in *I Never Sang For My Father*—an excruciatingly effective close-up of a selfish, domineering father who sabotaged his son's efforts at closeness. He also garnered a great deal of attention in his last great role as the dying tycoon in *Being There.*

FILMOGRAPHY

1931

Tonight or Never ★★★
Prestige ★★★
The Wiser Sex ★★★
Broken Wing ★★★
As You Desire Me ★★★★
The Old Dark House ★★★

1933

The Vampire Bat ★★★
Nagana ★★★
Counsellor-at-Law ★★★★

1934

Woman in the Dark ★★★
Dangerous Corner ★★★★

1935

The People's Enemy ★★★★
She Married Her Boss ★★★★
Mary Burns Fugitive ★★★
Annie Oakley ★★★★

1936

The Lone Wolf Returns ★★★★
And So They Were Married ★★★★
The Gorgeous Hussy ★★★
Theodora Goes Wild ★★★★

1937

Women of Glamour ★★★
Captains Courageous ★★★★
I Met Him in Paris ★★★★
Angel ★★★★
I'll Take Romance ★★★

1938

Arsene Lupin Returns ★★★
There's Always a Woman ★★★★
The Toy Wife ★★★
Fast Company ★★★
That Certain Age ★★★★
The Shining Hour ★★★
There's That Woman Again ★★★

1939

Tell No Tales ★★★
Good Girls Go to Paris ★★★
Ninotchka ★★★★
The Amazing Mr. Williams ★★★

Melvyn Douglas with Joan Blondell in *Good Girls Go to Paris.*

1940

Too Many Husbands ★★★★
He Stayed for Breakfast ★★★
Third Finger Left Hand ★★★

1941

This Thing Called Love ★★★
That Uncertain Feeling ★★★
A Woman's Face ★★★★
Our Wife ★★★
Two-Faced Woman ★★★

1942

We Were Dancing ★★★
They All Kissed the Bride ★★★

1943

Three Hearts for Julia ★★★

1947

The Sea of Grass ★★★
The Guilt of Janet Ames ★★★

1948

Mr. Blandings Builds His Dream House ★★★★

1949

My Own True Love ★★★
A Woman's Secret ★★★
The Great Sinner ★★★

1951

My Forbidden Past ★★★
On the Loose ★★★

1962

Billy Budd ★★★★

Melvyn Douglas in *Ghost Story.*

1963

Hud ★★★★

1964

Advance to the Rear ★★★
The Americanization of Emily ★★★★

1965

Rapture ★★★

1967

Hotel ★★★

1970

I Never Sang for My Father ★★★★

1972

One Is a Lonely Number ★★★★
The Candidate ★★★★

1976

The Tenant ★★★

1977

Twilight's Last Gleaming ★★★

1979

The Changeling ★★★
The Seduction of Joe Tynan ★★★★
Being There ★★★★

1981

Ghost Story ★★★

MICHAEL DOUGLAS
★★★ 2.89 STARS

Michael Douglas, the son of Kirk Douglas, lacks his father's brute power on the screen, but he has his own brand of amiable charm. The intelligence that made him capable of producing *One Flew Over the Cuckoo's Nest,* the winner of five major Oscars, can be felt in his performances.

Michael Douglas in *The China Syndrome*.

Douglas was born in New Jersey in 1944. He did a TV cop series, "The Streets of San Francisco," that ran for years and made Douglas well-known independently of his father. *Hail Hero!* was an unspectacular film debut, a dated 1960s tale of a hippie coping with his attitudes about Vietnam. He also co-starred with real-life girlfriend Brenda Vaccaro in another mediocre Vietnam drama, *Summertree.*

Douglas changed pace for a Disney comedy, *Napoleon and Samantha*, and his production of *Cuckoo's Nest* netted him industry respect and better parts. He performed well in a minor thriller, *Coma*, as the intern/boyfriend of Geneviève Bujold. Douglas' role in *The China Syndrome* was less showy than Jack Lemmon's, but he was convincingly intense as a cameraman. He also demonstrated comedic ease (something his father has yet to do) in an otherwise dreary romance with Jill Clayburgh, *It's My Turn.*

FILMOGRAPHY

1969

Hail, Hero! ★★★

1970

Adam at 6 A.M. ★★★

1971

Summertree ★★

1972

Napoleon and Samantha ★★★

1978

Coma ★★★★

1979

The China Syndrome ★★★
Running ★★

1980

It's My Turn ★★★

1983

The Star Chamber ★★★

RICHARD DREYFUSS
★★★ 3.08 STARS

Richard Dreyfuss is a pushy Dustin Hoffman. He barrels onto the screen taking command. He speaks rapidly and gives a charge to the most banal dialogue.

Dreyfuss was born in 1948, in Brooklyn, New York. His first interest was the stage. In Los Angeles, he got raves for a comic stage performance in "Aesop In Central Park," opposite Betty Garrett. He appeared frequently in off-Broadway shows and TV, and after a walk-on in the film *The Graduate*, he graduated to featured roles. In *Dillinger*, Dreyfuss's portrayal of Baby Face Nelson passed unnoticed, but *American Graffiti* made him a star. A study of aimless California teenagers, it was superficial but entertaining, and a huge hit.

The Apprenticeship of Duddy Kravitz was much less sympathetic. Dreyfuss played a conniving Jewish promoter in Montreal, projecting naked ambition more forcefully than anyone else had ever done on film.

Jaws was a better-than-the-book version of the Peter Benchley thriller, and Dreyfuss invested the scientist he portrayed with a scintillating combination of dedication and teddy bear humor. He also played in *Inserts*, a self-indulgent mistake, and *Close Encounters of the Third Kind* which rivaled *Star Wars* in popularity. His role in *Close Encounters* was too slow-paced and unexciting, however,. and Dreyfuss was overly subdued.

His energy poured out again in *The Goodbye Girl,* counteracting Marsha Mason's excessive teariness. He won an Oscar for his efforts. However, *The Big Fix* suggested he was giving in to egotism, with huge, sensual close-ups that sought to present him as a Paul Newman-type sex symbol. In *The Competition,* he was cast in a typically brash Dreyfuss role, but he was clearly too old to play a young pianist. *Whose Life Is It Anyway?* bottled his anger in a paraplegic's body. He garnered another Oscar nomination, but few audiences wanted to watch.

Dreyfuss represents the aggressive, go-getting side of all viewers, and he coats his energy with enough charm to make it palatable. As long as he maintains his dramatic integrity, he'll continue to be popular with audiences and critics alike.

Richard Dreyfuss in *Jaws.*

FILMOGRAPHY

1967

Valley of the Dolls (bit)
The Graduate (bit)

1968

The Young Runaways ★★★

1969

Hello Down There ★★

1973

Dillinger ★★★
American Graffiti ★★★

1974

The Apprenticeship of Duddy Kravitz ★★★★
The Second Coming of Suzanne ★★★

1975

Jaws ★★★★

1976

Inserts ★★

1977

Close Encounters of the Third Kind ★★★
The Goodbye Girl ★★★★

1978

The Big Fix ★★

1980

The Competition ★★★

1981

Whose Life is it Anyway? ★★★★

FAYE DUNAWAY
★★½ 2.54 STARS

An artificial, distant, WASPy actress, Faye Dunaway has managed through high-fashion looks and lucky casting to rise to the top of the heap.

Dunaway was born in Bascom, Florida, in 1941. As a member of the Lincoln Center Repertory Company, she appeared in "A Man for All Seasons" and "After the Fall." Then she played in the off-Broadway show, "Hogan's Goat."

She quarreled with director Otto Preminger while making *Hurry Sundown*, one of her first films, but hit solid gold with *Bonnie and Clyde*. Dunaway's grasping, sexual Bonnie revealed her as a strong emotional actress under the right conditions. However, she was bloodlessly chic and pretentious opposite Steve McQueen in *The Thomas Crown Affair.*

The Arrangement was based on Kazan's best-seller, an abrasive study of a failing marriage (Kirk Douglas was the man, Dunaway the other woman). However, the same public that had gobbled up the book ignored the picture. In *Puzzle of a Downfall Child* she was cast as a fashion model trying to put her life back together, an ordeal for the actors and viewers alike.

Little Big Man was director Arthur Penn's sprawling saga of the Old West, and she was slightly more animated. As in *The Three Musketeers,* she seemed to shine in smaller parts. *Oklahoma Crude* went by without arousing public interest, but director Roman Polanski (who called her "a maniac") used her neurotic acting style to advantage in *Chinatown* and she was Oscar-nominated. It was back to cool pretension for *The Towering Inferno* though a hotel fire kept her emoting to a minimum.

Faye Dunaway in *Mommie Dearest.*

Three Days of the Condor was a good thriller, and director Sidney Pollack heroically fought and succeeded in getting some humor into her role as Robert Redford's not-so-unwilling captive. *Network* brought the elusive Oscar; Dunaway's "style" was well suited for Paddy Chayefsky's satire of television. She was effective but again neurotic as the possessor of the *Eyes of Laura Mars.*

Maybe modern audiences like a fashion plate—as earlier viewers enjoyed Audrey Hepburn. The problem is where Hepburn was regally reserved, Dunaway is a beautiful block of ice.

FILMOGRAPHY

1967

The Happening ★★
Hurry Sundown ★★
Bonnie and Clyde ★★★★

1968

The Thomas Crown Affair ★★★

1969

The Arrangement ★★
The Extraordinary Seaman ★★
A Place for Lovers ★★

1970

Little Big Man ★★★
Puzzle of a Downfall Child ★★

1971

Doc ★★

1972

The Deadly Trap ★★

1973

Oklahoma Crude ★★★

1974

The Three Musketeers ★★★
Chinatown ★★★★
The Towering Inferno ★★

1975

Three Days of the Condor ★★★★
The Four Musketeers ★★★

1976

Network ★★★★
Voyage of the Damned ★★

1978

Eyes of Laura Mars ★★★

1979

The Champ ★★

1980

The First Deadly Sin ★★

1981

Mommie Dearest ★

1983

The Wicked Lady ★★

IRENE DUNNE
★★★ 3.15 STARS

Irene Dunne has to be applauded as a polished, versatile technician. She can be warm too but rarely does the warmth seem spontaneous.

She was born Irene Marie Dunn in 1898, in Louisville, Kentucky. The year 1929 was brightened by her stage appearance as Magnolia in "Show Boat," a role she later played successfully on the screen. Her second film, *Cimarron,* was a sprawling story of the Old West, but it clinched Dunne's stardom and won her an Oscar nomination.

She was a noble, long-suffering mistress in *Back Street,* but an Astaire-Rogers film, *Roberta,* temporarily dispensed with tears. They were back full force, however, in *Magnificent Obsession.* Dunne portrayed a woman accidentally blinded by playboy Robert Taylor; the roles were later re-done by Jane Wyman and Rock Hudson.

Show Boat reminded Hollywood

that she was a musical as well as dramatic star. She displayed her comic aptitude in the classic *The Awful Truth* with Cary Grant. This version can be doubly appreciated after seeing the musical update with Jane Wyman and Ray Milland, *Let's Do It Again*. *Love Affair*, with Charles Boyer, was touching and memorable, and she had another triumph with Grant again in *Penny Serenade*.

The White Cliffs of Dover was imitation *Mrs. Miniver* without the dramatic impact (her mechanical Great Lady performance didn't help), but *Anna and the King of Siam* showed that there was life in the story of a governess and a king even without Rodgers and Hammerstein songs. Dunne's career faded with *The Mudlark* and died after *Never a Dull Moment* and *It Grows on Trees*.

Unlike many stars who announced their retirement, she never returned to acting but her comedies and dramas are still rich in entertainment value. Irene Dunne's talent never leaped off the screen and grabbed the viewer by the shoulders. Hers was a quiet professionalism that seems more remarkable in retrospect than during her career.

FILMOGRAPHY

1930

Leathernecking ★★★

1931

Cimarron ★★★★
Bachelor Apartment ★★★
The Great Lover ★★★
Consolation Marriage ★★★

1932

Symphony of Six Million ★★★★
Back Street ★★★★
Thirteen Women ★★★

1933

No Other Woman ★★★
The Secret of Madame Blanche ★★★
The Silver Cord ★★★
Ann Vickers ★★★
If I Were Free ★★★

1934

This Man Is Mine ★★★
Stingaree ★★★
The Age of Innocence ★★★

Irene Dunne with Cary Grant in *My Favorite Wife*.

1935

Sweet Adeline ★★★
Roberta ★★★
Magnificent Obsession ★★★★

1936

Show Boat ★★★★
Theodora Goes Wild ★★★★

1937

High, Wide and Handsome ★★★
The Awful Truth ★★★★

1938

Joy of Living ★★★

1939

Love Affair ★★★★
Invitation to Happiness ★★
When Tomorrow Comes ★★

1940

My Favorite Wife ★★★

1941

Penny Serenade ★★★★
Unfinished Business ★★★

1942

Lady in a Jam ★★★

1943

A Guy Named Joe ★★★

1944

The White Cliffs of Dover ★★★
Together Again ★★★

1945

Anna and the King of Siam ★★★★

1947

Life With Father ★★★

1948

I Remember Mama ★★★

1950

Never a Dull Moment ★★
The Mudlark ★★★

1952

It Grows on Trees ★★

DAN DURYEA
★★★½ 3.26 STARS

Dan Duryea was one of Hollywood's most engaging bad guys. David Thomson once wrote, "In striped suit, bow-tie and straw hat, the Duryea of *Scarlet Street* is a delicious villain. A sly man, he creeps up on malice as if it were a cat to catch."

Duryea was born in New York, in 1907, and worked in advertising before his Broadway success in "The Little Foxes." He repeated his performance as the conniving weakling in William Wyler's film version of *The Little Foxes* and had another good part as a mob flunkie in *Ball of Fire* with Gary Cooper. *The Woman in the Window* permanently solidified his image as a cynical, grinning menace. *Another Part of the Forest* proved an absorbing sequel to *The Little Foxes* with Duryea more prominent, and he was particularly evil in *Johnny Stool Pigeon*.

Dan Duryea with James Stewart in *Thunder Bay*.

He pursued and tormented Lizabeth Scott for stolen money in *Too Late for Tears* and tried to pin a murder rap on Dorothy Lamour in *Manhandled*. He switched gears effectively to play Faith Domergue's crippled husband in the sudsy *This Is My Love*. Duryea died of cancer in 1968.

FILMOGRAPHY

1941

The Little Foxes ★★★★
Ball of Fire ★★★★

1942

The Pride of the Yankees ★★★

Dan Duryea.

1943

Sahara ★★★

1944

The Woman in the Window ★★★★
Ministry of Fear ★★★
Mrs. Parkington ★★★
None But the Lonely Heart ★★★★

1945

Main Street After Dark ★★★
The Great Flamarion ★★★
The Valley of Decision ★★★
Along Came Jones ★★★★
Lady on a Train ★★★★
Scarlet Street ★★★★

1946

Black Angel ★★★
White Tie and Tails ★★★

1948

Black Bart ★★★
Another Part of the Forest ★★★★
River Lady ★★★
Larceny ★★★★

1949

Criss Cross ★★★★
Manhandled ★★★★
Too Late for Tears ★★★★
Johnny Stool Pigeon ★★★★

1950

One Way Street ★★★★
Winchester '73 ★★★
The Underworld Story ★★★

1951

Al Jennings of Oklahoma ★★★
Chicago Calling ★★★

1953

Thunder Bay ★★★
Sky Commando ★★★

1954

Ride Clear of Diablo ★★★
Rails Into Laramie ★★★
World for Ransom ★★★
Silver Lode ★★★
This Is My Love ★★★

1955

The Marauders ★★★
Foxfire ★★★

1956

Storm Fear ★★★

1957

Battle Hymn ★★★
The Burglar ★★★
Night Passage ★★★
Slaughter on Tenth Avenue ★★★

1958

Kathy O' ★★★

1960

Platinum High School ★★★

1962

Six Black Horses ★★★

1964

He Rides Tall ★★★
Walk a Tightrope ★★★
Taggart ★★★

1965

The Bounty Killer ★★★
The Flight of the Phoenix ★★★

1966

Incident at Phantom Hill ★★★
The Hills Run Red ★★★

1968

The Bamboo Saucer ★★★

ROBERT DUVALL
★★★½ 3.50 STARS

In *Tender Mercies*, Robert Duvall's portrait of a down-and-out country singer was nothing less than astonishing. Furthermore, the film revolved around him so audiences could finally see the star quality that his masterly but self-effacing performances had disguised through the years.

Born in 1931, in San Diego, California, Duvall made his film debut in *To Kill a Mockingbird*. He disappeared so far into the character of a feeble-minded man that no traces of the actor were visible. Duvall also appeared in some good films including *The Detective*, *Bullitt*, and *True Grit*, but it wasn't until *The Godfather* that he imposed himself powerfully enough to be remembered afterward. His performance brought an Oscar nomination but not many showy roles. *The Great Northfield Minnesota Raid* was a so-so western in which he played Jesse James, *Lady Ice*, *The Outfit*, and *Badge 373* had such fleeting theatrical bookings that only TV viewers and fans of Duvall recall them today.

The Godfather, Part II was as riveting as the original, and Duvall was an important reason for its artistic success. However, no one stood out in *The Killer Elite*; there was too much bloodshed to accommodate any humanity. Duvall was too busy being quietly effective to garner much attention for himself in dramas like *Network*, *The Conversation*, *The Betsy*, *True Confessions*, and *The Seven Percent Solution*. He was the best part of Francis Ford Coppola's Vietnam epic, *Apocalypse Now*.

He had his first dazzling star part as *The Great Santini*, as an insensitive, brutally macho father who pushed his son to the breaking point. One moment—when Duvall bounced a basketball off his son's body—deserves a footnote in the cinema hall of fame.

If there's any justice in Hollywood, Duvall should win the Best Actor Oscar in 1984 for *Tender Mercies*.

Robert Duvall with Allan Hubbard in *Tender Mercies.*

FILMOGRAPHY

1963

To Kill a Mockingbird ★★★★

1964

Captain Newman M.D. ★★★★

1966

The Chase ★★★

1968

Bullitt ★★★
The Detective ★★★
Countdown ★★★

1969

True Grit ★★★★
The Rain People ★★★★

1970

M*A*S*H ★★★★
The Revolutionary ★★★

Robert Duvall in *True Confessions.*

1971

Lawman ★ ★ ★
THX 1138 ★ ★ ★

1972

The Godfather ★ ★ ★ ★
The Great Northfield Minnesota Raid ★ ★ ★ ★
Joe Kidd ★ ★ ★
Tomorrow ★ ★ ★ ★

1973

Badge 373 ★ ★ ★
Lady Ice ★ ★ ★
The Godfather, Part II ★ ★ ★ ★

1974

The Outfit ★ ★ ★
The Conversation (cameo)

1975

The Killer Elite ★ ★ ★
Breakout ★ ★ ★

1976

The Seven Percent Solution ★ ★ ★ ★
Network ★ ★ ★ ★

1977

The Greatest ★ ★ ★
The Eagle Has Landed ★ ★ ★

1978

The Betsy ★ ★ ★ ★

1979

Apocalypse Now ★ ★ ★ ★
The Great Santini ★ ★ ★ ★

1981

True Confessions ★ ★ ★ ★
The Pursuit of D.B. Cooper ★ ★ ★

1982

Tender Mercies ★ ★ ★ ★

SHELLEY DUVALL
★ ★ ★ 3.00 STARS

Shelley Duvall has had starring parts and played them well, but her peculiar appearance (so perfect in *Popeye*) is possibly too offbeat to represent ordinary American womanhood on the screen.

She was born in Houston, Texas in 1950. Director Robert Altman discovered her and cast her in his odd, erratic comedy *Brewster McCloud.* Duvall brought a little charm to the general tastelessness, and her part was bigger in Altman's next film, *McCabe and Mrs. Miller.* However, *Thieves Like Us*, a sensitive and often beautiful remake of the 1940s drama, *They Live by Night*, brought her to the fore. Duvall and Keith Carradine were the two doomed lovers (Farley Granger and Cathy O'Donnell played them in the original). It was certainly Altman's best film, but there were no audiences.

Nashville excited more interest but alienated country fans. Duvall didn't add much to *Buffalo Bill and the Indians*, but she was excellent in *Three Women.* She did a cameo in *Annie Hall* and played Olive Oyl in the ill-fated *Popeye.* Composer Harry Nilsson's songs were enough to sink any musical.

It's interesting that most of her films *(Brewster McCloud, McCabe and Mrs. Miller, Thieves Like Us, Buffalo Bill,* and *3 Women)* were directed by the "actor's director" Robert Altman. However, her one natural, totally lifelike performance came in a picture that the austere Stanley Kubrick directed, *The Shining.* Unfortunately, the director mangled Stephen King's original novel and Duvall didn't get the credit she deserved amid the clamor of hostility about the film itself.

Lately, Shelly Duvall has been wearing the hat of a producer, and she is responsible for the acclaimed "Faerie Tale Theatre" seen on cable television. Having created excellent performances for a decade, she is now creating that opportunity for other actors.

Shelly Duvall with Sissy Spacek in *3 Women.*

Shelly Duvall.

FILMOGRAPHY

1970

Brewster McCloud ★ ★

1971

McCabe and Mrs. Miller ★ ★ ★

1974

Thieves Like Us ★ ★ ★

1975

Nashville ★ ★

1976

Buffalo Bill and the Indians (cameo)

1977

Annie Hall (cameo)
3 Women ★ ★ ★ ★

1979

The Shining ★ ★ ★ ★

1980

Popeye ★ ★ ★

CLINT EASTWOOD
★★★ 2.94 STARS

Clint Eastwood's soft, toneless voice is not an ideal actor's instrument—but oddly enough, it has been a big asset in his roles. The whispery sound furnishes a humanizing contrast to Eastwood's tall, muscular strength and violent behavior, adding a needed element of sensitivity.

Born in San Francisco, in 1930, his early "physical" jobs as a lumberjack, swimming instructor, and athletic coach prepared him for the rugged roles he was to play later. His first movies were *Francis in the Navy, Tarantula,* and *Ambush at Cimarron Pass.* After these worthless experiences, his TV series, "Rawhide," was doubly welcome. It ran for eight years and made Eastwood enough of a star to play the "man with no name" in a cluster of Italian-made westerns for director Sergio Leone. They took the world by storm, and Eastwood's self-contained, potentially explosive bounty hunter made him a hot Hollywood property. His first western made in the states was *Hang 'em High,* an Americanized repeat of the spaghetti western formula. He had a charming leading lady in Inger Stevens.

Coogan's Bluff, expertly directed by Don Siegel, was an exciting, well-written story of an Arizona sheriff tracking down an escaped prisoner in Manhattan. Eastwood's seething cool worked better than ever, and the film later spawned the TV series, "McCloud." Although he was the only good thing about *Where Eagles Dare,* Eastwood still wanted to grow as an actor. However, he stumbled into alien territory with *Paint Your Wagon,* an elephant-sized musical with miniscule entertainment value. Neither of the other leads, Lee Marvin and Jean Seberg, could sing or dance, which didn't help. He did team amusingly with Shirley MacLaine in the enjoyable *Two Mules for Sister Sara.*

Clint Eastwood in *Coogan's Bluff.*

Eastwood made his best picture, and directed it as well, in 1971. In *Play Misty for Me,* a thriller that ranked with some of Hitchcock's finest, Eastwood was a disc jockey being mercilessly pursued by an unbalanced fan (Jessica Walter, in a classic performance).

In *Dirty Harry,* he played a tough cop who took the law into his own hands. The role provided him with another strong and identifiable image. *Magnum Force* brought back the Dirty Harry character, and the film was powerfully performed by Eastwood, Hal Holbrook, and David Soul. *Thunderbolt and Lightfoot* paired him with Jeff Bridges, who received an Oscar nomination. *The Eiger Sanction* milked a mountain-climbing plot for all possible thrills, and then he did his last Dirty Harry film, *The Enforcer.* The freshness of the first two was missing, but it had an endearing performance by Tyne Daly of "Cagney and Lacy."

Eastwood is often compared to Gary Cooper, and while there are similarities, Cooper may have had a wider range. However, Eastwood's excursions into comedy, *Every Which Way But Loose* and *Any Which Way You Can,* showed a lighter side. People believed Eastwood on the screen, possibly because as TV interviews suggested, he really *is* taciturn, nonverbal, and capable of letting emotion show only in tense situations.

Recent films have indicated his courage to test himself in different types of material. He's clearly not an actor to settle complacently into one groove and wear out his welcome. Because of his box-office power and his demonstrated desire to grow as an actor, Clint Eastwood is one of the most interesting actors to watch today.

Clint Eastwood in *Honky Tonk Man.*

FILMOGRAPHY

1955

Revenge of the Creature (bit)
Francis in the Navy (bit)
Lady Godiva (bit)
Tarantula (bit)

1956

Never Say Goodbye ★★
The First Traveling Saleslady ★★
Star in the Dust ★★

1957

Escapade in Japan ★★

1958

Ambush at Cimarron Pass ★★
Lafayette Escadrille ★★

1964

A Fistful of Dollars ★★★

1965

For a Few Dollars More ★★★

1966

The Good, the Bad and the Ugly ★★★

1967

The Witches ★★★

1968

Hang 'em High ★★★
Coogan's Bluff ★★★

1969

Where Eagles Dare ★★★
Paint Your Wagon ★★

1970

Two Mules for Sister Sara ★★★
Kelly's Heroes ★★★

1971

The Beguiled ★★★
Play Misty for Me (direction) ★★★★
Dirty Harry ★★★★

1972

Joe Kidd ★★

1973

High Plains Drifter (direction) ★★★
Magnum Force ★★★★

1974

Thunderbolt and Lightfoot ★★★★

1975

The Eiger Sanction (direction) ★★★

1976

The Outlaw Josey Wales (direction) ★★★
The Enforcer ★★★

1977

The Gauntlet (direction) ★★★

1978

Escape from Alcatraz ★★★★
Every Which Way But Loose ★★★

1980

Bronco Billy (direction) ★★★★
Any Which Way You Can ★★★

1982

Firefox (direction) ★★★
Honkytonk Man (direction) ★★★

NELSON EDDY
★★ 2.06 STARS

Legend says that Nelson Eddy and Jeanette MacDonald were bitter enemies off the screen although insiders claim the hostility was a cover-up for a tempestuous love affair. Whatever the truth, it had to be more dramatic than their saccharine entanglements on the screen.

Eddy was born in 1901, in Rhode Island, and sang in church choirs as a boy. He appeared in "Pagliacci" at the New York Metropolitan Opera and made his film debut with *Broadway to Hollywood. Naughty Marietta* was the first of a series of hugely popular operettas which today are considered camp. However, viewed in the right spirit, they *do* have a fairy-tale ebullience that provides refreshing escape from worldly realities. *Rose Marie, Maytime, The Girl of the Golden West,* and *Sweethearts* were some of their bigger hits, and they scored again in *New Moon* and *The Chocolate Soldier.*

Contemporary critics felt that Eddy was wooden when not singing, a view confirmed by reruns of his movies on TV. He had a final success without MacDonald in *The Phantom of the Opera.* Eddy died on stage of a stroke in 1967.

FILMOGRAPHY

1933

Broadway to Hollywood (cameo)
Dancing Lady (cameo)

1934

Student Tour ★★

1935

Naughty Marietta ★★

1936

Rose Marie ★★

1937

Maytime ★★
Rosalie ★★

1938

Sweethearts ★★
The Girl of the Golden West ★★

Nelson Eddy with Jeanette MacDonald in *Sweethearts.*

1939

Balalaika ★★
Let Freedom Ring! ★★

1940

New Moon ★★
Bittersweet ★★

1941

The Chocolate Soldier ★★

1942

I Married an Angel ★★

1943

The Phantom of the Opera ★★★

1944

Knickerbocker Holiday ★★

1946

Make Mine Music (voice only)

1947

Northwest Outpost ★★

DOUGLAS FAIRBANKS, JR.
★★★ 3.07 STARS

The old saying, "Like father, like son" applies to Douglas Fairbanks, Sr. and his son. Both displayed a hearty, engaging vitality in costume epics, but Douglas Fairbanks, Jr. demonstrated more range as a dramatic actor, partly due to opportunities provided by talkies.

Douglas Fairbanks, Jr. was born in 1909 in New York City. He made his first film *Stephen Steps Out* in 1923, against the wishes of his father who commented, "There can be only one Fairbanks!" Douglas, Jr. persisted although his first wife, Joan Crawford, criticized him in her autobiography for being "slipshod" and not caring enough.

After years of mainly forgotten movies including *Wild Horse Mesa, Padlocked, Broken Hearts of Hollywood,* and *Is Zat So?*, Douglas, Jr. had a hit with wife Crawford in *Our Modern Maidens.* He also inspired superlatives from critics for *The Dawn Patrol.* He paired with Bette Davis in the amusing *Parachute Jumper* and played Katharine Hepburn's fiance in *Morning Glory.*

The Prisoner of Zenda was a smash; Fairbanks made a dashing villain. He joined a British regiment with Cary Grant and Victor McLaglen in the exuberant *Gunga Din,* his best film. Fairbanks had his biggest hit with *Sinbad the Sailor* and then found himself stranded in a dull Betty Grable vehicle, *That Lady in Ermine.* After *Mr. Drake's Duck,* he retired from films. On the stage, he was a properly urbane Professor Higgins in "My Fair Lady."

Douglas Fairbanks, Jr.

He came back from retirement in 1981 to co-star with Melvyn Douglas and Fred Astaire in *Ghost Story*. One must regret that the vehicle wasn't worth the trip.

FILMOGRAPHY

1923

Stephen Steps Out ★★★

1925

The Air Mail ★★★
Wild Horse Mesa ★★★
Stella Dallas ★★★★

1926

The American Venus ★★★
Padlocked ★★★
Broken Hearts of Hollywood ★★★

1927

Man Bait ★★★
Women Love Diamonds ★★★
Is Zat So? ★★★
A Texas Steer ★★★

1928

Dead Man's Curve ★★★
Modern Mothers ★★★
The Toilers ★★★
The Power of the Press ★★★
The Barker ★★★
A Woman of Affairs ★★★

1929

The Jazz Age ★★★
Fast Life ★★★
Our Modern Maidens ★★★
The Careless Age ★★★
The Show of Shows ★★★
The Forward Pass ★★★

1930

Party Girl ★★★
Loose Ankles ★★★
The Dawn Patrol ★★★★
Little Accident ★★★★
One Night at Susie's ★★★
Outward Bound ★★★★
The Way of All Men ★★★★

1931

Little Caesar ★★★★
Chances ★★★
I Like Your Nerve ★★★

1932

Union Depot ★★★★
It's Tough to Be Famous ★★★
Love Is a Racket ★★★
Scarlet Dawn ★★★

1933

Parachute Jumper ★★★
The Life of Jimmy Dolan ★★★
The Narrow Corner ★★★
Morning Glory ★★★★
Captured ★★★

1934

Catherine the Great ★★★
Success at Any Price ★★★

1935

Mimi ★★

1936

The Amateur Gentleman ★★★
Accused ★★★

1937

The Prisoner of Zenda ★★★★
Jump for Glory ★★

1938

Joy of Living ★★★
The Rage of Paris ★★★
Having Wonderful Time ★★
The Young in Heart ★★★★

1939

Gunga Din ★★★★
The Sun Never Sets ★★★
Rulers of the Sea ★★★

Douglas Fairbanks, Jr. in *Ghost Story.*

1940

Green Hell ★★★
Safari ★★★
Angels Over Broadway ★★★

1941

The Corsican Brothers ★★★

1947

Sinbad the Sailor ★★★★
The Exile ★★★

1948

That Lady in Ermine ★★

1949

The Fighting O'Flynn ★★★

1950

State Secret ★★★★

1951

Mr. Drake's Duck ★★★

1981

Ghost Story ★★★

FRANCES FARMER
★★★ 3.00 STARS

The tragic deterioration of Frances Farmer has been dramatized in books and in two films, one made for TV, the other, a feature starring Jessica Lange. Gene Tierney, herself a victim of mental illness, recognized Farmer's symptoms when they were making *Son of Fury*, but Hollywood saw her only as a rebel. Her brilliant career was cut short from the beginning by clashes with studio executives.

She was born in 1913 in Seattle, Washington. Farmer wrote a controversial essay as a youngster and the prize—a trip to the Soviet Union—led to accusations of her being a communist. Stage work with the Group Theatre in "Golden Boy" led to film work in 1936. Her first pictures, *Too Many Parents* and *Border Flight*, meant little, but she had Bing Crosby as a co-star in *Rhythm on the Range*.

Come and Get It was her one powerful vehicle, the only Farmer performance most modern viewers have seen. She was brilliant, playing both mother and daughter, although Walter Brennan won the Oscar. She competed with newspaperman/boyfriend Fred MacMurray in the entertaining *Exclusive*, and did two undistinguished outdoor films, *South of Pago Pago* and *Badlands of Dakota*. *Among the Living* was low budget, but Albert Dekker's portrayal (as a deranged twin) created some suspense.

Frances Farmer with Jon Hall in *South of Pago Pago.*

She was attractive in the exotic *Son of Fury,* but after that, Farmer experienced years of alcoholism and barbaric treatment in various mental institutions. Whether she ever received a lobotomy is not known, but she recovered sufficiently to host a TV show in Indianapolis.

FILMOGRAPHY

1936

Too Many Parents ★★
Border Flight ★★★
Rhythm on the Range ★★★
Come and Get It ★★★★

1937

Exclusive ★★★
The Toast of New York ★★★
Ebb Tide ★★★

1938

Ride a Crooked Mile ★★★

1940

South of Pago-Pago ★★★
Flowing Gold ★★★

1941

World Premiere ★★★
Badlands of Dakota ★★★
Among the Living ★★★★

1942

Son of Fury ★★★

1958

The Party Crashers ★★

MIA FARROW
★★½ 2.47 STARS

In the mid-1960s, when Mia Farrow's romance and marriage to Frank Sinatra dominated the headlines, it seemed inevitable that she would become a big star. Sheilah Graham credited Farrow with the same talent and honesty as the young Audrey Hepburn. However, she lacked Hepburn's variety; no matter what the role, she seemed fey and fragile.

She was born in 1945, in Los Angeles, the daughter of director John Farrow and actress Maureen O'Sullivan. Her first important part, as Allison in TV's "Peyton Place" demanded that frail quality and so did director Roman Polanski's hair-raising *Rosemary's Baby.* She was superbly realistic as

Mia Farrow in *Rosemary's Baby.*

the unwitting victim of the devil's agents. It was a marked contrast to her bland, baby-doll performance in *John and Mary.* She was more human in *Follow Me,* but she lacked the charisma to make Robert Redford's obsession credible in *The Great Gatsby.*

Farrow's career has been prolonged by offscreen activities—as a 1960s flower child, as the "other woman" in the lives of Andre and Dory Previn, and as Woody Allen's wife. However, what she needs now is a movie more exciting than her publicity, meaty roles that will force her to abandon her old image. She may be finding just that under the smart direction of husband Woody Allen.

FILMOGRAPHY

1964

Guns at Batasi ★★

1968

A Dandy in Aspic ★★
Rosemary's Baby ★★★★
Secret Ceremony ★★★

1969

John and Mary ★★

1971

See No Evil ★★★

1972

Follow Me ★★★
Docteur Popaul ★★

1974

The Great Gatsby ★★

1975

The Tempest ★★

1977

The Haunting of Julia ★★★

1978

Avalanche ★★
A Wedding ★★
Death on the Nile ★★★

1979

The Hurricane ★

1982

A Midsummer Night's Sex Comedy ★★★
The Last Unicorn (voice only)

1983

Zelig ★★★

ALICE FAYE
★★★ 3.03 STARS

Alice Faye's biographers dwelled heavily on her feuds with producer Darryl F. Zanuck instead of her vulnerability and sensitivity on the screen. Her husky, contralto voice was also refreshing in an era of piercing sopranos.

Faye was born Alice Jeanne Leppert, in New York, in 1912. She first drew attention by singing on Rudy Vallee's radio show but kicked off her career at 20th Century Fox with a drama, *Now I'll Tell* with Spencer Tracy. A Shirley Temple film, *Poor Little Rich Girl,* focused more attention on her, and she had hits with *Wake Up and Live* and *You Can't Have Everything.*

In Old Chicago built a drama around the Great Chicago Fire of 1871 and featured an Oscar-winning

Alice Faye.

portrayal by Alice Brady. There was an Irving Berlin score to bolster *Alexander's Ragtime Band*. With her succession of hits, Faye made the Top 10 box-office attractions in 1938.

The story of Fanny Brice had its first fictionalized re-working in *Rose of Washington Square*, but the movie lacked the power of the later *Funny Girl*. After *That Night in Rio* and *Weekend in Havana*, Faye's popularity waned. She showed dramatic promise in *Fallen Angel*, and then went into a long retirement, broken (unfortunately) by 1962's *State Fair*.

FILMOGRAPHY

1934

Now I'll Tell ★★★
George White's Scandals ★★★
She Learned About Sailors ★★★
365 Nights in Hollywood ★★★

1935

George White's 1935 Scandals ★★★
Every Night at Eight ★★★
Music Is Magic ★★★

1936

King of Burlesque ★★★
Poor Little Rich Girl ★★★
Sing Baby Sing ★★★
Stowaway ★★★

1937

On the Avenue ★★★
Wake Up and Live ★★★★
You Can't Have Everything ★★★
You're a Sweetheart ★★★

1938

In Old Chicago ★★★★
Sally Irene and Mary ★★★
Alexander's Ragtime Band ★★★★

1939

Tail Spin ★★★
Rose of Washington Square ★★★★
Hollywood Cavalcade ★★★
Barricade ★★★

1940

Lillian Russell ★★
Little Old New York ★★★
Tin Pan Alley ★★★

1941

That Night in Rio ★★★
The Great American Broadcast ★★★
Weekend in Havana ★★★

1943

Hello Frisco Hello ★★★
The Gang's All Here ★★★

1944

Four Jills in a Jeep (cameo)

1945

Fallen Angel ★★★★

1962

State Fair ★★

1978

Every Girl Should Have One ★★
The Magic of Lassie ★★

JOSÉ FERRER
★★★ 3.08 STARS

José Ferrer can do anything and do it well—produce, direct, write, and act. He has star quality even in supporting roles and a natural ease in any period or costume drama.

Born in Puerto Rico, in 1912, and educated at Princeton, Ferrer's Broadway hits included "Brother Rat," "Key Largo," and "Charley's Aunt." His first film role was a small but effective part in Ingrid Bergman's version of *Joan of Arc*. He played the dauphin king. He got a bigger and better part in *Whirlpool*, as the sinister hypnotist who nearly murdered Gene Tierney. Ferrer received Hollywood acclaim for classical acting when he played *Cyrano de Bergerac*, and there was a third hit—*Moulin Rouge*, the story of Toulouse-Lautrec.

He reduced Humphrey Bogart to jelly on the witness stand in *The Caine Mutiny* and capitulated psychologically under June Allyson's domineering pressure in *The Shrike*. Although Ferrer's films varied in quality from the artistic high of *Lawrence of Arabia* to the low of *The Swarm*, his own contributions have seldom been less than excellent.

Jose Ferrer in *Moulin Rouge.*

FILMOGRAPHY

1948

Joan of Arc ★★★★

1950

Whirlpool ★★★★
Crisis ★★★
Cyrano de Bergerac ★★★★

1952

Anything Can Happen ★★★

1953

Moulin Rouge ★★★★
Miss Sadie Thompson ★★★

1954

The Caine Mutiny ★★★★
Deep in My Heart ★★★

1955

The Shrike ★★★★

1956

The Cockleshell Heroes ★★★

1957

The Great Man ★★★

1958

I Accuse! ★★★
The High Cost of Loving ★★★

1962

Lawrence of Arabia ★★★★

1963

Nine Hours to Rama ★★★
Stop Train 349 ★★★

1964

Cyrano et D'Artagnan ★★★

1965

The Greatest Story Ever Told ★★★
Ship of Fools ★★

1967

Enter Laughing ★★★
The Young Rebel ★★★

1974

Order to Kill ★★★

1976

Paco ★★★
The Big Bus ★★★
Voyage of the Damned ★★★★
Forever Young, Forever Free ★★

1977

The Sentinel ★★★
Who Has Seen the Wind ★★★
Zoltan Hound of Dracula ★★
The Private Lives of J. Edgar Hoover ★★

1978

The Swarm ★★
Fedora ★★★
The Amazing Captain Nemo ★★

1979

The Fifth Musketeer ★★★
Natural Enemies ★★★

1980

The Big Brawl ★★★

1982

A Midsummer Night's Sex Comedy ★★★★

MEL FERRER
★★½ 2.72 STARS

Mel Ferrer, like Laurence Harvey, is a critic's target. He can't seem to do anything right even when his performances merit approval. Ferrer is frequently referred to as "cold," but in many movies—*The Vintage*, for example—his warmth is the lifeblood of the film.

Ferrer was born into a wealthy family in New Jersey, in 1917. He had a fine acting debut in the conscientious *Lost Boundaries*, as a black doctor passing for white. His graceful touch helped the hard-breathing *Born to Be Bad*, and he made a convincing matador in *The Brave Bulls*. He and Stewart Granger were lively rivals in the colorful *Scaramouche*, and *Lili* paired him appealingly with Leslie Caron.

After that, the films dropped in artistic value. *The Sun Also Rises* was a talky version of the Hemingway novel, and Ferrer couldn't save either *Mayerling* or *Paris When It Sizzles* with then-wife Audrey Hepburn. He appeared in an episodic but popular war film, *The Longest Day*, and coped gamely with *Sex and the Single Girl*. Ferrer can now be seen weekly as Jane Wyman's lawyer in the TV series "Falcon Crest."

FILMOGRAPHY

1949

Lost Boundaries ★★★★

1950

Born to Be Bad ★★★

1951

The Brave Bulls ★★★★

Mel Ferrer in *The Brave Bulls.*

1952

Rancho Notorious ★★★
Scaramouche ★★★★

1953

Lili ★★★★

1954

Knights of the Round Table ★★★
Saadia ★★★

1955

Oh Rosalinda! ★★★
Forbidden ★★★

1956

War and Peace ★★★
Paris Does Strange Things ★★

1957

The Vintage ★★★★
The Sun Also Rises ★★★
Mayerling ★★

1958

Fraulein ★★

1959

The World, the Flesh, and the Devil ★★★

1960

L'Homme a Femmes ★★★
Blood and Roses ★★★

1961

The Hands of Orlac ★★★
Legge Di Guerra ★★★
I Lancieri neri ★★★

1962

The Devil and the Ten Commandments ★★
The Longest Day ★★★

1964

Paris When It Sizzles (cameo)
The Fall of the Roman Empire ★★
Sex and the Single Girl ★★
El Senor de la Salle ★★
El Greco ★★

1972

A Time For Loving ★★★

1975

Brannigan ★★
The Girl from the Red Cabaret ★★

1976

Das Netz ★★
Il Corsaro Nero ★★

1977

Eaten Alive ★★

1978

La Ragazza in Pigiama Giallo ★★
The Norseman ★★
The Tempter ★★

1979

Guyana: Cult of the Damned ★★

1980

Hi-Riders ★★★
The Chorus Girls ★★★
The Visitor ★★★
The Fifth Floor ★★★

1981

Lili Marleen ★★★

SALLY FIELD
★★★ 3.25 STARS

Once little more than the butt of jokes because of her "Flying Nun" TV series, Sally Field is now a highly respected dramatic actress.

Field was born in Pasadena, California in 1946. Her wholesome, pert features typed her as a Sandra Dee replacement—she did, in fact, play "Gidget" on TV. Her first film, *The Way West*, was a ponderous epic despite powerhouse leads like Kirk Douglas, Robert Mitchum, and Richard Widmark.

Field fared much better in *Stay Hungry*, a close-up of the body building scene, capturing the intensity and dedication of training. Of the three engaging principals—Jeff Bridges, Arnold Schwarzenegger, and Field—her performance stood out.

Field was presented with her first enormous acting challenge in *Sybil*, a TV movie which kept critic Pauline Kael home from theatres because "Sally Field's performance went beyond anything I was likely to see." As Sybil, she fragmented into sixteen personalities, and her psychiatrist was beautifully played by Joanne Woodward (a former Oscar winner for her multi-personality part in *The Three Faces of Eve*.)

Popular success was insured with the box-office smash, *Smokey and the Bandit*, and Field's offscreen romance with Burt Reynolds also lent color to her public profile. The movie itself, a protracted chase, had high spirits to compensate for the absence of a script.

Heroes was severely damaged by Henry Winkler's coy, oddball portrait of a Vietnam veteran, though Field's charm nearly saved it. Harrison Ford was also outstanding.

Beyond the Poseidon Adventure met the fate of most sequels, but Field gave a superb, Oscar-winning performance as a feisty factory worker in *Norma Rae*. That success led to another fine drama, *Absence of Malice*, with Paul Newman. *Back Roads* was a backfire by *Norma Rae* director Martin Ritt. It seems likely she'll continue to please and surprise her fans and critics alike.

Sally Field in *Absence of Malice*.

FILMOGRAPHY

1967

The Way West ★★★

1976

Stay Hungry ★★★★

1977

Smokey and the Bandit ★★★
Heroes ★★★★

1978

The End ★★★

1979

Beyond the Poseidon Adventure ★★
Norma Rae ★★★★
Hooper ★★★

1980

Smokey and the Bandit II ★★★
Back Roads ★★★

1981

Absence of Malice ★★★★

1982

Kiss Me Goodbye ★★★

W. C. FIELDS
★★★½ 3.53 STARS

Supreme misanthrope, great drinker, hen-pecked husband, con man, and braggart—W. C. Fields was all these things and more. He created—and *was*—a character so unique that it defies description. His witticisms, his temperament, his gripes, and his pleasures have all passed wholesale into American folklore. His persona still exists to be laughed at, identified with, or borrowed, but it hides a sad personal story that is indelibly linked to Fields' accomplishments.

He was born William Claude Dukenfield in 1879, in Philadelphia, a city he later referred to with great contempt. His family was very poor, and he left home at age eleven after a violent argument with his father. He knocked him out with a heavy wooden box. He bummed around, stealing and sleeping in jails until he got a job as a tramp juggler at age fourteen. He worked hard and traveled extensively and was a vaudeville comedy star by the time he was twenty. At age twenty-two, he gave a command performance at Buckingham Palace. For the next 20 years, he dominated vaudeville and made increasing inroads on Broadway. He appeared in "Ziegfeld's Follies" and "George White's Scandals."

In the mid 1920s he began to make silent films. He was funny, but the absence of sound deprived him of his greatest weapons—Fields was always a primarily verbal comic. *Sally of the Sawdust*, *It's the Old Army Game*, and *Two Flaming Youths* were funny in the vein of contemporary fare, but not the vintage Fields that was to come. With

W. C. Fields.

the advent of sound, however, he devoted himself full time to filmmaking.

Through a series of classic and not-so-classic films, he developed the W. C. Fields persona. His character, typically, starts off as a man drained by imposing in-laws, family, and other pests. Too weak-willed to fight, he tries to sneak out back for a cigarette or bolster himself with a drink. After getting caught, he tries to fabricate a lie that's as thin as a potato chip. And when that doesn't work, he comes forth with an oily compliment on his wife's attentiveness. Among his cronies, he manages a cloak of self-deprecating importance by entertaining them with florid monologues on nonexistent adventures—often forgetting where it was that he left off.

His character made guest appearances in rambling films like *International House*, *If I Had a Million*, and *The Big Broadcast of 1938*, as well as being the focus of his films (often authored by Fields himself under fanciful pseudonyms like Charles Bogle, Mahatma Kane Jeeves, or Otis J. Criblecoblis). His best films were: *Tillie and Gus*, *It's a Gift*, *Poppy*, *You Can't Cheat an Honest Man*, *My Little Chickadee*, *The Bank Dick*, and *Never Give a Sucker an Even Break*. In the few occasions when he stepped out of character to play another role he was also endearing and excellent. He was Humpty-Dumpty in *Alice in*

Wonderland and Micawber in *David Copperfield*.

There apparently was no real W. C. Fields *behind* the character he played—he *was* that bitter, tortured, fearful, drunken sourpuss everyone laughed at. He took no pleasure from his success and gave the world much more than he received.

FILMOGRAPHY

(features only)

1924

Janice Meredith ★★★

1925

Sally of the Sawdust ★★★★

1926

That Royle Girl ★★★
It's the Old Army Game ★★★
So's Your Old Man ★★★

1927

The Potters ★★★
Running Wild ★★★
Two Flaming Youths ★★★

1928

Tillie's Punctured Romance ★★★
Fools for Luck ★★★

1931

Her Majesty Love ★★★

1932

Million Dollar Legs ★★★★
If I Had a Million ★★★★

1933

International House ★★★★
Tillie and Gus ★★★★
Alice in Wonderland ★★★★

1934

Six of a Kind ★★★★
You're Telling Me ★★★★
The Old-Fashioned Way ★★★★
Mrs. Wiggs of the Cabbage Patch ★★★
It's a Gift ★★★★

1935

David Copperfield ★★★★
Mississippi ★★★
The Man on the Flying Trapeze ★★★★

1936

Poppy ★★★

1938

The Big Broadcast of 1938 ★★★

1939

You Can't Cheat an Honest Man ★★★★

1940

My Little Chickadee ★★★★
The Bank Dick ★★★★

1941

Never Give a Sucker an Even Break ★★★★

1944

Song of the Open Road (cameo)
Follow the Boys (cameo)
Sensations of 1945 (cameo)

PETER FINCH
★★★ 3.21 STARS

Peter Finch was always attractive, dependable, and distinctive on the screen, yet his distant and detached manner prevented American audiences from responding fully to him. It took *Network* to release his passion, but before he could play other roles with the same gusto, he died suddenly of a heart attack.

Finch (William Mitchell) was born in London, in 1916. He was a comedian's foil in vaudeville, and then acted in the theatre. Laurence Olivier encouraged and nurtured him (though Finch later had an affair with Vivien Leigh while she was still married to Olivier). His first film was *Dave and Dad Come to Town*, and he appeared briefly in *The Miniver Story*, a limp sequel to the Oscar-winning original.

Elephant Walk trapped him as Elizabeth Taylor's troubled husband—the actors were outshone by the elephants. *A Town Like Alice*, a grim tale of Japanese soldiers victimizing British women, fared better artistically. *The Nun's Story* made Finch well-known in the United States. As Audrey Hepburn's sympathetic doctor, he supplied force to an impeccably crafted but rather subtle and quiet picture.

Finch was Angie Dickinson's love interest in *The Sins of Rachel Cade*. He won the British equivalent of the Academy Award for *The Trials of Oscar Wilde* and *No Love for Johnnie*. He also contributed a fine, obsessive characterization to *Far from the Madding Crowd*.

Sunday Bloody Sunday was writer Penelope Gilliatt's overly restrained handling of a dramatic situation—the love of a homosexual man and a career woman for a young boy. Finch's thoughtful performance didn't create much excitement though he won another BFA award and an Oscar nomination. *Lost Horizon* was an atrocious musicalization of the James Hilton classic. He was excellent in a Graham Greene thriller, *England Made Me*, and again in *Network*, winning a posthumous Best Actor Oscar.

Peter Finch in *Network*.

FILMOGRAPHY

1936

Dave and Dad Come to Town ★★★

1937

Red Sky at Morning ★★★

1938

Mr. Chedworth Steps Out ★★★

1942

The Power and the Glory ★★★

1946

A Son Is Born ★★★★
The Rats of Tobruk ★★★★

1948

Massacre Hill ★★★★

1949

Train of Events ★★★

1950

The Wooden Horse ★★★
The Miniver Story ★★★

1951

The Story of Robin Hood ★★★★

1953

The Story of Gilbert and Sullivan ★★★
The Heart of the Matter ★★★

1954

Elephant Walk ★★
Father Brown ★★★

1955

Make Me an Offer ★★★
The Dark Avenger ★★★
Passage Home ★★★★
Josephine and Men ★★★
Simon and Laura ★★★

1956

A Town Like Alice ★★★★
The Battle of the River Plate ★★★

1957

The Shiralee ★★★★
Robbery Under Arms ★★★

1958

Windom's Way ★★★

1959

Operation Amsterdam ★★★
The Nun's Story ★★★★

1960

The Trials of Oscar Wilde ★★★★
Kidnapped ★★★★

1961

The Sins of Rachel Cade ★★★★
No Love for Johnnie ★★★★

1962

I Thank a Fool ★★★

1963

In the Cool of the Day ★★

1964

The Girl with Green Eyes ★★★★
First Men in the Moon (cameo)
The Pumpkin Eater ★★★★

1965

Judith ★★

1966

The Flight of the Phoenix ★★★★
10:30 P.M. Summer ★★★

1967

Far from the Madding Crowd ★★★★
The Legend of Lylah Clare ★★★

1971

The Red Tent ★★★
Sunday Bloody Sunday ★★★

1972

Something to Hide ★★★

1973

Lost Horizon ★
England Made Me ★★★
The Nelson Affair ★★★

1974

The Abdication ★★

1976

Network ★★★★

ALBERT FINNEY
★★★ 2.88 STARS

"Albee's wonderful—that's all there is to it," said co-star Audrey Hepburn. Critics agreed; it seemed Finney could do anything and play any kind of modern or classical role. His one handicap to continuous stardom is a kind of grim seriousness, a lack of lightness and humor.

Finney was born in 1936, in Salford, England. He played "Julius Caesar," "Henry V," and "Macbeth" on the stage, and made a worldwide impact on the screen with *Saturday Night and Sunday Morning*—a superb depiction of a working class rebel. Finney followed it up with an even stronger film, *Tom Jones*. The erotically funny eating scene pleased the public, but *Night Must Fall* was a letdown—a drab reworking of Robert Montgomery's 1940s classic. Finney, however, played the psychotic murderer with conviction. He was also believable as Audrey Hepburn's philandering, self-centered husband in *Two for the Road*. The pair definitely had a certain chemistry between them.

Albert Finney in *Wolfen.*

Charlie Bubbles presented him as a bored playwright though boredom fell even more heavily on viewers. He made a musical, *Scrooge*, seemingly at home in the world of Dickens. Agatha Christie's Hercule Poirot should have been a Finney triumph, but he hid behind layers of makeup and an unintelligible accent in *Murder on the Orient Express*. Any suspense was buried under a torrent of talk. His hostile writer role in *Shoot the Moon* was a powerful performance even though it was hard to find motivations for the character's erratic, vicious behavior.

His Daddy Warbucks in *Annie* was easier to understand, but Finney—like Carol Burnett and the other cast members—was defeated by John Huston's heavy-handed direction. While he remained more than competent in fluff like *Wolfen* or *Looker*, one has to long for the meaty material he tackled with such ease in his youth.

FILMOGRAPHY

1960

The Entertainer ★★★
Saturday Night and Sunday Morning ★★★★

1963

Tom Jones ★★★★
The Victors ★★★

1964

Night Must Fall ★★★

1967

Two for the Road ★★★
Charlie Bubbles ★★

1969

The Picasso Summer ★★

1970

Scrooge ★★★

1971

Gumshoe ★★★

1973

Alpha Beta ★★★

1974

Murder on the Orient Express ★★

1977

The Duellists ★★★

1981

Wolfen ★★★
Looker ★★

1982

Shoot the Moon ★★★★
Annie ★★

CARRIE FISHER
★★★ 2.89 STARS

Carrie Fisher is a pert-looking younger version of her mother, Debbie Reynolds. She has her mother's charm and comedic skill as well as a sexual allure that Reynolds never displayed.

Fisher was born in 1956, in Los Angeles. She inherited her father's

(Eddie Fisher's) voice and made a strong impression in her mother's Las Vegas nightclub act. *Shampoo* gave her a striking bit role as the precocious daughter of Lee Grant. However, she became a household word when she played in *Star Wars*. She was cast as Princess Leia, a part she assumed again in the smash sequel, *The Empire Strikes Back*. There was a brief appearance in *I Wanna Hold Your Hand* and a larger one in the offensive and tasteless *Under the Rainbow* with Chevy Chase.

In her final *Star Wars* sequel, she makes a lovely transition from a bratty, tom-boyish soldier to a mature and feminine beauty. It's a role she can play with ease.

Carrie Fisher in *Shampoo*.

FILMOGRAPHY

1975

Shampoo ★★★★

1977

Star Wars ★★★

1978

I Wanna Hold Your Hand ★★★

1979

Wise Blood ★★★

1980

The Empire Strikes Back ★★★
Mr. Mike's Mondo Video ★★

1981

Under the Rainbow ★★
The Blues Brothers ★★★

1983

Return of the Jedi ★★★

BARRY FITZGERALD
★★★½ 3.37 STARS

Barry Fitzgerald was the very best of that grand Hollywood fixture, the lovable old codger. His Irish charm gave needed transfusions to many films, and he won an Oscar for *Going My Way* (even beating out Clifton Webb's brilliant performance in *Laura*).

Fitzgerald was born William Joseph Shields, in Ireland, in 1888. Hitchcock's *Juno and the Paycock* (1930) was his first screen part, and he cemented his reputation as "the movie colony's Irishman-in-Residence" (Ephraim Katz) with *The Plough and the Stars*. He added to the fun in *Bringing Up Baby* and shone in the memorable *How Green Was My Valley. Going My Way* was his most famous role as the elderly priest who gradually accepts Bing Crosby, but another performance was even more outstanding—the ingratiating villain who assembled a group of people on a remote island and bumped them off in *And Then There Were None*.

He was at his most lovable and his most codgerly in John Ford's Irish fantasy, *The Quiet Man. Welcome Stranger* offered an agreeable reunion with Crosby, and there were other effective characterizations in *The Naked City, Top O' The Morning,* and *The Catered Affair*. Fitzgerald died in 1961.

Barry Fitzgerald in *San Francisco Docks*.

FILMOGRAPHY

1930

Juno and the Paycock ★★★

1936

When Knights Were Bold ★★★

1937

The Plough and the Stars ★★★★
Ebb Tide ★★★

1938

Bringing Up Baby ★★★★
Marie Antoinette ★★★
Four Men and a Prayer ★★★
The Dawn Patrol ★★★★

1939

The Saint Strikes Back ★★★
Pacific Liner ★★★
Full Confession ★★★

1940

The Long Voyage Home ★★★★

1941

The Sea Wolf ★★★★
San Francisco Docks ★★★
How Green Was My Valley ★★★★
Tarzan's Secret Treasure ★★★

1943

The Amazing Mrs. Halliday ★★★
Two Tickets to London ★★★
Corvette K-225 ★★★

1944

Going My Way ★★★★
I Love a Soldier ★★★
None But the Lonely Heart ★★★★

1945

Incendiary Blonde ★★★★
Duffy's Tavern ★★★★
And Then There Were None ★★★★
The Stork Club ★★★

1946

Two Years Before the Mast ★★★

1947

California ★★★
Easy Come Easy Go ★★★
Welcome Stranger ★★★★
Variety Girl ★★★

1948

The Naked City ★★★★
The Sainted Sisters ★★★★
Miss Tatlock's Millions ★★★

1949

Top O' The Morning ★★★
The Story of Seabiscuit ★★★

1950

Union Station ★★★★

1951

Silver City ★★★

1952

The Quiet Man ★★★★

1954

Happy Ever After ★★★

1956

The Catered Affair ★★★

1958

Rooney ★★★

1959

Broth of a Boy ★★★

ERROL FLYNN
★★★ 2.77 STARS

No one who has seen Errol Flynn on the screen will ever be satisfied with the other Robin Hoods, Musketeers, and buccaneers that followed. He was *born* to defend maids in distress or romance princesses. In looking back, one can see that he was also far more than the "mediocre talent" that producer Jack Warner accused him of being.

His real background was as lively as the plots for his films. Born in 1909, in Tasmania, he prospected for gold, smuggled diamonds, and worked on ships. His first movies were B's—*Don't Bet on Blondes* and *The Case of the Curious Bride*—but he found his permanent niche early in *Captain Blood* and *The Charge of the Light Brigade,* one of several teamings with Olivia De Havilland. In *The Perfect Specimen,* he indicated his ease with comedy, and he returned to action films with the classic *The Adventures of Robin Hood.* His athletic grace and obvious joy in cavorting was infectious.

He was also excellent in a Bette Davis vehicle, *The Sisters,* but Davis refused to consider costarring with Flynn in *Gone With the Wind.* "I wasn't going to be part of that package," she claimed in her autobiography. Flynn would have been much more appropriate for the Rhett Butler role than Davis would have been for Scarlett.

He did two vigorous westerns, *Dodge City* with De Havilland and *Virginia City.* There was plenty of piracy and swordplay in *The Sea Hawk,* and he was a fine Custer in *They Died With Their Boots On.*

Despite his popularity, Flynn's much-publicized trial for statutory rape threatened to ruin his career. It didn't; like Robert Mitchum's jail sentence for smoking marijuana, it only added further notoriety and public interest. He immediately made *Desperate Journey,* a fast-moving war drama. He was a boxer in *Gentleman Jim* and a member of the Norwegian underground movement in *Edge of Darkness.* There were more action films, *Northern Pursuit* and *Objective Burma!,* and a thriller, *Cry Wolf,* with Barbara Stanwyck.

Errol Flynn in *Captain Blood.*

There were two more capable portrayals before Flynn's alcoholism went totally out of control: *Adventures of Don Juan* and *That Forsyte Woman.* In *That Forsyte Woman,* he was particularly believable in an uncharacteristic part—Greer Garson's cold, unforgiving husband. *Adventures of Captain Fabian, Mara Maru,* and *The Master of Ballantrae* were sad echoes of vanished glory.

Like John Barrymore before him, Flynn wound up his screen career playing drunks. He was only too convincing as a souse in *The Sun Also Rises,* and his portrait of John Barrymore in *Too Much Too Soon* was the sole asset of a bleak and artificial biography. His last picture was *Cuban Rebel Girls* with teenager Beverly Aadland, a lover in real life.

He looked seventy when he died but was, in fact, only fifty—one of the more extreme and pathetic cases of Hollywood disintegration. Errol Flynn lived out his screen image in real life. While he inevitably paid the price for his fast living, it made him all the more a complete matinee idol.

FILMOGRAPHY

1935

Murder at Monte Carlo ★★
The Case of the Curious Bride ★★
Don't Bet on Blondes ★★
Captain Blood ★★★

1936

The Charge of the Light Brigade ★★★★

1937

Green Light ★★★
The Prince and the Pauper ★★★★
Another Dawn ★★★
The Perfect Specimen ★★★

1938

The Adventures of Robin Hood ★★★★
Four's a Crowd ★★★
The Sisters ★★★
The Dawn Patrol ★★★

1939

Dodge City ★★★
The Private Lives of Elizabeth and Essex ★★★

1940

Virginia City ★★★
The Sea Hawk ★★★
Santa Fe Trail ★★★

1941

Footsteps in the Dark ★★★
Dive Bomber ★★★

1942

They Died With Their Boots On ★★★
Desperate Journey ★★★
Gentleman Jim ★★★

1943

Edge of Darkness ★★★
Thank Your Lucky Stars (cameo)
Northern Pursuit ★★★

1944

Uncertain Glory ★★★

1946

Objective Burma! ★★★
San Antonio ★★★
Never Say Goodbye ★★★

1947

Cry Wolf ★★★★
Escape Me Never ★★★

1948

Silver River ★★★
Adventures of Don Juan ★★★

1949

It's a Great Feeling (cameo)
That Forsyte Woman ★★★★

Errol Flynn in *Virginia City*.

1950

Montana ★★★
Rocky Mountain ★★★

1951

Kim ★★★
Adventures of Captain Fabian ★★

1952

Mara Maru ★★
Against All Flags ★★

1953

The Master of Ballantrae ★★

1954

Crossed Swords ★★
William Tell ★
Lilacs in the Spring ★

1955

The Warriors ★★
King's Rhapsody ★★

1956

Istanbul ★★

1957

The Big Boodle ★★
The Sun Also Rises ★★★★

1958

Too Much Too Soon ★★★
The Roots of Heaven ★★★

1959

Cuban Rebel Girls ★

HENRY FONDA
★★★ 3.15 STARS

When Henry Fonda died recently, the press covered the event as if a part of America itself had passed away. Indeed, it had. In his legacy of films, Henry Fonda created America's ideal image of itself: honest, forthright, sincere, and struggling to be moral. Even his villains contained the same elements of truth. Henry Fonda portrayed our presidents, our common men, our soldiers, and our heroes. He was a hero himself.

Fonda was born in 1905, in Grand Island, Nebraska. He scored on Broadway in "New Faces of 1934" and went to Hollywood for a film remake of his stage success, *The Farmer Takes a Wife*, with Janet Gaynor. *The Trail of the Lonesome Pine* was the first full-color feature filmed outdoors and revealed Fonda as an ideal western hero. *The Moon's Our Home* was forgettable fluff, only interesting today because it teamed Fonda with his one-time wife Margaret Sullavan.

He had his next big dramatic challenge in *You Only Live Once*, as an ex-con fleeing the law. *That Certain Woman* was a soap opera with Bette Davis, and both stars fought to make something of flimsy material. They had more luck in a much better picture, William Wyler's engrossing *Jezebel*. Davis won her second Oscar and most of the attention, but Fonda's quiet underplaying provided the necessary balance.

The Mad Miss Manton was a nice comedy with Barbara Stanwyck, but *Jesse James* was one of his best westerns. He was convincing in *The Story of Alexander Graham Bell*, though the movie is remembered as Don Ameche's one notable hour. Fonda dominated *Young Mr. Lincoln*, a part tailor-made for his just-folks, Americana style. He struggled in colonial America with Claudette Colbert in *Drums Along the Mohawk*. Then he made the movie that should have won him an Oscar, *The Grapes of Wrath*. Fonda's portrayal of Tom Joad was his best performance until *On Golden Pond. The Lady Eve* reaffirmed his mastery of comedy; he was the rich bumpkin taken advantage of by scheming Barbara Stanwyck.

In *The Ox-Bow Incident*, an uncomfortably believable study of lynch mentality, Fonda played the lone voice of reason. However, his role in *Daisy Kenyon* was more engaging, as a soldier who tried to win Joan Crawford from married Dana Andrews. He was also outstanding in a pair of John Ford westerns, *My Darling Clementine* and *Fort Apache*.

After playing "Mister Roberts" on Broadway for five years, Fonda did the film version as well. A huge hit at the time, it seems curiously static and labored now. His professionalism was the only asset of *Stage Struck*, and he was bland in *Advise and Consent*, an otherwise juicy political drama. He was considerably stronger in another political story, *The Best Man*. Much of his work in this period was politically or socially conscious: *12 Angry Men*, *The Wrong Man*, and *Fail Safe*. He was always able to convey the issues involved in human terms. In *Fail Safe*, that meant playing the President of the United States who must order a nuclear attack on the city where his wife is staying.

His sense of comedy added greatly to *Yours, Mine and Ours*, a potentially corny sitcom saved by deft performances from Fonda and co-star Lucille Ball. He also milked *The Cheyenne Social Club* for all it was worth, even croaking through a title tune, "Rolling Stone." He was a sadistic villain in *Once Upon a Time in the West*.

It was his daughter Jane Fonda who produced *On Golden Pond* and gave her father his final triumph. As the cranky and frightened husband of Katharine Hepburn confronting senility, Fonda gave a performance that ranked with the best of Bogart and Tracy. He won his long-overdue Oscar and died shortly after, mourned by the entire film world.

FILMOGRAPHY

1935

The Farmer Takes a Wife ★★★
Way Down East ★★★
I Dream Too Much ★★★

1936

The Trail of the Lonesome Pine ★★★
The Moon's Our Home ★★★
Spendthrift ★★★

Henry Fonda in *The Grapes of Wrath.*

1937

You Only Live Once ★★★★
Wings of the Morning ★★★
Slim ★★★
That Certain Woman ★★★

1938

I Met My Love Again ★★★
Jezebel ★★★
Blockade ★★★
Spawn of the North ★★★
The Mad Miss Manton ★★★

1939

Jesse James ★★★
Let Us Live ★★★
The Story of Alexander Graham Bell ★★★
Young Mr. Lincoln ★★★★
Drums Along the Mohawk ★★★★

1940

The Grapes of Wrath ★★★★
Lillian Russell ★★★
The Return of Frank James ★★★
Chad Hanna ★★★

1941

The Lady Eve ★★★★
Wild Geese Calling ★★★
You Belong to Me ★★★

1942

The Male Animal ★★★
Rings on Her Fingers ★★★
The Magnificent Dope ★★★
Tales of Manhattan ★★★
The Big Street ★★★

1943

The Immortal Sergeant ★★★
The Ox-Bow Incident ★★★★

1946

My Darling Clementine ★★★★

1947

The Long Night ★★★
The Fugitive ★★★
Daisy Kenyon ★★★

1948

On Our Merry Way ★★★
Fort Apache ★★★★

1949

Jigsaw (cameo)

1955

Mister Roberts ★★★

1956

War and Peace ★★★★

1958

The Wrong Man ★★★★
12 Angry Men ★★★★
The Tin Star ★★★
Stage Struck ★★★

1959

Warlock ★★★
The Man Who Understood Women ★★★

1962

Advise and Consent ★★★★
The Longest Day ★★★
How the West Was Won ★★★

1963

Spencer's Mountain ★★

1964

The Best Man ★★★★
Fail Safe ★★★★
Sex and the Single Girl ★★

1965

The Rounders ★★★
In Harm's Way ★★★
Battle of the Bulge ★★★
The Dirty Game ★★★

1966

A Big Hand for the Little Lady ★★★

1967

Welcome to Hard Times ★★★

1969

Firecreek ★★★
Madigan ★★★★
Yours, Mine and Ours ★★★★
The Boston Strangler ★★★★
Once Upon a Time in the West ★★★★

1970

The Cheyenne Social Club ★★★
There Was a Crooked Man ★★★
Too Late the Hero ★★★

1971

Sometimes a Great Notion ★★★

1973

The Serpent ★★★
My Name Is Nobody ★★★
Ash Wednesday ★★

1974

Mussolini ★★★

1976

Midway ★★
The Great Smokey Roadblock ★★★

1977

Rollercoaster ★★★
Tentacles ★★★
The Last of the Cowboys ★★★

1978

The Swarm ★★
Meteor ★★
Fedora (cameo)

1979

City on Fire ★★★
Wanda Nevada ★★★

1982

The Man Who Loved Bears (narration)
On Golden Pond ★★★★

JANE FONDA
★★½ 2.67 STARS

It's not easy to live up to a famous parent, but Jane Fonda has equalled her father Henry's ability as a film actor and in box-office terms has surpassed him. Henry himself commented in 1968, "She isn't good, she is sensational....the best actress of her generation."

Born in 1937, her career got off to a faltering start in two flop Broadway plays, "There Was a Little Girl" and "The Fun Couple." Things improved slightly when she debuted in Josh Logan's trivial *Tall Story* opposite Tony Perkins.

Her early parts showed individuality, but the movies (*Walk on the Wild Side* and *The Chapman Report*) were too much for any actress to overcome. *Period of Adjustment*, featuring her as the naive bride of Jim Hutton, gave a hint of her comic talent and *Sunday in New York* showed it in full bloom.

When she married director Roger Vadim, he tried to shape her career in the image of his former wife, sexpot Brigitte Bardot. *The Game Is Over* was one mediocre example of this conversion, but *Cat Ballou*, a hilarious western spoof, repaired the damage. She hit bottom again in Arthur Penn's steamy melodrama, *The Chase*, a film that screenwriter Lillian Hellman later described as the death of a dream.

Hurry Sundown, Otto Preminger's warped view of the south, was even worse, but *Barefoot in the Park* gave her funny Neil Simon lines, and she delivered them beautifully. There was more Vadim cheesecake in *Barbarella*.

By this time, audiences were more preoccupied with Fonda's radical political views than her acting. Her strident activism on behalf of Black Panthers and Indians put off the public, and her struggles to end the war had detractors labeling her "Hanoi Hannah." This sort of criticism undoubtedly cost her jobs, but she got a great role in *They Shoot Horses Don't They?* as the bitter, hopeless marathon dancer Gloria. In *Klute*, she gave one of the finest portrayals in motion picture history. She won an Oscar on the basis of her talent despite her radical reputation.

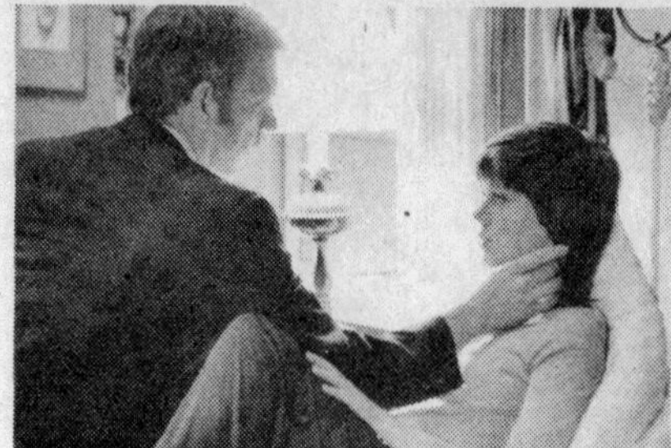

Jane Fonda with Donald Sutherland in *Klute*.

An all-star cast (Elizabeth Taylor, Ava Gardner, Cicely Tyson, and Fonda) went down with the Russian-made *The Blue Bird*, but *Julia* glowingly depicted Fonda as a girl who worshiped her activist friend (Vanessa Redgrave). *Coming Home* was a love story with a Vietnam background, but Fonda's Oscar-winning performance was better than the superficial screenplay. She ventured mild alarm to a reporter that the plots of her movies were "subservient to issues," and this description applied to the well-meaning but preachy *The China Syndrome*. *The Electric Horseman* was a pleasant western comedy with Robert Redford and *9 to 5* a foolish but funny tale of secretaries struggling with their boss.

Fonda then produced *On Golden Pond* and cast herself opposite her father. The film was her gesture of love to him, and audiences were deeply moved when they watched Jane and Henry, as battling father and daughter, stage a cinematic reconciliation. This was all the more poignant when remembering their years of conflict in real life.

Fonda will only grow. Like the indomitable Katharine Hepburn, she represents the independent woman. She is liberated, she is a fighter, yet she believes in standing beside her man. It's a modern example women will continue to applaud, enjoying exhibitions of the breathtaking Fonda talent in the meantime.

FILMOGRAPHY

1960
Tall Story ★★★

1962
Walk on the Wild Side ★★
The Chapman Report ★★
Period of Adjustment ★★

1963
In the Cool of the Day ★★

1964
Sunday in New York ★★★
The Love Cage ★★★
La Ronde ★★★

1965
Cat Ballou ★★★★

1966
The Chase ★★
The Game Is Over ★★★
Any Wednesday ★★★

1967
Hurry Sundown ★★
Barefoot in the Park ★★★★

Jane Fonda in *The Electric Horseman*.

1968
Barbarella ★★
Spirits of the Dead ★★

1969
They Shoot Horses Don't They? ★★★★

1971
Klute ★★★★

1972
F.T.A. (Free the Army) ★★★
Tout va bien ★★★

1973
Steelyard Blues ★★★
A Doll's House ★★★

1976
The Blue Bird ★★

1977
Fun With Dick and Jane ★★★
Julia ★★★★

1978

Coming Home ★★★★
Comes a Horseman ★★★
California Suite ★★★★

1979

The Electric Horseman ★★★
The China Syndrome ★★★

1980

9 to 5 ★★

1981

Rollover ★★

1982

On Golden Pond ★★★★

PETER FONDA
★★★ 2.89 STARS

When people think of Peter Fonda, they usually remember his feuds with his father or his well-publicized experiments with drugs. They rarely give much thought to his acting, yet Fonda appeared on Broadway at age twenty-two in "Blood, Sweat and Stanley Poole" and gave a comic performance that won over all the critics.

He was born in 1939, in New York City, two years after his sister Jane. *Tammy and the Doctor,* his first film, was bland and square, but he handled tougher material in *The Victors. Lilith* was a grim and unpopular close-up of mental patients. Fonda found his niche with *The Wild Angels* and *The Trip*. He defined the restlessness of his generation in *Easy Rider* (producing and writing as well as acting), though Jack Nicholson stole the spotlight in a supporting role. *Two People* cast him as a draft dodger in love with Lindsay Wagner, and he then went out west in *Wanda Nevada* with Brooke Shields.

His best performance came in a little-seen film called *Fighting Mad.* He played a loner who had to defend his family and his land against ruthless developers. Most of his movies since *Easy Rider* were mediocre, but it's only a matter of time until another notable part comes along.

Peter Fonda in *Fighting Mad.*

FILMOGRAPHY

1963

Tammy and the Doctor ★★
The Victors ★★★

1964

Lilith ★★★
The Young Lovers ★★★

1966

The Wild Angels ★★★

1967

The Trip ★★★

1968

Spirits of the Dead ★★★

1969

Easy Rider ★★★★

1971

The Hired Hand (direction) ★★★
The Last Movie ★★

1972

Two People ★★★

1974

Dirty Mary, Crazy Larry ★★
Open Season ★★

1975

Race with the Devil ★★
92 in the Shade ★★★
Killer Force ★★★

1976

Futureworld ★★★
Fighting Mad ★★★★

1977

Outlaw Blues ★★★

1978

High-Ballin' ★★★

1979

Wanda Nevada ★★★

1981

Triple Play ★★★

1982

The Cannonball Run ★★★

JOAN FONTAINE
★★★ 2.93 STARS

When Joan Fontaine began in films, she was a mousy, pallid creature, but her screen presence steadily gained in glamour and authority. Later roles were handicapped by a mannered coyness, but at her best she was "more versatile beneath the surface than her more famous sister, Olivia De Havilland," according to James Robert Parish in his book *The RKO Gals.*

Fontaine was born Joan de Beavoir de Havilland, in Tokyo, in 1917. Her sister Olivia De Havilland became a star first and Fontaine, with the competitive dedication so bluntly described in her autobiography *No Bed of Roses,* sought the same recognition. Fontaine was an inadequate partner for Fred Astaire in *A Damsel in Distress* and did a few pictures that nobody remembers including *Maid's Night Out* and *Blonde Cheat.* She was lost among the sharp-tongued principals, Joan Crawford and Rosalind Russell, in *The Women.*

Producer David O. Selznick decided to test her for *Rebecca,* and after a heated contest with rival applicant Anne Baxter, Fontaine won the part. She was superb as the timid, insecure girl who married Laurence Olivier and had to compete with the memory of his dead wife. *Suspicion,* made the following year, won her the Oscar she should have received for *Rebecca.* She had more fine roles in *The Constant Nymph, Jane Eyre,* and *The Affairs of Susan* which she tackled equally well. She was a murderess in *Ivy,* a slyly evil performance, and unforgettable as a young girl suffering unrequited love in Max Ophul's exquisite *Letter From an Unknown Woman.* The rest of her pictures varied sharply in quality, from the lush and enjoyable *September Affair* to the hokey *Island in the Sun.*

Her memoirs were brutally revealing (she called producer David O. Selznick a peddler of horseflesh), and she continued to pursue other interests—Fontaine is a golfer, licensed pilot, equestrienne, and interior decorator. She doesn't make movies now ("One of the reasons I stopped making pictures is so nobody could do to me what they did to poor Ray Milland in *Love Story.* He looked half dead...no toupee and those big closeups."). But *Rebecca, Suspicion, Letter From an Unknown Woman,* and *Ivanhoe* are classics that merit repeated viewing.

Joan Fontaine in *Kiss the Blood Off My Hands.*

FILMOGRAPHY

(billed as Joan Burfield)

1935

No More Ladies ★★

(billed as Joan Fontaine)

1937

Quality Street ★★
The Man Who Found Himself ★★
You Can't Beat Love ★★
Music for Madame ★★
A Damsel in Distress ★★★
A Million to One ★★

1938

Maid's Night Out ★★★
Blonde Cheat ★★
Sky Giant ★★
The Duke of West Point ★★★

1939

The Women ★★
Gunga Din ★★★
Man of Conquest ★★★

1940

Rebecca ★★★★

1941

Suspicion ★★★★

1942

This Above All ★★★

1943

The Constant Nymph ★★★★

1944

Jane Eyre ★★★★
Frenchman's Creek ★★

1945

The Affairs of Susan ★★★★

1946

From This Day Forward ★★★

1947

Ivy ★★★

1948

The Emperor Waltz ★★★
Kiss the Blood Off My Hands ★★★
Letter From an Unknown Woman ★★★★
You Gotta Stay Happy ★★★

1950

Born to Be Bad ★★★

1951

September Affair ★★★
Darling How Could You! ★★

1952

Ivanhoe ★★★
Something to Live For ★★★★

1953

The Bigamist ★★★
Flight to Tangier ★★★
Decameron Nights ★★

1954

Casanova's Big Night ★★★

1956

Serenade ★★★
Beyond a Reasonable Doubt ★★★

1957

Until they Sail ★★★★
Island in the Sun ★★★

1958

South Pacific (bit)
A Certain Smile ★★★

1961

Voyage to the Bottom of the Sea ★★★

1962

Tender Is the Night ★★★★

1966

The Devil's Own ★★★

GLENN FORD
★★★ 2.90 STARS

In his prime, Glenn Ford had an appealing tendency to underplay. He later carried this low-key sincerity to extremes as James Stewart sometimes does.

He was born Gwyllyn Samuel Newton Ford, in 1916, in Quebec. A contract with Columbia led to the films *Heaven with a Barbed Wire Fence, Convicted Woman,* and *Blondie Plays Cupid.* Ford's appeal was well captured in his first notable film, *So Ends Our Night,* a romantic anti-Nazi piece featuring Margaret Sullavan and Fredric March. He appeared with Rita Hayworth in *The Lady in Question,* but their chemistry didn't surface until *Gilda,* a sultry, erotic, and thoroughly enjoyable melodrama. Bette Davis requested him for *A Stolen Life,* and he was reunited with Hayworth a third time for *The Loves of Carmen.*

He was convincingly psychopathic as a trigger-happy sheriff in *The Man From Colorado,* and then the Ford-Hayworth combo sizzled one more time in *Affair in Trinidad.* This restraint also tensed up the time-bomb suspense of Fritz Lang's excellent thriller, *The Big Heat.* Ford's participation in *The Blackboard Jungle* was fortunate, since the movie acquired permanent relevance to a new rock-and-roll generation. "Rock Around the Clock" on the soundtrack was mainly responsible. In 1958, he was number one at the box office, and he sustained his popularity through 1959.

A reunion with Bette Davis in *Pocketful of Miracles* was depressingly maudlin, and most of his films afterward (*Love Is a Ball, Advance to the Rear,* and *The Money Trap,* his last with Hayworth) were either shabby dramas or strained comedies. He tried TV, appearing in "Cade's County" without success but showed up among several illustrious names in the episodic *Midway.* Today, Ford still does commercials and an occasional television feature.

FILMOGRAPHY

1939

Heaven with a Barbed Wire Fence ★★★
My Son Is Guilty ★★★

1940

Convicted Woman ★★★
Men Without Souls ★★★
Babies for Sale ★★★
Blondie Plays Cupid ★★
The Lady in Question ★★★

1941

So Ends Our Night ★★★★
Texas ★★★
Go West Young Lady ★★

1942

The Adventures of Martin Eden ★★★
Flight Lieutenant ★★★

1943

The Desperados ★★★
Destroyer ★★★★

1946

Gilda ★★★★
A Stolen Life ★★★★
Gallant Journey ★★★

1947

Framed ★★★

1948

The Mating of Millie ★★
The Loves of Carmen ★★★
The Return of October ★★★
The Man From Colorado ★★★★

1949

The Undercover Man ★★★
Lust for Gold ★★★★
Mr. Soft Touch ★★★
The Doctor and the Girl ★★★

1950

The White Tower ★★★
Convicted ★★★★
The Flying Missile ★★★

1951

Follow the Sun ★★★★
The Redhead and the Cowboy ★★★
The Secret of Convict Lake ★★

Glenn Ford in *Four Horsemen of the Apocalypse.*

1952

The Green Glove ★★★
Young Man with Ideas ★★★
Affair in Trinidad ★★★

1953

Terror on a Train ★★★
Plunder of the Sun ★★★
The Man From the Alamo ★★★
The Big Heat ★★★★
Appointment in Honduras ★★★

1954

Human Desire ★★★

1955

The Americano ★★★
The Violent Men ★★★
The Blackboard Jungle ★★★★
Interrupted Melody ★★★
Trial ★★★★

1956

Ransom ★★
Jubal ★★★
The Fastest Gun Alive ★★★
The Teahouse of the August Moon ★★

1957

3:10 to Yuma ★★★★
Don't Go Near the Water ★★★

1958

Cowboy ★★★
The Sheepman ★★★
Imitation General ★★
Torpedo Run ★★★

1959

It Started with a Kiss ★★★

1960

The Gazebo ★★★

1961

Cimarron ★★
Cry for Happy ★★
Pocketful of Miracles ★★

1962

Experiment in Terror ★★★
The Four Horsemen of the Apocalypse ★★

1963

The Courtship of Eddie's Father ★★★
Love Is a Ball ★

1964

Advance to the Rear ★★
Fate Is the Hunter ★★

1965

Dear Heart ★★★
The Rounders ★★★

1966

Rage ★★
The Money Trap ★★★
Is Paris Burning? ★★

1967

A Time for Killing ★★
The Last Challenge ★★

Glenn Ford with Ronnie Howard in *The Courtship of Eddie's Father.*

1968

Day of the Evil Gun ★★

1969

Smith! ★★★
Heaven with a Gun ★★★

1973

Santee ★★★

1976

Midway ★★★

1978

Goodbye and Amen ★★★
Superman ★★★

1979

The Visitor ★★★
Evening in Byzantium ★★

1981

Happy Birthday to Me ★★★

HARRISON FORD
★★★★ 3.27 STARS

Harrison Ford is an action hero with dimension—humorous, unpretentious, a superman who looks like an ordinary Joe. Many of his films have been gigantically popular, but his actual ability has hardly been tapped.

Ford was born in 1942, in Kansas City, Missouri, and began his career in the TV shows "Gunsmoke", "The Virginian", "Ironside", and "Leave it to Beaver." Nobody took much notice of him in the films *Dead Heat on a Merry-Go-Round, A Time for Killing,* and *Journey to Shiloh,* but critics singled him out in *American Graffiti.*

After playing in Coppola's artistically admired *The Conversation,* Ford hit pay dirt in *Star Wars.* He underplayed well in this lively comic strip that, incredibly, became

Harrison Ford in *Blade Runner*.

the biggest box-office grosser of its day. An even better performance—as the burned-out Vietnam vet in *Heroes*—was overlooked. His presence added freshness to *Force 10 From Navarone* and a dated love story, *Hanover Street*. He marked time with Gene Wilder in *The Frisco Kid* and then did *The Empire Strikes Back*.

Raiders of the Lost Ark was a breathtaking, fast-paced send-up of Saturday matinee serials, and even among the dizzying cinematic effects, Ford managed to retain his humanity. He went from the Orient to outer-space with *Blade Runner*, playing a film-noirish type who hunted down fake humans in a futuristic Los Angeles. In the long-awaited finale to the *Star Wars* trilogy, *Return of the Jedi*, his Han Solo predictably but entertainingly beat the bad guys and got the girl. Audiences await further adventures from this new matinee idol.

FILMOGRAPHY

1966

Dead Heat on a Merry-Go-Round (bit)

1967

A Time for Killing ★★★

1968

Journey to Shiloh ★★★

1970

Getting Straight ★★★

1973

American Graffiti ★★★

1974

The Conversation ★★★★

1977

Star Wars ★★★★
Heroes ★★★★

1978

Apocalypse Now ★★★
Force 10 From Navarone ★★★

1979

Hanover Street ★★★
The Frisco Kid ★★★

1980

The Empire Strikes Back ★★★

1981

Raiders of the Lost Ark ★★★★

1982

Blade Runner ★★★

1983

Return of the Jedi ★★★

JODIE FOSTER
★★★½ 3.27 STARS

As the motivation for John Hinckley's assassination attempt against President Reagan, Jodie Foster has had more than her share of lurid publicity. Throughout, she has maintained a graceful dignity, displaying the kind of maturity and strength so evident in her film appearances.

Foster was born in 1963, in the Bronx, New York. She was already performing at age three and appeared on the screen at nine in Disney's *Napoleon and Samantha* with Michael Douglas. In *Tom Sawyer*, she was cast as Mark Twain's Becky Thatcher—a warm and precocious performance in an engaging musical. The script in *Alice Doesn't Live Here Anymore* gave her less to do, but she stole all her scenes as Alfred Lutter's deep-voiced, older-than-her-years girlfriend.

In *Echoes of a Summer*, Foster bravely faced an agonizing death. Everyone else, including Lois Nettleton and Richard Harris, overacted, but she handled the sentiment straightforwardly. A few better scripts turned up, notably *Taxi Driver*, even though one flinched at her participation in the sordid events depicted—she was a teenage prostitute addicted to drugs. *Bugsy Malone* was a peculiar musical in which kids played gangsters. With the exception of Foster's performance, it all seemed forced and self-consciously clever. She returned to Disney for *Freaky Friday*, a shallow farce based on Mary Rodgers' best-seller about a mother and daughter who exchanged roles. Foster and Barbara Harris were funny in spite of the script contrivances.

She murdered Alexis Smith in a weak thriller, *The Little Girl Who Lived Down the Lane* and she continued to play older-than-her-years roles as a teenage rock 'n' roller in *Foxes*. A TV movie, *Svengali*, with Peter O'Toole, gave a recent indication that Foster will one day rise to the forefront of American actresses.

Jodie Foster in *Carny*.

FILMOGRAPHY

1972

Napoleon and Samantha ★★★
Kansas City Bomber ★★★

1973

Tom Sawyer ★★★★
One Little Indian ★★★

1975

Alice Doesn't Live Here Anymore ★★★★
Echoes of a Summer ★★★

1976

Taxi Driver ★★★★
Bugsy Malone ★★★

1977

Freaky Friday ★★★★
The Little Girl Who Lived Down the Lane ★★★
Il Cosotto ★★★
Moi, Fleur bleue ★★★

1978

Candle Shoe ★★★

1980

Foxes ★★★

1981

Carny ★★★

ANNETTE FUNICELLO
★★1.62 STARS

From the day she put on her Mickey Mouse ears, through her Beach Party film days to today, Annette Funicello has stood for wholesome, clean fun as much as Pat Boone or milk. The fact that she couldn't act any better than Pat Boone (or milk) has rather hampered her career, though.

Born in 1944, she was the last of the original Mouseketeers rounded up for "The Mickey Mouse Club" back in 1955. The popular TV show made her nationally known, as America watched her grow up into a teenager. When most of the original cast members faded from the spotlight, Funicello went on to greater heights as a recording artist and movie star.

When American International Pictures wanted to tap into the then-current teenage fad of surfing, they chose her to co-star with singing idol Frankie Avalon in a series of Beach Party movies which, by underestimating the intelligence of the average teen, made their makers rich. While the rest of the cast frolicked and went sex-crazy, it was Funicello's job to mumble inanities about love and marriage as she, in a clinging bathing suit, sang about Frankie. Though her scripts were awful, she performed the seemingly incredible feat of being worse than everybody else.

Annette Funicello as a Mouseketeer.

FILMOGRAPHY

1959

The Shaggy Dog ★★

1961

Babes in Toyland ★★

1963

Beach Party ★★

1964

The Misadventures of Merlin Jones ★★
Muscle Beach Party ★
Bikini Beach ★★
Pajama Party ★

1965

The Monkey's Uncle ★★
How to Stuff a Wild Bikini ★
Beach Blanket Bingo ★★

1966

Jet Breed ★
Fireball 500 ★★

1967

Thunder Alley ★

1968

Head (cameo)

CLARK GABLE
★★★ 3.12 STARS

No one else could have played Rhett Butler with Clark Gable's dash and virile charm. No other actor could have brought more magnetism and humor to *It Happened One Night*. However, despite all the cinematic evidence, critics still refer to Gable as a personality rather than an actor, but his accomplishments deserve better.

Gable was born in Cadiz, Ohio, in 1901 (although his first wife Josephine Dillon once put the birth date ten years earlier). For a "personality," he started off with solid acting crendentials in the theatre in "Love, Honor and Obey" and "The Last Mile." MGM, initially doubtful, finally put him under contract and cast him in two gangster movies, *The Finger Points* and *The Secret Six. Dance Fools Dance* with Joan Crawford started a screen partnership that continued amorously off the screen, despite the fact that they were both married. Crawford later remarked, "No matter how offhand he was about it, his career meant more than anything else." He worked hard to perfect his craft and made a powerful impression in *A Free Soul*, especially when he slapped Norma Shearer. He also proved a capable leading man opposite Greta Garbo in the steamy *Susan Lennox-Her Fall and Rise*.

Clark Gable.

He gained greater recognition in *Red Dust* with Jean Harlow and Mary Astor, playing an adventurer with blunt good humor. There were more hits: *No Man of Her Own* with Carole Lombard and *Dancing Lady*, with Joan Crawford. *It Happened One Night* was forced on him, and co-star Claudette Colbert was equally resentful. However, their chemistry jelled with Frank Capra's brisk direction and a witty script and captured both crowds and awards. He played a gangster again in *Manhattan Melodrama*, and a magnificent Fletcher Christian in the first, and best, version of *Mutiny on the Bounty*. He was voted The King of Hollywood in 1936 and then ironically had his worst failure with *Parnell*.

Gone With the Wind brought him his greatest fame. Everybody was superb (Leigh, De Havilland, and Howard) but Gable's Rhett Butler is the only portrayal that seemed fresh enough to have been filmed yesterday. He didn't win an Oscar, because his own studio promoted Robert Donat in *Goodbye, Mr. Chips* to boost that film's box office. *Strange Cargo* was his last film with Crawford, a peculiar adventure story with Ian Hunter as a modern Christ. *Boom Town* didn't exert any demand on his talent, although the all-star cast including Tracy, Colbert, and Lamarr, made it popular.

After the war his luck faltered, and he teamed incongruously with Greer Garson in the dreary *Adventure. The Hucksters* was a sharp satire of the ad game, but *Command Decision* was too talky to command public attention. He was a gambler in the tired *Any Number Can Play* and a racing car driver in *To Please a Lady* with Barbara Stanwyck. *Mogambo* brought him back—a colorful drama of extra-marital intrigue set in Africa. It was a remake of his *Red Dust* with Ava Gardner and Grace Kelly. A few mildly appealing comedies followed: *But Not for Me, It Started in Naples,* and *Teacher's Pet* with Doris Day. His final picture was *The Misfits,* Arthur Miller's windy and pretentious modern western. Among the notable cast, Marilyn Monroe, Montgomery Clift, Thelma Ritter, and Eli Wallach, Gable got the best reviews. He died shortly after.

Gable's image of total manhood may have been one of the chemical accidents of the screen. In real life, he was reputed to be a less-than-ideal lover; his third wife Carole Lombard admitted as much. However, it's still good to watch a male image unencumbered by neurosis, fear, or self-doubt. Even with the current emphasis on psychology, viewers need exposure to men who reflect their fantasies.

Clark Gable with Joan Crawford in *Possessed.*

FILMOGRAPHY

1931

The Painted Desert ★★
The Easiest Way ★★
Dance Fools Dance ★★★
The Secret Six ★★★
The Finger Points ★★★
Laughing Sinners ★★★
A Free Soul ★★★★
Night Nurse ★★★
Sporting Blood ★★★
Susan Lenox-Her Fall and Rise ★★★
Possessed ★★★★
Hell Divers ★★★

1932

Polly of the Circus ★★
Red Dust ★★★★
Strange Interlude ★★★
No Man of Her Own ★★★

1933

The White Sister ★★★
Hold Your Man ★★★
Night Flight ★★★
Dancing Lady ★★★★

1934

It Happened One Night ★★★★
Men in White ★★★
Manhattan Melodrama ★★★★
Chained ★★★
Forsaking All Others ★★★

1935

After Office Hours ★★★
The Call of the Wild ★★★
China Seas ★★★
Mutiny on the Bounty ★★★★

1936

Wife vs. Secretary ★★★
San Francisco ★★★★
Cain and Mabel ★★★
Love on the Run ★★★

1937

Parnell ★
Saratoga ★★★

1938

Test Pilot ★★★
Too Hot to Handle ★★★

1939

Idiot's Delight ★★★★
Gone With the Wind ★★★★

1940

Strange Cargo ★★★
Boom Town ★★★★
Comrade X ★★★

1941

They Met in Bombay ★★★
Honky Tonk ★★★

1942

Somewhere I'll Find You ★★★

1945

Adventure ★

1947

The Hucksters ★★★★

1948

Command Decision ★★★
Homecoming ★★★★

1949

Any Number Can Play ★★★

1950

Key to the City ★★★
To Please a Lady ★★

1951

Across the Wide Missouri ★★★
Callaway Went Thataway (cameo)

1952

Lone Star ★★★

1953

Never Let Me Go ★★★
Mogambo ★★★★

1954

Betrayed ★★★

1955

Soldier of Fortune ★★★
The Tall Men ★★★

1956

The King and Four Queens ★★★

1957

Band of Angels ★★★

1958

Run Silent Run Deep ★★★
Teacher's Pet ★★★★

1959

But Not for Me ★★★

1960

It Started in Naples ★★★

1961

The Misfits ★★★★

EVA GABOR
★★★ 2.76 STARS

Zsa Zsa Gabor fills up more gossip columns than her sister Eva, but Eva is the one with acting ability. The key to her success, however—her love of clothes, jewels, and men—is also her chief liability when it comes to gaining serious respect as an actress.

Reputedly born in 1924, in Budapest, as Sari Gabor, Eva began her career as a singer and professional ice skater and then won applause for her Broadway appearance in "The Happy Time". She was only a decoration in her first films, *A Royal*

Eva Gabor.

Scandal, The Wife of Monte Cristo, and *Paris Model,* but she proved strikingly effective in *The Last Time I Saw Paris* with Elizabeth Taylor. *My Man Godfrey* was an anemic remake of the sparkling original.

Gabor had her best role in Minnelli's classic *Gigi* as Louis Jourdan's two-timing mistress, and her comedic expertise proved an asset to *It Started With a Kiss* and *A New Kind of Love. Youngblood Hawke* conferred credit on no one, and after that, she did voice-overs for two Disney films, *The Aristocats* and *The Rescuers.* Eva is best known for her work with Eddie Albert in the TV series, "Green Acres," which is still popular in syndication.

FILMOGRAPHY

1941

Forced Landing ★★

1945

A Royal Scandal ★★★

1946

The Wife of Monte Cristo ★★

1949

Song of Surrender ★★★

1953

Paris Model ★★

1954

The Mad Magician ★★
The Last Time I Saw Paris ★★★

1955

Artists and Models ★★★

1957

My Man Godfrey ★★★
Don't Go Near the Water ★★★

1958

Gigi ★★★★
The Truth About Women ★★★

1959

It Started With a Kiss ★★★

1960

Love Island ★★★

1963

A New Kind of Love ★★★

1964

Youngblood Hawke ★★

1970

The Aristocats (voice only)

1977

The Rescuers (voice only)

1979

Nutcracker Fantasy ★★★

GRETA GARBO
★★★½ 3.67 STARS

Critic Bosley Crowther once wrote, "The mystique of Greta Garbo is such that the mere mention of her name, even among those people who weren't alive when she was active in films, triggers a flood of luxuriant and anomalous images that put in the shade most of the legends of other great and near-great movie stars." Greta Garbo is the movie star by which the term will always be defined.

Garbo (Greta Louisa Gustafsson) was born in 1905, in Stockholm. She grew up in a Swedish slum, and her father was a struggling laborer. A couple of film modeling jobs encouraged her to study acting at the Royal Dramatic Theatre training school. She was discovered there by Mauritz Stiller who was the pre-

Greta Garbo with the U.S.C. Swim Team.

eminent director of Swedish filmmaking at the time. Stiller cast her in *The Story of Gösta Berling,* and they began a Svengali-Trilby relationship ("I immediately noticed how easily one could dominate her by looking straight into her eyes," said Stiller).

Hollywood beckoned, in the form of Louis B. Mayer, and Garbo made her first MGM film, *The Torrent,* without Stiller. She inspired critical superlatives, and Stiller found himself in a humiliating, secondary position. Though he directed her second film, *The Temptress,* Stiller returned to Sweden two years later, in 1928, reportedly heartbroken over the unexpected turn of events. Garbo continued to blaze in *Flesh and the Devil, A Woman of Affairs,* and *Wild Orchids.*

Talkies came, threatening many a foreign star's career, but Garbo's voice had a husky magic that made her a natural for the new medium. *Anna Christie* was her introduction to sound films, and the ads read "Garbo Talks!" Gable was her leading man in *Susan Lenox-Her Fall and Rise,* and she danced a spell on Ramon Navarro as the spy *Mata Hari.* She never did say, "I vant to be alone"; a publicity man said it, and Garbo adopted the phrase as her trademark. No one was allowed on the sets of her pictures, including *Grand Hotel*—co-star Joan Crawford treasured the memory of the one tea they shared together. Other performers, like Bette Davis, idolized her talent, and so did her loyal fans.

Queen Christina was a somewhat stodgy, historical drama except for a famous close-up of Garbo at the end. *The Painted Veil,* a hokey tale of infidelity, was based on one of Somerset Maugham's hokier novels. She brought magnetism to these weak vehicles, however, a feat she accomplished again in *Anna Karenina.* She won a New York Critics Award but no Oscar, an omission historians still speak of with horror. Then Garbo played *Camille,* usually considered to be her best performance. She also played Marie Walewska opposite Charles Boyer's Napoleon in *Conquest.*

Her finest film featured her most atypical role. She played a cold and aloof communist in the delightful comedy *Ninotchka.* The witty script by Billy Wilder and Charles Brackett and smart direction finally gave her a vehicle worthy of her talents. She had been carrying inferior films on the strength of her magnetic presence for a decade.

Unfortunately, the failure of her next film, *Two-Faced Woman,* a weak imitation of *Ninotchka,* precipitated an early retirement. Quitting films at the height of her power only added to her mystique. Greta Garbo has continued to hold the rapt attention of film fans as she lives out the rest of her life in quiet seclusion.

Greta Garbo.

FILMOGRAPHY

1922

Luffar Peter ★★★

1924

The Legend of Gösta Berling ★★★

1925

Die Freudlose Gasse ★★★

1926

The Torrent ★★★★
The Temptress ★★★★

1927

Flesh and the Devil ★★★★
Love ★★★★

1928

The Divine Woman ★★★★
The Mysterious Lady ★★★★
A Woman of Affairs ★★★★

1929

Wild Orchids ★★★★
A Man's Man (cameo)
The Single Standard ★★★★
The Kiss ★★★★

Greta Garbo in *Queen Christina.*

1930

Anna Christie ★★★★
Romance ★★★★

1931

Inspiration ★★★★
Susan Lenox-Her Fall and Rise ★★★★
Mata Hari ★★★★

1932

As You Desire Me ★★★★
Grand Hotel ★★★

1933

Queen Christina ★★★

1934

The Painted Veil ★★★

1935

Anna Karenina ★★★★

1937

Camille ★★★★
Conquest ★★★

1939

Ninotchka ★★★★

1941

Two-Faced Woman ★★

AVA GARDNER
★★½ 2.67 STARS

"Everytime I tried to act they stepped on me," Ava Gardner once complained to Rex Reed. "They" was a euphemism for Louis B. Mayer, and judging by some of her scripts, Gardner was probably right. However, when she had a good role, she was haunting—a creature who embodied every male fantasy.

The woman Elizabeth Taylor once cited as the epitome of beauty was born in 1922, in Smithfield, North Carolina. She started inauspiciously at MGM in 1942, with a bit part in *We Were Dancing,* and nobody noticed her in *Calling Dr. Gillespie, Hitler's Madman,* and *Ghosts on the Loose.* She was still a decorative nonentity by the time she married and divorced her second husband Artie Shaw (Mickey Rooney was her first). The vehicle that established her as a star was *The Killers* with Burt Lancaster. It was a popular and critical success, but *Singapore* and *One Touch of Venus* failed to capture the smouldering sensuality that *The Killers* had ignited.

Gardner stood out as Clark Gable's friend in *The Hucksters* and was particularly striking in *East Side, West Side* as the "other woman" who broke up James Mason's marriage to Barbara Stanwyck. Her beauty carried viewers through the wordier passages of *Pandora and the Flying Dutchman,* and *Show Boat* was a marked improvement in material. Gardner was "exquisitely ravaged," according to critic Douglas McVay, as the tragic mulatto Julie. She was bitter when the studio forced her to dub her songs and even more bitter when they jeopardized her success by casting her in a Clark Gable western, *Lone Star.*

Gardner's best period began with *The Snows of Kilimanjaro;* she was Gregory Peck's unattainable love, and the movie caught Hemingway's particular flavor. Her performance was convincing though she mispronounced "Seine," a mistake critics have derisively referred to for 30 years. *Mogambo* was MGM's lusty remake of *Red Dust* with Gardner a knockout in the role originally slated for Gene Tierney. Later, in her biography, Tierney was quoted as saying, "I thought Ava Gardner stole the movie."

There was nothing to steal in *Knights of the Round Table,* but she was ideally cast in *The Barefoot Contessa.* Even though the censors forced Joseph Mankiewicz to compromise his script (the Count who kills Gardner, Rossano Brazzi, was a homosexual in Mankiewicz's original), the film remained powerful. Mankiewicz offended Gardner when he called her "the sittingest actress he'd ever worked with," but critics liked her performance.

The Little Hut was an unbearable comedy with Stewart Granger, and *On the Beach* was Stanley Kramer's bloated version of author Nevil Shute's tight, exciting novel about the end of the world. Gardner and co-star Gregory Peck were effective together, but the movie was one of Kramer's biggest flops. *Seven Days in May* was much better, and Gardner brought a much-needed earthiness to *The Night of the Iguana.* She didn't get along with Charlton Heston on the set of *Earthquake,* and it showed.

Gardner recently celebrated her sixtieth birthday and referred to herself as "an old broad." Maybe—but at one time she was the most electrifyingly glamorous of them all.

FILMOGRAPHY

1942

We Were Dancing (bit)
Joe Smith, American (bit)
Sunday Punch (bit)
Kid Glove Killer (bit)
This Time for Keeps (bit)
Calling Dr. Gillespie (bit)

1943

Pilot No. 5 (bit)
Ghosts on the Loose ★★
Hitler's Madman ★★
Du Barry Was a Lady (bit)
Reunion in France (bit)
Young Ideas (bit)
Lost Angel (bit)

1944

Swing Fever (bit)
Music for Millions (bit)
Three Men in White ★★★
Blonde Fever ★★
Maisie Goes to Reno ★★
Two Girls and a Sailor ★★

Ava Gardner with Laurence Naismith in *Mogambo.*

1945

She Went to the Races ★★

1946

Whistle Stop ★★★
The Killers ★★★★

1947

The Hucksters ★★★★
Singapore ★★★

1948

One Touch of Venus ★★★

1949

The Bribe ★★★
The Great Sinner ★★
East Side, West Side ★★★

1951

My Forbidden Past ★★
Show Boat ★★★★
Pandora and the Flying Dutchman ★★★

1952

Lone Star ★★★
The Snows of Kilimanjaro ★★★★

1953

Ride Vaquero! ★★★
The Band Wagon (cameo)
Mogambo ★★★★

1954

Knights of the Round Table ★★
The Barefoot Contessa ★★★★

1956

Bhowani Junction ★★★

1957

The Little Hut ★★
The Sun Also Rises ★★★

1959

The Naked Maja ★★★
On the Beach ★★★

1960

The Angel Wore Red ★★

1963

55 Days at Peking ★★

1964

Seven Days in May ★★★
The Night of the Iguana ★★★★

1966

The Bible ★★

1968

Mayerling ★★

1971

The Devil's Widow ★★

1972

The Life and Times of Judge Roy Bean ★★★

1974

Earthquake ★★

1975

Permission to Kill ★★★

1976

The Blue Bird ★

1977

The Cassandra Crossing ★★
The Sentinel ★★

1979

City on Fire ★★

1980

The Kidnapping of the President ★★

1981

Priest of Love ★★★

JOHN GARFIELD
★★★½ 3.44 STARS

John Garfield was "funky" long before Brando and had a street-smart exterior before McQueen. He was honest and believable and did wonders with several run-of-the-mill roles.

He was born Julius Garfinkle in New York, in 1913 and found his first recognition there on stage. The play was "Golden Boy" which led to a Warner Brothers contract and a hit film, *Four Daughters.* Two sequels followed, *Four Wives* and the underrated *Daughters Courageous.* Garfield's portrait of a fugitive boxer lent power to *They Made Me a Criminal,* but he could do little with the hackneyed prison story, *Castle on the Hudson. East of the River* was more formula prison stuff, but Garfield was superb in *The Sea Wolf* up against tyrannical Edward G. Robinson.

John Garfield.

He was excellent in *Pride of the Marines,* playing a blind ex-soldier. However, his first great film was *The Postman Always Rings Twice,* as the handyman who helped Lana Turner kill her husband. He made an entertaining contrast to the regal Joan Crawford in *Humoresque,* an outrageously corny but entertaining melodrama. Garfield was the sole authentic aspect of *Gentleman's Agreement* as Gregory Peck's Jewish friend, although critic Bosley Crowther, in a bizarre pronouncement, cited him as the only weak member of the cast. His prizefighter in *Body and Soul* merited its Oscar nomination and should have won.

During the McCarthy hearings he was blacklisted for suspected communist leanings. Garfield was reportedly heartbroken over his black listing. He loved acting and lost his will when he couldn't continue. He died in 1952, the first of the young rebel heroes and in many ways the best.

FILMOGRAPHY

1933

Footlight Parade (bit)

1938

Four Daughters ★★★★

1939

They Made Me a Criminal ★★★★
Blackwell's Island ★★★
Juarez ★★★
Daughters Courageous ★★★★
Four Wives ★★★
Dust Be My Destiny ★★★

1940

Castle on the Hudson ★★★
Saturday's Children ★★★★
Flowing Gold ★★★
East of the River ★★★

1941

The Sea Wolf ★★★★
Out of the Fog ★★★★

1942

Dangerously They Live ★★★
Tortilla Flat ★★★

John Garfield with Lana Turner in *The Postman Always Rings Twice.*

1943

Air Force ★★★
The Fallen Sparrow ★★★
Thank Your Lucky Stars ★★★

1944

Between Two Worlds ★★★
Destination Tokyo ★★★
Hollywood Canteen ★★★

1945

Pride of the Marines ★★★★

1946

Humoresque ★★★★
The Postman Always Rings Twice ★★★★
Nobody Lives Forever ★★★

1947

Body and Soul ★★★★
Gentleman's Agreement ★★★★

1948

Force of Evil ★★★★

1949

We Were Strangers ★★★

1950

Under My Skin ★★★
The Breaking Point ★★★★

1951

He Ran All the Way ★★★★

JUDY GARLAND
★★★½ 3.31 STARS

Judy Garland was a genius. It wasn't just her voice, although her singing could break your heart. It wasn't simply her dancing, even though she demonstrated enormous skill in her films with Fred Astaire and Gene Kelly. Critic Penelope Houston put it best when she wrote, "No one has been able to match the high-strung vitality, the tensely gay personality that made Miss Garland such a uniquely stimulating performer."

She was born Frances Gumm, in 1922, in Grand Rapids, Minnesota. She first attracted attention with her sisters in their singing act and was put under contract to MGM at the age of thirteen! Garland started out at MGM with Deanna Durbin in a short, *Every Sunday.* When Durbin's contract was accidentally allowed to lapse, Louis B. Mayer decided angrily, "I'll take this fat one, Garland, and make her a bigger star than Durbin." She charmed audiences and critics in *Listen Darling* and *Love Finds Andy Hardy* but almost lost *The Wizard of Oz* to Shirley Temple. Once she got it, her legendary status was assured. It still ranks as one of her greatest performances and perhaps *the* greatest performance by any seventeen-year-old.

Judy Garland.

Mary Astor, in her book A Life on Film, claimed that Garland was a giggly, normal teenager during these years, but her bitter fights with her mother ("the wicked witch of the West," in Garland's words) were escalating. Shattered romances with Artie Shaw and Joseph Mankiewicz undermined her confidence, though she had full command of herself on the screen. Her first co-starring nonjuvenile vehicle with Gene Kelly, *For Me and My Gal,* was one of the year's biggest hits, and *Meet Me in St. Louis* was, and still is, one of the most enchanting musicals in movie history. Garland was against the part until she was pressured by the studio, but she blossomed under Vincente Minnelli's direction. They later married, and he also directed *The Clock,* a nonmusical romance featuring another troubled soul, Robert Walker.

Judy Garland in *A Star Is Born.*

Her health problems were becoming public knowledge, and fans sympathized and cast her as the victim of a manipulative, exploitative studio. She had her first box-office failure with *The Pirate* but quickly bounced back in *Easter Parade.* An Irving Berlin score and Fred Astaire were added bonuses, and a follow-up with Astaire was planned in *The Barkleys of Broadway.* However, Garland collapsed and Ginger Rogers replaced her.

She gave one of her best performances in *In the Good Old Summertime,* but she failed to even show up during the shooting of *Annie Get Your Gun.* A highly publicized firing and suicide attempt gathered fans to her side, but after *Summer Stock* she and MGM parted company.

Before she died of alcoholism and drug addiction, there were a few more triumphs. Her in-person appearances drove audiences to the edge of hysteria, and she was magnificent in the powerful remake of *A Star Is Born* with James Mason. Lauren Bacall said that Garland was bitter that she lost the Oscar to Grace Kelly, and instinctively knew it was then or never.

There were no more great film roles. *A Child Is Waiting* was an unpopular drama about mongoloid children, and she was high-strung and actressy in director Stanley Kramer's *Judgment At Nuremberg. I Could Go On Singing* was a soap opera about an unwed mother's fight to reclaim her child. Garland shouted rather than sang her songs, but her acting was superb.

In tragic cases like Judy Garland's, one is tempted to "what if" about their careers. However, Garland's brilliant performances were born out of the personal problems that created her intensity. She might have had better luck, but her blazing-comet career could not have been altered.

FILMOGRAPHY

1936

Pigskin Parade ★★★

1937

Broadway Melody of 1938 ★★★
Thoroughbreds Don't Cry ★★★

1938

Everybody Sing ★★★
Love Finds Andy Hardy ★★★
Listen Darling ★★★

1939

The Wizard of Oz ★★★★
Babes In Arms ★★★

1940

Andy Hardy Meets Debutante ★★★
Strike Up the Band ★★★
Little Nellie Kelly ★★★

1941

Ziegfeld Girl ★★★★
Life Begins for Andy Hardy ★★★

1942

Babes On Broadway ★★★
For Me and My Gal ★★★★

1943

Presenting Lily Mars ★★★
Thousands Cheer ★★★
Girl Crazy ★★★

1944

Meet Me in St. Louis ★★★★

Judy Garland in *The Wizard of Oz.*

1945

The Clock ★★★★

1946

The Harvey Girls ★★★★
Ziegfeld Follies ★★★
Till the Clouds Roll By ★★★

1947

The Pirate ★★★
Easter Parade ★★★★
Words and Music ★★★

1949

In the Good Old Summertime ★★★★

1950

Summer Stock ★★★★

1954

A Star Is Born ★★★★

1960

Pepe (cameo)

1961

Judgment At Nuremberg ★★

1962

Gay Purr-ee (voice only)

1963

A Child Is Waiting ★★★
I Could Go On Singing ★★★★

JAMES GARNER
★★★ 3.03 STARS

Whether pitching cameras for Polaroid, riding a horse, or sparring with Doris Day, James Garner is one of the most lethargically agreeable presences on film or television. He's Bing Crosby with sex appeal.

Garner (James Baumgarner) was born in 1928, in Norman, Oklahoma. He was awarded the Purple Heart while serving in Korea and then worked as a male model. The TV show "Maverick" made him a star, establishing his genial, unaffected persona. His film career began with *Toward the Unknown* and *The Girl He Left Behind* although neither these nor *Shoot-Out at Medicine Bend* did much for his movie career.

He was effective as the lead opposite Natalie Wood in a weak comedy about finance, *Cash McCall*, and believable as Audrey Hepburn's boyfriend in Wyler's pallid remake of *The Children's Hour.* He finally got his star-making part in director John Sturges' exciting *The Great Escape.* It was a box-office bonanza, and Garner followed it with another hit, *The Thrill of It All.* The film was Doris Day's best comedy and a hilarious spoof of the ad game. *Move Over, Darling* was one of her worst although the Day-Garner team rode smoothly over the rough spots.

Garner played a likable and logical military coward in writer Paddy Chayefsky's *The Americanization of Emily* and was the only leading man to bring out Julie Andrew's sexuality. (He did it again in 1982's *Victor Victoria.)* After he completed the fine thriller *36 Hours*, the quality of his pictures dropped for a while *(The Art of Love, Duel at Diablo, How Sweet It Is*, and the unbearable *Mister Buddwing.) Support Your Local Sheriff* turned the tide, and Garner reaffirmed his reputation as King of TV with the long-running "The Rockford Files."

He continues to ply his affable manner with ease. One suspects he will age admirably into character parts.

FILMOGRAPHY

1956

The Girl He Left Behind ★★
Toward the Unknown ★★★

1957

Sayonara ★★★
Shoot-Out at Medicine Bend ★★★

1958

Darby's Rangers ★★★

1959

Up Periscope ★★★

1960

Cash McCall ★★★

1962

The Children's Hour ★★★★
Boys' Night Out ★★★

1963

Move Over, Darling ★★
The Great Escape ★★★★
The Thrill of It All ★★★★
The Wheeler Dealers ★★

1964

The Americanization of Emily ★★★★

1965

36 Hours ★★★
The Art of Love ★★

James Garner in *Marlowe.*

1966

A Man Could Get Killed ★★★
Duel at Diablo ★★★
Mister Buddwing ★★
Grand Prix ★★★

1967

Hour of the Gun ★★★

1968

How Sweet It Is ★★★
The Pink Jungle ★★★

1969

Marlowe ★★★
Support Your Local Sheriff ★★★

1970

A Man Called Sledge ★★★

1971

Skin Game ★★★★
Support Your Local Gunfighter ★★★

1972

They Only Kill Their Masters ★★★

1973

One Little Indian ★★★

1974

The Castaway Cowboy ★★★

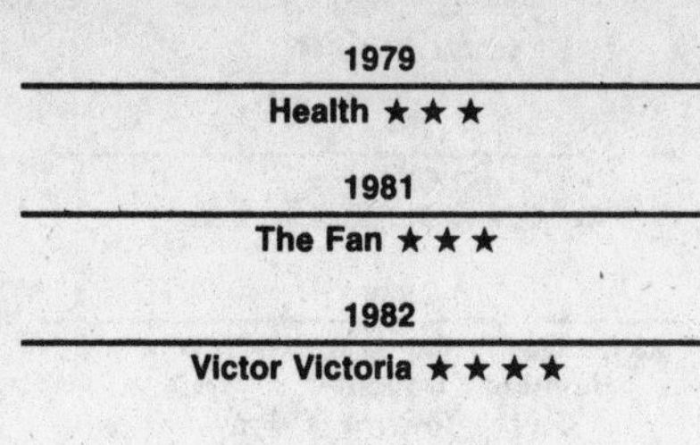

1979

Health ★★★

1981

The Fan ★★★

1982

Victor Victoria ★★★★

TERI GARR
★★★ 3.06 STARS

A lively, natural, unstagy performer, Teri Garr lights up the screen whenever she appears.

Garr came from a show business family—her father (Eddie Garr) was an actor-comic and her mother (Phyllis Lind) was a Rockette. Born in 1952, in Lakewood, Ohio, she attended dancing school though her parents were dead set against her theatrical aspirations. Garr did a Los Angeles tour of "West Side Story," commercials, and finally TV ("Star Trek," "The Sonny and Cher Show," and "McCloud"), maintaining a determined and positive attitude.

Her first movie was the offbeat *Head* ("I played a girl who died of a snake bite") and she went on to do *Young Frankenstein* although she had wanted the part Madeline Kahn finally played. It brought some critical and public attention, and more good films followed including: *Close Encounters of the Third Kind, One From the Heart* (a romantic but unsuccessful love story), and *The Sting II*.

Teri Garr with Jackie Gleason in *The Sting II.*

Her own attitude about men was perfectly consistent with the Oscar-nominated part she played in *Tootsie* ("I got my pain from men—I was always in love and these boyfriends would treat me bad or leave me after one night"). Dustin Hoffman was the one who left her in the picture, and her reactions were both comedic and touching.

Garr once again exhibited her mastery of light comedy in the delightful *Mr. Mom*. Though co-star Michael Keaton stole the film, she showed an intelligent awareness of when to underplay and when to grab her laugh. Garr's versatility is already admirable and she's just beginning.

FILMOGRAPHY

1968

Head (bit)

1969

Changes ★★★

1970

The Moonshine War ★★★

1975

Young Frankenstein ★★★★
The Conversation ★★★★

1976

Won Ton Ton - the Dog Who Saved Hollywood ★★★

1977

Close Encounters of the Third Kind ★★★
Oh God! ★★★

1979

Mr. Mike's Mondo Video ★★
The Black Stallion ★★★

1981

Honky Tonk Freeway ★★★

1982

Tootsie ★★★★
One From the Heart ★★★
The Escape Artist ★★★

1983

Mr. Mom ★★★
The Sting II ★★
The Black Stallion Returns ★★★

BETTY GARRETT
★★★½ 3.29 STARS

Betty Garrett was a bright, witty and vivacious presence in musicals. Her sharp wit and effervescent talent allowed her to poke fun at her average looks. She was a comedienne in the vein of Fanny Brice.

Born in 1919, in St. Joseph, Missouri, she started acting in her teens. She acted with the Mercury Theater, danced with Martha Graham, and sang in nightclubs. When Betty Garrett conquered Broadway in "Call Me Mister," it was inevitable that movies would come begging, and they did. In her second film, *Words and Music*, she brought humanity to a highly fictional character, the girlfriend of lyricist Larry Hart (Mickey Rooney). She was joyously energetic in *On The Town* as a pushy lady cab driver who pursued Frank Sinatra. She was equally engaging chasing Sinatra again in *Take Me Out to the Ballgame*, singing "It's Fate, Baby, It's Fate."

Unfortunately, fate was cruel to Garrett off the screen. Her actor husband Larry Parks (*The Jolson Story*) was branded a communist in 1951, and Garrett's career collapsed along with his. Four years later, she returned long enough to steal *My Sister Eileen* from Janet Leigh. Since then, viewers can only enjoy her on TV in "All in the Family" and "Laverne and Shirley" and regret the circumstances that deprived musical movies of an enduring superstar.

Betty Garrett.

FILMOGRAPHY

1948

Big City ★★
Words and Music ★★★★

1949

Take Me Out to the Ballgame ★★★★
Neptune's Daughter ★★★
On the Town ★★★★

1955

My Sister Eileen ★★★

1957

The Shadow on the Window ★★★

GREER GARSON
★★★ 2.88 STARS

During her days as Queen of the MGM lot (1940-1946), Greer Garson was the epitome of noble, self-sacrificing charm. She acted impeccably in a series of handsome, if synthetic, costume dramas, but her roles became dated after films adopted a new, postwar realism.

Garson was born in 1908, in County Down, Ireland. She appeared on stage in "Twelfth Night" and "School for Scandal" and made her movie debut in *Goodbye, Mr. Chips*. She confided to columnists that "it's a very small role, and my friends will think I'm a failure," but world fame resulted instead.

Garson was a perfect Elizabeth Bennett in *Pride and Prejudice*, one of the few film versions of a classic that did justice to its source. In *Mrs. Miniver,* she was typecast as a strong, capable wife who remained unruffled, whether confronting a lazy maid or a murderous Nazi. She was at her best in *Random Harvest*, playing the wife whom Ronald Colman didn't remember. After three more big hits, *Madame Curie*, *Mrs. Parkington*, and *The Valley of Decision*, she was sabotaged by poor films. *Desire Me* prompted director George Cukor to remove his name from the credits and *The Miniver Story* was a lame and teary sequel to the original. By this time Garson was affecting "great lady" speech patterns and mannerisms, a tendency that was particularly jarring in the western *Strange Lady in Town*. *Sunrise at Campobello* accommodated these pretensions more comfortably as she played Eleanor Roosevelt.

Some actors are frozen in time more rigidly than others. To appreciate Garson's grace and beauty, one has to see her for what she was—an elegant but impossible ideal for war-weary audiences who wanted to escape reality through their cinematic idols.

Greer Garson in *Random Harvest*.

FILMOGRAPHY

1939

Goodbye, Mr. Chips ★★★★
Remember? ★★

1940

Pride and Prejudice ★★★★

1941

Blossoms in the Dust ★★★
When Ladies Meet ★★★

1942

Mrs. Miniver ★★★★
Random Harvest ★★★★

1943

The Youngest Profession ★★★
Madame Curie ★★★

1944

Mrs. Parkington ★★★

1945

The Valley of Decision ★★★

1946

Adventure ★★

1947

Desire Me ★★

1948

Julia Misbehaves ★★★

1949

That Forsyte Woman ★ ★ ★

1950

The Miniver Story ★ ★

1951

The Law and the Lady ★ ★

1953

Julius Caesar ★ ★ ★
Scandal at Scourie ★ ★ ★

1954

Her Twelve Men ★ ★ ★

1955

Strange Lady in Town ★ ★

1960

Sunrise at Campobello ★ ★ ★
Pepe ★ ★ ★

1966

The Singing Nun ★ ★

1967

The Happiest Millionaire ★ ★

JANET GAYNOR
★ ★ ★ 3.11 STARS

Janet Gaynor always tended to be overly sentimental but her wholesome charm appealed to the audiences of the 1930s.

Gaynor (Laura Gainor) was born in 1906, in Philadelphia. After making shorts and two-reelers, she landed a good part in *The Johnstown Flood*. A ghost story, *The Return of Peter Grimm*, increased her popularity, and *Seventh Heaven* made her an automatic box-office draw. She played a Paris streetwalker redeemed by sewer worker Charles Farrell. They quickly co-starred in another hit, *Street Angel*. Gaynor had a solo triumph in *Sunrise*, as a wife who lost her husband. These three performances were rewarded with an Oscar in 1928.

Gaynor sang in *Sunny Side Up*, played a junkie in *The Man Who Came Back*, and secured more hits with Charles Farrell in *Merely Mary Ann, Delicious*, and *The First Year*. Gaynor starred in the first of three versions of *State Fair*—she was appealing, but the homespun folksiness got a little thick. Her loyal hankie-holding fans began defecting

Janet Gaynor with Charles Farrell in *Seventh Heaven.*

after *Servants' Entrance* with Lew Ayres and *The Farmer Takes a Wife* with Henry Fonda, but Janet Gaynor had one final triumph left. The 1937 version of *A Star Is Born* brought her an Oscar nomination, and her performance still brings tears to the eyes of soap opera fans. She *was* convincing, but anyone who has seen Judy Garland's Vicki Lester would have to rank Gaynor second.

Gaynor retired in 1940 and returned only once—as Pat Boone's mother in *Bernadine*. Her performance indicated that retirements, once undertaken, should sometimes be permanent.

FILMOGRAPHY

1926

The Johnstown Flood ★ ★ ★
The Shamrock Handicap ★ ★ ★
The Midnight Kiss ★ ★ ★
The Blue Eagle ★ ★ ★
The Return of Peter Grimm ★ ★ ★

1927

Seventh Heaven ★ ★ ★ ★
Sunrise ★ ★ ★ ★
Two Girls Wanted ★ ★ ★

1928

Street Angel ★ ★ ★ ★
Four Devils ★ ★ ★

1929

Christina ★ ★ ★
Sunny Side Up ★ ★ ★
Lucky Star ★ ★ ★
The River ★ ★ ★ ★

1930

High Society Blues ★ ★ ★
Happy Days ★ ★ ★

1931

The Man Who Came Back ★ ★ ★
Daddy Long Legs ★ ★ ★ ★
Merely Mary Ann ★ ★ ★
Delicious ★ ★ ★

1932

The First Year ★ ★ ★
Tess of the Storm Country ★ ★ ★

1933

State Fair ★ ★ ★
Adorable ★ ★ ★
Paddy the Next Best Thing ★ ★ ★

1934

Carolina ★ ★ ★
Change of Heart ★ ★ ★
Servants' Entrance ★ ★ ★

1935

One More Spring ★ ★ ★
The Farmer Takes a Wife ★ ★ ★

1936

Small Town Girl ★ ★ ★
Ladies in Love ★ ★ ★

1937

A Star Is Born ★ ★ ★

1938

Three Loves Has Nancy ★ ★ ★
The Young in Heart ★ ★ ★ ★

1957

Bernadine ★

BEN GAZZARA
★ ★ ★ 3.14 STARS

After a strong start, Ben Gazzara's movie career ran out of steam. The trouble isn't his acting, which is always good, but his material. He seems to lack judgment in choosing scripts.

New York-born in 1930, Gazzara had two Broadway hits, "Cat on a Hot Tin Roof" and "A Hatful of Rain," and performed superbly in both. He played a sadistic cadet in his first film, *The Strange One*, and although he gave another great performance, the film was too depressing for mass interest. He was equally unlikable as the defendant saved by James Stewart in *Anatomy of a Murder.* He was good in *The Young Doctors*, though the film was an ordinary soap opera.

Gazzara's well-executed performance in *A Rage to Live*, as the victim of nympho Suzanne Pleshette,

Ben Gazzara in *Capone.*

was lost amid critical hatchet jobs for the film itself. He "improvised" in John Cassavetes' meandering *Husbands* and fought the gangster movie clichés in *Capone*.

He was truly excellent in two Peter Bogdanovich features, *Saint Jack* and *They All Laughed*, but they both bombed at the box office and no one saw his performances.

Sidney Sheldon's Bloodline, a big-budget version of the Sidney Sheldon best-seller, should have stopped the run of bad luck, but direction and script were pure cardboard.

Gazzara has a relaxed manner and a weathered face that seems to hint at experience. He'll be a marvelous leading man if he ever finds a hit.

FILMOGRAPHY

1957

The Strange One ★★★★

1959

Anatomy of a Murder ★★★★

1960

The Passionate Thief ★★★

1961

The Young Doctors ★★★

1962

Convicts Four ★★★
Conquered City ★★★

1965

A Rage to Live ★★★

1970

The Bridge at Remagen ★★★
Husbands ★★

1973

The Neptune Factor ★★★

1975

Capone ★★★

1976

The Killing of a Chinese Bookie ★★★
Voyage of the Damned ★★★

1978

The Sicilian Connection ★★★
High Velocity ★★★
Opening Night ★★★

1979

Saint Jack ★★★★
Sidney Sheldon's Bloodline ★★★

1981

They All Laughed ★★★★

1982

Inchon ★★★

1983

Tales of Ordinary Madness ★★★

RICHARD GERE
★★★ 3.00 STARS

The major sex symbol of the 1980s appears to be Richard Gere. Gere's appeal is not merely good looks but animal sexuality with a threat built into it. Newsweek said, "He first made his name synonymous with erotic danger in *Looking for Mr. Goodbar,* leaping across Diane Keaton's bedroom in a jockstrap with phallic knife in hand. No one expresses more clearly . . . the delights of violence, the overtones of a semiconscious sadism . . . which is the basis of American sex appeal."

Gere was born in Syracuse, New York, in 1949. He played a pimp in his first movie, *Report to the Commissioner,* and had his first important lead in the photographically beautiful but dramatically thin *Days of Heaven.* His chilling portrayal of a homosexual Nazi victim in Broadway's "Bent" was the first indication of his explosive power. Gere's borderline psychotic in *Looking for Mr. Goodbar* was the only element that suggested the tawdriness of the novel, and he also stole *Bloodbrothers* as a young man trying to cut loose from his family. He took on a conventional romantic role in John Schlesinger's *Yanks.* The script was low-key and listless, but his performance as the soldier afraid to get involved with Lisa Eichhorn struck the sole note of passion in the picture.

American Gigolo seemed to be a perfect vehicle for Gere to finally establish his star power, but the dialogue and direction were glossy and pretentious. The movie that finally highlighted his uniqueness was *An Officer and a Gentleman.* As the slum kid who joined the service and fought to become an officer, Gere was brilliant. He was inexplicably overlooked in the Oscar race, although co-stars Debra Winger and Lou Gossett, Jr. were both nominated and Gossett won. Gere was sensitive in the love scenes and heart-wrenching when he broke down in tears before Gossett, sobbing, "I've got no place to go!" But after *Officer* and the hyperactive *Breathless,* Gere is going only one place, and that's up.

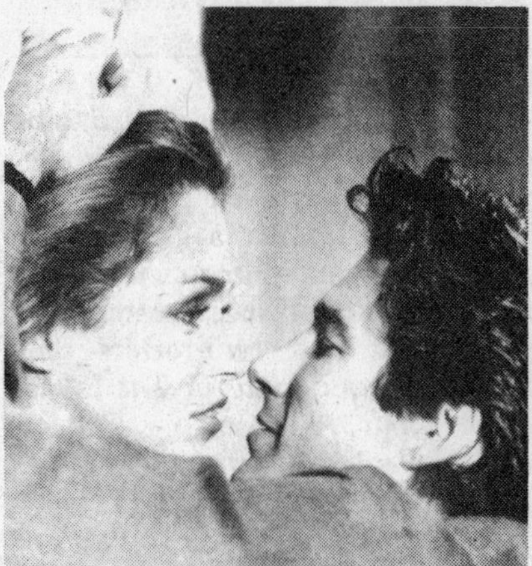

Richard Gere with Lauren Hutton in *American Gigolo.*

FILMOGRAPHY

1975

Report to the Commissioner ★★

1976

Baby Blue Marine ★★

1977

Looking for Mr. Goodbar ★★★★

1978

Days of Heaven ★★★
Bloodbrothers ★★★★

1979

Yanks ★★★
American Gigolo ★★★

1982

An Officer and a Gentleman ★★★★

1983

Breathless ★★

MEL GIBSON
★★★ 3.17 STARS

Road Warrior has been compared to the classic western *Shane*, and it's easy to compare Mel Gibson to the young Alan Ladd. Gibson projects both vulnerability and toughness, classic traits of romantic heroes.

Although he is known as the most promising actor to come out of the New Australian Cinema, Mel Gibson is actually an American citizen. Born in upstate New York in 1956, the sixth of eleven children, he emigrated with his railroad worker father to Australia at the age of twelve. After high school, he studied at Australia's National Institute of Dramatic Art. Gibson prefers stage to film acting. He won Australia's best-new-talent award for his role in *Tim*. His introduction to a wide American audience came with *Mad Max*, a futuristic road western, and its sequel *Road Warrior*. He played a soldier in *Gallipoli* and a journalist in turbulent Jakarta in *The Year of Living Dangerously*. Most of his films thus far have cast him as an inexperienced but charming young man who is hardened by his experiences in the cruel world. But he seems destined to become one of the the major romantic leads of the 1980s.

Mel Gibson in *Road Warrior*.

FILMOGRAPHY

1979

Tim ★★★

1980

Mad Max ★★★

1981

Attack Force Z ★★★
Gallipoli ★★★

1982

Road Warrior ★★★★

1983

The Year of Living Dangerously ★★★

JOHN GIELGUD
★★★½ 3.42 STARS

In the Celebrity Register, John Gielgud was quoted as saying, "I've at last learned to relax. The emotional crises are finished so one can concentrate more on one's work which is all, finally, I care about." This dedication has been responsible for a breathtaking gallery of characterizations.

Gielgud was born in 1904, in London. By his mid-twenties, he was regarded as one of the foremost interpreters of Shakespeare. His film career began with a couple of silents, *Who Is the Man?* and *The Clue of the New Pin*. He had an excellent part in the Hitchcock thriller *Secret Agent*, with Madeleine Carroll, and in 1941 he was Disraeli in *The Prime Minister*.

Gielgud was absent from the screen for 12 years until he returned to play in a series of Shakespearean adaptations: *Julius Caesar, Richard III*, and *Romeo and Juliet*, which he narrated. He stole *The Barretts of Wimpole Street* as Elizabeth Barrett Browning's dictatorial father. There was a cameo in *Around the World in 80 Days*, and he was the only authoritative and authentic thing about Otto Preminger's *Saint Joan*, the film fiasco that nearly wrecked Jean Seberg's career at the outset.

John Gielgud with Diana Wynward in *The Prime Minister*.

Gielgud participated in another version of *Julius Caesar*, this time playing the title role. He also tried, without success, to pump life into the stillborn *Lost Horizon* and the equally bloodless *11 Harrowhouse* and *Murder on the Orient Express*. He was brilliant, though, in the enigmatic *Providence*.

It took *Arthur* to rescue him from anemic, uncommercial enterprises. He was superb as Dudley Moore's wry and understanding butler, and for the first time an Oscar winner. Seldom has a nominee been so deserving. Like his Shakespearean counterpart, Laurence Olivier, John Gielgud seems willing to tackle character roles in films in his old age. Having achieved complete success on the stage, he seems eager to create a lasting impression on film.

FILMOGRAPHY

1924

Who Is the Man? ★★★

1929

The Clue of the New Pin ★★★

1932

Insult ★★★

1933

The Good Companions ★★★

1936

Secret Agent ★★★★

1941

The Prime Minister ★★★★

1953

Julius Caesar ★★★★

1954

Romeo and Juliet (voice only)

1955

Richard III ★★★★

1956

The Barretts of Wimpole Street ★★★★
Around the World in 80 Days (cameo)

1957

Saint Joan ★★★★

1964

Becket ★★★★

1965

The Loved One ★★★

1966

Falstaff ★★★★

1968

Sebastian ★★★
The Charge of the Light Brigade ★★★★
The Shoes of the Fisherman ★★★

1969

Assignment to Kill ★★★
Oh! What a Lovely War ★★★

1970

Julius Caesar ★★★★

1971

Eagle in a Cage ★★★

1973

Lost Horizon ★★

1974

11 Harrowhouse ★★★
Gold ★★★
Murder on the Orient Express ★★★

1976

Aces High ★★★

1977

Providence ★★★★
Caligula ★★★

John Gielgud in *Murder on the Orient Express.*

1979

Murder by Decree ★★★★
Omar Mukhtar—Lion of the Desert ★★★
A Portrait of the Artist as a Young Man ★★★

1980

The Formula ★★★
The Elephant Man ★★★★
The Human Factor ★★★★

1981

Arthur ★★★★
Sphinx ★★★
Chariots of Fire ★★★★
Priest of Love ★★★

1982

Gandhi ★★★★

PAULETTE GODDARD
★★★ 2.81 STARS

Paulette Goddard was vivacious and appealing in a host of popular pictures, but only the two she did with ex-husband Charlie Chaplin, *Modern Times* and *The Great Dictator,* seem likely to have significance for future generations.

Born Marion Levy, in 1911, in New York, Goddard was a Ziegfeld girl by the age of fourteen. *Modern Times* was her first major film, and she was "shiny and attractive," according to critic Pauline Kael in *The Young in Heart.*

The Cat and the Canary, a comedy with Bob Hope, was so well received that they teamed again in *Nothing But the Truth.* She was a favorite of director Cecil B. DeMille, and he cast her in his *North West Mounted Police* and *Reap the Wild Wind.* She also held her own with veteran Claudette Colbert in *So Proudly We Hail* and then reached her height in a Pygmalion-type tale *Kitty* with Ray Milland.

After that, a dizzyingly fast decline in the quality of her scripts was apparent in *Bride of Vengeance, Hazard,* and *The Torch.* In *Anna Lucasta,* she was cast as a goldenhearted whore who defied her strict father (Oscar Homolka). Although she was convincing, her audiences turned a cold shoulder. After *Vice Squad,* Goddard virtually retired.

Paulette Goddard in *Kitty.*

FILMOGRAPHY

1929

City Streets (bit)
The Girl Habit (bit)
Berth Marks (bit)

1931

The Mouthpiece (bit)
The Kid from Spain (bit)

1936

Modern Times ★★★★

1938

The Young in Heart ★★★★
Dramatic School ★★★

1939

The Women ★★★
The Cat and the Canary ★★★

1940

The Ghost Breakers ★★★
The Great Dictator ★★★★
North West Mounted Police ★★★

1941

Second Chorus ★★
Pot O'Gold ★★★
Hold Back the Dawn ★★★
Nothing But the Truth ★★★

1942

The Lady Has Plans ★★★
Reap the Wild Wind ★★★
The Forest Rangers ★★★
Star Spangled Rhythm (cameo)

1943

The Crystal Ball ★★★
So Proudly We Hail ★★★

1944

Standing Room Only ★★★
I Love a Soldier ★★★

1945

Duffy's Tavern (cameo)

1946

Kitty ★★★★
The Diary of a Chambermaid ★★★

1947

Suddenly It's Spring ★★
Variety Girl (cameo)
Unconquered ★★★

1948

Hazard ★ ★ ★
An Ideal Husband ★ ★ ★
On Our Merry Way ★ ★ ★

1949

Bride of Vengeance ★ ★
Anna Lucasta ★ ★ ★

1950

The Torch ★ ★

1952

Babes in Baghdad ★ ★

1953

Sins of Jezebel ★ ★ ★
Vice Squad ★ ★
Paris Model ★ ★

1954

The Charge of the Lancers ★ ★
The Stranger Came Home ★ ★

1964

Time of Indifference ★ ★

RUTH GORDON
★ ★ ★ 3.16 STARS

Nobody can accuse Ruth Gordon of lacking individuality. Her distinctive speech and Peter-Pan-grown-old face have enlivened dozens of films.

She was born Ruth Jones, in Massachusetts, in 1896. After carving out a solid reputation on the stage, she made a few silent films, including *Camille* and *The Wheel of Life*, and then stayed away from Hollywood until her performance in 1940's *Abe Lincoln in Illinois.* There were other good pictures, *Dr. Ehrlich's Magic Bullet* and *Edge of Darkness*, but she made her greatest impact in the 1960s with *Inside Daisy Clover, Lord Love a Duck*, and particularly in *Rosemary's Baby.* She played Mia Farrow's seemingly warmhearted neighbor who turned out to be a witch. Gordon won a Best Supporting Actress Oscar for her role in *Rosemary's Baby* and followed it with another excellent thriller, *What Ever Happened to Aunt Alice?*

Where's Poppa? and *Harold and Maude* were too far out for general taste though they have devoted cult followings now. Gordon occasionally went overboard, as in *Every Which Way But Loose* and *My Bodyguard*, but she was always entertaining to watch.

Ruth Gordon is also a successful playwright and has written several screenplays with Garson Kanin.

FILMOGRAPHY

1915

Camille ★ ★ ★

1916

The Wheel of Life ★ ★ ★

1940

Abe Lincoln in Illinois ★ ★ ★
Dr. Ehrlich's Magic Bullet ★ ★ ★

1941

Two-Faced Woman ★ ★ ★

1943

Edge of Darkness ★ ★ ★ ★
Action in the North Atlantic ★ ★ ★ ★

1966

Inside Daisy Clover ★ ★ ★ ★
Lord Love a Duck ★ ★ ★ ★

1968

Rosemary's Baby ★ ★ ★ ★

Ruth Gordon in *What Ever Happened to Aunt Alice?*

1969

What Ever Happened to Aunt Alice? ★ ★ ★ ★

1970

Where's Poppa? ★ ★ ★

1971

Harold and Maude ★ ★ ★

1976

The Big Bus ★ ★ ★

1978

Every Which Way But Loose ★ ★

1979

Boardwalk ★ ★ ★
Scavenger Hunt ★ ★ ★

1980

My Bodyguard ★ ★
Any Which Way You Can ★ ★

LOU GOSSETT, JR.
★ ★ ★ 3.25 STARS

Lou Gossett, Jr. once said, "I'm still only earning half of what I deserve." Judging from his recent work on film and television, the situation should change shortly. Gossett is an impressive actor, versatile and strong. He makes baldness as eloquent as Yul Brynner did years ago.

He was born in Brooklyn, in 1936, and studied for a while to become a brain surgeon. A leading role in the stage version of "Take a Giant Step" altered those plans, and he gave other fine portrayals in "Desk Set" (with Shirley Booth), "Lost in the Stars," and "A Raisin in the Sun." He repeated his part on screen in the film version of *A Raisin in the Sun* and reviewers were impressed. However, the movie itself was too talky and too much like a photographed stage play for wide acceptance. An apprenticeship on TV included "The Partridge Family," "Mod Squad," and "The Young Rebels."

Gossett was particularly notable in *The Landlord*, an outstanding tale of tenement life. His vigorous presence also compensated for Maggie Smith's mannered portrayal in *Travels With My Aunt*, and he won superlatives for his role as Fiddler in TV's "Roots."

He usually played second banana, though in steadily more important vehicles like *Skin Game, The Laughing Policeman*, and *The Deep*. His part in *An Officer and a Gentleman* brought his career to a new height. Gossett's portrait of a tough but human drill sergeant had power and wit and was the overwhelming favorite to win the 1982 Best Supporting Actor Oscar.

With the leverage of this superb, award-winning performance, his future in leading roles is unlimited. He definitely chose the wrong vehicle to follow up this success, however. Not even Lou Gossett, Jr. had the depth to act competently in *Jaws 3-D*.

Lou Gossett, Jr. with David Janssen in "Harry O."

FILMOGRAPHY

1961

A Raisin in the Sun ★★★★

1970

The Landlord ★★★

1971

Skin Game ★★★

1972

Travels With My Aunt ★★★

1973

The Laughing Policeman ★★★★

1974

The White Dawn ★★★★

1976

The River Niger ★★★
J.D.'s Revenge ★★★

1977

The Choirboys ★★★
The Deep ★★★

1982

An Officer and a Gentleman ★★★★

1983

Jaws 3-D ★★

ELLIOTT GOULD
★★½ 2.32 STARS

Elliott Gould's career has followed the pattern of a roller coaster. He was a Broadway leading man, and then married to become "Mr. Barbra Streisand." After their divorce, he found superstardom. Today, after a run of failures, he's struggling once again to scale the ladder.

Gould was born Elliott Goldstein, in 1938. He was the focal point of "I Can Get It for You Wholesale" on stage, but Streisand, who had only a small part, received the attention. After a slow start in movies in *The Night They Raided Minsky's*, he virtually stole *Bob & Carol & Ted & Alice* from co-stars Natalie Wood, Robert Culp, and Dyan Cannon. M*A*S*H kept the momentum going, and *Getting Straight* turned out to be the only worthwhile film made about student unrest.

Gould made the mistake of appearing in an Ingmar Bergman picture, *The Touch*, and after that the scripts dropped disastrously in quality (*Busting*, *S*P*Y*S*, and *Whiffs*). He gave a shuffling, idiosyncratic charm to Raymond Chandler's *The Long Goodbye* but played second fiddle to a kangaroo in *Matilda*.

Elliott Gould's low-keyed manner is really ill-equipped for lead playing, and Gould should be exercising far more judgment in script selection to build a credible image. Sometimes, he even has the disconcerting ability to make his co-stars look bad as well.

Elliott Gould in *Little Murders*.

FILMOGRAPHY

1968

The Night They Raided Minsky's ★★

1969

Bob & Carol & Ted & Alice ★★★

1970

M*A*S*H ★★★
Getting Straight ★★★★
Move ★★
I Love My Wife ★★

1971

The Touch ★★
Little Murders ★★★

Elliott Gould with Stephanie Powers in *Escape to Athena*.

1973

The Long Goodbye ★★★

1974

Busting ★★
S*P*Y*S ★★
California Split ★★★

1975

Who? ★★
Nashville (cameo)
Whiffs ★★

1976

I Will, I Will...For Now ★
Harry and Walter Go to New York ★
Mean Johnny Barrows ★

1977

A Bridge Too Far ★★

1978

The Silent Partner ★★★
Capricorn One ★★★
Matilda ★

1979

The Lady Vanishes ★★★
Escape to Athena ★★
The Muppet Movie (cameo)

1980

The Last Flight of Noah's Ark ★★
Falling in Love Again ★★

1981

The Devil and Max Devlin ★★

BETTY GRABLE
★★★ 2.86 STARS

Betty Grable once said: "I'm in show business for two good reasons, and I'm standing on both of them. Put me in a long dress and I'd starve to death." She underrated herself. While it was true that her singing and dancing were merely adequate and her acting wasn't brilliant, she projected a friendly approachability that wartime audiences found impossible to resist. She performed admirably considering the poor quality of nearly all of her movies.

She was born in 1916, in St. Louis, and was strongly pushed by a determined stage mother. Mrs. Grable once commented, "It was like a poker game in which you know you're holding four aces. I knew Betty had what they wanted." Nobody noticed the "it" quality in her early films such as *New Movietone Follies of 1930*, but her parts got bigger in *Thrill of a Lifetime* and *Give Me a Sailor.* Still, she remained a minor supporting player until her appearance on Broadway in "Du Barry Was a Lady."

Her Broadway success stimulated new studio interest, and Grable made her first color musical, *Down Argentine Way.* She also played in *Tin Pan Alley,* a film about struggling songwriters, and *Moon Over Miami,* with Don Ameche. She looked luscious in all three.

Later in her career, producer Darryl F. Zanuck asked Grable to appear in a serious film, *The Razor's Edge,* in a role that eventually won Anne Baxter an Oscar. Grable refused, claiming she wasn't a good enough actress for drama. She might have been right, considering her performance in *I Wake Up Screaming* as the sister of murder victim Carole Landis. *A Yank in the R.A.F.* with Tyrone Power was also a non-musical, but was lighter and more within her range. She also made a series of highly attended but innocuous musicals, including *Song of the Islands, Sweet Rosie O'Grady,* and *Diamond Horseshoe.*

The Dolly Sisters was exceptionally successful, and she got her first rave reviews for *Mother Wore Tights,* a featherweight tale of two vaudeville performers. It teamed her with Dan Dailey for the first time, and the two had good chemistry together. Critics went too far, however, when they compared the Grable/Dailey combination to Rogers and Astaire.

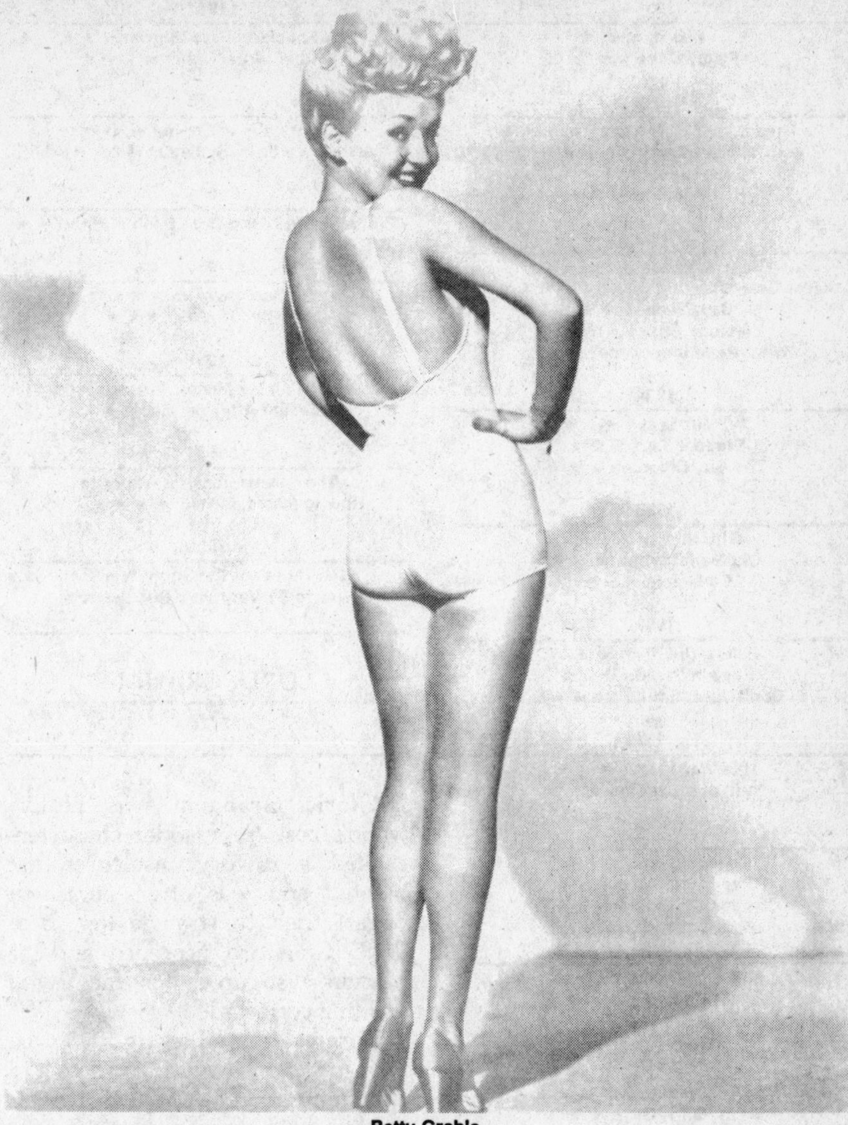

Betty Grable.

My Blue Heaven (about Grable's struggle to adopt a child) was stickier than usual, and *The Beautiful Blonde from Bashful Bend* was a surprisingly strained comedy directed by the usually excellent Preston Sturges. Grable's unparalleled box-office power took a dip when she made *The Farmer Takes a Wife.* She rebounded briefly with *How to Marry a Millionaire,* holding her own with Marilyn Monroe and Lauren Bacall. However, *How to Be Very Very Popular* was another detour that proved unpopular with viewers. It also prompted her retirement.

The clue to Grable's appeal—aside from her famous legs—was that, in Hollywood writer Jeanine Basinger's words, "She appealed to both sexes...She offered men everything. She seemed like a girl you could take home to mother, but with that body and mouth, anything might be posssible." This message came over loud and clear to the GIs who loved her during the war years, and all the audiences who followed afterward.

FILMOGRAPHY

1930

Happy Days ★★
Let's Go Place's ★★
New Movietone Follies of 1930 ★★
Whoopee ★★

1931

Kiki ★★★
Palmy Days ★★★

1932

The Greeks Had a Word for Them ★★★
The Kid from Spain ★★★
Probation ★★★
Hold 'Em Jail ★★★

1933

Child of Manhattan ★★★
The Sweetheart of Sigma Chi ★★★
Cavalcade ★★★
Melody Cruise ★★★
What Price Innocence? ★★★

1934

By Your Leave ★★★
Student Tour ★★★
The Gay Divorcee ★★★

1935

The Nitwits ★★★
Old Man Rhythm ★★★
Collegiate ★★★

1936

Follow the Fleet ★★★
Pigskin Parade ★★★
Don't Turn 'Em Loose ★★★

1937

This Way Please ★★★
Thrill of a Lifetime ★★★

1938

College Swing ★★★
Give Me a Sailor ★★★
Campus Confessions ★★★

1939

Man About Town ★★★
Million Dollar Legs ★★★
The Day the Bookies Wept ★★★

1940

Down Argentine Way ★★★
Tin Pan Alley ★★★

1941

Moon Over Miami ★★★
A Yank in the R.A.F. ★★★
I Wake Up Screaming ★★

1942

Footlight Serenade ★★★
Song of the Islands ★★★
Springtime in the Rockies ★★★

1943

Coney Island ★★★
Sweet Rosie O'Grady ★★★

1944

Four Jills in a Jeep ★★★
Pin-Up Girl ★★★

1945

Diamond Horseshoe ★★★
The Dolly Sisters ★★★

1946

Do You Love Me? (cameo)

1947

The Shocking Miss Pilgrim ★★★
Mother Wore Tights ★★★★

1948

That Lady in Ermine ★★★
When My Baby Smiles at Me ★★★

1949

The Beautiful Blond from Bashful Bend ★★

1950

Wabash Avenue ★★★
My Blue Heaven ★★★

1951

Call Me Mister ★★★
Meet Me After the Show ★★

1953

The Farmer Takes a Wife ★★
How to Marry a Millionaire ★★★★

1955

Three for the Show ★★
How to Be Very Very Popular ★★

GLORIA GRAHAME
★★★ 2.97 STARS

Gloria Grahame was Hollywood's best tramp. Her characters exuded a tawdry insolence that taunted and was often punished: Bogart tried to strangle her, Broderick Crawford succeeded, and Lee Marvin disfigured her face with scalding coffee.

Born in Los Angeles, in 1925, to a former actress, she grew up acting in community theatre and high school. Curiously, she appeared on Broadway before returning to her hometown to make films. Her first memorable part was in *It's a Wonderful Life*. She was the town tramp to whom James Stewart gave money to leave town and start anew.

Gloria Grahame with Lee Marvin in *The Big Heat*.

In 1950, she played Laurel in *In a Lonely Place*, the blonde-across-the-courtyard who provided murder-suspect Humphrey Bogart with an alibi. In the film, she fell in love with Bogart, but offscreen she fell for the director instead. She married Nicholas Ray shortly afterward. She won a Best Supporting Actress Oscar for *The Bad and the Beautiful*. Grahame played Dick Powell's spoiled Southern belle wife who gets killed in a plane crash while running away with her lover.

She was gangster Lee Marvin's girlfriend in *The Big Heat*. Face bandaged and conscience stricken, she had a memorable line when she killed the wife of a crooked cop: "We're sisters under the mink." With no musical credits to her background, she surprised everyone as Ado Annie in *Oklahoma!* with her version of "I'm Just a Girl Who Can't Say No."

When good roles dried up, she played schlock films and worked on the British stage. Before dying of cancer in 1981, she had one final good role as John Heard's loony but foxy mother in *Chilly Scenes of Winter*.

FILMOGRAPHY

1944

Blonde Fever ★★

1945

Without Love ★★

1946

It's a Wonderful Life ★★★

1947

It Happened in Brooklyn ★★★
Crossfire ★★★★
Song of the Thin Man ★★★
Merton of the Movies ★★★

1949

A Woman's Secret ★★★★
Roughshod ★★★

1950

In a Lonely Place ★★★★

1952

The Greatest Show on Earth ★★★
Macao ★★★
Sudden Fear ★★★★
The Bad and the Beautiful ★★★★

Gloria Grahame.

1953

The Glass Wall ★ ★ ★
Man on a Tightrope ★ ★ ★
The Big Heat ★ ★ ★ ★
Prisoners of the Casbah ★ ★

1954

Human Desire ★ ★ ★ ★
Naked Alibi ★ ★ ★

1955

The Good Die Young ★ ★ ★
Not as a Stranger ★ ★ ★
The Cobweb ★ ★ ★
Oklahoma! ★ ★ ★ ★

1956

The Man Who Never Was ★ ★ ★

1957

Ride Out for Revenge ★ ★

1959

Odds Against Tomorrow ★ ★ ★

1966

Ride Beyond Vengeance ★ ★

1971

The Todd Killings ★ ★
Chandler ★ ★ ★
Blood and Lace ★ ★ ★

1972

The Loners ★ ★ ★

1973

Tarot ★ ★ ★

1974

Mama's Dirty Girls ★ ★

1976

Mansion of the Doomed ★

1979

Chilly Scenes of Winter ★ ★ ★ ★
A Nightingale Sang in Berkeley Square ★ ★

1982

The Nesting (cameo)

FARLEY GRANGER
★ ★ ★ 2.88 STARS

Listen to the current actor Barry Bostwick and then watch an old Farley Granger movie—the voices are identical. Granger had perhaps less acting range than Bostwick, but he was a competent, likable performer, and well-suited to the romantic leads he played.

He was born in 1925, in San Jose, California. At eighteen he debuted in *The North Star* and then convincingly projected moral weakness in Hitchcock's *Rope. Enchantment* was an episodic and colorless love story, but *They Live by Night*, as directed by Nicholas Ray, was a sensitive and beautifully acted drama of two lovers fleeing the law. The movie was overlooked in the United States, but made a strong impression on British audiences.

Side Street was a pale reprise of *They Live by Night*—Granger co-starred in both with Cathy O'Donnell. He had his strongest role in another Hitchcock picture, *Strangers on a Train*, a classic—though Robert Walker's performance was more showy. A dull comedy, *Behave Yourself*, and a soap opera, *I Want You*, followed before Granger had another chance to shine in *Hans Christian Andersen*. Written by Frank Loesser, it was a sentimental but engaging musical.

Farley Granger with Robert Walker in *Strangers on a Train.*

His sincerity also did something to boost the trivial script of *Small Town Girl*, a picture memorable only for Ann Miller's dancing. However, its box-office failure weakened his popularity. The pictures which destroyed it included *The Naked Street, The Girl in the Red Velvet Swing*, and *They Call Me Trinity.* Years later, he took over the lead role in Broadway's "Deathtrap," reminding audiences of an acting talent that had too rarely been exploited in movies.

FILMOGRAPHY

1943

The North Star ★ ★ ★

1944

The Purple Heart ★ ★ ★

1948

Rope ★ ★ ★
Enchantment ★ ★ ★

1949

Roseanna McCoy ★ ★
They Live by Night ★ ★ ★ ★

1950

Side Street ★ ★ ★
Our Very Own ★ ★ ★
Edge of Doom ★ ★

1951

Strangers on a Train ★ ★ ★ ★
Behave Yourself ★ ★
I Want You ★ ★ ★

1952

Hans Christian Andersen ★ ★ ★
O. Henry's Full House ★ ★ ★

1953

The Story of Three Loves ★ ★ ★
Small Town Girl ★ ★ ★

1954

Senso ★ ★ ★ ★

1955

The Girl in the Red Velvet Swing ★ ★
The Naked Street ★ ★

1967

Rogue's Gallery ★ ★ ★

1971

They Call Me Trinity ★ ★ ★

1973

The Man Called Noon ★ ★
The Serpent ★ ★ ★

1975

La Polizia Chiede Aiuto ★ ★ ★

CARY GRANT
★ ★ ★ ½ 3.31 STARS

The screen's most handsome and self-effacing playboy, Cary Grant has fashioned one of Hollywood's greatest careers by applying a single screen image to a wide variety of situations and genres. Perenially playing the urbane super-sophisticate who can tackle any of life's problems with a chuckle and a well-timed witticism, Grant has made every one of his performances seem natural and easy.

Grant was born Archibald Alexander Leach in 1904, in Bristol, England. He was an acrobat, dancer, and juggler in his early years, then appeared on Broadway in "Golden Dawn," "Polly," and "Boom-Boom." His film debut was in *This Is the Night*, a musical with Roland Young. He was already typecast as the wastrel playboy by the time he played in *Blonde Venus* with Marlene Dietrich. He first gained attention as Mae West's suitor in *She Done Him Wrong*, a role he reprised with her in *I'm No Angel*. His first important dramatic part was as a young World War I pilot in *The Eagle and the Hawk*.

Sylvia Scarlett was so bad that Katharine Hepburn admitted fleeing to the ladies room before the preview was over, but Grant's cockney rogue came off quite well on screen. He was hilarious in the much more successful *Topper*, and demonstrated impeccable timing in *The Awful Truth* with Irene Dunne, who said: "I wish all aspiring actors could have witnessed Cary's concentration and preparedness during the production—an object lesson in professionalism." *Bringing Up Baby* showed him off in an equally positive light, and he matched well with Hepburn again in suitable *Holiday*.

Even in his action dramas like *Gunga Din* and *Only Angels Have Wings*, he relied upon his affable wit to charm cohorts, enemies, and audiences. *His Girl Friday* was an adaptation of Ben Hecht's "The Front Page," changing the sex of one of the characters (Rosalind Russell). It garnered raves, and so did the talky and now-dated *The Philadelphia Story*. *Suspicion* belonged to Joan Fontaine (who won an Oscar), but Grant brought much-needed charm to the sluggish *Talk of the Town*. He returned to cockney portrayals for the moving *None But the Lonely Heart*. He played the prodigal son of long-suffering Ethel Barrymore.

Cary Grant.

He was trapped in the worst of all musical biographies, *Night and Day*, but at his best in Hitchcock's masterful *Notorious*. He was the American agent in love with beautiful spy Ingrid Bergman. His straight-faced reactions to the absurd situations in *The Bachelor and the Bobby-Soxer* had audiences rolling in the aisles, particularly during the race. *I Was a Male War Bride* found him pretending to be a woman, which he did as easily as Jack Lemmon and Tony Curtis managed years later in *Some Like It Hot*. He had no shortage of light, delightful comedies during this period: *Arsenic and Old Lace*, *Mr. Blandings Builds His Dream House*, *Monkey Business*, and *Indiscreet*, a long-awaited reunion with Ingrid Bergman.

A few movies threatened his superstar status: *Crisis*, a morbid political drama, and *People Will Talk*, an only-too-accurate title. But he was perfect as the reformed cat burglar in *To Catch a Thief*, trading

Noel Cowardish banter with a radiant Grace Kelly. *North By Northwest* was also classic Hitchcock, featuring the famous crop dusting scene. *Operation Petticoat* was a weak comedy, but also a big moneymaker at the time. The concluding scene in *An Affair to Remember* where Cary Grant discovers that, Deborah Kerr has been hurt, contains some of the most beautiful acting anyone has ever committed to film.

He continued to be the epitome of sophistication in one of Doris Day's better comedies, *That Touch of Mink*, but after the static *The Grass Is Greener* and the forgettable *Walk Don't Run*, he retired.

"I am a pseudo-sophisticate," Grant protested. "But I play my idea of a sophisticate. Really, I play myself." Whatever he does, it's enough to make him, as Joan Crawford once said, "the most charming man to ever appear on the screen."

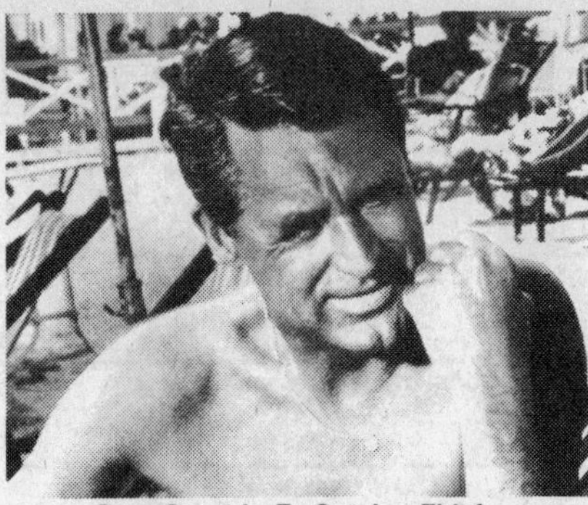
Cary Grant in *To Catch a Thief*.

FILMOGRAPHY

1932

This Is the Night ★★★
Sinners in the Sun ★★★
Merrily We Go to Hell ★★★
The Devil and the Deep ★★★
Blonde Venus ★★★★
Hot Saturday ★★★★
Madame Butterfly ★★★

1933

She Done Him Wrong ★★★★
The Woman Accused ★★★
The Eagle and the Hawk ★★★★
Gambling Ship ★★★
I'm No Angel ★★★
Alice in Wonderland ★★

1934

Thirty Day Princess ★★★
Born to Be Bad ★★★
Kiss and Make-Up ★★★
Ladies Should Listen ★★★

1935

Enter Madame ★★★
Wings in the Dark ★★★
The Last Outpost ★★★

1936

Sylvia Scarlett ★★★★
Big Brown Eyes ★★★
Suzy ★★★
Wedding Present ★★★
The Amazing Quest of Ernest Bliss ★★★

1937

When You're in Love ★★★
Topper ★★★★
The Toast of New York ★★★
The Awful Truth ★★★★

1938

Bringing Up Baby ★★★★
Holiday ★★★★

1939

Gunga Din ★★★★
Only Angels Have Wings ★★★★
In Name Only ★★★★

1940

His Girl Friday ★★★★
My Favorite Wife ★★★
The Howards of Virginia ★★

1941

The Philadelphia Story ★★★
Penny Serenade ★★★★
Suspicion ★★★★

1942

Talk of the Town ★★★
Once Upon a Honeymoon ★★★

1943

Mr. Lucky ★★★

1944

Destination Tokyo ★★★
Once Upon a Time ★★★
None But the Lonely Heart ★★★★
Arsenic and Old Lace ★★★★

1946

Without Reservations (cameo)
Night and Day ★★
Notorious ★★★★

1947

The Bachelor and the Bobby-Soxer ★★★★
The Bishop's Wife ★★★

1948

Mr. Blandings Builds His Dream House ★★★★
Every Girl Should Be Married ★★★

1949

I Was a Male War Bride ★★★★

1950

Crisis ★★★

1951

People Will Talk ★★★

1952

Room for One More ★★★
Monkey Business ★★★

1953

Dream Wife ★★★

1955

To Catch a Thief ★★★★

1957

The Pride and the Passion ★★
An Affair to Remember ★★★★
Kiss Them for Me ★★★

1958

Indiscreet ★★★★
Houseboat ★★★

1959

North By Northwest ★★★★
Operation Petticoat ★★★

1961

The Grass Is Greener ★★★

1962

That Touch of Mink ★★★★

1963

Charade ★★★★

1964

Father Goose ★★★

1966

Walk Don't Run ★★★

KATHRYN GRAYSON
★★½ 2.65 STARS

MGM had two popular sopranos under contract during the 1940s—Kathryn Grayson and Jane Powell. Powell was possibly more appealing and versatile, but Grayson could show great charm when given a good role.

She was born Zelma Kathryn Hedrick, in 1922, in Winston-Salem, North Carolina. After singing on Eddie Cantor's radio show, she went to MGM to play in *Andy Hardy's Private Secretary*. She was saddled with *The Vanishing Virginian* before finding a good role in an Abbott and Costello film *Rio Rita*.

Van Heflin was her leading man in a pleasant musical, *Seven Sweethearts*, and she teamed with Gene Kelly in the all-star extravaganza, *Thousands Cheer*. She made a couple of guest appearances in revue-like films—*Ziegfeld Follies* and *Till the Clouds Roll By*—and was the object of Frank Sinatra's affections in *It Happened in Brooklyn*.

Grayson shared the spotlight with June Allyson in the entertaining *Two Sisters from Boston.* She made two films that indulged her fondness for grand opera, *Toast of New Orleans* and *That Midnight Kiss,* both with Mario Lanza. However, she had her one great part in *Show Boat.* Kathryn Grayson and Howard Keel made an effective team, both dramatically and melodically, and the picture was a huge success. *Kiss Me Kate* (again with Keel) was also first-rate, but Grayson was arch in *So This Is Love* (the Grace Moore story) and a featherweight farce, *Grounds for Marriage.*

Her sweetness somewhat disguised her sex appeal. She was known as Hollywood's bustiest leading lady. "She should have had breast surgery," commented Joan Crawford. However, she insisted on loose-fitting costumes to conceal her bosom. It's a shame because a little more spice and a little less sugar might have prolonged her career.

Kathryn Grayson with Mario Lanza in *Toast of New Orleans.*

FILMOGRAPHY

1941

Andy Hardy's Private Secretary ★★

1942

The Vanishing Virginian ★★
Rio Rita ★★
Seven Sweethearts ★★★

1943

Thousands Cheer ★★★

1945

Anchors Aweigh ★★★

1946

Ziegfeld Follies ★★★
Two Sisters from Boston ★★★
Till the Clouds Roll By ★★★

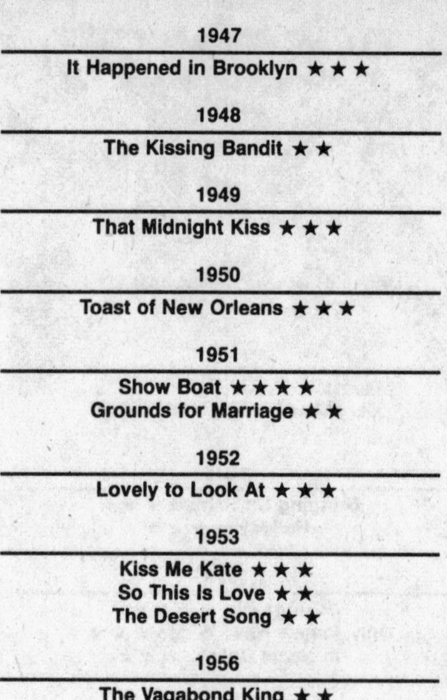

1947

It Happened in Brooklyn ★★★

1948

The Kissing Bandit ★★

1949

That Midnight Kiss ★★★

1950

Toast of New Orleans ★★★

1951

Show Boat ★★★★
Grounds for Marriage ★★

1952

Lovely to Look At ★★★

1953

Kiss Me Kate ★★★
So This Is Love ★★
The Desert Song ★★

1956

The Vagabond King ★★

SYDNEY GREENSTREET
★★★½ 3.55 STARS

Sydney Greenstreet was the screen's most stylized menace—fat, genial, and with a voice like an asthmatic hiccup.

He was born in 1879, in Sandwich, England. His first stage role, as a murderer in "Sherlock Holmes," indicated the direction of his later career. There were more stage parts, ranging from musicals to Shakespeare, before his spectacular film debut in John Huston's *The Maltese Falcon,* with Humphrey Bogart. He was likably sinister again in another Bogart vehicle, *Across the Pacific,* and added his distinct flair into the wonderful mix of elements that was *Casablanca.* He played a black marketeer and Bogart's rival casino owner.

Peter Lorre and Greenstreet were a match made in heaven—or hell—in the exciting *The Mask of Dimitrios.*

He played the lead in *The Verdict,* a combination melodrama/mystery perfectly suited to his talents. Again, he was paired with Peter Lorre.

A poor comedy, *Pillow to Post,* with Ida Lupino, made little use of his peculiarly individual qualities,

Sydney Greenstreet in *Across the Pacific.*

but he was an asset to *Conflict* as Bogart's psychiatrist friend. The wild inaccuracies of *Devotion,* a so-called biography of the Bronte sisters, condemned it to critical failure, despite Greenstreet's fine performance.

He was a different kind of villain in *The Hucksters*—a monstrously egomanical advertising executive who tried unsuccessfully to intimidate Clark Gable. He killed Zachary Scott in *Ruthless* and played the menacing Count Fosco in *The Woman in White.* However, Greenstreet's most rounded villain was the southern sheriff in *Flamingo Road.* His collisions with defiant carnival dancer Joan Crawford were terrifyingly potent, a classic clash of good and evil. *It's a Great Feeling* and *Malaya,* his last two films, were disappointing after this mesmerizing characterization. Greenstreet died in 1954.

Sydney Greenstreet's career is indelibly linked to the careers of Humphrey Bogart and Peter Lorre. Much more than just the chance pairing of fellow contract players at Warner Brothers, these actors created a chemistry together that was subtle, powerful, and totally convincing. Sydney Greenstreet rarely received credit in his own right. Though he deserved praise, he was part of an acting whole that was greater than each of its parts.

FILMOGRAPHY

1941

The Maltese Falcon ★★★
They Died with Their Boots On ★★★

1942

In This Our Life (cameo)
Across the Pacific ★★★

1943

Casablanca ★★★
Background to Danger ★★★

1944

Passage to Marseilles ★★★
Between Two Worlds ★★★
The Mask of Dimitrios ★★★★
The Conspirators ★★★★
Hollywood Canteen (cameo)

1945

Pillow to Post ★★★
Conflict ★★★★
Christmas in Connecticut ★★★

1946

Three Strangers ★★★
Devotion ★★★
The Verdict ★★★★

1947

The Hucksters ★★★★
That Way with Women ★★★

1948

The Woman in White ★★★★
The Velvet Touch ★★★★
Ruthless ★★★★

1949

Flamingo Road ★★★★
It's a Great Feeling (cameo)

1950

Malaya ★★★

ALEC GUINNESS
★★★½ 3.30 STARS

Alec Guinness was once asked if he enjoyed acting and he replied, "Yes, I do. It's happy agony." Watching him, one should only be glad he feels that the agony is worth it. Few, if any, actors have given so many dazzling performances in such a wide variety of roles.

Guinness was born in London, in 1914. After doing "Hamlet" at the Old Vic ("the egomaniac part of all time"), David Lean cast him in *Great Expectations* as John Mills's loyal friend. His part was small, but the film was a masterpiece, the best screen version of any Dickens novel. He returned to Dickens in *Oliver Twist*, this time in a major part as the thieving Fagin. Jewish protest hurt the picture's commercial prospects in the United States, but Guinness was recognized as superlative.

He dared to portray eight different characters in *Kind Hearts and Coronets*. To get a sense of his accomplishments, one need only think of Jerry Lewis attempting the same gambit in *The Family Jewels*. He was a dying man living up his last few months in the pleasant comedy *Last Holiday*, and made an impressive Disraeli to a miscast Irene Dunne (as Queen Victoria) in *The Mudlark*.

The Captain's Paradise benefited from his amusing performance as a skipper who shuttled back and forth between two wives (Yvonne De Carlo and Celia Johnson), though the script was mild stuff. *The Ladykillers* was funnier, but *The Swan* (Grace Kelly's last film) proved dull and unsuccessful, despite massive publicity concerning Kelly's wedding. Guinness' career got a needed dramatic boost with *The Bridge on the River Kwai*, a magnificent wartime drama about British soldiers in a Japanese prison camp. Director David Lean had wanted Charles Laughton, and Guinness turned down the role three times before accepting. "You can make a mistake," he said later, "I thought the film was anti-British." Fortunately, he was prevailed upon to play the role and won a Best Actor Oscar.

Alec Guinness in *The Bridge on the River Kwai*.

His follow-up, *The Scapegoat*, was weak, and he clashed with co-star Bette Davis. He wrote his own starring role in *The Horse's Mouth*, a delightful comedy about an eccentric painter and he had an actor's field day opposite John Mills in the mesmerizing *Tunes of Glory*. From these high notes he accepted the *worst* role of his career—as the Japanese widower who fell in love with a Jewish matron (Rosalind Russell) in *A Majority of One*.

Alec Guinness with director George Lucas in *Star Wars*.

The lapse was temporary. A series of skillful characterizations followed: an Arab in *Lawrence of Arabia*; a Commissar in the memorably romantic *Doctor Zhivago*; and a butler in Neil Simon's sophomoric but enjoyable spoof of crime movies, *Murder by Death*. For all of his outstanding screen portraits, he *deserved* the unexpected gift of *Star Wars*. Like the other players in the picture, he took a percentage and when the film became the top-grossing box-office hit of all time (until beaten by *E.T.*), he made millions. It's ironic, because the part demanded so much less of him than his other roles, dramatically speaking, yet they didn't draw a fraction of the attention.

Guinness is both a character actor and a star. He's the best proof movies have that an actor can be both.

FILMOGRAPHY

1946

Great Expectations ★★★

1948

Oliver Twist ★★★★

1949

Kind Hearts and Coronets ★★★★
A Run for Your Money ★★★

1950

Last Holiday ★★★★
The Mudlark ★★★★

1951

The Lavender Hill Mob ★★★★
The Man in the White Suit ★★★★

1952

The Promoter ★★★

1953

The Captain's Paradise ★★★★
The Malta Story ★★★

1954

The Detective ★★★
To Paris With Love ★★★

1955

The Prisoner ★★★
The Ladykillers ★★★★

1956

The Swan ★★★

1957

All At Sea ★★★
The Bridge on the River Kwai ★★★★

1958

The Horse's Mouth ★★★★

1959

The Scapegoat ★★★
Our Man in Havana ★★★

1960

Tunes of Glory ★★★★

1962

A Majority of One ★★
Damn the Defiant ★★★
Lawrence of Arabia ★★★★

1964

The Fall of the Roman Empire ★★★

1965

Situation Hopeless but Not Serious ★★★
Doctor Zhivago ★★★

1966

Hotel Paradiso ★★★
The Quiller Memorandum ★★★

1967

The Comedians ★★★

1970

Cromwell ★★★
Scrooge ★★★★

1973

Brother Sun, Sister Moon ★★★
Hitler: The Last Ten Days ★★★

1976

Murder by Death ★★★

1977

Star Wars ★★★

1980

Raise the Titanic ★★★
The Empire Strikes Back ★★★

1983

Lovesick ★★★
Return of the Jedi (cameo)

GENE HACKMAN
★★★ 2.94 STARS

Few would downgrade Gene Hackman's acting ability. He can bring conviction to the most contrived dialogue. He's equally capable of being sympathetic or villainous, but he lacks sex appeal. A clue to his problem is contained in his own remark, "Errol Flynn was my idol. I'd come out of a theatre and be startled when I looked in a mirror because I didn't look like Flynn. I *felt* like him!"

Hackman was born in San Bernardino, California, in 1931. Two plays on Broadway made him well known, "Barefoot in the Park," and "Any Wednesday." Both were comedies, but his first major movie was a serious psychological drama, *Lilith.* He was effective, but the film had no audience support. A few unimportant pictures including *A Covenant With Death* and *First To Fight* preceded the vehicle that really established him, *Bonnie and Clyde.* Many critics thought his was the best performance in a picture riddled with outstanding performances (Warren Beatty, Faye Dunaway, and Estelle Parsons). Hackman was a coach in the pictorially-vivid-but-dramatically-drab *Downhill Racer. The Gypsy Moths* was a gripping, underrated study of skydivers, and he stole the film from Burt Lancaster and Scott Wilson.

I Never Sang for My Father showcased a relentlessly painful study of a son trying to make contact with an egocentric father. Hackman played the son, and only the steel-hearted could remain unmoved by his scenes with his father, played by Melvyn Douglas. *Doctors' Wives* was another story, a grotesque and gory soap opera, in which he played Rachel Roberts's understanding husband. *Prime Cut* pitted him against Lee Marvin in a confused, rancid gangster film.

Hackman needed a good picture, and *The French Connection* supplied it. He energetically portrayed the crazy detective Popeye and won an Oscar. *The Poseidon Adventure* gave him a strange role, as a dedicated preacher leading people to safety aboard an upside-down ocean liner. His authority was an asset to an original and gripping thriller. He followed this performance with *Zandy's Bride*, an old-fashioned love story about a neglectful husband and his immigrant wife (Liv Ullmann). Unfortunately, the script required a 1940s type of romantic magnetism which neither star provided.

He also performed well in a magnificent role in Francis Ford Coppola's *The Conversation.* He played a nebbishy, guilt-ridden Catholic whose guilt was worsened by his profession of wire-tapping. The film has been hailed as one of the finest American movies of the 1970s.

The films that followed, *Night Moves* and *Bite the Bullet*, were moderately entertaining but failed to find a public. Nobody liked *Lucky Lady,* a disastrous "comedy" that stranded Burt Reynolds and Liza Minnelli. Everyone in the cast received more than their usual salaries, but their acting reputations diminished.

A disjointed thriller, *The Domino Principle,* continued his downward trend. Hackman tried to play a villain in *Superman*, but he mugged too broadly even for a comic strip. He did the same thing in *Superman II*, but both movies boosted him at the box office again.

Gene Hackman in *Bonnie and Clyde.*

Hackman is a fine actor, but he lacks the charisma to carry mediocre films. When the script is good, he can be brilliant, but unlike Bogart, Cooper, Flynn, and Tracy, he's totally dependent on his materials.

FILMOGRAPHY

1961

Mad Dog Coll (bit)

1964

Lilith★★★

1966

Hawaii★★★

1967

A Covenant With Death★★★
First To Fight★★★
Banning★★★
Bonnie and Clyde★★★★

1968

The Split★★★

1969

The Gypsy Moths★★★★
Downhill Racer★★★
Riot★★
Marooned★★★

1970

I Never Sang for My Father★★★★

1971

Doctors' Wives★★
The Hunting Party★★
The French Connection★★★★

1972

Cisco Pike★★★★
Prime Cut★★★
The Poseidon Adventure★★★★

1973

Scarecrow★★

1974

The Conversation★★★★
Zandy's Bride★★
Young Frankenstein (cameo)

1975

French Connection II★★★
Bite the Bullet★★★
Night Moves★★★
Lucky Lady★★

1976

The Domino Principle★★
A Bridge Too Far★★
March or Die★★★

1978

Superman★★

1980

Superman II★★
A Look at Liv★★★

1981

All Night Long★★★

1982

Reds★★★

1983

Eureka★★★★

JEAN HARLOW
★★★ 3.22 STARS

One of the earliest and most talented of the platinum blondes, Jean Harlow had a brash, down-to-earth appeal that enhanced all her films. Critics panned her at first but gradually reversed themselves in a unanimous storm of praise.

Jean Harlow.

Harlow (Harlean Carpenter) was born in 1911, in Kansas City, Missouri. She began as an extra in the film, *Moran of the Marines*, then worked her way into shorts directed by Hal Roach. A good role in the hit drama *Hell's Angels* established her at the box office, and she appeared in *The Secret Six* with Lew Ayres and *Platinum Blonde* with Loretta Young.

The 1932 classic *Red Dust* teamed her with Clark Gable, and their sexy images blended perfectly. In fact, the film was considered immoral at the time. She easily portrayed a sexy movie star in *Bombshell*. *Dinner at Eight* was a witty comedy of social types, and Harlow vied with Marie Dressler for acting honors—there was a triumphant tie. She was *The Girl from Missouri* who fell for Franchot Tone, and she was a chorus girl in *Reckless*, an unsatisfying and thinly veiled account of the Libby Holman murder case. In *China Seas*, an adventure yarn, she co-starred opposite Gable again. Harlow and Tracy were in the fishing business in *Riffraff*, a routine melodrama. Even her presence couldn't save *Suzy*. *Libeled Lady* was her best vehicle, a hilarious comedy with William Powell and Myrna Loy.

She died young at twenty-six and her life story became the subject of several books and movies. All the gossip concerning Harlow harped on her scandalous marriage to Paul Bern who committed suicide shortly after their wedding. However, this one-dimensional approach was as trite as morning soap operas.

FILMOGRAPHY

1928

Moran of the Marines (bit)

1929

The Love Parade (bit)
City Lights (bit)
The Saturday Night Kid★★★

1930

Hell's Angels★★★

1931

The Secret Six★★★
The Iron Man★★★
The Public Enemy★★★
Goldie★★★
Platinum Blonde★★★

1932

Three Wise Girls★★★
The Beast of the City★★★
Red-Headed Woman★★★
Red Dust★★★★

1933

Hold Your Man★★★★
Bombshell★★★★

1934

Dinner at Eight★★★★
The Girl from Missouri★★★★

1935

Reckless★★
China Seas★★★
Riffraff★★★★

1936

Wife vs. Secretary★★★
Suzy★★
Libeled Lady★★★★

1937

Personal Property★★★
Saratoga★★★

RICHARD HARRIS
★★★ 2.89 STARS

Richard Harris, like Peter O'Toole, is reputed to be a hell-raiser in real life. This rugged, pugnacious quality comes through on the screen, adding drive to his performances.

Harris was born in Limerick, Ireland, in 1932. He registered strongly in *The Wreck of the Mary Deare*, holding his own with Gary Cooper and Charlton Heston. He overshadowed Marlon Brando's prissy Fletcher Christian in *Mutiny on the Bounty.* Harris bulled his way brilliantly through *This Sporting Life*, still his best role, as a determined rugby player.

There were a few failures including, *Major Dundee* and *The Heroes of Telemark* and then a successful, if grueling and distasteful, western, *A Man Called Horse.* He was charismatic in the otherwise heavy-handed version of *Camelot*, which he repeated on stage in 1983 to great acclaim. None of his subsequent vehicles has been good enough to sustain a consistent box-office following.

FILMOGRAPHY

1958
Alive and Kicking ★★★

1959
Shake Hands with the Devil ★★★
The Wreck of the Mary Deare ★★★★

1960
A Terrible Beauty ★★★

1961
The Long and the Short and the Tall ★★★
Mutiny on the Bounty ★★★
The Guns of Navarone ★★★

1963
This Sporting Life ★★★★

1964
Red Desert ★★★★

1965
I Tre Volti ★★★
Major Dundee ★★
The Heroes of Telemark ★★

Richard Harris in *Camelot*.

1966
The Bible ★★
Hawaii ★★★

1967
Caprice ★★★
Camelot ★★★

1970
The Molly Maguires ★★★★
A Man Called Horse ★★★★
Cromwell ★★★
The Lady in the Car with Glasses and a Gun ★★

1971
The Hero ★★★
Man in the Wilderness ★★★

1973
The Deadly Trackers ★★★

1974
99 and 44/100% Dead ★★★
Juggernaut ★★

1975
Echoes of a Summer ★★

1976
The Return of a Man Called Horse ★★★
Robin and Marian ★★★

1977
The Cassandra Crossing ★★★
Gulliver's Travels ★★★
Orca ★★
Golden Rendezvous ★★★

1978
The Wild Geese ★★★

1979
The Number ★★★
Game for Vultures ★★★

1981
The Last Word ★★★
Tarzan, The Ape Man ★

REX HARRISON
★★★ 3.21 STARS

Rex Harrison was never one of the top box-office attractions, though he has had a long and prolific career. Despite his impeccable performances, his cool, aristocratic manner placed a barrier between himself and his audiences. He did try some Cary Grant-like roles, but he lacked Grant's underlying common touch.

Rex Harrison was born in 1908, in Huyton, England. At the age of sixteen, he joined the Liverpool Repertory Theatre. From then on, he worked continuously on the stage, and his dedication showed in his first successes, "French Without Tears" and "Man of Yesterday." He showed his comedy technique on film in *Storm in a Teacup* opposite Vivien Leigh, and had a good role with Leigh again in *St. Martin's Lane. Night Train* is still a classic thriller from the 1940s. The screen version of Shaw's *Major Barbara* was too literally adapted from the play, but Harrison made his long speeches sound less verbose than they really were.

Anna and the King of Siam was the basis for the musical, *The King and I*, and Harrison's king was just as commanding and charismatic as Yul Brynner's was in the musical version. He gave that same power and dimension to his dead sea captain in *The Ghost and Mrs. Muir*, a memorable comedy with Gene Tierney. The clichés were thick in *The Foxes of Harrow*, but Harrison was convincing as a wrongfully convicted prisoner in *Escape. Unfaith-*

Rex Harrison with Audrey Hepburn in *My Fair Lady*.

fully Yours has become a cult film, but at the time the public stayed home.

Harrison's greatest film achievement came when he repeated his stage role of Professor Henry Higgins in *My Fair Lady.* His expertise was sorely needed. Director George Cukor brought no movement or cinematic imagination to the numbers, leading lady Audrey Hepburn was miscast, and Harrison was all alone with his sheer, volatile charm. He won an Oscar and followed up with *The Agony and the Ecstasy.* He played Pope Julius II to Charlton Heston's Michelangelo in a talky spectacle about the painting of the Sistine Chapel. His suaveness was again badly needed in *The Honey Pot,* a talk laden update of *Volpone.* Among a cadre of inadequate performances given by Susan Hayward, Capucine, and Edie Adams, Harrison and Maggie Smith shone like diamonds.

The remainder of his films were depressing. It wasn't his fault that *Doctor Dolittle* failed, nor could he have done anything to save *Staircase.* He played an aging homosexual living with Richard Burton. However, it was understandable that he should retire from films to tour with "My Fair Lady." His performance wasn't what it had been, but enough magic remained to make it a lovely experience.

Second wife Lilli Palmer said in a 1983 interview that Rex "doesn't exist offstage. His life is the theatre."

FILMOGRAPHY

1930

The Great Game ★★★
School for Scandal ★★★

1934

Get Your Man ★★★
Leave It To Blanche ★★★

1935

All at Sea ★★★

1936

Men Are Not Gods ★★★

1937

Storm in a Teacup ★★★
School for Husbands ★★★
Over the Moon ★★★

1939

St. Martin's Lane ★★★
The Citadel ★★★
Continental Express ★★★

1940

Ten Days in Paris ★★★
Night Train ★★★★

1941

Major Barbara ★★★★

1945

Blithe Spirit ★★★★
A Yank in London ★★★
The Rake's Progress ★★★

1946

Anna and the King of Siam ★★★★

1947

The Ghost and Mrs. Muir ★★★★
The Foxes of Harrow ★★★

Rex Harrison with Gene Tierney in *The Ghost and Mrs. Muir.*

1948

Escape ★★★★
Unfaithfully Yours ★★★★

1951

The Long Dark Hall ★★★

1952

The Fourposter ★★★

1953

Main Street to Broadway (cameo)

1954

King Richard and the Crusaders ★★★

1955

The Constant Husband ★★★

1958

The Reluctant Debutante ★★★

1960

Midnight Lace ★★★★

1962

The Happy Thieves ★★★

1963

Cleopatra ★★★★

Rex Harrison in *Night Train.*

1964

The Yellow Rolls-Royce ★★★
My Fair Lady ★★★★

1965

The Agony and the Ecstasy ★★★

1967

The Honey Pot ★★★★
Doctor Dolittle ★★★

1968

A Flea in Her Ear ★★

1969

Staircase ★★

1977

The Prince and the Pauper ★★★

1978

Shalimar ★★★

1979

Ashanti ★★★
The Fifth Musketeer ★★★

LAURENCE HARVEY
★★½ 2.62 STARS

Although Elizabeth Taylor respected Laurence Harvey's abilities, Jane Fonda claimed that "acting with Harvey is like acting by yourself—only worse." While it is true that his acting was sometimes stiff and cold, Harvey had the charisma to be a leading man and the ability to extract subtleties from a part.

Harvey (Lauruska Mischa Skikne) was born in 1928, in Yomishkis, Lithuania. He was already acting on stage by his midteens and made his screen debut at twenty in *House of Darkness.* Uninteresting roles kept him glued to the bottom rung for a while, but he was a convincing juvenile delinquent in *I Believe in You* with Joan Collins. An important Hollywood role in *King Richard and the Crusaders* made him an international name. He did an enjoyable version of *Romeo and Juliet* and was well matched with Julie Harris in *I Am a Camera,* later musicalized as *Cabaret.*

Critics were still not in Harvey's corner. They finally cheered as did the Academy, when they nominated him Best Actor for *Room at the Top.* He portrayed a calculating social climber who deserts girlfriend Simone Signoret. In 1958, he played in "Henry V" at the Old Vic, and his screen roles kept pace with *Butterfield 8,* a marvelously hammy melodrama. He also overplayed a good role as a show business promoter in *Expresso Bongo.*

He had two more outstanding parts, in *The Manchurian Candidate,* as a programmed assassin, and in *Darling,* as the playboy who helped Julie Christie destroy her life. There was also a reunion with *Butterfield 8* co-star Elizabeth Taylor in *Night Watch,* a dull thriller. On this professional low note, Harvey died of cancer at the age of forty-five.

FILMOGRAPHY

1948

House of Darkness ★★★
The Dancing Years (bit)

1949

Man on the Run ★★★
Landfall ★★
The Man from Yesterday ★★

1950

Cairo Road ★★★
The Black Rose ★★

1951

There Is Another Sun ★★★
The Scarlet Thread ★★

1952

I Believe in You ★★★
A Killer Walks ★★★
Women of Twilight ★★

1953

Innocents in Paris ★★★

Laurence Harvey with Heather Sears in *Room at the Top.*

1954

Romeo and Juliet ★★★
The Good Die Young ★★★
King Richard and the Crusaders ★★★

1955

I Am a Camera ★★★
Storm Over the Nile ★★★

1956

Three Men in a Boat ★★★

1957

After the Ball ★★★

1958

The Truth About Women ★★★
The Silent Enemy ★★★
Room at the Top ★★★★

1959

Expresso Bongo ★★★★

1960

The Alamo ★★
Butterfield 8 ★★★★

1961

Two Loves ★★
The Long and the Short and the Tall ★★

1962

Walk on the Wild Side ★★
The Wonderful World of the Brothers Grimm ★★
The Manchurian Candidate ★★★★

1963

A Girl Named Tamiko ★★
The Running Man ★★
The Ceremony ★★

1964

The Outrage ★★
Of Human Bondage ★★

1965

Life at the Top ★★★
Darling ★★★★

1966

The Spy with the Cold Nose ★★

1968

A Dandy In Aspic ★★
Kampf um Rom ★★

1969

L'Assoluto Naturale ★★
The Magic Christian ★★

1970

WUSA ★★★

1972

Escape to the Sun ★★

1973

Night Watch ★★

1974

Welcome to Arrow Beach ★★

GOLDIE HAWN
★★★ 3.07 STARS

Goldie Hawn is currently one of our most appealing comediennes. She possesses a giddy, disarming manner and a naughty giggle, but her strength lies in the intelligence beneath. One senses a firm command of concept and characterization even when she's at her silliest.

Hawn was born in Washington, D.C., in 1945, and started studying ballet and tap dancing at three. She acted professionally at sixteen, playing Juliet with the Virginia Stage Company, and later, she performed as a can-can dancer. She did little more than giggle in her first film, Disney's forgettable *The One and Only Genuine Original Family Band.* After that, television was a welcome improvement. It gave her an identity and national popularity when she starred in "Laugh-In." She managed to upstage such other bright comediennes as Ruth Buzzi, Judy Carne, and Joanne Worley.

Fame offered a second shot at feature films, and this time she was lucky—Columbia signed her for *Cactus Flower.* She played the record store salesgirl with a mad crush on married Walter Matthau. The movie had its weaknesses, for Ingrid Bergman was too mature for her part, and some of the scenes were stagy. However, Hawn's daffiness was right on target, and she won a Best Supporting Actress Oscar.

There's a Girl in My Soup, a strained farce with Peter Sellers, had a funny title but little else. *Butterflies Are Free* was far superior. Hawn was the sympathetic girl who gave Edward Albert the confidence to cope with his blindness. Both stars were excellent, though Eileen Heckart won the Oscar and the plaudits. Even those who didn't like her comedy had to agree that *The Sugarland Express* contained some fine dramatic acting. The downbeat

Goldie Hawn in *The Sugarland Express.*

nature of the material kept audiences away, and sheer lack of quality discouraged anyone from seeing *The Girl from Petrovka.* The film was a creaky romantic comedy with Hawn as the Russian girl having an affair with American correspondent Hal Holbrook.

One of Hawn's biggest successes came in *Shampoo,* a kinky story of superficial Californians. She was touching as Warren Beatty's loyal lover, the one totally human note in an otherwise phony enterprise. She played a western hooker in *The Duchess and the Dirtwater Fox,* but all her skill—and the comic mastery of co-star George Segal—couldn't mask the forced gags and below-par script.

Up until the mid-1970s, Hawn's material zigzagged wildly. She began a more consistent pattern with *Foul Play,* a comedy-thriller that gave her an ideal teammate in Chevy Chase. She was the producing hand behind *Private Benjamin,* her most successful movie to date. It was a variation on the old service comedies (particularly Rosalind Russell's *Never Wave at a Wac*), but Hawn's freshness gave it a modern feeling. Eileen Brennan was also outstanding as the tough officer who forced Hawn to prove herself.

For all her talent, Hawn can occasionally go overboard on cuteness. She'll mug too much if she has to compensate for weak material, such as in *Seems Like Old Times.* However, with the right material, she brilliantly carries the banner once held by another "dumb" blonde, Judy Holliday.

FILMOGRAPHY

1968

The One and Only Genuine Original Family Band (bit)

1969

Cactus Flower ★★★★

1970

There's a Girl in My Soup ★★★

1972

Butterflies Are Free ★★★★
$ ★★

1974

The Sugarland Express ★★★
The Girl from Petrovka ★★

1975

Shampoo ★★★★

1976

The Duchess and the Dirtwater Fox ★★

1978

Foul Play ★★★★

1979

Lovers and Liars ★★

1980

Private Benjamin ★★★★

Goldie Hawn in *Private Benjamin.*

1981

Seems Like Old Times ★★★

1982

Best Friends ★★★

1983

Swing Shift ★★★

STERLING HAYDEN
★★★ 2.93 STARS

Hulking and handsome, Sterling Hayden never found his niche in films. In the beginning, he was just too big and brutish to be a romantic leading man. And later on, he was just too handsome and fair-featured to make a memorable villain. However, he did develop into a capable and compelling character actor.

Sterling Hayden with Joan Crawford in *Johnny Guitar.*

He was born John Hamilton on March 26, 1916, in New Jersey. At age sixteen he shipped out as a mate on a schooner, and by twenty-two he was a captain. In 1940, Paramount Studios signed him and billed him as "the most beautiful man in the movies"; for a while they spelled his name as Stirling. The publicity, including his marriage to actress Madeleine Carroll, made little impact, and he shipped out after only two films to serve in World War II.

After the war, he returned to films and was increasingly cast as a suave criminal. He proved himself with an excellent performance in John Huston's *The Asphalt Jungle.* In 1951, he was called before the House Un-American Activities Committee where he confessed to Communist ties and named other party members—an action that still haunts him. At the time, however, his career did not suffer. He had a curiously emasculating role in the oddball western *Johnny Guitar* and the lead in Stanley Kubrick's *The Killing*, where he cool-headedly masterminds a race-track heist. Hayden's demand dwindled with the fading of the 1950s-style crime drama, but he continued to find effective roles in widely divergent films: *Dr. Strangelove*, *The Godfather*, *The Long Goodbye*, *1900*, *King of the Gypsies*, and *Winter Kills*.

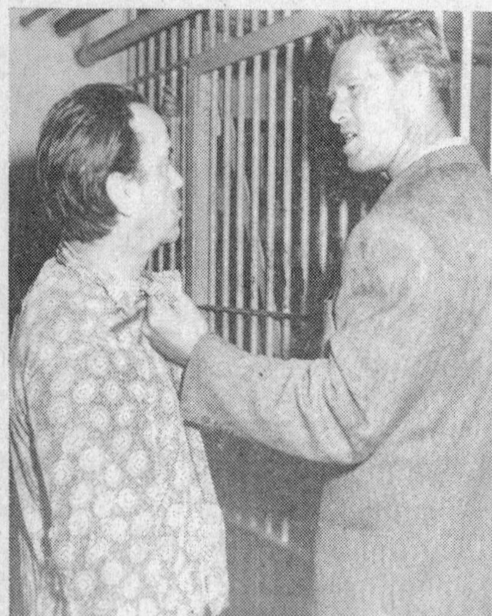

Sterling Hayden in *Crime Wave*.

FILMOGRAPHY

1941

Virginia ★★
Bahama Passage ★★

1947

Variety Girl ★★
Blaze of Noon ★★★

1949

El Paso ★★★
Manhandled ★★★

1950

The Asphalt Jungle ★★★★

1951

Journey Into Light ★★★

1952

Flaming Feather ★★★
The Denver and Rio Grande ★★★
Hellgate ★★★
The Golden Hawk ★★★
Flat Top ★★★

1953

The Star ★★★★
Take Me to Town ★★★
Kansas Pacific ★★★
Fighter Attack ★★★
So Big ★★★

1954

Crime Wave ★★★
Prince Valiant ★★
Arrow in the Dust ★★
Johnny Guitar ★★★★
Naked Alibi ★★★
Suddenly ★★★★

1955

Battle Taxi ★★★
Timberjack ★★★
Shotgun ★★★
The Eternal Sea ★★★
The Last Command ★★★
Top Gun ★★★

1956

The Come On ★★★
The Killing ★★★★

1957

Crime of Passion ★★★
Five Steps to Danger ★★★
The Iron Sheriff ★★
Valerie ★★★
Gun Battle at Monterey ★★
Zero Hour ★★★

1958

Terror in a Texas Town ★★★
Ten Days to Tulara ★★★

1964

Dr. Strangelove or How I Learned to Stop Worrying and Love the Bomb ★★★★

1969

Hard Contract ★★★
Sweet Lovers ★★★

1970

Loving ★★★

1971

Cobra ★★

1972

The Godfather ★★★★

1976

The Long Goodbye ★★★★
Last Days of Man on Earth ★★★

1976

1900 ★★★

1979

King of the Gypsies ★★★
Winter Kills ★★★
9 to 5 ★★★

1980

The Outsider ★★★
Cry Onion ★★

1981

Gas ★★

HELEN HAYES
★★★ 3.12 STARS

Helen Hayes is always interesting and individual on film, but a hint of Broadway clings to her acting. She enunciates and gestures as though she is playing to the balcony.

Hayes was born Helen Hayes Brown, in Washington D.C., in 1900. She acted from earliest childhood and achieved so many successes ("Ceasar and Cleopatra," "What Every Woman Knows," and "The Touch of the Poet") that she was inevitably tagged The First Lady of the Theatre. She won an Oscar for her first starring role in *The Sin of Madelon Claudet*. After *Arrowsmith* with Ronald Colman, she did the first and best version of *A Farewell to Arms*, performing touching and memorable scenes opposite Gary Cooper.

With the completion of *The White Sister* and *Night Flight*, Hayes returned to Broadway and didn't make any movies for 18 years. Her greatest screen performance was the queen in *Anastasia* who refused to accept niece Ingrid Bergman. *Airport* won her a second Oscar, but her cutesiness only intruded on the action. She has frequent guest appearances on TV, and starred in a short-lived TV series, "The Snoop Sisters."

FILMOGRAPHY

1917

The Weavers of Life ★★★

1920

Babs ★★★

1931

The Sin of Madelon Claudet ★★★★
Arrowsmith ★★★★

1932

A Farewell to Arms ★★★★
The Son-Daughter ★★★

1933

The White Sister ★★★
Another Language ★★★
Night Flight ★★★

1934

Crime Without Passion (cameo)
What Every Woman Knows ★★★

Helen Hayes.

1935

Vanessa: Her Love Story ★★★

1943

Stage Door Canteen (cameo)

1952

My Son John ★★

1953

Main Street to Broadway (cameo)

1956

Anastasia ★★★★

1959

Third Man on the Mountain (cameo)

1970

Airport ★★

1974

Helen Hayes: Portrait of an American Actress (documentary)
Herbie Rides Again ★★★

1975

One of Our Dinosaurs Is Missing ★★★

1978

Candleshoe ★★★

SUSAN HAYWARD
★★★ 2.98 STARS

During her lifetime, Susan Hayward contributed a gallery of great dramatic portrayals, won an Oscar, and made the Exhibitor's Top 10 regularly. However, her death failed to stimulate any media attention. Perhaps there were no tributes or retrospectives because of her lack of personal popularity, which once led an observer to comment, "She's smart . . . but cold as a Polar Bear's foot."

Hayward was born Edythe Marrener, in Brooklyn, in 1918. She modeled for awhile and then made an unbilled appearance in *Girls on Probation*. After a minor part in *Beau Geste*, director Gregory Ratoff hired her to play a bad girl in *Adam Had Four Sons*. She was strikingly effective, and her reviews were equally good for *Among the Living*, a melodrama about a deranged killer.

She graduated to second leads in *The Forest Rangers* and *I Married a Witch* and then gave another riveting unsympathetic performance in *The Hairy Ape*. *Smash-Up: The Story of a Woman* showed how powerfully she could play an alcoholic, something she reaffirmed in 1956's *I'll Cry Tomorrow*. In *The Saxon Charm*, a fascinating study of a manipulative producer, Robert Montgomery had all the big scenes. She made a stronger impression in *Tulsa* with Robert Preston.

Susan Hayward with Richard Conte in *I'll Cry Tomorrow*.

In *House of Strangers*, Mankiewicz's magnificent melodrama about a banking family, Hayward was convincing, if strident, as Richard Conte's girlfriend. Her best part came next in *My Foolish Heart* as the pregnant girl who lost her lover (Dana Andrews) in a flying accident. Although it proved conclusively that she could project vulnerability and warmth, her cutting edge returned in *I Can Get It for You Wholesale*, a sharp, no-holds-barred close-up of the garment business. When she tried historical spectacle in *David and Bathsheba*, the production values were epic enough but the script stubbornly refused to come to life.

Her warmth was an asset to *With a Song in My Heart*, a romanticized version of the life of singer Jane Froman. In *The Snows of Kiliminjaro*, one of the best cinematic attempts to capture Hemingway, Hayward's role was pallid and subsidiary to Ava Gardner's. She continued to perform competently even with a temporary dip in material in *The Lusty Men*, *The President's Lady*, *White Witch Doctor*, and *Demetrius and the Gladiators*.

Soldier of Fortune with Clark Gable was a clinker of a film that rang bells at the box office. Her best opportunity for genuine acting came one year later, with *I'll Cry Tomorrow*. As she showed in *Smash-Up: The Story of a Woman*, Hayward had a gift of getting under the skin of an alcoholic. A favorite to win the Oscar in 1955, she lost to Anna Magnani. *I Want to Live* miraculously handed her a second once-in-a-lifetime role. Hayward played Barbara Graham, a real-life call girl convicted of murder. Her vividly delineated anxiety brought her the Oscar she had nearly won before.

A Woman Obsessed, *Thunder in the Sun*, and *I Thank a Fool* were undistinguished. *Where Love Has Gone* "was a piece of crap," said costar Davis, "but it paid for my daughter's wedding." Hayward appeared in a huge hit, *Valley of the Dolls*, but her performance was sadly inferior to her earlier work. After a long bout with cancer, she died in 1975. Susan Hayward was a great film actress, but she never managed to acquire the aura and mystique that is supposed to accompany Hollywood stardom.

FILMOGRAPHY

1937

Hollywood Hotel (bit)

1938

The Sisters (bit)
Comet Over Broadway (bit)
Girls on Probation ★★★

1939

Our Leading Citizen ★★
Beau Geste ★★★
$1,000 a Touchdown ★★★

Susan Hayward.

1941

Adam Had Four Sons ★★★★
Sis Hopkins ★★★
Among the Living ★★★★

1942

Reap the Wild Wind ★★★
The Forest Rangers ★★
I Married a Witch ★★★
Star Spangled Rhythm (cameo)

1943

Hit Parade of 1943 ★★★
Young and Willing ★★★
Jack London ★★★

1944

The Fighting Seabees ★★★
The Hairy Ape ★★★★
And Now Tomorrow ★★

1946

Deadline at Dawn ★★★★
Canyon Passage ★★★

1947

Smash-Up: The Story of a Woman ★★★★
They Won't Believe Me ★★★
The Lost Moment ★★★

1948

Tap Roots ★★★
The Saxon Charm ★★★

1949

Tulsa ★★★
House of Strangers ★★★

1950

My Foolish Heart ★★★★

1951

I'd Climb the Highest Mountain ★★★
Rawhide ★★★
I Can Get It for You Wholesale ★★★★
David and Bathsheba ★★★

1952

With a Song in My Heart ★★★★
The Snows of Kiliminjaro ★★★
The Lusty Men ★★★★

1953

The President's Lady ★★★
White Witch Doctor ★★★

1954

Demetrius and the Gladiators ★★
Garden of Evil ★★★

1955

Untamed ★★★
Soldier of Fortune ★★★

1956

I'll Cry Tomorrow ★★★★
The Conqueror ★★

1957

Top Secret Affair ★★

1958

I Want to Live ★★★★

1959

A Woman Obsessed ★★
Thunder in the Sun ★★

1961

The Marriage-Go-Round ★★
Ada ★★★
Back Street ★★★

1962

I Thank a Fool ★★★

1963

Stolen Hours ★★★

1964

Where Love Has Gone ★★

1967

The Honey Pot ★★
Valley of the Dolls ★★

1972

The Revengers ★★★

RITA HAYWORTH
★★★ 3.00 STARS

A colleague of Rita Hayworth's once commented, "When she walked on the set she looked like nothing in the world, but in front of a camera, one looked at nothing else. It wouldn't have been possible to make her look uninteresting."

Hayworth was born Margarita Carmen Cansino, in 1918, in New York, the daughter of a well-known Latin dancer. Her training began at age three and a half, and she later said, "Rehearse, rehearse, rehearse. That was my childhood." A minor decoration in her first films, *Charlie Chan in Egypt* and *Human Cargo*, the B pictures continued through *Girls Can Play, Paid to Dance, Juvenile Court*, and *Homicide Bureau*. Her only good part in this period was in *Only Angels Have Wings*. After *Special Inspector* and *Blondie on a Budget*, director George Cukor thought her "attractive and gifted" enough to put her in *Susan and God*.

Strawberry Blonde began her spectacular ascent as the epitome of a "Love Goddess," and she was magnetic as the shallow beauty James Cagney loved and lost. In fact, the New York Telegram raved, "When it comes to oomph, Miss Hayworth possesses an 18-karat variety and she certainly tosses it around to good advantage here." In *Blood and Sand*, a full color remake of a Rudolph Valentino film, Hayworth was called "devastating" by the New York Herald Tribune. Finally, she was teamed with Fred Astaire and kicked off the pair of musicals that best utilized her talents. Astaire said admiringly, "She learned steps faster than anyone I've ever known." They made *You'll Never Get Rich* and *You Were Never Lovelier* together, two charming and underrated musicals.

Rita Hayworth in *Gilda*.

Cover Girl, her first acknowledged classic, featured innovative dance routines by Gene Kelly and Hayworth at her loveliest. *Cover Girl*'s songs were written by Gershwin, Kern, and Harburg, but *Tonight and Every Night* had a less memorable score and a more serious wartime theme. Her next classic was *Gilda*, an erotic love triangle, featuring Hayworth's famous striptease to the tune of "Put the Blame on Mame, Boys." Glenn Ford and George Macready understandably fought for her affections. *The Lady From Shanghai* has become a cult film, but at the time this weird, experimental effort by Orson Welles, Hayworth's husband, alienated her fans.

None of her follow-ups had the steamy sensuality of *Gilda*, although Hayworth brought a crisp magnetism to the "older" woman in *Pal Joey*. In *Separate Tables*, she was cast as a woman terrified of loneliness and middle age who maneuvered to win back husband Burt Lancaster. She was surprisingly effective, and she gave a performance of Oscar caliber in Clifford Odets' somber courtroom study, *The Story On Page One*. *Circus World*, with John Wayne, centered on a mother-daughter conflict (Claudia Cardinale was Hayworth's daughter) but the spectacle dwarfed her performance.

Hayworth has been called dull and uninteresting off the screen. She said somewhat wistfully to Virginia Van Upp, author of *Gilda*, "It's your fault. . . . Every man has gone to bed with Gilda and wakened with me."

FILMOGRAPHY

(billed as Rita Cansino)

1935

Under the Pampas Moon ★★
Charlie Chan in Egypt ★★
Dante's Inferno ★★
Paddy O'Day ★★

1936

Human Cargo ★★
Meet Nero Wolfe ★★
Rebellion ★★

1937

Trouble in Texas ★★
Old Louisiana ★★
Hit the Saddle ★★★

Rita Hayworth in *Salome*.

(billed as Rita Hayworth)

1937

Girls Can Play ★★★
The Game That Kills ★★★
Criminals of the Air ★★★
Paid to Dance ★★★
The Shadow ★★★

1938

Who Killed Gail Preston? ★★★
There's Always a Woman ★★★
Convicted ★★★
Juvenile Court ★★★

1939

Homicide Bureau ★★★
The Renegade Ranger ★★★
The Lone Wolf Spy Hunt ★★★
Only Angels Have Wings ★★★★
Special Inspector ★★★

1940

Music in My Heart ★★★
Blondie on a Budget ★★★
Susan and God ★★★
The Lady in Question ★★★
Angels Over Broadway ★★★

1941

Strawberry Blonde ★★★★
Affectionately Yours ★★★
Blood and Sand ★★★★
You'll Never Get Rich ★★★★

1942

My Gal Sal ★★★
Tales of Manhattan ★★★
You Were Never Lovelier ★★★★

1944

Cover Girl ★★★★

1945

Tonight and Every Night ★★★★

1946

Gilda ★★★★

1947

Down to Earth ★★★

1948

The Lady From Shanghai ★★★★
The Loves of Carmen ★★★

1952

Champagne Safari (documentary)
Affair in Trinidad ★★★

1953

Salome ★★★
Miss Sadie Thompson ★★★

1957

Fire Down Below ★★★
Pal Joey ★★★★

1958

Separate Tables ★★★★
They Came to Cordura ★★★★

1960

The Story On Page One ★★★★

1962

The Happy Thieves ★★

1964

Circus World ★★★

1966

The Money Trap ★★★★
The Poppy Is Also a Flower ★★

1967

The Rover ★★★

1969

Sons of Satan ★★

1970

The Road to Salina ★★

1971

The Naked Zoo ★★

1972

The Wrath of God ★★★

AUDREY HEPBURN
★★★ 3.14 STARS

Audrey Hepburn's delicate, high-fashion beauty is a totally individual creation; she projects sensitivity and refinement but never weakness. Like Loretta Young and Jeanette MacDonald, she has a bit of the iron butterfly about her but not enough to endanger her charm.

She was born Audrey Hepburn-Ruston, in Belgium in 1929, the daughter of a wealthy baroness. After studying ballet and modeling, she appeared briefly in a short film, *Nederlands In Zeven Lessen*, and a few other minor parts in *Laughter in Paradise*, *One Wild Oat*, and *The Lavender Hill Mob*. Her Broadway appearance in "Gigi" brought raves and the leading role in *Roman Holiday.* Critical reaction was ecstatic ("Miss Hepburn is a thing of beauty—in comedy, romance, drama and farce"—Cue magazine), and the Academy declared its agreement by awarding her an Oscar.

Sabrina, which followed, was even more enchanting than *Roman Holiday.* Hepburn played a chauffeur's daughter who had to choose between playboy William Holden and his older, more serious-minded brother (Humphrey Bogart). It was unanimously agreed that grown-up fairy tales were her natural element.

In *War and Peace,* an elaborate but superficial adaptation of the Tolstoy classic, Hepburn was singled out for praise. The more entertaining Gershwin musical *Funny Face* spotlighted her dancing talents and her ability to wear chic clothes. Fred Astaire was a perfect match despite the difference in their ages. The May-December romance didn't work with Gary Cooper in Billy Wilder's *Love in the Afternoon.* Both players were at their best, but only the Maurice Chevalier sequences sparkled.

Audrey Hepburn in *War and Peace.*

The Nun's Story, a more dramatically challenging vehicle, gave Hepburn the opportunity to prove her acting strength, and she rose brilliantly to the challenge. Without resorting to broad histrionics, she conveyed all the conflict and emotional strains of flesh vs. spirit. She was helped enormously by Peter Finch in the Congo sequences. Her sprite image wasn't able to make much out of *Green Mansions;* Hepburn played Rima, the Bird Girl. A western, *The Unforgiven,* brought her down to earth.

Breakfast at Tiffany's was a witty, way-out (for 1961) tale of Holly Golightly, a game-playing kook stabilized by the love of George Peppard. However, author Truman Capote disapproved of her interpretation of the role, "They made a big, boring Audrey Hepburn thing out of it." It was true that the immoral aspects of Holly's character were removed, but audiences applauded, and the Academy nominated Hepburn for another award.

Director William Wyler tried to remake *The Children's Hour,* reinstating the lesbian theme that had been removed from the first version, *These Three.* It seemed like much ado about nothing, and Hepburn was revived by *Charade,* a delightful Hitchcock-like thriller with Cary Grant. Her appearance in *My Fair Lady,* however, backfired; critics grumbled busily about Julie Andrews' exclusion, and Hepburn's performance *was* a letdown. She was elegant after her transformation into a lady but disturbingly miscast as the dirty-faced flower girl.

She retired in the late 1960s but returned to do *Robin and Marian,* a surprisingly sordid reworking of the Robin Hood legend. She had similar bad luck in the messy screen version of *Sidney Sheldon's Bloodline.* However, she regained her airy charm as a reclusive millionaire's wife (well matched with co-star Ben Gazzara) in the light comedy *They All Laughed.*

Audrey Hepburn with Ben Gazzara in *They All Laughed.*

FILMOGRAPHY

1951

One Wild Oat (bit)
The Lavender Hill Mob (bit)
Laughter in Paradise (bit)
Young Wives' Tale ★★★

1952

Monte Carlo Baby ★★★
The Secret People ★★★

1953

Roman Holiday ★★★★

1954

Sabrina ★★★★

1956

War and Peace ★★★

1957

Funny Face ★★★★
Love in the Afternoon ★★★

1959

Green Mansions ★★
The Nun's Story ★★★★

1960

The Unforgiven ★★★

1961

Breakfast at Tiffany's ★★★★

1962

The Children's Hour ★★★

1963

Charade ★★★★

1964

Paris When It Sizzles ★★
My Fair Lady ★★

1966

How to Steal a Million ★★

1967

Two for the Road ★★★★
Wait Until Dark ★★★★

1976

Robin and Marian ★★

1979

Sidney Sheldon's Bloodline ★★

1981

They All Laughed ★★★

KATHARINE HEPBURN
★ ★ ★ 3.14 STARS

Katharine Hepburn's achievements are so impressive that few people would dare to criticize her today. She has won four Best Actress Oscars, an unparalleled record, for her performances in *Morning Glory, Guess Who's Coming To Dinner, The Lion in Winter,* and *On Golden Pond*. Yet, every now and then, Joseph Mankiewicz's comment on her acting applies, "She's the greatest amateur actress in the world, most of whose performances—though remarkably effective—are fake."

Fake is the wrong word; stylized is more appropriate. She was born to wealthy parents in Connecticut, in 1909, and Hepburn was always mannered, her accent upper class. Throughout her film career, she has remained distinctly herself, no matter what the character. Her own personality was mesmerizing in her first screen role, *Bill of Divorcement*, and equally brilliant in *Morning Glory* and the hugely successful *Little Women*.

The public was intrigued, but Hepburn never became a popular favorite, making the box office top ten only once in 1969. Viewers sympathized with her desperate wallflower in *Alice Adams* but rejected her in *Spitfire, Break of Hearts, A Woman Rebels, Sylvia Scarlett, Mary of Scotland,* and *The Little Minister*. Labeled box-office poison along with Joan Crawford and Fred Astaire in the late 1930s, *Stage Door* was a delightful but temporary plus. *Bringing Up Baby,* a screwball comedy with Cary Grant, was a commercial disappointment despite fine reviews.

She fought to play Scarlett O'Hara in *Gone With the Wind* but producer Selznick wisely vetoed her as not sexy enough. Her comeback was *The Philadelphia Story* originally a success for her on Broadway. Everyone was enchanted in 1940, but today the movie is talky and synthetic, notable only for James Stewart's Oscar-winning performance.

Hepburn's mass appeal increased when she teamed with Spencer Tracy for *Adam's Rib*. Other successes with Tracy included the delightful *Pat and Mike* (featuring her as a champion athlete) and the topical but slow-moving *Woman of the Year. The African Queen* was a total triumph. Her mannerisms as the "skinny, psalm-singing old maid Rosie" worked perfectly for the character, and she blended surprisingly well with Humphrey Bogart.

Katharine Hepburn with Humphrey Bogart in *The African Queen*.

Summertime, hauntingly photographed in Venice and meticulously directed by David Lean, was soap opera of the highest grade, and she projected tomboyish magnetism in *The Rainmaker* opposite Burt Lancaster. Critics applauded her portrayal of a drug-addicted mother in *Long Day's Journey Into Night*. After this gallery of great screen portraits, the Academy saw fit to honor an infinitely less distinguished performance in *Guess Who's Coming To Dinner*. A ludicrous, patronizing look at interracial marriage, it is unwatchable today except for one breathtaking monologue by Spencer Tracy at the end.

Hepburn's uniqueness lay in her independence, her aristocratic strength. She was the very model of a woman who could cope, but after *Guess Who's Coming To Dinner* she developed an excessively tearful quality. The lump stayed in her throat during *The Lion in Winter*.

It was *On Golden Pond* that reconfirmed her special genius. As the loving but realistic wife of dying Henry Fonda, she was sensible, strong, humorous, and vulnerable—a well-rounded character. It was heartening evidence that the quality of one's film performance can be maintained even after 51 years of constant filmmaking.

FILMOGRAPHY

1932

Bill of Divorcement ★ ★ ★ ★

1933

Christopher Strong ★ ★
Morning Glory ★ ★ ★ ★
Little Women ★ ★ ★ ★

1934

Spitfire ★ ★
The Little Minister ★ ★ ★

1935

Break of Hearts ★ ★ ★
Alice Adams ★ ★ ★ ★

1936

Sylvia Scarlett ★ ★
Mary of Scotland ★ ★ ★
A Woman Rebels ★ ★ ★

1937

Quality Street ★ ★ ★
Stage Door ★ ★ ★ ★

1938

Bringing Up Baby ★ ★ ★ ★
Holiday ★ ★ ★ ★

1940

The Philadelphia Story ★ ★ ★

1942

Woman of the Year ★ ★ ★
Keeper of the Flame ★ ★

1943

Stage Door Canteen ★ ★ ★

1944

Dragon Seed ★ ★ ★

1945

Without Love ★ ★ ★

Katharine Hepburn with James Stewart in *The Philadelphia Story*.

1946

Undercurrent ★★★

1947

Sea of Grass ★★
Song of Love ★★

1948

State of the Union ★★★★

1949

Adam's Rib ★★★★

1951

The African Queen ★★★★

1952

Pat and Mike ★★★★

1955

Summertime ★★★★

Katharine Hepburn in *Little Women.*

1956

The Rainmaker ★★★★
The Iron Petticoat ★★

1957

Desk Set ★★★

1959

Suddenly Last Summer ★★★★

1962

Long Day's Journey Into Night ★★★★

1967

Guess Who's Coming To Dinner ★★★

1968

The Lion in Winter ★★★

1969

The Madwoman of Chaillot ★★

1971

The Trojan Women ★★

1973

A Delicate Balance ★★★★

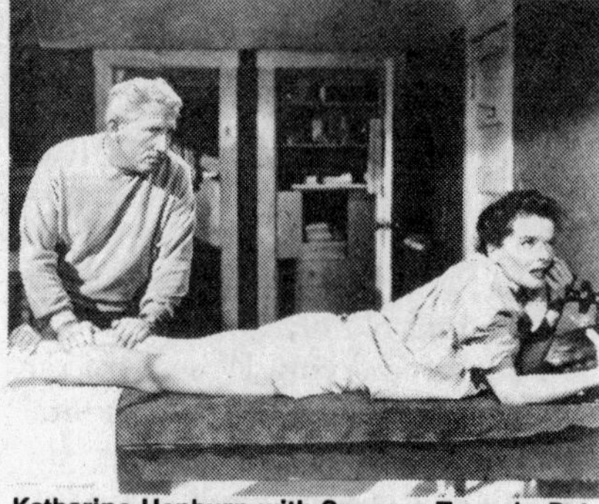

Katharine Hepburn with Spencer Tracy in *Pat and Mike.*

1975

The Glass Menagerie ★★★

1976

Rooster Cogburn ★★

1978

Olly, Olly, Oxen Free ★★

1982

On Golden Pond ★★★★

CHARLTON HESTON
★★★ 2.77 STARS

Charlton Heston was shaped by nature to be a hero. Tall and muscular with a low, commanding voice, he's always been perfectly at home commanding armies or leading biblical crowds over land and sea. Unfortunately, more intimate backdrops expose a tight-jawed somberness and a lack of humor.

Heston (Charles Carter) was born in 1923, in Evanston, Illinois. In 1947 he appeared on Broadway with Katherine Cornell in "Anthony and Cleopatra." He was also active on TV in "Julius Caesar" and "Jane Eyre" before doing his first Hollywood movie, an insignificant gambling drama *Dark City.* His next film, *The Greatest Show on Earth,* was vastly different in size and quality—an Oscar winner for best picture and an excellent vehicle for Heston who played a circus manager.

His authoritative performance insured steady work though his next pictures were less than outstanding. The best of the bunch, *Ruby Gentry,* featured an uncharacteristically sexy Jennifer Jones. *Pony Express, Arrowhead,* and *The Far Horizons* just filled time until he played in his next epic, *The Ten Commandments,* a huge money-maker. Heston portrayed a convincing Moses, but the lively fun of another De Mille biblical spectacle *Samson and Delilah* was missing.

A soap opera with Jane Wyman, *Lucy Gallant,* followed along with an Orson Welles thriller, *Touch of Evil,* that impressed critics more than audiences. Heston dominated William Wyler's *The Big Country,* a popular western though co-star Burl Ives won the Oscar.

Heston's time for Oscar recognition came with *Ben Hur.* This epic made Heston a superstar, and he said, rather pompously, "It will probably not only be the most important film I'll ever make, but should also either finally push me into thin, airless reaches where the supernovae drift, or demonstrate conclusively that my orbit is a different one." *The Wreck of the Mary Deare* with Gary Cooper was another hit, but *The Pigeon That Took Rome* demonstrated that comedy wasn't his forte.

Spectacle followed spectacle: *El Cid, Diamond Head, 55 Days at Peking* (with Ava Gardner, an actress he loathed), *The Greatest Story Ever Told, The Agony and the Ecstasy, The War Lord,* and *Khartoum.* These films were big, but not entertaining, and his box-office appeal began to wane.

Suffering from epic-itis, the public ignored Heston in a pair of fine westerns that happened to escape his inclination to pomposity. *Major Dundee* and *Will Penny* were artistic successes that failed at the box office. Heston bitterly complained that *Will Penny* was sold short by the studio.

Planet of the Apes was a smash, however, and so was the sequel, *Beneath the Planet of the Apes.* He bolstered his appeal with these simplistic science fictions, and remained stiff and uninteresting in his later films. However, a costume drama (*The Three Musketeers*) was good fun, and he was appropriately typecast as a captain in the episodic *Midway.*

Heston isn't a flexible actor, but he deserves credit for trying all sorts of classical and modern parts. Filmgoers need an old-fashioned Superman to provide contrast to the small, average-looking Hoffmans, Pacinos, and De Niros.

FILMOGRAPHY

1950

Dark City ★★★

1952

The Greatest Show on Earth ★★★★
The Savage ★★★
Ruby Gentry ★★★★

1953

The President's Lady ★★★
Pony Express ★★
Arrowhead ★★
Bad for Each Other ★★

1954

The Naked Jungle ★★★
Secret of the Incas ★★

1955

The Far Horizons ★★★
The Private War of Major Benson ★★
Lucy Gallant ★★★

1956

The Ten Commandments ★★★★

1957

Three Violent People ★★★

1958

Touch of Evil ★★★★
The Big Country ★★★★
The Buccaneer ★★★

1959

The Wreck of the Mary Deare ★★★
Ben Hur ★★★★

1961

El Cid ★★

Charlton Heston with Sophia Loren in *El Cid*.

Charlton Heston.

1962

The Pigeon That Took Rome ★★

1963

Diamond Head ★★
55 Days at Peking ★★

1965

The Greatest Story Ever Told ★★★
Major Dundee ★★★
The Agony and the Ecstasy ★★
The War Lord ★★

1966

Khartoum ★★★

1968

Will Penny ★★★★
Planet of the Apes ★★★
Counterpoint ★★

1969

Number One ★★★

1970

Julius Caesar ★★★
Beneath the Planet of the Apes ★★★
The Hawaiians ★★

1971

The Omega Man ★★

1972

Call of the Wild ★★★
Anthony and Cleopatra ★★★
Skyjacked ★★★

1973

Soylent Green ★★★

1974

Earthquake ★★
Airport 1975 ★★★
The Three Musketeers ★★★

1975

The Four Musketeers ★★

1976

The Last Hard Men ★★★
Midway ★★
Two-Minute Warning ★★★

1977

Crossed Swords ★★★

1978

Gray Lady Down ★★★

1980

The Mountain Men ★★
The Awakening ★★

WENDY HILLER
★★★½ 3.71 STARS

A crisp, no-nonsense actress, Wendy Hiller literally took command of the screen whenever she appeared on film.

Hiller was born in 1912, in Bramshall, Cheshire, England and took London by storm in 1936 with "Love on the Dole." She scored her first major film triumph as Eliza Doolittle in *Pygmalion*, and her authority cut through the incessant chatter of *Major Barbara*. Hiller was also a touchingly tragic victim of Mau Mau terrorism in the bloody *Something of Value*.

In *Separate Tables*, Hiller played the proprietress of a secluded hotel who lost Burt Lancaster to his scheming ex-wife (Rita Hayworth). Hiller resisted making an obvious soap-opera bid for sympathy yet moved audiences everywhere (including the Academy, who voted her Best Supporting Actress in 1958). She was the nice sister, Geraldine Page was the nasty one, in Lillian Hellman's *Toys in the Attic*. And her portrayals in *Sons and Lovers* and *Murder on the Orient Express* were the strongest elements of both films. She was given the title of Dame in 1975.

FILMOGRAPHY

1937

Lancashire Lad ★★★

1938

Pygmalion ★★★★

1941

Major Barbara ★★★★

1945

I Know Where I'm Going ★★★★

1951

Outcast of the Islands ★★★★
Singlehanded ★★★

1957

Something of Value ★★★★
How to Murder a Rich Uncle ★★★★

1958

Separate Tables ★★★★

Wendy Hiller in *Voyage of the Damned.*

1960

Sons and Lovers ★★★★

1963

Toys in the Attic ★★★

1966

A Man for All Seasons ★★★★

1970

David Copperfield ★★★★

1974

Murder on the Orient Express ★★★★

1976

Voyage of the Damned ★★★★

1978

The Cat and the Canary ★★★

1981

The Elephant Man ★★★

DUSTIN HOFFMAN
★★★ 3.24 STARS

Dustin Hoffman is typical of modern stars. He offers no sex appeal, good looks, or traditional masculinity, yet he is sensational because of his ability to play average guys with sensitivity. His great acting skill is always at the fore of every role. Rarely, if ever, will he try to carry a weak film on the basis of his personality.

Born in Los Angeles, in 1937, Dustin Hoffman's acting career took wing in a New York play, "Harry Noon and Night," in which he played a German homosexual. His first film was a forgettable Spanish-Italian affair, *Un Dollaro Per Sette Vigliacchi* with Cesar Romero. No one noticed his debut, even when the film was retitled *Madigan's Millions* in the States.

The Graduate launched him as a symbol of misunderstood youth to an entire generation. Brilliantly directed by Mike Nichols, Hoffman brought pathos and comedic flair to his role as the floundering Benjamin. Critics typed him as a callow adolescent, a notion he buried immediately with *Midnight Cowboy.* He played the crippled, scheming Ratso with uncomfortable conviction, matched by Jon Voight's portrayal of a naive male hustler.

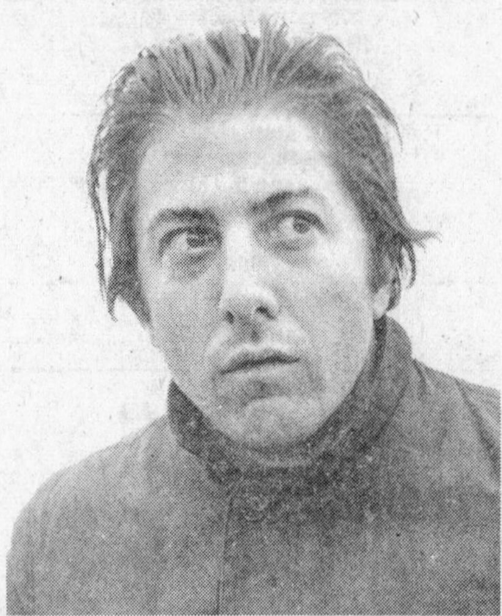

Dustin Hoffman in *Midnight Cowboy.*

His dedication to versatility temporarily derailed him in *John and Mary,* a pallid "hip" comedy about two people (Mia Farrow was the girl) who spent a night together before learning each other's names. Hoffman played a disturbed songwriter in *Who is Harry Kellerman and Why Is He Saying All Those Terrible Things About Me?* and his portrayal was pure self-indulgence. His performance helped hold together *Little Big Man,* Arthur Penn's sprawling over-ambitious look at the old West.

In *Papillon,* a minor improvement, Hoffman was Steve McQueen's prison buddy, and his eccentric mannerisms enlivened a grim, repetitive adventure. *Lenny* brought him an Oscar nomination, and he made a conscientious attempt to convey the contradiction of Lenny Bruce's character. His basic amiability worked against the concept, but it showed his eagerness to take on new challenges.

All the President's Men, Alan Pakula's meticulous recreation of the Watergate investigation, teamed him effectively with Robert Redford. In *Marathon Man,* a disjointed but exciting thriller, Hoffman had a spine-chilling scene as the victim of sadistic Nazi dentist Laurence Olivier. His career meandered a bit with *Straight Time* and *Agatha,* but he had his finest moment and his long-sought-after Oscar with *Kramer vs. Kramer.*

Tootsie, the most successful film in Columbia Pictures' history, offered him a seemingly impossible role—a male actor masquerading as a woman to get a part—and he brought it off. He accomplished this feat by getting inside the role, not spoofing it or subliminally whispering to audiences, "I'm a man, don't take this seriously." Curiously, it gave him a sexual allure absent from some of his earlier work. Hoffman, more than anyone today, is willing to take chances and to experiment, and this dedication can only bring new and unexpected dividends to all moviegoers.

FILMOGRAPHY

1967

The Tiger Makes Out ★★★
The Graduate ★★★★

1968

Madigan's Millions ★★

1969

Midnight Cowboy ★★★★
John and Mary ★★

1970

Little Big Man ★★★

1971

Who is Harry Kellerman and Why Is He Saying All Those Terrible Things About Me? ★★
Straw Dogs ★★★★

1972

Alfredo, Alfredo ★★★

1973

Papillon ★★★

1974

Lenny ★★★

1976

All The President's Men ★★★★
Marathon Man ★★★★

Dustin Hoffman with Sydney Pollack in *Tootsie*.

1978

Straight Time ★★★

1979

Agatha ★★★
Kramer vs. Kramer ★★★★

1982

Tootsie ★★★★

WILLIAM HOLDEN
★★★ 3.21 STARS

Great actors like William Holden are often overlooked because their portrayals are accomplished simply through honesty without gimmicks and cosmetic aids. Holden was a consummate actor and never less than believable. Humphrey Bogart once said of Spencer Tracy, "He's the best, because you don't see the wheels turning." The same was true of William Holden.

He was born William Franklin Beedle, Jr., in 1918, in O'Fallon, Illinois, and began acting at an early age. He played Madame Curie's eighty-year-old father-in-law on stage when he was nineteen. With minimum experience, he did a superb job in *Golden Boy* and credited star Barbara Stanwyck for his performance. Most of his subsequent early roles were innocuous: *Invisible Stripes*, *Those Were the Days*, and *I Wanted Wings*. John Huston summed it up when he called Holden, "that nice young man who played second lieutenants." He showed a knack for comedy in *Dear Ruth*, a big hit, and stole *Rachel and the Stranger* from Robert Mitchum. *Dear Wife* was an amusing sequel to *Dear Ruth*, but Holden had little to do.

He had a great deal to do in *Sunset Boulevard*, Billy Wilder's classic study of desperation and vanquished stardom in Hollywood. Gloria Swanson was flashy and theatrical as an over-the-hill actress attempting a comeback, but Holden's gigolo was equally compelling. He played Judy Holliday's tutor in the hilarious *Born Yesterday*. His next movies, *Force of Arms*, *Submarine Command*, and *Boots Malone*, pleasant though they were, represented an artistic setback.

Stalag 17 brought Holden the Oscar he should have received for *Sunset Boulevard*, and he began to dominate the box-office lists. *The Moon Is Blue* was a supposedly daring comedy because it used the word "virgin," and *Forever Female* was inconsequential backstage stuff. *Executive Suite* allowed him room to demonstrate his excellence again, and his charm was an asset to the wonderful *Sabrina*. In *Love Is a Many-Splendored Thing*, he was uninteresting, but he clashed dynamically with domineering Grace Kelly in *The Country Girl*.

For a while everything went right. *Picnic* was a smash, and Holden was convincing as the womanizing drifter who fell for Kim Novak. *The Bridge on the River Kwai* represented an artistic and financial triumph, and Holden's percentage brought him a lifetime annuity. After *The World of Suzie Wong*, his luck changed. *Satan Never Sleeps*, *The Lion*, *Paris When It Sizzles*, *The Seventh Dawn*, *Alvarez Kelly*, and *The Devil's Brigade* were all dismal failures. *The Wild Bunch*, an incredibly violent Sam Peckinpah western, was the box-office hit that rescued him.

After *The Wild Bunch*, there were a few more bonanzas, such as *The Towering Inferno*, Irwin Allen's record-breaking disaster movie, and *Network*. Holden played an honest, idealistic TV producer, giving human weight to writer Paddy Chayefsky's windy diatribes on the evils of television. *Damien—Omen II* wasn't up to the gory but exciting original, and *Fedora* was a fuzzy, *Sunset Boulevard*-like drama with a lackluster co-star, Marthe Keller.

The mean-spirited gossip regarding Holden's death—believed to be the result of a fall induced by drunkenness—showed Hollywood at its least admirable. Whatever his private devils, he always had the utmost integrity on screen.

FILMOGRAPHY

1938

Prison Farm (bit)

1939

Million Dollar Legs (bit)
Golden Boy ★★★★

1940

Invisible Stripes ★★★
Our Town ★★★
Those Were the Days ★★★
Arizona ★★★

1941

I Wanted Wings ★★★
Texas ★★★

1942

The Remarkable Andrew ★★★
The Fleet's In ★★★
Meet the Stewarts ★★★

1943

Young and Willing ★★★

1947

Blaze of Noon ★★★
Dear Ruth ★★★★
Variety Girl (cameo)

1948

Rachel and the Stranger ★★★★
Apartment for Peggy ★★★
The Man from Colorado ★★★★

1949

The Dark Past ★★★★
Streets of Laredo ★★★
Miss Grant Takes Richmond ★★★

1950

Dear Wife ★★★
Father Is a Bachelor ★★★
Sunset Boulevard ★★★★
Union Station ★★★★

1951

Born Yesterday ★★★★
Force of Arms ★★★
Submarine Command ★★★

1952

Boots Malone ★★★
The Turning Point ★★★

1953

Stalag 17 ★★★★
The Moon Is Blue ★★★
Escape From Fort Bravo ★★★

1954

Forever Female ★★★
Executive Suite ★★★
Sabrina ★★★★

William Holden with Kim Novak in *Picnic.*

1955

The Country Girl ★★★★
The Bridges at Toko-Ri ★★★
Love Is a Many-Splendored Thing ★★★

1956

Picnic ★★★★
The Proud and the Profane ★★★
Toward the Unknown ★★★

1957

The Bridge on the River Kwai ★★★★

1958

The Key ★★★

1959

The Horse Soldiers ★★★

1960

The World of Suzie Wong ★★★

1962

Satan Never Sleeps ★★★
The Counterfeit Traitor ★★★★
The Lion ★★★

1964

Paris When It Sizzles ★★★
The Seventh Dawn ★★★

1966

Alvarez Kelly ★★★

1967

Casino Royale ★★★

1968

The Devil's Brigade ★★★

1969

The Wild Bunch ★★★
The Christmas Tree ★★★

1971

Wild Rovers ★★★

1972

The Revengers ★★★

1973

Breezy ★★

1974

Open Season ★★★
The Towering Inferno ★★★

1976

Network ★★★★

1978

Damien—Omen II ★★★
Fedora ★★★

1979

Ashanti ★★★
When Time Ran Out ★★★

1981

S.O.B. ★★★
The Earthling ★★★

JUDY HOLLIDAY
★★★½ 3.45 STARS

Judy Holliday almost didn't become Billie Dawn in *Born Yesterday*—twice. She was a last-minute replacement for Jean Arthur on stage, and Harry Cohn at Columbia Pictures was dead set against her when the film was scheduled to be made. Fortunately for audiences, she triumphed both times and created what is still the definitive "dumb blonde" stock character.

Holliday was born Judith Tuvim, in 1922, in New York. She began as part of a comedy team, The Revuers, with Adolph Comden and Betty Green. She made *Winged Victory* with Jeanne Crain in 1944. Harry Cohn had wanted *Born Yesterday* for Rita Hayworth and remarked crudely about Holliday's "fat ass" (she had a lifelong complex about her weight). Nevertheless, after she appeared in *Adam's Rib* with Tracy and Hepburn, she won the part with the combined support of these two co-stars. Her Oscar for *Born Yesterday* was a surprise, for Bette Davis in *All About Eve* and Gloria Swanson in *Sunset Boulevard* had been considered more likely candidates.

Unfortunately *Born Yesterday* also typed her, and none of her parts varied much from the character of Billie Dawn. She was appealing, however, in *The Marrying Kind. It Should Happen to You* prompted co-star Jack Lemmon to praise her talent and call her "one of the nicest people I've ever met."

There was also another Broadway hit, "The Bells Are Ringing," which netted her fine reviews—and personal grief after a romance with leading man Sidney Chaplin collapsed. His father Charles Chaplin had voted thumbs down on the match, and Holliday recuperated by making *The Solid Gold Cadillac*—failure-proof material which cast her as a small stockholder challenging the crooked policies of a major corporation. Her last picture, *The Bells Are Ringing,* was a disappoint-

Judy Holliday with Paul Douglas in *The Solid Gold Cadillac.*

ing Vincente Minnelli-directed adaptation of the Broadway play.

Holliday had a few stage flops, "Hot Spot" and "Laurette", and another unhappy romance (with musician Gerry Mulligan) before succumbing to cancer at age forty-three. Her death in 1965 robbed the motion picture and theatrical world of a giant talent who was just beginning to reach her full potential.

FILMOGRAPHY

1944

Greenwich Village ★★★
Something for the Boys ★★★
Winged Victory ★★★

1949

Adam's Rib ★★★★

1950

Born Yesterday ★★★★

1952

The Marrying Kind ★★★

1954

It Should Happen to You ★★★
Phffft ★★★★

1956

The Solid Gold Cadillac ★★★★

1957

Full of Life ★★★★

1960

The Bells Are Ringing ★★★

BOB HOPE
★★★ 3.02 STARS

Bob Hope's brand of comedy was perfect for the screen. He knew just how to deliver lines for their maximum effect, and he maintained an actor's control throughout the most bizarre slapstick situations. Unlike some comedians, he was unwilling to expand his image by playing drama, just as he can't sit through an interview without lapsing into one liners.

Hope was born Leslie Townes Hope, in England, in 1903. He came from a poor background and was even pulled in by police once for stealing items from a sporting goods store. After a period of amateur boxing, he concentrated on vaudeville. His stage appearances included "Roberta," "Ziegfeld Follies," and "Red Hot and Blue," after which he made his first film, *The Big Broadcast of 1938.* The film featured a song that became solely identified with him, "Thanks For the Memory."

His popularity swelled after only a few pictures—*College Swing, Give Me a Sailor,* and *Never Say Die.* He made *Road to Singapore* in 1940 and dominated the box-office top ten for the rest of the decade. The interplay between Hope and his partner, Bing Crosby, in the road pictures was eagerly accepted by audiences, and *Road to Zanzibar* did even better than the first one. Hope co-starred with another "Road" player, Dorothy Lamour, in an army farce called *Caught in the Draft,* and then consolidated his comedic position with *Road to Morocco, Road to Utopia,* and *The Princess and the Pirate.*

One of Hope's writers, Mel Shavelson (also his director on *The Seven Little Foys* and *Beau James),* claimed that "Bob Hope's staff has usually been large, sleepless and prolific. He may call you at any hour from any place in the world for material on any subject." This relentless quest for perfection produced a score of enjoyable vehicles including: *Road to Rio, My Favorite Brunette,* and *Monsieur Beaucaire.* He was ideal in the superior remake of *Little Miss Marker,* and Lucille Ball, his only female comedic equal, made a perfect partner. He also matched well with Jane Russell in *The Paleface.*

After *Fancy Pants, Son of Paleface,* and *My Favorite Spy,* Hope's comedy writers seemed to lose their touch. *The Iron Petticoat* with Katharine Hepburn was disastrous. Director Ralph Thomas called him "uncertain and insecure" and added, "Hope and Hepburn were playing in two different pictures. She was a mistress of light, sophisticated romantic comedy; he was much broader." The *Seven Little Foys* was better, and Hope actually showed some acting ability. Mel Shavelson said, "I was able to force him away from his standard one-dimensional character and make him attempt difficult acting."

Paris Holiday and *That Certain Feeling* were only mildly entertaining, but they ranked as masterpieces beside the frantic farces that followed, *Bachelor in Paradise* with Lana Turner, *Critic's Choice, Call Me Bwana,* and *Boy, Did I Get a Wrong Number!*

In Hope's heyday, there had been some shred of characterization, as well as plenty of wit. Both were dismally absent in his later films, and Hope wouldn't (or couldn't) compensate for the omissions. He followed his scripts to the letter, never deviating, never adding anything of his own. But when the scripts were good, Hope richly earned his reputation as the funniest man in films.

FILMOGRAPHY

1938

The Big Broadcast of 1938 ★★★
College Swing ★★★
Give Me a Sailor ★★★
Thanks for the Memory ★★★

1939

Never Say Die ★★★
Some Like It Hot ★★★
The Cat and the Canary ★★★★

Bob Hope.

1940

Road to Singapore ★★★★
The Ghostbreakers ★★★★

1941

Road to Zanzibar ★★★★
Caught in the Draft ★★★
Nothing But the Truth ★★★
Louisiana Purchase ★★★

1942

My Favorite Blonde ★★★★
Road to Morocco ★★★★
Star Spangled Rhythm ★★★

1943

They Got Me Covered ★★★
Let's Face It ★★★

1944

The Princess and the Pirate ★★★

1946

Road to Utopia ★★★★
Monsieur Beaucaire ★★★★

1947

My Favorite Brunette ★★★★
Where There's Life ★★★
Variety Girl (cameo)

1948

Road to Rio ★★★★
The Paleface ★★★★

1949

Sorrowful Jones ★★★★
The Great Lover ★★★

1950

Fancy Pants ★★★★

1951

The Lemon Drop Kid ★★★
My Favorite Spy ★★★

1952

The Greatest Show on Earth (cameo)
Son of Paleface ★★★

1953

Road to Bali ★★★
Off Limits ★★★
Scared Stiff (cameo)
Here Come the Girls ★★★

1954

Casanova's Big Night ★★★

1955

The Seven Little Foys ★★★

1956

That Certain Feeling ★★★
The Iron Petticoat ★

1957

Beau James ★★★

1958

Paris Holiday ★★

1959

The Five Pennies (cameo)
Alias Jesse James ★★★★

Bob Hope with Bing Crosby in *The Road to Morocco.*

1960

The Facts of Life ★★★★

1961

Bachelor in Paradise ★★

1962

The Road to Hong Kong ★★★

1963

Critic's Choice ★★
Call Me Bwana ★

1964

A Global Affair ★★

1965

I'll Take Sweden ★★

1966

The Oscar (cameo)
Not With My Wife You Don't (cameo)
Boy, Did I Get a Wrong Number! ★

1967

Eight on the Lam ★★

1968

The Private Navy of Sergeant O'Farrell ★★

1969

How to Commit Marriage ★★★

1972

Cancel My Reservation ★★

1979

The Muppet Movie (cameo)

ANTHONY HOPKINS
★★★ 3.13 STARS

Even in his happier parts, Anthony Hopkins manages to suggest inner conflict and suffering. This pent-up tension gives a unique flavor to his characterizations.

Hopkins was born in 1937, in Port Talbot, South Wales. He attended the Cardiff College of Drama and made a striking film debut in *The Lion in Winter* with Katharine Hepburn and Peter O'Toole. He was Claudius in *Hamlet* in 1969, and later moved dully through a boring film version of John Le Carre's best-seller, *The Looking Glass War.*

He played in *When Eight Bells Toll,* written by Alistair MacLean, but this tale of adventurers in search of gold did nothing for its talented cast (Robert Morley and Jack Hawkins). A plodding historical hodgepodge, *Young Winston,* also put Hopkins' talent on hold. He had a much more suitable part as the unforgiving husband in *A Doll's House,* with Claire Bloom. He also played in *The Girl From Petrovka,* actually old-fashioned drivel, and *Juggernaut,* merely a thinking man's *Poseidon Adventure.* Critic Pauline Kael applauded *Juggernaut* for leaving out routine action clichés, but unfortunately this inventiveness also canceled any suspense.

Anthony Hopkins in *A Change of Seasons.*

As the concerned father of a possessed young girl in *Audrey Rose,* Hopkins' anguish was convincing but the film wasn't. He got lost amidst director Richard Attenborough's overinflated *A Bridge Too Far,* but Hopkins managed to insert some flesh and blood into *International Velvet,* an old-fashioned update of *National Velvet.* He emoted strenuously in *Magic* as a schizophrenic puppeteer.

A TV remake of *Dark Victory* was the most effective demonstration of his talents. As the concerned lover of the dying Elizabeth Montgomery, he displayed an aching tenderness that singlehandedly made the film worth watching. He was also noteworthy in another sprawling TV movie, *QBVII*, as a sympathetic doctor with a guilty past. Anthony Hopkins is much too good an actor to languish in feature films much longer.

FILMOGRAPHY

1968
The Lion in Winter ★★★★

1969
Hamlet ★★★★

1970
The Looking Glass War ★★★

1971
When Eight Bells Toll ★★★

1972
Young Winston ★★★

1973
A Doll's House ★★★★

1974
The Girl From Petrovka ★★
Juggernaut ★★★

1975
All Creatures Great and Small ★★★

1977
Audrey Rose ★★★
A Bridge Too Far ★★★

1978
Magic ★★
International Velvet ★★★

1979
Red, White and Zero ★★★

1980
A Change of Seasons ★★★
The Elephant Man ★★★★

DENNIS HOPPER
★★½ 2.54 STARS

Dennis Hopper developed from the beautiful youth who could play the son of Elizabeth Taylor and Rock Hudson in *Giant*, to the volatile, shaggy hippie of *Easy Rider*. His reputation as a loner and troublemaker is earned, not affected. Like many of the film industry's most in-

Dennis Hopper in *The Last Movie*.

tense personalities, he now plays the role that is himself.

He was born in 1936, in Dodge City, Kansas. His first film appearance, as a gang member in *Rebel Without a Cause*, had a profound effect on his development. Under the influence of co-star James Dean, he acquired the rebelliousness that would plague and sustain him. Between *Giant* and *Easy Rider*, he had small roles in several films (*Key Witness, The Sons of Katie Elder, Cool Hand Luke*) but his intensity always shone through.

When he shocked Hollywood with the phenomenal success of *Easy Rider*, which he directed and co-authored, he was allowed to write his own ticket for his next film. His own ticket was very bizarre indeed. *The Last Movie* was shot in Peru, featured a large cast, no script, a movie-within-a-movie, and was considered virtually unreleasable. Critics were too dumbfounded to even pan it.

This failure cut short his meteoric rise and relegated him to sporadic bits in an odd assortment of films. In *The American Friend* he was a footloose, ingratiating con man of the art world who poisoned Bruno Ganz's life with his friendship. He played the wild-eyed photographer in Francis Ford Coppola's *Apocalypse Now*, and an Australian outlaw in *Mad Dog Morgan*.

His roles often call for emotional violence or a loss of control, yet he still displays a touching, boyish vulnerability. Even in a film like *Out of the Blue* where Hopper plays a truck driver who molests his own daughter, he manages to make the character sympathetic.

FILMOGRAPHY

1955
Rebel Without a Cause (bit)

1956
Giant ★★

1957
Gunfight at the O.K. Corral (bit)
The Story of Mankind ★★

1958
From Hell to Texas ★★

1959
The Young Land ★★

1960
Key Witness ★★

1963
Night Tide ★★★★

1964
Tarzan and Jane Regained Sort Of ★★

1965
The Sons of Katie Elder ★★

1966
Queen of Blood ★★

1967
Cool Hand Luke (cameo)
The Trip ★★
The Glory Stompers ★★

1968
Panic in the City ★★
Hang 'Em High ★★

1969
Easy Rider (direction) ★★★
True Grit (cameo)

1971
The American Dreamer (documentary)
The Last Movie (direction) ★★★★

1973
Kid Blue ★★★

Dennis Hopper.

1975

The Sky Is Falling ★★

1976

Mad Dog Morgan ★★★
Tracks ★★★★

1977

Les Apprentis Sorciers (cameo)
The American Friend ★★★★
Couleur Chair ★★

1978

L'Ordre et la Securité du Monde (cameo)

1979

Apocalypse Now ★★★

1981

King of the Mountain ★

1982

Human Highway ★★
Out of the Blue (direction) ★★★★
Reborn ★★★

JOHN HOUSEMAN
★★★ 2.82 STARS

John Houseman is marvelously hammy, the way Charles Laughton used to be. Laughton had more acting strings to his bow, but Houseman is flamboyant and entertaining. Occasionally, as in *The Paper Chase*, his amusing one-upmanship can show humility and vulnerability as well.

Houseman (Jacques Haussman) was born in 1902, in Bucharest. His talent for writing, directing, and producing led to a prolific stage career, and he founded the Mercury Theater with Orson Welles in 1937. They had a tempestuous, burningly-close relationship (everything but sex, according to People magazine). This artistic marriage produced the famous "War of the Worlds" on radio, a program that reportedly sent people racing hysterically into the streets. He also participated in the making of *Citizen Kane* before bitterly splitting with Welles.

Houseman produced many superb films—*The Blue Dahlia, Letter From an Unknown Woman, The Bad and the Beautiful*, and *Lust for Life*—before embarking at age seventy on a busy acting career. His first leading role as the pedantic, intimidating Professor Kingsfield in *The Paper Chase* won a Best Supporting Actor Oscar. He played a devious CIA agent in Robert Redford's confusing but suspenseful *Three Days of the Condor*, and costarred with Charles Bronson in another disjointed thriller, *St. Ives*.

The Cheap Detective exploited his flair for comedy, but Houseman now seems content to do variations on his pompous *The Paper Chase* performance in every picture. Lately, he has carried that pose to amusing, if ridiculous, extremes in a series of Smith Barney commercials.

John Houseman in *Ghost Story*.

FILMOGRAPHY

1964

Seven Days in May ★★★

1973

The Paper Chase ★★★★

1975

I'm a Stranger Here Myself (documentary)
Rollerball ★★★
Three Days of the Condor ★★★

1976

St. Ives ★★

1978

The Cheap Detective ★★★

1979

Old Boyfriends ★★

1980

The Fog ★★★
My Bodyguard ★★★
Wholly Moses ★★

1981

Ghost Story ★★★

LESLIE HOWARD
★★★★ 3.76 STARS

The test of an actor is his ability to breathe life into cardboard roles. Leslie Howard's Ashley in *Gone With the Wind* is a perfect example. This paragon of self-sacrifice is almost comedic, but Howard seems to *believe* in Ashley's conflicts, making audiences willing to believe in them too.

Howard (Leslie Stainer) was born in London, in 1893. He suffered from shell shock after World War I and turned to acting for therapy. Four years later (in 1922) he was on Broadway in "Just Suppose," following that with "Outward Bound" and "Escape." When Howard was recruited to star in the movie version of *Outward Bound*, he was superb. The film itself was a fascinating tale of ship passengers who gradually realized that they were dead. Watch the remake, *Between Two Worlds*, to see how good the first version was. *A Free Soul*, with Norma Shearer, increased his reputation, and he was paired with Shearer again in *Smilin' Through*. He also played in *Berkeley Square*, a romantic and haunting tale of an American transported back to 18th century London.

According to Bette Davis, Howard ignored her while filming *Of Human Bondage* until informed that "the kid is walking off with the picture." Seen today, both actors are evenly matched, though Davis had the advantage of big melodramatic moments. *Bondage* did only so-so at the box office, but *The Scarlet Pimpernel* was a huge success. Howard's conventional Englishman leading a double life in *Pimpernel* brought acclaim and a Picturegoer Gold Medal. In *The Petrified Forest*, a moderately engrossing talky piece, Bogart, who had played his part on the stage with Howard, stole the show as a gangster. However, Howard and Bette Davis were excellent as well. Howard also garnered prestige with Norma Shearer in the lead roles of *Romeo and Juliet*.

Leslie Howard in *Romeo and Juliet.*

A third teaming with Bette Davis was less serious than the earlier two in *It's Love I'm After,* and Howard and Davis were lovers off-camera as well as on. His understated elegance blended amusingly with Joan Blondell's brassiness in *Stand-In.* He played Professor Henry Higgins in *Pygmalion* and was perfectly cast in a movie that holds up much more effectively than the musical version, *My Fair Lady.*

Gone With the Wind proved to be the only timeless vehicle of his career. He didn't want to do it, but capitulated under studio pressure. He and Olivia De Havilland made their niceness seem charismatic, and he accomplished the same miracle with an even more magnetic co-player, Ingrid Bergman. He played opposite Bergman in *Intermezzo: A Love Story* in her American movie debut. The rest of his pictures were entertaining though less distinguished (*Pimpernel Smith, The 49th Parallel,* and *The First of the Few*). He died in 1943, when his plane was shot down by Nazis.

Oddly enough, Howard had a reputation in private life as a champion seducer. This quality was never utilized on screen, but possibly some of it came through—just enough, perhaps, to humanize his polished, classy exterior and give him sex appeal.

FILMOGRAPHY

1930

Outward Bound ★★★★

1931

Never the Twain Shall Meet ★★★
A Free Soul ★★★★
Five and Ten ★★★★
Devotion ★★★★

1932

Service for Ladies ★★★★
Smilin' Through ★★★★
The Animal Kingdom ★★★★

1933

Secrets ★★★
Captured ★★★★
Berkeley Square ★★★★

1934

The Lady Is Willing ★★★
Of Human Bondage ★★★★
British Agent ★★★★

1935

The Scarlet Pimpernel ★★★★

1936

The Petrified Forest ★★★★
Romeo and Juliet ★★★

1937

It's Love I'm After ★★★
Stand-In ★★★

1938

Pygmalion (co-direction) ★★★★

1939

Intermezzo: A Love Story ★★★★
Gone With the Wind ★★★★

1941

Pimpernel Smith (direction) ★★★★
The 49th Parallel ★★★★

1942

The First of the Few (direction) ★★★★

TREVOR HOWARD
★★½ 2.52 STARS

Trevor Howard is a perfectionist. He once said, "I won't do anything unless I know it's right." All of Howard's performances are "right" and sometimes—as in *Brief Encounter*—perfect. In fact, a strong case could be made for Howard as the finest actor ever to appear in films.

He was born in 1916, in Cliftonville, England. In his third picture and first leading part, he played opposite Celia Johnson in *Brief Encounter.* Howard and Johnson played a couple secretly meeting in a train station cafe and their affair was touching, subtle, and quite believable. He followed that triumph with a gripping thriller, *I See a Dark Stranger,* and Howard was the elusive other man in David Lean's sparkling romantic drama, *The Passionate Friends.* He was excellent in his next film, author Graham Greene's classic spy story *The Third Man.* Most of Howard's early pictures were good, but even when they weren't, for example, *Odette* and *Glory at Sea,* he was superb. Another Graham Greene piece, *The Heart of the Matter,* benefited from Howard's thoughtful characterization—he played a police officer.

After *The Cockleshell Heroes, Run for the Sun,* and *Interpol,* he stole scenes from William Holden and Sophia Loren in *The Key. Sons and Lovers* brought his one Oscar nomination, an appalling illustration of Academy neglect. His tyrannical Captain Bligh made co-star Marlon Brando look like a prissy amateur in the inferior remake of *Mutiny on the Bounty.* He played second fiddle to Cary Grant in *Father Goose* and did a fine job as a priest in *Ryan's Daughter,* though John Mills won the Oscar.

Most of his subsequent pictures—*11 Harrowhouse, The Last Remake of Beau Geste, The Hurricane,* and *Meteor*—have wasted his talent and acting skills. Hopefully, he hasn't been discouraged by these roles and will continue searching for another part worthy of his stature.

FILMOGRAPHY

1944

The Way Ahead ★★★★

1945

The Way to the Stars ★★★★
Brief Encounter ★★★★

1946

I See a Dark Stranger ★★★★
Green for Danger ★★★★

1947

They Made Me a Fugitive ★★★★
So Well Remembered ★★★★

1948

The Passionate Friends ★★★★

1949

The Third Man ★★★★
The Golden Salamander ★★★★

1950

Odette ★★★★
The Clouded Yellow ★★★★

1951

Outcast of the Islands ★★★★

Trevor Howard in *I Became a Criminal.*

1952

Glory at Sea ★★★★

1953

The Heart of the Matter ★★★★
The Stranger's Hand ★★★★

1955

Lovers' Net ★★★★
The Cockleshell Heroes ★★★★

1956

Run for the Sun ★★★★
Around the World in 80 Days ★★★★

1957

Interpol ★★★
Manuela ★★★

1958

The Key ★★★★
The Roots of Heaven ★★★★

1960

Moment of Danger ★★★
Sons and Lovers ★★★★

1962

The Lion ★★★
Mutiny on the Bounty ★★★★

1963

Man in the Middle ★★★★

1964

Father Goose ★★★★

1965

Operation Crossbow ★★★
Von Ryan's Express ★★★★
Morituri ★★★

1966

The Poppy Is Also a Flower ★★★
The Liquidator ★★★
Triple Cross ★★★

1967

The Long Duel ★★★
A Matter of Innocence ★★★★

1968

The Charge of the Light Brigade ★★★★

1969

Battle of Britain ★★★

1970

Twinky ★★★
Ryan's Daughter ★★★★

1971

The Night Visitor ★★★★
Catch Me a Spy ★★★
Kidnapped ★★★★
Mary Queen of Scots ★★★★

1972

Pope Joan ★★★
Something Like the Truth ★★★

1973

Ludwig ★★★
The Offense ★★★
A Doll's House ★★★★

1974

Craze ★★★
11 Harrowhouse ★★★
Persecution ★★★

1975

Who? ★★★
Hennessy ★★★★
Conduct Unbecoming ★★★★

1976

The Bawdy Adventures of Tom Jones ★★★
Whispering Death ★★★
The Count of Monte Cristo ★★★
Aces High ★★★
Eliza Fraser ★★★

1977

The Last Remake of Beau Geste ★★★

1978

Meteor ★★★
Stevie ★★★★
Superman ★★★

1979

The Hurricane ★★★

1980

Sir Henry at Rawlinson End ★★★
Windwalker ★★★
The Sea Wolves ★★★

1982

The Missionary ★★★

ROCK HUDSON
★★½ 2.71 STARS

Rock Hudson was never a critic's favorite. He began as a male sex symbol, and he never made pretentious noises to interviewers about "acting," as Marilyn Monroe did. No one could believe him in classical roles, but Hudson is a master of one thing—underplaying. He instinctively knows how to scale down his speech and movements to the needs of the camera.

He was born Roy Scherer, Jr., in Illinois, in 1925. Despite the lack of any formal training, agent Henry Wilson, who also handled Tab Hunter, Rory Calhoun, and Robert Wagner, took him on. His first film appearance was a small role in *Fighter Squadron* (a single line that required 38 takes), and he gradually improved in *Undertow, One Way Street,* and *The Iron Man.* He worked up to the lead in a James Stewart western, *Bend of the River* and did several others including, *The Lawless Breed, Seminole,* and *Horizons West.*

The Magnificent Obsession made Hudson more than a routine action hero. As the playboy who fell in love with the woman (Jane Wyman) he accidentally blinded, he was sincere and gentle, an effective contrast to his height and rugged good looks. The popularity of the picture led to another teaming with Wyman in *All That Heaven Allows.* Hudson played a gardener who communed with nature and rejected false material values. It was an unactable part, but his whispery and undramatic approach made it work. He was also believable as the gambler who learned (almost too late) that he loved Anne Baxter in *One Desire,* an engrossing western.

Giant, Hudson's personal favorite among his films, brought him his only Oscar nomination. His calm, unaffected performance brought out the best in co-star Elizabeth Taylor. The movie was one of Hollywood's few interesting three-hour-plus spectaculars. *Written on the Wind* was stolen by Dorothy Malone who won a Best Supporting Actress Academy Award, and *Something of Value* centered on Sidney Poitier. Hudson couldn't do much with the dated, overblown remake of *A Farewell to Arms,* but he held his own with Jean Simmons, Claude Rains, and Dorothy McGuire in *This Earth Is Mine.* He displayed a relaxed sense of comedy in *Pillow Talk* with Doris Day, a skill once again evident in their follow-up, *Lover Come Back.* Some of his scripts, *Man's Favorite*

Sport?, A Very Special Favor, and *Come September,* required every bit of comic flair he could muster and then some.

Hudson's box-office power dimmed through a succession of mediocre pictures. *Send Me No Flowers* was his last and worst with Doris Day, and *Strange Bedfellows* substituted slapstick for wit. He had a challenging dramatic part in *Seconds,* as a man who regained his youth, but it was peculiarly depressing and nobody went to see it. After *Tobruk, Ice Station Zebra,* and *Darling Lili,* he desperately needed television to revive his career. "MacMillan and Wife" was a ratings blockbuster and started him on a whole new phase of his career.

Hudson is a more current version of Gregory Peck. Neither actor set the screen on fire, but both were comfortable and clean-cut. Both project, in writer Michael Stern's words, "reserved dignity." Sometimes a quiet leading man can be soothing to audiences inundated with histrionics.

Rock Hudson.

FILMOGRAPHY

1948

Fighter Squadron ★★

1949

Undertow ★★

1950

I Was a Shoplifter ★★
One Way Street ★★
Winchester '73 ★★★
Peggy ★★
Desert Hawk ★★
Shakedown ★★
Double Crossbones ★★

1951

Tomahawk ★★
Air Cadet ★★
The Fat Man ★★
The Iron Man ★★
Bright Victory ★★★

1952

Here Come the Nelsons ★★★
Bend of the River ★★★
Scarlet Angel ★★★
Has Anybody Seen My Gal? ★★★
Horizons West ★★★

1953

The Lawless Breed ★★★
Seminole ★★★
Sea Devils ★★★
The Golden Blade ★★★
Gun Fury ★★★
Back to God's Country ★★★

1954

Taza, Son of Cochise ★★
The Magnificent Obsession ★★★★
Bengal Brigade ★★★

1955

Captain Lightfoot ★★★
One Desire ★★★

1956

All That Heaven Allows ★★★★
Never Say Goodbye ★★★
Giant ★★★★

1957

Written on the Wind ★★★
Battle Hymn ★★★
Something of Value ★★★
A Farewell to Arms ★★

1958

The Tarnished Angels ★★★
Twilight for the Gods ★★★

1959

Pillow Talk ★★★★
This Earth Is Mine ★★★

1961

The Last Sunset ★★
Come September ★★★

1962

Lover Come Back ★★★
The Spiral Road ★★★

1963

Marilyn (narration)
A Gathering of Eagles ★★★

1964

Man's Favorite Sport? ★★
Send Me No Flowers ★★
A Very Special Favor ★★

1965

Strange Bedfellows ★★

1966

Blindfold ★★★
Seconds ★★★★

1967

Tobruk ★★★
Ice Station Zebra ★★★

1969

A Fine Pair ★★
The Undefeated ★★

1970

The Hornet's Nest ★★★
Darling Lili ★★

1971

Pretty Maids All in a Row ★★★

1973

Showdown ★★★

1976

Embryo ★★★

1978

Avalanche ★★

1980

The Mirror Crack'd ★★

JEFFREY HUNTER
★★½ 2.62 STARS

Jeffrey Hunter was a handsome, competent actor who had a strange identity problem in films. He was never quite a fan-magazine pretty boy or a ruggedly virile action hero. After swinging back and forth between romantic leads and westerns, he finally found his niche as Jesus in *King of Kings.*

He was born Henry Herman McKinnies, Jr., in 1925. Hunter performed on radio during high school and had a good early role in *Dreamboat,* Claude Binyon's clever satire about silent films. He performed in a number of outdoor sagas, *Princess of the Nile, White Feather, Seven Cities of Gold,* and one classic, *The Searchers.*

Hunter was convincing as the nice guy who suspected Robert Wagner of murder in *A Kiss Before Dying,* and *In Love and War* gave him another of his few strong parts. Despite his seeming incongruity for the part, Hunter had just the right serene intensity for the role of Christ in Nicholas Ray's bible epic *King of Kings.* He dropped his sympathetic image to play a demented murderer in *Brainstorm* and was on the edge of finally breaking through when he died in 1969 following a brain operation.

FILMOGRAPHY

1946

A Boy, a Girl and a Dog ★★

1948

A Date with Judy ★★

1951

14 Hours ★★★
Call Me Mister ★★★
Take Care of My Little Girl ★★★
The Frogmen ★★

1952

Red Skies of Montana ★★★
Belles on Their Toes ★★★
Lure of the Wilderness ★★
Dreamboat ★★★

1953

Sailor of the King ★★

1954

Three Young Texans ★★
Princess of the Nile ★★

1955

White Feather ★★
Seven Angry Men ★★
Seven Cities of Gold ★★

1956

The Searchers ★★★★
The Proud Ones ★★★
A Kiss Before Dying ★★★
The Great Locomotive Chase ★★★

1957

The Way to the Gold ★★★
No Down Payment ★★★★
The True Story of Jesse James ★★★
Gun for a Coward ★★★

1958

In Love and War ★★★★
The Last Hurrah ★★★★
Count Five and Die ★★★

1960

Key Witness ★★★
Hell to Eternity ★★★
Sergeant Rutledge ★★★

Jeffrey Hunter with Susan Harrison in *Key Witness.*

1961

King of Kings ★★★★
Man Trap ★★

1962

No Man Is an Island ★★
The Longest Day ★★★

1964

The Man From Galveston ★★
Gold for the Caesars ★★

1965

Brainstorm ★★★★
Vendetta ★★★
The Woman Who Wouldn't Die ★★★
Murieta ★★

1966

Dimension 5 ★★
A Witch Without a Broom ★★★

1967

A Guide for the Married Man ★★★

1968

The Private Navy of Sgt. O'Farrell ★★
The Christmas Kid ★★
Joe, Find a Place to Die ★★
Sexy Susan at the King's Court ★★
Custer of the West ★★

1969

The Hostess Also Has a Count ★★
Make Love Not War ★★

TAB HUNTER
★★½ 2.32 STARS

Tab Hunter was always underrated. He was too pretty and overpublicized to get much respect. For the most part he had impossible roles, but he did surprisingly well in the better ones.

He was born Arthur Gelien, in New York, in 1931. Hunter started in films at age twenty-one in the ludicrous *Island of Desire* opposite Linda Darnell. Publicity helped him to survive such vehicles as *Gun Belt, The Steel Lady,* and *Return to Treasure Island,* but he improved in *Track of the Cat* opposite Robert Mitchum. Hunter was likable and convincing as a soldier having an affair with the older Dorothy Malone in the entertaining *Battle Cry,* and competent in *The Sea Chase* with John Wayne.

Cast against type as Van Heflin's murderous younger brother in *Gunman's Walk,* he was superb. *Damn Yankees* pointed up his limitations as a musical star despite a million-selling hit record, "Young Love." He was charming as Debbie Reynolds' bewildered boyfriend in *The Pleasure of His Company,* but bad pictures such as *Ride the Wild Surf, City Under the Sea,* and *Birds Do It* finally did him in.

Hunter is a sad illustration of how a teenage buildup can backfire. Even when the idol shows ability, derisive critics won't forget his beginnings and accept him as a talent.

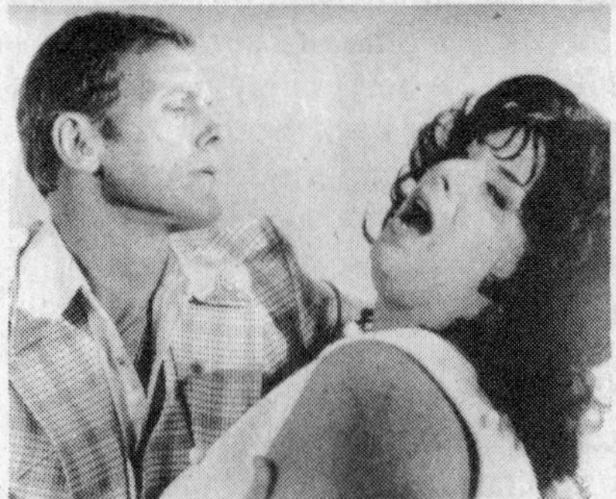

Tab Hunter with Divine in *Polyester.*

FILMOGRAPHY

1952

Island of Desire ★★

1953

Gun Belt ★★
The Steel Lady ★★

1954

Track of the Cat ★★★
Return to Treasure Island ★★

1955

Battle Cry ★★★
The Sea Chase ★★★

1956

The Burning Hills ★★
The Girl He Left Behind ★★

1958

Lafayette Escadrille ★★
Gunman's Walk ★★★★
Damn Yankees ★★★

1959

That Kind of Woman ★★
They Came to Cordura ★★★

1961

The Pleasure of His Company ★★★

1962

The Golden Arrow ★★

1963

Operation Bikini ★★

1964

Ride the Wild Surf ★★

Tab Hunter with Gwen Verdon in *Damn Yankees.*

1965

The Loved One ★★
City Under the Sea ★★

1966

Birds Do It ★★

1967

Hostile Guns ★★
The Fickle Finger of Fate ★★★

1969

Quel Maledetto Ponte sull' Elba ★★
La Porta del Cannone ★★

1971

A Kiss From Eddie ★★

1972

The Life and Times of Judge Roy Bean ★★★

1973

The Arousers ★★

1975

Timber Tramps ★★

1976

Won Ton Ton—the Dog Who Saved Hollywood (cameo)

1981

Polyester ★★★

1982

Grease 2 ★

JOHN HURT
★★★½ 3.26 STARS

John Hurt can play anything. He appears to have as many contrasting characters locked inside him as Laurence Olivier.

Hurt was born in 1940, in Chesterfield, England. His father was a clergyman, his brother a Roman Catholic priest, but "from the first role in the first play I knew there was no other career for me than acting." His parents objected, insisting he couldn't survive financially. Persistence led to an RADA (Royal Academy of Dramatic Arts) scholarship, and he made his film debut at age twenty-two in *The Wild and the Willing*.

A Man for All Seasons followed and critics applauded; they also voted him Most Promising Newcomer for his work in a Harold Pinter play, "The Dwarfs." *Sinful Davey* and *Before Winter Comes* were mild comedy-dramas, but *10 Rillington Place* was a gripping true-life murder yarn, and Hurt was superb. He won a Best Supporting Actor Oscar nomination for his participation in the grim *Midnight Express*, and he had another fine part in *Night Crossing*, the tale of two East German families escaping to freedom in a homemade balloon.

John Hurt in *Partners.*

He gave an incredible, nearly miraculous portrayal of the deformed John Merrick in the moving *The Elephant Man*. Other roles that displayed his versatility were television dramas: "I, Claudius" and "The Naked Civil Servant."

Hurt claims, "I always try to follow my instincts," and sometimes this can backfire as it did with Michael Cimino's *Heaven's Gate*. He actually stated, "I didn't even read the script." One thing is certain, however, when Hurt is in a picture, viewers can be sure the results will be offbeat and interesting.

FILMOGRAPHY

1962

The Wild and the Willing ★★★

1966

A Man for All Seasons ★★★★

1967

The Sailor from Gibraltar ★★★

1969

Before Winter Comes ★★★
Sinful Davey ★★★
East of Elephant Rock ★★★

1970

In Search of Gregory ★★★

1971

Forbush and the Penguins ★★★
10 Rillington Place ★★★★

1972

The Pied Piper ★★★

1977

The Disappearance ★★★
The Shout ★★★

1979

Midnight Express ★★★★
Heaven's Gate ★★★
Alien ★★★★

1980

The Elephant Man ★★★★
Watership Down (voice only)

1981

Night Crossing ★★★★

1982

Partners ★★
History of the World Part I ★★★

WALTER HUSTON
★★★★ 3.85 STARS

Unlike his son John, whose acting stints are enjoyable but mannered, Walter Huston had a glowing, accessible warmth. Villain or hero, he turned all his co-stars into cardboard whenever he walked on the screen.

Huston (Walter Houghston) was born in 1884, in Toronto. His first triumphs were in the theatre in "Mr. Pitt" and "Desire Under the Elms." He was already forty-five when he made his first movies (*Gentlemen of the Press, The Lady Lies*, and *The Virginian*). He played the lead in *Abraham Lincoln* in 1930, and had a good part as a judge in *Night Court*.

Walter Huston with Constance Cummings in *The Criminal Code.*

Rain was one of Joan Crawford's few failures, but it wasn't Huston's fault. His performance as the judgmental Reverend Davidson was the picture's only satisfying ingredient.

He did "Dodsworth" on the stage and then starred in the screen adaptation. As the loving but bewildered husband of status-seeking Ruth Chatterton, Huston touched every emotional base—confusion, pride, anger, and tenderness. Unfortunately, his portrayal lost to Paul Muni's affected portrayal of Louis Pasteur in the Oscar race.

He returned to Broadway again for "Knickerbocker Holiday," then did *All That Money Can Buy* and *Swamp Water.* In *Yankee Doodle Dandy,* he was featured as James Cagney's father, and he was a convincing Doc Holliday in Jane Russell's scandalous debut film, *The Outlaw.* His performance in author Agatha Christie's *And Then There Were None,* as a murderer trapped with several others on a deserted island, was one of the best in the film.

Huston's legendary moment came with *The Treasure of the Sierra Madre*, directed by his son John. He played the wily old prospector who kept his wits when his partners caught gold-fever. His performance finally brought him an Oscar. He died after doing a grim western, *The Furies,* in 1950, but fortunately his performances survive as inspirations to every aspiring actor.

FILMOGRAPHY

1929

Gentlemen of the Press ★★★★
The Lady Lies ★★★★
The Virginian ★★★★

1930

Abraham Lincoln ★★★★
The Bad Man ★★★
The Virtuous Sin ★★★★

1931

The Criminal Code ★★★★
The Star Witness ★★★★
The Ruling Voice ★★★★

1932

The Woman from Monte Carlo ★★★★
A House Divided ★★★★
Law and Order ★★★★
The Beast of the City ★★★★
The Wet Parade ★★★★
Night Court ★★★★
American Madness ★★★★
Rain ★★★★
Kongo ★★★★

1933

Gabriel Over the White House ★★★★
Hell Below ★★★★
Storm at Daybreak ★★★★
Ann Vickers ★★★★
The Prizefighter and the Lady ★★★★

1934

Keep 'Em Rolling ★★★★

1935

The Tunnel ★★★★

1936

Rhodes of Africa ★★★★
Dodsworth ★★★★

1938

Of Human Hearts ★★★★

1940

The Light That Failed ★★★★

1941

The Maltese Falcon (bit)
All That Money Can Buy ★★★
Swamp Water ★★★

1942

In This Our Life (bit)
The Shanghai Gesture ★★★★
Always in My Heart ★★★★
Yankee Doodle Dandy ★★★★

1943

The Outlaw ★★★★
Edge of Darkness ★★★★
Mission to Moscow ★★★★
The North Star ★★★★

Walter Huston in *Kongo.*

Walter Huston with Katherine Byron in *The Bad Man.*

1944

Dragon Seed ★★★

1945

And Then There Were None ★★★★

1946

Dragonwick ★★★

1947

Duel in the Sun ★★★★

1948

The Treasure of Sierra Madre ★★★★
Summer Holiday ★★★

1949

The Great Sinner ★★★

1950

The Furies ★★★★

BETTY HUTTON
★★★ 3.11 STARS

"Volatile" is a passive description of Betty Hutton. She didn't just act in a film—she gobbled up her parts with a zest that either repelled or enchanted viewers.

Hutton (Betty June Thornburg) was born in 1921, in Battle Creek, Michigan. In 1940 she appeared on Broadway in "Two for the Show," and Paramount cast her with Eddie Bracken in the film, *The Fleet's In.* Her talents were fully utilized in a clever Preston Sturges comedy, *The Miracle of Morgan's Creek.* She and Dorothy Lamour played a sister singing act in *And the Angels Sing,* and Hutton played twins in *Here Come the Waves,* a Bing Crosby musical.

Incendiary Blonde was a biography of nightclub star Texas Guinan and a big hit. Having become a guaranteed box-office attraction, she maintained that state as serial queen Pearl White in *The Perils of Pauline.* She was the *Dream Girl,* but her nonstop fantasies were too dull to sustain viewer interest.

When Judy Garland was fired from *Annie Get Your Gun,* Hutton replaced her and did a superb job. The story and score were foolproof, and Howard Keel made a likable leading man. She reportedly infuriated Fred Astaire with her inability to dance in *Let's Dance,* but she seemed at home on the high wire in

Betty Hutton with Eddie Bracken in *The Miracle of Morgan's Creek.*

director Cecil B. De Mille's Oscar-winning circus extravaganza, *The Greatest Show on Earth.* Hutton did one more musical, *Somebody Loves Me,* and was then unofficially blacklisted for walking out on her Paramount contract.

Her sister Marion Hutton, a former band singer, said later that Betty's downfall came about because she blamed everyone else for her problems. In 1974 she was discovered to be broke and working in a Catholic rectory, a definitive example of what stardom can do to the unrealistic and immature.

FILMOGRAPHY

1942

The Fleet's In ★★★
Star Spangled Rhythm ★★★

1943

Happy Go Lucky ★★★
Let's Face It ★★★

1944

The Miracle of Morgan's Creek ★★★★
And the Angels Sing ★★★
Here Come the Waves ★★★

1945

Incendiary Blonde ★★★★
Duffy's Tavern ★★★
The Stork Club ★★★

1946

Cross My Heart ★★★

1947

The Perils of Pauline ★★★★

1948

Dream Girl ★★★

1949

Red Hot and Blue ★★

1950

Annie Get Your Gun ★★★★
Let's Dance ★★

1952

Sailor Beware (cameo)
The Greatest Show on Earth ★★★★
Somebody Love Me ★★★

1957

Spring Reunion ★★

TIMOTHY HUTTON
★★★½ 3.67 STARS

It's too soon to know if Timothy Hutton will become a consistently great actor. However, his first performance as the troubled young son in *Ordinary People* indicates a talent full of sensitivity and promise.

Hutton was born in California, near Malibu, in 1960. His father was Jim Hutton, a gifted light comedian who died at age forty-five without ever receiving the roles he deserved. Tim Hutton's creativity surfaced first in music (flute, drums, guitar, and piano) and then acting. He played Nathan Detroit in a Fairfax High School production of "Guys and Dolls" and TV was the next step in *Friendly Fire,* an Emmy-winning drama about Vietnam. Other TV roles included *The Best Place To Be* and *Young Love First Love.* He was superb in all of them and equally notable in a Los Angeles stage pre-

Timothy Hutton with Valerie Bertinelli in the TV movie, *Young Love, First Love.*

sentation, "The Oldest Living Graduate" with Henry Fonda.

Ordinary People brought him worldwide acclaim; he was every youngster unable to communicate with his parents. His suffering was more real, more open than the inward torture displayed by early Method actors in similar parts, and he won an Oscar for Best Supporting Actor and a Golden Globe. For *Taps,* his second film, Hutton spent four weeks living and rehearsing at Valley Forge Military Academy.

Timothy Hutton sums up his acting approach this way, "When I take on a role I look around among real people for something like the character I'm portraying and creatively try to identify with him." Whatever his method, the results are brilliant.

FILMOGRAPHY

1980

Ordinary People ★★★★

1981

Taps ★★★★

1983

Daniel ★★★

BURL IVES
★★★ 3.12 STARS

Burl Ives is a man of impressive stature in physical size and histrionic weight.

Ives was born Burle Icle Ivanhoe, in 1909, in Illinois. Before embarking on a film career, he established a reputation as a first-rate folksinger. He started as a genial presence in two westerns, *Smoky* and *Green Grass of Wyoming*, and had a powerful acting part in the unforgettable *East of Eden*. In *Desire Under the Elms*, he was cast as the older husband whom Sophia Loren rejected in favor of Anthony Perkins. However, Ives's fine performance was lost amid the theatrical dialogue and staginess.

He won an Oscar for his part in director William Wyler's large-scale, absorbing western, *The Big Country*. He played a ranching father who fought along with his sons for watering rights. He made an excellent Big Daddy in the diluted but entertaining version of author Tennessee Williams' play "Cat on a Hot Tin Roof." Ives invested the gruff, old patriarch with humanity and power. This performance makes one regret that his later films, *Summer Magic, Ensign Pulver, Baker's Hawk*, and *Just You and Me, Kid* never again gave him the opportunity for greatness.

Burl Ives with Shelley Winters in *Let No Man Write My Epitaph*.

FILMOGRAPHY

1946

Smoky ★★★

1948

Green Grass of Wyoming ★★★
Station West ★★★
So Dear to My Heart ★★★

1950

Sierra ★★★

1955

East of Eden ★★★★

1956

The Power and the Prize ★★★

1958

Desire Under the Elms ★★★
The Big Country ★★★★
Wind Across the Everglades ★★★
Cat on a Hot Tin Roof ★★★★

1959

Day of the Outlaw ★★★
Our Man in Havana ★★★★

1960

Let No Man Write My Epitaph ★★★

1962

The Spiral Road ★★★
Mediterranean Holiday (narration)

1963

Summer Magic ★★★

1964

The Brass Bottle ★★★
Ensign Pulver ★★★

1966

The Daydreamer (voice only)

1967

Those Fantastic Flying Fools ★★★

1968

The Other Side of Bonnie and Clyde (narration)

1970

The McMasters ★★★
The Only Way Out Is Dead ★★★

1976

Hugo the Hippo (voice only)
Baker's Hawk ★★★

1979

Heidi ★★★

1980

Just You and Me, Kid ★★

1981

Earthbound ★★★

GLENDA JACKSON
★★★ 2.95 STARS

Glenda Jackson uses hostility as a come-on. She seems to say, "All right, try to win me over if you want to, but I won't make it easy." Men find her attitude a challenge, and women like her because she's shrewd and independent.

Jackson was born in 1936, in England. Early stage training with Peter Brook's Experimental Group led to a Broadway role in "Marat-Sade." She co-starred with Diane Cilento, Sean Connery's ex-wife, in *Negatives* but clinched her hold on stardom with director Ken Russell's *Women in Love*. Based on a D.H. Lawrence novel, the movie was less

Glenda Jackson in *Sunday Bloody Sunday*.

prone to hysterical excesses than Russell's later work, and Jackson established her image as the woman-no-man-can-own. It won her an Oscar.

She was Tchaikovsky's insane wife in a perverted "biography" of the composer's problems *The Music Lovers*. The film seemed designed to point out that homosexuals were deranged, but *Sunday, Bloody Sunday* compensated. It was, again, based on a homosexual theme—gay Peter Finch and straight Glenda Jackson competed for a young boy's affections (Murray Head). In fact, director John Schlesinger's treatment was too tasteful, almost undramatic.

She was "great," according to Pauline Kael in a TV mini-series *Elizabeth R* and at ease playing the same part in *Mary, Queen of Scots*. Jackson also showed her flair for comedy in the hilarious *A Touch of Class* with George Segal. Against powerful competition, Ellen Burstyn, Marsha Mason, Barbra Streisand, and Joanne Woodward, she won her second Academy Award. Director Joseph Losey's tart dialogue fell naturally off her tongue in the unjustly neglected *The Romantic Englishwoman*, but she couldn't pump any life into a stodgy film version of *Hedda*.

The Incredible Sarah was flamboyant but phony (including her performance), and *House Calls*, a terrific comedy with Walter Matthau, provided welcome relief from her "serious" emoting. She teamed with Matthau in another, less entertaining film, *Hopscotch* and crudely but effectively parodied herself in director Robert Altman's sprawling farce, *Health*.

She continues to make one picture after another, all commendable experiments even when their goals are unrealized.

FILMOGRAPHY

1967

The Persecution and Assassination of Jean-Paul Marat as Performed by the Inmates of the Asylum of Charenton Under the Direction of the Marquis de Sade ★★★

1969

Tell Me Lies ★★★
Negatives ★★★
Women in Love ★★★★

1971

The Music Lovers ★★★
Sunday, Bloody Sunday ★★★★
Mary, Queen of Scots ★★★
The Boy Friend (cameo)

1973

Triple Echo ★★★
The Nelson Affair ★★
A Touch of Class ★★★★

1974

The Maids ★★★

1975

The Romantic Englishwoman ★★★★
The Devil Is a Woman ★★★
Hedda ★★

1976

The Incredible Sarah ★★
Nasty Habits ★★

1978

House Calls ★★★★
Stevie ★★★
The Class of Miss MacMichael ★★★

1979

Lost and Found ★★★
Health ★★★

1980

Hopscotch ★★

DEAN JAGGER
★★★ 3.11 STARS

Actors who play leaders on the screen tend to seem pompous and one-dimensional. Dean Jagger had enough warmth to make his cardboard figures credible and even moving.

Jagger was born in 1903, in Lima, Ohio. He began inauspiciously in films like *Woman from Hell* but brought authority and religious conviction to the otherwise bloodless *Brigham Young—Frontiersman.* A good western, *Western Union,* and an exciting thriller, *When Strangers Marry,* followed before Jagger reached the height of his career as an officer in *Twelve O'Clock High.* It won him a Best Supporting Oscar.

He was quite moving as the fearful father of a communist in a tawdry propaganda film, *My Son John.* Jagger was perfectly at home in the *Executive Suite,* a tale of corporate intrigue. He also gave a notable portrayal of a tobacco man defending his crop against the manipulations of rival Karl Malden in *Parrish.* This performance showed what he could do to elevate weak material, a trick he pulled off again and again in: *Cash McCall, King Creole, Bernadine, God Bless Dr. Shagetz,* and *Tiger By the Tail.*

FILMOGRAPHY

1929

Woman from Hell ★★★
Handcuffed ★★★

1934

College Rhythm ★★★
You Belong to Me ★★★

1935

Home on the Range ★★★
Wings in the Dark ★★★
Car No. 99 ★★★
Behold My Wife ★★★
People Will Talk ★★★
Men Without Names ★★★
Wanderer of the Wasteland ★★★

1936

Woman Trap ★★★
Thirteen Hours By Air ★★★
Revolt of the Zombies ★★★
Pepper ★★★
Star for a Night ★★★

1937

Woman in Distress ★★★
Escape by Night ★★★
Dangerous Number ★★★
Undercover of Night ★★★
Exiled to Shanghai ★★★

1940

Brigham Young—Frontiersman ★★★★

1941

Western Union ★★★
Men in Her Life ★★★

1942

Valley of the Sun ★★★
The Omaha Trail ★★★

1943

I Escaped from the Gestapo ★★★
The North Star ★★★★
No Escape ★★★

1944

Alaska ★★★
When Strangers Marry ★★★★

1945

I Lived in Grosvenor Square ★★★

1946

Sister Kenny ★★★

1947

Pursued ★★★
Driftwood ★★★

1949

Twelve O'Clock High ★★★★
C-Man ★★★

1950

Sierra ★★★
Dark City ★★★

1951

Rawhide ★★★
War Path ★★★

1952

The Denver and Rio Grande ★★★
My Son John ★★★★
It Grows on Trees ★★★

1953

The Robe ★★★

1954

Executive Suite ★★★
Private Hell No. 36 ★★★
White Christmas ★★★
Bad Day at Black Rock ★★★★

1955

The Eternal Sea ★★★
It's a Dog's Life ★★★

1956

On the Threshold of Space ★★★
Red Sundown ★★★
The Great Man ★★★

1957

Three Brave Men ★★★
X—the Unknown ★★★
Forty Guns ★★★
Bernadine ★★★

Dean Jagger.

1958

The Proud Rebel ★★★★
King Creole ★★★

1959

The Nun's Story ★★★
Cash McCall ★★★

1960

Elmer Gantry ★★★★

1961

Parrish ★★★★
The Honeymoon Machine ★★★

1962

Jumbo ★★★

1967

First to Fight ★★★

1968

Firecreek ★★★
Day of the Evil Gun ★★★
Tiger By the Tail ★★★

1969

Smith! ★★★
The Kremlin Letter ★★★
The Savarona Syndrome ★★★

1971

Vanishing Point ★★★

1975

The Great Lester Boggs ★★★

1977

God Bless Dr. Shagetz ★★★
End of the World ★★★
Game of Death ★★★

1980

Alligator ★★★

BEN JOHNSON
★★★ 3.18 STARS

Sooner or later, most actors are pushed into the saddle and forced to make westerns. Some of them look notably ill at ease; Rock Hudson once said, "Horses don't like me." One of the few who always seemed to really blend in with the prairie landscape was Ben Johnson.

Johnson was born in 1920, in Pawhuska, Oklahoma. His ease with the western genre stemmed from his early experiences as a rodeo performer. Hollywood used him mostly as a stuntman until he made his acting mark in an unpretentious western *Wagonmaster.* He brought authenticity to *She Wore a Yellow Ribbon, Rio Grande, Fort Defiance,* and *Shane.* There were more supporting parts in *Major Dundee, The Rare Breed,* and *Will Penny* in which he provided solid, consistent performances. Then he got a role that allowed him to draw on the enormous reserve of strength that years of support had given him. He played Sam the Lion in *The Last Picture Show* and won an Oscar for Best Supporting Actor.

Ben Johnson in *The Last Picture Show.*

Larger, but not better, roles followed in *Junior Bonner, The Getaway,* and *The Train Robbers.* However, good script (*The Sugarland Express*) or bad (*Hustle* and *The Swarm*), Johnson is a flesh-and-blood presence—you never catch him "acting."

FILMOGRAPHY

1948

Fort Apache (stuntman)

1949

She Wore a Yellow Ribbon ★★★
Mighty Joe Young ★★★
Three Godfathers ★★★

1950

Wagonmaster ★★★★
Rio Grande ★★★★

1951

Fort Defiance ★★★

1952

Wild Stallion ★★★

1953

Shane ★★★★

1956

Rebel in Town ★★★

1957

War Drums ★★★
Slim Carter ★★★

1958

Fort Bowie ★★★

1960

Ten Who Dared ★★★

1961

The Cowboy and the Champ ★★★
One-Eyed Jacks ★★★

1965

Major Dundee ★★★
War Party (stuntman)

1966

The Rare Breed ★★★

1968

Will Penny ★★★★
Hang 'Em High ★★★

1969

The Undefeated ★★★
The Wild Bunch ★★★★

1970

Chisum ★★★

1971

The Last Picture Show ★★★★
Something Big ★★★

1972

Junior Bonner ★★★
The Getaway ★★★

1973

The Train Robbers ★★★
Kid Blue ★★★
Dillinger ★★★

1974

The Sugarland Express ★★★★

1975

Bite the Bullet ★★★★
Hustle ★★★

1976

Breakheart Pass ★★★

1977

The Greatest ★★★
The Town That Dreaded Sundown ★★★
Greyeagle ★★★

1978

The Swarm ★★

1980

The Hunter ★★★

1981

Ruckus ★★★

VAN JOHNSON
★★★ 2.90 STARS

Film historians will probably dismiss Van Johnson as the innocuous one-time rage of impressionable bobby-soxers. Freckles and all-American features were no asset to his acting reputation, yet Johnson was always convincing and sometimes outstanding.

He was born Charles Van Johnson in 1916, in Newport, Rhode Island. After some chorus boy appearances on Broadway, he began his screen career in *Murder in the Big House*. The film *Dr. Gillespie's New Assistant* did little for him, but he shot to stardom in *A Guy Named Joe*. In *Two Girls and a Sailor,* he was teamed with June Allyson, and did a few other lightweight but popular pictures (*Thrill of a Romance* with Esther Williams and *Weekend at the Waldorf* with Lana Turner). Two reunions with Allyson in *High Barbaree* and *The Bride Goes Wild* didn't achieve the acclaim of their first pairing, but *State of the Union* was a substantial script for a change. Van Johnson played a campaign manager in this typically literate Hepburn and Tracy vehicle. He was likable as an orderly in the otherwise somber *Command Decision.* In *Mother Is a Freshman,* he was cast as an English professor who fell in love with student Loretta Young.

He had his best part, as Judy Garland's pen pal, in *In the Good Old Summertime.* A delightful remake of *The Shop Around the Corner* with music, it showed what Johnson could do with witty dialogue. The funny lines weren't there in a so-called comedy, *The Big Hangover,* nor did they surface in *Grounds for Marriage* and *Three Guys Named Mike.*

It took another strong role in *The Caine Mutiny,* as the officer who relieved Humphrey Bogart of command, to remind viewers of his ability. He didn't have the ability, however, to make the forced cynicism of his character in *Brigadoon* seem believable; it was an otherwise delightful musical. He was also fine in *The Last Time I Saw Paris* and *The End of the Affair* though he himself was mortified by his performance at the Cannes Film Festival.

Johnson keeps busy in summer stock and on TV, still freckled, still youthful, and always pleasant to watch.

Van Johnson.

FILMOGRAPHY

1942

Too Many Girls (bit)
Murder in the Big House ★★
Somewhere I'll Find You (bit)
The War Against Mrs. Hadley ★★
Dr. Gillespie's New Assistant ★★★

1943

The Human Comedy ★★★
Pilot No. 5 ★★★
Madame Curie ★★
A Guy Named Joe ★★★
Dr. Gillespie's Criminal Case ★★★

1944

The White Cliffs of Dover ★★★
Three Men in White ★★★
Two Girls and a Sailor ★★★
Thirty Seconds Over Tokyo ★★★

1945

Between Two Women ★★★
Thrill of a Romance ★★★
Weekend at the Waldorf ★★★

1946

Ziegfeld Follies (cameo)
Easy to Wed ★★★
No Leave No Love ★★★
Till the Clouds Roll By (cameo)

1947

High Barbaree ★★
The Romance of Rosy Ridge ★★★

1948

State of the Union ★★★★
The Bride Goes Wild ★★★

1949

Command Decision ★★★★
Mother Is a Freshman ★★★★
Scene of the Crime ★★★
In the Good Old Summertime ★★★★
Battleground ★★★★

1950

The Big Hangover ★★
Duchess of Idaho ★★★

1951

Grounds for Marriage ★★
Three Guys Named Mike ★★★
Go for Broke ★★
Too Young to Kiss ★★★

1952

It's a Big Country ★★★
Invitation ★★★
When in Rome ★★
Washington Story ★★★
Plymouth Adventure ★★★

1953

Confidentially Connie ★★★
Remains to Be Seen ★★
Easy to Love ★★★

1954

The Siege at Red River ★★★
Men of the Fighting Lady ★★★
The Caine Mutiny ★★★★
Brigadoon ★★★
The Last Time I Saw Paris ★★★★

1955

The End of the Affair ★★★

1956

The Brass Bottle ★★
Miracle in the Rain ★★★★
23 Paces to Baker Street ★★★

1957

Slander ★★★
Kelly and Me ★★
Action of the Tiger ★★★

1959

The Last Blitzkrieg ★★
Subway in the Sky ★★★
Beyond This Place ★★★

1960

The Enemy General ★★★

1961

The Pied Piper of Hamelin ★★★

1963

Wives and Lovers ★★★

1967

Divorce American Style ★★★★

1968

Yours, Mine and Ours ★★★
Where Angels Go . . . Trouble Follows ★★★

1969

Battle Squadron ★★★

1970

Il Prezzo del Potere ★★★
Company of Killers ★★

1971

L'Occhio del Ragno ★★★

1979

Concorde Affaire ★★★
Da Corleone ad Brooklyn ★★

JAMES EARL JONES
★★★ 2.93 STARS

With his resonant voice and his commanding presence, James Earl Jones is probably most at home in the theatre. However, for generations to come, it is probably as the disembodied bass voice of Darth Vader in the *Star Wars* trilogy that Jones will be best remembered.

Born in 1931, in Arkabutla, Mississippi, Jones became an overnight sensation in the Broadway production of "The Great White Hope," after years of performing the classics and avant-garde plays of the theatre. A veteran of Joseph Papp's New York Shakespeare Festival, Jones won the Tony Award for Best Actor in 1969 for the lead in "Hope." The play dealt with the life of Jack Johnson, the first Negro to win the heavyweight championship. As Jack Johnson, he was harassed by whites unable to accept the defeat of a white by a black in the ring. Jones recreated the stage role on film opposite Jane Alexander.

His best film role since that triumph was a moving comedy about the Negro Baseball League called *The Bingo Long Traveling All-Stars and Motor Kings*. He has also used his commanding bravado to create memorable villains in the Charles Laughton tradition in *Exorcist II: The Heretic*, *Swashbuckler*, and *Conan the Barbarian*.

Jones returned to the stage in recent years, appearing as the jealous Othello in Shakespeare's tragedy and in Athol Fugard's metaphorical play about life in South Africa, "Master Harold and the Boys."

FILMOGRAPHY

1964

Dr. Strangelove (bit)

1967

The Comedians ★★★

1970

King (documentary)
End of the Road ★★★
The Great White Hope ★★★★

James Earl Jones with Jane Alexander in *The Great White Hope.*

1972

Malcolm X (documentary, narration)
The Man ★★★

1975

Claudine ★★★

1976

Deadly Hero ★★★
The River Niger ★★★
The Bingo Long Traveling All-Stars and Motor Kings ★★★★
Swashbuckler ★★

1977

The Greatest ★★
Exorcist II: The Heretic ★★
The Last Remake of Beau Geste ★★★
Star Wars (voice only)
A Piece of the Action ★★★

1980

The Empire Strikes Back (voice only)

1982

Conan the Barbarian ★★★

1983

Return of the Jedi (voice only)

JENNIFER JONES
★★½ 2.58 STARS

In retrospect, Newsweek was over-enthusiastic when it called Jennifer Jones a "cinematic Cinderella" for her performance in *The Song of Bernadette*. Critic Kate Cameron added, "she not only reaches stardom, but she must be counted a phenomenon." Jones *was* a sensitive actress in good vehicles, but too often she resorted to neurotic, lip-twisting mannerisms.

She was born Phyllis Lee Isley, in Tulsa, Oklahoma, in 1919. Despite painful shyness, she sought an acting career. She appeared under her own name in Republic Pictures low-budgeters *New Frontier* and *Dick Tracy's G-Men* until producer David O. Selznick decided to make her a star. He cast her in the spectacularly successful *The Song of Bernadette*, and she won an Oscar for her part.

She was lively and touching in *Since You Went Away*, as the girl who lost her soldier-boyfriend Robert Walker. Their real-life marriage also collapsed, and Jones married mentor Selznick, who put her in a series of varied pictures. She was sexier than ever again in *Duel in the Sun*, and appealing fey as an amnesia victim in *Love Letters*. Critic Howard Barnes found her "artful and attractive" in *Cluny Brown*, an Ernst Lubitsch-directed comedy, but *Portrait of Jennie* was too ethereal to make a box-office impact.

Director Vincente Minnelli had originally wanted Lana Turner for *Madame Bovary*, but he settled for Jones. The rigid censorship of the 1940s prevented her from frankly portraying a loose lady, and the point of Flaubert's novel was blunted. The public was indifferent, and they also avoided *Carrie*, a grim and disturbing drama adapted from Theodore Dreiser's classic. She was adequate in the lush *Love Is a Many Splendored Thing*, and maddeningly pretentious in *The Man in the Gray Flannel Suit*.

Selznick's death brought her professional decline and a suicide attempt, but Jones made a fine comeback in *The Towering Inferno*. She married art collector and millionaire businessman Norton Simon in 1971.

FILMOGRAPHY

(billed as Phyllis Isley)

1939

New Frontier ★★
Dick Tracy's G-Men (serial) ★★

(billed as Jennifer Jones)

1944

The Song of Bernadette ★★★
Since You Went Away ★★★

1945

Love Letters ★★★

1946

Cluny Brown ★★★★

1947

Duel in the Sun ★★★

1949

Portrait of Jennie ★★★
We Were Strangers ★★
Madame Bovary ★★

1950

The Wild Heart ★★

1952

Carrie ★★★

Jennifer Jones in *The Song of Bernadette*.

1953

Ruby Gentry ★★★

1954

Beat the Devil ★★★★
Indiscretion of an American Wife ★★★

1955

Love Is a Many Splendored Thing ★★★
Good Morning Miss Dove ★★★

1956

The Man in the Gray Flannel Suit ★

1957

The Barretts of Wimpole Street ★★★★
A Farewell to Arms ★★

1962

Tender Is the Night ★★

1966

The Idol ★★

1969

Angel, Angel, Down We Go ★

1974

The Towering Inferno ★★

SHIRLEY JONES
★★★ 3.05 STARS

Shirley Jones began her film career as a sweet and wholesome ingenue. She was always pleasing, rarely saccharine, but few expected her to develop into such a capable actress.

Jones was born in 1934, in Smithton, Pennsylvania. Her screen debut was spectacular—she was Rodgers and Hammerstein's personal choice for the lead in *Oklahoma!* Jones's winsome charm was ideal for the role, although the movie itself had a labored feeling. Gordon MacRae was her co-star, and they were paired again in *Carousel* after Frank Sinatra refused the male lead. The sentimental weaknesses of the script were apparent when blown up to cinemascope size, and MacRae's song "Soliloquy" dwarfed any of Jones's contributions. A frail musical drama, *Never Steal Anything Small,* did nothing for her or co-star James Cagney.

She shocked the movie industry with her superb portrait of a prostitute in *Elmer Gantry,* and her Best Supporting Oscar released her permanently from the straitjacket of sugary musical parts. *Two Rode Together* was a fair western; John Ford directed and male stars included James Stewart and Richard Widmark. Jones was also appealing in a cutesy family comedy, *The Courtship of Eddie's Father* and right at home with Robert Preston in *The Music Man.*

Shirley Jones in *The Cheyenne Social Club*.

She decorated *A Ticklish Affair* and struggled gamely through *Bedtime Story,* a leaden comedy mutilated by Marlon Brando's heavy hand. *Beyond the Poseidon Adventure* showed how low a sequel can sink. Currently, Jones appears regularly on TV in a variety of roles, consistently demonstrating professionalism and sensitivity.

FILMOGRAPHY

1955

Oklahoma! ★★★★

1956

Carousel ★★★

1957

April Love ★★★

1959

Never Steal Anything Small ★★

1960

Bobbikins ★★
Elmer Gantry ★★★★
Pepe ★★

1961

Two Rode Together ★★★

1962

The Music Man ★★★★

1963

The Courtship of Eddie's Father ★★
A Ticklish Affair ★★★

1964

Dark Purpose ★★★
Bedtime Story ★★★

1965

Fluffy ★★★
The Secret of My Success ★★

1969

The Happy Ending ★★★

1970

The Cheyenne Social Club ★★★

1979

Beyond the Poseidon Adventure ★★
Evening in Byzantium ★★★

LOUIS JOURDAN
★★★ 2.97 STARS

As a young man, Louis Jourdan could only be described as beautiful—perfect features, warm but not-too-thick French accent, and a winning smile. However, he was more than the stereotype of a lover for he showed remarkable ease with urbane dialogue and had the proper intensity for heavy melodrama.

Jourdan (Louis Gendre) was born in 1919, in Marseille, France. During the war, he and his brother were members of the underground. He also starred in some French films, *Le Corsaire* and *La Vie de Boheme*, before coming to the U.S. He was effective in *The Paradine Case* as the young man who incited Valli to commit murder though Hitchcock had wanted Robert Newton for the part.

Letter from an Unknown Woman was probably his finest hour as an actor; Jourdan played the self-centered musician who broke Joan Fontaine's heart. He played in *No Minor Vices*, a very minor comedy, and was appropriately romantic in *Madame Bovary.* Two costume pictures, *Bird of Paradise* and *Anne of the Indies*, slid by without creating a stir. In *Three Coins in the Fountain*, a light but likable tale of girls husband-hunting in Rome, Jourdan was the target of Maggie McNamara's pursuit. His polish and grace enlivened *The Swan*, and his portrayal of a maniacally jealous husband out to murder Doris Day in *Julie* showed what he could do with an unsympathetic role.

In *Gigi*, his most popular picture, Jourdan seemed to be born to play the man about town who slowly awakened to Leslie Caron's charms. Now aging but still attractive, he should be able to switch to young girl/older man romantic parts without any trouble.

FILMOGRAPHY

1939
Le Corsaire ★★★

1941
Premier Rendez-Vous ★★★

1942
L'Arlesienne ★★★
Felicie Nanteuil ★★★
La Vie de Bohème ★★★

1943
Untel Perè et Fils ★★★

1945
La Belle Aventure ★★★

1948
The Paradine Case ★★★★
Letter from an Unknown Woman ★★★★
No Minor Vices ★★

1949
Madame Bovary ★★★★

1951
Bird of Paradise ★★
Anne of the Indies ★★

Louis Jourdan with Elizabeth Taylor and Richard Burton in *The V.I.P. s.*

1952
The Happy Time ★★★

1953
Rue de l'Estrapade ★★★
Decameron Nights ★★★

1954
Three Coins in the Fountain ★★★

1956
Julie ★★★★
The Swan ★★★
The Bride Is Much Too Beautiful ★★★

1957
Dangerous Exile ★★

1958
Gigi ★★★★

1959
The Best of Everything ★★★★

1960
Can-Can ★★★

1961
The Story of Monte Cristo ★★★
Amazons of Rome ★★★

1962
Disorder ★★★

1963
The V.I.P.s ★★★

1966
Made in Paris ★★★

1967
To Commit a Murder ★★★

1968
A Flea in Her Ear ★★
The Young Rebel ★★★

1976
The Count of Monte Cristo ★★★

1977
Silver Bears ★★★

1982
Swamp Thing ★★

1983
Octopussy ★★

BORIS KARLOFF
★★★ 3.17 STARS

In private life, arch-villain Boris Karloff was known as a gentle, even-tempered individual, yet he excelled in horror roles, adding dimension to the most macabre parts.

Karloff (William Henry Pratt) was born in 1887, in Dulwich, England. He was a successful stage actor by the time he debuted as an extra in *The Dumb Girl of Portici.* After several silents, *Without Benefit of Clergy, Cheated Hearts*, and *The Woman Conquers*, he did his first talkie, *The Unholy Night*, playing a Hindu servant.

He established his permanent image in *Frankenstein*, assuming the part of the Creature after Bela Lugosi rejected it. He was murderous in *The Old Dark House*, then starred in *The Mask of Fu Manchu.* Karloff abandoned monsterdom for John Ford's *The Lost Patrol* and portrayed an anti-Semite in *The House of Rothschild.*

Then he went back to familiar territory in *The Bride of Frankenstein* and *The Raven* with Lugosi. He later did *Son of Frankenstein, The Invisible Menace*, and *the Man They Could Not Hang. The Body Snatcher* was based on a Robert Lewis Stevenson story and generally conceded to be as Leonard Maltin put it, "one of the classic Val Lewton thrillers."

He showed his range in comedy *(The Secret Life of Walter Mitty)*, westerns *(Unconquered)*, and straight thrillers *(Lured)* and then made *Abbott and Costello Meet the Killer Boris Karloff*. In that film he tried to kill Costello. He was excellent in *The Raven* along with other horror specialists Vincent Price and Peter Lorre. AIP Studios cast him in *Bikini Beach* and *The Ghost in the Invisible Bikini*, among others, but his class and style stood out even in silly vehicles like these.

Karloff's triumph on stage in "Peter Pan" told those detractors prejudiced against the horror genre that he was a fine actor, something he proved again in *Targets*, one of his last films.

Boris Karloff in *The Black Cat*.

FILMOGRAPHY

(features only)

1919

His Majesty the American ★★★
The Prince and Betty ★★★

1920

The Deadlier Sex ★★★
The Courage of Marge O'Doone ★★★
The Last of the Mohicans ★★★

1921

The Hope Diamond Mystery (serial) ★★★
Without Benefit of Clergy ★★★
Cheated Hearts ★★★
The Cave Girl ★★★

1922

The Man From Downing Street ★★★
The Infidel ★★★
The Altar Stairs ★★★
Omar the Tentmaker ★★★
The Woman Conquers ★★★

1923

The Prisoner ★★★

1924

The Hellion ★★★
Dynamite Dan ★★★

1925

Parisian Nights ★★★
Forbidden Cargo ★★★
The Prairie Wife ★★★
Lady Robinhood ★★★
Never the Twain Shall Meet ★★★

1926

The Greater Glory ★★★
Her Honor the Governor ★★★
The Bells ★★★
Eagle of the Sea ★★★
Flames ★★★
The Golden Web ★★★
Flaming Fury ★★★
Valencia (bit)
Man in the Saddle ★★★
Old Ironsides ★★★

1927

Tarzan and the Golden Lion ★★★
Let It Rain ★★★
The Meddlin' Stranger ★★★
The Princess From Hoboken ★★★
The Phantom Buster ★★★
Soft Cushions ★★★
Two Arabian Knights ★★★
The Love Mart ★★★

1928

Vultures of the Sea (serial) ★★★
The Little Wild Girl ★★★

1929

Devil's Chaplain ★★★
Two Sisters ★★★
The Phantom of the North ★★★
Anne Against the World ★★★
King of the Kongo (serial) ★★★
Behind That Curtain ★★★
The Unholy Night ★★★★
Burning the Wind ★★★

1930

The Band One (bit)
The Sea Bat ★★★
The Utah Kid ★★★

1931

Mother's Cry (bit)
The Criminal Code ★★★★
Cracked Nuts ★★★
Donovan's Kid ★★★
King of the Wild (serial) ★★★
Smart Money ★★★
The Public Defender ★★★
I Like Your Nerve ★★★
Five Star Final ★★★★
Pardon Us ★★★
Graft ★★★
The Mad Genius ★★★★
The Yellow Ticket ★★★
The Guilty Generation ★★★
Frankenstein ★★★★
Tonight or Never ★★★

1932

Business and Pleasure ★★★
Alias the Doctor ★★★
Behind the Mask ★★★★
Scarface ★★★★
The Miracle Man ★★★
The Cohens and Kellys in Hollywood (cameo)
Night World ★★★
The Old Dark House ★★★★
The Mask of Fu Manchu ★★★★
The Mummy ★★★★

1933

The Ghoul ★★★★

1934

The Lost Patrol ★★★★
The House of Rothschild ★★★★
The Black Cat ★★★★
The Gift of Gab (cameo)

1935

The Bride of Frankenstein ★★★★
The Black Room ★★★
The Raven ★★★

1936

The Invisible Ray ★★★★
The Walking Dead ★★★
The Man Who Lived Again ★★★★
Juggernaut ★★★★

1937

Charlie Chan at the Opera ★★★
Night Key ★★★
West of Shanghai ★★★

1938

The Invisible Menace ★★★★
Mr. Wong-Detective ★★★

1939

Son of Frankenstein ★★★★
The Mystery of Mr. Wong ★★★
Mr. Wong in Chinatown ★★★
The Man They Could Not Hang ★★★★
Tower of London ★★★★

1940

The Fatal Hour ★★★
British Intelligence ★★★
Black Friday ★★★
The Man With Nine Lives ★★★
Devil's Island ★★★
Doomed to Die ★★★
Before I Hang ★★★
You'll Find Out ★★★

1941

The Devil Commands ★★★

1942

The Boogie Man Will Get You ★★★

1944

The Climax ★★★★
House of Frankenstein ★★★★

1945

The Body Snatcher ★★★★
Isle of the Dead ★★★★

1946

Bedlam ★★★★

1947

The Secret Life of Walter Mitty ★★★★
Lured ★★★★
Unconquered ★★★
Dick Tracy Meets Gruesome ★★★

1948

Tap Roots ★★★

1949

Abbott and Costello Meet the Killer Boris Karloff ★★

1951

The Strange Door ★★★

1952

The Black Castle ★★★

1953

Abbott and Costello Meet Dr. Jekyll and Mr. Hyde ★★
Monster of the Island ★★★
The Hindu ★★★

1957

Voodoo Island ★★★

1958

The Haunted Strangler ★★★
Frankenstein 1970 ★★★

1962

Corridors of Blood ★★★★

1963

The Raven ★★★★
The Terror ★★★
Black Sabbath ★★★
The Comedy of Terrors ★★

1964

Bikini Beach (cameo)

1965

Die Monster Die! ★★★

1966

The Ghost in the Invisible Bikini ★★
The Daydreamer (voice only)

1967

The Venetian Affair ★★★
The Sorcerers ★★★
Mad Monster Party (voice only)

1968

Targets ★★★★
Curse of the Crimson Altar ★★★
The Snake People ★★

1971

The Incredible Invasion ★★
Cauldron of Blood ★★

DANNY KAYE
★★★ 2.94 STARS

Danny Kaye's statements make him sound *serious*, almost stuffy: "I guess what I had to be, I am—an entertainer." or, "We who have been fortunate to make people laugh should be satisfied being comedians. I don't mean to boast, but there do not seem to be too many of us." Fortunately, his screen presence was everything these pronouncements were not: lively, free-wheeling, and bursting with energy and talent.

Danny Kaye in *Hans Christian Andersen*.

Kaye (David Daniel Kaminski) was born in 1913, Brooklyn, New York. He left school at age thirteen to work in the Catskill Mountains, toured the Orient at age twenty ("I was getting my education around the world"), and then married Sylvia Fine who supplied his best material in the years to come. A Broadway success, Cole Porter's "Let's Face It," preceded his first film, *Up in Arms*, a hit comedy with Dinah Shore.

Excellent reviews and audience response led to *Wonder Man*, in which he was cast as twins, and he was a milkman-turned-prizefighter in *The Kid from Brooklyn. The Secret Life of Walter Mitty* was a smash, and Kaye had a field day as a young man given to extravagant fantasizing. However, something went wrong with *A Song Is Born*, a musical update of *Ball of Fire*, costarring Virginia Mayo. It was overlong and labored, lacking the energy of his previous vehicles. The box office reflected these deficiencies.

The Inspector General was also tedious though critic Steven H. Scheuer spoke for the minority group that reveres this film, "It's a Danny Kaye romp, and one of those rare times when the story comes close to matching his artistry." *Hans Christian Andersen* earned the approval of most observers, more for Frank Loesser's delightful score than for the dramatic situations depicted. He was hilarious in *Knock on Wood* as a puppeteer who got embroiled with spies including the lovely Mai Zetterling.

Kaye's biggest commercial hit was *White Christmas* with Bing

Crosby. The sentiment was laid on thickly, but the Irving Berlin score made it all palatable. The Academy certified his achievements in 1954 with a Special Oscar "for his unique talents, his Service to the Academy, the Motion Picture Industry and the American People."

The American people didn't see him on screen again for two years, but he was *The Court Jester* in 1956. This film included his famous "the pellet with the poison's in the vessel with the pestle" monologue. *Merry Andrew* found him somewhat more subdued, and he erased his wackiness totally in the glum *Me and the Colonel. The Five Pennies* compensated, an entertaining, if clichéd, biography of bandleader Red Nichols. His screen career disintegrated overnight in *The Man from the Diner's Club* and *The Madwoman of Chaillot*, so he went to Broadway in a Richard Rodgers musical "Two by Two" and scored a success.

TV also proved fruitful. "The Danny Kaye Show" ran from 1963-1967 and garnered him an Emmy and a Peabody Award. His filmography includes many enjoyable pictures, but no classics. Kaye's routines, however—his double-talk, impersonations, and slapstick—are classic, and will be quoted after the films themselves have been forgotten.

FILMOGRAPHY

1944

Up in Arms ★★★

1945

Wonder Man ★★★★

1946

The Kid from Brooklyn ★★★

1947

The Secret Life of Walter Mitty ★★★★

1948

A Song Is Born ★★★

1949

The Inspector General ★★★
It's a Great Feeling (cameo)

1951

On the Riviera ★★★

1952

Hans Christian Andersen ★★★★

1954

Knock on Wood ★★★
White Christmas ★★★

1956

The Court Jester ★★★★

1958

Merry Andrew ★★★
Me and the Colonel ★★

1959

The Five Pennies ★★

1961

On the Double ★★

1963

The Man From the Diner's Club ★★

1969

The Madwoman of Chaillot ★★

DIANE KEATON
★★★ 3.07 STARS

Diane Keaton's endearing helplessness is ideal for comedy, and her *Annie Hall* Oscar was well deserved. You can't fault her dramatic ability either, although she seems miscast in some of her serious roles. She lacks the earthy core that would have made her, for example, a credible nymphomaniac in *Looking for Mr. Goodbar.*

Keaton was born Diane Hall, in Los Angeles in 1946. Theatre-goers first saw her in "Hair," and she made a strong impression opposite Woody Allen in his Broadway hit, "Play It Again, Sam." Her first film was an enjoyable comedy, *Lovers and Other Strangers*, and she was lucky with her second, *The Godfather.* Keaton played Al Pacino's girlfriend, and she became his wife in the sequel, *The Godfather, Part II.* Both films seemed to dilute her energy; she was competent but mechanical, contrasting with the full-blooded work of Pacino and the other principals.

Keaton's radiance was first glowingly apparent in the screen version of *Play it Again, Sam.* She had all the comedic flair of Woody Allen's first partner, Louise Lasser, and a more feminine leading-lady appeal. Her hesitant charm was an asset to another Allen movie, *Sleeper*, although critic Pauline Kael remained "on the verge of responding to her...She's just there to be Woody's girl." *Love and Death* was their third teaming and even zanier than the earlier two. Allen played a Russian trying to avoid the draft, and she was the sex-starved cousin he yearned for.

The merit of Allen's material was emphasized when Keaton made two comedies without him. One, *I Will, I Will...For Now* with Elliott Gould was a limpid but sincere satire. The other, *Harry and Walter Go to New York*, with Gould again was even worse: "a lavish but lopsided period farce," according to critic Leonard Maltin.

Allen quickly arrived to undo the damage with *Annie Hall.* It was a bittersweet, evidently autobiographical study of their personal relationship and beyond the wit—there was plenty of it—all the insecurity, hope, and final disillutionment of a love affair was beautifully captured. The film won a Best Picture Oscar and Keaton won for Best Actress.

Looking for Mr. Goodbar was a problem from the start. Writer-director Richard Brooks vulgarized and distorted the original novel, and Keaton never made the viewer believe in her promiscuity. Part of the problem was the nice-girl image she had built up in former films. Just the same, critics like Rex Reed raved, "If Diane Keaton doesn't win an Oscar, there is no God."

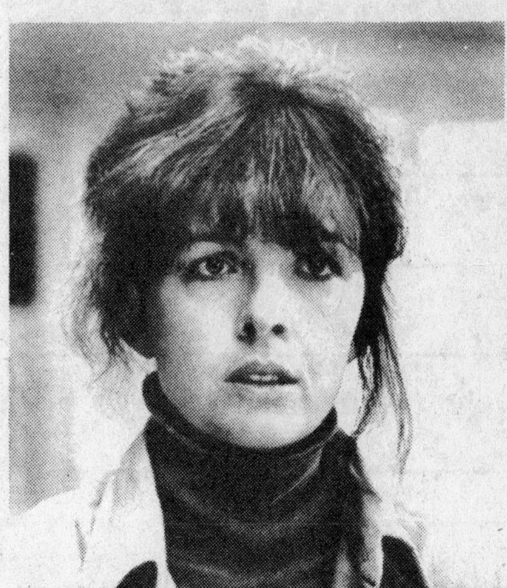

Diane Keaton in *Shoot the Moon.*

There were also good reviews for her contribution to *Interiors,* Allen's first serious film. Though less successful than his comedies, it had strong moments, especially when Geraldine Page and Maureen Stapleton were on the screen. Audiences much preferred *Manhattan,* which was funnier than *Annie Hall* but not quite as deep.

Keaton gave her best serious performance in *Shoot the Moon.* As the estranged wife of Albert Finney, she burst beyond her "la-de-dah" *Annie Hall* persona, projecting all the accumulated despair and violence of a frustrated marriage. The movie was destroyed by a grotesquely melodramatic ending, however, and she was similarly weighed down by the verbose ambitiousness of *Reds. Reds* was Warren Beatty's (another of her boyfriends) attempts at epic seriousness. Diane Keaton couldn't penetrate any further into her character of Louise Bryant than an "Annie-Hall-goes-to-Russia" portrayal.

Like all talented and popular actresses, Diane Keaton seems to want out of her defined niche. She has the talent to break out but not the vehicle. It would be a shame, though, if she never plays The Further Adventures of Annie Hall.

FILMOGRAPHY

1970

Lovers and Other Strangers ★★

1972

The Godfather ★★★
Play It Again, Sam ★★★★

1973

Sleeper ★★★

1974

The Godfather, Part II ★★★

1975

Love and Death ★★★

1976

I Will, I Will...For Now ★★
Harry and Walter Go to New York ★★

1977

Looking for Mr. Goodbar ★★
Annie Hall ★★★★

1978

Interiors ★★★★

1979

Manhattan ★★★★

1981

Reds ★★★

1982

Shoot the Moon ★★★★

HOWARD KEEL
★★★ 2.92 STARS

If you tune in to an old musical starring Howard Keel, you'll hear immediately something that today's musicals have lost. His voice is warm, rich and virile, capable of either tenderness or soaring power.

Keel was born Harry Clifford Leek, in 1917, in Gillespie, Illinois. He made his mark in a 1947 London production of "Oklahoma!" and after an unnoticed appearance in *The Small Voice* as an escaped convict, he signed for MGM's *Annie Get Your Gun.* He didn't care for co-star Betty Hutton who replaced Judy Garland, but they both triumphed. Keel was equally good as the gambling Gaylord Ravenal in *Show Boat.* His singing couldn't save *Lovely to Look At,* but *Calamity Jane* offered him a part (and a score) on par with *Annie Get Your Gun,* and he solidified his success. *Seven Brides for Seven Brothers* was superb, and he was superb in it—too imposing to be overshadowed by the dazzling Michael Kidd choreography.

When times grew lean, he played in a number of second rate films including *Floods of Fear, The Big Fisherman,* and *Waco.* However, Keel returned to the stage, eliciting standing ovations for "Man of La Mancha," "South Pacific," and the hit theatrical version of "Seven Brides." TV viewers can also see him regularly on "Dallas."

FILMOGRAPHY

1948

The Small Voice ★★

1950

Annie Get Your Gun ★★★★
Pagan Love Song ★★★

Howard Keel.

1951

Three Guys Named Mike ★★★
Show Boat ★★★★
Texas Carnival ★★★

1952

Callaway Went Thataway ★★★
Lovely to Look At ★★★
Desperate Search ★★

1953

Ride Vaquero! ★★★
Fast Company ★★
Calamity Jane ★★★
Kiss Me Kate ★★★★

1954

Rose Marie ★★★
Seven Brides for Seven Brothers ★★★★
Deep in My Heart (cameo)

1955

Jupiter's Darling ★★★
Kismet ★★★

1959

Floods of Fear ★★★
The Big Fisherman ★★

1961

Armored Command ★★★

1963

Day of the Triffids ★★

1965

The Man From Button Willow (voice only)

1966

Waco ★★★

1967

The War Wagon ★★★
Red Tomahawk ★★★

1968

Arizona Bushwhackers ★★

GENE KELLY
★★★ 3.18 STARS

Gene Kelly and Fred Astaire have been compared for over 40 years. Except for the obvious fact that they both dance, the two have little in common. Kelly is warm and outgoing, Astaire aloof and cool. Kelly is earthy, Astaire refined. Kelly's dramatic style is expansive; Astaire underplays to the point of self-effacement. Their only similarity, beside dancing, is their talent for delivering superb entertainment.

Kelly was born in Pittsburgh, in 1912. He claims he started dancing as "strictly a case of male ego. I'd do a buck-and-wing and they all thought it was nifty...it was just a way to meet girls." After working as a dancing instructor with his brother Fred, Kelly appeared in a Broadway revue, "One For the Money" and then made his biggest impact as the conniving gigolo in "Pal Joey." His success led to an excellent film debut in *For Me and My Gal* opposite Judy Garland.

He was competent in the dramatic *The Cross of Lorraine*, although his dancing was missed. He compensated by conceiving a series of fresh, imaginative dance routines for *Cover Girl* and had another lovely partner in Rita Hayworth. *Christmas Holiday* offered a change of pace—Kelly was a killer married to the unsuspecting Deanna Durbin.

He was Oscar-nominated for *Anchors Aweigh*, a lively musical that seems dated today, except for his dance with a cartoon mouse.

Gene Kelly in *Thousands Cheer.*

Ziegfeld Follies presented what is now a collector's item—Astaire and Kelly dancing together. A reunion with Judy Garland in *The Pirate* fell short of commercial hopes. At the time the New York Herald Tribune called this period satire about pirates "scrambled entertainment," although film historian Joel Siegel years later found it "above all an exuberant parody of operetta conventions with dividend winks at Victorian melodrama and swashbuckler romance. The Garland and Kelly performances are extremely ambitious attempts at extending their usual ranges."

Gene Kelly in *Singin' in the Rain.*

His "Slaughter on Tenth Avenue" ballet in *Words and Music* was the high point of that film, and he made a dashingly athletic D'Artagnan in *The Three Musketeers. Take Me Out to the Ball Game* was an underrated but delightful spoof about ballplayers, and then he extended his range still further when tackling *An American in Paris.* The 20-minute ballet to George Gershwin's music insured Kelly's cinematic immortality, although the plot now looks threadbare. *On the Town,* in retrospect, was less pretentious, more joyful and less straining for "art."

But art was achieved in full measure with *Singin' in the Rain.* This time the script, a takeoff on silent movies, matched the level of the dancing and the score. Every number has become legendary, from Kelly's ballet with Cyd Charisse to his own dancing of the title tune in the rain.

Anything after that was found to be anticlimactic, and *It's Always Fair Weather* ran afoul of box-office expectations. It had merits—a clever concept about three GIs meeting ten years after World War II—but the comedy was heavy-handed and the score uninspired. *Brigadoon* was stagy, and Kelly was glaringly miscast as the Jewish Noel Airman in *Marjorie Morningstar.*

He was in the dramatic *Inherit the Wind* and thoroughly likable in *40 Carats.* However, these aren't the roles to remember him for. Gene Kelly's brilliance is well defined by his special Oscar, "in appreciation of his versatility as an actor, singer, director and dancer, and specifically for his brilliant achievements in the art of choreography on film."

FILMOGRAPHY

1942

For Me and My Gal ★★★

1943

Pilot No. 5 ★★★
Du Barry Was a Lady ★★★
Thousands Cheer ★★★
The Cross of Lorraine ★★★

1944

Cover Girl ★★★★
Christmas Holiday ★★★

1945

Anchors Aweigh ★★★

1946

Ziegfeld Follies ★★★★

1947

Living in a Big Way ★★★

1948

The Pirate ★★★★
The Three Musketeers ★★★
Words and Music ★★★★

1949

Take Me Out to the Ball Game ★★★★
On the Town ★★★★

1950

The Black Hand ★★
Summer Stock ★★★★

1951

An American in Paris ★★★★

1952

It's a Big Country ★★
Singin' in the Rain ★★★★
The Devil Makes Three ★★★

Gene Kelly with Van Johnson in *Brigadoon.*

1954

Brigadoon ★★★
Crest of the Wave ★★★
Deep in My Heart (cameo)

1955

It's Always Fair Weather ★★★

1956

Invitation to the Dance ★★★

1957

The Happy Road ★★★
Les Girls ★★★

1958

Marjorie Morningstar ★★★

1960

Let's Make Love (cameo)
Inherit the Wind ★★★

1964

What a Way to Go ★★★

1967

The Young Girls of Rochefort ★★★

1973

40 Carats ★★★

1974

That's Entertainment (narration)

1976

That's Entertainment, Part II (narration)

1977

Viva Knievel ★★

1980

Xanadu ★★★

GRACE KELLY
★★★½ 3.45 STARS

There's a scene in *To Catch a Thief* where Grace Kelly surprised Cary Grant with a quiet, sensual kiss, then closed the door while he stared after her, stunned. David Thompson, in A Biographical Dictionary of Film, analyzed her approach further, "Her asking him (Grant) to choose between breast and leg is indelible. No wonder her future husband did what he could to keep the finished film under wraps."

Kelly was born in Philadelphia, in 1928. Her striving for achievement was due to a prolific and talented family. Her father John Kelly was a prominent businessman, her Uncle George was a famous playwright ("Craig's Wife"), and another uncle, Walter, was well known in vaudeville. She modeled and appeared on television and then made a brief, unnoticed appearance in *14 Hours.* In *High Noon* she was cast in her first leading part, but after director Fred Zinnemann shot an abundance of loving close-ups, the film was reedited to concentrate on Gary Cooper. Not until *Mogambo,* a remake of *Red Dust,* did her icy fire become obvious. Even pitted against the colorful earthiness of Ava Gardner, Kelly was exciting in Mary Astor's old role.

Alfred Hitchcock saw what writer Robert Osborne referred to as "her puzzling personality . . . on the one hand she was distant, cool and frigid. On the other, rumors of red-hot romances with Clark Gable, Ray Milland . . . made her somewhat of a female fatale." He cast her in *Dial M for Murder* as the rich wife Ray Milland tried to kill, and she dominated the proceedings with her refined magnetism. The movie itself now ranks as one of Hitchcock's talkiest, but *Rear Window* was beyond criticism—a classic Hitchcock chiller with Kelly playing James Stewart's endangered fiancee.

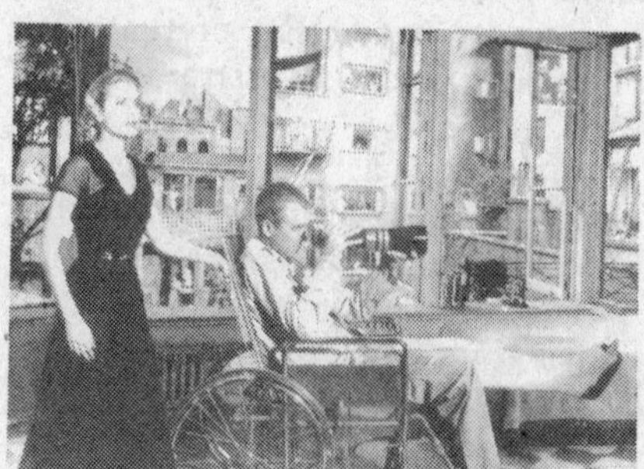

Grace Kelly with James Stewart in *Rear Window.*

She did an uninspired adventure film with Stewart Granger, *Green Fire,* the one box-office disappointment during this golder period, and then tackled a character part in *The Country Girl.* She attempted to deglamorize herself to become the wife of alcoholic Bing Crosby, and it *almost* worked; her incisive and touching portrait of a trapped woman won an Oscar. Most journalists feel, in retrospect, that the Oscar should have gone to Judy Garland for *A Star Is Born.*

Grace Kelly with Bing Crosby in *High Society.*

To Catch a Thief, her last film with Hitchcock, had enough wit and sexuality to make people forget the lack of mystery and tension. Kelly's love scene with Grant to the accompaniment of fireworks is a visual classic. She made one musical, *High Society,* that was a remake of *The Philadelphia Story.* Although she was more alluring and less mannered than Katharine Hepburn had been, the film's real pleasures were Frank Sinatra, Bing Crosby, and the Cole Porter score. Her last picture was *The Swan,* an old-fashioned romance about a Princess forced to choose between a commoner (Louis Jourdan) and a Prince (Alec Guiness). She retired to marry the Prince of Monaco in real life.

For years there were rumors of a comeback (*Marnie* was planned, till her subjects objected), and then she passed into Hollywood legend. She died in 1982, the victim of a car accident. She was mourned as a Queen, but it was much more pleasant to remember Grace Kelly as the matchless vision of beauty she had been in the 1950s.

Grace Kelly.

FILMOGRAPHY

1951

14 Hours ★★

1952

High Noon ★★★

1953

Mogambo ★★★★

1954

Dial M for Murder ★★★★
Rear Window ★★★★
The Country Girl ★★★★
Green Fire ★★★

1955

The Bridges at Toko-Ri ★★★
To Catch a Thief ★★★★

1956

High Society ★★★★
The Swan ★★★

DEBORAH KERR
★★★½ 3.27 STARS

For popularity and longevity, Deborah Kerr's career in America is unequaled by any other British actress. The reasons are clear: warmth, wit, beauty, versatility and all-around acting skill.

Kerr (Deborah J. Kerr-Trimmer) was born in 1921, in Helensburgh, Scotland, She studied to be dancer but abandoned dancing for drama in her teens. A small role in *Major Barbara* led to larger ones in *Hatter's Castle* and *The Life and Death of Colonel Blimp*. In her first American film, *The Hucksters,* she was cast as the proper heroine Clark Gable unsuccessfully tried to seduce. She had that typical English reserve, as well as a subtle sensuality. Kerr was one of the few actresses to overshadow Spencer Tracy. The picture was *Edward, My Son,* and she played a devoted mother who watched her son come to ruin through parental indulgence.

Her talent wasn't particularly taxed by *King Solomon's Mines* although it was an exciting and popular African adventure, nor was acting essential to *Quo Vadis,* another giant commercial success. She proved an expert comedienne in director Sidney Sheldon's amusing *Dream Wife* with Cary Grant. Then, she played the part that fully spotlighted her sexuality as Burt Lancaster's married mistress in *From Here to Eternity.* She was superb, but her next roles were ladylike as the understanding Laura in *Tea and Sympathy,* the governess in *The King and I,* and the religious fanatic in *The End of the Affair.*

Kerr was irresistible (with Cary Grant again) in *An Affair to Remember,* an exquisite remake of *Love Affair.* With the exception of her actressy Sheilah Graham impersonation in *Beloved Infidel,* her every performance was on target including those in *Separate Tables, The Innocents, The Chalk Garden,* and *The Night of the Iguana.* She retired in 1969, less from choice than from refusal to do unsuitable roles.

FILMOGRAPHY

1941

Major Barbara ★★★
Love on the Dole ★★★
Penn of Pennsylvania ★★★
Hatter's Castle ★★★★

1942

The Day Will Dawn ★★★

Deborah Kerr with Robert Mitchum in *The Sundowners.*

1943

The Life and Death of Colonel Blimp ★★★★

1945

Vacation from Marriage ★★★★

1946

I See a Dark Stranger ★★★★

1947

Black Narcissus ★★★★
The Hucksters ★★★

1948

If Winter Comes ★★★

1949

Edward, My Son ★★★★

1950

Please Believe Me ★★★
King Solomon's Mines ★★★★

1951

Quo Vadis ★★★

1952

The Prisoner of Zenda ★★★

1953

Dream Wife ★★★★
Thunder in the East ★★★
Young Bess ★★★
Julius Caesar ★★★
From Here to Eternity ★★★★

1954

The End of the Affair ★★★

1956

The Proud and the Profane ★★★
The King and I ★★★★
Tea and Sympathy ★★★★

1957

Heaven Knows Mr. Allison ★★★
An Affair to Remember ★★★★

1958

Bonjour Tristesse ★★★
Separate Tables ★★★★

1959

The Journey ★★
Count Your Blessings ★★
Beloved Infidel ★★

1960

The Grass Is Greener ★★★
The Sundowners ★★★★

1961

The Innocents ★★★★
The Naked Edge ★★★

1963

The Chalk Garden ★★★★

1964

The Night of the Iguana ★★★★

1965

Marriage on the Rocks ★★

1967

Eye of the Devil ★★★
Casino Royale ★★★

1968

Prudence and the Pill ★★

1969

The Gypsy Moths ★★★★
The Arrangement ★★

MARGOT KIDDER
★★★ 2.76 STARS

Margot Kidder, a strong, intriguing actress, has a certain toughness, a street-wise directness in her manner that sets her apart from more conventional leading ladies.

She was born in 1948, in Yellow Knife, Canada. Her first movie, *Gaily, Gaily,* wasn't quite a gay experience for the viewer, nor did *Quackser Fortune Has a Cousin in the Bronx* do much to endear her to audiences. *Sisters* was much better, a bloody, almost unbearably graphic thriller about a mentally disturbed twin with a penchant for knifing people. Brian De Palma directed *Sisters,* but wasn't around to rescue *Black Christmas,* another horror story set in a sorority house although Kidder stood out.

She was impressive playing the mother of a grown daughter in *The Reincarnation of Peter Proud,* but an unsatisfactory conclusion marred the picture. *Gravy Train* gave her two lackluster leading men, Stacy Keach and Frederic Forrest, and she added little to a Robert Redford vehicle, *The Great Waldo Pepper.* She was good in *92 in the Shade,* a sometimes diverting tale of Florida fishing boat captains.

Commercial success came with *Superman;* she was Lois Lane, a per-

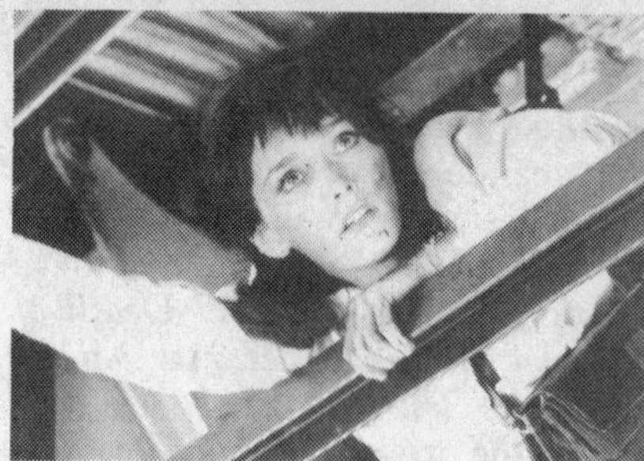

Margot Kidder in *Superman II.*

fect, worldly counterpart to Christopher Reeve's naive Clark Kent. Kidder also played in the popular but poor thriller, *The Amityville Horror,* which was supposedly based on fact, and then Kidder did *Superman II.* Although it was better than the original, she reluctantly appeared in a third *Superman* picture because of a salary dispute. She has had some starring vehicles in *Trenchcoat, Heartaches,* and *Willie and Phil* but has been unable to carry off such weak material.

FILMOGRAPHY

1969

Gaily, Gaily ★★

1970

Quackser Fortune Has a Cousin in the Bronx ★★

1973

Sisters ★★★

1974

Black Christmas ★★★
Gravy Train ★★★

1975

The Great Waldo Pepper ★★★
The Reincarnation of Peter Proud ★★★★
92 in the Shade ★★★

1978

Superman ★★★★

1979

The Amityville Horror ★★
Mrs. Mike's Mondo Video ★★

1980

Superman II ★★★
Willie and Phil ★★★

1981

Heartaches ★★★

1982

Some Kind of Hero ★★★

1983

Superman III ★★
Trenchcoat ★

BEN KINGSLEY
★★★★ 4.00 STARS

"If Paul Newman doesn't win an Oscar for *The Verdict* there is no justice," said People Magazine. In any other year, the six-time-nominated Newman would have been an automatic choice; but Ben Kingsley emerged from relative obscurity, gave an unforgettable performance as *Gandhi,* and captured the prize.

Kingsley (Krisha Bhanji) was born in Yorkshire, England, in 1943. His father was an Indian doctor, his mother an English model. Kingsley became enchanted with acting after seeing a production of "Richard III," saying "I was so overcome that I fainted and they had to carry me out."

In 1968 he appeared in "A Smashing Day" (he also wrote the songs), and then did a number of Shakespearean plays, including: "Much Ado About Nothing," "A Midsummer Night's Dream," and "Hamlet." A number of major actors fought to play the title role of *Gandhi,* but di-

Ben Kingsley in *Gandhi.*

rector Richard Attenborough saw Kingsley in the London production of "Nicholas Nickleby" and asked him to test. His familiarity with film technique came from television appearances, but his portrait of the legendary peacemaker went beyond mechanical prowess. The role required him to age from twenty-three to seventy-nine and to change from a vain young lawyer to a compassionate, self-sacrificing leader. Few actors have ever succeeded in externalizing *spirituality* for moviegoers to "see"; Kingsley did it with newsreel-like reality and precision.

He was totally different in his second picture, *Betrayal*, a clever Harold Pinter drama about infidelity. Kingsley is obviously a performer (like Olivier) who can illuminate the inner lives of a thousand characters.

FILMOGRAPHY

1981

Gandhi ★★★★

1982

Betrayal ★★★★

NASTASSIA KINSKI
★★½ 2.38 STARS

She has been compared to Ingrid Bergman, Brigitte Bardot, and even Audrey Hepburn, and dubbed "the thinking man's Brooke Shields." Kinski is, for all her ethereal presence, more of a model than an actress. However, if she continues to turn in more of the poor performances that have plagued her recently, she may quickly become the Kim Novak of the 1980s.

Born in 1961 to a German mother and Polish-born actor father Klaus Kinski, Nastassia Kinski made her first film appearance at age thirteen, playing a deaf-mute in Wim Wenders' *False Movement*. A few years later, in the midst of a scandalous relationship with director Roman Polanski, she got her first big part in *Tess*, Polanski's version of Thomas Hardy's novel, Tess of the D'Urbevilles (a role Polanski had once intended for the ill-fated Sharon Tate).

Nastassia Kinski in *Tess*.

Her seductive innocence has graced several less-than-successful films, including *Cat People*, *One From the Heart*, *Exposed*, and *The Moon in the Gutter*. Though she is bewitching to watch, audiences may soon grow tired of waiting for her talent to blossom. With her natural grace, perfect European features, and command of languages, she has the potential to become a great international star.

Nastassia Kinski in *Cat People*.

FILMOGRAPHY

1978

False Movement ★★★

1979

Stay As You Are ★★

1980

Tess ★★★

1982

One From the Heart ★★
Cat People ★★

1983

Exposed ★★★
Symphony of Love ★★
The Moon in the Gutter ★★

KRIS KRISTOFFERSON
★★½ 2.67 STARS

When Kris Kristofferson is clean-shaven, he's bland—but a beard miraculously transforms him into an exciting romantic star. His low-key affable acting style can also be colorless until he has a vivid leading lady to play against.

Born in 1936, in Brownsville, Texas, Kristofferson was a Rhodes scholar before devoting his attention to songwriting. He was soon recognized as one of the finest composer/lyricists of his generation for his songs, "Me and Bobby McGee" and "Sunday Morning Coming Down." His film career began with a bit part in *The Last Movie*, Dennis Hopper's egofest, and *Pat Garrett and Billy the Kid* paired him with another musical great, Bob Dylan. In *Blume in Love*, his role captured his easy-going sex-appeal, a feat not accomplished in Sam Peckinpah's gory *Bring Me the Head of Alfredo Garcia*. A fine co-star (Ellen Burstyn) and a great script encouraged Kristofferson to shine in *Alice Doesn't Live Here Anymore*. Although he played a convincing part in *The Sailor Who Fell From Grace With the Sea*, co-star Sarah Miles didn't, and the script was alternately pretentious and distasteful.

A Star Is Born was a huge success; and critics who decimated Barbra Streisand ("A bore is starred," etc.) pointed out that Kristofferson's self-effacing portrayal became the film's sole asset. He seemed lost in *Semi-Tough*, a Burt Reynolds vehicle about pro football, but more comfortable in another Sam Peckinpah film, *Convoy*, about renegade truckers. However, his co-star Ali MacGraw didn't give him much to underplay.

A TV movie, *Freedom Road*, drew much attention because Muhammad Ali was in it. However, the script mangled Howard Fast's novel, and Ali was so wooden that Kristofferson couldn't save the day. Nevertheless, his friendly presence is refreshing and with any luck, he should have a long and successful career.

FILMOGRAPHY

1971

The Last Movie (bit)

1972

Cisco Pike★★★

1973

Pat Garrett and Billy the Kid★★
Blume in Love★★★★

Kris Kristofferson with Ali MacGraw in *Convoy.*

1974

Bring Me the Head of Alfredo Garcia★★

1975

Alice Doesn't Live Here Anymore★★★★

1976

The Sailor Who Fell from Grace With the Sea★★★
Vigilante Force★★
A Star Is Born★★★

1977

Semi-Tough★★

1978

Convoy★★★

1980

Heaven's Gate★★

1981

Rollover★★

ALAN LADD
★★½ 2.68 STARS

Alan Ladd was always underrated even though he had genuine star quality, a deep, resonant voice, and coldly compelling good looks. Critics ridiculed his low-key acting style, but today his performances look less mannered than many of his contemporaries.

Ladd was born in 1913, in Hot Springs, Arkansas. He never studied drama; his early years were devoted to becoming a lifeguard and diving champion, but former silent star, Sue Carol, saw his potential and took him under her wing (she also married him). Ladd worked his way through the ranks in *Gangs of Chicago, The Green Hornet* (a serial), *Meet the Missus,* and *Petticoat Politics.*

This Gun for Hire caught the grimly effective atmosphere of Graham Greene's novel, and Ladd surprised everyone with his adept performance as a hired killer. He was equally charismatic in *The Glass Key.* Veronica Lake was in both, and they became recognized as a team.

They were also a good physical match. Ladd was abnormally sensitive about his height. Some sources say 5'6", others say 5'2" and Lake was petite. He also did two films with Loretta Young, *China,* an action drama plus *And Now Tomorrow,* a soapy tale of a woman going deaf (Ladd played her doctor). He seemed out of place in the latter, but he was right at home in *Salty O'Rourke,* an enjoyable horse racing yarn with Gail Russell.

The Blue Dahlia was author Raymond Chandler's absorbing thriller about an ex-serviceman who returned to find his wife murdered. Lake was the girl standing by to help, and Ladd's box-office potency continued in *Two Years Before the Mast* and *Calcutta* (again with Gail Russell, a haunting and tragic actress who died of alcoholism at thirty-six). *Beyond Glory* and *Whispering Smith* were ordinary, but Ladd was excellent as *The Great Gatsby.* He managed to suggest the vulgarity and classlessness behind the veneer of pretense—qualities Robert Redford was incapable of projecting in the remake.

Gatsby was a box-office disappointment. *Chicago Deadline, Captain Carey U.S.A.* (which yielded an Oscar-winning song, "Mona Lisa"), *Appointment with Danger,* and *The Iron Mistress* recaptured fans, though critics were indifferent. Fans and critics were united, however, for one of the few times in Ladd's entire career about *Shane,* George Stevens' exquisitely made western. Ladd played an enigmatic gunman who helped a family (Van Heflin, Jean Arthur, and Brandon De Wilde) and then left (producing a historic moment on film) as the son chased hysterically after him, crying, "Shane, come back, Shane!"

By this time, Ladd was drinking heavily. He found momentary happiness while making *The McConnell Story* with June Allyson. They fell in love, according to her autobiography, and his height obsession also eased around Allyson. In *Boy on a Dolphin,* with Sophia Loren, he had been made to stand on a box during their love scenes. He did one more fine picture, *The Proud Rebel,* and one more box-office smash, *The Carpetbaggers.* Director Edward Dymytrk claimed that the performance was difficult to obtain, given Ladd's drinking, but he was more than adequate in the role of Nevada Smith. Ladd died in 1964, of alcohol combined with sedatives, a tragic case of insecurity that neither stardom nor wealth could alleviate.

Alan Ladd with William Bendix in *China.*

FILMOGRAPHY

1932

Once in a Lifetime★★

1936

Pigskin Parade★★

1937

Last Train from Madrid★★
Souls at Sea★★
Hold 'Em Navy★★
Born to the West★★

1938

The Goldwyn Follies★★
Come On Leathernecks★★★
Freshman Year★★

1939

Beasts of Berlin★★
Rulers of the Sea★★

1940

The Green Hornet (serial)★★
Light of the Western Stars★★
Gangs of Chicago★★★
In Old Missouri★★
The Howards of Virginia★★★
Those Were the Days★★
Captain Caution★★★
Wildcast Bus★★
Meet the Missus★★
Her First Romance★★

1941

Great Guns★★
Citizen Kane★★★
Cadet Girl★★
Petticoat Politics★★
The Black Cat★★
The Reluctant Dragon★★
Paper Bullets★★★

1942

Joan of Paris★★
This Gun for Hire★★★★
The Glass Key★★★★
Lucky Jordan★★★
Star Spangled Rhythm (cameo)

1943

China★★★

1944

And Now Tomorrow★★★

1945

Salty O'Rourke★★★
Duffy's Tavern (cameo)

1946

The Blue Dahlia★★★★
O. S. S. ★★★
Two Years Before the Mast★★★★

1947

Calcutta★★★
Variety Girl (cameo)
Wild Harvest★★★
My Favorite Brunette (cameo)

1948

Saigon★★★
Beyond Glory★★★
Whispering Smith★★★

1949

The Great Gatsby★★★★
Chicago Deadline★★★★

1950

Captain Carey U.S.A.★★★

1951

Branded★★★
Appointment with Danger★★★

1952

The Iron Mistress★★★★
Red Mountain★★★

1953

Thunder in the East★★★
Desert Legion★★
Shane★★★★
Botany Bay★★★

1954

The Red Beret★★★
The Black Knight★★
Saskatchewan★★
Hell Below Zero★★★
Drum Beat★★

1955

The McConnell Story★★★
Hell on Frisco Bay★★

1956

Santiago★★

Alan Ladd with Veronica Lake in *This Gun for Hire.*

1957

The Big Land★★★★
Boy on a Dolphin★★★

1958

The Deep Six★★★
The Proud Rebel★★★★
The Badlanders★★★

1959

The Man in the Net★★★

1960

Guns of the Timberland★★
All the Young Men★★★
One Foot in Hell★★

1961

Duel of Champions★★

1962

13 West Street★★★

1964

The Carpetbaggers★★★

VERONICA LAKE
★★½ 2.52 STARS

Veronica Lake became the prisoner of a gimmick—her long, blonde hair, combed over one eye. She had more talent than she was given credit for, but when she cut her hair, critics wrote her off and the good roles stopped coming.

She was born Constance Frances Marie Ockelman in Brooklyn, in 1919, and began in films with small roles under the name Constance Keane. When she changed her name to Veronica Lake and her image to the sultry glamour girl, her career finally took off. *I Wanted Wings* in 1941 was her first hit, but it wasn't until director Preston Sturges cast her in *Sullivan's Travels* that she displayed her acting ability. She teamed with Alan Ladd for two successful thrillers, *This Gun for Hire* and *The Glass Key,* and her provocative, independent-minded femme fatale image paved the way for Lauren Bacall, Lizabeth Scott, and other self-possessed sirens.

At that high point, she trimmed her famous long locks on government request since girls imitating her hairstyle were getting their hair mangled in factory machines, and her career dipped overnight. *The Hour Before the Dawn* presented her as a Nazi spy, but the film was tedious. She was then trapped in second-rate musicals like *Bring on the Girls,* and *Hold That Blonde. The Blue Dahlia,* again with Alan Ladd, temporarily provided rescue, but neither *Ramrod,* a forgettable Joel McCrea western, nor *Slattery's Hurricane* brought back her old public.

Veronica Lake.

She was never a docile actress, feuding with co-stars like Fredric March ("Mr. March is lucky he didn't get my knee in his groin") and eventually succumbing to alcoholism. As a result of her 1971 autobiography, many people only remember the sordid details of her life. However, along the course of her career she showed genuine comic promise in *I Married a Witch* and strong dramatic potential in *So Proudly We Hail.*

Veronica Lake.

FILMOGRAPHY

(billed as Constance Keane)

1939

All Women Have Secrets★★
Sorority House★★

1940

Young as You Feel★★
Forty Little Mothers★★

(billed as Veronica Lake)

1941

I Wanted Wings★★★
Hold Back the Dawn★★★

1942

Sullivan's Travels★★★★
This Gun for Hire★★★★
The Glass Key★★★★
I Married a Witch★★★★

1943

Star Spangled Rhythm (cameo)
So Proudly We Hail★★★

1944

The Hour Before the Dawn★★

1945

Bring on the Girls★★
Out of This World★★
Duffy's Tavern (cameo)
Hold that Blonde★★

1946

Miss Susie Slagle's★★★
The Blue Dahlia★★★

1947

Ramrod★★
Variety Girl (cameo)

1948

Saigon★★★
The Sainted Sisters★★★
Isn't It Romantic?★★

1949

Slattery's Hurricane★★

1952

Stronghold★★

1966

Footsteps in the Snow★

1970

Flesh Feast★

HEDY LAMARR
★★½ 2.45 STARS

When Hedy Lamarr first appeared on film, she was considered by many to be the most beautiful girl in the world. She had a built-in notoriety as well since her European movie, *Ecstasy,* featured scandalous nude shots. But even though Lamarr was a competent actress, she rarely set the screen on fire.

Lamarr (Hedwig Eva Maria Kiesler) was born in 1913, in Vienna. Before coming to the United States, she did *Die Blumenfrau von Lindenau* and *Die Koffer des Herrn O.F.* as well as *Ecstasy.* Her American debut in *Algiers* was a big success, and for a while MGM sought to make her Greta Garbo's successor. Their excitement cooled after *Lady of the Tropics* and *I Take This Woman.*

She co-starred with Gable, Tracy, and Colbert in the enjoyable *Boom Town* (though her part was colorless) and she played the least interesting *Ziegfeld Girl* (Judy Garland and Lana Turner were the others). *H.M. Pulham Esq.* featured her finest performance as Robert Young's true love.

Lamarr was puzzling; she seemed sultry, but her sex appeal was curiously bland. She gave one vivid portrayal, as Delilah, in De Mille's fast-moving and lively *Samson and Delilah.* By her own admission she was "difficult," and with her box office fast falling, producers lost interest. *Copper Canyon* was an ordinary western, and she took a backseat to Bob Hope in one of his weaker comedies, *My Favorite Spy.* She and Jane Powell were both miscast in *The Female Animal.*

Hedy Lamarr.

Hedy Lamarr drifted out of films in the 1950s and was plagued by misfortune and bad press in her retirement. She was accused of shoplifting (later cleared) and published a lurid autobiography, which she claimed was misrepresented by her collaborators.

FILMOGRAPHY

1931

Die Blumenfrau von Lindenau★★
Man braucht kein Geld★★
Die Koffer des Herrn O.F.★★

1933

Ecstasy★★★

1938

Algiers★★★★

1939

Lady of the Tropics★★

1940

I Take This Woman★★
Boom Town★★★
Comrade X★★

1941

Come Live With Me★★
Ziegfeld Girl★★
H. M. Pulham Esq.★★★★

1942

Tortilla Flat★★★
Crossroads★★
White Cargo★★

1944

Experiment Perilous★★★
The Heavenly Body★★
The Conspirators★★★

1945

Her Highness and the Bellboy★★

1946

The Strange Woman★★

1947

Dishonored Lady★★★

1948

Let's Live a Little★★

1949

Samson and Delilah★★★★

1950

A Lady Without a Passport★★
Copper Canyon★★

Hedy Lamarr.

1951

My Favorite Spy★★★

1954

Loves of Three Queens★★

1957

The Story of Mankind★★

1958

The Female Animal★★

DOROTHY LAMOUR
★★★ 2.81 STARS

Dorothy Lamour was merely a passable dramatic actress, but she had a lively, good-natured sense of comedy.

Born Mary Leta Dorothy Kaumeyer in 1914, in New Orleans, Lamour was a beauty contest winner (Miss New Orleans, 1931) and band singer before making *The Jungle Princess*. Her early pictures included *College Holiday, High Wide and Handsome*, and *The Last Train from Madrid. The Hurricane* capitalized on her exotic looks, as did *Her Jungle Love* with Ray Milland.

She had an offbeat part, as a gangster's moll, in *Johnny Apollo* and did a creditable job, but her sarong became a permanent trademark after *Road to Singapore*. The success of that film with Bing Crosby and Bob Hope led to an even funnier sequel, *Road to Zanzibar*. She was with Hope alone in the amusing *Caught in the Draft*, and *Road to Morocco* continued the winning trend. She also gave a convincing performance as one half of a singing sister act (the other half was Betty Hutton) in *And the Angels Sing*.

She traveled the *Road to Utopia* and then did the excellent *A Medal for Benny*. After *Road to Rio* came a trite melodrama, *Lulu Belle*, and a thriller, *The Lucky Stiff*, that proved a stiff at the box office. *The Greatest Show on Earth* was 1952's Oscar winner for Best Picture though Lamour's role was minor, and *Road to Bali* was strained compared to the quality of previous "Road" pictures. When Crosby and Hope did their last "Road" film in 1962, Lamour was given only a supporting role; Joan Collins had the lead.

Pajama Party was her cinema swan song, and she wisely decided to tour with "Hello Dolly." Lamour was never a great actress, but she was always pleasing, professional, and unaffected, characteristics that make most of her movies on TV relaxing to watch.

Dorothy Lamour.

FILMOGRAPHY

1936

The Jungle Princess★★★

1937

Swing High Swing Low★★★
College Holiday★★★
The Last Train from Madrid★★★
High Wide and Handsome★★★
The Hurricane★★
Thrill of a Lifetime★★★

1938

The Big Broadcast of 1938★★★
Her Jungle Love★★
Spawn of the North★★★
Tropic Holiday★★★

1939

St. Louis Blues★★★
Man About Town★★★
Disputed Passage★★★

1940

Johnny Apollo★★★
Typhoon★★★
Road to Singapore★★★
Moon Over Burma★★★
Chad Hanna★★★

1941

Road to Zanzibar★★★
Caught in the Draft★★★
Aloma of the South Seas★★★

1942

The Fleet's In★★★
Beyond the Blue Horizon★★★
Road to Morocco★★★

1943

Star Spangled Rhythm (cameo)
They Got Me Covered★★★
Dixie★★★
Riding High★★★

1944

And the Angels Sing★★★
Rainbow Island★★★

1945

A Medal for Benny★★★
Duffy's Tavern★★★
Masquerade in Mexico★★★

1946

Road to Utopia★★★

1947

My Favorite Brunette★★★★
Road to Rio★★★★
Wild Harvest★★
Variety Girl (cameo)

1948

On Our Merry Way★★
Lulu Belle★★
The Girl From Manhattan★★

1949

Slightly French★★
Manhandled★★
The Lucky Stiff★★

1951

Here Comes the Groom (cameo)

1952

The Greatest Show on Earth★★★

1953

Road to Bali★★★

1962

The Road to Hong Kong★★

1963

Donovan's Reef★★★

1964

Pajama Party★★

1970

The Phynx (cameo)

BURT LANCASTER
★★★½ 3.26 STARS

Burt Lancaster seems to thrive on challenge, running the gamut from acrobat to dramatic actor, villain to hero. He isn't always inspired, but his intelligence and magnetism make most of his performances interesting.

Born in 1913, in New York City, he broke into show business with a short-lived Broadway play that netted him some good personal reviews. According to the New York Journal American, "Burt Lancaster, as Mooney, is the non-com every private prays for." He was superb in his screen debut, *The Killers*, and equally strong as a convict in *Brute Force*.

In *Desert Fury* he was "merely a romantic prop" (The New York Herald Tribune), but he clashed potently with Edward G. Robinson in the absorbing *All My Sons*, a film based on Arthur Miller's award-winning play. He also made his presence felt, though Barbara Stanwyck had the spotlight, in *Sorry, Wrong Number.* Lancaster's acrobatics in *The Flame and the Arrow* boosted his box-office value, and so did another swashbuckler, *The Crimson Pirate*.

Burt Lancaster in *Birdman of Alcatraz.*

Come Back Little Sheba was an engrossing, though downbeat, study of an unhappy marriage; Lancaster was much too young and virile as Shirley Booth's husband even though he had the proper intensity. The New York Film Critics cited him their Best Actor for *From Here to Eternity,* an award he richly deserved. He was also outstanding pitted against Gary Cooper in *Vera Cruz*, an excellent western.

Lancaster struck sparks with Anna Magnani in a colorful version of author Tennessee Williams' drama, *The Rose Tattoo*, and his acrobatic training bolstered his performance in *Trapeze. The Rainmaker* paired him with Katharine Hepburn—an odd combination that worked—and he made a box-office killing in *Gunfight at the O.K. Corral.* In *The Sweet Smell of Success* he was cast as a ruthless Broadway columnist, spectacularly capturing all the Walter Winchell viciousness required by the role. However, the public found the subject matter too depressing. He was Rita Hayworth's ex-husband in *Separate Tables*, a good performance considerably underrated by those who knew Laurence Olivier had originally been cast. *Elmer Gantry* won him a Best Actor Oscar. In his own words, "Some parts you fall into like an old glove. Elmer really wasn't acting—that was me!"

In an all-star cast (Maximillian Schell, Spencer Tracy, Montgomery Clift, and Judy Garland) Lancaster dominated his scenes as a Nazi war criminal in *Judgment at Nuremberg.* He played the *Birdman of Alcatraz* with subtlety and feeling, matched by Thelma Ritter as his mother. That performance garnered him a Venice Film Festival award, and he had more hits with *The Train* and *The Professionals. Seven Days in May,* a political thriller, should have done better commercially.

Lancaster was given the lead in *Airport*, the first "disaster" film to become a blockbuster. He also had several good small parts in unconventional films like *1900* and *Buffalo Bill and the Indians* as well as leads in unpopular films like *Twilight's Last Gleaming* and *The Island of Dr. Moreau.*

Then, Lancaster turned in the portrayal of his life in Louis Malle's *Atlantic City.* Even his detractors admitted that he showed greatness as an aging loser who lived on illusions. His career as a character actor may just be beginning.

FILMOGRAPHY

1946

The Killers★★★

1947

Variety Girl (cameo)
Brute Force★★★
Desert Fury★★★

1948

I Walk Alone★★★
All My Sons★★★
Sorry, Wrong Number★★★
Kiss the Blood Off My Hands★★★

1949

Criss Cross★★★
Rope of Sand★★★

1950

The Flame and the Arrow★★★
Mister 880★★★

1951

Vengeance Valley★★★
Jim Thorpe-All American★★★
Ten Tall Men★★★

1952

The Crimson Pirate★★★
Come Back Little Sheba★★★

1953

South Sea Woman★★★
From Here to Eternity★★★

1954

His Majesty O'Keefe★★★
Apache★★★
Vera Cruz★★★

1955

The Kentuckian (direction)★★
The Rose Tattoo★★★

1956

Trapeze★★★
The Rainmaker★★★

1957

Gunfight at the O.K. Corral★★★
The Sweet Smell of Success★★★

1958

Run Silent Run Deep★★★
Separate Tables★★★

1959

The Devil's Disciple★★

1960

The Unforgiven★★★
Elmer Gantry★★★

1961

The Young Savages★★★
Judgment at Nuremburg★★★

1962

Birdman of Alcatraz★★★

1963

A Child Is Waiting★★★
The List of Adrian Messenger★★★
The Leopard★★★

Burt Lancaster in *Elmer Gantry.*

1964

Seven Days in May★★★
The Train★★★

1965

The Hallelujah Trail★★★

1966

The Professionals★★★

1968

The Scalphunters★★★
The Swimmer★★★

1969

Castle Keep★★★
The Gypsy Moths★★★

1970

King (documentary)
Airport★★★

1971

Lawman★★★
Valdez Is Coming★★★

1972

Ulzana's Raid★★★

1973

Scorpio★★
Executive Action★★

1974

The Midnight Man★★

1975

Conversation Piece★★★

1976

Moses★★★
1900★★★
Buffalo Bill and the Indians★★★

1977

The Cassandra Crossing★★
Twilight's Last Gleaming★★
The Island of Dr. Moreau★★

1978

Go Tell the Spartans★★★

1979

Zulu Dawn★★★
Cattle Annie and Little Britches★★★

1980

Atlantic City★★★

1982

Local Hero★★★

ELSA LANCHESTER

★★★½ 3.39 STARS

Elsa Lanchester was never the focal point of the films she was in, as her husband Charles Laughton always was in his, but she was delightfully eccentric, engaging, and humorous. She added immeasurably to the films in which she appeared.

Born Elizabeth Sullivan in Lewisham, England, in 1902, Lanchester toured as a dancer during her childhood. When she made her movie debut in 1927, in *One of the Best*, she met her future husband Laughton in the cast. *The Private Life of Henry VIII* teamed her memorably with Laughton (she was Anne of Cleves). In *The Bride of Frankenstein*, she was "created" in the doctor's lab to become the ill-fated bride.

Laughton was her teammate again, and they had other happy outings together in *Rembrandt* and *The Big Clock*. Lanchester received an Oscar nomination for her sticky performance in *Come to the Stable* and another for *Witness for the Prosecution*. In the latter film, a sparkling courtroom drama, her portrayal of a nagging nurse stood out. Her sense of humor also enlivened *Mary Poppins; Bell, Book and Candle*; and *Murder by Death*.

FILMOGRAPHY

1927

One of the Best ★★★

1928

The Constant Nymph ★★★

1930

Comets ★★★
The Love Habit ★★★

1931

The Stronger Sex ★★★
Potiphar's Wife ★★★
The Officers' Mess ★★★

1933

The Private Life of Henry VIII ★★★

1935

David Copperfield ★★★
Naughty Marietta ★★★
The Bride of Frankenstein ★★★

Elsa Lanchester in *Murder by Death.*

1936

The Ghost Goes West ★★★★
Rembrandt ★★★

1938

The Beachcomber ★★★

1941

Ladies in Retirement ★★★★

1942

Son of Fury ★★★
Tales of Manhattan ★★★

1943

Forever and a Day ★★★★
Thumbs Up ★★★
Lassie Come Home ★★★

1944

Passport to Adventure ★★★

1946

The Spiral Staircase ★★★★
The Razor's Edge ★★★★

1947

The Bishop's Wife ★★★
Northwest Outpost ★★★

1948

The Big Clock ★★★★

1949

The Secret Garden ★★★
Come to the Stable ★★★★
The Inspector General ★★★★

1950

Buccaneer's Girl ★★★
Mystery Street ★★★★
The Petty Girl ★★★

1951

Frenchie ★★★

1952

Dreamboat ★★★★
Les Miserables ★★★★

1953

Androcles and the Lion ★★★★
The Girls of Pleasure Island ★★★

1954

Hell's Half Acre ★★★

1955

Three-Ring Circus ★★★
The Glass Slipper ★★★

1958

Witness for the Prosecution ★★★★
Bell, Book and Candle ★★★★

1964

Honeymoon Hotel ★★★
Mary Poppins ★★★★
Pajama Party ★★★

1965

That Darn Cat ★★★

1967

Easy Come Easy Go ★★★

1968

Blackbeard's Ghost ★★★

1969

Rascal ★★★
Me, Natalie ★★★

1971

Willard ★★★

1973

Terror in the Wax Museum ★★★
Arnold ★★★

1976

Murder by Death ★★★

JESSICA LANGE
★★★ 3.00 STARS

Jessica Lange is one of movietown's most engaging surprises. When she began, she was little more than an attractively ordinary blonde, until a couple of performances pointed out a superb acting ability.

Lange was born in 1950, in Cloquet, Minnesota. She studied mime in Paris and danced in the chorus of the Opera Comique. Her acting talent was irrelevant in the bloated remake of *King Kong;* insurmountable problems included an unbelievable gorilla and a silly tongue-in-cheek approach. *All That Jazz* was better, although Roy Scheider dominated.

She was the calculating Cora in another remake, *The Postman Always Rings Twice.* The sexual details were more explicit, the atmosphere more sordid than the 1946 version, but all the humanity seemed to disappear in the modernization. Co-star Jack Nicholson was panned though critics liked Lange and thought she deserved better roles.

Then, in an unexpected and startling switch of fate, she became a hot property. The commercial smash that did it was *Tootsie.* Lange played an actress who befriends soap star Dustin Hoffman (masquerading as a woman). Her delicacy and sweetness were revealed on screen for the first time, and she won a Best Supporting Oscar.

Jessica Lange in *Frances.*

She was also brilliant as *Frances,* though the picture itself, a supposed biography of Frances Farmer, had loose ends and heavy doses of invented romantic fiction. Sheila Benson in the L.A. Times took the script and direction to task, but added that it was "worth seeing for the performance of Jessica Lange." On the basis of these last two portrayals, Lange should inevitably become a superstar.

FILMOGRAPHY

1976

King Kong ★★

1979

All That Jazz ★★★

1980

How to Beat the High Cost of Living★★

1981

The Postman Always Rings Twice★★★

1982

Frances★★★★
Tootsie★★★★

ANGELA LANSBURY
★★★½ 3.34 STARS

Angela Lansbury is a great actress whose roles were rarely worthy of her. But she took the good with the bad, commenting, "In Hollywood you're either a member of the working group or not, and if not, you're easily forgotten. I've had high spots, medium spots and a couple of low spots, but I've always been in there pitching."

Angela (Brigid) Lansbury was born in London, in 1925. She started strongly in films playing a maid and earning an Oscar nomination in *Gaslight*, and she was nominated again for *The Picture of Dorian Gray. The Harvey Girls* marked a change of pace, Lansbury was the singer who fought Judy Garland for John Hodiak's love. Even up against Garland at full blast, she made her scenes stand out. She was even more vicious in *If Winter Comes* as Walter Pidgeon's selfish wife. *State of the Union* and *The Three Musketeers* offered varied parts (career woman and Queen), and she played them perfectly.

Lansbury was Delilah's sister in *Samson and Delilah*, but she died too early in the story. There were a series of unimportant pictures, *Mutiny, The Key Man*, and *The Purple Mask*, before another juicy role came along as Orson Welles' marriage-minded mistress in the enjoyable *The Long Hot Summer.* As Robert Preston's devoted friend, who wanted to be more than a friend, she almost stole *The Dark at the Top of the Stairs.*

Her performance as Warren Beatty's clutching mother in *All Fall Down* was breathtaking, and she should have won an Oscar for *The Manchurian Candidate*, a definitive portrait of political evil. No other role has come along to match that one, but Lansbury was fine in *Death on the Nile* and *The Mirror Crack'd*, both Agatha Christie thrillers. On Broadway she has triumphed in "Mame," "A Taste of Honey," "Gypsy," and "Sweeney Todd."

Angela Lansbury with Walter Pidgeon in *If Winter Comes.*

FILMOGRAPHY

1944

Gaslight★★★★
National Velvet★★★★

1945

The Picture of Dorian Gray★★★★

1946

The Harvey Girls★★★★
The Hoodlum Saint★★★
Till the Clouds Roll By (cameo)

1947

The Private Affairs of Bel Ami★★★★

1948

If Winter Comes★★★
Tenth Avenue Angel★★★
State of the Union★★★★
The Three Musketeers★★★

1949

The Red Danube★★★
Samson and Delilah★★★★

1951

Kind Lady★★★★

1952

Mutiny★★★

1953

Remains to Be Seen★★★

1955

A Lawless Street★★★
The Purple Mask★★★

1956

Please Murder Me★★★
The Court Jester★★★★

1957

The Key Man★★★

1958

The Long Hot Summer★★★★
The Reluctant Debutante★★★

1959

Season of Passion★★★

1960

The Dark at the Top of the Stairs★★★★
A Breath of Scandal★★★
Blue Hawaii★★★

1961

All Fall Down★★★★
The Manchurian Candidate★★★★

1963

In the Cool of the Day★★★

1964

The World of Henry Orient★★★

1965

Dear Heart★★★
The Greatest Story Ever Told★★★
The Amorous Adventures of Moll Flanders★★
Harlow★★★

1966

Mister Buddwing★★

1970

Something for Everyone★★★★

1971

Bedknobs and Broomsticks★★★

1978

Death on the Nile★★★★

1979

The Lady Vanishes★★★★

1980

The Mirror Crack'd★★★

1982

The Last Unicorn (voice only)

1983

The Pirates of Penzance★★★

CHARLES LAUGHTON
★★★½ 3.66 STARS

Charles Laughton was a brilliant, versatile actor. He concentrated very hard on perfecting his craft (widow Elsa Lanchester says, "Charles and I never went out much"), and the results are still a pleasure to watch.

Laughton was born in 1899, in Scarborough, England. His father was a hotel man, but after working briefly as a hotel clerk, Laughton studied at the Royal Academy of Dramatic Art. Stage successes on the West End of London included "The Greater Love," "The Man With Red Hair," and "Mr. Pickwick." He and Lanchester were married in 1929 after working together in one of his early British silent films.

Laughton's first notable film role was in *Devil and the Deep* with Gary Cooper, as a submarine commander married to Tallulah Bankhead. Although the film wasn't very good, Laughton's acting ability came across well. The budget was bigger in De Mille's *The Sign of the Cross* though it took *The Private Life of Henry VIII* to make him a star. He won an Oscar for his lively, flamboyant portrayal of the title character. It didn't matter that his own self-definition was accurate, "I have a face that would stop a sundial and that frightens small children"; audiences loved him even in trivia like *White Woman* with Carole Lombard. He almost played Wilkins Micawber in *David Copperfield* and would have been perfect (W.C. Fields got the part).

He *was* perfect in *The Barretts of Wimpole Street* as Elizabeth Barrett Browning's tyrannical father. There were more hits including: *Ruggles of Red Gap* (he was an English butler in the American West), *Les Misérables,* and *Mutiny on the Bounty* (as the monstrous Captain Bligh). Largely because of his portrayal, which was Oscar-nominated, the Academy voted *Mutiny* 1935's Best Picture.

Laughton switched gears again as *Rembrandt,* and the critics raved. According to the New York Times, "Mr. Laughton becomes Rembrandt as nobody else in the world could—of this we are firmly and unmistakably convinced." From this triumph he went on to what should have been his greatest role—as the lead in *I, Claudius.* Production was halted, however, due to an illness and the film was never completed. Observers claimed that it was his finest hour as an actor. He was equally superb in *Sidewalks of London* with Vivien Leigh and made an impressive Quasimodo in the *Hunchback of Notre Dame.*

They Knew What They Wanted was a touching tale of an immigrant and his mail-order bride (the basis for Frank Loesser's musical, "The Most Happy Fella"). More fine performances followed with *It Started With Eve,* one of Deanna Durbin's best pictures, and *The Canterville Ghost.* He was also magnificent as the murderer in *The Big Clock.* After that the quality of his pictures temporarily declined in *The Girl from Manhattan, The Bribe,* and *Abbott and Costello Meet Captain Kidd.*

It's hard to pick a favorite Laughton performance, but this observer would choose his barrister in *Witness for the Prosecution.* He seemed to relish every second of the role, defending murderess Marlene Dietrich and disobeying the orders of his overly-strict nurse (Elsa Lanchester). He was nominated for an Oscar for that role. *Spartacus* was a rousing version of Howard Fast's best-seller, and he was slyly engaging as a senator in Otto Preminger's *Advise and Consent.* Laughton died in 1962, but fortunately his work lives on.

FILMOGRAPHY

1929

Piccadilly★★★

1930

Comets★★★
Wanted Men★★★

1931

Down River★★★

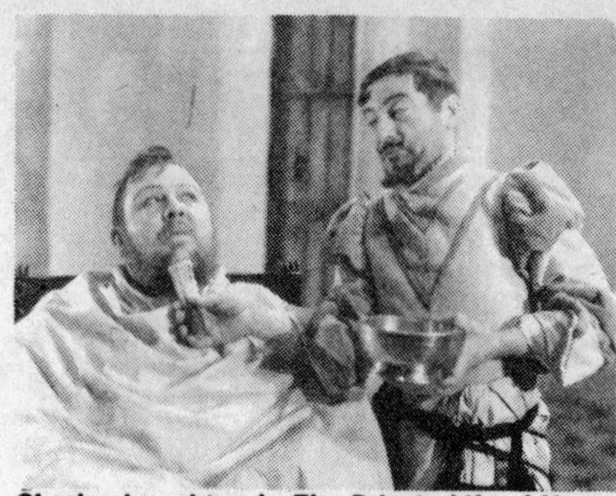

Charles Laughton in *The Private Life of Henry VIII.*

1932

Devil and the Deep★★★
The Old Dark House★★★
Payment Deferred★★★★
The Sign of the Cross★★★★
If I Had a Million★★★★
Island of Lost Souls★★★★

1933

The Private Life of Henry VIII★★★★
White Woman★★★★

1934

The Barretts of Wimpole Street★★★★

1935

Ruggles of Red Gap★★★★
Les Misérables★★★★
Mutiny on the Bounty★★★★

1936

Rembrandt★★★★

1937

I, Claudius (unfinished)

1938

The Beachcomber★★★★
Sidewalks of London★★★★

1939

Jamaica Inn★★★
The Hunchback of Notre Dame★★★★

1940

They Knew What They Wanted★★★★

1941

It Started With Eve★★★★

1942

The Tuttles of Tahiti★★★
Tales of Manhattan★★★
Stand By for Action★★★

1943

Forever and a Day★★★★
This Land Is Mine★★★★
The Man From Down Under★★★★

1944

The Canterville Ghost★★★★

1945

The Suspect★★★★
Captain Kidd★★★

1946

Because of Him★★★★

1948

The Paradine Case★★★★
Arch of Triumph★★★
The Big Clock★★★★
The Girl from Manhattan★★★

1949

The Bribe★★★

1950

The Man on the Eiffel Tower★★★★

1951

The Blue Veil★★★★
The Strange Door★★★

1952

O'Henry's Full House★★★★
Abbott and Costello Meet Captain Kidd★★★

1953

Salome★★★★
Young Bess★★★★

1954

Hobson's Choice★★★★

1958

Witness for the Prosecution★★★★

1960

Under Ten Flags★★★
Spartacus★★★★

1962

Advise and Consent★★★★

LAUREL AND HARDY
★★★ 2.83 STARS

Rivaled only by the Marx Brothers as the movies' greatest comedy team, Stan Laurel and Oliver Hardy have always been the people's choice rather than that of the critics. Their films for the Hal Roach Studios from 1927 to 1940 bridge the great era of silent comedy and the maturity of dialogue comedy. Laurel and Hardy made this transition more smoothly than all other comics who began in the silent days.

Stan Laurel was born Arthur Stanley Jefferson in England in 1890. Like Charlie Chaplin, he moved from music hall to slapstick comedies, playing in 76 films before teaming up with Hardy. Oliver Hardy was born in Harlem, Georgia in 1892. He played bit and supporting roles for the Hal Roach Studios until 1926 when he and Laurel officially became a team at director Leo McCarey's urging.

In the way that they dressed, Laurel—the thin, rubber-limbed innocent and Hardy—the genially pompous fat man, they bore a false dignity reminiscent of Chaplin's Tramp. Sporting derbies, suits, and ties, Laurel and Hardy always aspired to a certain middle class respectability. In their films, they often had wives and jobs; Hardy especially saw himself as a model citizen. Their short comedies from the late 1920s to the mid-1930s were sharp caricatures of middle class society in disintegration, inevitably involving the breakdown of the pair's social pretensions. In classic silents such as *Two Tars* (1927) and *Big Business* (1929), their personal exchanges with others would begin with minor affronts and escalate to widespread mayhem. Sound added a dimension to their characters—British-accented Laurel's childlike confusion of language and Hardy's melodious Southern purr. Throughout their prime, however, they remained essentially visual comedians.

Laurel and Hardy in the short, *Big Business*.

Convinced of the economic advantages of features over short film production, Hal Roach began to experiment with full-length Laurel and Hardy films with *Pardon Us*, a parody of prison dramas like *The Big House*. Started as a short before expansion into feature length, *Pardon Us* has strong material, but betrays its episodic quality. *Pack Up Your Troubles* also suffers from a patchwork conception.

Their features can be divided between those with well-constructed stories (*Sons of the Desert*, *Our Relations*, *Way Out West*) and episodic yet charming operettas, in which the team's routines alternate with musical numbers.

Stan and Ollie fit snugly in the wigs and period dress of *The Devil's Brother, Babes in Toyland*, and *The Bohemian Girl*, and these operettas are among their most felicitous efforts. *Sons of the Desert* remains one of their very best films. Its title is the name of a fraternity whose silly yet innocent activities they must hide from their rather domineering wives. They are outguessed by their wives at every turn—only logical, since they were never really more sophisticated than a couple of naughty boys. Their projection of innocence probably explains why *Way Out West* (1937), another of their best films, is more a parody of gaslight melodramas than of real westerns.

Although made for Roach, *Way Out West* was "A Stan Laurel Production." Laurel was the more aggressive and creative force behind the camera in terms of writing, direction, and editing. He had many contractual disputes with Roach, although he never seriously wanted to break up the team.

By the time of *Swiss Miss*, the team had begun to show signs of age. Youth was an asset to both, but essential to Laurel. Following the expiration of their Hal Roach contracts, they made several films that ranged from bad to atrocious, and they finally retired in 1950. It was a sad demise to a great team.

Remarking on their universal appeal, Oliver Hardy once said, "There are plenty of Laurel and Hardys in the world. I used to see them in my mother's hotel when I was a kid: the dumb, dumb guy who never has anything bad happen to him and the smart guy who's dumber than the dumb guy only he doesn't know it."

FILMOGRAPHY

(features only)

1929

The Hollywood Revue of 1929 (cameo)

1930

The Rogue's Song ★★★

1931

Pardon Us ★★★

1932

Pack Up Your Troubles ★★★

1933

The Devil's Brother ★★★
Sons of the Desert ★★★★

1934

Hollywood Party ★★★
Babes in Toyland ★★★★

1935

Bonnie Scotland ★★★★

1936

The Bohemian Girl ★★★
Our Relations ★★★★

1937

Way Out West ★★★★
Pick a Star (cameo)

1938

Swiss Miss ★★★

1940

A Chump at Oxford ★★★★
Saps at Sea ★★★

1941

Great Guns ★★

1942

A-Haunting We Will Go ★★

1943

Air Raid Wardens ★★
Jitterbugs ★★★
The Dancing Masters ★★

1944

The Big Noise ★
Nothing But Trouble ★★

1945

The Bullfighters ★★

1950

Utopia ★

PETER LAWFORD
★★½ 2.62 STARS

It's hard to know what Peter Lawford could have accomplished as an actor—he never had a difficult or dramatically challenging role. However, he played all his middle-of-the-road parts with ease, grace, and an understated British charm.

Lawford was born in 1923, in London. He first appeared on film in 1931, in *Poor Old Bill,* but didn't do an "A" picture until 1942, *Mrs. Miniver.* He failed to impose his personality on any of his subsequent movies, *Random Harvest, The Immortal Sergeant,* or *The White Cliffs of Dover* but was likable as Frank Sinatra's friend in the enjoyable *It Happened in Brooklyn.*

Good News was a star part and Lawford, though not much of a singer or dancer, threw himself energetically into the spirit of things with co-star June Allyson. The picture made "nothing but money" according to producer Arthur Freed, and he was in another huge-grossing musical, *Easter Parade,* as the playboy Judy Garland rejected for Fred Astaire.

Esther Williams was his romantic interest in *On an Island with You,* and he romanced Elizabeth Taylor in the tedious *Julia Misbehaves.* He gave his best performance in *Little Women* as Laurie, again in love with June Allyson, and the film's big box-office reception insured other parts in *The Red Danube, Please Believe Me,* and *Just This Once. Royal Wedding* paired him with Jane Powell, and they made an appealing team.

His image changed when he joined Sinatra's Rat Pack and participated in a group of tongue-in-cheek movies, *Sergeants 3* and *Ocean's Eleven.* Lawford was smooth and relaxed in three TV series: "Dear Phoebe," "The Thin Man," and "The Doris Day Show." However, he was ineffectual in *The April Fools* and *They Only Kill Their Masters.*

Peter Lawford's career is curious—unlike many great stars, he never gave a bad performance, but he never had a single moment on screen that made audiences sit up and say, "Good, well done!"

FILMOGRAPHY

1931

Poor Old Bill ★★

1938

Lord Jeff ★★

1942

Mrs. Miniver ★★
Eagle Squadron ★★
Thunder Birds ★★

Peter Lawford with Roland Culver in *The Hour of 13.*

Junior Army ★★
A Yank at Eton ★★
London Blackout Murders ★★
Random Harvest ★★

1943

Girl Crazy ★★
The Purple V ★★
The Immortal Sergeant ★★★
Pilot No. 5 ★★★
Above Suspicion ★★★
Someone to Remember ★★★
The Man from Down Under ★★★
Sherlock Holmes Faces Death ★★
The Sky's the Limit ★★
Paris After Dark ★★
Flesh and Fantasy ★★★
Assignment in Brittany ★★★
Sahara ★★★
West Side Kid ★★★
Corvette K-225 ★★

1944

The White Cliffs of Dover ★★★
The Canterville Ghost ★★★
Mrs. Parkington ★★★

1945

Son of Lassie ★★★
The Picture of Dorian Gray ★★★

1946

Two Sisters from Boston ★★★
Cluny Brown ★★★
My Brother Talks to Horses ★★★

1947

It Happened in Brooklyn ★★★
Good News ★★★★

1948

On an Island with You ★★★
Easter Parade ★★★
Julia Misbehaves ★★★

1949

Little Women ★★★★
The Red Danube ★★★

1950

Please Believe Me ★★★

1951

Royal Wedding ★★★

1952

Just This Once ★★
Kangaroo ★★
You for Me ★★
The Hour of 13 ★★
Rogue's March ★★★

1954

It Should Happen to You ★★★

1959

Never So Few ★★

1960

Ocean's Eleven ★★
Exodus ★★
Pepe ★★

1962

Sergeants 3 ★★★
Advise and Consent ★★★
The Longest Day ★★★

1964

Dead Ringer ★★★

1965

Sylvia ★★★
Harlow ★★★

1966

The Oscar ★★
A Man Called Adam ★★★

1968

Salt and Pepper ★★★
Buona Sera Mrs. Campbell ★★★
Skidoo ★

1969

The April Fools ★
Hook, Line and Sinker ★★★

1970

One More Time ★★★

1971

Clay Pigeon (cameo)

1972

Return to the Land of Oz (voice only)
They Only Kill Their Masters ★★

1974

That's Entertainment (narration)

1975

Rosebud ★★

1979

Seven From Heaven (cameo)

1981

Body and Soul ★★★

CLORIS LEACHMAN
★★★ 2.95 STARS

Cloris Leachman's versatility is astonishing. She excels in heavy drama, light comedy and can even sing; she performed the title tune for a popular TV drama, *Someone I Touched.*

Leachman was born in 1926, in Des Moines, Iowa. Though she eventually found her niche as a plain-looking character actress, she was a runner-up in the 1946 Miss America Pageant. Her early pictures rarely focused on her (*Kiss Me Deadly, The Rack*, and *Butch Cassidy and the Sundance Kid*), but Peter Bogdanovich gave her a good part as the lonely older woman in *The Last Picture Show* and she was breathtaking. A Best Supporting Oscar confirmed her brilliance, and Mel Brooks utilized her comedic gifts in *Young Frankenstein* and *High Anxiety.* Leachman stole a clever Disney comedy, *The North Avenue Irregulars,* from Susan Clark and Karen Valentine and won an Emmy for a TV movie, *A Brand New Life.*

FILMOGRAPHY

1955

Kiss Me Deadly ★★★★

1956

The Rack ★★★

Cloris Leachman.

1962

The Chapman Report ★★★

1969

Butch Cassidy and the Sundance Kid ★★★

1970

WUSA ★★
Lovers and Other Strangers ★★★
The People Next Door ★★

1971

The Steagle ★★★
The Last Picture Show ★★★★

1973

Charley and the Angel ★★
Dillinger ★★★
Happy Mother's Day-Love George ★★★

1974

Young Frankenstein ★★★★
Daisy Miller ★★★

1975

Crazy Mama ★★★

1977

High Anxiety ★★★★

1978

The North Avenue Irregulars ★★★★

1979

The Muppet Movie (cameo)
Foolin' Around ★★
Yesterday ★★
S. O. S. Titanic ★★★
Scavenger Hunt ★★

1982

History of the World-Part I ★★★

JANET LEIGH
★★★ 3.15 STARS

Janet Leigh claims she was dismayed when given the lead in *The Romance of Rosy Ridge* because she lacked training as an actress. However, some performers are naturally skillful, having what Robert Mitchum calls "an ear." Leigh belonged to that select group.

She was born Jeanette Helen Morrison in 1927, in Merced, California. She had already married twice in 1942 and 1946 before Norma Shearer recommended her for a screen test. After *Rosy Ridge* she gave a good performance in *If Winter Comes,* and later played Richard Rodgers' girlfriend (Tom Drake was Rodgers) in the factually fraudulent *Words and Music.*

All her early pictures show a warmly appealing girl-to-bring-home-to-mother type, an image she sustained through *Holiday Affair* with Robert Mitchum. *Scaramouche* glamorized her, but she was outshone by a flamboyant Eleanor Parker. Leigh eloped in 1951 with Tony Curtis and they became the darlings of the fan magazines. A series of co-starring vehicles (*The Black Shield of Falworth, The Perfect Furlough,* and *Houdini*), enhanced Curtis's stature but seemed to diminish Leigh.

The legendary shower sequence helped to secure an Oscar nomination, and she was also effective in Orson Welles' *Touch of Evil.* One felt she was worthy of better things

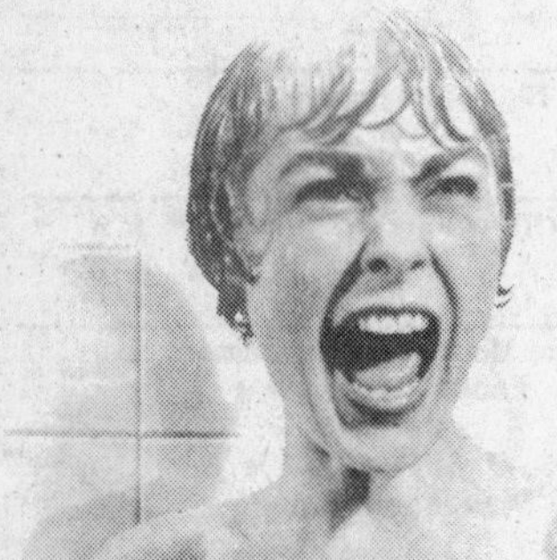

Janet Leigh in *Psycho.*

though it took Hitchcock's horrifying *Psycho* to finally show her full dimension as an actress.

Her role in *The Manchurian Candidate* was purely decorative, but *Harper* and *One Is a Lonely Number* offered better parts. Leigh has the capacity to be a brilliant actress, rather than just a good one, and she may yet find roles that fulfill her potential.

Janet Leigh with Tony Curtis and Dean Martin in *Who Was That Lady?*

FILMOGRAPHY

1947

The Romance of Rosy Ridge★★★

1948

If Winter Comes★★★★
Hills of Home★★★
Words and Music★★★

1949

Act of Violence★★★★
Little Women★★★
The Doctor and the Girl★★★
That Forsyte Woman★★★★
The Red Danube★★
Holiday Affair★★★★

1951

Strictly Dishonorable★★★
Angels in the Outfield★★★
Two Tickets to Broadway★★★

1952

It's a Big Country★★★
Just This Once★★★
Scaramouche★★★★
Fearless Fagan★★★

1953

The Naked Spur★★★
Confidentially Connie★★★
Houdini★★★
Walking My Baby Back Home★★★

1954

Rogue Cop★★★★
Prince Valiant★★★
Living It Up★★★
The Black Shield of Falworth★★

1955

Pete Kelly's Blues★★★
My Sister Eileen★★★★

1956

Safari★★★

1957

Jet Pilot★★★

1958

Touch of Evil★★★★
The Vikings★★★

1959

The Perfect Furlough★★★

1960

Psycho★★★★
Who Was That Lady?★★★
Pepe★★

1962

The Manchurian Candidate★★★★

1963

Bye Bye Birdie★★★
Wives and Lovers★★★

1966

Kid Rodelo★★★
Harper★★★
Three on a Couch★★
An American Dream★★★

1968

Grand Slam★★★

1969

Hello Down There★★★

1972

One Is a Lonely Number★★★★
Night of the Lepus★★★

1979

The Fog★★★
Boardwalk★★★

VIVIEN LEIGH
★★★ 3.21 STARS

English leading ladies who make it in American films are usually reserved and genteel in the mold of Greer Garson and Deborah Kerr. Vivien Leigh was the exception. Her delicate, china-doll-like beauty never masked a blazing inner fire. Director George Cukor, viewing tests for *Gone With the Wind,* commented, "There was an indescribable wildness to her."

She was born Vivian Mary Hartley, in Darjeeling, India, in 1913, and convent-educated in England. Her acting ambitions surfaced early, to the surprise of her first husband, a barrister who later said, "She did not seem to me at that time to have those qualities that brought her fame." Early films such as *The Village Squire* and *Gentleman's Agreement* did little to contradict him. It was a play, "The Mask of Virtue" by Ashley Dukes, that insured stardom and a movie contract.

Laurence Olivier (also married) fell in love with Leigh and recognized her potential. They co-starred in *Fire Over England* and *21 Days* without making much of a splash, but *Yank at Oxford* with Robert Taylor offered the meaty role she needed to gain worldwide attention. In *Sidewalks of London* she was an

Vivien Leigh.

ambitious street singer. Although she lacked strong musical talents (a deficiency noticeable later in her Broadway musical "Tovarich"), she made the character affecting and powerful.

When producer David O. Selznick chose her to play Scarlett in *Gone With the Wind*, there was a huge outcry, especially from front-runner Bette Davis. Shooting was stormy (director George Cukor, whom Leigh trusted, was fired and replaced by Victor Fleming). Leigh had no rapport with Gable personally, but their onscreen chemistry was ideal. She won a Best Actress Oscar, and a glittering future in films appeared inevitable.

However, her career stumbled unevenly along with only occasional artistic peaks to remind audiences of her brilliance. She finally married Laurence Olivier, who stood by her through all the troubled times to come. Although theatre work claimed much of her time, she had to begin dealing with a growing mental illness that the press carefully concealed. *Waterloo Bridge* was her peak, and Leigh was exquisite as the ballerina who turned to prostitution when she believed her soldier boyfriend dead. After the sluggish *Caesar and Cleopatra* and the uninspired remake of *Anna Karenina*, Leigh returned to top form with *A Streetcar Named Desire*. She won a second Oscar and praise from critics like Pauline Kael who called her Blanche Du Bois, "the best feminine performance you're ever likely to see." Her own manic-depressive tendencies undoubtedly lent an added reality to this haunting portrayal of madness.

Subsequent films were disappointing. *The Deep Blue Sea* was talky and uninvolving, and *The Roman Spring of Mrs. Stone* saddled her with a wildly miscast Warren Beatty. In *Ship of Fools*, she was touching but secondary to Simone Signoret and Oskar Werner. Two years later she died, in early 1967. Leigh's list of films is paltry when compared to the filmographies of Davis or Hepburn. But artistic accomplishment is not a game of numbers. If she had never played any characters except Scarlett O'Hara and Blanche Du Bois her reputation would still be permanently secure.

FILMOGRAPHY

1934

Things Are Looking Up ★★

1935

The Village Squire ★★
Gentleman's Agreement ★★★
Look Up and Laugh ★★★

1937

Fire Over England ★★★
Dark Journey ★★★
Storm in a Teacup ★★★

1938

Yank at Oxford ★★★★
Sidewalks of London ★★★★

1939

21 Days ★★★
Gone With the Wind ★★★★

1940

Waterloo Bridge ★★★★

Vivien Leigh in *Gone With the Wind.*

1941

That Hamilton Woman ★★★★

1945

Caesar and Cleopatra ★★★

1948

Anna Karenina ★★★

1951

A Streetcar Named Desire ★★★★

1955

The Deep Blue Sea ★★★

1961

The Roman Spring of Mrs. Stone ★★★

1965

Ship of Fools ★★★

JACK LEMMON
★★★ 3.03 STARS

Jack Lemmon is the screen's best nice guy. In comedies, he dithers and fumbles, but it never seems affected; he's more like a person thinking out his next move. He is also non-threatening, yet convincing as a romantic lead.

Lemmon (John Uhler Lemmon III) was born in 1925, in Boston. His father ran a doughnut company, but Jack preferred acting to business and concentrated on dramatics at Harvard. A long TV apprenticeship led to a fine debut in *It Should Happen to You* with Judy Holliday. Then, he played in *Three for the Show*, a weak film with Betty Grable whose career was in decline. However, his portrayal of Ensign Pulver in *Mister Roberts* brought him a Best Supporting Oscar, and he was the brightest thing about that stagy comedy.

Fire Down Below also featured Lemmon opposite a star (Rita Hayworth) on the skids and did nothing to halt Hayworth's downward course. He blamed a bad title for the failure of *It Happened to Jane*, telling the press he loved working with Doris Day.

Some Like It Hot was Lemmon's first classic; he and Tony Curtis masqueraded as girls, and director Billy Wilder maintained a semblance of good taste amid the general craziness. *The Apartment*, also directed by Wilder, won a Best Picture Oscar. Lemmon was the businessman with the apartment that accommodated executives and their mistresses. Shirley MacLaine was his co-star and both were superb. *The Notorious Landlady* was a second unmemorable teaming with Kim Novak—the first was *Bell, Book and Candle*. He gave his best performance in *The Days of Wine and Roses*, a study of an alcoholic marriage. The final shot with Lemmon staring out of the window while the light of a liquor store flickered was unforgettable.

It was much easier to forget *Irma La Douce*. He was again paired with Shirley MacLaine, but the script was vulgar and the directing heavy-handed. Commercially it succeeded, but his next films didn't: *Under the Yum Yum Tree*, *Good Neighbor Sam*, and *The Great Race*. *The Fortune Cookie* won an Oscar for frequent teammate Walter Matthau, and both were hilarious in *The Odd Couple*. Matthau and Lemmon also had a field day in Wilder's less-than-subtle remake of *The Front Page*.

Save the Tiger dealt with a dress manufacturer who set fire to his factory for the insurance. The film had a downbeat subject with preachy dialogue and an unconscionably prolonged "nervous breakdown" sequence. Critics thought it was "saying something," and so did the Academy because it won Lemmon a Best Actor Oscar. Ironically, his portrayal in *The Days of Wine and Roses* was infinitely superior. Other commanding performances included roles in *The Entertainer* (a TV adaptation of the Laurence Olivier vehicle), *The China Syndrome*, and *Missing*.

Jack Lemmon in *Mister Roberts.*

It's not often one can say of an actor that after 27 years of constant stardom and exposure, he's better than ever.

FILMOGRAPHY

1954

It Should Happen to You ★★★
Phffft ★★★

1955

Three for the Show ★★★
Mister Roberts ★★★★
My Sister Eileen ★★★

1956

You Can't Run Away from It ★★★

1957

Fire Down Below ★★★
Operation Mad Ball ★★★

1958

Cowboy ★★★

1959

Bell, Book and Candle ★★★
Some Like It Hot ★★★★
It Happened to Jane ★★★

1960

The Apartment ★★★★
Pepe ★★
The Wackiest Ship in the Army ★★★

1962

The Notorious Landlady ★★★
The Days of Wine and Roses ★★★★

1963

Irma La Douce ★★★
Under the Yum Yum Tree ★★★

1964

Good Neighbor Sam ★★★

1965

How to Murder Your Wife ★★★
The Great Race ★

1966

The Fortune Cookie ★★★

1968

The Odd Couple ★★★★

1969

The April Fools ★★

1970

The Out-of-Towners ★★

1972

The War Between Men and Women ★★★
Avanti! ★★★

1973

Save the Tiger ★★★

Jack Lemmon with Sissy Spacek in *Missing.*

1974

The Front Page ★★★

1975

The Prisoner of Second Avenue ★★★

1976

The Entertainer ★★★★
Alex and the Gypsy ★★★

1977

Airport '77 ★★

1979

The China Syndrome ★★★★

1980

Tribute ★★★

1981

Buddy Buddy ★★

1982

Missing ★★★★

OSCAR LEVANT
★★★ 3.00 STARS

With the possible exception of George Sanders, no other performer ever turned witty cynicism to such good advantage as Oscar Levant. Despite an offhand attitude toward acting, he took his profession seriously. Director Vincente Minnelli recalled his "vanity-wounded roar" when one of his scenes was cut from *An American in Paris*.

Levant was born in 1906, in Pittsburgh, Pennsylvania. He was a fine pianist and built a reputation as the foremost interpreter of Gershwin's music. His pianist skills were utilized in films, and he played Gershwin's "Concerto in F" in *An American in Paris*. His droll wit gave a sparkling edge to Clifford

Odet's dialogue in *Humoresque*. Levant's acerbic presence gave a lift to several other good musicals including: *The Barkleys of Broadway, Romance on the High Seas*, and *The Band Wagon*.

After making Minnelli's disjointed *The Cobweb*, Levant retired from the screen, slowly succumbing to pill addiction. In his later years he found his perfect niche as a cynical guest on late-night TV talk shows. He died in 1972.

Oscar Levant.

FILMOGRAPHY

1929

Dance of Life ★★★

1935

In Person ★★

1940

Rhythm on the Range ★★★

1945

Rhapsody in Blue ★★★★

1946

Humoresque ★★★★

1948

You Were Meant for Me ★★★
The Barkleys of Broadway ★★★
Romance on the High Seas ★★

1951

An American in Paris ★★★

1952

O'Henry's Full House ★★★

1953

The Band Wagon ★★★
The I Don't Care Girl ★★★

1955

The Cobweb ★★

JERRY LEWIS
★★ 2.02 STARS

Attitudes on Jerry Lewis vary widely. Some French critics revere him and Dean Martin, after their bitter partnership ended, said, "God gave him the gift to be the funniest comic the world ever saw." However, many others agree with the Harvard Lampoon which appraised him in 1952, "Jerry Lewis...by dint of incessant struggle, has unquestionably established himself as the Worst Comedian of All Time."

Lewis was born Joseph Levitch in 1926, in Newark, New Jersey. His parents were entertainers in New York's Catskill Mountains—the Borscht Circuit—and he was a seasoned performer by the time he met Dean Martin at age 20. Following a successful engagement at Manhattan's Copacabana nightclub, Martin and Lewis signed to do *My Friend Irma*. They stole the film and did the sequel, *My Friend Irma Goes West*, which wasn't nearly as funny. Children, in particular, loved Lewis's goofy grimacing and vocal inflections though Groucho Marx dismissed him as a "puller of faces."

In any case, Martin and Lewis were box-office magic in *That's My Boy, Sailor Beware*, and *The Stooge*—which netted Martin good personal reviews as an actor. Lewis and Carmen Miranda hammed it up to advantage in *Scared Stiff*. *The Caddy* had a witless script (Lewis was teaching Martin how to play golf) and one decent song, "That's Amore." Better than any of these was *You're Never Too Young*, a remake of the old Ginger Rogers hit, *The Major and the Minor*.

Jerry Lewis.

Pardners and *Hollywood or Bust* marked the end of a golden partnership. The break was bitter, but Hollywood expected Lewis to weather it more successfully than Martin, and at first he did. As *The Delicate Delinquent*, he became a policeman with Darren McGavin's help. *The Sad Sack* put him in the army, and he fathered triplets in the dreary *Rock-a-Bye Baby*. *The Geisha Boy* cast him as a magician. Director Frank Tashlin gave some bounce to the proceedings, but the movie was mainly notable because Suzanne Pleshette made her cinema debut. Lewis's vehicles, which never were very strong, became unbearable in *The Bellboy, Cinderfella*, and *It's Only Money*.

However, audiences were still responding. Lewis had a smash hit with *The Nutty Professor*, and even a few critics felt it was inventive. Nobody found much merit in *The Patsy* or *The Family Jewels*—he played seven characters, none of which bore the slightest resemblance to a human being. Most of his films after Martin centered solely around Lewis. *Boeing Boeing* gave him an important co-star in Tony Curtis, removing Lewis from the direct light of center stage. It was too late; audiences were sick of his moronic, strident shennanigans. Unfortunately, the films got worse, *Three on a Couch, Way...Way Out, Don't Raise the Bridge—Lower the River*, and *Which Way to the Front?*

Lewis stayed in the news through his charity work for muscular dystrophy. Martin appeared on one of the telethons, giving rise to rumors of a reteaming, but nothing ever developed. Lewis may yet surprise, however. He did a picture for Martin Scorsese, *King of Comedy*, as a TV talk show host and got better reviews than critic's pet Robert De Niro.

FILMOGRAPHY

1949

My Friend Irma ★★★

1950

My Friend Irma Goes West ★★

Jerry Lewis in *The Big Mouth.*

1951

That's My Boy ★★
At War With the Army ★★★

1952

Jumping Jacks ★★★
Road to Bali (cameo)
Sailor Beware ★★

1953

The Stooge ★★
Scared Stiff ★★
The Caddy ★★★

1954

Money from Home ★★
Living It Up ★★
Three Ring Circus ★★

1955

You're Never Too Young ★★
Artists and Models ★★★

1956

Pardners ★★
Hollywood or Bust ★★★

1957

The Delicate Delinquent ★★★
The Sad Sack ★★

1958

Rock-a-Bye Baby ★
The Geisha Boy ★★

1959

Don't Give Up the Ship ★

1960

Visit to a Small Planet ★★
The Bellboy ★★
Cinderfella ★

1961

The Ladies Man ★★
The Errand Boy ★

1962

It's Only Money ★★

1963

Who's Minding the Store? ★★
The Nutty Professor ★★★★
It's a Mad Mad Mad Mad World (cameo)

1964

The Disorderly Orderly ★★★
The Patsy ★★

1965

The Family Jewels ★
Boeing Boeing ★★

1966

Way...Way Out ★
Three on a Couch ★

1967

The Big Mouth ★

1968

Don't Raise the Bridge—Lower the River ★

1969

Hook Line and Sinker ★

1970

Which Way to the Front? ★

1979

Hardly Working ★

1983

King of Comedy ★★★★

GINA LOLLOBRIGIDA
★★★ 2.81 STARS

Gina Lollobrigida has talent and beauty, but like many European stars, such as Maria Schell and Alida Valli, her special quality didn't work well on American shores.

Lollobrigida was born in 1927, in Subiaco, Italy, a town about 50 miles from Rome. A carpenter's daughter, she began as a model under the name Diana Loris. Director Mario Costa discovered her and cast her in *Elisir d'Amore*, and she made several other popular films, (*Campane A Martello, La Sposa non puo Attendare, Alina*) all of which showcased her physical charms. Her first American picture of note was the spoof adventure *Beat the Devil* with Humphrey Bogart. Now a cult film, it was one of Bogart's few movies to fail at the time of release.

The vehicle that established her as an American star was *Trapeze*. Lollobrigida was the aerialist loved by Burt Lancaster and Tony Curtis, and she portrayed a convincing blend of love and ambition. *Solomon and Sheba* was a boring biblical spectacle, but she excelled in *Woman of Straw* as a potential murderess. There were two weak comedies, *Come September* and *Strange Bedfellows*, both with Rock Hudson.

Since the mid-1970s, Lollobrigida has been off the screen pursuing her other creative passion, photography.

FILMOGRAPHY

1946

Aquila Nera ★★
Elisir d'Amore ★★
Lucia di Lammermoor ★★

1947

Il Delitto di Giovanni Episcopo ★★
Il Segreto di Don Giovanni ★★
Follie per l'Opera ★★

1948

I Pagliacci ★★

1949

Campane A Martello ★★
La Sposa no puo Attendare ★★★★
Alina ★★★

1950

Miss Italia ★★★
Cuori senza Frontiere ★★★
Vita de Cani ★★★

1951

A Tale of Five Cities ★★★
Achtung! Banditi ★★★
The Young Caruso ★★★
La Citta si difende ★★★
Altri Tempi ★★★
Amor non ho...Però Però ★★★

1952

Fanfan la Tulipe ★★★
Les Belles de Nuit ★★★
Moglie per una Notte ★★★
Le Infideli ★★★

Gina Lollobrigida in *Come September.*

1953

La Provinciale ★★★
Il Maestro di Don Giovanni ★★★
Pane Amore e Fantasia ★★★

1954

Beat the Devil ★★★★
Le Grand Jeu ★★★
La Romana ★★★
Pane Amore e Gelosia ★★★

1955

La Donna piu Bella del Mondo ★★

1956

Trapeze ★★★★
Notre Dame de Paris ★★★

1958

Anna di Brooklyn ★★★

1959

Where the Hot Wind Blows ★★
Solomon and Sheba ★★
Never So Few ★★

1961

Go Naked in the World ★★
Come September ★★★

1962

Venus imperiale ★★★
Bellezza d'Ippolita ★★★

1963

Mare Matto ★★★

1964

Woman of Straw ★★★★

1965

The Dolls ★★★
Strange Bedfellows ★★★

1966

Hotel Paradiso ★★★

1967

Cervantes ★★★
Io lo lo. . . e gli Altri ★★★
Les Sultans ★★★
Le Morte ha Fatto l'Uovo ★★★

1968

The Private Navy of Sgt. O'Farrell ★★
Un Bellissimo Novembre ★★★
Buona Sera Mrs. Campbell ★★★

1971

Bad Man's River ★★

1973

King, Queen Knave ★★★
Where the Bullets Fly ★★★
No Encontre Rosas para Mi Madre ★★★

1975

The Lonely Woman ★★★
Portrait of Fidel Castro (documentary)

CAROLE LOMBARD
★★★½ 3.33 STARS

Carole Lombard was known in private life for her outspoken tongue and bawdy language. Censorship prohibited off-color screen talk in the 1930s, but Lombard's honest, earthy quality penetrated beneath her glamorous facade making her seem "real" to her millions of fans.

She was born Jane Alice Peters in 1908, in Fort Wayne, Indiana. Her early work included 13 two-reelers for comedy producer Mack Sennett, and her first talkies (*High Voltage, Big News, The Racketeer*) were heavily melodramatic. She appeared with husband-to-be William Powell in *Man of the World* and played in *No Man of Her Own* with Clark Gable. According to the London Film Weekly, her performance opposite Gable was "cool, sincere and intelligent...makes the perfect heroine." Their love affair didn't develop off the set until later; Lombard was still married to Powell. At this time though, she was involved with bandleader Russ Colombo, who died in a freak shooting accident.

Her transformation from leading lady to star began with her role in *Twentieth Century*, a frenetic farce that also featured John Barrymore. Barrymore later called her "perhaps the greatest actress I ever worked with." Great acting wasn't required in a Shirley Temple film, *Now and Forever*, but several comedies showed her off to good advantage (*Hands Across the Table, Love Before Breakfast*, and notably *My Man Godfrey* (with now ex-husband Powell).

She switched to soap opera in the film *In Name Only*, then did Hitchcock's only attempt at comedy, *Mr. and Mrs. Smith*, though the script was bad. Later, Lombard and Jack Benny matched perfectly as two temperamental actors in Nazi-occupied Poland in *To Be or Not To Be*. She married Gable and lived happily with him for three years before an air crash took her life.

Carole Lombard with Zazu Pitts in *The Gay Bride*.

FILMOGRAPHY

1921

A Perfect Crime ★★★

1925

Marriage in Transit ★★★
Hearts and Spurs ★★★
Durand of the Badlands ★★★

1926

The Road to Glory (bit)

1928

The Divine Sinner ★★★
Power ★★★
Me Gangster ★★★
Show Folks ★★★
Ned McCobb's Daughter ★★★

1929

High Voltage ★★★
Big News ★★★
The Racketeer ★★★

1930

The Arizona Kid ★★★
Safety in Numbers ★★★
Fast and Loose ★★★★

1931

It Pays to Advertise ★★★★
Man of the World ★★★★
Ladies' Man ★★★★
Up Pops the Devil ★★★
I Take This Woman ★★★

1932

No One Man ★★★
Sinners in the Sun ★★★
Virtue ★★★
No More Orchids ★★★
No Man of Her Own ★★★★

1933

From Hell to Heaven ★★★
Supernatural ★★★
The Eagle and the Hawk ★★★
Brief Moment ★★★
White Woman ★★★

1934

Bolero ★★★★
We're Not Dressing ★★★★
Twentieth Century ★★★★
Now and Forever ★★★
Lady by Choice ★★★
The Gay Bride ★★★

Carole Lombard.

1935

Rumba ★★★★
Hands Across the Table ★★★★

1936

Love Before Breakfast ★★★
The Princess Comes Across ★★★★
My Man Godfrey ★★★★

1937

Swing High Swing Low ★★★
Nothing Sacred ★★★★
True Confession ★★★★

1938

Fools for Scandal ★★★

1939

Made for Each Other ★★★★
In Name Only ★★★

1940

Vigil in the Night ★★★
They Knew What They Wanted ★★★★

1941

Mr. and Mrs. Smith ★★★

1942

To Be or Not To Be ★★★★

SOPHIA LOREN
★★½ 2.73 STARS

Sophia Loren admitted that her third great passion, after family and performing, is gambling: "It's a very beautiful game, exciting, unpredictable and courageous." Her description of the game might have been a description of Loren herself. Luscious loveliness and steely determination enabled her to achieve stardom against overwhelming odds.

Loren (Sofia Villani Scicolone) was born in 1934, in Rome—illegitimate—to a mother with unrealized acting ambitions. A beauty contest winner at fourteen and nicknamed Stechetto—the stick—she entered another (The Miss Italy competition) and was named Miss Elegance. This exposure and her fashion modeling brought her to the attention of Carlo Ponti, who dedicated his life thereafter to making her a star.

Early pictures *Il Mago per Forza* and *E'Arrivato l'Accordatore*, led to a fine role in *La Favorita*. Fame escalated through *La Domenica della Buona Gente, Two Nights With Cleopatra*, and *Attila* with Anthony Quinn.

Eventually Hollywood showed interest and launched her in *Boy on a Dolphin* (a ludicrous pairing with Alan Ladd). The film itself, about a search for sunken treasure, became oblivious quickly. Her second American venture, *The Pride and the Passion*, was even worse—the star turned out to be a huge cannon. Loren was out of place in the film, as were co-stars Frank Sinatra and Cary Grant. Grant fell in love with her although she was deeply involved with Ponti. A third failure *The Legend of the Lost*, cast her as an Arab slave girl, and it was one of John Wayne's rare misfires.

Loren's special charms—her energy, her sexuality, her "life force" earthiness—were all ignored in these three films, and *Desire Under The Elms* squashed them entirely. Anthony Perkins was her ill-chosen co-star. *The Key* was an improvement though co-star Trevor Howard was its one notable ingredient. Loren did a second film with Grant, *Houseboat*, a moderately amusing comedy and her only big hit in Hollywood. Another unsuitable leading man (Tab Hunter) destroyed her potential in *That Kind of Woman*.

Her career was box-office shambles by the time *Two Women* came along, a gripping, realistic study of a widow and her daughter during wartime. Loren won an Oscar, but artistic respectability didn't improve her vehicles. In *El Cid* with Charlton Heston, they had no rapport on or off the screen, and *Five Miles to Midnight*, a so-called thriller with Anthony Perkins and *The Fall of the Roman Empire* were both second rate films.

Loren finally married Carlo Ponti in 1966, after years of legal wrangling with the Italian Government. Ponti had been divorced, and divorce wasn't recognized in Italy. Her personal life stayed on an even keel—two children were born after many miscarriages—though her movie career continued its wayward course.

Judith was so tasteless it "bordered on the obscene," according to critic Judith Crist, and *A Countess From Hong King* demonstrated that director Charlie Chaplin had lost his touch. She was also out of place in the travesty made of *Man Of La Mancha*. However, her touching portrayal in *A Special Day* as a housewife trying to seduce homosexual Marcello Mastroianni showed a talent too often buried in bad product.

Loren is admirable—she has remained a superstar by studying, working, and diversifying. She even won a Golden Globe Award as the World's Most Popular Star when the box-office results of her movies proclaimed just the opposite.

FILMOGRAPHY

1950

Cuori sul Mare ★★
Il Voto ★★
Le Sei Moglie di Barbablu ★★
Io Sono il Capataz ★★
Milano Miliardaria ★★

1952

Il Mago per Forza ★★
Il Sogno di Zorro ★★
E'Arrivato l'Accordatore ★★
Era Lui Si Si ★★
La Favorita ★★★
La Tratta della Bianche ★★★

1953

Africa Sotto i Mari ★★★
Aida ★★★
The Anatomy of Love ★★★
Ci Troviamo in Galleria ★★★

1954

Carosello Napolitano (bit)
Two Nights With Cleopatra ★★★
Atilla ★★★
Gold of Naples ★★★
A Day in Court ★★★
La Domenica della Buona Gente ★★★
Il Paese dei Campanelli ★★★
Pellegrini d'Amore ★★★

1955

La Donna del Fiume ★★★
Too Bad She's Bad ★★★
Il Segno di Venere ★★★
The Miller's Beautiful Wife ★★★
Scandal in Surrento ★★★
L'Oro di Napoli ★★★

1956

Lucky to Be a Woman ★★★
Peccato che Sia Una Canaglia ★★★

1957

Boy on a Dolphin ★★

1958

The Pride and Passion ★★
The Legend of the Lost ★★
Desire Under the Elms ★★
The Key ★★★
Houseboat ★★★

1959

The Black Orchid ★★★
That Kind of Woman ★★

1960

Heller in Pink Tights ★★★

Sophia Loren.

It Started in Naples ★★★
A Breath of Scandal ★★★
The Millionairess ★★★
Two Women ★★★★

1961

El Cid ★★
Madame ★★

1962

Boccaccio '70 ★★★★
Five Miles to Midnight ★★★
The Condemned of Altona ★★★

1963

Yesterday, Today and Tomorrow ★★★★

1964

The Fall of the Roman Empire ★★
Marriage Italian Style ★★★★

1965

Operation Crossbow ★★
Lady L ★★

1966

Judith ★★
Arabesque ★★★

1967

A Countess From Hong Kong ★★
Cinderella Italian Style ★★★

1968

Ghosts Italian Style ★★

1969

Sunflower ★★★

1970

The Priest's Wife ★★★

1971

Lady Liberty ★★★

1972

Man of La Mancha ★★

1973

White Sister ★★

1974

The Voyage ★★

1975

The Verdict ★★★

1977

A Special Day ★★★★
The Cassandra Crossing ★★★

1978

Angela ★★★
Brass Target ★★★
Shimmy Lugano e Tarantelle e Vino ★★★

1979

Revenge ★★★
Firepower ★★★
Vengeance ★★★
Blood Feud ★★★

1981

Oopsie Poopsie ★★★

PETER LORRE
★★★½ 3.62 STARS

Sneaky, weasel-like, deceitful, and sometimes monstrously evil, Peter Lorre was usually the best thing about his dozens of films.

Lorre (Laszlo Löwenstein) was born in 1904, in Rosenberg, Hungary. His first major picture is still one many regard as his best, Fritz Lang's *M*. Lorre was cast as a child murderer, and he made the character both pathetic and repulsive. He was also in the first version of Hitchcock's *The Man Who Knew Too Much* and then did *Secret Agent*, another Hitchcock film, before immigrating to Hollywood.

His first Hollywood role was a classic portrayal as the evil Dr. Gogol in *Mad Love*. A series of *Mr. Moto* pictures followed: *Think Fast Mr. Moto*, *Mr. Moto's Gamble*, *The Mysterious Mr. Moto of Devil's Island* and many more. Lorre's clashes with Mary Astor in *The Maltese Falcon* had a comically evil edge. His whining cowardice was again amusing in *Casablanca*, and he teamed with Bogart again in *All Through the Night*. He switched from heavy to hero in *The Constant Nymph* and *The Mask of Dimitrios*. Sydney Greenstreet was his co-star, and they also did a *Casablanca* imitation, *The Conspirators*, as well as a competent thriller, *The Verdict*.

Peter Lorre with Mary Astor and Humphrey Bogart in *The Maltese Falcon*.

He was strangled by a disembodied hand in *The Beast With Five Fingers*, a film highly regarded by horror buffs. His villainous image was spoofed in *My Favorite Brunette* with Bob Hope. *Casbah* was a remake of *Algiers* undone by the casting of Tony Martin and Yvonne De Carlo. There were some mediocre ventures, *Black Angel*, *The Chase*, and *Quicksand*, and finally a worthy part in Bogart's *Beat the Devil*. However, the unrewarding roles continued through *The Story of Mankind*, *Hell Ship Mutiny*, *The Sad Sack*, and *The Big Circus*. Lorre died of a stroke in 1964.

Lorre, unfortunately, became a parody of himself in his twilight roles in the early 1960s. But this ignominy was possible only because he had created such a strong and identifiable character in his earlier roles. Peter Lorre was one of the greatest character actors of all time.

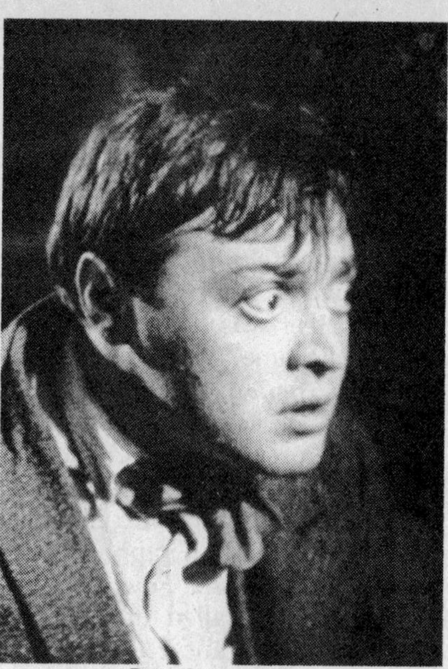

Peter Lorre in *M*.

FILMOGRAPHY

1928

Pionier in Inoplastadt ★★★

1929

Fruhlings Erwachen ★★★

1931

Die Koffer des Herrn O. F. ★★★
M ★★★★
Monte Carlo Madness ★★★★

1932

F. P. I antwortet nicht ★★★★
Schuss im Morgengrauen ★★★★
Funf von der Jazzband ★★★★
Der Weisse Damon ★★★★

1933

Was Frauen träumen ★★★★
Unsichtbare Gegner ★★★★

1934

Du Haut en Bas ★★★★
The Man Who Knew Too Much ★★★★

1935

Mad Love ★★★★
Crime and Punishment ★★★★

1936

Secret Agent ★★★★

1937

Crack-Up ★★★
Nancy Steele Is Missing ★★★
Think Fast Mr. Moto ★★★★
Lancer Spy ★★★★
Thank You Mr. Moto ★★★★

1938

Mr. Moto in Danger Island ★★★★
Mr. Moto's Gamble ★★★★
Mr. Moto Takes a Chance ★★★★
I'll Give a Million ★★★★
The Mysterious Mr. Moto of Devil's Island ★★★★

1939

Mr. Moto's Last Warning ★★★★
Mr. Moto Takes a Vacation ★★★★

1940

Strange Cargo ★★★★
I Was an Adventuress ★★★★
Island of Doomed Men ★★★★
Stranger on the Third Floor ★★★★
You'll Find Out ★★★

1941

The Face Behind the Mask ★★★★
Mr. District Attorney ★★★★
They Met in Bombay ★★★
The Maltese Falcon ★★★★

1942

All Through the Night ★★★★
In This Our Life (cameo)
The Boogie Man Will Get You ★★★
Invisible Agent ★★★
Casablanca ★★★★

1943

The Constant Nymph ★★★★
Background to Danger ★★★★
The Cross of Lorraine ★★★

1944

Passage to Marseilles ★★★★
The Mask of Dimitrios ★★★★
Arsenic and Old Lace ★★★★
The Conspirators ★★★★
Hollywood Canteen (cameo)

1945

Hotel Berlin ★★★★
Confidential Agent ★★★★

1946

Three Strangers ★★★★
Black Angel ★★★★
The Chase ★★★★
The Verdict ★★★★
The Beast With Five Fingers ★★★★

1947

My Favorite Brunette ★★★

1948

Casbah ★★★

1949

Rope of Sand ★★★

1950

Double Confession ★★★
Quicksand ★★★

1951

The Lost One ★★★

1954

20,000 Leagues Under the Sea ★★★★
Beat the Devil ★★★

1956

Congo Crossing ★★★
Meet Me in Las Vegas (cameo)
Around the World in 80 Days ★★★

Peter Lorre with Rochelle Hudson in *Island of Doomed Men.*

1957

The Buster Keaton Story ★★★
Silk Stockings ★★★
The Story of Mankind ★★★
The Sad Sack ★★★
Hell Ship Mutiny ★★★

1959

The Big Circus ★★★

1960

Scent of Mystery ★★★

1961

Voyage to the Bottom of the Sea ★★★

1962

Tales of Terror ★★★★
Five Weeks in a Balloon ★★★

1963

The Raven ★★★★
The Comedy of Terrors ★★★

1964

Muscle Beach Party (cameo)
The Patsy ★★★

MYRNA LOY
★★★ 3.18 STARS

More than contemporaries Rosalind Russell or Claudette Colbert, Myrna Loy was the screen's "perfect wife." She had a sophisticated, graceful way with a witty line that enhanced all her comedies, and she was also a highly skilled dramatic actress.

Loy was born Myrna Williams, in 1905, in Raidersburg, Montana. She started in silent films in *Pretty Ladies* in 1925, and had a bit part in the first talkie, *The Jazz Singer.* In her early pictures *(The Squall, Rebound,* and *Consolation Marriage)* she played a vamp seductress, and her biographer Karyn Ray pointed out, "The fact that Loy began her career not as a quintessential homemaker...but as a devious home*wrecker,* is often forgotten." She had a good part in *Night Flight* with Clark Gable and teamed with him again in *Manhattan Melodrama.*

The Thin Man ushered in her best period. She established a rapport with co-star William Powell that made many theorize that their screen relationship constituted the ideal marriage—they were more than spouses, they were *buddies.* There were several entertaining sequels and two hilarious comedies with Cary Grant, *Mr. Blandings Builds His Dream House* and *The Bachelor and the Bobby-Soxer.* Her finest dramatic opportunity was Wyler's memorable *The Best Years of Our Lives.* Her warmth and devotion to Fredric March were the most touching aspects of the movie. Her role in *The Red Pony* was slow going, except for Aaron Copland's superb score, but *Cheaper by the Dozen* gave her a great teammate in Clifton Webb. She had a powerful scene as Paul Newman's alcoholic mother in *From the Terrace* and added a feyly engaging touch to *The April Fools.*

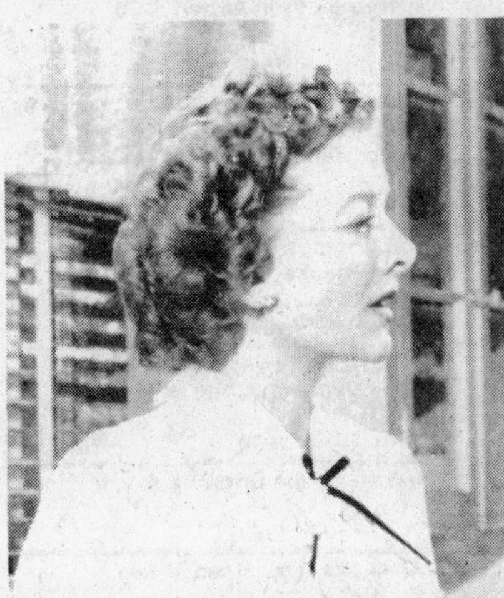

Myrna Loy in *The Best Years of Our Lives.*

Loy's consistent and engaging contribution to over a hundred pictures is a remarkable achievement. Even more remarkable, she was never nominated for an Oscar. Like all great performers, she never made her efforts seem enough like work to garner attention.

FILMOGRAPHY

1925

Pretty Ladies (bit)

1926

Ben-Hur (bit)
The Cave Man ★★
The Gilded Highway ★★
Across the Pacific ★★★
Why Girls Go Back Home ★★★
Don Juan ★★★
The Exquisite Sinner ★★★
So This Is Paris ★★★

1927

Finger Prints ★★
Ham and Eggs at the Front ★★
Bitter Apples ★★★
The Heart of Maryland ★★★
The Jazz Singer (bit)
If I Were Single ★★★
The Climbers ★★★
Simple Sis ★★
A Sailor's Sweetheart ★★★
The Girl From Chicago ★★★

1928

What Price Beauty (bit)
Beware of Married Men ★★★
Turn Back the Hours ★★★
The Crimson City ★★★
Pay As You Enter ★★★
State Street Sadie ★★★
The Midnight Taxi ★★★

1929

Noah's Ark ★★★
Fancy Baggage ★★★
The Desert Song ★★★★
The Black Watch ★★★
The Squall ★★★
Hardboiled Rose ★★★
Evidence ★★★
The Show of Shows ★★★
The Great Divide ★★★

Myrna Loy with Pat O'Brien in *Consolation Marriage.*

1930

Cameo Kirby ★★★
Isle of Escape ★★★
Under a Texas Moon ★★★
Cock o' the Walk ★★★★
Bride of the Regiment ★★★
Last of the Duanes ★★★
Renegades ★★★
The Jazz Cinderella ★★
The Truth About Youth ★★★
The Devil to Pay ★★★
Rogue of the Rio Grande ★★

1931

Body and Soul ★★★
The Naughty Flirt ★★★
A Connecticut Yankee ★★★
Hush Money ★★★
Transatlantic ★★★
Rebound ★★★
Skyline ★★★★
Consolation Marriage ★★★
Arrowsmith ★★★★

1932

Emma ★★★
The Wet Parade ★★★
Vanity Fair ★★★
The Woman in Room 13 ★★★
New Morals for Old ★★★
Love Me Tonight ★★★
Thirteen Women ★★★
The Mask of Fu Manchu ★★★
The Animal Kingdom ★★★★

1933

Topaze ★★
The Barbarian ★★
When Ladies Meet ★★★★
Penthouse ★★★★
Night Flight ★★★★
The Prizefighter and the Lady ★★★★

1934

Men in White ★★★★
Manhattan Melodrama ★★★★
The Thin Man ★★★★
Stamboul Quest ★★
Evelyn Prentice ★★★★
Broadway Bill ★★★★

1935

Wings in the Dark ★★★
Whipsaw ★★★★

1936

Wife vs. Secretary ★★★★
Petticoat Fever ★★★
The Great Ziegfeld ★★★
To Mary—With Love ★★★★
Libeled Lady ★★★★
After the Thin Man ★★★★

1937

Parnell ★★
Double Wedding ★★★★

1938

Man-Proof ★★★
Test Pilot ★★★★
Too Hot to Handle ★★★★

1939

Lucky Night ★★★
The Rains Came ★★★
Another Thin Man ★★★★

1940

I Love You Again ★★★★
Third Finger Left Hand ★★★

1941

Love Crazy ★★★
Shadow of the Thin Man ★★★★

1944

The Thin Man Goes Home ★★★

1946

So Goes My Love ★★★
The Best Years of Our Lives ★★★★

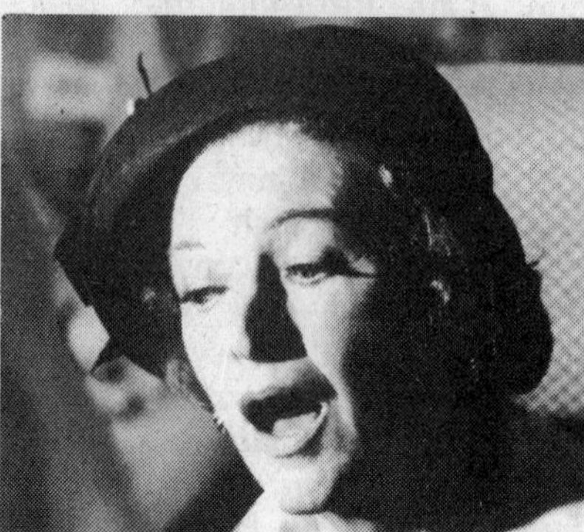

Myrna Loy in *Airport 1975.*

1947

The Bachelor and the Bobby-Soxer ★★★★
The Senator Was Indiscreet (cameo)
Song of the Thin Man ★★★

1948

Mr. Blandings Builds His Dream House ★★★★

1949

The Red Pony ★★★
That Dangerous Age ★★★

1950

Cheaper by the Dozen ★★★★

1952

Belles on Their Toes ★★★

1956

The Ambassador's Daughter ★★★

1959

Lonelyhearts ★★★

1960

Midnight Lace ★★★
From the Terrace ★★★★

1969

The April Fools ★★★

1974

Airport 1975 ★★★

1978

The End (cameo)

1979

Just Tell Me What You Want ★★★

BELA LUGOSI
★★ 1.90 STARS

Moviegoers rarely saw the real Bela Lugosi. The Hungarian-born actor was usually required to play villains and monsters who sported severe makeup and contorted facial expressions. But Lugosi's countenance as Dracula is easily one of the most recognizable in the Hollywood canon of screen characters.

He was born Bela Blasko in Lugos, Hungary in 1882. Gaining experience on the European stage and screen, Lugosi came to the United States where in New York he appeared in numerous stage productions, including "The Red Poppy," "Arabesque," and "Dracula."

He then repeated the role of the vampire count from Transylvania in the movie version in 1931. Lugosi breathed life into the character created by Bram Stoker, while his Dracula drained blood out of his victims' necks.

He did appear in some non-horror films, most notably opposite Greta Garbo in the 1939 MGM classic *Ninotchka.* But from the titles of some of his other movies—*Mark of the Vampire, Dracula's Daughter, The Return of the Vampire,* and *Devil Bat*—it's easy to see the type of vehicles to which he was relegated.

Over the years, Universal Studios lost interest in the Dracula series, and Lugosi was forced to make vampire films for lower and lower budgets at smaller and smaller independent production companies. He even dipped into self-parody when he consented to appear in the 1948 film, *Abbott and Costello Meet Frankenstein*.

Dracula was a role he would play until his death in 1956. In fact, he was working on another bloodsucker at the time of his demise, and another actor was forced to double for Lugosi by covering his ill-matched resemblance with the infamous Dracula cape. However, it wasn't even the genuine article of clothing for, according to his wishes, Lugosi was buried in the Dracula cloak.

Bela Lugosi.

FILMOGRAPHY

1917

A Leopard (bit)

1918

Lulu (bit)
Casanova (bit)

1919

Sklaven fremden Willens (bit)

1920

Der Tanz auf dem Vulkan (bit)
Der Januskopf (bit)

1923

The Silent Command (bit)

1924

The Rejected Woman (bit)

1925

The Midnight Girl (bit)

1929

Prisoners (bit)
The Thirteenth Chair (bit)

1930

Such Men Are Dangerous (bit)
Renegades (bit)

1931

Dracula ★★★★
Women of All Nations ★★
The Black Camel ★★

1932

Murders in the Rue Morgue ★★★
White Zombie ★★★
Chandu the Magician ★★★
Island of Lost Souls ★★
The Death Kiss ★★

1933

The Whispering Shadow ★★
International House ★★
Night of Terror ★★

1934

The Black Cat ★★★★
The Return of Chandu ★★

1935

Best Man Wins ★★
The Mysterious Mr. Wong ★★
Murder by Television ★
Mark of the Vampire ★★★★
The Raven ★★★

1936

Shadow of Chinatown ★★
The Invisible Ray ★★★

1937

S.O.S. Coast Guard ★

1939

The Phantom Creeps ★★
Son of Frankenstein ★★★★
The Gorilla ★
Ninotchka ★★★
The Dark Eyes of London ★★★

1940

The Saint's Double Trouble ★★
Black Friday ★★
You'll Find Out ★
Devil Bat ★

1941

The Black Cat ★★
The Invisible Ghost ★
Spooks Run Wild ★
The Wolf Man ★★

1942

Black Dragons ★
The Ghost of Frankenstein ★★
The Corpse Vanishes ★
Bowery at Midnight ★
Night Monster ★★

1943

Frankenstein Meets the Wolf Man ★★
Ghosts on the Loose ★
The Return of the Vampire ★
The Ape Man ★

Bela Lugosi with Boris Karloff in *The Raven*.

1944

The Voodoo Man ★
Return of the Ape Man ★
One Body Too Many ★

1945

Zombies on Broadway ★
The Body Snatcher ★★★

1946

Genius at Work ★

1947

Scared to Death ★

1948

Abbott and Costello Meet Frankenstein ★★★

1952

Mother Riley Meets the Vampire ★
Bela Lugosi Meets a Brooklyn Gorilla ★

1956

Bride of the Monster ★
The Black Sleep ★★
Plan 9 From Outer Space (cameo)

IDA LUPINO
★★★ 3.11 STARS

Though less publicized in her heyday than either Bette Davis or Joan Crawford, Ida Lupino was often better than either of them. She was intense, believable, and totally without affectation.

She was born in 1918, in London, and came by her talent naturally—her father, Stanley Lupino, was a comedian in revues and films. After training at the Royal Academy of Dramatic Arts, she began her film career with *Her First Affair* in 1933. Neither that, nor the pictures that followed, *High Finance*, *Prince of Arcadia*, *Come on Marines*, or *Paris in Spring*, brought stardom. A comedy, *Artists and Models*, focused on co-star Jack Benny, but she was excellent in *The Light That Failed* with Ronald Colman.

She was even better in *They Drive by Night*, an exciting drama about truckers with Bogart and George Raft and she later played Bogart's moll in the classic *High Sierra*. *The Sea Wolf* offered two strong leading men, Edward G. Robinson and John Garfield, and a terrific script based on a Jack London novel that has been remade seven times to date. *Ladies in Retirement* cast Lupino as a housekeeper who murdered to keep her two feebleminded sisters from being institutionalized.

Ida Lupino with Louis Hayward in *Ladies in Retirement*.

She was never nominated for an Oscar, but the New York critics chose her as Best Actress for *The Hard Way*. She played an ambitious woman who pushed sister Joan Leslie to stardom (an amazing feat, considering Leslie's lack of star quality). *In Our Time* with Paul Henreid had good moments, and Lupino's Emily Bronte in *Devotion* added a note of humanity to a synthetic "biography." She also turned in a perfect performance in *On Dangerous Ground*, an underrated thriller that had her protecting her feebleminded brother. Lupino had the ability to play strong women with ease.

Directing seemed the next logical step, and Lupino helmed *The Hitchhiker*, *Never Fear*, and *Hard Fast and Beautiful*. She wrote as well as directed *Outrage* and acted in and directed *The Bigamist*. Most of these were low-budget and awkwardly acted, but she gave them pace and a sense of urgency. In the late 1950s she and husband Howard Duff had their own TV series, "Mr. Adams and Eve." She continued to direct in the 1960s, including the raggedy but delightful *The Trouble with Angels*. The strong woman image that Ida Lupino excelled at in performances proved true of herself in real life. She has become the most significant female director that Hollywood has yet produced.

FILMOGRAPHY

1933

Her First Affair ★★★
Money for Speed ★★★
High Finance ★★★
Prince of Arcadia ★★★
The Ghost Camera ★★★
I Lived With You ★★★

1934

Search for Beauty ★★★
Come on Marines ★★★
Ready for Love ★★★

1935

Paris in Spring ★★★
Smart Girl ★★★
Peter Ibbetson ★★★

1936

Anything Goes ★★
One Rainy Afternoon ★★★
Yours for the Asking ★★★
The Gay Desperado ★★★

1937

Sea Devils ★★★
Let's Get Married ★★★
Artists and Models ★★★
Fight for Your Lady ★★★

1939

The Lone Wolf Spy Hunt ★★
The Lady and the Mob ★★
The Adventures of Sherlock Holmes ★★★

1940

The Light That Failed ★★★★
They Drive by Night ★★★★

1941

High Sierra ★★★★
The Sea Wolf ★★★★
Out of the Fog ★★★★
Ladies in Retirement ★★★★

1942

Moontide ★★★
Life Begins at Eight Thirty ★★★

1943

The Hard Way ★★★★
Forever and a Day ★★★
Thank Your Lucky Stars ★★

1944

In Our Time ★★★★
Hollywood Canteen ★★★

1945

Pillow to Post ★★

1946

Devotion ★★★

1947

The Man I Love ★★★
Deep Valley ★★★★
Escape Me Never ★★★

1948

Road House ★★★★

1949

Lust for Gold ★★★★

1950

Woman in Hiding ★★★

1952

On Dangerous Ground ★★★★
Beware, My Lovely ★★★

1953

Jennifer ★★★
The Bigamist (direction) ★★★★

1954

Private Hell 36 ★★★

1955

Women's Prison ★★★
The Big Knife ★★★

1956

While the City Sleeps ★★★
Strange Intruder ★★★

1969

Backtrack ★★★

1972

Junior Bonner ★★★

1975

The Devil's Rain ★★
The Food of the Gods ★★

MERCEDES MCCAMBRIDGE
★★★½ 3.41 STARS

Orson Welles once called Mercedes McCambridge, "the world's greatest living radio actress." The compliment is accurate. McCambridge's sharp, nasal, yet strangely *warm* voice is one of the most unique tools an actress has ever possessed.

She was born Carlotta Mercedes Agnes McCambridge in 1918, in Joliet, Illinois. Her radio successes led to Broadway and then Hollywood where she won an Oscar for her first film role in *All the King's Men*. It was her best vehicle artistically although *Lightning Strikes Twice* with

Mercedes McCambridge with Ward Bond in *Johnny Guitar.*

Richard Todd was an entertaining thriller. She played a murderess in *Lightning Strikes Twice* and she was superbly campy as Joan Crawford's deadly gun-toting rival in *Johnny Guitar*. McCambridge was a rival off the screen too; Sterling Hayden claimed that Crawford's treatment of McCambridge was "a shameful thing." *Giant* offered a juicy role as Rock Hudson's jealous sister, and she made her scenes count in *Suddenly, Last Summer.*

Only her voice was used in *The Exorcist*, but the weird, terrifying sounds she made (she was the Devil) were integral to the film. She has recently conquered a long battle with alcoholism and will now, possibly, increase her movie activity.

FILMOGRAPHY

1949

All the King's Men ★★★★

1951

The Scarf ★★★
Inside Straight ★★★
Lightning Strikes Twice ★★★★

1954

Johnny Guitar ★★★★

1956

Giant ★★★★

1957

A Farewell to Arms ★★★

1958

Touch of Evil ★★★★

1959

Suddenly, Last Summer ★★★★

1960

Cimarron ★★★

1961

Angel Baby ★★★★

1965

Run Home Slow ★★★

1968

The Counterfeit Killer ★★★

1969

99 Women ★★★

1973

The Exorcist (voice only)

1974

Like a Crow on a June Bug ★★★

1977

Thieves ★★★

1979

The Concorde—Airport '79 ★★★

JOEL MCCREA
★★★½ 3.27 STARS

Director Preston Sturges called Joel McCrea "one of the most underrated actors in Hollywood," and Danny Peary in his book Close-Ups, placed McCrea in a chapter called The Professionals. Even though McCrea himself said with typical modesty, "I should have tried harder to be a better actor," he was one of Hollywood's finest.

He was born in 1905, in Los Angeles. McCrea acted in school plays at Pomona State College, worked as an extra in films, and finally landed a good part in the 1929 film *The Jazz Age*. Early pictures included *Kept Husbands, Girls About Town*, and *The Lost Squadron*, but it wasn't until *Private Worlds*, a study of life in a mental institution, that he had a meaty acting part. He was excellent and equally convincing as one of *These Three* (his two co-stars were Merle Oberon and Miriam Hopkins). He also played a lumberjack opposite Frances Farmer in the absorbing *Come and Get It*. A couple of exciting westerns, *Wells Fargo* and *Union Pacific*, with Barbara Stanwyck showed his ease in the saddle. McCrea cited Stanwyck as the best actress he ever worked with.

He was billed over Bogart in director William Wyler's *Dead End*, but the picture he dominated totally was Hitchcock's classic *Foreign Correspondent*. In *Sullivan's Travels*—one of director Preston Sturges' most highly regarded comedies— he was cast as a director who took to the road and met Veronica Lake. He was fine in the lead of *Buffalo Bill* and seemed comfortable in a ghost story called *The Unseen*. After that McCrea did mostly second-feature westerns, and all of them benefited from his untheatrical, low-key presence, including: *Ramrod, Colorado Territory, Stars in My Crown, Saddle Tramp, Frenchie*, and *Trooper Hook* (a reunion with Stanwyck).

He retired for three years and then did the finest film of his career, *Ride the High Country* with Randolph Scott. Like the later Jeff Bridges, McCrea never "acted," he just became the character and let it live.

FILMOGRAPHY

1923

Penrod and Sam (bit)

1924

A Self-Made Failure (bit)

1929

The Jazz Age ★★★
So This Is College ★★★
The Single Standard ★★★
Dynamite ★★★

1930

The Silver Horde ★★★
Lightnin' ★★★★

1931

Once a Sinner ★★★
Kept Husbands ★★★★
Born to Love ★★★
The Common Law ★★★
Girls About Town ★★★

1932

Business and Pleasure ★★★
The Lost Squadron ★★★★
Bird of Paradise ★★★
The Most Dangerous Game ★★★
Rockabye ★★★
The Sport Parade ★★★

1933

The Silver Cord ★★★
Bed of Roses ★★★
One Man's Journey ★★★
Chance at Heaven ★★★

1934

Gambling Lady ★★★★
Half a Sinner ★★★
The Richest Girl in the World ★★★★

Joel McCrea in *Our Little Girl.*

1935

Private Worlds ★★★★
Our Little Girl ★★★
Barbary Coast ★★★★
Splendor ★★★
Woman Wanted ★★★

1936

These Three ★★★★
Two in a Crowd ★★★
Adventure in Manhattan ★★★
Come and Get It ★★★★
Banjo on My Knee ★★★

1937

Dead End ★★★★
Interns Can't Take Money ★★★
Woman Chases Man ★★★
Wells Fargo ★★★★

1938

Three Blind Mice ★★★
Youth Takes a Fling ★★★

1939

Union Pacific ★★★★
They Shall Have Music ★★★
Espionage Agent ★★★

1940

He Married His Wife ★★★
Primrose Path ★★★★
Foreign Correspondent ★★★★

1941

Reaching for the Sun ★★★
Sullivan's Travels ★★★★

1942

The Great Man's Lady ★★★
The Palm Beach Story ★★★★

1943

The More the Merrier ★★★★

1944

Buffalo Bill ★★★
The Great Moment ★★★

1945

The Unseen ★★★★

1946

The Virginian ★★★

1947

Ramrod ★★★

1948

Four Faces West ★★★

1949

South of St. Louis ★★★
Colorado Territory ★★★

1950

Stars in My Crown ★★★★
The Outriders ★★★
Saddle Tramp ★★★

1951

Frenchie ★★★★
The Hollywood Story (cameo)
Cattle Drive ★★★★

1952

The San Francisco Story ★★★

1953

Rough Shoot ★★★
Lone Hand ★★★

1954

Border River ★★★
Black Horse Canyon ★★★

1955

Wichita ★★★
Stranger on Horseback ★★★

1956

The First Texan ★★★

1957

Trooper Hook ★★★
Gunsight Ridge ★★★
The Tall Stranger ★★★
The Oklahoman ★★★

1958

Cattle Empire ★★★
Fort Massacre ★★★

1959

Gunfight in Dodge City ★★★

1962

Ride the High Country ★★★★

1970

Cry Blood-Apache ★★★

JEANETTE MACDONALD
★★★ 3.07 STARS

Jane Powell once remarked, "Everyone talks about Garland, but they forget how much money Jeanette MacDonald made for MGM." MacDonald's beauty, charm, and singing ability entranced audiences through the 1930s, and seen today, the star impact is there although her operatic vehicles have become horribly dated.

MacDonald was born in 1901, in Philadelphia. She began as a chorus girl on Broadway and then made *The Love Parade* with Maurice Chevalier for director Ernst Lubitsch. Reaction was positive, so she followed that with *The Vagabond King* and *Monte Carlo*. Two more teamings with Maurice Chevalier in *One Hour With You* and *Love Me Tonight* yielded good entertainment but limited patronage. Her career got into high gear when she signed with MGM in 1934, and did *The Merry Widow*, again with Chevalier. *Naughty Marietta* kicked off the legendary MacDonald-Nelson Eddy series and remains their best picture.

A happy change of pace occurred when MacDonald and the studio convinced Clark Gable to co-star in *San Francisco*, an exciting drama with its famous earthquake finale. MacDonald and Eddy then made *Maytime* (her personal favorite among her films). After *The Firefly* she quarreled with producer Louis B. Mayer, and his refusal to forgive her hurt her status at the studio. There were more popular operettas, *The Girl of the Golden West*, *Sweethearts*, *New Moon*, and *Bitter Sweet* but *I Married an Angel* failed, indicating that the MacDonald-Eddy vogue was past.

Jeanette MacDonald with Maurice Chevalier in *The Love Parade.*

She did stage work in "The King and I" and "Faust" with the Chicago Civic Opera Company and a couple of picture appearances six years later in *Three Daring Daughters* and *The Sun Comes Up*. However, nobody went to see them, and MacDonald retired. She died in 1965, never knowing the kind of crowds her films continued to draw in revivals.

FILMOGRAPHY

1929

The Love Parade ★★★

1930

The Vagabond King ★★★
Monte Carlo ★★★
Let's Go Native ★★★
The Lottery Bride ★★★
Oh for a Man! ★★★

1931

Don't Bet on Women ★★★
Annabelle's Affairs ★★★
One Hour With You ★★★
Love Me Tonight ★★★

1934

The Cat and the Fiddle ★★★
The Merry Widow ★★★

1935

Naughty Marietta ★★★★

1936

Rose Marie ★★★
San Francisco ★★★★

1937

Maytime ★★★
The Firefly ★★★

1938

The Girl of the Golden West ★★★
Sweethearts ★★★

1939

Broadway Serenade ★★★

1940

New Moon ★★★★
Bitter Sweet ★★★

1941

Smilin' Through ★★★

1942

I Married an Angel ★★★
Cairo ★★

1944

Follow the Boys (cameo)

1948

Three Daring Daughters ★★★

1949

The Sun Comes Up ★★★

RODDY MCDOWALL
★★★ 3.01 STARS

Roddy McDowall has always been one of Hollywood's busiest actors, first as a child star, then as a polished supporting actor. He never stole the show but always improved the film.

McDowall (Roderick Andrew Anthony Jude McDowall) was born in London, in 1928. He shared in the general acclaim awarded the great picture, *How Green Was My Valley,* and followed it with another success, *Lassie Come Home*. He switched from dogs to horses in *My Friend Flicka* and *Thunderhead, Son of Flicka,* then attempted to extend his range in Orson Welles' *Macbeth*.

He did a few time-fillers, *Tuna Clipper, Black Midnight*, and *Killer Shark*, but had an attention-getting role in *Cleopatra*. McDowall was more convincing than Burton or Taylor (not a great achievement) and later showed his versatility in widely contrasting vehicles, *The Greatest Story Ever Told, That Darn Cat*, and *Lord Love a Duck*.

Planet of the Apes was a big plus, since he managed to seem human in a monkey suit. Moreover, he was warmly natural in some of the hokier segments of *The Poseidon Adventure*. There were more ape pictures, and then he added needed sincerity to the overwrought *Funny Lady.* He has recently shown his ability to stand out in small roles, as in *Evil Under the Sun* and especially *Class of 1984*. McDowall deserves an accolade that's more impressive than it sounds: a busy, working actor who knows his trade.

FILMOGRAPHY

1936

Murder in the Family ★★★
You Will Remember ★★★

1937

Scruffy ★★★
I See Ice ★★★
Just William ★★★

1938

The Outsider ★★★
Hey! Hey! U.S.A. ★★★
John Halifax—Gentleman ★★★
Convict 99 ★★★
Sarah Seddons ★★★
Poison Pen ★★★
Dead Man's Shoes ★★★

1939

His Brother's Keeper ★★★
Dirt ★★★
Saloon Bar ★★★

1940

This England ★★★

1941

How Green Was My Valley ★★★★
Confirm or Deny ★★★
Man Hunt ★★★

1942

Son of Fury ★★★
The Pied Piper ★★★★
On the Sunny Side ★★★

1943

My Friend Flicka ★★★★
Lassie Come Home ★★★★

1944

White Cliffs of Dover ★★★
Keys of the Kingdom ★★★

1945

Molly and Me ★★★
Thunderhead, Son of Flicka ★★★★

1946

Holiday in Mexico ★★★

1948

Green Grass of Wyoming ★★★★
Rocky ★★★
Kidnapped ★★★★
Macbeth ★★★

1949

Tuna Clipper ★★★
Black Midnight ★★★

1950

Big Timber ★★★
Killer Shark ★★★

1952

The Steel Fist ★★★

1960

The Subterraneans ★★★
Midnight Lace ★★★

1961

The Power and the Glory ★★★

1962

The Longest Day ★★★

1963

Cleopatra ★★★

1964

Shock Treatment ★★★

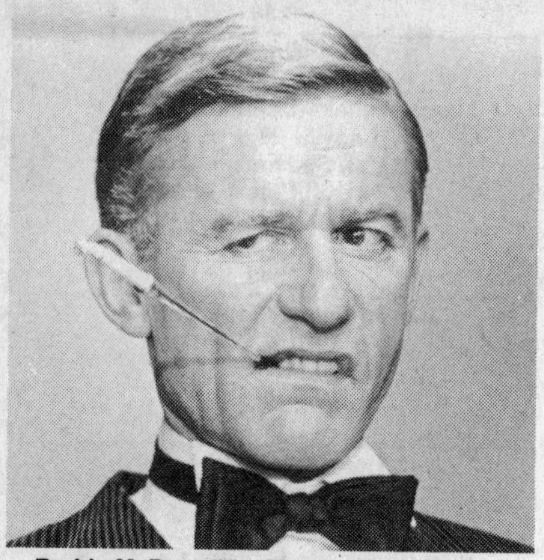

Roddy McDowall in *Charlie Chan and the Curse of the Dragon Queen.*

1965

The Greatest Story Ever Told ★★★
The Third Day ★★★
That Darn Cat ★★★
The Loved One ★★★
Inside Daisy Clover ★★★

1966

Lord Love a Duck ★★★
The Defector ★★★

1967

The Adventures of Bullwhip Griffin ★★
The Cool Ones ★★★

1968

Planet of the Apes ★★★★
The Midas Run ★★★
Five Card Stud ★★★

1969

Giovanni ★★
Angel, Angel, Down We Go ★★★
Hello Down There ★★★

1970

Cult of the Damned ★★★

1971

Escape from the Planet of the Apes ★★★
Bedknobs and Broomsticks ★★★
Pretty Maids All in a Row ★★

1972

Conquest of the Planet of the Apes ★★★
The Poseidon Adventure ★★★
The Life and Times of Judge Roy Bean ★★★

1973

Battle for the Planet of the Apes ★★★
The Legend of Hell House ★★★
Arnold ★★

1974

Dirty Mary, Crazy Larry ★★★

1975

Funny Lady ★★★

1976

Embryo ★★★
Mean Johnny Barrows ★★★

1979

Circle of Iron ★★
Nutcracker Fantasy (voice only)
Scavenger Hunt ★★
Rabbit Test ★★
The Cat from Outer Space ★★

1981

Charlie Chan and the Curse of the Dragon Queen ★★

1982

Evil Under the Sun ★★★

1983

Class of 1984 ★★★★

MALCOLM MCDOWELL
★★★ 3.33 STARS

Malcolm McDowell is a cross between a thug and a pixie. Not handsome by conventional standards, he nevertheless has a wonderfully expressive face, a hint of rebellion in his voice and manner, and an offbeat charisma.

He was born in 1943, in Leeds, England and became a salesman for a coffee factory before joining the Royal Shakespeare Company. He began his career with TV parts and a screen appearance with Carol White (a Julie Christie lookalike) in the drab *Poor Cow*. *If...*was a gripping study of boarding school students and McDowell was superb. Despite an unsatisfying ending, most critics applauded the movie and McDowell's work in it. He was also convincing in an otherwise labored soap opera, *Long Ago Tomorrow*—as a paraplegic in love with Nanette Newman. *A Clockwork Orange* was Stanley Kubrick's adaptation of Anthony Burgess' novel, a grim glimpse into the future. It was violent, upsetting, and definitely not for all tastes, but McDowell played the central part brilliantly.

He was the glue that held together *O Lucky Man!*, a jumbled, tuneful, and generally entertaining saga of a coffee salesman based on McDowell's own experiences at that job. Richard Lester's *Royal Flash* was an amusing costume epic, and *Voyage of the Damned* was a long, serious tale of German-Jewish refugees denied access to the United States. The subject matter and McDowell's performance were assets, especially when the screenplay slowed down to a snail's pace. He was top-billed in the dramatic *Aces High* as a squadron leader.

He got bogged down in the artistic quagmire of *Caligula*. It was *supposed* to be chic pornography, but it was neither. However, *Time After Time* was the vehicle that showed him to best advantage...as H. G. Wells transported to modern day San Francisco via a time machine. He projected just the right combination of bewilderment, excitement, and passion. The script was illogical but witty, and he also had a delightful chemistry with Mary Steenburgen (whom he later married in real life.)

Malcolm McDowell continues to turn in expert performances like clockwork. His villainous army colonel in the smash *Blue Thunder* made a real person out of a cardboard character. He has the untapped intensity to shock the world when the perfect part comes along.

Malcolm McDowell with Nastassia Kinski in *Cat People.*

FILMOGRAPHY

1967

Poor Cow ★★★

1968

If... ★★★★

1970

Figures in a Landscape ★★★

1971

Long Ago Tomorrow ★★★
A Clockwork Orange ★★★★

1973

O Lucky Man! ★★★★

1975

Royal Flash ★★★

1976

Voyage of the Damned ★★★★
Aces High ★★★★

1977

Caligula ★★

1979

The Passage ★★★
Time After Time ★★★★

1980

Look Back in Anger ★★★★

1982

Britannia Hospital ★★★
Cat People ★★

1983

Blue Thunder ★★★
Cross Creek ★★★
Get Crazy ★★★★

ALI MACGRAW
★½ 1.67 STARS

If reviews are any indication, Ali MacGraw certainly ranks as one of the worst actresses in Hollywood. No matter what character she played, she pouted and grimaced petulantly like a spoiled child. Even Kim Novak, in her day, had more variety.

MacGraw (Alice MacGraw) was born in 1938, in Pound Ridge, New York. After attending Wellesley College, she became a famous fashion model. The head of production at Paramount Studios, Bob Evans, discovered and groomed her, and she had a choice role in *Goodbye Columbus*. Except for the last scene, she managed to capture the shallowness of Brenda, the Jewish princess who enticed Richard Benjamin.

Love Story was an overly sensitive screen version of the Eric Segal best-seller. Ryan O'Neal's performance held it together though MacGraw had a few effective moments. However, critic Pauline Kael called her "horribly smug and smirky."

Ali McGraw with Ryan O'Neal in *Love Story*.

The Getaway co-starred her with real-life lover Steve McQueen. It was a vicious, senseless bloodbath, but even the sight of corpses littering the screen couldn't prevent one from noticing MacGraw's amateurish emoting. *Convoy* was about truckers and MacGraw had little to do, which was fortunate.

In *Players*, critic Leonard Maltin commented, "There's something wrong with any movie where Pancho Gonzalez gives the best performance." She was a little better in *Just Tell Me What You Want*, and then stayed away from the screen until 1983's highly publicized TV mini-series, *The Winds of War*. Nobody was up to their best (Robert Mitchum, Jan-Michael Vincent, and John Houseman), but even surrounded by such mediocrity, MacGraw came across as the most strikingly inept performer.

FILMOGRAPHY

1968

A Lovely Way to Die (bit)

1969

Goodbye Columbus ★★★

1970

Love Story ★★

1972

The Getaway ★

1978

Convoy ★

1979

Players ★
Just Tell Me What You Want ★★

DOROTHY MCGUIRE
★★★½ 3.38 STARS

After scoring a tremendous Broadway success as "Claudia" in 1941, Dorothy McGuire signed with producer David O. Selznick. It was during this period that Selznick considered his protégée, Jennifer Jones, for every good role first, and McGuire nearly lost the chance to repeat her stage role in the film version of *Claudia*. Audiences would have lost out too, because McGuire's appearances on screen were one of the great pleasures of moviegoing during the 1940s and 1950s.

Dorothy McGuire with Robert Young in *Claudia*.

She was born in 1918, in Omaha, Nebraska. She started acting at an early age and had 10 years of experience by the time she starred in "Claudia." Her warmth made *Claudia* as popular on film as on the stage, and she revealed sensitivity and power in Elia Kazan's *A Tree Grows in Brooklyn*. In *The Enchanted Cottage*, she was teamed effectively with Robert Young. This tale of two "ugly" (by Hollywood standards only) people who saw each other as beautiful through the eyes of love was pure sentiment—but her sincerity miraculously saved it. She displayed versatility again, playing a mute servant girl marked for murder in Robert Siodmak's breathtakingly suspenseful *The Spiral Staircase*.

Till the End of Time was less interesting, but *Gentleman's Agreement* offered a complex part as the seemingly liberal society woman who was bigoted underneath.

After that, the quality of her roles temporarily fell off with a strained comedy, *Mother Didn't Tell Me* and an artificial soap opera, *Invitation*. She stole *Three Coins in the Fountain* from her younger co-stars Jean Peters and Maggie McNamara and accomplished the same feat in *A Summer Place*. She was glowing in the unforgettable *Friendly Persuasion* and deeply affecting in *The Dark at the Top of the Stairs*. Even in a pitifully contrived teenage romance like *Susan Slade*, she brought humanity to a shallow character.

She returned to the stage in 1976 to play in "The Night of the Iguana," but she has shied away from films for the last decade. It's a loss to moviegoers because Dorothy McGuire is one of the film industry's very best actresses.

FILMOGRAPHY

1943

Claudia ★★★★

1945

A Tree Grows in Brooklyn ★★★★
The Enchanted Cottage ★★★★

1946

The Spiral Staircase ★★★★
Claudia and David ★★★
Till the End of Time ★★★

1947

Gentleman's Agreement ★★★★

1950

Mister 880 ★★★★
Mother Didn't Tell Me ★★★

1951

Callaway Went Thataway ★★★
I Want You ★★★

1952

Invitation ★★★

1954

Make Haste to Live ★★★
Three Coins in the Fountain ★★★

1955

Trial ★★★

1956

Friendly Persuasion ★★★★

1957

Old Yeller ★★★

1959

The Remarkable Mr. Pennypacker ★★★
This Earth Is Mine ★★★★
A Summer Place ★★★★

1960

The Dark at the Top of the Stairs ★★★★
Swiss Family Robinson ★★★

1961

Susan Slade ★★★

1963

Summer Magic ★★★

1965

The Greatest Story Ever Told ★★★

1971

Flight of the Doves ★★★

1973

Jonathan Livingston Seagull (voice only)

SHIRLEY MACLAINE
★★★ 2.90 STARS

Shirley MacLaine has always been unique—a warm, natural, attractively average girl with a subtle "hippie" streak. As she grew older, her beauty and talent deepened. From a pleasing actress, she became a brilliant one.

She was born Shirley MacLean Beatty, in 1934, in Richmond, Virginia, and her brother, Warren Beatty, came along three years later. She studied ballet and got her big break with a stroke of luck in "Pajama Game." Carol Haney was the star of the show and couldn't go on, and MacLaine, her understudy, filled in. Hal Wallis, who was in the audience that particular night, cast her in one of Hitchcock's few financial disasters, *The Trouble with Harry. Artists and Models* with Jerry Lewis didn't push her forward either, and she tested unsuccessfully for *Marjorie Morningstar.* However, she gave a superb performance as Anthony Quinn's daughter in *Hot Spell.*

Some Came Running was the movie that solidified her stardom; she was the not-too-bright hooker who sacrificed her life to save Frank Sinatra. An Oscar nomination and glowing reactions brought other fine parts (Laurette Taylor's son expressed sorrow that his mother, the author of *Some Came Running,* hadn't been alive to see the performance). *Ask Any Girl* demonstrated her flair for comedy though the script wasn't up to the breezy bestseller version. *Can-Can* had been one of Cole Porter's weakest Broadway musicals despite some good songs, and it didn't work on film either. . . though MacLaine and Frank Sinatra gave it their best.

Shirley MacLaine with Jack Lemmon in *The Apartment*.

She was expected to win an Academy Award for *The Apartment*, a touching and original tale about an executive who lent his apartment to married businessmen for their secret trysts. Elizabeth Taylor had just recovered from a near-fatal pneumonia, however, and the Academy gave her the Oscar, a sympathy nod for *Butterfield 8*. MacLaine was heard to comment at the ceremonies, "I lost to a tracheotomy." Neither *All in a Night's Work* nor *Two Loves* offered a similar opportunity, nor did *The Children's Hour*, a sluggish drama about repressed lesbianism complete with a suicide ending. MacLaine was miscast in *Two for the Seesaw* though she brought in the crowds to *Irma La Douce* ("a monstrous mutation," critic Pauline Kael called it). *What a Way To Go!* also, inexplicably, made money. *Sweet Charity* was Bob Fosse's first major directorial effort and drove him back to Broadway when the public ignored the picture. After *Charity,* MacLaine wrote a brilliant autobiography, Don't Fall Off the Mountain, and shrewdly expanded her artistic agenda with an outstanding Las Vegas act.

Hit movies still eluded her, despite *Desperate Characters*, which got raves and *The Possession of Joel Delaney,* which didn't. *The Turning Point* provided rescue, and she revealed a fire, a depth, and a tenderness not apparent in her other work. She played a former dancer, jealous of friend Anne Bancroft's success. She followed with a similar artistic and commercial success in *Being There*, opposite co-star Peter Sellers.

MacLaine's talent is limitless. Like her brother Warren Beatty, she has more than mere ability—she has intelligence, imagination, and business acumen.

FILMOGRAPHY

1955

The Trouble with Harry ★★★
Artists and Models ★★

1956

Around the World in 80 Days ★★

1958

The Sheepman ★★★
The Matchmaker ★★★
Hot Spell ★★★★

1959

Some Came Running ★★★★
Ask Any Girl ★★★★
Career ★★★

1960

Ocean's 11 (cameo)
Can-Can ★★★
The Apartment ★★★★

1961

All in a Night's Work ★★★
Two Loves ★★

1962

The Children's Hour ★★
My Geisha ★★
Two for the Seesaw ★★

1963

Irma La Douce ★★★

Shirley MacLaine in *Being There.*

1964

What a Way to Go! ★★
The Yellow Rolls Royce ★★★

1965

John Goldfarb, Please Come Home ★★

1966

Gambit ★★★

1967

Woman Times Seven ★★

1968

The Bliss of Mrs. Blossom ★★

1969

Sweet Charity ★★★

1970

Two Mules for Sister Sara ★★★

1972

Desperate Characters ★★★★
The Possession of Joel Delaney ★★★

1973

The Year of the Woman (documentary)

1975

The Other Half of the Sky: A China Memoir (documentary: screenplay, co-direction)

1977

The Turning Point ★★★★

1979

Being There ★★★★

1980

Loving Couples ★★★
A Change of Seasons ★★★

FRED MACMURRAY
★★★ 3.06 STARS

Fred MacMurray never won an Oscar, possibly because he made acting look easy. He was equally nimble in comedy and drama, and when he grew older, he managed the transition gracefully to Robert Young-like "daddy" roles.

MacMurray was born in 1908, in Kankakee, Illinois. He concentrated initially on being a saxophone player (his father was a concert violinist), and he also sang. His saxophone skill was utilized in a Broadway show, "Roberta," but acting took precedence after a co-starring appearance with Claudette Colbert in *The Gilded Lily.* He was the regular Joe; Ray Milland played the aristocrat. In *Alice Adams*, another notable advance, he and Katharine Hepburn were excellent in one of the best (and most underrated) comedy-dramas of the 1930s. The MacMurray/Colbert combination worked again in *The Bride Comes Home*, and he was comfortable out west in *Trail of the Lonesome Pine* and *The Texas Rangers.*

He and Colbert tried something more serious in *Maid of Salem*, and he co-starred with Frances Farmer in one of her few good vehicles, *Exclusive*. Several good pictures with Carole Lombard followed, including: *Hands Across the Table*, *The Princess Comes Across*, and *True Confession*. He had more of an acting chance than usual in *Remember the Night* opposite Barbara Stanwyck, as a D.A. who looked after and then fell in love with a shoplifter. Both stars had the advantage of working with a fine Preston Sturges script. He marked time with his next few films, *Rangers of Fortune*, *One Night in Lisbon*, *New York Town*, and *The Forest Rangers*.

MacMurray had to be talked into making *Double Indemnity.* He and Stanwyck were absolutely superb as the two calculating killers who did away with Stanwyck's husband. MacMurray wasn't nominated for an Oscar but Stanwyck was. Both should have won. After this high, he did a couple of mediocre vehicles, *Practically Yours*, *Murder He Says*, *Where Do We Go From Here?* and *Suddenly It's Spring*. He rebounded with a hilarious comedy, *The Egg and I*, playing opposite Claudette Colbert as chicken farmers. The plot was based on fact and turned out to be one of the largest grossers of 1947. *Family Honeymoon*, again with Colbert, was also pleasant but less popular. The movies that followed were *neither* pleasant nor popular: *Singapore*, *The Miracle of the Bells* (which hastened Sinatra's demise at the box office), *Don't Trust Your Husband*, and *Fair Wind to Java*.

The winds shifted in a more positive direction when he did *The Caine Mutiny*, giving an outstanding performance as the slimy troublemaker who incited the mutiny.

He appeared with Kim Novak in *Pushover* and had one more fine part as the married man who drove Shirley MacLaine to near-suicide in *The Apartment*. A series of Disney pictures, *The Absent-Minded Professor, Bon Voyage!*, and *Son of Flubber*, sustained his popularity.

He lives quietly today with second wife June Haver, enjoying a wealthy retirement and indulging in one of his favorite hobbies ("I fix stuff...got the only workshop in Brentwood with wall-to-wall carpeting").

Fred MacMurray in *At Gunpoint*.

FILMOGRAPHY

1928

Girls Gone Wild (bit)

1934

Friends of Mr. Sweeney★★★

1935

Grand Old Girl★★★
The Gilded Lily★★★★
Car 99★★
Men Without Names★★
Alice Adams★★★★
Hands Across the Table★★★★
The Bride Comes Home★★★★

1936

Champagne Waltz★★★
Maid of Salem★★★
Swing High-Swing Low★★★
Exclusive★★★
True Confession★★★
Trail of the Lonesome Pine★★★
Thirteen Hours By Air★★★

1938

Cocoanut Grove★★★
Sing You Sinners★★★★
Men With Wings★★★
The Princess Comes Across★★★★
The Texas Rangers★★★

1939

Cafe Society★★★
Invitation to Happiness★★★
Honeymoon in Bali★★★★

1940

Remember the Night★★★★
Little Old New York★★★
Too Many Husbands★★★
Rangers of Fortune★★★

1941

Virginia★★★
One Night in Lisbon★★★
Dive Bomber★★★
New York Town★★★

1942

The Lady Is Willing★★★
Take A Letter Darling★★★
The Forest Rangers★★★
Star Spangled Rhythm★★★

1943

Flight For Freedom★★★
Above Suspicion★★★
No Time for Love★★★

1944

Standing Room Only★★★
And the Angels Sing★★★★
Double Indemnity★★★★

1945

Practically Yours★★★
Where Do We Go From Here?★★★
Murder He Says★★★
Captain Eddie★★★

1946

Pardon My Past★★★
Smoky★★★

1947

Suddenly It's Spring★★★
The Egg and I★★★★
Singapore★★★

1948

On Our Merry Way★★
The Miracle of the Bells★★
Don't Trust Your Husband★★★

1949

Family Honeymoon★★★
Father Was a Fullback★★★

1950

Borderline★★★
Never a Dull Moment★★

1951

A Millionaire for Christy★★★
Callaway Went Thataway★★★

1953

Fair Wind to Java★★
The Moonlighter★★★

1954

The Caine Mutiny★★★★
Pushover★★★★
A Woman's World★★★

Fred MacMurray in *Pushover*.

1955

The Fair Horizons★★★
The Rains of Ranchipur★★★
At Gunpoint★★★

1956

There's Always Tomorrow★★★

1957

Guns for a Coward★★★
Quantez★★★

1958

Day of the Badman★★★

1959

Good Day For a Hanging★★★
The Shaggy Dog★★★
Face of a Fugitive★★★
The Oregon Trail★★★

1960

The Apartment★★★★

1961

The Absent-Minded Professor★★★

1962

Bon Voyage!★★★

1963

Son of Flubber★★★

1964

Kisses for My President★★

1966

Follow Me Boys!★★★

1967

The Happiest Millionaire★★

1973

Charley and the Angel★★★

1978

The Swarm★★

KRISTY MCNICHOL
★ ★ ★ 3.17 STARS

Kristy McNichol has already been showered with more praise than many actors receive in a lifetime. Director Ronald F. Maxwell said she was "incapable of a false move or gesture," and co-star Tatum O'Neal in *Little Darlings* added, "She's a perfectionist...and she's absolutely right."

McNichol was born in 1962, and her mother Carolynne, a secretary at the William Morris Agency, concentrated on promoting Kristy's career. Her efforts resulted in TV work in "Apple's Way," "Love, American Style," "The Bionic Woman," and "Starsky and Hutch." She also had a long-running role as Buddy Lawrence in "Family," still perhaps the most haunting, beautifully acted series television has ever presented.

McNichol was excellent in the TV movies *Like Mom Like Me* with Linda Lavin and *The Summer of My German Soldier* with Bruce Davison. Burt Reynolds selected her to play his daughter in *The End*; they had a strong personal chemistry which, unfortunately, did not show up in the film. *Little Darlings* gave her a star part as the tough kid who competed with rich girl Tatum O'Neal to see who could lose her virginity first. It was a silly situation rescued by McNichol's work, particularly in scenes with Matt Dillon. She then appeared in *The Night the Lights Went Out in Georgia*, playing the sister of a country singer. She was fine in *Only When I Laugh* and tried to laugh through the critically panned *The Pirate Movie*. She has also made *White Dog*, but U.S. distributors have been reluctant to release it, despite good European reviews. McNichol's dream is to be a rock star—unfortunately, since her ability in this area appears less striking than her acting talent.

Kristy McNichol in *Only When I Laugh*.

FILMOGRAPHY

1978

The End ★ ★ ★

1980

Little Darlings ★ ★ ★ ★

1981

The Night the Lights Went Out in Georgia ★ ★ ★

1982

The Pirate Movie ★ ★
Only When I Laugh ★ ★ ★
White Dog ★ ★ ★ ★

STEVE MCQUEEN
★ ★ ★ 3.04 STARS

Steve McQueen was an ideal rebel-hero and his first wife Neile called him "a wild man." He himself said, "A lot of people think that actors are a little strange, unmasculine, not like the guys who are riveters at Lockheed and things like that. I had to beat the actor's image."

The man whom Hedda Hopper praised for his don't-give-a-damn manner was born Terrence Steven McQueen, in 1930, in Slater, Missouri. He was a lumberjack, bartender, and numbers runner before joining New York's Neighborhood Playhouse. He replaced Ben Gazzara on Broadway in "Hatful of Rain" and then made some poor movies *Somebody Up There Likes Me* and *The Blob*. Fortunately, Frank Sinatra saw him on TV in his series "Wanted: Dead or Alive," and cast him in *Never So Few*. Sammy Davis, Jr. had been slated for the role but was removed by Sinatra after an argument between them. He was an excellent seventh of *The Magnificent Seven* and superb as *The War Lover*. Screenwriter Howard Koch was dissatisfied with the final product, but he still admired McQueen's work in *The War Lover*.

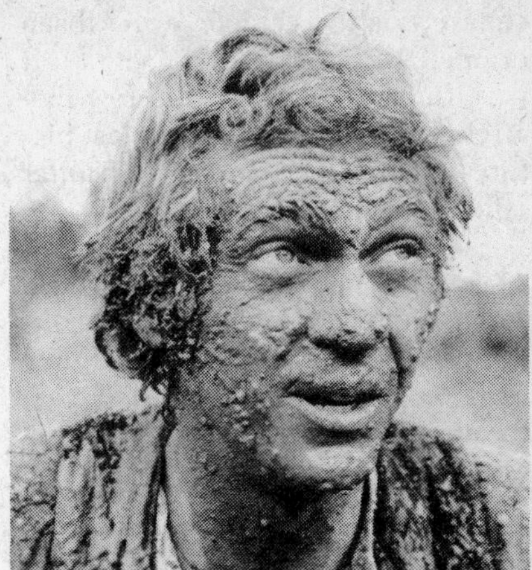
Steve McQueen in *The Reivers*.

The Great Escape made him a star, and *Love With the Proper Stranger* was a flavorful romance. McQueen played a shiftless musician who impregnated Natalie Wood. *Soldier in the Rain* failed, but moviegoers heartily approved of *The Cincinnati Kid*. Edward G. Robinson stole the picture, but McQueen was also excellent. He dominated in *Nevada Smith* and *The Sand Pebbles*. Although saddled with a mechanical leading lady in *The Thomas Crown Affair* (Faye Dunaway), he still gave the film a posh, glossy quality that made it worth watching.

Bullitt was the first smash that he carried singlehandedly. It's also the first film to concentrate heavily on car chases, setting a style for thrillers that has lasted to this day. He was hard on directors, and according to critic Sheilah Graham, "McQueen will never forget an injury." Everyone endured his temperament because he had become (along with Paul Newman) a box-office king. He co-starred with Newman in the record-breaking *The Towering Inferno*. *Papillon* was also a hit, an overlong and mercilessly depressing study of a prisoner who kept escaping and getting caught by authorities.

He left films after his divorce and remarriage to Ali McGraw, whom he met during the filming of *The Getaway*. When that union broke up, he returned to films in an uncharacteristic vehicle (an Ibsen drama, *An Enemy of the People*). It was too slow-moving, and few theatres booked it. McQueen's last pictures, *Tom Horn* and *The Hunter* failed to attract his old public.

Steve McQueen was only fifty years old when he died of cancer in 1980. Surprisingly, he has no cult, no posthumous reputation; for a man of his popularity and image, the absence of lingering public interest is inexplicable.

Steve McQueen with Aneta Corseaut in *The Blob.*

FILMOGRAPHY

1956

Somebody Up There Likes Me (bit)

1958

Never Love a Stranger★★★
The Blob★★

1959

Never So Few★★★
The Great St. Louis Bank Robbery★★★

1960

The Magnificent Seven★★★★

1961

The Honeymoon Machine★★

1962

Hell Is For Heroes★★★
The War Lover★★★★

1963

The Great Escape★★★★
Soldier in the Rain★★★
Love With the Proper Stranger★★★★

1965

Baby the Rain Must Fall★★★
The Cincinnati Kid★★★★

1966

Nevada Smith★★★
The Sand Pebbles★★★

1967

The Thomas Crown Affair★★★
Bullitt★★★★

1969

The Reivers★★★

1971

On Any Sunday (documentary)
Le Mans★★★

1972

Junior Bonner★★★
The Getaway★★

1973

Papillon★★★

1974

The Towering Inferno★★★

1979

An Enemy of the People★★

1980

Tom Horn★★
The Hunter★★★

ANNA MAGNANI
★★★½ 3.42 STARS

An unidentified actress once commented about Anna Magnani: "It isn't necessary to look so crummy." By the bejeweled, minkcovered standards of a Joan Crawford, Magnani was certainly an eyesore, but she could act rings around every Hollywood fashion plate.

She was born in Alexandria, Egypt, in 1908. Early stage work led to a film, *La Cieca di Sorrento*, and she continued working on the stage in "The Petrified Forest" and "Anna Christie." Magnani marked time in *Cavalleria, Teresa Venerdi,* and *La Fortuna viene dal Cielo*, before conquering world audiences with director Rossellini's *Open City.* She also played in a comedy, *Abbasso La Miseria*, and a drama, *L'Onorevole Angelina*, that won her a Best Actress Award at the Venice Film Festival.

She was personally involved with Roberto Rossellini until Ingrid Bergman appeared on the scene. An embittered Magnani went off on her own to make Luchino Visconti's *Bellissima*, playing a Rome stage mother.

Her debut in American movies came when playwright Tennessee Williams persuaded her to do *The Rose Tattoo*. Judith Crist summed up the general attitude when she said, "Magnani...ah!!" She won an Oscar, a New York Film Critics award, and a BFA award. Her lusty portrait of a grieving widow who found love with Burt Lancaster led to another Paramount picture, *Wild Is the Wind*. It was at least as good as its predecessor, but somehow the public failed to respond. She tried another Tennessee Williams piece, *The Fugitive Kind*, a dreary, endless drama with Marlon Brando. It wasn't her fault, but the movie was a critical and financial disaster.

She returned to Europe and did *The Passionate Thief, Mamma Roma,* and *Le Magot de Josefá.* Though *The Secret of Santa Vittoria* was a fairly feeble tale of Italian villagers hiding bottles of wine from the Germans, Magnani and Anthony Quinn were properly lusty and passionate. She died in 1973, just as her vogue was winding down.

FILMOGRAPHY

1927

Scampolo (bit)

1934

La Cieca di Sorrento ★★★
Tempo Massimo ★★★

1936

Cavalleria ★★★
Trenta Secondi d'Amore ★★★

1938

Tarakanova ★★★★

1940

Una Lampada alla Finestra ★★★

1941

Finalmente Soli ★★★
La Fuggitiva ★★★
Teresa Venerdi ★★★

1942

La Fortuna viene dal Cielo ★★★★

1943

L'Avventura di Annabella ★★★
Campo dè Fiori ★★★
L'Ultima Carrozzella ★★★★
T'amero sempre ★★★

1944

Il Fiore sotto gli Occhi ★★★

1945

Open City ★★★★
Abbasso la Miseria ★★★★

Anna Magnani in *The Secret of Santa Vittoria*.

1946

Un Uomo ritorna ★★★
Davanti a lui tremava tutta Roma ★★★★
Il Bandito ★★★★
Abbasso la Ricchezza ★★★

1947

Lo Sconosciuto de San Marino ★★★★
Quartetto Pazzo ★★★★
L'Onorevole Angelina ★★★★
Assunta Spina ★★★★

1948

L'Amore ★★★★
Molti Sogni per le Strade ★★★★

1950

Vulcano ★★★★

1951

Bellissima ★★★★

1952

Camicie rosse ★★★

1953

The Golden Coach ★★★★
Siamo Donne ★★★★

1955

The Rose Tattoo ★★★★

1956

The Awakening ★★★

1957

Wild Is the Wind ★★★★

1958

Hell in the City ★★★

1960

The Fugitive Kind ★★
The Passionate Thief ★★★

1962

Mamma Roma ★★★

1963

Le Magot de Joséfa ★★★

1964

Volles Herz und leere Taschen ★★★

1965

Made in Italy ★★★

1969

The Secret of Santa Vittoria ★★★

1972

1870 ★★★
Fellini's Roma (cameo)

DOROTHY MALONE
★★★ 3.13 STARS

Dorothy Malone has accomplished a near-impossible feat, maintaining a lengthy career in the face of third-rate material.

Malone (Dorothy Eloise Maloney) was born in 1925, in Chicago. She pursued modeling as well as acting and was discovered by a talent scout at Southern Methodist University. Her film debut, *The Falcon and the Co-Eds*, was, unfortunately, an accurate indicator of what was to follow: *One Mysterious Night*, *Too Young to Know*, and *Janie Gets Married*. She had a small but striking part as a sex-starved bookseller in *The Big Sleep*, but *Two Guys from Texas*, *South of St. Louis*, and *Colorado Territory* pulled her back down again. Malone brought charm to the indifferent musical remake of *Strawberry Blonde*, *One Sunday Afternoon*, though co-stars Don Defore and Dennis Morgan were a problem. Not much acting was required in *The Killer That Stalked New York* and *Loophole*.

Her big chance came in *Written on the Wind* as Robert Stack's nymphomaniac sister—a steamy, pulsating performance which won her an Oscar. She made a gallant attempt to pump life into the story of Diana Barrymore's life, *Too Much, Too Soon*, but the script was a formidable obstacle. TV came to the rescue with "Peyton Place," and when the show wound up, Malone continued in features in *The Man Who Would Not Die* and *Golden Rendezvous*. Unless a good script comes along, Dorothy Malone may continue playing second rate melodramas.

FILMOGRAPHY

(billed as Dorothy Maloney)

1943

The Falcon and the Co-Eds ★★

1944

One Mysterious Night ★★
Show Business ★★
Hollywood Canteen ★★

(billed as Dorothy Malone)

1945

Too Young to Know ★★★

1946

The Big Sleep ★★★★
Janie Gets Married ★★
Night and Day ★★★

1948

Two Guys from Texas ★★★
To the Victor ★★★
One Sunday Afternoon ★★★★

1949

Colorado Territory ★★★
Flaxy Martin ★★★
South of St. Louis ★★★

1950

Mrs. O'Malley and Mr. Malone ★★
The Killer That Stalked New York ★★★
The Man From Nevada ★★★
Convicted ★★★

1951

Saddle Legion ★★★

1952

The Bushwackers ★★★

1953

Law and Order ★★★
Scared Stiff ★★★
Jack Slade ★★★
Torpedo Alley ★★★

1954

The Lone Gun ★★★
Loophole ★★★
The Pushover ★★★
Security Risk ★★★
Private Hell No. 36 ★★★
Young at Heart ★★★★
Fast and Furious ★★★

1955

Battle Cry ★★★★
At Gunpoint ★★★
Five Guns West ★★★
Tall Man Riding ★★★
Sincerely Yours ★★
Artists and Models ★★

1956

Pillars of the Sky ★★★
Written on the Wind ★★★★
Tension at Table Rock ★★★

1957

Man of a Thousand Faces ★★★★
Tip Off on a Dead Jockey ★★★
Quantez ★★★
Tarnished Angels ★★★★

Dorothy Malone with Robert Stack in *Written on the Wind.*

1958

Too Much, Too Soon ★★★

1959

Warlock ★★★

1960

The Last Voyage ★★★

1961

The Last Sunset ★★★

1963

Beach Party ★★

1964

Fate Is the Hunter ★★★

1969

The Exhibition ★★★

1975

The Man Who Would Not Die ★★★
Abduction ★★★

1977

Golden Rendezvous ★★★

1979

Good Luck, Miss Wyckoff ★★★
Winter Kills ★★★

1980

The Day Time Ended ★★★

JAYNE MANSFIELD
★½ 1.63 STARS

Many glamour girls climb to the top on their curves. Once they do, however, they generally make an effort to learn their craft to insure their staying power after their physical charms have faded. Jayne Mansfield, however, was too busy chasing publicity and fame to give this possibility much attention.

She was born Vera Jayne Palmer, in 1933, in Bryn Mawr, Pennsylvania. After a stormy adolescence, she fought and clawed her way into movies. Her measurements—40-18½-36—got her started in the film *Pete Kelly's Blues*. She showed a glimmer of promise as a moll in Edward G. Robinson's *Illegal*, and *The Girl Can't Help It* was a fun if brainless farce. Broadway provided a hit vehicle with *Will Success Spoil Rock Hunter?*, the only film that ever brought her good reviews.

The Wayward Bus was an indifferent version of a Steinbeck novel, even though she calmed down and tried to play a character. A Cary Grant comedy, *Kiss Them for Me*, offered momentary prestige, but after that, she made only failures like *Panic Button* and *The Fat Spy*. She died in a car accident in 1967.

Jayne Mansfield.

FILMOGRAPHY

1955

Pete Kelly's Blues ★★
Illegal ★★

1956

Hell on Frisco Bay ★★
Female Jungle ★★
The Girl Can't Help It ★★★

1957

The Burglar ★★
The Wayward Bus ★★★
Will Success Spoil Rock Hunter? ★★★
Kiss Them for Me ★★

1958

The Sheriff of Fractured Jaw ★★

1960

Gli Amori di Ercole ★
It Takes a Thief ★★
Too Hot to Handle ★

1961

The George Raft Story ★★

1962

It Happened in Athens ★

1963

Promises! Promises! ★

1964

Panic Button ★
Dog Eat Dog ★
Primitive Love ★

1966

The Fat Spy ★
Las Vegas Hillbillies ★

1967

A Guide for the Married Man (cameo)
Las Vegas by Night ★

1968

The Wild Wild World of Jayne Mansfield ★
Single Room Furnished ★

FREDRIC MARCH
★★★½ 3.36 STARS

Fredric March once commented, "To me, characterizing is the whole fun of acting . . . *every* part is a character part." The results have been memorable. March attempted a wide variety of roles, and he was excellent in nearly all of them.

March (Ernest Frederick McIntyre Bickel) was born in 1897, in Racine, Wisconsin. He was a bank teller for a while ("Inside me there was a bursting love of the theatre"), then a model, until progressing to a featured role in a 1927 play, "The Devil in the Cheese." His solid, firm, self-possessed air was beneficial in his early films, *The Dummy, The Wild Party, Footlights and Fools*, and *Manslaughter*. He did the definitive screen version of *Dr. Jekyll and Mr. Hyde* which, years later, would be praised lavishly by critics unhappy with Spencer Tracy's interpretation. He won an Academy Award for the part. There was a De Mille spectacle, *The Sign of the Cross* and a drawing room comedy, *Design for Living* with co-stars Gary

Cooper and Miriam Hopkins. However, out of the trio, he was the only believable element. Norma Shearer was Elizabeth to his Robert Browning in *The Barretts of Wimpole Street*, another vehicle that buffs remembered more fondly after the 1957 remake. March was an excellent "Browning" and a fine Vronsky in *Anna Karenina*. His wife, Florence Eldridge, played opposite him in *Mary of Scotland*. Although they were a celebrated stage team, they lacked the proper chemistry on film.

The 1937 version of *A Star Is Born* was a success, due almost entirely to his superb portrait of an actor on the skids. Then, Broadway claimed him for a while in "The Skin of Our Teeth," "The American Way," and "Years Ago." He made a couple of fair pictures, *Susan and God*, *Victory*, and *So Ends Our Night* and then a great one, *The Best Years of Our Lives*. Among an excellent cast—Dana Andrews, Myrna Loy, and Teresa Wright—his performance had the most authority, the strongest correlation to real life. The movie won him his second Best Actor Oscar.

Fredric March in *Executive Suite*.

March gave another one of his greatest portrayals as Willy Loman in Stanley Kramer's adaptation of *Death of a Salesman*. He captured all the pathos and disillusionment of the title character, living under fantasies of his success and basically knowing better. Puzzlingly, the universality of this protagonist which made it a Broadway hit didn't pull in moviegoers. *Executive Suite* and *The Desperate Hours* offered meaty parts, and he was convincing as a businessman married to his work in the otherwise stilted *The Man in the Gray Flannel Suit*. Broadway kept him busy for two years in his greatest triumph, "Long Day's Journey Into Night." His film comeback, unfortunately, was disappointing; he played the Edward G. Robinson stage part in *Middle of the Night*. He was somehow unbelievable as the aging Jewish man in love with a young girl. His co-star Kim Novak was a further problem; Gena Rowlands had done it on Broadway. However, his clashes with Spencer Tracy were exciting to watch in *Inherit the Wind*, and he was effective as the President in *Seven Days in May*. March died in 1975.

FILMOGRAPHY

1929

The Dummy ★★★
The Wild Party ★★★
The Studio Murder Mystery ★★★
Jealousy ★★★
Paris Bound ★★★
Footlights and Fools ★★★
The Marriage Playground ★★★

1930

Sarah and Son ★★★
Ladies Love Brutes ★★★
True to the Navy ★★★
Paramount on Parade ★★★
Manslaughter ★★★
Laughter ★★★

1931

The Royal Family of Broadway ★★★
Honor Among Lovers ★★★
The Night Angel ★★★
My Sin ★★★

1932

Dr. Jekyll and Mr. Hyde ★★★★
Strangers in Love ★★★
Merrily We Go to Hell ★★★
Make Me a Star (cameo)
Smilin' Through ★★★★
The Sign of the Cross ★★★

1933

Tonight Is Ours ★★★
The Eagle and the Hawk ★★★★
Design for Living ★★★★

1934

All of Me ★★★
Death Takes a Holiday ★★★★
Good Dame ★★★
The Affairs of Cellini ★★★
The Barretts of Wimpole Street ★★★★
We Live Again ★★★

1935

Les Miserables ★★★★
Anna Karenina ★★★★
The Dark Angel ★★★★

1936

Mary of Scotland ★★★
The Road to Glory ★★★
Anthony Adverse ★★★

1937

A Star Is Born ★★★★
Nothing Sacred ★★★★

1938

The Buccaneer ★★★
There Goes My Heart ★★★

1939

Trade Winds ★★★★

1940

Susan and God ★★★
Victory ★★★★

1941

So Ends Our Night ★★★★
One Foot in Heaven ★★★★
Bedtime Story ★★★

1942

I Married a Witch ★★★★

1944

The Adventures of Mark Twain ★★★
Tomorrow the World ★★★★

1946

The Best Years of Our Lives ★★★★

1948

Another Part of the Forest ★★★★
An Act of Murder ★★★★

1949

Christopher Columbus ★★★

1951

Death of a Salesman ★★★★

1952

It's a Big Country ★★★

1953

Man on a Tightrope ★★★

1954

Executive Suite ★★★

1955

The Desperate Hours ★★★★
The Bridges at Toko-Ri ★★★

1956

Alexander the Great ★★★
The Man in the Gray Flannel Suit ★★★★

1959

Middle of the Night ★★

1960

Inherit the Wind ★★★

1961

The Young Doctors ★★★

1962

The Condemned of Altona ★★★

1964

Seven Days in May ★★★★

1967

Hombre ★★★★

1970

Tick Tick Tick ★★★

1973

The Iceman Cometh ★★★★

HERBERT MARSHALL
★★★½ 3.28 STARS

An elegant, urbane, and eminently polished leading man, Herbert Marshall defined Hollywood's image of aristrocratic breeding and class.

He was born in London, in 1890, and became a business manager before trying the stage. A war wound forced amputation of his right leg, but he overcame the handicap and went on to make a string of notable pictures including: *Blonde Venus* with Marlene Dietrich, *Four Frightened People* with Claudette Colbert, and *Riptide* with Norma Shearer. His mannered willfulness was put to its most well-suited use in director Ernst Lubitsch's continental farce, *Trouble in Paradise*.

He was Greta Garbo's leading man in the tedious film version of Somerset Maugham's novel about an unfaithful wife, *The Painted Veil*, and again coped with adultery (with Bette Davis) in *The Letter*. Marshall's performance was superb, and he also made a strong impression in a Hitchcock thriller, *Foreign Correspondent*. Bette Davis betrayed him again and even killed him in *The Little Foxes*, and he underplayed beautifully in the face of her snarling mannerisms. Joan Fontaine's *Ivy* dispatched him with poison, but he was on safer ground with the young Margaret O'Brien in *The Secret Garden*.

In the 1950's, Marshall was relegated to character parts, which he accomplished with ease. His later films were mostly low-grade costume epics and murder mysteries. He continued to act until his death in 1966.

FILMOGRAPHY

1927

Mumsie ★★★

1928

Dawn ★★★

1929

The Letter ★★★

1930

Murder ★★★★

1931

The Calendar ★★★
Michael and Mary ★★★
Secrets of a Secretary ★★★

1932

The Faithful Heart ★★★
Blonde Venus ★★★★
Trouble in Paradise ★★★★
Evenings for Sale ★★★

1933

Clear All Wires ★★★
The Solitaire Man ★★★
I Was a Spy ★★★

1934

Four Frightened People ★★★
Riptide ★★★★
Outcast Lady ★★★
The Painted Veil ★★★★

1935

The Good Fairy ★★★★
The Flame Within ★★★
Accent on Youth ★★★★
The Dark Angel ★★★★
If You Could Only Cook ★★★

1936

The Lady Consents ★★★
Till We Meet Again ★★★★
Forgotten Faces ★★★
Girls' Dormitory ★★★
A Woman Rebels ★★★
Make Way for a Lady ★★★

1937

Angel ★★
Breakfast for Two ★★★

1938

Mad About Music ★★★★
Always Goodbye ★★★
Woman Against Woman ★★★

Herbert Marshall in *Evenings for Sale.*

1939

Zaza ★★★

1940

A Bill of Divorcement ★★★
Foreign Correspondent ★★★
The Letter ★★★★

1941

Adventure in Washington ★★★
The Little Foxes ★★★★
When Ladies Meet ★★★
Kathleen ★★★

1943

The Moon and Sixpence ★★★★
Forever and a Day ★★★
Flight for Freedom ★★★
Young Ideas ★★★

1944

Andy Hardy's Blonde Trouble ★★★

1945

The Unseen ★★★★
The Enchanted Cottage ★★★★

1946

Crack-Up ★★★
The Razor's Edge ★★★

1947

Duel in the Sun ★★★★
Ivy ★★★★

1948

High Wall ★★★

1949

The Secret Garden ★★★★

1950

The Underworld Story ★★★

1951

Anne of the Indies ★★★

1952

Captain Blackjack ★ ★ ★

1953

Angel Face ★ ★ ★

1954

Riders to the Stars ★ ★ ★
Gog ★ ★ ★
The Black Shield of Falworth ★ ★ ★

1955

The Virgin Queen ★ ★ ★ ★

1956

Wicked As They Come ★ ★ ★

1957

The Weapon ★ ★ ★

1958

Stage Struck ★ ★ ★
The Fly ★ ★ ★

1960

College Confidential ★ ★ ★
Midnight Lace ★ ★ ★ ★

1961

Fever in the Blood ★ ★ ★

1962

Five Weeks in a Balloon ★ ★ ★

1963

The List of Adrian Messenger ★ ★ ★
The Caretakers ★ ★ ★

1965

The Third Day ★ ★ ★ ★

DEAN MARTIN
★ ★ ½ 2.42 STARS

When Jerry Lewis and Dean Martin broke up, most people expected Dean Martin's career to collapse. Few could have predicted his emergence as a fine dramatic actor. Fewer still would have expected the absence of Lewis to *improve* Martin's comedy gifts.

Martin (Dino Paul Crocetti) was born in 1917, in Steubenville, Ohio. A former prizefighter and steel mill laborer, he sang in local nightclubs until the Martin-Lewis partnership was forged. They stole their first movie, *My Friend Irma*, and went on to make a series of farces that delighted children and adults alike—*My Friend Irma Goes West* (not as good as the original), *At War With the Army*, *Sailor Beware*, *Jumping Jacks*, and *The Stooge*, which cast Martin as a drunk.

Hollywood or Bust was their last vehicle together, and Martin appeared in a strained farce, *Ten Thousand Bedrooms*, that failed badly at the box office. He compensated with *Some Came Running*, and co-star Shirley MacLaine commented, "Frank (Sinatra) should have tried harder, but Dean was marvelous." He was perfectly cast as the playwright Judy Holliday loved in *Bells Are Ringing* and gave an admirable dramatic account of himself as a dreamer stifled by two sisters, Wendy Hiller and Geraldine Page, in *Toys in the Attic*.

Kiss Me Stupid was an incredibly tasteless "comedy" and a flop, but Martin became Matt Helm in a successful action series including: *The Silencers*, *Murderers' Row*, and *The Ambushers*. His biggest hit was *Airport*, as the pilot who left Barbara Hale for Jacqueline Bisset. Martin gave the film's most natural performance even though Helen Hayes won the Oscar. Subsequent movies let him down (*Something Big*, *The Wrecking Crew*, and *Mr. Ricco*), but Martin has remained a surefire draw on TV.

Dean Martin in *Airport*.

FILMOGRAPHY

1949

My Friend Irma ★ ★ ★

1950

My Friend Irma Goes West ★ ★

1951

At War With the Army ★ ★
That's My Boy ★ ★

1952

Sailor Beware ★ ★ ★
Jumping Jacks ★ ★

1953

The Stooge ★ ★ ★
Scared Stiff ★ ★
The Caddy ★ ★ ★

1954

Money From Home ★ ★
Living It Up ★ ★
Three Ring Circus ★ ★

1955

You're Never Too Young ★ ★
Artists and Models ★ ★ ★

1956

Pardners ★ ★ ★
Hollywood or Bust ★ ★ ★

1957

Ten Thousand Bedrooms ★ ★

1958

The Young Lions ★ ★ ★

1959

Some Came Running ★ ★ ★ ★
Rio Bravo ★ ★ ★
Career ★ ★ ★

1960

Who Was That Lady? ★ ★ ★
Bells Are Ringing ★ ★ ★
Ocean's Eleven ★ ★

1961

All in a Night's Work ★ ★
Ada ★ ★

1962

Who's Got the Action? ★ ★
Sergeants 3 ★ ★

1963

Toys in the Attic ★ ★ ★
Four for Texas ★ ★
Who's Been Sleeping in My Bed? ★ ★ ★

1964

Kiss Me Stupid ★
What a Way to Go! ★ ★
Robin and the 7 Hoods ★ ★

1965

The Sons of Katie Elder ★ ★ ★
Marriage on the Rocks ★ ★

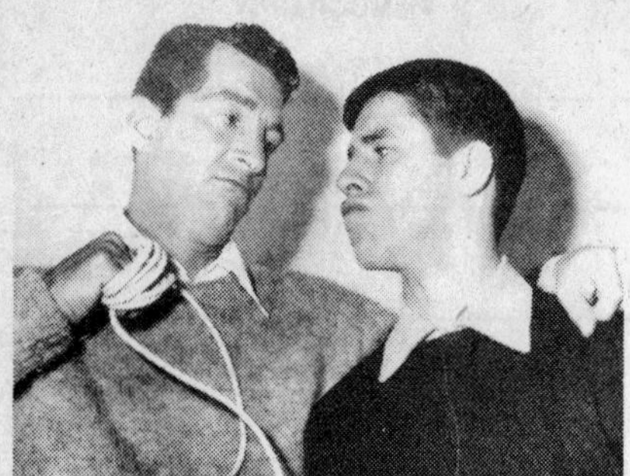

Dean Martin with Jerry Lewis.

1966

The Silencers★★★
Texas Across the River★★★
Murderers' Row★★★

1967

Rough Night in Jericho★★
The Ambushers★★

1968

How to Save a Marriage—and Ruin Your Life★★
Bandolero!★★
Five Card Stud★★

1969

The Wrecking Crew★★

1970

Airport★★★

1971

Something Big★★★
Showdown★★★

1975

Mr. Ricco★★

1982

The Cannonball Run★

STEVE MARTIN
★★★ 3.00 STARS

The L.A. Times said of Steve Martin, "His character is selfish, amoral, pompous, inept, garish, crude, rude, and allows the audience to delight in their superiority over the fool before them." However you define it, though, this Wild and Crazy Guy is hilariously funny.

Martin was born in Waco, Texas, probably in 1945, (he's evasive about his age). He first made his mark with a short film, *The Absent-Minded Waiter*, which was nominated for an Oscar. When he was twenty-one, he wrote for TV's "Smothers Brothers Comedy Hour," as well as "The Sonny and Cher Comedy Hour," "The Glen Campbell Goodtime Hour," "John Denver," and "Van Dyke and Company" (which brought an Emmy nomination). Guest appearances on the "Tonight Show" and stints on "NBC's Saturday Night Live" made him nationally known.

A few cameos followed in *The Muppet Movie* and *Sgt. Pepper's Lonely Hearts Club Band*. As a feature film star, he could have done better than *The Jerk*, playing the adopted son of a black sharecropping family. He had a challenging role in *Pennies From Heaven*. This peculiar, fanciful, sordid blend of melodrama and musical comedy showed his abilities as a dancer and actor but otherwise afforded little entertainment. He was more at home in *Dead Men Don't Wear Plaid* and the zany *The Man With Two Brains*. Critics have shrugged off his movies so far with a disdainful "excuuuu-se me," but the time will come when the vehicles are equal to his talent.

Steve Martin in *The Man With Two Brains*.

FILMOGRAPHY

(features only)

1978

Sgt. Pepper's Lonely Hearts Club Band (cameo)

1979

The Muppet Movie (cameo)
The Jerk ★★

1981

Pennies From Heaven ★★★★
Dead Men Don't Wear Plaid ★★★

1983

The Man With Two Brains ★★★

LEE MARVIN
★★★½ 3.28 STARS

Rugged and white-haired, with a low, gritty voice, Lee Marvin is a total original. No hero or villain has ever resembled him. Bogart had his kind of uniqueness, and though Marvin isn't quite Bogie's equal as an actor, his versatility is enjoyable.

Marvin was born in 1924, in New York City. He began as a plumber's assistant and then took up acting at New York's American Theatre Wing. Stage appearances included "Billy Budd" on Broadway and "A Streetcar Named Desire" on tour. His first noteworthy film part came in *Eight Iron Men*, and there were many action films that followed: *Down Among the Sheltering Palms*, *Seminole*, and *The Stranger Wore a Gun*. He murdered Gloria Grahame in the gripping *The Big Heat* and rode motorcycles with Marlon Brando in *The Wild One*. His warmth in *Pete Kelly's Blues* pointed out co-star Jack Webb's coldness, and he was mesmerizing as Paul Newman's army enemy in *The Rack*.

Marvin's popularity escalated with *Pillars of the Sky*, *Attack!*, and *Raintree County*, reaching a crescendo when he took on a dual role in the hilarious *Cat Ballou*. It won him an Oscar and more prestigious movies. *The Professionals* was a smash and *The Dirty Dozen* even bigger, a stirring tale of ex-cons molded into soldiers during World War II.

There was public applause for a thriller, *Point Blank*, though Marvin made a mistake when he attempted *Paint Your Wagon*, a hopeless musical undermined further by non-singing leads. He jumped back to action territory in *Monte Walsh* and *Pocket Money*.

In the last decade, Lee Marvin has turned in a host of memorable performances as the lead in John Frankenheimer's *The Iceman Cometh*; world-famous hobo in *Emperor of the North Pole*; ubiquitous sarge in *The Big Red One*; and the level-

Lee Marvin in *Paint Your Wagon*.

headed Mountie coolly chasing Charles Bronson in *Death Hunt*. Marvin is a marvel of consistency; one can only complain that he doesn't work more often.

FILMOGRAPHY

1951

You're in the Navy Now ★★★

1952

Hong Kong ★★★
We're Not Married ★★★
Diplomatic Courier ★★★
Duel at Silver Creek ★★★
Hangman's Knot ★★★
Eight Iron Men ★★★

1953

Seminole ★★★
The Glory Brigade ★★★
Down Among the Sheltering Palms ★★★
The Stranger Wore a Gun ★★★
The Big Heat ★★★★
Gun Fury ★★★

1954

The Wild One ★★★★
Gorilla at Large ★★★
The Caine Mutiny ★★★
The Raid ★★★

1955

Bad Day at Black Rock ★★★★
Violent Saturday ★★★
Not as a Stranger ★★★
A Life in the Balance ★★★
Pete Kelly's Blues ★★★★
I Died a Thousand Times ★★★
Shack Out on 101 ★★★

1956

Seven Men from Now ★★★
Pillars of the Sky ★★★
The Rack ★★★★
Attack! ★★★★

1957

Raintree County ★★★

1958

The Missouri Traveler ★★★

1961

The Comancheros ★★★

1962

The Man Who Shot Liberty Valance ★★★★

1963

Donovan's Reef ★★★

1964

The Killers ★★★★

1965

Cat Ballou ★★★★
Ship of Fools ★★★★

1966

The Professionals ★★★★

1967

The Dirty Dozen ★★★★
Point Blank ★★★★
Tonite Let's All Make Love in London (documentary)

1968

Hell in the Pacific ★★★

1969

Paint Your Wagon ★★

1970

Monte Walsh ★★★

1972

Pocket Money ★★★
Prime Cut ★★★

Lee Marvin with Gene Hackman in *Prime Cut*.

1973

Emperor of the North Pole ★★★★
The Iceman Cometh ★★★★

1974

The Spikes Gang ★★★
The Klansmen ★★★

1976

Shout at the Devil ★★★
Great Scout and Cathouse Thursday ★★★

1979

The Big Red One ★★★★
Avalanche Express ★★★

1981

Death Hunt ★★★

THE MARX BROTHERS
★★★½ 3.43 STARS

It took a long time for the Marx Brothers to make it to the top ("We played in towns," Groucho commented in his autobiography, "I would refuse to be buried in today even if the funeral was free and they tossed in a tombstone for lagniappe.") Fortunately, with the aid of a very determined mother, they persevered and became the funniest group of comics the screen has ever known.

Chico (Leonard Marx) was born in 1886; Harpo (Adolph, but also known as Arthur Marx), was born in 1888; Groucho (Julius Henry Marx) was born in 1890; and Zeppo (Herbert) was born in 1901. Their father was a tailor ("Misfit Sam," Groucho called him). Mother Minna, dramatized in a weak Broadway musical, "Minnie's Boys," got them started as "The Three Nightingales," then "The Six Musical Mascots." Their mother was one of the Mascots. Years of struggle finally resulted in a series of Broadway successes, "I'll Say She Is," "The Cocoanuts," and "Animal Crackers."

In 1929, they repeated their roles in the film adaptation of *The Cocoanuts.* A tedious musical subplot got in the way, but their zany routines delighted audiences. *Animal Crackers* featured the classic song, "Hooray for Captain Spaulding." Their best foil, Margaret Dumont, was in both films. In *Horse Feathers,* Groucho was cast as a college dean. Sentiments like his "Whatever it is, I'm against it" are partly responsible for his appeal to modern youthful audiences. Groucho was back in office again as president of a banana republic in *Duck Soup*, sharing the inspired lunacy with Harpo and Chico (as secret agents).

A Night at the Opera was their biggest box-office smash. Kitty Carlisle and Allan Jones offered some "dreadful duets" (critic Pauline Kael), but it just gave the brothers more to spoof. This film also fea-

The Marx Brothers.

tured the screamingly funny stateroom sequence. *A Day at the Races* was also enjoyable despite dreary romantic interludes, and *Room Service* had a semblance of a plot (producer and cohorts fought eviction from their hotel room). Most observers agreed that *At the Circus* was their weakest vehicle up to that time, but Groucho sang "Lydia the Tattooed Lady," and the Harold Arlen score helped. It has been generally conceded that the Marx Brothers lost heart in making movies after their mentor, famed producer Irving Thalberg, died.

There were a few more amusing pictures, *Go West, The Big Store*, and particularly *A Night in Casablanca. Love Happy* was a major disappointment; Groucho appeared only briefly, and his wit was sorely missed (Marilyn Monroe also had a bit part). The Marxes were also wasted in *The Story of Mankind*

Chico and Harpo worked sparingly after that, but Groucho kept busy, writing autobiographies (Groucho and Me, Memoirs of a Mangy Lover, The Groucho Letters) and hosted the popular television quiz show, "You Bet Your Life." He won a special Oscar shortly before he died and expressed sadness that his deceased brothers (Chico and Harpo who died, respectively, in 1961 and 1964) were not around to share it.

FILMOGRAPHY

1929

The Cocoanuts ★★★★

1930

Animal Crackers ★★★★

1931

Monkey Business ★★★

1932

Horse Feathers ★★★

1933

Duck Soup ★★★★

1935

A Night at the Opera ★★★★

1937

A Day at the Races ★★★

1938

Room Service ★★★★

1939

At the Circus ★★★

1940

Go West ★★★

1941

The Big Store ★★★★

1946

A Night in Casablanca ★★★★

1950

Love Happy ★★

1957

The Story of Mankind ★★★

The Marx Brothers and friend.

GROUCHO MARX ONLY

1947

Copacabana ★★★

1950

Mr. Music (cameo)

1951

Double Dynamite ★★★

1952

A Girl in Every Port ★★★

1957

Will Success Spoil Rock Hunter? (cameo)

1968

Skidoo ★★★

HARPO MARX ONLY

1925

Too Many Kisses ★★★

1943

Stage Door Canteen (cameo)

JAMES MASON
★★★ 3.18 STARS

James Mason isn't a flashy actor. He never had fan clubs or sex appeal. But he is a consummate performer, improving every film with his presence. James Mason has made a more lasting contribution to film than the dozens of showy actors who call attention to themselves.

Mason was born in 1909, in Huddersfield, England. After studying architecture at Cambridge, he drifted into acting. He quickly rose to leading parts, proving his talent in films generally unworthy of it. He was number one at the British box office from 1944 to 1947, mostly in evil roles in films like *The Man in Grey* and *Fanny by Gaslight*. But he gave a totally original performance in *The Seventh Veil* as Ann Todd's cold, neurotic, and yet oddly sympathetic piano teacher. Brilliant is the only word for his wounded fugitive in *Odd Man Out*. When he moved to Hollywood, he brought equal shadings of good and evil to his role of the blackmailer in *The Reckless Moment*. He made an excellent Field Marshall Rommel in *The Desert Fox. Five Fingers* was a superlatively written spy thriller using his dry wit to advantage, and he was a well-received Brutus in *Julius Caesar*. Critic Pauline Kael thought he stole *A Star Is Born* from Judy Garland. He was nominated for an Oscar for his role as an alcoholic falling star.

For over three decades since, James Mason has continued to turn in quietly effective performances in a wide variety of films: as a pill addict in *Bigger Than Life*; as Captain Nemo in *20,000 Leagues Under the Sea*; as the art-collecting leader of a spy ring in *North by Northwest*; as an explorer in *Journey to the Center of the Earth*; as the lecherous and betrayed Humbert Humbert in *Lolita*; as Gentleman Brown in *Lord Jim*; as a crook in *11 Harrowhouse*; as a refugee in *Voyage of the Damned*; as an angel in *Heaven Can Wait*; and as Holmes' Dr. Watson in *Murder by Decree*. He was nominated for an Oscar again for his most recent performance—as a cunning lawyer in *The Verdict*.

FILMOGRAPHY

1935

Late Extra ★ ★ ★

1936

Twice Branded ★ ★ ★
Troubled Waters ★ ★ ★
Blind Man's Bluff ★ ★ ★
Prison Breaker ★ ★ ★

1937

The Secret of Stamboul ★ ★ ★
The Mill on the Floss ★ ★ ★
The High Command ★ ★ ★
Fire Over England ★ ★ ★
Catch as Catch Can ★ ★ ★

1938

The Return of the Scarlet Pimpernel ★ ★ ★

1939

I Met a Murderer ★ ★ ★ ★

1941

This Man Is Dangerous ★ ★ ★

1942

Hatter's Castle ★ ★ ★ ★
The Night Has Eyes ★ ★ ★
Alibi ★ ★ ★
Secret Mission ★ ★ ★

1943

Thunder Rock ★ ★ ★
The Man in Grey ★ ★ ★ ★
They Met in the Dark ★ ★ ★
The Bells Go Down ★ ★ ★
Candlelight in Algeria ★ ★ ★

1944

Fanny by Gaslight ★ ★ ★
Hotel Reserve ★ ★ ★

1945

A Place of One's Own ★ ★ ★
They Were Sisters ★ ★ ★
The Seventh Veil ★ ★ ★ ★

1946

The Wicked Lady ★ ★ ★

1947

The Upturned Glass ★ ★ ★
Odd Man Out ★ ★ ★ ★

James Mason in *The Upturned Glass.*

1949

The Reckless Moment ★ ★ ★ ★
Madame Bovary ★ ★
Caught ★ ★ ★

1950

One Way Street ★ ★ ★
East Side, West Side ★ ★ ★

1951

The Desert Fox ★ ★ ★ ★
Pandora and the Flying Dutchman ★ ★ ★

1952

Lady Possessed ★ ★ ★
Five Fingers ★ ★ ★ ★
The Prisoner of Zenda ★ ★ ★
Face to Face ★ ★ ★

1953

The Story of Three Loves ★ ★ ★
The Desert Rats ★ ★ ★ ★
Julius Caesar ★ ★ ★ ★
Botany Bay ★ ★ ★
The Man Between ★ ★ ★

1954

Prince Valiant ★ ★ ★
A Star Is Born ★ ★ ★ ★
20,000 Leagues Under the Sea ★ ★ ★ ★

1956

Bigger Than Life ★ ★ ★ ★
Forever Darling ★ ★ ★

1957

Island in the Sun ★ ★ ★

1958

Cry Terror ★ ★ ★
The Decks Ran Red ★ ★ ★

1959

North By Northwest ★ ★ ★ ★
Journey to the Center of the Earth ★ ★ ★ ★

1960

A Touch of Larceny ★ ★ ★
The Trials of Oscar Wilde ★ ★ ★

1961

The Marriage-Go-Round ★ ★

James Mason in *The Desert Fox.*

1962

Hero's Island ★ ★ ★
Lolita ★ ★ ★ ★
Escape From Zahrain ★ ★ ★
Tiara Tahiti ★ ★ ★

1963

Torpedo Bay ★ ★ ★

1964

The Pumpkin Eater ★ ★ ★ ★
The Fall of the Roman Empire ★ ★ ★

1965

Lord Jim ★ ★ ★
The Uninhibited ★ ★ ★
Genghis Khan ★ ★ ★

1966

The Blue Max ★ ★ ★
Georgy Girl ★ ★ ★ ★

1967

The Deadly Affair ★ ★ ★ ★
Stranger in the House ★ ★ ★

1968

The Sea Gull ★ ★ ★

1969

Mayerling ★ ★
The London Nobody Knows (documentary)
Age of Consent ★ ★ ★

1970

Spring and Port Wine ★ ★ ★
Cold Sweat ★ ★ ★

1971

Kill! Kill! Kill! Kill! ★ ★ ★
Bad Man's River ★ ★ ★

1972

Child's Play ★ ★ ★ ★

1973

The Last of Sheila ★ ★ ★
The Mackintosh Man ★ ★ ★

1974

The Marseilles Contract ★ ★ ★
11 Harrowhouse ★ ★ ★
Trikimia ★ ★ ★
Nostro Nero in Casa Nichols ★ ★ ★

1975

Autobiography of a Princess ★ ★ ★
The Schoolmistress and the Devil ★ ★ ★
Inside Out ★ ★ ★
Mandingo ★ ★ ★
La Polizia interviene ★ ★ ★

1976

Voyage of the Damned ★ ★ ★
People on the Wind (narration)

1977

Homage to Chagall (narration)
Cross of Iron ★ ★ ★
Hot Stuff ★ ★ ★

1978

Heaven Can Wait ★ ★ ★ ★
The Boys from Brazil ★ ★ ★

1979

The Passage ★ ★ ★
Murder by Decree ★ ★ ★
Sidney Sheldon's Bloodline ★ ★ ★
The Waterbabies ★ ★ ★
North Sea Hijack ★ ★ ★

1980

Ffolkes ★ ★ ★

1982

The Verdict ★ ★ ★ ★

MARSHA MASON
★ ★ ★ 2.90 STARS

Neil Simon has been both a blessing and a liability to Marsha Mason. He wrote tailor-made vehicles for her, which guaranteed stardom, but most of them emphasized a sniveling helplessness that detracted from her sexuality.

Mason was born in 1942, in St. Louis, Missouri. She did a forgettable action film, *Hot Rod Hullabaloo* in 1966, and kept busy on Broadway before returning to the screen in 1973. In *Blume in Love*, she was cast as an unhappy divorcee and she was touching, but *Cinderella Liberty* offered an even richer part as a hard-living whore who attempted to straighten out her life for sailor James Caan. She was lusty and exciting, and Oscar-nominated. Her follow-up film was the dreary *Audrey Rose,* which managed to remove all the thrills that had made the book a best-seller.

The Goodbye Girl brought another nomination, although she was overshadowed by Richard Dreyfuss' frenetic performance. By this time, she was speaking with a permanent lump in her throat. Fortunately, the red eyes and quivering chin were abandoned in Neil Simon's silly *The Cheap Detective*. She played a doctor tending to a dying cancer patient (played by Kathleen Beller) in the relentlessly upsetting *Promises in the Dark*. The lighter material of *Chapter Two* came as a welcome relief. This time Mason kept her tearfulness under firmer control, except during the climactic sequences.

As of this writing, with *Max Dugan Returns* in general release, Mason and Simon have separated. Whatever detrimental effects this has on their personal lives, it can only be a positive influence on her acting development.

Marsha Mason in *Chapter Two.*

FILMOGRAPHY

1966

Hot Rod Hullabaloo ★ ★

1973

Blume in Love ★ ★ ★
Cinderella Liberty ★ ★ ★ ★

1977

Audrey Rose ★ ★
The Goodbye Girl ★ ★ ★

1978

The Cheap Detective ★ ★ ★

1979

Promises in the Dark ★ ★ ★
Chapter Two ★ ★

1981

Only When I Laugh ★ ★ ★ ★

1982

Max Dugan Returns ★ ★ ★

WALTER MATTHAU
★★★ 3.15 STARS

Walter Matthau once neatly summed his image with: "Most people on the street...usually look at me and say, Who the hell is that guy? Was I in the army with him?" Matthau looks less like a box-office star than any other actor in movies, but people identify with Matthau; they like him. This he's-one-of-us charm, plus his enormous talent for comedy and drama, have contributed to his huge success.

Matthau (Walter Matuschanskavasky) was born in 1920, on the Lower East Side of New York. Stopgap work—as a boxing instructor and a basketball coach—ceased as his acting career gained momentum, notably in "Will Success Spoil Rock Hunter?" on the stage. His first film was a mediocre western, *The Kentuckian*, poorly directed by Burt Lancaster. However, he followed it with some good pictures: *Bigger Than Life* (as a friend of drug addict James Mason) and *A Face in the Crowd*, playing a reporter. He did the only acting in an Elvis Presley vehicle, *King Creole*, as a villain. He made a convincing lecher in *Strangers When We Meet*; his short part showed up Kirk Douglas' inadequacies.

A Tony award on Broadway for "A Shot in the Dark" garnered further respect although he was still saving mediocre pictures (*Who's Got the Action?*, *Island of Love*, and *Ensign Pulver*). *Charade* gave him a superb role as a murderer, and he stole his scenes from Cary Grant and Audrey Hepburn. In the witty thriller, *Mirage*, he put Gregory Peck in the shade.

The Fortune Cookie brought him an Oscar, and he teamed delightfully with Jack Lemmon—a partnership that continued in several enjoyable films. They were outstanding in *The Odd Couple*. Matthau dominated *A Guide for the Married Man* as a husband being taught the finer points of infidelity. He hated working with Barbra Streisand in *Hello Dolly!*, calling her a "complete megalomaniac." They were both miscast, which didn't help the situation. He was more comfortable in *Cactus Flower*, even though Ingrid Bergman was too mature as his love interest. Best of all was his pairing with Elaine May in *A New Leaf*.

Walter Matthau with Glenda Jackson in *House Calls*.

Pete 'n' Tillie, with Carol Burnett, had amusing moments until the drama took a tragic turn (their son died of leukemia). It was uneven but moving. He was the best thing about Billy Wilder's noisy remake of *The Front Page*, but decidedly second-fiddle to George Burns in the schmaltzy, slow-moving *The Sunshine Boys*. Even so, he won a Golden Globe for Best Actor, an award that might more appropriately have gone to his portrayal in *The Bad News Bears* as coach of a youngster's baseball team.

With the exception of *House Calls*, Matthau's recent movies (*Casey's Shadow* and *California Suite*) have been uninteresting.

He had fun as a goofy CIA agent in *Hopscotch*, an improbable but enjoyable farce. Although he had a good chemistry with co-star Ann Margret in *I Ought to Be in Pictures*, the film was lousy.

Matthau is at his best when teamed with a strong foil, such as Robin Williams in the recent *Survivors* (a film that *should* have been better than it was).

FILMOGRAPHY

1955

The Kentuckian★★★
The Indian Fighter★★★

1956

Bigger Than Life★★★

1957

A Face in the Crowd★★★★
Slaughter on Tenth Avenue★★★★

1958

King Creole★★★★
Voice in the Mirror★★★
Onionhead★★★
Ride a Crooked Trail★★★

1960

Gangster Story★★★
Strangers When We Meet★★★★

1962

Lonely are the Brave★★★★
Who's Got the Action?★★★★

1963

Island of Love★★★
Charade★★★★

1964

Ensign Pulver★★★
Fail Safe★★★
Goodbye Charlie★★★

1965

Mirage★★★★

1966

The Fortune Cookie★★★★

1967

A Guide for the Married Man★★★★

1968

The Odd Couple★★★★
The Secret Life of an American Wife★★★
Candy★★★

1969

Hello Dolly!★★
Cactus Flower★★★

1971

A New Leaf★★★★
Plaza Suite★★
Kotch★★★

1972

Pete 'n' Tillie★★★★

1973

Charlie Varrick★★★
The Laughing Policeman★★

1974

The Taking of Pelham One Two Three★★★★
The Front Page★★★★

1975

The Sunshine Boys★★

1976

The Bad News Bears★★★★

1978

Casey's Shadow★★★
House Calls★★★★
California Suite★★★

1979

Little Miss Marker★★★
Sunburn★★

1980

Hopscotch★★★

1981

First Monday in October★★★
Buddy Buddy★★

1982

I Ought to Be in Pictures★★★

1983

The Survivors★★★

VICTOR MATURE
★★½ 2.38 STARS

In the 1940s, Victor Mature was what women today would call a "hunk." He was a competent actor, but an aura of self-love and egotism robbed even his sympathetic performances of charm.

Mature was born in Louisville, Kentucky, in 1915. His second film, *One Million B.C.*, with Carole Landis was popular, and he did a succession of major movies with an emphasis on his leading ladies: *I Wake Up Screaming* (Betty Grable), *The Shanghai Gesture* (Gene Tierney), and *Song of the Islands* (Grable again). He was much better in two strong suspense pictures, *Moss Rose* and *Kiss of Death*, though Richard Widmark stole the latter as the villain who pushed a wheelchair-bound old lady down the stairs.

Victor Mature in *Kiss of Death*.

Samson and Delilah was his biggest success, a fast-paced, enjoyable and dubiously biblical epic by Cecil B. De Mille. It led to more large-scale action films, *The Robe*, with Richard Burton, and *Demetrius and the Gladiators*. He wasn't bad in *Betrayed*, a Clark Gable vehicle, but Gable was in the midst of a career decline and audiences stayed home. Mature played out the rest of his career in mindless adventure films, *The Sharkfighters*, *Escort West*, and *The Last Frontier*.

FILMOGRAPHY

1939

The Housekeeper's Daughter★★

1940

One Million B.C.★★
Captain Caution★★
No No Nanette★★

1941

I Wake Up Screaming★★★
The Shanghai Gesture★★

1942

Song of the Islands★★
My Gal Sal★★★
Footlight Serenade★★★
Seven Days' Leave★★★

1946

My Darling Clementine★★★

1947

Moss Rose★★★
Kiss of Death★★★★

1948

Fury at Furnace Creek★★★
Cry of the City★★★

1949

Easy Living★★★
Red Hot and Blue★★
Samson and Delilah★★★

1950

I'll Get By (cameo)
Stella★★★

1951

Gambling House★★★

1952

The Las Vegas Story★★
Something for the Birds★★
Million Dollar Mermaid★★

1953

Androcles and the Lion★★
Affair With a Stranger★★★
The Glory Brigade★★
The Robe★★★
The Veils of Bagdad★★★

1954

Dangerous Mission★★★
Demetrius and the Gladiators★★
The Egyptian★★
Betrayed★★★

1955

Chief Crazy Horse★★
Violent Saturday★★★
The Last Frontier★★★

1956

The Sharkfighters★★
Zarak★★
Safari★★★

Victor Mature.

1957

Interpol ★★
The Long Haul ★★

1958

No Time to Die ★★
China Doll ★★

1959

Escort West ★★
The Bandit of Zhobe ★★
The Big Circus ★★
Timbuktu ★★

1960

Hannibal ★★

1961

The Tartars ★★

1966

After the Fox ★★★

1968

Head (cameo)

1972

Every Little Crook and Nanny ★★

1976

Won Ton Ton-the Dog Who Saved Hollywood (cameo)

1979

Firepower ★★

BURGESS MEREDITH
★★★ 3.17 STARS

Short, slight, and nondescript-looking, Burgess Meredith still manages to fill the screen with power. Part of the reason is his intensity; another is his raspy distinctive voice.

Meredith was born in 1908, in Cleveland, Ohio. He did a Broadway play in 1935 and repeated it on film (*Winterset*). His performance holds up more effectively than the movie, but his portrayal in *Of Mice and Men* moved Joel Greenberg to write in Hollywood in the Forties: "Burgess Meredith's George... could hardly be bettered." He was amusing as one of Ginger Rogers' three suitors in *Tom, Dick and Harry,* and powerful as an unqualified psychiatrist who triggered disaster in *Mine Own Executioner.*

Two Preminger pictures, *Advise and Consent* and *The Cardinal*, benefited from his presence, although a third Preminger film, *Such Good Friends*, was superfluous. Television audiences will never forget his waddling, cackling caricature of The Penguin on the "Batman" series.

He had an excellent short scene with Robert De Niro in *True Confessions*, and Meredith is still active as an integral part of the *Rocky* films. Age seems to add to his talent, rather than diminish it.

FILMOGRAPHY

1936

Winterset ★★★★

1937

There Goes the Groom ★★★

1938

Spring Madness ★★★

1939

Idiot's Delight ★★★

1940

Of Mice and Men ★★★★
Castle on the Hudson ★★★★

1941

Second Chorus ★★★
San Francisco Docks ★★★
That Uncertain Feeling ★★★
Tom, Dick and Harry ★★★★

Burgess Meredith in *Of Mice and Men.*

1942

Street of Chance ★★★

1945

The Story of G.I. Joe ★★★★

1946

The Diary of a Chambermaid ★★★
Magnificent Doll ★★★

1947

Mine Own Executioner ★★★★

1948

On Our Merry Way ★★★

1949

The Man on the Eiffel Tower (direction) ★★★

1953

The Gay Adventure ★★★

1957

Joe Butterfly ★★

1962

Advise and Consent ★★★

1963

The Cardinal ★★★

1964

The Kidnappers ★★★

1965

In Harm's Way ★★★

1966

Madame X ★★★
A Big Hand for the Little Lady ★★★★
Crazy Quilt (narration)

1967

Hurry Sundown ★★★
Torture Garden ★★

1968

Stay Away Joe ★★
Skidoo ★★★

1969

Mackenna's Gold ★★★
Hard Contract ★★★
The Reivers (narration)

1970

There Was a Crooked Man ★★★

1971

Such Good Friends ★★★
Clay Pigeon ★★★

1972

A Fan's Notes ★★★
The Man ★★★

1974

Golden Needles ★★★

1975

The Day of the Locust ★★★
92 in the Shade ★★★
The Hindenburg ★★★

Burgess Meredith in *True Confessions.*

1976

Burnt Offerings ★★★
Rocky ★★★★

1977

The Sentinel ★★★
Shenanigans ★★★
Golden Rendezvous ★★★

1978

The Monitor ★★★
Foul Play ★★★★
A Wedding ★★★
Magic ★★★★

1979

When Time Ran Out ★★
Rocky II ★★★★

1981

True Confessions ★★★
The Last Chase ★★★
Clash of the Titans ★★★

1982

Rocky III ★★★★

1983

Twilight Zone-the Movie (narration)

ETHEL MERMAN
★★½ 2.53 STARS

Some Broadway stars are dismissed by studio heads as unsuitable for film material. Ethel Merman, like her contemporary Mary Martin, failed to conform to Hollywood standards of beauty. But when she was given a good opportunity, she burst through onto the screen with flying colors.

Merman (Ethel Zimmerman) was born in 1909, in Astoria, Queens, New York. She had a strong, unforgettable stage presence...Irving Berlin warned once, "Don't give Ethel a bad song, because you'll *hear* it." Audiences heard her in *The Big Broadcast of 1936,* and *Anything Goes* with Bing Crosby. She was too strident, but given a chance to repeat one of her Broadway hits, *Call Me Madam,* Merman flooded the screen with energy and warmth.

There's No Business Like Show Business was a hit, basically on the strength of Marilyn Monroe's name, and neither *It's a Mad Mad Mad Mad World* or *The Art of Love* made use of Merman's unique personality. Like Barbra Streisand, Merman is too powerful to stay in the background; she has to dominate. One only regrets that she lost the part of Mama Rose in *Gypsy* to Rosalind Russell. It could have been the role that captured fully on film all the charisma she's always had on stage.

Ethel Merman and Billy De Wolfe in *Call Me Madam.*

FILMOGRAPHY

1930

Follow the Leader ★★

1934

We're Not Dressing ★★
Kid Millions ★★

1936

The Big Broadcast of 1936 ★★★
Anything Goes ★★
Strike Me Pink ★★

1938

Happy Landing ★★★
Alexander's Ragtime Band ★★★
Straight Place and Show ★★★

1943

Stage Door Canteen (cameo)

1953

Call Me Madam ★★★★

1954

There's No Business Like Show Business ★★★

1963

It's a Mad Mad Mad Mad World ★★

1965

The Art of Love ★★

1979

Rudolph and Frosty's Christmas in July (voice only)

1980

Airplane (cameo)

BETTE MIDLER
★★★ 3.00 STARS

Bette Midler defines herself as "trash with flash...sleaze with ease." Newsweek's Charles Michener adds, "Burlesque? Parody? Camp? Yes—but only on the surface." Beneath her wild theatrics is a recognizable human being, a funny, needy, anxious human being that everyone can respond to.

Midler was born in Honolulu, Hawaii, in 1945. She sang in Greenwich Village coffeehouses and worked as a go-go dancer before moving up to Broadway—playing Tevye's oldest daughter in "Fiddler on the Roof." Word got around of her prodigious talent when she appeared at the Continental Baths on New York's Upper East Side, and "The Divine Miss M" proceeded to break Broadway records in one-woman shows and do likewise as a recording artist.

When Mark Rydell decided to direct *The Rose* (a thinly veiled portrait of Janis Joplin), he chose Midler, and she came through with an intense, stirring (if occasionally hysterical) performance. "I see Rose as a human being living emotionally close to the edge," Midler commented, and her characterization caught that desperation. This eccentric, gifted Grammy and Tony winner was also the focal point of her filmed one-woman show *Divine Madness.* She showed talent in her next dramatic film, *Jinxed,* but the plot was too convoluted for anybody to care. Clearly she has talent. The trick now is to find vehicles that accommodate her idiosyncratic personality.

Bette Midler in *Jinxed.*

FILMOGRAPHY

1980

The Rose ★★★

1981

Divine Madness ★★★★

1983

Jinxed ★★

RAY MILLAND
★★★3.13 STARS

He complains of embarrassment while performing, yet Ray Milland has appeared in more than 200 films since 1929. His films run the gamut from adventures and mysteries to romantic comedies. Perhaps not as flamboyant as some of his colleagues, Milland always gave his directors professionalism rather than showy star turns.

Born Reginald Truscott-Jones in 1903, in Neath, Wales. He entered British films in 1929, and went to Hollywood in 1930. Although he served as a contract player at Paramount for some years, it was not until *The Doctor Takes a Wife,* with Loretta Young, that Milland was considered a powerful box-office draw. This led to a string of films opposite Claudette Colbert *(Arise My Love, Skylark)* and a role as Ginger Rogers' musical partner in *Lady in the Dark*.

But it was in 1945 that Milland received his Best Actor Oscar for *The Lost Weekend*, Billy Wilder's study of an alcoholic writer. Critics said he plumbed the "depths of degradation and shame, revealing the inner torment of a weak, yet respectable man." He was also honored by the New York Film Critics.

Following this success, Milland worked with Grace Kelly in Alfred Hitchcock's *Dial M for Murder.* He has since written an autobiography, Wide-Eyed in Babylon, and is probably best known to younger audiences as the actor who played Ryan O'Neal's father in *Love Story* and its sequel, *Oliver's Story.*

FILMOGRAPHY

1929

The Plaything ★★★
The Informer ★★★
The Flyng Scotsman ★★★
The Lady From the Sea ★★★

1930

Way for a Sailor ★★★
Passion Flower ★★★

1931

The Bachelor Father ★★★
Just a Gigolo ★★★
Bought ★★★
Ambassador Bill ★★★
Blonde Crazy ★★★

1932

The Man Who Played God ★★★
Polly of the Circus ★★
Payment Deferred ★★★★

1933

Orders Is Orders ★★★
This Is The Life ★★★

1934

Bolero ★★★
We're Not Dressing ★★★
Many Happy Returns ★★★
Charlie Chan in London ★★★
Menace ★★★

1935

One Hour Late ★★★
The Gilded Lily ★★★★
Four Hours to Kill ★★★
The Glass Key ★★★★
Alias Mary Dow ★★★

1936

Next Time We Love ★★★
The Return of Sophia Lang ★★★
The Big Broadcast of 1937 ★★★
The Jungle Princess ★★★
Three Smart Girls ★★★★

1937

Bulldog Drummond Escapes ★★★
Wings Over Honolulu ★★★
Easy Living ★★★★
Ebb Tide ★★★★
Wise Girl ★★★

Ray Milland.

1938

Her Jungle Love ★★★
Tropic Holiday ★★★
Men With Wings ★★★
Say It in French ★★★

1939

French Without Tears ★★★
Hotel Imperial ★★★
Beau Geste ★★★★
Everything Happens at Night ★★★★

1940

Irene ★★★
The Doctor Takes a Wife ★★★
Untamed ★★★
Arise My Love ★★★

1941

I Wanted Wings ★★★★
Skylark ★★★★

1942

The Lady Has Plans ★★★★
Reap the Wild Wind ★★★
Are Husbands Necessary? ★★★
The Major and the Minor ★★★★
Star Spangled Rhythm ★★★

1943

The Crystal Ball ★★★
Forever and a Day ★★★

1944

The Uninvited ★★★★
Lady in the Dark ★★★
Till We Meet Again ★★★
Ministry of Fear ★★★★

1945

The Lost Weekend ★★★★

1946

Kitty ★★★★
The Well Groomed Bride ★★★

1947

California ★★★
The Imperfect Lady ★★★
The Trouble with Women ★★★
Variety Girl (cameo)
Golden Earrings ★★★

1948

The Big Clock ★★★★
So Evil My Love ★★★★
Miss Tatlock's Millions (cameo)
Sealed Verdict ★★★

1949

Alias Nick Beal ★★★★
It Happens Every Spring ★★★

1950

A Woman of Distinction ★★★
A Life of Her Own ★★★
Copper Canyon ★★

1951

Circle of Danger ★★★
Night Into Morning ★★★★
Rhubarb ★★★
Close to My Heart ★★★

Ray Milland in *The Lost Weekend.*

1952

Bugles in the Afternoon ★★
Something to Live For ★★★★
The Thief ★★★★

1953

Jamaica Run ★★★
Let's Do It Again ★★

1954

Dial M for Murder ★★★★

1955

The Girl in the Red Velvet Swing ★★★
A Man Alone (direction) ★★★

1957

Lisbon (direction) ★★★
Three Brave Men ★★★
The River's Edge ★★★
High Flight ★★★

1958

The Safecracker (direction) ★★★

1962

Premature Burial ★★★
Panic in the Year Zero! (direction) ★★★★

1963

X—the Man With the X-Ray Eyes ★★★★

1967

Hostile Witness (direction) ★★★

1968

Rose Rosse per il Fuhrer ★★★

1970

Company of Killers ★★★
Love Story ★★

1972

The Big Game ★★★
Frogs ★★
The Thing With Two Heads ★
Embassy ★★★

1973

The House in Nightmare Park ★★★
Terror in the Wax Museum ★★★

1974

Gold ★★★

1975

Escape to Witch Mountain ★★

1976

Aces High ★★★
The Last Tycoon ★★★

1977

Slavers ★★★
Oil ★★★
The Swiss Conspiracy ★★★
The Uncanny ★★★

1978

La Ragazza in Pigiama Giallo ★★★
Blackout ★★★
Spree ★★★
Oliver's Story ★★

1979

Game for Vultures ★★★

ANN MILLER
★★½ 2.38 STARS

Ann Miller's acting is one-dimensional. Her dancing, however—aided by sleek, long legs—is extraordinary, a major asset to some of MGM's best musicals.

Miller (Lucille Ann Collier) was born in 1919, in Chireno, Texas. She trained from early childhood to be a dancer and then appeared on the screen in a series of forgotten pictures including *The Life of the Party, Radio City Revels,* and *The Devil on Horseback*. Miller was first widely seen and noticed in an

Ann Miller in *The Thrill of Brazil.*

Oscar-winning film, *You Can't Take It With You.*

Having Wonderful Time was also an "A," but after that she muddled through *Too Many Girls, Melody Ranch* with Gene Autry, and *Time Out for Rhythm.* Not much could be said for *Reveille With Beverly, What's Buzzin' Cousin?,* and *Hey Rookie* although she was lively and graceful in all of them.

Rescue and prestige finally came with *Easter Parade.* Miller played the dance partner Fred Astaire lost before turning to Judy Garland. She had some superb numbers and a chance to show her acting ability. *The Kissing Bandit* was almost her kiss of death along with Frank Sinatra's, so *On the Town* was a welcome uplift—an effervescent, irresistible concoction about three sailors on leave. Miller, Betty Garrett, and Vera-Ellen played the girlfriends. *Watch the Birdie* with Red Skelton was a poor follow-up, and her co-stars in *Two Tickets to Broadway* (Gloria DeHaven and Tony Martin) weren't in the Astaire or Kelly class.

Kiss Me Kate brought raves for Miller's dancing, and she added zest to *Deep in My Heart* and *Hit the Deck.* She made her last film, *The Great American Pastime,* in 1956 and later conquered Broadway in "Mame" and "Sugar Babies." Ann Miller continues to dance away, in road tours of "Sugar Babies."

FILMOGRAPHY

1936

The Devil on Horseback ★★

1937

New Faces of 1937 ★★★
Stage Door ★★★
The Life of the Party ★★

1938

Radio City Revels ★★
Having Wonderful Time ★★
You Can't Take It With You ★★★
Room Service ★★
Tarnished Angel ★★

1940

Too Many Girls ★★
Hit Parade of 1941 ★★
Melody Ranch ★★

1941

Time Out for Rhythm ★★
Go West Young Lady ★★

Ann Miller with Victor Moore in *Carolina Blues*.

1942

True to the Army ★★
Priorities on Parade ★★

1943

Reveille With Beverly ★★
What's Buzzin' Cousin? ★★

1944

Jam Session ★★
Hey Rookie ★★
Carolina Blues ★★

1945

Eve Knew Her Apples ★★
Eadie Was a Lady ★★

1946

The Thrill of Brazil ★★

1948

The Kissing Bandit ★★
Easter Parade ★★★

1949

On the Town ★★★★

1950

Watch the Birdie ★★

1951

Two Tickets to Broadway ★★
Texas Carnival ★★★

1952

Lovely to Look At ★★★

1953

Small Town Girl ★★★
Kiss Me Kate ★★★★

1954

Deep in My Heart ★★★

1955

Hit the Deck ★★★

1956

The Opposite Sex ★★★
The Great American Pastime ★★

JOHN MILLS
★★★½ 3.35 STARS

David Lean's *Great Expectations* is still the best movie version of Dickens material, and the major reason is John Mills. His sensitive, obsessed Pip is only one characterization in a gallery of memorable screen portraits.

Born in 1908, in North Elmham, England, Mills was a chorus boy before moving to straight acting. He played a sailor in his first movie, *The Midshipmaid,* and an appearance in the classic *Goodbye Mr. Chips* enhanced his reputation. He was also effective with Robert Donat in *The Young Mr. Pitt.*

In Noel Coward's *In Which We Serve,* he was again cast as a sailor and his portrayal in a realistic wartime drama was believable. His characterization and the film itself were opposed to the romanticization of *Mrs. Miniver,* popular at the same time. More hits followed: *The Way to the Stars,* a close-up of the R.A.F., and *The October Man.*

The Rocking Horse Winner from a D. H. Lawrence story was too downbeat for public approval, but Mills was brilliant and the movie itself underrated. In fact he was always good, whether the picture succeeded (*Hobson's Choice*) or failed (*The End of the Affair*). *Tunes of Glory* pitted him against Alec Guinness, presenting a spectacularly absorbing contrast of types (callous Colonel, sensitive young officer).

He appeared with daughter Hayley in *The Chalk Garden* and then stole *The Family Way* as a macho father who ridiculed his son (Hywel Bennett). Oddly enough, he won an Oscar for *Ryan's Daughter,* a performance far below his best work. *Young Winston* was a historical charade that brought no credit to anyone, so Mills returned to the stage in "Power of Persuasion" and "Veterans."

He was knighted in 1976, a richly deserving recipient of this honor, and continues to make films (*The 39 Steps, The Big Sleep,* and *Zulu Dawn*).

John Mills.

FILMOGRAPHY

1932

The Midshipmaid ★★★

1933

Britannia of Billingsgate ★★★
The Ghost Camera ★★★

1934

River Wolves ★★★
A Political Party ★★★
Those Were the Days ★★★
The Lash ★★★
Blind Justice ★★★
Doctor's Orders ★★★

1935

Royal Cavalcade ★★★★
Forever England ★★★★
Charing Cross Road ★★★★

1936

First Offense ★★★
Tudor Rose ★★★

1937

OHMS ★★★
The Green Cockatoo ★★★★

1939

Goodbye, Mr. Chips ★★★★

1941

Old Bill and Son ★★★
Cottage to Let ★★★★
The Black Sheep of Whitehall ★★★

1942

The Young Mr. Pitt ★★★★
The Big Blockade ★★★★
In Which We Serve ★★★★

1943

We Drive at Dawn ★★★

1944

This Happy Breed ★★★
Waterloo Road ★★★★

1945

The Way to the Stars ★★★★

1946

Great Expectations ★★★★

1947

So Well Remembered ★★★★
The October Man ★★★★

1948

Scott of the Antarctic ★★★

1949

The History of Mr. Polly ★★★
The Rocking Horse Winner ★★★★

1950

Morning Departure ★★★★

1951

Mr. Denning Drives North ★★★

1952

The Gentle Gunman ★★★★
The Long Memory ★★★★

1954

Hobson's Choice ★★★★

1955

The Colditz Story ★★★
The End of the Affair ★★★
Above Us the Waves ★★★
Escapade ★★★

1956

War and Peace ★★★
It's Great to Be Young ★★★
The Baby and the Battleship ★★★
Around the World in 80 Days (cameo)

1957

Dunkirk ★★★
Ice Cold in Alex ★★★
I Was Monty's Double ★★★

1959

Tiger Bay ★★★★

John Mills in *The Truth About Spring.*

1960

Summer of the 17th Doll ★★★
Tunes of Glory ★★★★
Swiss Family Robinson ★★★★

1961

The Singer Not the Song ★★★

1962

Flame in the Streets ★★★
The Valiant ★★★
Tiara Tahiti ★★★

1963

The Chalk Garden ★★★★

1964

The Truth About Spring ★★★

1965

Operation Crossbow ★★★
King Rat ★★★★

1966

The Wrong Box ★★★

1967

The Family Way ★★★★
Africa-Texas Style! ★★★
Chuka ★★★

1968

Lady Hamilton ★★★
The Making of a Lady ★★★

1969

Oh! What a Lovely War ★★★
Run Wild Run Free ★★★
A Black Veil for Lisa ★★★

1970

Adam's Woman ★★★
Ryan's Daughter ★★★

1971

Dulcima ★★★

1972

Young Winston ★★★
Lady Caroline Lamb ★★★

1975

Oklahoma Crude ★★★

1976

Dirty Knights' Work ★★★

1978

The Big Sleep ★★★

1979

Zulu Dawn ★★★
The 39 Steps ★★★★

1980

The Human Factor ★★★★

1982

Gandhi (cameo)

SAL MINEO
★★★ 3.05 STARS

Rebel Without a Cause is still the best drama ever filmed about youth. But it has a special poignancy; James Dean, Natalie Wood, and Sal Mineo all died tragic, violent, and senseless deaths.

Mineo (Salvatore Mineo) was born in the Bronx, New York, in 1939. He appeared on Broadway in "The Rose Tattoo" and "The King and I" and then made a national impact with *Rebel*, a superb, Oscar-nominated portrait of a lonely outcast in the throes of hero worship. *Somebody Up There Likes Me* offered him another fine part, as Paul Newman's loser friend. *Crime in the Streets* and *Dino* were run-of-the-mill, but *Giant* brought acclaim and *Exodus* a second Oscar nomination.

He was well cast as Gene Krupa in *The Gene Krupa Story* though the script demolished him with clichés. Mineo had an even weaker script in his next film, *Who Killed Teddy Bear?* In spite of the script, he managed to project the fear, uncertainty, and rage of a sex pervert. His last pictures did nothing for him (*80 Steps to Jonah; Krakatoa, East of Java*), but a stage appearance in "Fortune and Men's Eyes," as a homosexual in prison who raped another inmate, showed the range and power of his acting ability. He was mysteriously stabbed to death in 1976 as he was in the midst of rehearsing another play.

FILMOGRAPHY

1955
Six Bridges to Cross ★★★
Rebel Without a Cause ★★★★

1966
Crime in the Streets ★★★
Somebody Up There Likes Me ★★★★
Giant ★★★★

1957
The Young Don't Cry ★★★
Dino ★★★

1958
Tonka ★★★

1959
A Private's Affair ★★
The Gene Krupa Story ★★

1960
Exodus ★★★★

1962
Escape From Zahrain ★★★
The Longest Day ★★★

1964
Cheyenne Autumn ★★★

1965
The Greatest Story Ever Told ★★
Who Killed Teddy Bear? ★★★

1969
80 Steps to Jonah ★★★
Krakatoa, East of Java ★★★

1971
Escape From the Planet of the Apes ★★★

Sal Mineo with Ralph Meeker in the TV movie, *The Magic Horn*.

LIZA MINNELLI
★★★ 2.88 STARS

Liza Minnelli inspires violent reaction for or against her. Critic Pauline Kael called her "electrifying" while John Simon said, "as for Miss Minnelli, she is herself a perfect ménage à trois in which lack of talent, lack of looks, and lack of a speaking voice cohabit blissfully." The truth lies in between.

Minnelli was born in 1946, in Los Angeles, California. She appeared as a baby with her mother, Judy Garland, *In the Good Old Summertime*. Although Garland discouraged her ambitions, she persevered landing the lead in an off-Broadway revival of "Best Foot Forward." She collected a Tony for her appearance in "Flora, the Red Menace"—the first in a series of lucrative collaborations with composers Kander and Ebb. *Charlie Bubbles* was the wrong debut film for her intense charm—a humdrum, introspective tale of a writer (Albert Finney) fighting boredom.

Her second picture *The Sterile Cuckoo* was much better though—Minnelli was superb as a needy loser who latched on to a naive and unsuspecting Wendell Burton. Despite later acclaim, it still remains her best performance, and she was nominated for an Oscar.

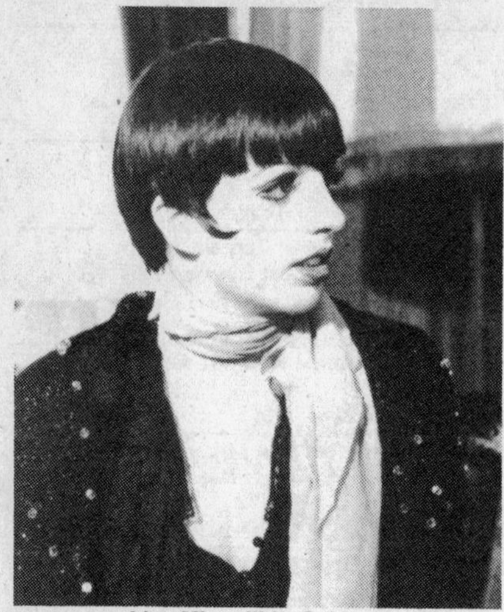

Liza Minnelli in *Cabaret.*

The Oscar nomination meant more leading parts, but *Tell Me That You Love Me, Junie Moon* distorted a good novel. Otto Preminger's heavy direction was to blame, but there was no directing problem when Bob Fosse took over *Cabaret*. Minnelli played the "divinely decadent" Sally Bowles asking no sympathy and living life to its fullest. Minnelli explained, "I saw Julie Harris play Sally in the film, *I Am a Camera* and she was great, but she played her like a campy butterfly ....I saw Sally as a girl with an element of terrible selfishness and meanness." The Academy saw it that way too and voted her an Oscar over Diana Ross' work in *Lady Sings the Blues*.

Stardom seemed assured, but Variety felt she was well on her way to being box-office poison after her next films. *Lucky Lady* was a horrendous "comedy" with Gene Hackman and Burt Reynolds, and *A Matter of Time*, directed by dad Vincente Minnelli also proved to be second rate. *New York, New York* received extensive coverage, but audiences were faced with a grim and overlong musical-drama about a band singer and the boor she married (Robert De Niro). It was really De Niro's neurotic and noisy portrayal that destroyed the picture. Minnelli had some touching moments despite the repetitive script. Her willingness to mimic her mother's mannerisms and style were unnerving, though.

Roddy McDowall predicted that she would be as big as ever with one good vehicle, and he was right. After *Arthur*, a hilarious comedy with Dudley Moore, she was heavily in demand. Meanwhile, her stage career soars along in its surefire standing-room-only way. Her overdramatization and emotional excesses, which sometimes misfired on the screen, create guaranteed excitement for live audiences.

FILMOGRAPHY

1967

Charlie Bubbles ★★

1969

The Sterile Cuckoo ★★★★

Liza Minnelli with Wendell Burton in *The Sterile Cuckoo.*

1970

Tell Me that You Love Me, Junie Moon ★★★

1972

Cabaret ★★★★

1974

Journey Back to Oz (voice only)
That's Entertainment (narration)

1975

Lucky Lady ★

1976

Silent Movie (cameo)
A Matter of Time ★★

1977

New York, New York ★★★

1981

Arthur ★★★★

ROBERT MITCHUM
★★★ 3.11 STARS

In his book The Tough Guys, James Robert Parish wrote, "He (Mitchum) has always been a deceptively simplistic actor. Robert Mitchum's solid beefcake nature has been confused for stolid and his lackadaisical persona misinterpreted as laziness. In sharp contrast, he is one of the most consummate Hollywood performers...his individuality of character and style shines through every performance, making one constantly marvel at how he has salvaged so many trashy projects in his long career."

Mitchum was born in 1917, in Bridgeport, Connecticut. His background was perfect material for modern day country music songwriters. Before becoming established as an actor, he was a nightclub bouncer, engine wiper on a freighter, and hobo rider on trains and trucks. He began his movie career with bit parts in *Hoppy Serves a Writ* and *Border Patrol*, and then was cast in an absorbing suspense-drama, *When Strangers Marry*. Director Mervyn LeRoy cast him into *Thirty Seconds Over Tokyo* and stated, "You're either the lousiest actor in the world or the best."

The Story of G.I. Joe brought an Oscar nomination for Best Supporting Actor, and Mitchum's lazy ease was an asset to *Till the End of Time*. Katharine Hepburn reportedly told him, "you know you can't act," when they made *Undercurrent*, but he didn't quit. He went on to do *The Locket*, a confused but fascinating study of a psychopathic jewel thief (played by Laraine Day). Mitchum was one of the several men she destroyed (the others were Brian Aherne and Gene Raymond).

He got an even stronger role in *Crossfire*. This hard-hitting tale of anti-Semitism proved popular, and he had good luck with *Out of the Past*, an outstanding thriller that gains power every time you see it. He was overshadowed by William Holden in *Rachel and the Stranger*, but dominated a western, *Blood on the Moon*.

However, bad pictures (*My Forbidden Past, The Big Steel*) began to pile up. *Holiday Affair*, though enjoyable, lacked the strength to bolster his box office. Around this time he was arrested for smoking marijuana. He told the police officers, "I'm ruined. I'm all washed up in pictures now, I guess," but the reverse proved to be the case. He costarred with Marilyn Monroe in the lame but well-attended *River of No Return* and had his biggest smash as a selfish doctor in *Not as a Stranger*.

Some of Mitchum's best pictures, such as *The Night of the Hunter*, failed, while more mediocre efforts like *Heaven Knows Mr. Allison* brought in the crowds. Although the majority of his 1960s entries were undistinguished, *Home from the Hill* was an outstanding exception. He was saddled with a Noel Coward-type comedy in *The Grass Is Greener*, and the script lacked wit. The drab and talky *Two for the Seesaw* followed. In *Cape Fear* he was cast as a vengeful murderer, a terrifying characterization in a gripping thriller. He supplied the only emotional intensity to *Ryan's Daughter*, a padded, over-extended love story. However, Mitchum was well-cast in some Raymond Chandler remakes, *Farewell, My Lovely* and *The Big Sleep*.

Possibly discouraged by the movie material available to him, Mitchum starred in a television mini-series, *The Winds of War*, based on Herman Wouk's best-seller. His expressionless portrayal carried underplaying to a fault. Fortunately, reruns of *Out of the Past* and *Crossfire* appear regularly to remind audiences how good he was at his best.

Robert Mitchum with Lizabeth Scott in *The Racket*.

FILMOGRAPHY

1943

Hoppy Serves a Writ (bit)
The Leather Burners (bit)
Border Patrol (bit)
Follow the Band (bit)
Colt Comrades (bit)
Bar 20 (bit)
We've Never Been Licked (bit)
Doughboys in Ireland (bit)
Corvette K-225 (bit)
Aerial Gunner (bit)
The Lone Star Trail (bit)
The Dancing Masters (bit)
False Colors (bit)
Riders of the Deadline (bit)
Minesweeper (bit)
Beyond the Last Frontier★★★
Cry Havoc★★
Gung Ho!★★
The Human Comedy (bit)

1944

Johnny Doesn't Live Here Any More★★★
When Strangers Marry★★★★
The Girl Rush★★★
Thirty Seconds Over Tokyo★★★
Nevada★★★

1945

West of the Pecos★★★
The Story of G. I. Joe★★★★

1946

Till the End of Time★★★
Undercurrent★★★
The Locket★★★★

1947

Pursued★★★
Crossfire★★★★
Desire Me★★
Out of the Past★★★★

1948

Rachel and the Stranger★★★
Blood on the Moon★★★★

1949

The Red Pony★★★
The Big Steal★★★
Holiday Affair★★★★

1950

Where Danger Lives★★★

1951

My Forbidden Past★★★
His Kind of Woman★★★★
The Racket★★★

1952

Macao★★★
One Minute to Zero★★★
The Lusty Men★★★★

1953

Second Chance★★★
Angel Face★★★★
White Witch Doctor★★★

1954

She Couldn't Say No★★★
River of No Return★★★
Track of the Cat★★★

1955

Not as a Stranger★★★★
The Night of the Hunter★★★★
Man With the Gun★★★

Robert Mitchum in *His Kind of Woman.*

1956

Foreign Intrigue★★★
Bandido★★★

1957

Heaven Knows Mr. Allison★★★
Fire Down Below★★★
The Enemy Below★★★

1958

Thunder Road★★★
The Hunters★★★

1959

The Angry Hills★★★
The Wonderful Country★★★

1960

Home from the Hill★★★★
The Sundowners★★★★
The Night Fighters★★★
The Grass Is Greener★★★

1961

The Last Time I Saw Archie★★★

1962

Cape Fear★★★★
The Longest Day★★★
Two for the Seesaw★★

1963

The List of Adrian Messenger★★★
Rampage★★★

1964

Man in the Middle★★★
What a Way to Go!★★

1965

Mister Moses★★★

1967

The Way West★★★
El Dorado★★★★

1968

Villa Rides★★★
Anzio★★★
5 Card Stud★★★
Secret Ceremony★★

1969

Young Billy Young★★★
The Good Guys and the Bad Guys★★★

1970

Ryan's Daughter★★★★

1971

Going Home★★★★

1972

The Wrath of God★★★

1973

The Friends of Eddie Coyle★★★

1975

The Yakuza★★
Farewell, My Lovely★★★★

1976

Midway★★
The Last Tycoon★★★

1977

The Amsterdam Kill★★

1978

Matilda★★
The Big Sleep★★★

1979

Sergeant Steiner★★★
Agency★★★

1982

That Championship Season★★★

MARILYN MONROE
★★★ 2.81 STARS

Marilyn Monroe was a beautiful mirror for the feelings of all moviegoers. She represented the success they all aspired to, yet experienced the pain of loneliness and rejection they all felt. Those with tormented childhoods could identify with Monroe's bitter life in a foster home. Those who suffered in love could say, "Poor Marilyn, she has everything except a good man to really care about her."

From the moment of her birth in 1926, in Los Angeles, California, she was unquestionably a victim—raped at eight years old, illegitimate, abandoned by her father. However, Monroe (born Norma Jean Mortenson) was ambitious too, and she sought a film career with single-minded intensity. Powerful friends, such as agent Johnny Hyde and columnist Sidney Skolsky, helped her to land good roles in *The Asphalt Jungle* and *All About Eve*. Her memorable cameo in *All About Eve* as a "graduate of the Copacabana School of Dramatic Art" lit up the screen, surprising dissenters such as co-star Celeste Holm, who confessed, "I saw nothing special in her. I thought she was just another dumb blonde."

Niagara, casting her as Joseph Cotten's unfaithful wife, began Monroe's evolution into what critic Judith Crist called "that rare creature that reigns undisputed in Everyman's Desire." She found her forte in comedy with *Gentlemen Prefer Blondes* and *How to Marry a Millionaire*. Her box-office magic even triumphed over poor musicals like *There's No Business Like Show Business*.

Unfortunately, she began to think of herself as a "serious artist, attending Actor's Studio classes and blindly following every direction of drama coach Paula Strasberg. This resulted in endless retakes and habitual lateness. Columnist Hedda Hopper blamed her growing inferiority complex on a "clutch of nudgers, prodders, counselors, and advisers." Her screen sparkle was still unaffected, and she revealed faultless comedic timing in *The Seven Year Itch. Bus Stop* brought acclaim, but not the Oscar nomination she desperately wanted.

Laurence Olivier directed and costarred with Monroe in *The Prince and the Showgirl* and has spoken re-

Marilyn Monroe.

cently of her rudeness and lack of cooperation. In retrospect, her beauty is the only palatable feature of an otherwise talky, witless film. Her best and most successful vehicle was the hilarious *Some Like It Hot*. Probably her worst was *Let's Make Love*. Her affair with married Yves Montand dominated the world headlines, but the notoriety was no help at the box office. *The Misfits*, written by estranged husband Arthur Miller, was a stagy and downbeat drama. Monroe was unconvincing, causing one to reconsider Hedda Hopper's assessment: "In spite of her talk about playing Dostoevski heroines. . .the sexy blonde remained her stock in trade."

But she is still remembered, discussed, and analyzed decades after her death in August, 1962. This is partly due to her movie appearance, her beauty, the quality of her innocence caught by a loving camera. But more significantly, Monroe represents, as does Judy Garland, the classic victim. She is the Cinderella who made it to the ball, and found no love or security there.

FILMOGRAPHY

1948

Scudda Hoo! Scudda Hay! (bit)
Dangerous Years (bit)
Ladies of the Chorus (bit)

1950

Love Happy (bit)
A Ticket to Tomahawk (bit)
The Asphalt Jungle (bit)
All About Eve ★★★★
Right Cross (bit)
The Fireball (bit)

1951

The Hometown Story ★★
As Young As You Feel ★★★
Love Nest ★★★
Let's Make It Legal ★★★

1952

Clash by Night ★★★
We're Not Married ★★★
Don't Bother to Knock ★
Monkey Business ★★★
O. Henry's Full House ★★

1953

Niagara ★★★
Gentlemen Prefer Blondes ★★★
How to Marry a Millionaire ★★★

1954

River of No Return ★★
There's No Business Like Show Business ★★

Marilyn Monroe.

1955

The Seven Year Itch ★★★★

1956

Bus Stop ★★★★

1957

The Prince and the Showgirl ★★★

1959

Some Like It Hot ★★★★

1960

Let's Make Love ★★

1961

The Misfits ★★

MARIA MONTEZ
★½ 1.58 STARS

Maria Montez was Universal Studio's symbol of the exotic. No matter how flimsy the sets, or how ludicrously inappropriate the dialog, Montez's presence in and of itself guaranteed that a story took place in Tahiti, or Africa, or even Atlantis.

She was born Maria Africa Vidal de Santos Silas in 1920, in the Dominican Republic. As an actress, Montez put her early convent education to good use; her fabulously sexy, otherworldy characters usually "discovered" (or were informed about) the passion which burned within them in the course of the narrative. Much could probably be made of the links between the exotic locales and Montez's continual rediscovery of her sensuality in film after film. As an actress, she was pathetically bad, but she trudged through her playacting with such mindless conviction that it didn't seem to matter. Her definitive performance, such as it was, was surely *Cobra Woman*, the inspiration for the later underground classic *Flaming Creatures*. The fact that she produced as well as starred in *Siren of Atlantis*, one of the more delirious exercises in conscious camp ever assembled, hints that Montez was perhaps well aware of the peculiarity of her appeal.

FILMOGRAPHY

1941

Lucky Devils ★
The Invisible Woman ★★
Boss of Bullion City ★
That Night in Rio ★★
Raiders of the Desert ★
Moonlight in Hawaii ★
South of Tahiti ★

1942

Bombay Clipper ★★
The Mystery of Marie Roget ★★
Arabian Nights ★

1943

White Savage ★★★

1944

Ali Baba and the Forty Thieves ★★
Follow the Boys ★
Cobra Woman ★★★
Gypsy Wildcat ★
Bowery to Broadway ★

1945

Sudan ★

1946

Tangier ★★

1947

The Exile ★★
Pirates of Monterey ★

Maria Montez.

1949

Siren of Atlantis ★ ★ ★
Portrait d'un Assassin ★

1950

Hans le Marin ★
Il Ladro di Venezia ★ ★

1951

Amore e Sangue ★
La Vendetta del Corsaro ★ ★

ROBERT MONTGOMERY
★ ★ ★ ½ 3.27 STARS

Robert Montgomery was a polished light comedian, a proficient dramatic actor and, briefly, an imaginative, risk-taking director.

Montgomery (Henry Montgomery, Jr.) was born in 1904, in Beacon, New York, and got into acting after failing to make his mark as an author. His Broadway appearances in "Dawn," "One of the Family," and "Possession," led to an MGM contract and a group of now-forgotten films (*Three Live Ghosts*, *Untamed*, and *Father's Day*). A successful teaming with Norma Shearer in *Their Own Desire* helped him turn the corner, and he made *Our Blushing Brides* with Joan Crawford. Shearer was his leading lady again in the compelling *Riptide*.

Because Montgomery's participation as president of the Screen Actor's Guild antagonized studio bosses, he was pushed into an uncharacteristic role as a homicidal maniac in *Night Must Fall*. Ironically, he was superb, and the movie did surprisingly well. There were other enjoyable parts: as a bootlegger in *The Earl of Chicago*, the detective Lord Peter Wimsey in *Busman's Honeymoon*, and as Mr. Smith in Alfred Hitchcock's *Mr. and Mrs. Smith*. Then came his first classic, *Here Comes Mr. Jordan*. He played a dead boxer who gets a new body instead of going straight to heaven. The film was remade as *Heaven Can Wait*, and Montgomery was as spryly engaging as Warren Beatty was in the later version.

Montgomery switched gears after World War II by moving into film direction as well as acting. His first effort, *Lady in the Lake*, was a splashy and entertaining experiment. He played the detective Phillip Marlowe and told the entire story in first person point-of-view shots. He appeared only when his character crossed in front of mirrors. His next film as director/actor was less showy but more accomplished, *Ride the Pink Horse*. Later, *The Saxon Charm* featured one of Montgomery's most brilliant performances, as a manipulative, egomaniacal producer who controls playwright John Payne.

TV took up most of his time from then on in "Robert Montgomery Presents" and "Lucky Strike Theatre." It was a loss to films, for he quit films just as he was showing his greatest promise. His early work for television ranks as some of that medium's finest.

Robert Montgomery with Edward Everett Horton in *Here Comes Mr. Jordan.*

FILMOGRAPHY

1929

The Single Standard (bit)
So This Is College ★ ★ ★
Three Live Ghosts ★ ★ ★
Untamed ★ ★ ★
Their Own Desire ★ ★ ★

1930

Free and Easy ★ ★ ★
The Divorcee ★ ★ ★
The Big House ★ ★ ★ ★
Sins of the Children ★ ★ ★
Our Blushing Brides ★ ★ ★ ★
Love in the Rough ★ ★ ★
War Nurse ★ ★ ★

1931

Inspiration ★ ★ ★
The Easiest Way ★ ★ ★
Strangers May Kiss ★ ★ ★
Shipmates ★ ★ ★
The Man in Possession ★ ★ ★
Private Lives ★ ★ ★ ★

Robert Montgomery with Ingrid Bergman in *Rage in Heaven.*

1932

Lovers Courageous ★ ★ ★
But the Flesh Is Weak ★ ★ ★
Letty Lynton ★ ★ ★
Blondie of the Follies ★ ★ ★
Faithless ★ ★ ★

1933

Hell Below ★ ★ ★
When Ladies Meet ★ ★ ★
Made on Broadway ★ ★ ★
Another Language ★ ★ ★
Night Flight ★ ★ ★ ★

1934

Fugitive Lovers ★ ★ ★
The Mystery of Mr. X ★ ★ ★ ★
Riptide ★ ★ ★ ★
Hide-Out ★ ★ ★
Forsaking All Others ★ ★ ★

1935

Biography of a Bachelor Girl ★ ★ ★ ★
Vanessa: Her Love Story ★ ★ ★
No More Ladies ★ ★ ★

1936

Petticoat Fever ★ ★ ★
Trouble for Two ★ ★ ★
Piccadilly Jim ★ ★ ★ ★

1937

The Last of Mrs. Cheyney ★ ★ ★
Night Must Fall ★ ★ ★ ★
Ever Since Eve ★ ★ ★
Live, Love and Learn ★ ★ ★

1938

The First 100 Years ★ ★ ★
Yellow Jack ★ ★ ★ ★
Three Loves Has Nancy ★ ★ ★

1939

Fast and Loose ★ ★ ★

1940

The Earl of Chicago ★ ★ ★ ★
Busman's Honeymoon ★ ★ ★

1941

Mr. and Mrs. Smith ★ ★ ★
Rage in Heaven ★ ★ ★ ★
Here Comes Mr. Jordan ★ ★ ★ ★
Unfinished Business ★ ★ ★

1945

They Were Expendable (direction) ★ ★ ★ ★

1947

Lady in the Lake (direction) ★★★★
Ride the Pink Horse (direction) ★★★★

1948

The Saxon Charm ★★★★
June Bride ★★★★

1949

Once More My Darling ★★

1950

Eye Witness ★★★

1960

The Gallant Hours (direction, cameo)

MONTY PYTHON
★★★3.00 STARS

Graham ChapmanJohnCleeseTerryGilliamEricIdleTerryJonesMichaelPalin or just Monty Python—this zany British comedy group assaults its fans with its debauched good humor in group or solo movies, telecasts, record albums, and books. They burst at the seams with creativity—and bad taste.

Graham Chapman (Brian in *Monty Python's Life of Brian* and creator of the all-star *Yellowbeard*) claims the roots of their popularity are based on "sex and violence." The six Pythons are close in age, all in their early forties, and except for Terry Gilliam, the token American, products of either a Cambridge or Oxford education.

The members met while writing for David Frost's BBC comedy show, "The Frost Report." They pitched the concept for their own show, and the program, "Monty Python's Flying Circus," was born. The group performed its skits about twit contests, silly walks, and penguins on the telly for four years. Although the jokes were perhaps too British for the English, it caught on with American college students, who were still watching reruns long after Python had stopped filming new episodes.

The television series was followed by *And Now For Something Completely Different*, a compilation of Python's greatest skits released to movie theaters. Then came the spoof of the Arthurian legend, *Monty Python and the Holy Grail*, a collection of loosely related skits and such grotesqueries as blood spewing from dismembered limbs.

Life of Brian followed, denounced by Jewish, Catholic, and Protestant leaders as "blasphemous" and "immoral." The controversy translated into lines at the box office. If Python had had its way, a more offensive scene edited out would have been restored.

Cleese (most famous for his "dead parrot" sketch) says the days of making sketch films, a la *Grail*, are past. "You've got to keep the audience on the hop a bit." And except for films based on live performances that resurrect old material, such as *Monty Python Live at the Hollywood Bowl*, the group is entering different areas.

The most successful effort to date has been Gilliam and Palin's *Time Bandits*. It made twice as much money as any group Python film. Palin calls Gilliam the workaholic of the six. Not one to wait around for the other Pythons, Gilliam is now at work on a screenplay with playwright Tom Stoppard. Palin says, "If Python was made up of six Gilliams, there would be this total explosion of creativity."

Eric Idle ("wink, wink, nudge, nudge") hosted "Saturday Night Live" several times and was the mastermind behind the Beatles spoof, "The Rutles." He has been influential in obtaining financing for Python's projects through such friends as George Harrison, who produced *Life of Brian* and *Time Bandits*.

Jones recently directed Python in its current hit *Monty Python's The Meaning of Life*. Its most stomach-churning scene features a glutton who gorges himself and then vomits repeatedly, while the waiter (Cleese) acts blase and makes small talk. The easily offended or squeamish know best to stay away.

Monty Python in *The Meaning of Life.*

With all of the individual and collective deals the group cooks up, what does the future hold for Python? Michael Palin once said, "It's nice to think we'll be making a film in the year 2000: Monty Python's 2001."

Graham Chapman in *Monty Python and the Holy Grail.*

FILMOGRAPHY

1972

And Now For Something Completely Different ★★★

1975

Monty Python and the Holy Grail ★★★

1979

Monty Python's Life of Brian ★★★★

1982

Monty Python Live at the Hollywood Bowl ★★
The Secret Policeman's Other Ball ★★

1983

Monty Python's The Meaning of Life ★★★★

GRAHAM CHAPMAN ONLY

1983

Yellowbeard ★★

JOHN CLEESE ONLY

1968

Interlude ★★★

1970

The Magic Christian ★★★

1981

Time Bandits ★★★

1982

Pirates On Parade ★★

1983

Yellowbeard ★★

ERIC IDLE ONLY

1981

Time Bandits ★★★

1983

Yellowbeard ★★★

MICHAEL PALIN ONLY

1977

Jabberwocky ★★★

1981

Time Bandits ★★★

1982

The Missionary ★★★

DUDLEY MOORE
★★★ 3.08 STARS

Although British, Dudley Moore is really Woody Allen's cousin under the skin. He flaunts his hangups and asks to be loved in spite of them.

Moore was born in 1935, in London. He received extensive training as a pianist while perfecting his skills as a writer and comic. A Broadway success with his partner Peter Cook in "Good Evening" preceded several unsuccessful but extremely funny movies, *The Wrong Box*, *Bedazzled* (which he also cowrote), and *30 Is a Dangerous Age, Cynthia*. Up to this point, his only interesting part was in *Foul Play* as an orchestra conductor. He married and divorced two actresses—Suzy Kendall and Tuesday Weld—and remarked on marriage: "I don't flourish with that institution."

His big break came when George Segal backed out of *10*. "When I saw the rough cut I wanted to shoot myself," Moore commented later, but the picture was a smash. Bo Derek's incredible beauty helped, and stardom was finally within his reach.

Arthur cemented his popularity. He was nominated for an Oscar, and his performance indicated his ability to dig deep into a characterization. Headlines about his private life, a romance with the much-taller Susan Anton, kept him in the news. Through disastrous follow-up films, *Six Weeks* with Mary Tyler Moore and *Lovesick* with Elizabeth McGovern, he has almost sunk his career at the onset. However, Moore has the wit, charm, and audience rapport to maintain his success despite temporary setbacks.

Dudley Moore in *Lovesick*.

FILMOGRAPHY

1966

The Wrong Box ★★★

1967

Bedazzled ★★★

1968

30 Is a Dangerous Age, Cynthia ★★★

1969

Monte Carlo or Bust ★★★
The Bed Sitting Room ★★★

1972

Alice's Adventures in Wonderland ★★★

1978

Foul Play ★★★★
The Hound of the Baskervilles ★★

1980

10 ★★★★

1981

Wholly Moses ★★

1982

Arthur ★★★★
Six Weeks ★★★

1983

Lovesick ★★★

MARY TYLER MOORE
★★½ 2.57 STARS

Mary Tyler Moore has always been one of TV's most engaging comediennes, until *Ordinary People*, but Hollywood always saddled her with poor scripts.

She was born in 1937, in Brooklyn, New York. Her debut film, *X-15*, a sober tail of researchers on a missile base, wasted her talent. *Thoroughly Modern Millie* had a much bigger budget, a solid box-office draw in Julie Andrews and a belabored script that none of the gifted actors (Beatrice Lillie, Carol Channing, and James Fox) could overcome. Moore teamed with Robert Wagner in a forgettable comedy, *Don't Just Stand There!*, and had even worse luck opposite George Peppard in *What's So Bad About Feeling Good?* She also tried to play a nun in an Elvis Presley misfire, *Change of Habit*. It seemed that the Moore talent, so brilliantly displayed in TV movies like *First You Cry*, would never be unveiled in theatres until *Ordinary People* finally turned the trick. As the waspy wife/mother seemingly enslaved by the need to preserve appearances, Moore was faultless. There is one moment, when she turned a huge smile on a waitress in the midst of arguing with husband Donald Sutherland, that alone justified her Oscar nomination.

Mary Tyler Moore with Elvis Presley in *Change of Habit*.

Although she still retains her inability to choose good scripts, as evidenced by *Six Weeks*, she does display great talent when she has a decent role.

FILMOGRAPHY

1961

X-15 ★★

1967

Thoroughly Modern Millie ★★★

1968

Don't Just Stand There! ★★
What's So Bad About Feeling Good? ★★

1969

Change of Habit ★★

1980

Ordinary People ★★★★

1982

Six Weeks ★★★

ROGER MOORE
★★½ 2.44 STARS

Judy Garland once called Robert Goulet "an eight by ten glossy," and this description applies to Roger Moore as well. Moore's attempts at Cary Grant-like suavity are always sunk by a cardboard shallowness. However, his saving grace is a sense of humor, an easy charm that says, "don't take any of this too seriously."

Moore was born in 1928, in London. TV shows like "The Persuaders" and "The Saint" gave him a measure of popularity, but he was bland in early film roles in *Interrupted Melody, The King's Thief*, and *Diane*. There was one excellent part in *The Sins of Rachel Cade* as Angie Dickinson's lover and a few good ones in the minor efforts, *Il Ratto delle Sabine* and *Crossplot*.

Stardom came when Sean Connery left the James Bond series, and Moore was cast in *Live and Let Die* and *The Man With the Golden Gun*. He was more urbane and polished but not quite as forceful as Connery in the role. However, his tongue-in-cheek manner pleased audiences. After a tired thriller, *Gold*, he returned for his best Bond outing, *The Spy Who Loved Me*. *Moonraker* and *Octopussy* continued the winning Bond pattern, and it seems likely that Moore has a secure hold on stardom whether he remains James Bond or not.

Roger Moore in *Octopussy*.

FILMOGRAPHY

1948

The Fuller Brush Man ★★

1951

As Young As You Feel ★★

1954

The Last Time I Saw Paris ★★★

1955

Interrupted Melody ★★★
The King's Thief ★★

1959

Diane ★★

1961

The Sins of Rachel Cade ★★★
Gold of the Seven Saints ★★

1962

Il Ratto delle Sabine ★★

1969

Crossplot ★★

1970

The Man Who Haunted Himself ★★

1973

Live and Let Die ★★★

1974

Gold ★★
The Man With the Golden Gun ★★★

1975

That Lucky Touch ★★

1976

Shout at the Devil ★★
Street People ★★

1977

The Spy Who Loved Me ★★★★

1978

The Wild Geese ★★

1979

Moonraker ★★★
Escape From Athena ★★★

1980

ffolkes ★★

1981

The Cannonball Run ★★
For Your Eyes Only ★★★
The Sea Wolves ★★★
Sunday Lovers ★★★

1982

Octopussy ★★

AGNES MOOREHEAD
★★★½ 3.48 STARS

It is very hard to praise Agnes Moorehead enough. Even her five Oscar nominations don't convey the power and scope she gave to every role, no matter how badly some of the scripts were written.

Born in 1906 in Clinton, Massachusetts, Moorehead was a proficient singer and ballet dancer, as well as a drama coach. Her efforts in radio drama encouraged Orson Welles to cast her in *Citizen Kane*. Although she had a small part, she was stunning as Kane's mother. She was also magnificent as a spinster aunt in *The Magnificent Ambersons*. A radio performance in "Sorry, Wrong Number" had more tension than the screen version with Barbara Stanwyck and brought additional acclaim.

Moorehead was a convincing murderess in a Bogart vehicle, *Dark Passage*, and her portrayal of Charles Bickford's shrewish sister in *Johnny Belinda* was, and remains, among the finest performances ever put on the screen. Another shrewish role, as Kathryn Grayson's mother in *Show Boat*, gave her less to sink her teeth into, but she was amazingly good. When Moorehead played Kim Novak's acting teacher in *Jeanne Eagles*, none of the talent Moorehead displayed rubbed off on Novak. She proved at home with horror *(Hush, Hush . . . Sweet Charlotte)* and her presence as Endora on TV's "Bewitched" was the brightest aspect of an entertaining series.

Though she rarely got lead roles, Agnes Moorehead was uniformly excellent in her roles. She remains one of the finest character actresses that Hollywood has yet produced.

FILMOGRAPHY

1941

Citizen Kane ★★★★

1942

The Magnificent Ambersons ★★★★
The Big Street ★★★

1943

Journey Into Fear ★★★★
The Youngest Profession ★★★
Government Girl ★★★

1944

Jane Eyre ★★★★
Since You Went Away ★★★★
Dragon Seed ★★★
The Seventh Cross ★★★
Mrs. Parkington ★★★★
Tomorrow the World ★★★★

1945

Keep Your Powder Dry ★★★
Our Vines Have Tender Grapes ★★★★
Her Highness and the Bellboy ★★★

1947

Dark Passage ★★★★
The Lost Moment ★★★★

1948

The Woman in White ★★★
Summer Holiday ★★★
Johnny Belinda ★★★★
Station West ★★★

1949

The Stratton Story ★★★★
The Great Sinner ★★★
Without Honor ★★★

1950

Caged ★★★★

1951

Fourteen Hours ★★★★
Show Boat ★★★★
The Blue Veil ★★★★
The Adventures of Captain Fabian ★★★

1952

Captain Black Jack ★★★
The Blazing Forest ★★★

Agnes Moorehead in *Captain Black Jack*.

1953

The Story of Three Loves ★★★★
Scandal at Scourie ★★★
Those Redheads From Seattle ★★★
Main Street to Broadway ★★★

1954

Magnificent Obsession ★★★★

1955

Untamed ★★★
The Left Hand of God ★★★

1956

All that Heaven Allows ★★★★
Meet Me in Las Vegas ★★★
The Conqueror ★★★
The Swan ★★★★
The Revolt of Mamie Stover ★★★
Pardners ★★★
The Opposite Sex ★★★★

1957

The True Story of Jesse James ★★★
Jeanne Eagels ★★★★
The Story of Mankind ★★★
Raintree County ★★★★

1959

Night of the Quarter Moon ★★★
Tempest ★★★
The Bat ★★★★

1960

Pollyanna ★★★★

1961

Twenty Plus Two ★★★
Bachelor in Paradise ★★★★

1962

Jessica ★★★
How the West Was Won ★★★★

1963

Who's Minding the Store? ★★★

1965

Hush, Hush . . . Sweet Charlotte ★★★★

1966

The Singing Nun ★★★

1971

What's the Matter With Helen? ★★★★

1973

Charlotte's Web (voice only)

1975

Dear Dead Delilah ★★★★

ROBERT MORLEY
★★★ 3.06 STARS

Robert Morley is the best thing about nearly all his films. His talent and wit, like his bulk, spread out in all directions.

Morley was born in Semley, England, in 1908. He made a name for himself on the stage, playing such roles as Professor Higgins in "Pygmalion," and then debuted on screen in *Marie Antoinette*, a marvelous performance in an otherwise dreary spectacle. He was superb again in *Outcast of the Islands* and hilarious with Humphrey Bogart in *Beat the Devil*. A suspense drama, *Murder at the Gallop* with Margaret Rutherford, suited his acerbic style, and so did the tense, well-directed *Topkapi* with Melina Mercouri and Peter Ustinov. Morley was a wickedly prissy critic in *Theatre of Blood*, forced to eat his beloved poodle as a punishment for giving the mad actor Vincent Price bad reviews. He played the part with relish and made a meal out of *Who Is Killing the Great Chefs of Europe?*, as one of the title characters.

FILMOGRAPHY

1938

Marie Antoinette ★★★

1941

Major Barbara ★★★★

1942

This Was Paris ★ ★ ★
The Big Blockade ★ ★ ★
The Foreman Went to France ★ ★ ★
The Young Mr. Pitt ★ ★ ★ ★

1945

I Live in Grosvenor Square ★ ★ ★ ★

1949

The Small Back Room ★ ★ ★

1951

Outcast of the Islands ★ ★ ★ ★

1952

The African Queen ★ ★ ★
Curtain Up ★ ★ ★

1953

The Final Test ★ ★ ★
The Story of Gilbert and Sullivan ★ ★ ★
Melba ★ ★ ★

1954

The Good Die Young ★ ★ ★
Rainbow Jacket ★ ★ ★
Beau Brummel ★ ★ ★
Beat the Devil ★ ★ ★ ★

1955

The Adventures of Quentin Durward ★ ★ ★

1956

Around the World in 80 Days (cameo)
Loser Takes All ★ ★ ★

1958

Law and Disorder ★ ★ ★
The Sheriff of Fractured Jaw ★ ★ ★

1959

The Journey ★ ★ ★
The Doctor's Dilemma ★ ★ ★ ★
Libel ★ ★ ★ ★
The Battle of the Sexes ★ ★

1960

Oscar Wilde ★ ★ ★ ★
Giuseppe venduto dai Fratelli ★ ★ ★
The Young One ★ ★ ★

1962

Go to Blazes ★ ★ ★
Road to Hong Kong (cameo)
The Boys ★ ★ ★

1963

Nine Hours to Rama ★ ★ ★
Murder at the Gallop ★ ★ ★
The Old Dark House ★ ★
Take Her—She's Mine ★ ★

1964

Hot Enough for June ★ ★ ★
Topkapi ★ ★ ★ ★
Of Human Bondage ★ ★ ★ ★

1965

Genghis Kahn ★ ★ ★
Those Magnificent Men in Their Flying Machines ★ ★ ★
A Study in Terror ★ ★ ★
Life at the Top ★ ★ ★ ★
The Loved One ★ ★ ★

Robert Morley in *Scavenger Hunt.*

1966

The Alphabet Murders ★ ★ ★
Hotel Paradiso ★ ★
Tender Scoundrel ★ ★
Way . . . Way Out ★ ★

1967

Woman Times Seven ★ ★ ★
The Trygon Factor ★ ★

1968

Hot Millions ★ ★ ★

1969

Some Girls Do ★ ★ ★
Sinful Davey ★ ★

1970

Cromwell ★ ★ ★
Song of Norway ★ ★
Twinky ★ ★
Doctor in Trouble ★ ★ ★

1971

When Eight Bells Toll ★ ★ ★

1973

Theatre of Blood ★ ★ ★ ★

1976

The Blue Bird ★ ★ ★

1978

Who Is Killing the Great Chefs of Europe? ★ ★ ★ ★

1979

Scavenger Hunt ★ ★ ★

1980

Oh Heavenly Dog ★ ★ ★
The Human Factor ★ ★ ★ ★

1981

The Great Muppet Caper (cameo)

VIC MORROW
★ ★ ★ 3.00 STARS

Vic Morrow was such a brutally convincing villain that audiences never quite accepted him in sympathetic parts. His eyes and smile had built-in menace.

Born in 1932, in the Bronx of New York, Morrow was a knife-wielding delinquent in his first film, *The Blackboard Jungle.* His performance stayed in the minds of audiences long after the image of Glenn Ford, who played a nice, victimized teacher, faded. His next pictures were ordinary, *Tribute to a Bad Man, Men in War,* and *God's Little Acre,* but he was back on comfortable ground in *Portrait of a Mobster* as gangster Dutch Schultz. *The Bad News Bears* gave him a chance at comedy, and he was excellent in the fast company of Walter Matthau.

Morrow had a hit TV series, "Combat," and appeared frequently in television movies. One of these, *The Glass House,* showed him at the height of his villainy; he was a prison ringleader who instigated the gang rape of an inmate. He died in 1982 during a freak plane accident while filming *Twilight Zone—the Movie.*

FILMOGRAPHY

1955

The Blackboard Jungle ★ ★ ★ ★

1956

Tribute to a Bad Man ★ ★ ★

1957

Men in War ★ ★ ★

1958

God's Little Acre ★ ★ ★ ★
Hell's Five Hours ★ ★ ★
King Creole ★ ★ ★

1960

Cimarron ★ ★ ★

1961

Portrait of a Mobster ★ ★ ★ ★
Posse From Hell ★ ★ ★

1967

Survival ★ ★ ★

Vic Morrow in *Twilight Zone—The Movie.*

1969

A River of Diamonds ★★★
How to Make It ★★

1974

Dirty Mary Crazy Larry ★★★
The Take ★★

1975

Babysitter ★★★

1976

The Bad News Bears ★★★★
Treasure of Matecumbe ★★★

1977

Funeral for an Assassin ★★★

1978

Message From Space ★★★

1979

The Evictors ★★

1980

Humanoids from the Deep ★★

1983

Twilight Zone—the Movie ★★★

ZERO MOSTEL
★★★ 2.83 STARS

Critic Pauline Kael called Mostel, "the one-man obstacle course that has broken the back of every movie director." It's true that Mostel had a larger-than-life quality that sometimes swamped the camera. However, he also had the talent and intelligence to adapt to any medium, and it's regrettable he was denied the opportunity to do the screen version of "Fiddler on the Roof."

Mostel (Samuel Joel Mostel) was born in 1915, in Brooklyn, New York. His talent for painting surfaced early, but financial security came with standup comedy appearances in nightclubs and his radio and vaudeville appearances led to films. He was a heavy in *Panic in the Streets* and *The Enforcer* but touching as the lonely man who came to see marriage broker Thelma Ritter in *The Model and the Marriage Broker.* He played too broad in *A Funny Thing Happened on the Way to the Forum* but was ideal as one of the *The Producers* who set out to sabotage a Broadway show and wound up with a smash.

He had his greatest triumph on Broadway as the Russian peasant Tevye in the hit musical "Fiddler on the Roof," but his tendency to overplay cost him the role in the movie version. He couldn't triumph over the schmaltzy sentimentality of *The Angel Levine*, but director Martin Ritt toned him down effectively for *The Front.* Mostel played a victim of the blacklist, a role he also played in real life during the 1950s. He died in 1977, just as his movie career was at last gaining impetus.

Zero Mostel in *The Hot Rock.*

FILMOGRAPHY

1943

Du Barry Was a Lady ★★★

1950

Panic in the Streets ★★★★

1951

The Enforcer ★★★
Sirocco ★★★
The Guy Who Came Back ★★★
Mr. Belvedere Rings the Bell ★★

1952

The Model and the Marriage Broker ★★★★

1966

A Funny Thing Happened on the Way to the Forum ★★

1967

The Producers ★★★★

1968

Great Catherine ★★

1969

The Great Bank Robbery ★★

1970

The Angel Levine ★★

1972

The Hot Rock ★★★

1973

Marco ★★

1974

Rhinoceros ★★★

1975

Foreplay ★★★
Journey Into Fear ★★

1976

The Front ★★★★

1978

Watership Down (voice only)

PAUL MUNI
★★★ 3.09 STARS

Paul Muni won a Best Actor Oscar in 1936 for *The Story of Louis Pasteur.* In his heyday, he was widely acclaimed for his meticulous acting, which he worked on "like a scientist who works on an invention." However, there were dissenters, like Mary Astor, who felt, "I didn't approve of his method of working...his total attention to externals, makeup, hair, clothing, manner of walking, gesturing. Every word of the script memorized and actually recorded and rerecorded before he ever went on the set."

Muni was born Muni Weiserfreund in Austria, in 1895. He acted in the Yiddish theatre and then garnered an Oscar nomination for his first picture, *The Valiant*, playing a murderer. *Scarface* and *I Am a Fugitive From a Chain Gang*, both classics, followed and Muni went on to make a string of other highly regarded films: *Bordertown* with Bette Davis, *The Story of Louis Pasteur* and *The Life of Emile Zola*. They were all prestigious costume epics that seem stiff and remote today, but *We Are Not Alone* was a touching tale of a man unjustly executed for murder that still seems fresh. He was mannered and unintentionally comedic as Chopin's teacher in *A Song to Remember*, but warmly human as *The Last Angry Man*, a Brooklyn doctor.

Unfortunately, Mary Astor was right. Muni sank so completely into each individual part that he has no distinct star identity for modern moviegoers.

FILMOGRAPHY

1929

The Valiant ★★★
Seven Faces ★★★

1932

Scarface ★★★★
I Am a Fugitive From a Chain Gang ★★★★

1933

The World Changes ★★★

1934

Hi Nellie! ★★★

1935

Bordertown ★★★★
Black Fury ★★★
Dr. Socrates ★★★

1936

The Story of Louis Pasteur ★★★

1937

The Good Earth ★★
The Woman I Love ★★★
The Life of Emile Zola ★★★

Paul Muni with Ann Carter in *The Commandos Strike at Dawn*.

1939

Juarez ★★★★
We Are Not Alone ★★★★

1941

Hudson's Bay ★★

1943

The Commandos Strike at Dawn ★★★
Stage Door Canteen (cameo)

1945

A Song to Remember ★
Counter-Attack ★★★

1946

Angel on My Shoulder ★★★

1952

Stranger on the Prowl ★★★

1959

The Last Angry Man ★★★★

EDDIE MURPHY
★★★★ 4.00 STARS

Eddie Murphy recently told a reporter, "I put 100% into my comedy. You just gotta have no doubts. I think that even the ugliest bitch in the world can say, 'I want to be a model' and be one!" This driving inner confidence, coupled with charisma and sex appeal, has propelled the youthful comic to superstardom after just two films.

Murphy was born in 1961, in Long Island, New York. By the age of fifteen he was trying out self-written routines at youth centers and bars. His talent and ego ("I'm cocky—there's no such thing as a humble entertainer") got him a spot on "Saturday Night Live" before his twentieth birthday. He proved an expert impressionist and his parodies of ad-pitchman Velvet Jones, film critic Abdul Muhammed, and exercise king Little Richard Simmons made him the undisputed ratings draw of that TV show.

Murphy's popularity soared with a Grammy-nominated album, and movies beckoned. In his first film, *48 Hours*, he played a convict who helped Nick Nolte track down a killer. He lit up the screen, demonstrating what Dan Aykroyd called "inbred talent . . . talent you can't teach, like the dexterity in the fingers of Barney Clark's surgeons." He also had the kind of ease before a camera that usually comes after ten years of training and effort. His follow-up film, *Trading Places*, proved that *48 Hours* was no accident and allowed him more room for comedy and improvising. He proved up to the challenge, displaying the kind of expert timing and explosiveness that will eventually propel him past the inevitable comparisons to Richard Pryor.

Eddie Murphy with Dan Aykroyd in *Trading Places*.

At the root of his appeal is a comment his stepfather, Vernon Lynch, made; Lynch was once a boxer and he wanted Eddie to become one too. His words were, "Heart is what makes a boxer, and it seems like it's what makes a comedian. Eddie has tremendous heart."

FILMOGRAPHY

1981

48 Hours ★★★★

1982

Trading Places ★★★★

PATRICIA NEAL
★★★ 3.14 STARS

Poor films, a tragic romance with Gary Cooper, debilitating strokes, and the illnesses of her children have continually sabotaged Patricia Neal's career. It's amazing—and a tribute to her talent—that she contributed as much to cinema as she did.

She was born in 1926, in Packard, Kentucky. Her Broadway success in "The Voice of the Turtle" and "Another Part of the Forest" led to a starring part in the film, *John Loves Mary*. She struggled to adapt the unadaptable in the movie version of Ayn Rand's novel, The Fountainhead. She was warm and sympathetic in *The Hasty Heart*, though Richard Todd walked away with all the reviews.

One of Neal's best early performances was in *Bright Leaf*—she was the selfish beauty who destroyed tobacco man Gary Cooper. She was also good in *Three Secrets*, and superb in *The Breaking Point*, one of the few screenplays to capture Hemingway's original flavor. *Raton Pass*, *Weekend With Father*, and *Something for the Birds* prompted Warner Brothers to let her go. The talent Hollywood had misused was brilliantly spotlighted on Broadway when she substituted for Barbara Bel Geddes in "Cat on a Hot Tin Roof." However, her next film, the outstanding *A Face in the Crowd*, still didn't bring in the public.

She finally had a commercial break with *Breakfast at Tiffany's*, as the woman who maintained George Peppard. There were both critical and box-office responses to *Hud*. Her Alma was "unsurpassable," according to critic John Simon, and the Academy awarded her an Oscar. She struggled through a near-fatal illness and then did *The Subject Was Roses*, which brought another Oscar nomination.

A TV movie of her ordeal was made starring Glenda Jackson. It inspired awe and admiration, and a hope that she will stay well enough to grace many future films.

FILMOGRAPHY

1949

John Loves Mary ★★
The Fountainhead ★★
It's a Great Feeling ★★★

1950

Bright Leaf ★★★
The Hasty Heart ★★★★
Three Secrets ★★★★
The Breaking Point ★★★★

1951

Operation Pacific ★★★
Raton Pass ★★★
The Day the Earth Stood Still ★★★★
Weekend With Father ★★

Patricia Neal with Paul Newman in *Hud*.

1952

Diplomatic Courier ★★★★
Something for the Birds ★★★
Washington Story ★★★

1954

La Tua Donna ★★
Stranger From Venus ★★

1957

A Face in the Crowd ★★★★

1961

Breakfast at Tiffany's ★★★★

1963

Hud ★★★★

1964

Psyche 59 ★★★

1965

In Harm's Way ★★★

1968

The Subject Was Roses ★★★★

1971

The Night Digger ★★★

1972

Baxter ★★★

1973

Happy Mother's Day-Love George ★★★

1977

Widow's Nest ★★★

1978

Nido de Viudas ★★★

1979

The Passage ★★★

1981

Ghost Story ★★★

PAUL NEWMAN
★★★ 3.05 STARS

Paul Newman's box-office power and striking blue eyes sometimes tended to obscure his genuine talent as an actor. Only now—in his late fifties and silver-haired—is everyone recognizing his ability to get beneath the skin of a character.

Newman was born in 1925, in Cleveland, Ohio. After training at the Yale School of Drama, he performed in TV and became part of the Actor's Studio. Though married to actress Jacqueline Witte, he fell in love with Joanne Woodward when they appeared on Broadway in "Picnic." His film debut in *The Silver Chalice* almost finished him, and he was accused of copying Brando in *The Rack*.

Somebody Up There Likes Me was the turning point, a tremendously enjoyable biography of boxer Rocky Graziano. *The Helen Morgan Story* and *Until They Sail* were less satisfying, but William Faulkner's *The Long Hot Summer* was, and remains, one of his most enjoyable pictures. He played a drifter and suspected barn burner bribed by Orson Welles to marry his daughter Joanne Woodward. The screenplay had wit and tension though a silly Hollywood ending almost spoiled it.

Cat on a Hot Tin Roof inspired critic Bosley Crowther to say, "Newman is perhaps the most resourceful and dramatically restrained of the lot...he gives an ingratiating picture of a tortured young man." He was equally good as an ambitious

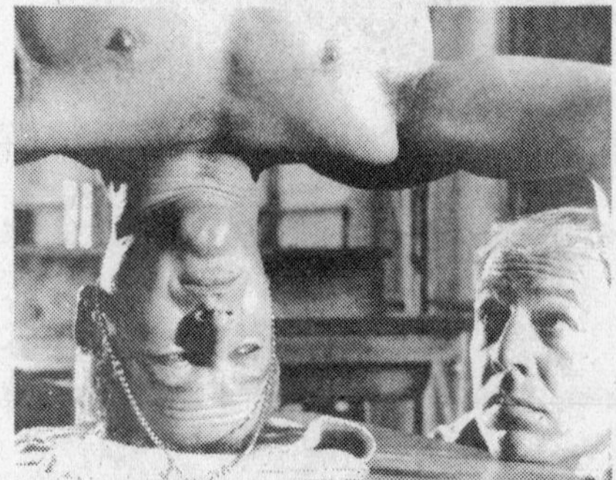

Paul Newman with George Kennedy in *Cool Hand Luke*.

lawyer in *The Young Philadelphians*. He headed the cast of Leon Uris' *Exodus*, a spectacular but somewhat artificial rendering of life in postwar Israel.

There was nothing but praise, however, for his portrayal of *The Hustler*, a brilliant tale of pool players. The other performances, by George C. Scott, Piper Laurie, and Jackie Gleason, were also superb. Newman's luck held through *Sweet Bird of Youth* and *Hud*, an acrid reworking of John Frankenheimer's earlier *All Fall Down*.

Newman's box-office power directed viewers toward *Torn Curtain*, but it was Hitchcock's worst film. He played *Harper*, a down-and-out private eye, and was very effective. His performance as a member of a chain gang in the colorful *Cool Hand Luke* made that film a classic. Best of all was his venture with Robert Redford in *Butch Cassidy and the Sundance Kid*, a tongue-in-cheek western that was initially panned only to find huge audiences anyway.

When *Sometimes a Great Notion*, *WUSA*, *Pocket Money*, and *The Life and Times of Judge Roy Bean* flopped, people began writing Newman off, till he rebounded with two enormous hits, *The Sting* and *The Towering Inferno*. More mediocre pictures (*The Drowning Pool*, *Quintet*) threatened his status before he established his supremacy as a character actor in two excellent vehicles, *Absence of Malice* and *The Verdict*. These performances (both Oscar-nominated), should bring a whole new surge of popularity and critical respect to a richly deserving actor.

FILMOGRAPHY

1955

The Silver Chalice ★★

1956

Somebody Up There Likes Me ★★★★
The Rack ★★★

1957

The Helen Morgan Story ★★★
Until They Sail ★★★

1958

The Long Hot Summer ★★★★
The Left-Handed Gun ★★★
Cat on a Hot Tin Roof ★★★★
Rally 'Round the Flag Boys! ★★

1959

The Young Philadelphians ★★★★

1960

Exodus ★★★
From the Terrace ★★★

1961

Paris Blues ★★★
The Hustler ★★★★

Paul Newman in *The Hustler.*

1962

Sweet Bird of Youth ★★★
Hemingway's Adventures of a Young Man ★★★

1963

Hud ★★★★
A New Kind of Love ★★
The Prize ★★★

1964

What a Way to Go! ★★★
The Outrage ★★

1965

Lady L ★★

1966

Harper ★★★
Torn Curtain ★★★

1967

Hombre ★★★
Cool Hand Luke ★★★★

1968

The Secret War of Harry Frigg ★★

1969

Winning ★★★
Butch Cassidy and the Sundance Kid ★★★★

1970

WUSA ★★
King (documentary)

1971

Sometimes a Great Notion (direction) ★★★

Paul Newman in *The Verdict.*

1972

Pocket Money ★★★
The Life and Times of Judge Roy Bean ★★★

1973

The Sting ★★★★
The Mackintosh Man ★★★

1974

The Towering Inferno ★★

1975

The Drowning Pool ★★★

1976

Silent Movie (cameo)
Buffalo Bill and the Indians ★★★

1977

Slap Shot ★★★

1979

Quintet ★★★
When Time Ran Out ★★★

1981

Absence of Malice ★★★
Fort Apache, The Bronx ★★★

1982

The Verdict ★★★★

JACK NICHOLSON
★★★ 2.97 STARS

Jack Nicholson spent 11 years in low-budget quickies before becoming an "overnight success." Now that his brilliance has been demonstrated so many times, it's somewhat of a mystery that such strong talent could have been ignored.

Born in 1937, in Neptune, New Jersey, his TV work led to a film part in *Attack of the Crab Monsters*. He could only go up after that, and he did, slightly, with *Too Soon to Love*, *Studs Lonigan*, and *The Wild Ride*.

The Little Shop of Horrors didn't help, though it was later used as the basis for an award-winning musical, nor did *Ride the Whirlwind* and *Hell's Angels on Wheels*. Nicholson co-wrote the script for *Head*, a comedy featuring the Monkees. Although it fared badly at the time of release, film buffs like it today.

Easy Rider was more than a box-office success; it triggered a whole trend of youth films. Nicholson was delightful as the middle-class worker who tossed security aside to join his hippie friends (Peter Fonda and Dennis Hopper). A minor role in *On a Clear Day You Can See Forever* passed unnoticed, but *Five Easy Pieces* gave him the triumph he needed for top stardom. He played a drifter who returned to his rich family and tried to make sense of his ambivalent feelings about them. One particularly beautiful scene had him struggling to communicate with his father, a stroke victim.

Carnal Knowledge analyzed the sexual immaturity of the male, and Nicholson embodied this part perfectly. *A Safe Place* was an incomprehensible stab at "art" with Tuesday Weld. Fortunately, *The Last Detail* was considerably livelier; Nicholson played a softhearted sailor taking Randy Quaid to jail. He won the New York Film Critics Award for *Chinatown* and was expected to win the Oscar too, but at the last minute Art Carney scored a surprise victory for *Harry and Tonto*.

Entrenched as a top 10 box-office attraction, he attempted to stretch a bit in Michelangelo Antonioni's *The Passenger*. Though he was excellent, it was nearly a passport to oblivion. *The Fortune*, directed by Mike Nichols, didn't work either, despite the presence of Warren Beatty and Stockard Channing. The elusive Oscar finally fell into his hands for *One Flew Over the Cuckoo's Nest*. He was perfect for the role of the sane man trapped in a lunatic asylum.

As often happens, the Oscar proved a jinx. He paired with Marlon Brando in a distasteful western, *The Missouri Breaks*, certainly Brando's worst performance, and stayed outdoors for *Goin' South*, which he also directed. John Belushi and the delightful Mary Steenburgen were co-starred. *The Shining* had a strong Stephen King novel as its source, but director Stanley Kubrick rewrote much of it, destroying the author's original intentions. Nicholson was, for the first time, monotonous as an insane, possessed hotel caretaker. He repaired the damage with an excellent characterization of playwright Eugene O'Neill in Warren Beatty's epic, *Reds*. There are years of superb roles and future awards waiting for this gifted, charismatic actor.

Jack Nicholson in *The Postman Always Rings Twice*.

FILMOGRAPHY

1957

Attack of the Crab Monsters (bit)

1958

The Cry Baby Killer ★★

1960

Too Soon to Love ★★
The Wild Ride ★★
Studs Lonigan ★★★

1961

The Little Shop of Horrors ★★★

1962

The Broken Land ★★★

1963

The Raven ★★★
The Terror ★★★

1964

Ensign Pulver ★★★
Back Door to Hell ★★★

1966

The Shooting ★★★
Ride the Whirlwind ★★★
Flight to Fury ★★★

1967

The St. Valentine's Day Massacre (bit)
Hell's Angels on Wheels ★★★

1968

Psych-Out ★★★

1969

Easy Rider ★★★★

1970

Rebel Rousers ★★
On a Clear Day You Can See Forever ★★
Five Easy Pieces ★★★★

1971

Carnal Knowledge ★★★★
A Safe Place ★★

1972

The King of Marvin Gardens ★★★

1973

The Last Detail ★★★★

1974

Chinatown ★★★★

1975

Tommy ★★★
The Passenger ★★★★
The Fortune ★★
One Flew Over the Cuckoo's Nest ★★★★

1976

The Missouri Breaks ★★
The Last Tycoon ★★★

1978

Goin' South (direction) ★★★

1979

The Shining ★★

1982

The Postman Always Rings Twice ★★★
Reds ★★★★

DAVID NIVEN
★★★ 2.93 STARS

"I have a face that is a cross between 2 lbs. of halibut and an explosion in an old clothes closet," David Niven once said. "If it isn't mobile, it's dead." This remark sounds like just the sort of witticism Niven performed best on screen. None can surpass him in the area of light comedy.

Niven (James David Graham Niven) was born in 1909, in Kirriemuir, Scotland. His first notable break came with *Dodsworth* as a gigolo. He apparently hated working with director William Wyler but agreed to be Edgar Linton in Wyler's *Wuthering Heights*. The role was too pallid to do his career much good, but *Bachelor Mother* established him as a Cary Grant-type comedian. He was equally relaxed in a soap opera, *The Other Love*, playing the doctor who fell in love with mortally ill Barbara Stanwyck.

Niven played a bishop in *The Bishop's Wife*, a pleasant piece of whimsy—Cary Grant was an angel. He had to tolerate a teenage Shirley Temple in *A Kiss for Corliss*, though *The Moon Is Blue* struck a spark with audiences. It was a pseudo-suggestive, overly talky vehicle, remembered now only because co-star Maggie McNamara later committed suicide.

Niven's biggest box-office success was, and remains, *Around the World in 80 Days*. After that peak, he hit bottom in *The Little Hut*, a hopeless farce with Ava Gardner. He was perfect as the aging rogue in *Bonjour Tristesse*, though Jean Seberg's middle-American charms destroyed all plausibility.

An overdue Oscar arrived with *Separate Tables*. An equal number of successes (*Please Don't Eat the Daisies* and *The Guns of Navarone*) were balanced against his failures (*Bedtime Story* and *Eye of the Devil*), but Niven maintained his polish and authority whatever the circumstances. He died in 1983.

FILMOGRAPHY

1935

Without Regret (bit)
Mutiny on the Bounty (bit)
Barbary Coast (bit)
A Feather in Her Hat (bit)
Splendor (bit)

1936

Rose Marie (bit)
Palm Springs ★★
Thank You Jeeves ★★★
Dodsworth ★★★
The Charge of the Light Brigade ★★★★
Beloved Enemy ★★★

1937

We Have Our Moments ★★★
The Prisoner of Zenda ★★★
Dinner at the Ritz ★★★★

1938

Bluebeard's Eighth Wife ★★★
Four Men and a Prayer ★★★
Three Blind Mice ★★★
Dawn Patrol ★★★★

1939

Wuthering Heights ★★★
Bachelor Mother ★★★★
The Real Glory ★★★
Eternally Yours ★★★

1940

Raffles ★★★★

1942

The First of the Few ★★★★

1944

The Way Ahead ★★★★

1946

Stairway to Heaven ★★★★
Magnificent Doll ★★★

1947

The Perfect Marriage ★★★
The Other Love ★★★
The Bishop's Wife ★★★

1948

Bonnie Prince Charlie ★★★
Enchantment ★★★

1949

A Kiss in the Dark ★★

David Niven with Kathryn Grayson in *The Toast of New Orleans.*

1950

The Elusive Pimpernel ★★★
A Kiss for Corliss ★★
The Toast of New Orleans ★★★

1951

Soldiers Three ★★★
Happy Go Lovely ★★
Appointment With Venus ★★★

1952

The Lady Says No ★★★

1953

The Moon Is Blue ★★★

1954

The Love Lottery ★★★
Happy Ever After ★★★

1955

Court Martial ★★★
The King's Thief ★★★

1956

The Birds and the Bees ★★★
Around the World in 80 Days ★★★

1957

Oh Men! Oh Women! ★★
The Little Hut ★★
My Man Godfrey ★★★
The Silken Affair ★★

1958

Bonjour Tristesse ★★★
Separate Tables ★★★★

1959

Ask Any Girl ★★★★
Happy Anniversary ★★★

1960

Please Don't Eat the Daisies ★★★★

1961

The Guns of Navarone ★★★★
The Best of Enemies ★★★

1962

The Road to Hong Kong ★★★
Guns of Darkness ★★★
Conquered City ★★★

1963

55 Days at Peking ★★★

1964

The Pink Panther ★★★★
Bedtime Story ★★

1965

Lady L ★★★

1966

Where the Spies Are ★★★

1967

Casino Royale ★★★
Eye of the Devil ★★★

1968

Prudence and the Pill ★★
The Impossible Years ★★

1969

The Extraordinary Seaman ★★
Before Winter Comes ★★★
The Brain ★★★

1971

The Statue ★★
King Queen Knave ★★★

1974

Old Dracula ★★★

1975

Paper Tiger ★★★

1976

No Deposit-No Return ★★
Murder by Death ★★

1978

Candleshoe ★★★
Death on the Nile ★★★

1979

A Man Called Intrepid ★★
Escape to Athena ★★
A Nightingale Sang in Berkeley Square ★★★

1980

Rough Cut ★★

1981

The Sea Wolves ★★

1982

Trail of the Pink Panther ★★

1983

Curse of the Pink Panther ★★★

NICK NOLTE
★★★ 3.00 STARS

Nick Nolte always looks like a laborer sweating under a hot sun, and a Los Angeles magazine described him as "a beer drinker." However, this surface appearance masks an individual dedication to his craft, a dedication that kept him on the stage in repertory and stock for 13 years before reaching the screen.

Nolte was born in 1941, in Omaha, Nebraska. He had his heart set on being a football player in college, but was kicked out after sneaking into the women's dorm. He was a steelworker for a while before his first big splash came with Irwin Shaw's "Rich Man Poor Man" on TV. According to Nolte, "Whatever I am today in this business I owe to Irwin Shaw."

His breakthrough film, *The Deep*, was a huge success and made him a star, though his acting was mediocre. *Who'll Stop the Rain?* was much better, and Nolte was brilliant as a drug smuggler. He took other chances, playing a bisexual dreamer in *Heart Beat* and an irresponsible pro-footballer in *North Dallas Forty*. Critical raves didn't bring in the crowds. He made headlines when his long-time girlfriend Karen Eklund slapped him with a palimony suit. There were also rumors of a romance with Jacqueline Bisset.

Nick Nolte.

He starred in *Cannery Row*, an unexpected disappointment, and his career seemed seriously threatened until *48 Hours*, a brutal but hilarious thriller co-starring the delightful Eddie Murphy. Fans cheered, and Nolte went immediately into the forthcoming *Under Fire* with Gene Hackman. His own code: "Survival is not fighting, it's adapting." It appears that Nolte has adapted and is beginning a second climb to the top.

FILMOGRAPHY

1975

Return to Macon County ★★★

1977

The Deep ★★

1978

Who'll Stop the Rain? ★★★★

1979

North Dallas Forty ★★★
Heart Beat ★★★

1982

Cannery Row ★★★
48 Hours ★★★

KIM NOVAK
★★ 2.08 STARS

The late Harry Cohn, head of Columbia Pictures, once said of Kim Novak: "This girl has had five hit pictures. If you wanna bring me your wife or your aunt, we'll do the same for them." In her heyday, Novak was hauntingly beautiful, with a low, sensual voice and "the sort of face," according to Life magazine, "that looks as if the rest of her body is making love." If she had ever learned to act, she could have been a great movie star.

Born Marilyn Pauline Novak, in Chicago, in 1933, she came to Hollywood to escape the attentions of a persistent suitor. Cohn trained her as Rita Hayworth's replacement, and she was cast in *Pushover* with Fred MacMurray. Over director Josh Logan's bitter protests, Novak was cast in *Picnic* and managed to create a *few* sparks with co-star William Holden. She was also magnetic in *The Man With the Golden Arm* as the girl who saved junkie Frank Sinatra from going under.

Kim Novak with Frank Sinatra in *The Man With the Golden Arm.*

Unfortunately, her lack of acting skill was beginning to surface, and she was brutally exposed in the disastrous melodrama, *Jeanne Eagels*. However she insisted, "I know people don't agree with me, but I think I got what I saw in the character." In Hitchcock's *Vertigo*, despite the appearance of having been heavily coached, she *was* effective. But *Of Human Bondage* and *Kiss Me Stupid* only confirmed Time magazine's evaluation of her: "Since she will never be an actress, the time to enjoy her is now."

FILMOGRAPHY

1954

The French Line (bit)
Pushover ★★★
Phffft ★★★

1955

Son of Sinbad (bit)
Five Against the House ★★★
The Man With the Golden Arm ★★★

1956

Picnic ★★★
The Eddy Duchin Story ★★

Kim Novak in *The Legend of Lylah Clare.*

1957

Jeanne Eagels ★
Pal Joey ★ ★

1958

Vertigo ★ ★ ★
Bell Book and Candle ★ ★

1959

Middle of the Night ★ ★

1960

Strangers When We Meet ★ ★
Pepe (cameo)

1962

Boy's Night Out ★ ★
The Notorious Landlady ★ ★

1964

Of Human Bondage ★
Kiss Me Stupid ★ ★

1965

The Amorous Adventures of Moll Flanders ★ ★

1968

The Legend of Lylah Clare ★ ★

1969

The Great Bank Robbery ★

1973

Tales That Witness Murder ★

1976

Massacre at Blood Bath Drive-In ★

1977

The White Buffalo ★ ★ ★

1979

Just a Gigolo ★ ★

1980

The Mirror Crack'd ★ ★

WARREN OATES
★ ★ ★ 3.24 STARS

"My face looks like two miles of country road. Every night I've stayed up late, every woman I ever chased, every drink I've taken—shows. But, hell, man, I don't work in spite of my face, I work *because* of it—and I know that to be true," Warren Oates once told the Hollywood Reporter. Warren Oates belonged to that select group of actors known as "actors' actors." Like Harry Dean Stanton or Robert Duvall, Oates was able to humanize loners and malcontents. Not having the pretty-boy appearance for leading actor status, Oates forged a supporting career in more than 200 television roles and several dozen movie appearances.

He was born in Depoy, Kentucky, in 1928. He did odd jobs before breaking into live television drama. Director Sam Peckinpah gave Oates his start in early TV westerns and promoted him to appear in such feature films as *Ride the High Country* and *The Wild Bunch*. In the latter he played Lyle Gorch, the most rebellious and unpredictable of the bunch.

In the Heat of the Night is the film for which Oates will probably best be remembered. In it, he played a bumbling officer with the Sparta Police Department who also happens to be a Peeping Tom. Oates was less successful when he was elevated to starring roles, as in John Milius' *Dillinger* or Peckinpah's *Bring Me the Head of Alfredo Garcia*.

He carved a second career out of roles in such strictly-for-laughs features as *Stripes* with Bill Murray and Steven Spielberg's *1941*. His last role, as a good-natured policeman in *Blue Thunder*, was released after his death at age fifty-two of a heart attack.

FILMOGRAPHY

1959

Up Periscope! ★ ★ ★
Yellowstone Kelly ★ ★ ★

1960

The Rise and Fall of Legs Diamond ★ ★ ★
Private Property ★ ★ ★

1961

Lover Come Back ★ ★ ★

1962

Ride the High Country ★ ★ ★ ★
Hero's Island ★ ★ ★

1964

Mail Order Bride ★ ★ ★

1965

Major Dundee ★ ★ ★ ★
The Rounders ★ ★ ★

1966

Return of the Seven ★ ★ ★ ★

1967

The Terrornauts ★ ★ ★
Welcome to Hard Times ★ ★ ★ ★
In the Heat of the Night ★ ★ ★ ★

1968

The Wild Bunch ★ ★ ★ ★
The Split ★ ★ ★

1969

Smith! ★ ★ ★
Barquero ★ ★ ★
Crooks and Coronets ★ ★ ★
There Was a Crooked Man ★ ★ ★ ★
Trog ★ ★

1971

The Hired Hand ★ ★ ★
Two Lane Blacktop ★ ★ ★ ★

1972

Chandler ★ ★ ★

1973

Tom Sawyer ★ ★ ★
Kid Blue ★ ★ ★
The Thief Who Came to Dinner ★ ★ ★
Dillinger ★ ★ ★ ★

1974

Badlands ★ ★ ★ ★
The White Dawn ★ ★ ★
Bring Me the Head of Alfredo Garcia ★ ★ ★
Cockfighter ★ ★ ★

Warren Oates in *The Border.*

1975

Race With the Devil ★★★
92 in the Shade ★★★

1976

Dixie Dynamite ★★★
Drum ★★★

1977

Sleeping Dogs ★★★★

1978

The Brinks Job ★★★
China 9, Liberty 37 ★★★

1979

1941 ★★★

1981

Stripes ★★★

1982

The Border ★★★

1983

Blue Thunder ★★★★
Tough Enough ★★★
White Dog ★★★

MERLE OBERON
★★½ 2.70 STARS

Merle Oberon once confessed to Eddie Fisher, "I can have anything I want, but I don't have love. I've chosen the wrong friends." This reality is a considerable contrast to her screen image. Onscreen, Oberon was most often wealthy, glamorous, and totally in command of her life. She was also, when the script permitted, a capable actress.

She was born Estelle Merle O'Brien, in 1911, and raised in India. Film stardom came with *The Private Life of Henry VIII*, and she was excellent in *These Three*, a screen version of Lillian Hellman's "The Children's Hour." In *Wuthering Heights*, she was cast as the willful, passionate Cathy, and she was convincing though slightly bland. It still became a classic, and Oberon appeared in other popular ventures: *'Til We Meet Again*, a tearjerker, and *The Lodger*, with co-star Laird Cregar.

She was a ludicrously modern George Sand in *A Song to Remember*, but the rest of her credits (*Night Song, Berlin Express*, and *Desiree*) are easily forgotten. She had a fine role in *Hotel* and made the most of it. She died in November, 1979.

FILMOGRAPHY

1930

Alf's Button (bit)

1931

Never Trouble Trouble (bit)
Fascination (bit)

1932

Service for Ladies (bit)
For the Love of Mike (bit)
Ebb Tide (bit)
Aren't We All? (bit)
Wedding Rehearsal ★★
Men of Tomorrow ★★

1933

The Private Life of Henry VIII ★★★

Merle Oberon in *Night in Paradise.*

1934

The Battle ★★★
The Broken Melody ★★★
The Private Life of Don Juan ★★★

1935

The Scarlet Pimpernel ★★★
Folies-Bergère ★★★
The Dark Angel ★★★

1936

These Three ★★★★
Beloved Enemy ★★★

1937

I, Claudius (unfinished)
Over the Moon ★★

1938

The Divorce of Lady X ★★
The Cowboy and the Lady ★★★

1939

Wuthering Heights ★★★
The Lion Has Wings ★★★

1940

'Til We Meet Again ★★★

1941

That Uncertain Feeling ★★★
Affectionately Yours ★★★
Lydia ★★★

1943

Forever and a Day ★★★
Stage Door Canteen (cameo)
First Comes Courage ★★★

1944

The Lodger ★★★★
Dark Waters ★★★★

1945

A Song to Remember ★★
This Love of Ours ★★★

1946

Night in Paradise ★★
Temptation ★★

1947

Night Song ★★

1948

Berlin Express ★★★

1951

Pardon My French ★★

1952

24 Hours of a Woman's Life ★★

1954

Todo es Posible en Granada ★★★
Desiree ★★★
Deep in My Heart ★★★

1956

The Price of Fear ★★

1963

Of Love and Desire ★★

1966

The Oscar ★★

1967

Hotel ★★★

1973

Interval ★

EDMOND O'BRIEN
★★★ 3.21 STARS

Edmond O'Brien had the appearance of a character actor rather than a star, but his personality was so forceful that he often stole films from their leading players.

He was born in New York, in 1915. After a few minor Broadway appearances, he joined Orson

Welles' Mercury Players at age twenty-two. His presence enhanced a number of quality films, *The Killers, A Double Life, Another Part of the Forest*, and *White Heat*, and then he was given the lead in an exciting murder mystery *D.O.A.* O'Brien was excellent as the ordinary businessman mistakenly given a dose of slow-acting poison. He returned to supporting roles but carried *The Bigamist*, an absorbing study of a man with two wives, played by Ida Lupino and Joan Fontaine.

His sharp-talking press agent in *The Barefoot Contessa* won an Oscar, and he was nominated again for *Seven Days in May*. O'Brien was also memorable as a drunken newspaperman in *The Man Who Shot Liberty Valance*, an inmate in *Birdman of Alcatraz*, and an aging outlaw in *The Wild Bunch*.

FILMOGRAPHY

1939

The Hunchback of Notre Dame ★★★

1941

Parachute Battalion ★★★

1942

Obliging Young Lady ★★★
Powder Town ★★★

1943

The Amazing Mrs. Holliday ★★★

1944

Winged Victory ★★★

1946

The Killers ★★★★

1947

The Web ★★★★

1948

A Double Life ★★★★
Another Part of the Forest ★★★★
For the Love of Mary ★★★
An Act of Murder ★★★
Fighter Squadron ★★★

1949

White Heat ★★★★

1950

Backfire ★★★
D.O.A. ★★★★
711 Ocean Drive ★★★
Between Midnight and Dawn ★★★
The Admiral Was a Lady ★★★

Edmond O'Brien in *Julius Caesar.*

1951

The Redhead and the Cowboy ★★★
Two of a Kind ★★★
Warpath ★★★
Silver City ★★★

1952

The Denver and the Rio Grande ★★★
The Turning Point ★★★

1953

Man in the Dark ★★★
The Hitch-Hiker ★★★★
Julius Caesar ★★★
The Bigamist ★★★★

1954

Shield for Murder ★★★
The Shanghai Story ★★★
The Barefoot Contessa ★★★★

1955

Pete Kelly's Blues ★★★★

1956

D-Day the Sixth of June ★★★
A Cry in the Night ★★★
1984 ★★★
The Rack ★★★
The Girl Can't Help It ★★★

1957

The Big Land ★★★

1958

The World Was His Jury ★★★
Sing Boy Sing ★★★

1959

The Climbers ★★★
Up Periscope ★★★

1960

The Last Voyage ★★★
The Third Voice ★★★★

1961

The Great Imposter ★★★

1962

Moon Pilot ★★★
The Man Who Shot Liberty Valance ★★★
Birdman of Alcatraz ★★★
The Longest Day ★★★

1964

Seven Days in May ★★★★
Rio Conchos ★★★

1965

Sylvia ★★★
Synanon ★★★

1966

Fantastic Voyage ★★★

1967

The Viscount ★★★
To Commit a Murder ★★★

1969

The Wild Bunch ★★★★

1972

They Only Kill Their Masters ★★★

1974

Lucky Luciano ★★★
99 44/100% Dead ★★★

MAUREEN O'HARA
★★★ 2.87 STARS

Maureen O'Hara's stock in trade was good-natured Irish charm. Unmemorable costume pictures diminished her credibility as an actress, but she was always competent (and occasionally excellent) when the role allowed.

O'Hara (Maureen FitzSimons) was born in 1920, in Millwall, near Dublin, Ireland. After a few innocuous parts in *Kicking the Moon Around* and *My Irish Molly*, she did *Jamaica Inn* for Alfred Hitchcock. It was one of the few Hitchcock pictures to suffer from slow pacing. She was lovely but seemed out of place in *The Hunchback of Notre Dame*. Her performance in *A Bill of Divorcement* in the Katharine Hepburn part wasn't nearly as bad as critics at the time implied. She was

Maureen O'Hara with John Wayne in *The Quiet Man.*

appealing and strong in the Oscar-winning *How Green Was My Valley.* Her ability proven, it was promptly ignored in *To the Shores of Tripoli, The Black Swan,* and *The Spanish Main.* In *Sentimental Journey* she was cast as a dying wife who adopted a child, an artificial situation played by O'Hara and John Payne. She related more naturally to another movie child, Natalie Wood, in the ever-fresh fantasy, *Miracle on 34th Street.* Another comedy, *Sitting Pretty,* was even funnier, thanks to Clifton Webb's hilarious Mr. Belvedere.

The Quiet Man won director John Ford his fourth Oscar, but everybody concerned was at their best. It was O'Hara's finest performance, and she showed a true romantic chemistry with John Wayne. She did *The Magnificent Matador* because, "I felt Anthony Quinn and I would be thoroughly convincing lovers on screen." Yet, the whole enterprise smacked of phoniness, as did *Lady Godiva* and the tasteless *Spencer's Mountain. The Parent Trap* was a smash, however, and *Big Jake* (with Wayne again) also scored well at ticket windows. O'Hara may never be singled out for cult status, but she always offered pleasure to the eye and ear.

FILMOGRAPHY

1938

Kicking the Moon Around (bit)

1939

My Irish Molly ★★
Jamaica Inn ★★★
The Hunchback of Notre Dame ★★★

1940

A Bill of Divorcement ★★★
Dance Girl Dance ★★

1941

They Met in Argentina ★★★
How Green Was My Valley ★★★★

1942

To the Shores of Tripoli ★★
Ten Gentlemen From West Point ★★★
The Black Swan ★★★

1943

The Immortal Sergeant ★★★
This Land Is Mine ★★★
The Fallen Sparrow ★★★

1944

Buffalo Bill ★★★

1945

The Spanish Main ★★★

1946

Sentimental Journey ★★★
Do You Love Me? ★★

1947

Sinbad the Sailor ★★★
The Homestretch ★★★
Miracle on 34th Street ★★★★
The Foxes of Harrow ★★★

1948

Sitting Pretty ★★★★

1949

Forbidden Street ★★★
A Woman's Secret ★★★
Father Was a Fullback ★★★
Bagdad ★★

Maureen O'Hara in *The Rare Breed.*

1950

Comanche Territory ★★
Tripoli ★★★
Rio Grande ★★★★

1951

Flame of Araby ★★

1952

At Sword's Point ★★★
Kangaroo ★★
The Quiet Man ★★★★
Against All Flags ★★★

1953

The Redhead From Wyoming ★★

1954

War Arrow ★★
Malaga ★★

1955

The Long Gray Line ★★★
The Magnificent Matador ★★
Lady Godiva ★★

1956

Lisbon ★★★
Everything But the Truth ★★★

1957

The Wings of Eagles ★★★

1959

Our Man in Havana ★★★

1961

The Parent Trap ★★★
The Deadly Companions ★★★★

1962

Mr. Hobbs Takes a Vacation ★★★

1963

Spencer's Mountain ★★★
McLintock! ★★★

1965

The Battle of the Villa Fiorita ★★★

1966

The Rare Breed ★★★

1970

How Do I Love Thee? ★★★

1971

Big Jake ★★★

LAURENCE OLIVIER
★★★ 3.19 STARS

If versatility means greatness, Laurence Olivier is the finest actor in the world. He began in films as a brooding hero (Maxim in *Rebecca*), went on to make Shakespeare palatable to the masses (*Hamlet*), and has since played arch villains, weaklings, and intellectuals with equal authority.

Olivier was born in 1907, in Dorking, England. He was already a stage star when he did his first movie, *The Temporary Widow.* Early vehicles (*Friends and Lovers* and *Westward Passage*) were generally innocuous. Garbo refused to accept him as her leading man in *Queen Christina.* (Olivier now feels she was right.) He played in two ordinary movies with real-life love Vivien Leigh (*21 Days* and *Fire Over England*) and then William Wyler cast him as Heathcliff in *Wuthering Heights.* He was brilliant. Seldom, if ever, has an agonized, unquenchable love been projected with such force and pathos on the screen. He

Laurence Olivier.

was equally impressive as the coldly reserved Maxim in *Rebecca*. *Pride and Prejudice* made it three hits in a row. Greer Garson was Elizabeth Bennett to his delightful Mr. Darcy, and he played the Lord in love with Lady Hamilton (Vivien Leigh) in *That Hamilton Woman*.

Firmly established as a star, he took his first film stab at Shakespeare in *Henry V.* His work as director, actor, and producer received raves. So did *Hamlet*, which won a Best Picture Oscar, and Olivier won for Best Actor. On this high note he accepted another offer from William Wyler to play in *Carrie*. He was obsessively in love again, this time with Jennifer Jones, but the production was too grim and painful for public enthusiasm. Olivier's performance, though, ranks with his best.

He did more Shakespeare, *Richard III*, and then teamed with Marilyn Monroe in the puzzlingly slow-moving and witless *The Prince and the Showgirl*. Ironically, Olivier found it "enchanting." Audiences didn't agree, despite heavy publicity. They also avoided *The Entertainer*, but his Archie Rice was one of his greatest film portrayals. *Spartacus* was a smash. *Bunny Lake Is Missing*, *Khartoum*, *The Shoes of the Fisherman* and *Oh! What a Lovely War* were uncommercial subjects, yet, he himself, remained consistently excellent.

It took *Sleuth* (a clever duel of wits between Olivier and Michael Caine) to bring viewers in. *Marathon Man* allowed him to be breathtakingly evil as a sadistic Nazi dentist. In recent vehicles (*The Boys From Brazil* and *The Jazz Singer*), he seemed to be hamming it up a little too much and employing a corny accent, but minor lapses of that kind hardly matter. Like Bette Davis, who has done a parody of herself for the last ten years, Olivier's contribution is too vast to be threatened at this late date. Even geniuses can falter occasionally, but the body of their work remains great.

FILMOGRAPHY

1930

The Temporary Widow ★★★
Too Many Crooks ★★★

1931

Potiphar's Wife ★★★
The Yellow Ticket ★★★
Friends and Lovers ★★★

1932

Perfect Understanding ★★
No Funny Business ★★★
Westward Passage ★★★

1935

Moscow Nights ★★★

1936

Conquest of the Air (documentary)
As You Like it ★★★★

1937

Fire Over England ★★★

1938

The Divorce of Lady X ★★★

1939

Clouds Over Europe ★★★
Wuthering Heights ★★★★

1940

21 Days ★★★
Rebecca ★★★★
Pride and Prejudice ★★★★

1941

That Hamilton Woman ★★★★
49th Parallel ★★★
Words for Battle (voice only)

1943

Adventure for Two ★★★

Laurence Olivier with Merle Oberon in *Wuthering Heights*.

Laurence Olivier in *Hamlet.*

1944

Henry V ★★★★

1948

Hamlet ★★★★

1951

The Magic Box (cameo)

1952

Carrie ★★★★

1953

The Beggar's Opera ★★★
A Queen Is Crowned (voice only)

1955

Richard III ★★★★

1957

The Prince and the Showgirl ★★

1959

The Devil's Disciple ★★★

1960

The Entertainer ★★★★
Spartacus ★★★★

1962

Term of Trial ★★★★

1963

Uncle Vanya ★★★★

1965

Bunny Lake Is Missing ★★★
Othello ★★★★

1966

Khartoum ★★★★

1968

Romeo and Juliet (narration)
The Shoes of the Fisherman ★★★

1969

Oh! What a Lovely War ★★★
The Dance of Death ★★★
Battle of Britain ★★★

1970

The Three Sisters ★★★

1971

Nicholas and Alexandra ★★★

1972

Sleuth ★★★★
Lady Caroline Lamb ★★★

1976

Marathon Man ★★★★
The Seven Percent Solution ★★★★

1977

A Bridge Too Far ★★

1978

The Betsy ★★
The Boys From Brazil ★★★

1979

A Little Romance ★★★
Dracula ★★

1980

The Jazz Singer ★★

1981

Clash of the Titans★★★

1982

Inchon★

RYAN O'NEAL
★★★ 2.80 STARS

Unlike Warren Beatty, Ryan O'Neal hasn't benefited from his off-screen ladies' man image. The fan magazines romanticize Beatty and criticize O'Neal for narcissism, but there's more to him than swim trunks and a suntan, as several performances have indicated.

O'Neal was born Patrick O'Neal in Los Angeles, California, in 1941. A former lifeguard and amateur boxer, he gained popularity via TV's "Peyton Place," and then entered movies with *The Big Bounce*. It led nowhere, as did an Olympic tale, *The Games*. In *Love Story*, O'Neal played the husband of doomed Ali MacGraw with total honesty and selflessness, and established himself as an actor. He was also good, if miscast, opposite Barbra Streisand in *What's Up, Doc?*, and scored his third bull's-eye in *Paper Moon*.

It wasn't his fault that director Stanley Kubrick's elaborate conception of *Barry Lyndon* overwhelmed the actors. Nor could he have done anything to save *Oliver's Story*, a limp sequel to *Love Story*. He was little more than a generic model in Walter Hill's *The Driver*—his character didn't even have a name. He paired with Streisand again in *The Main Event*, and although it was less enjoyable than their other teaming, O'Neal made excellent use of the comic material at hand. Lately, he has kept to light comedy, being mildly enjoyable in *So Fine* and *Partners*.

Ryan O'Neal with Barbra Streisand in *What's Up, Doc?*

FILMOGRAPHY

1969

The Big Bounce ★★

1970

The Games ★★★
Love Story ★★★

1971

Wild Rovers ★★

1972

What's Up, Doc? ★★★

1973

The Thief Who Came to Dinner ★★★
Paper Moon ★★★★

1975

Barry Lyndon ★★★

1976

Nickelodeon ★★★

1977

A Bridge Too Far ★★

1978

The Driver ★★★
Oliver's Story ★★

1979

The Main Event ★★★

1981

So Fine ★★★

1982

Partners ★★★

TATUM O'NEAL
★★★ 3.00 STARS

Tatum O'Neal was a true original when she first debuted in *Paper Moon*—a tough, independent kid who knew her way around better than most adults. She's since gone through that inevitable awkward phase encountered by child actors in transition, but her talent is strong enough to see her through.

Tatum was born in Los Angeles, California, in 1963, the daughter of Ryan O'Neal and actress Joanna Moore. As noted, she was perfect in *Paper Moon*, the youngest Oscar winner in Hollywood history. *The Bad News Bears* was a worthy follow-up, and O'Neal was amusing as the Little Leaguer coping with beer-drinking coach Walter Matthau. The material was thinner in director Peter Bogdanovich's tribute to early moviemaking, *Nickelodeon*.

Dad Ryan urged her to do *International Velvet*—a mistake commercially, although the film built up to an exciting climax and had excellent support by Anthony Hopkins. *Little Darlings* dealt with an entertaining rivalry between O'Neal and Kristy McNichol. McNichol emerged the more finished actress, though Newsweek's David Ansen said O'Neal was developing a definite allure. This allure augurs well for her future in films.

Tatum O'Neal in *International Velvet.*

FILMOGRAPHY

1973

Paper Moon ★★★★

1976

The Bad News Bears ★★★★
Nickelodeon ★★★

1978

International Velvet ★★

1979

Little Darlings ★★★

1980

Circle of Two ★★

PETER O'TOOLE
★★★ 3.04 STARS

Peter O'Toole is theatrical and flamboyant, but also believable. He brims with vitality, yet he can tone down and play a subdued, reclusive character when required to.

Born in 1932, in Connemara, Ireland, O'Toole tried journalism for awhile and then concentrated on the stage. Some early successes in "The Holiday," "Hamlet," and "The Long and the Short and the Tall" led to the Disney film *Kidnapped*. He played in *The Day They Robbed the Bank of England*, a well-made but routine caper picture, but stardom was inevitable when David Lean cast him as *Lawrence of Arabia*. The movie and his portrayal were universally admired, and he received an Oscar nomination, even though *Becket* was far more enjoyable. O'Toole's obsessed King Henry II outshone Richard Burton's Becket, and the relationship between the two men gave a human center to the spectacular backdrops.

He had bad luck with *Lord Jim*, a tedious adaptation of Conrad's novel about a British officer discredited as a coward. Critic Leonard Maltin observed accurately that "the film's great moments are provided by an outstanding supporting cast." The cast included James Mason. Curt Jurgens, Eli Wallach, Jack Hawkins, and Paul Lukas. *What's New, Pussycat?* was a box-office hit, but the movie turned out to be a strained, unfunny farce. It was scripted by Woody Allen before he hit his stride. *How to Steal a Million* with Audrey Hepburn was pleasant but uninspired, and *The Night of the Generals* died onscreen and at ticket windows.

O'Toole needed a worthwhile picture and he got it with *The Lion in Winter.* His vivid portrayal of King

Peter O'Toole in *My Favorite Year.*

Henry II dominated throughout although Katharine Hepburn won the undeserved Oscar. His drinking reportedly caused delays and O'Toole's producer Joseph E. Levine refused to pay his star a percentage until ordered by the courts to do so. *Goodbye, Mr. Chips* was a commercial disaster—unfortunately, since it contained O'Toole's most sensitive and detailed performance. As the crusty old schoolmaster humanized by love, he managed to suggest the man's repressed need for affection even when hiding behind a cold, guarded exterior.

Most of his subsequent pictures have been disappointing. *Brotherly Love* was a forgettable mishmash about incest, and he was wildly out of place in the dark, drab film version of *Man of La Mancha. The Ruling Class* brought an Oscar nomination, but few paying customers cared to find out why.

His comeback part was in a comedy, *My Favorite Year.* Directed by actor Richard Benjamin, the script was an affectionate satire of early TV. He had formidable competition, for Joe Bologna did a magnificent takeoff of Sid Caesar, but O'Toole carried the picture, playing a drunk old actor recruited to star on a television show. The character could have been irritating and abrasive, but in O'Toole's hands he was recognizably human and even moving (as well as hilarious). This performance, in fact, stands as a definitive example of how to invest multiple shadings into a part.

FILMOGRAPHY

1960

The Savage Innocents ★ ★ ★
The Day They Robbed the Bank of England ★ ★ ★
Kidnapped ★ ★ ★

1962

Lawrence of Arabia ★ ★ ★ ★

1964

Becket ★ ★ ★ ★

1965

Lord Jim ★ ★
What's New Pussycat? ★ ★
The Sandpiper (voice only)

1966

The Bible ★ ★ ★

Peter O'Toole in *Lawrence of Arabia.*

How to Steal a Million ★ ★ ★
The Night of the Generals ★ ★

1967

Casino Royale ★ ★

1968

The Lion in Winter ★ ★ ★ ★
Great Catherine ★ ★ ★

1969

Goodbye, Mr. Chips ★ ★ ★ ★

1970

Brotherly Love ★ ★ ★

1971

Murphy's War ★ ★ ★
Under Milk Wood ★ ★

1972

The Ruling Class ★ ★ ★ ★
Man of La Mancha ★ ★

1975

Rosebud ★ ★ ★
Man Friday ★ ★ ★

1976

Other Side of Paradise ★ ★ ★

1977

Caligula ★ ★ ★

1978

The Stuntman ★ ★ ★ ★
Power Play ★ ★ ★

1979

Zulu Dawn ★ ★ ★

1982

My Favorite Year ★ ★ ★ ★

AL PACINO
★ ★ ★ 2.83 STARS

Al Pacino is a man-on-the-street type of star like Dustin Hoffman. Both have intensity and power, but Pacino lacks the humor and charm needed for romantic roles.

Pacino (Alberto Pacino) was born in 1940, in New York City. Though cited by Variety as a graduate of the High School of Performing Arts, he actually dropped out at age seventeen and began appearing off-Broadway. "The Indian Wants the Bronx" won him an Obie award, and he won a Tony for his next stage effort in "Does a Tiger Wear a Necktie?" *Me Natalie,* his first movie, was a soap opera with Patty Duke, and though the star was entranced with the film, audiences showed less enthusiasm.

Pacino's debut was unmemorable, but his next role as a junkie in *Panic in Needle Park* was quite meaty. The script took a relentlessly realistic and sordid view of drug addiction, and Pacino captured all the pettiness and anxiety of the main character. *The Godfather* was grim too, an epic study of gangsters who liked their work, and he was superb as son and successor to Mafia Don Marlon Brando. Brando's performance (despite a Best Actor Oscar)

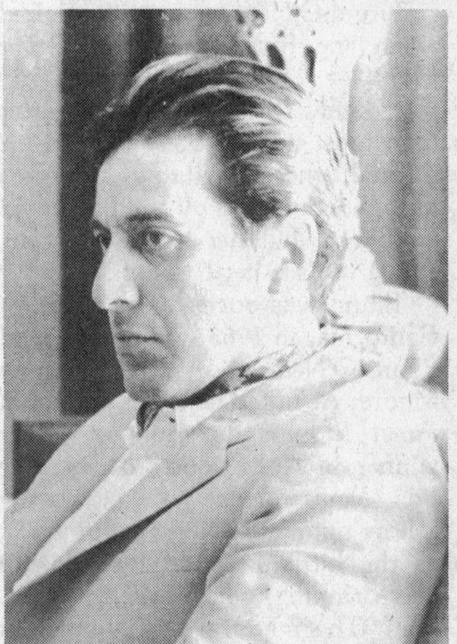

Al Pacino in *The Godfather, Part II.*

was mannered and his vocal tricks irritating; Pacino played it straight, drawing emotion from the inside and stealing the picture.

A string of strong vehicles made him a sure box-office attraction. The first was *Serpico;* he played a cop who expressed his outrage about the corruption within the police department and incurred resentment from co-workers. The single-mindedness of his character became tedious before the fadeout, but Pacino invested it with conviction. *Dog Day Afternoon* was more

Al Pacino with John Cazale in *Dog Day Afternoon.*

peculiar, a bizarre comedy-drama about a gay bank robber who wanted to finance a sex-change operation for his male lover. Both films garnered him Oscar nominations, but he was even more brilliant in *The Godfather, Part II.* His performance was almost motionless except around the eyes, but viewers saw the slow buildup of murderous evil that finally eroded his soul. Like its predecessor, the movie won a Best Picture Oscar.

Unfortunately, he chose to follow with a ludicrous romantic drama, *Bobby Deerfield.* He played a race car driver in love with dying Marthe Keller and proved that soap operas weren't as easy to pull off as most critics supposed. As a crusading lawyer battling injustice in the form of corrupt Judge John Forsythe in *And Justice For All,* he returned to form. A few more Broadway hits, "The Basic Training of Pavlo Hummel" and "Richard III," offset the ugly, unpleasant, and unpopular *Cruising.* Pacino was a detective who gradually turned psychotic while seeking the killer of gays. He took the part, undoubtedly, because it presented a challenge.

Challenges can backfire, but when they work, as in *Dog Day Afternoon,* they allow an actor to show new facets of his talent. Those high moments from performers of Pacino's stature are worth the occasional failures.

FILMOGRAPHY

1969

Me Natalie ★★

1971

Panic in Needle Park ★★★

1972

The Godfather ★★★★

1973

Scarecrow ★★
Serpico ★★★★

1974

The Godfather, Part II ★★★★

1975

Dog Day Afternoon ★★★★

1977

Bobby Deerfield ★

1979

And Justice for All ★★★

1980

Cruising ★★

1982

Author! Author! ★★

1983

Scarface ★★★

GREGORY PECK
★★★ 3.04 STARS

Critic Pauline Kael called Gregory Peck "competent but always a little boring—a leading man disguised as a star." Peck was rarely exciting, but in his youth he had looks and sexuality. The sexuality has gone, but his earnestness still lends conviction to his later work.

Peck (Eldred Gregory Peck) was born in 1916, in La Jolla, California. He made a strong impression on Broadway in Emlyn Williams' "The Morning Star," and then did his first picture, *Days of Glory.* It was a slow-moving war story though reaction to Peck was positive. His sincerity was appropriate for *The Keys of the Kingdom,* even if A. J. Cronin's mesmerizing novel lost its punch in screen translation. *The Valley of Decision* was his third film, and aided by the box-office potency of Greer Garson, it was a hit. Years later, he complained that Garson was always well lit, while shots of him were mysteriously out of focus. He held his own with "Big Red" anyway (his nickname for Garson), and he won additional plaudits as a mental patient in Hitchcock's *Spellbound. The Yearling* was a classic tale of a boy and his fawn, and Peck supplied authority as Claude Jarman, Jr.'s, father. *Duel in the Sun* was producer Selznick's attempt to top his own *Gone With the Wind.* He didn't, although co-stars Peck and Jennifer Jones blended effectively.

Gentlemen's Agreement won a Best Picture Oscar and added "prestige" to his career. He played a Gentile posing as a Jew, and the film examined the subtler aspects of anti-Semitism—the "nice people who protest it and help it grow." The hero's horrified naivete over discriminatory practices taxed viewer credulity, and Peck was more mechanical than co-stars John Garfield and Dorothy McGuire. He didn't seem convincingly British either, as a London barrister defending a murderess in *The Paradine Case.* However, he made an effective General

Gregory Peck with Deborah Kerr in *Beloved Infidel.*

in *Twelve O'Clock High* and was superb as *The Gunfighter.*

Other successes included *The Snows of Kilimanjaro*, a touching version of a Hemingway story, and *Roman Holiday*, the romantic fantasy that launched Audrey Hepburn. He fumbled as Ahab in John Huston's *Moby Dick*, and walked woodenly through *The Man in the Gray Flannel Suit*, a weak version of a good novel by Sloan Wilson.

Beloved Infidel cast him as F. Scott Fitzgerald, a mistake on all counts as Sheilah Graham (the author) felt even before shooting began. *The Guns of Navarone* compensated, and *To Kill a Mockingbird* won him his first Oscar after five nominations. The role required strength, sincerity, and kindness—qualities Peck projected exceptionally well. He followed this triumph with a few other entertaining vehicles, *Captain Newman M.D.*, the amusing *Mirage*, and a somber western, *The Stalking Moon*.

A long line of flops, *I Walk the Line*, *Shoot-Out*, and *Billy Two Hats*, seemed to indicate that his career was finished. However, he suddenly had the biggest financial smash of his whole career: *The Omen*, a bloody but engrossing horror yarn. *The Boys From Brazil* was popular too, although Peck was an odd choice to play a Nazi sadist. Still, his basic niceness which worked against creating evil characters should sustain him as long as he cares to make films.

Gregory Peck.

FILMOGRAPHY

1944

The Days of Glory ★★★

1945

The Keys of the Kingdom ★★★★
The Valley of Decision ★★★
Spellbound ★★★★

1946

The Yearling ★★★★

1947

The Macomber Affair ★★★★
Duel in the Sun ★★★
Gentleman's Agreement ★★

1948

The Paradine Case ★★
Yellow Sky ★★★

1949

The Great Sinner ★★★

1950

Twelve O'Clock High ★★★★
The Gunfighter ★★★★

1951

Only the Valiant ★★★
David and Bathsheba ★★★
Captain Horatio Hornblower ★★★

1952

The Snows of Kiliminjaro ★★★★
The World in His Arms ★★★

1953

Roman Holiday ★★★★

1954

Night People ★★★
The Million Pound Note ★★★
The Purple Plain ★★★

1956

The Man in the Gray Flannel Suit ★★
Moby Dick ★★

1957

Designing Woman ★★★

1958

The Bravados ★★★
The Big Country ★★★

1959

Pork Chop Hill ★★★
Beloved Infidel ★
On the Beach ★★★

1961

The Guns of Navarone ★★★★

1962

To Kill a Mockingbird ★★★★
Cape Fear ★★★★
How the West Was Won ★★★

1964

Captain Newman M.D. ★★★★
Behold a Pale Horse ★★

1965

Mirage ★★★

1966

Arabesque ★★

1969

The Stalking Moon ★★★
MeKenna's Gold ★★★
The Chairman ★★
Marooned ★★★

1970

I Walk the Line ★★

1971

Shoot-Out ★★★

1974

Billy Two Hats ★★★

1976

The Omen ★★★

1977

MacArthur ★★★

1978

The Boys From Brazil ★★★

1980

The Sea Wolves ★★★

SEAN PENN
★★★½ 3.33 STARS

A highly versatile teen star, Sean Penn can play a stoned-out surfer or a brooding killer with equal skill. Rolling Stone Magazine has called him the next James Dean, but he is much too detached and ironic an actor for that.

He was born in Santa Monica, California in 1963. His father was a television director and he was encouraged to act in the theatre. His Broadway debut in a short-lived play attracted the attention of a casting director. He made his film debut in 1981 with *Taps*. As the wry voice of reason when his fellow cadets take up arms, he possessed a relaxed quality that clashed well with star Timothy Hutton's conventional good looks and rigid demeanor.

Sean Penn in *Bad Boys*.

Penn stretched his relaxed quality to quaalude proportions in *Fast Times at Ridgemont High*. As surfer Jeff Spicolli, he stole the film and immortalized the line, "Hey Bud, let's party!" In his third film, *Bad Boys*, he starred as a misunderstood young hoodlum who must learn to cope in a reform school. It is an intense, aware performance that is the beginning of a mature career. Sean Penn recently returned to Broadway in "Slab Boys," and is currently engaged to rock singer Bruce Springsteen's sister Pam.

FILMOGRAPHY

1981

Taps ★★★

1982

Fast Times at Ridgemont High ★★★

1983

Bad Boys ★★★★

GEORGE PEPPARD
★★★ 2.88 STARS

Viewing George Peppard's beautiful performance as Rafe in *Home From the Hill* gives one a sad sense of talent wasted. Never again did he display the haunting eloquence and sincerity contained in that role.

Peppard was born in 1928, in Detroit, Michigan. He debuted in Jack Garfein's grimly effective but unpopular cadet drama, *The Strange One*, and then played in *Pork Chop Hill*, another depressing vehicle. Vincente Minnelli cast him in *Home From the Hill*, and stardom seemed a certainty. He was comfortable in the zany *Breakfast at Tiffany's* opposite Audrey Hepburn, no mean feat in a cast where everyone (particularly Mickey Rooney) overplayed.

How the West Was Won drew huge audiences, and Peppard was commercially lucky again with *The Victors*, although the script wandered until it lost all sense of direction. Director Edward Dmytryk is on record as praising Peppard's performance in *The Carpetbaggers*; his steely stare and tight-jawed intensity were peculiarly right for the Howard Hughes-like part.

Problems surfaced when he did *The Third Day* with wife Elizabeth Ashley (who also appeared in *The Carpetbaggers*). Ashley's acting style, ideal for the stage, was gratingly affected on film. *Pendulum* was an improvement, a neat crime story that stated both a pro and con case for capital punishment.

The *House of Cards* caved in, however, and he couldn't save a silly comedy with Mary Tyler Moore, *What's So Bad About Feeling Good?* Peppard had—still has—it all; the looks, the camera presence, and the acting equipment. However, he couldn't overcome the low quality of his recent pictures. *One More Train to Rob, Newman's Law, Damnation Alley,* and *Five Days From Home* are simply second-rate.

George Peppard is now a star at last—on television for the camp/violent "The 'A' Team." This must surely be the strangest twist in his whole career.

George Peppard in *How the West Was Won.*

FILMOGRAPHY

1957

The Strange One ★★★

1959

Pork Chop Hill ★★★

1960

Home From the Hill ★★★★
The Subterraneans ★★

1961

Breakfast at Tiffany's ★★★★

1962

How the West Was Won ★★★

1963

The Victors ★★★★

1964

The Carpetbaggers ★★★

1965

The Third Day ★★★
Operation Crossbow ★★★

1966

The Blue Max ★★★

1967

Rough Night in Jericho ★★★
Tobruk ★★★

1968

P.J. ★ ★ ★
What's So Bad About Feeling Good ★ ★

1969

House of Cards ★ ★
Pendulum ★ ★ ★

1970

The Executioner ★ ★ ★
Cannon for Cordoba ★ ★

1971

One More Train to Rob ★ ★

1972

The Groundstar Conspiracy ★ ★ ★

1974

Newman's Law ★ ★ ★

1977

Damnation Alley ★ ★

1978

Five Days From Home ★ ★ ★

1979

Da Dunkerque alla Vittoria ★ ★ ★

1980

Battle Beyond the Stars ★ ★ ★

ANTHONY PERKINS
★ ★ ½ 2.64 STARS

When Anthony Perkins first appeared on the screen, everyone thought he would become one of Hollywood's hottest stars. Because he played too many neurotic weaklings, it didn't work out that way, despite his charm and talent. When he was matched up with important female co-stars (Ingrid Bergman, Melina Mercouri, and Sophia Loren), they were physically and temperamentally inappropriate for his personality.

Perkins was born in 1932, in New York City, and made an inauspicious film debut in *The Actress* with Jean Simmons. He remedied that with *Friendly Persuasion*, and his sensitive portrait of a boy questioning his pacifist beliefs was the best thing about that brilliant picture. *Desire Under the Elms* and *Green Mansions* were disasters, but he created a legendary character—one that he can never escape—as the maniacal killer Norman Bates in Alfred Hitchcock's *Psycho*.

After that, *Tall Story* and *On the Beach* were bland indeed, and *Phaedra* was merely ludicrous. *Pretty Poison* with Tuesday Weld gave him a chance to show his skill, but it was his last lead role for quite awhile.

Perkins turned in excellent supporting performances in *Catch-22*, *The Life and Times of Judge Roy Bean*, *Murder on the Orient Express*, and *Winter Kills*. He didn't receive another starring role until called upon to repeat Norman Bates in *Psycho II*. Though he was good, the film wasn't. The contrast to his performance 23 years earlier did point out how he had matured through his career.

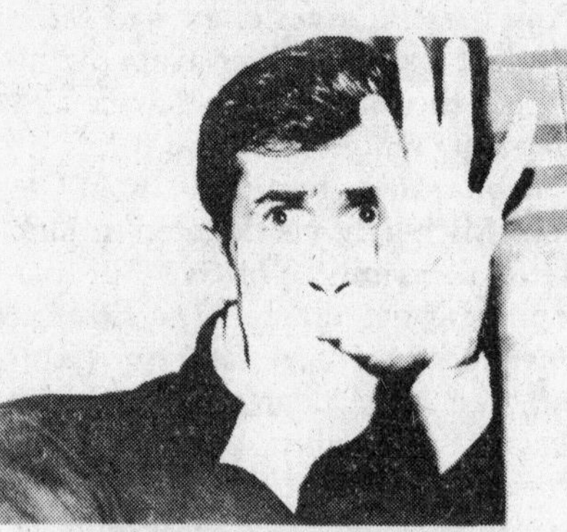

Anthony Perkins in *Psycho*.

FILMOGRAPHY

1953

The Actress ★ ★ ★

1956

Friendly Persuasion ★ ★ ★ ★

1957

Fear Strikes Out ★ ★ ★ ★
The Lonely Man ★ ★ ★
The Tin Star ★ ★ ★

1958

Desire Under the Elms ★ ★
This Angry Age ★ ★ ★
The Matchmaker ★ ★ ★

1959

Green Mansions ★ ★
On the Beach ★ ★ ★

1960

Tall Story ★ ★
Psycho ★ ★ ★ ★

1961

Goodbye Again ★ ★

1962

Phaedra ★ ★
The Trial ★ ★ ★
Five Miles to Midnight ★ ★ ★

Anthony Perkins with Tuesday Weld in *Pretty Poison.*

1963

Two Are Guilty ★ ★ ★

1964

A Ravishing Idiot ★ ★

1965

The Fool Killer ★ ★ ★

1966

Is Paris Burning? ★ ★

1967

The Champagne Murders ★ ★ ★

1968

Pretty Poison ★ ★ ★ ★

1970

Catch-22 ★ ★ ★ ★
WUSA ★ ★ ★

1971

Someone Behind the Door ★ ★ ★

1972

Ten Days' Wonder ★ ★ ★
Play It As It Lays ★ ★ ★
The Life and Times of Judge Roy Bean ★ ★ ★

1974

Lovin' Molly ★ ★ ★
Murder on the Orient Express ★ ★ ★

1975

Mahagony ★ ★

1978

Remember My Name ★ ★ ★

1979

The Black Hole ★ ★ ★
Twice a Woman ★ ★ ★
Double Negative ★ ★
Winter Kills ★ ★ ★

1980

Blind Love ★ ★ ★
Ffolkes ★ ★ ★

1983

Psycho II ★ ★ ★

WALTER PIDGEON
★ ★ ★ 3.08 STARS

In the 1940s, Walter Pidgeon and Greer Garson were the definitive examples of domestic harmony on film. Pidgeon was agreeable without being passive, heroic without histrionics. The word that best described his acting style was "comfortable."

Born in 1897, in East St. John, New Brunswick, Canada, Pidgeon was a singer and vaudeville entertainer before embarking on a screen career. Early silents included *Mannequin, Old Loves and New, The Girl From Rio,* and *The Thirteenth Juror.* His reputation rose with a Jeanette MacDonald vehicle, *The Girl of the Golden West,* and *Too Hot to Handle* with Clark Gable and Myrna Loy. He was believable in a thriller, *Man Hunt,* and then made the movie that solidified his stardom, *Blossoms in the Dust,* with Greer Garson.

How Green Was My Valley, an Oscar winner for Best Picture, cast him effectively as a priest. He was the perfect husband for Greer Garson in *Mrs. Miniver,* and his reassuring strength made wartime viewers feel the situation with Hitler was well in hand. There were also more hits with Garson in *Madam Curie* and *Mrs. Parkington.* He waited patiently for Claudette Colbert to resolve her family crises in *The Secret Heart,* an absorbing woman's picture. He rescued Garson from the selfish domination of Errol Flynn in *That Forsyte Woman.* He was particularly notable as a studio boss in *The Bad and the Beautiful* and played a powerful confrontation scene with son Paul Newman in *The Rack.* In the same year, he starred in a science-fiction classic, *Forbidden Planet.*

After doing "The Happiest Millionaire" on Broadway, Pidgeon played Ziegfeld opposite Barbra Streisand's Fanny Brice in *Funny Girl.* Now unofficially retired, he still dominates the late-night movies on TV, dispensing his brand of solid, unthreatening masculinity to new generations.

FILMOGRAPHY

1926

Mannequin ★ ★ ★
The Outsider ★ ★ ★
Old Loves and New ★ ★ ★
Miss Nobody ★ ★ ★
Marriage License? ★ ★ ★

1927

The Heart of Salome ★ ★ ★
The Girl From Rio ★ ★ ★
The Gorilla ★ ★ ★
The Thirteenth Juror ★ ★ ★

1928

The Gateway of the Moon ★ ★ ★
Woman Wise ★ ★ ★
Turn Back the Hours ★ ★ ★
Clothes Make the Woman ★ ★ ★
Melody of Love ★ ★ ★

1929

The Voice Within ★ ★ ★
Her Private Life ★ ★ ★
A Most Immoral Lady ★ ★ ★

1930

Showgirl in Hollywood (cameo)
Bride of the Regiment ★ ★ ★
Sweet Kitty Bellairs ★ ★ ★
Viennese Nights ★ ★ ★

1931

Kiss Me Again ★ ★ ★
Going Wild ★ ★ ★
The Gorilla ★ ★ ★
The Hot Heiress ★ ★ ★

1932

Rockabye ★ ★ ★

1933

The Kiss Before the Mirror ★ ★ ★

1934

Journal of a Crime ★ ★ ★

1936

Big Brown Eyes ★ ★ ★
Fatal Lady ★ ★ ★

1937

She's Dangerous ★ ★ ★
Girl Overboard ★ ★ ★
As Good As Married ★ ★ ★
Saratoga ★ ★ ★
My Dear Miss Aldrich ★ ★ ★
A Girl With Ideas ★ ★ ★

1938

Man-Proof ★ ★ ★
The Girl of the Golden West ★ ★ ★
The Shopworn Angel ★ ★ ★
Too Hot to Handle ★ ★ ★
Listen Darling ★ ★ ★

1939

Society Lawyer ★ ★ ★
6,000 Enemies ★ ★ ★
Stronger Than Desire ★ ★ ★
Nick Carter-Master Detective ★ ★ ★

Walter Pidgeon with Ann Harding in *The Unknown Man.*

1940

The House Across the Bay ★ ★ ★
It's a Date ★ ★ ★
Dark Command ★ ★ ★
Phantom Raiders ★ ★ ★
Sky Murder ★ ★ ★

1941

Flight Command ★ ★ ★
Man Hunt ★ ★ ★ ★
Blossoms in the Dust ★ ★ ★ ★
How Green Was My Valley ★ ★ ★ ★
Design for Scandal ★ ★ ★

1942

Mrs. Miniver ★ ★ ★ ★
White Cargo ★ ★ ★

1943

The Youngest Profession ★ ★ ★
Madame Curie ★ ★ ★

1944

Mrs. Parkington ★ ★ ★

1945

Weekend at the Waldorf ★ ★ ★

1946

Holiday in Mexico ★ ★ ★
The Secret Heart ★ ★ ★ ★

1948

Cass Timberlane (cameo)
If Winter Comes ★ ★ ★
Julia Misbehaves ★ ★ ★

1949

Command Decision ★ ★ ★ ★
The Red Danube ★ ★ ★
The Forsyte Woman ★ ★ ★ ★

1950

The Miniver Story ★ ★

1951

Soldiers Three ★ ★ ★
The Unknown Man ★ ★ ★
Calling Bulldog Drummond ★ ★ ★

1952

The Sellout ★★★
Million Dollar Mermaid ★★★
The Bad and the Beautiful ★★★★

1953

Dream Wife ★★★
Scandal at Scourie ★★★

1954

Executive Suite ★★★
Men of the Fighting Lady ★★★
The Last Time I Saw Paris ★★★
Deep in My Heart ★★★

1955

Hit the Deck ★★★

1956

Forbidden Planet ★★★★
These Wilder Years ★★★
The Rack ★★★★

1961

Voyage to the Bottom of the Sea ★★★

1962

Advise and Consent ★★★
Big Red ★★★

1963

Two Colonels ★★★
Il Giorno piu Corto ★★★

1967

Warning Shot ★★★

1968

Funny Girl ★★★

1969

Rascal ★★★

1972

Skyjacked ★★★

1973

The Neptune Factor ★★★
Harry in Your Pocket ★★★

1976

Two-Minute Warning ★★★

1978

Sextette ★★

CHRISTOPHER PLUMMER
★★★ 2.94 STARS

Some "classical" actors loosen up on the screen as they progress in their careers. Christopher Plummer was stiff, regal and formidable in his early films, but his later performances reveal an increasing warmth.

Born Arthur Christopher Orme Plummer, in Toronto, Canada, in 1927, Plummer built up a strong acting reputation in his native Canada and then conquered Broadway. His first film, *Stage Struck*, was hampered by Susan Strasberg's amateurish acting, but he struck gold in *The Sound of Music*. Although, as the harsh baron, he was a little *too* tight-lipped. His rigidity made him ideal for military casting and he marched through *Night of the Generals*, *Battle of Britain*, *Waterloo*, *Conduct Unbecoming*, and *The Man Who Would Be King*. He has also made himself perfectly at home in comedies like *The Return of the Pink Panther.* And he made a likable Sherlock Holmes in *Murder by Decree*.

Christopher Plummer in *Murder by Decree.*

FILMOGRAPHY

1958

Stage Struck ★★★
Wind Across the Everglades ★★

1964

The Fall of the Roman Empire ★★★

1965

The Sound of Music ★★★

1966

Inside Daisy Clover ★★★
Triple Cross ★★★

1967

Night of the Generals ★★

1968

Oedipus the King ★★★★
The High Commissioner ★★★

1969

The Royal Hunt of the Sun ★★★
Battle of Britain ★★★
Lock Up Your Daughters ★★★

1970

Waterloo ★★★

1973

The Pyx ★★★

1975

The Return of the Pink Panther ★★★★
Conduct Unbecoming ★★★
The Man Who Would Be King ★★★

1976

Aces High ★★★
Assassination at Sarajevo ★★★

1977

The Assignment ★★★
The Disappearance ★★★

1978

Murder by Decree ★★★
International Velvet ★★★
The Silent Partner ★★★★

1979

Hanover Street ★★
Reil ★★★
Starcrash ★★

1980

Arthur Miller on Home Ground ★★★

1981

Somewhere in Time ★★★
Eyewitness ★★

1982

The Amateur ★★★

SIDNEY POITIER
★★★ 3.13 STARS

Sidney Poitier became the first black superstar for many reasons. He was handsome, gifted, versatile, and charismatic. He was also middle-of-the-road enough in the pre-*Shaft* days to avoid making white viewers uncomfortable.

Poitier was born in 1924, in Miami, Florida. After serving in World War II, he worked his way up through various roles until he found himself on Broadway in a Negro production of "Lysistrata." His first film, *No Way Out*, dealt inevitably with racial prejudice. He played a doctor who tended to bigot Richard Widmark. Unlike *Pinky* and *Lost Boundaries*, which glossed over the issue and cast white actors in the racial leads, *No Way Out* was possibly too raw, and box-office reaction was weak. *Cry the Beloved Country* was gripping, but *Red Ball Express* and *Go Man Go!* vanished immediately.

His breakthrough came with his portrayal of a student in *The Blackboard Jungle*, and Poitier's sincerity and magnetism put co-star Glenn Ford in the shade. Poitier's finest performance came in 1957, in *Edge of the City.* Adapted from a TV play, "A Man Is Ten Feet Tall," it cast him as a waterfront worker who befriended misfit John Cassavetes and had to cope with the vicious prejudice of foreman Jack Warden. Archer Winsten of the New York Post offered one minor objection: ". . . not a perfect picture. There's a feeling that the wrong guy gets killed" (Poitier).

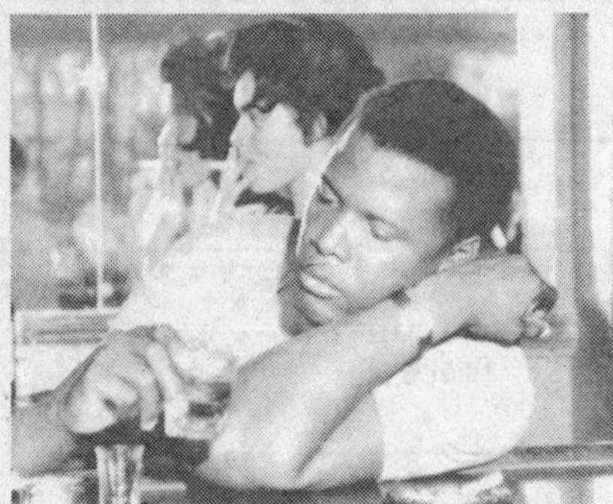

Sidney Poitier in *A Raisin in the Sun.*

Something of Value was an almost unbearably grim close-up of African unrest, but Poitier easily outshone Rock Hudson. He couldn't bring to life *Band of Angels*, a trashy melodrama set in antebellum New Orleans. (He even mispronounced "Monsieur.") However, he made no mistakes in *The Defiant Ones*, a powerful tale about two escaped convicts bound by shackles and hatred. He got an Oscar nomination for that role. *Porgy and Bess* proved to be "a dull, photographed opera with no heart or finesse," according to critic Hedda Hopper. Otto Preminger's plodding direction was responsible, though the Gershwin score still provided pleasure. *Paris Blues* had a stellar cast (Paul Newman, Joanne Woodward, Poitier, and Diahann Carroll—his offscreen interest for many years) and a fairly solid script, but even Newman's fans were unimpressed. Poitier stood out among other excellent cast members in *A Raisin in the Sun*, a sensitive drama about a Chicago family.

Poitier's superstardom began with *Lilies of the Field*, a pleasant comedy about a young man helping a group of nuns. He won an Oscar, the first black performer to win as Best Actor, and the hits increased. In *A Patch of Blue*, he incurred the wrath of bigot Shelley Winters, and in *To Sir With Love*, he played a beloved schoolteacher. His best performance of all was in *In the Heat of the Night*, working with sheriff Rod Steiger on a murder case down South. Steiger carried home the prize this time, but both were superb. Moviegoers made *Guess Who's Coming to Dinner* one of the biggest smashes of 1967, though it's patronizing tone and sentiment now look embarrassing.

Poitier gained directing control over his movies, a satisfaction to him but an artistic loss as well, in *Buck and the Preacher* and *A Warm December.* He has continued to be an important star, but none of his recent films, *The Wilby Conspiracy* or *Let's Do It Again*, matched the quality of the early ones. Most of them have been comedies requiring him to mug, but none test his dramatic ability. Even if he never makes another *Edge of the City*, Poitier's position as leader and trailblazer is secure. He also seems to be moving more comfortably towards directing and may become well-established in that field as well.

FILMOGRAPHY

1949

From Whence Cometh Help (documentary)

1950

No Way Out★★★

1952

Cry the Beloved Country★★★
Red Ball Express★★★

1954

Go Man Go!★★★

1955

The Blackboard Jungle★★★

1956

Goodbye My Lady★★★

1957

Edge of the City★★★
Something of Value★★★
Band of Angels★★

1958

The Mark of the Hawk★★★
The Defiant Ones★★★

1959

Porgy and Bess★★

1960

All the Young Men★★★
Virgin Island★★★

1961

A Raisin in the Sun★★★
Paris Blues★★★

1962

Pressure Point★★★

1963

Lilies of the Field★★★

1964

The Long Ships★★

1965

The Bedford Incident★★★
The Greatest Story Ever Told★★★
A Patch of Blue★★★
The Slender Thread★★★

1966

Duel at Diablo★★★

1967

In the Heat of the Night★★★
To Sir With Love★★★
Guess Who's Coming to Dinner★★★

Sidney Poitier in *To Sir With Love.*

1968

For Love of Ivy★★★

1969

The Lost Man★★★

1970

They Call Me Mister Tibbs★★★
King (documentary)

1971

The Organization★★★

1972

Buck and the Preacher (direction)★★★
Brother John★★★

1973

A Warm December (direction)★★

1974

Uptown Saturday Night (direction)★★★

1975

The Wilby Conspiracy★★
Let's Do It Again (direction)★★

1977

A Piece of the Action (direction)★★

DICK POWELL
★★★ 3.02 STARS

"What counts in this profession is survival," Dick Powell once said. By that standard, Powell has fared well. He attained popularity as a singing idol, then a private eye (Philip Marlowe), and finally a TV actor and producer.

Powell was born Richard E. Powell in 1904, in Mountain View, Arkansas. His early years as instrumentalist and singer made him ideal for musicals. One of these, *42nd Street*, with Ruby Keeler, is a cult favorite; others included *Twenty Million Sweethearts* and *Shipmates Forever*. He had several hit records in the 1930s, and his box office held solidly through *Gold Diggers of 1937*, *On the Avenue*, and *Naughty But Nice*.

Powell wanted meatier parts, and he got one in Rene Clair's fantasy, *It Happened Tomorrow*; he played a reporter who received news a day before it ocurred. A complete change of image came in *Murder My Sweet*; Powell was convincingly hardboiled as Marlowe, "a realistic, sweaty and exciting performance" according to Judith M. Kass, author of Closeups. Some other strong melodramas included *Johnny O'Clock*, *Cornered*, and *To the Ends of the Earth*. He was at his best in *Pitfall*, protecting Lizabeth Scott against the loathsome attentions of Raymond Burr. He was also at home in an Alaskan soap opera, *Mrs. Mike*.

The Reformer and the Redhead paired him with wife June Allyson, and then Powell went into TV, creating the "Four Star Playhouse," with David Niven and Charles Boyer. He produced and directed, but found time to do one more classic picture, *The Bad and the Beautiful*, as the playwright who lost Gloria Grahame to Gilbert Roland. He died in 1963 a thoroughly professional and polished actor who survived the changing trends while he was alive, but who somehow has not survived the test of time.

Dick Powell with Signe Hasso in *To the Ends of the Earth*.

FILMOGRAPHY

1932

Blessed Event★★★
Too Busy to Work★★★

1933

The King's Vacation★★
42nd Street★★★
Gold Diggers of 1933★★★
Footlight Parade★★★
College Coach★★
Convention City★★★

1934

Wonder Bar★★★
Dames★★
Twenty Million Sweethearts★★
Happiness Ahead★★★
Flirtation Walk★★

1935

Gold Diggers of 1935★★★
Page Miss Glory★★★
Broadway Gondolier★★
Shipmates Forever★★★
Thanks a Million★★★
A Midsummer Night's Dream★★

1936

Colleen★★★
Hearts Divided★★★
Stage Struck★★★
Gold Diggers of 1937★★

1937

On the Avenue★★★
The Singing Marine★★
Varsity Show★★
Hollywood Hotel★★★

1938

Cowboy From Brooklyn★★
Hard to Get★★★
Going Places★★★

1939

Naughty But Nice★★★

1940

Christmas in July★★★★
I Want a Divorce★★★

1941

Model Wife★★★
In the Navy★★★

1943

Star Spangled Rhythm★★★
Happy Go Lucky★★★
True to Life★★★
Riding High★★★

1944

Meet the People★★★
It Happened Tomorrow★★★★

1945

Murder My Sweet★★★★
Cornered★★★★

1947

Johnny O'Clock★★★

1948

To the Ends of the Earth★★★
Station West★★★
Pitfall★★★★
Rogue's Regiment★★★

1949

Mrs. Mike★★★

1950

The Reformer and the Redhead★★★
Right Cross★★★

1951

Cry Danger★★★★
The Tall Target★★★★
You Can Never Tell★★★

1952

The Bad and the Beautiful★★★★

1954

Susan Slept Here★★★

WILLIAM POWELL
★★★½ 3.30 STARS

William Powell made nearly a hundred pictures, but his reputation today rests on one role, in *The Thin Man*. Powell's wit, sophistication, and elegance were all perfectly suited to Dashiell Hammett's detective.

He was born in 1892, in Pittsburgh. He appeared on Broadway in "Within the Law" and "Spanish Love" and debuted on film in *Sherlock Holmes*. Then Powell worked solidly for eight years in silents, *When Knighthood Was in Flower, The Beautiful City, Beau Geste, The Great Gatsby,* and *She's a Sheik*. An early talkie, *One Way Passage*, became a classic tearjerker. Co-star Kay Francis was fatally ill, and Powell was the con man who loved her. *Manhattan Melodrama* teamed him with Myrna Loy, and though MGM saw them both as heavies, they were paired again at director W. S. Van Dyke's pleading in *The Thin Man*. They made one of Hollywood's greatest screen couples. He co-starred with fiancee Jean Harlow in *Reckless*, and then reteamed with Loy for the hilarious *Libeled Lady. The Great Ziegfeld* was boring but a success, and Powell was ideal as the butler in *My Man Godfrey.* He lost *Ninotchka* to Melvyn Douglas because of illness, though *Another Thin Man* and *Shadow of the Thin Man* compensated.

After a cancer operation, he worked more sparingly. However, the peak of his career came when he played the title part in *Life With Father.* Although the picture seems slow and dated today, it was embraced warmly in 1947. Powell received an Oscar nomination for his performance and a New York Film Critics Award.

A silly comedy, *Mr. Peabody and the Mermaid*, and a western, *The Treasure of Lost Canyon*, were unworthy of him, but he was superb as Doc in *Mister Roberts*, his last film. Now in his nineties, he lives with third wife Diana Lewis in Palm Springs.

William Powell in *The Senator Was Indiscreet.*

FILMOGRAPHY

1922

Sherlock Holmes ★★★
When Knighthood Was In Flower ★★★
Outcast ★★★

1923

The Bright Shawl ★★★
Under the Red Robe ★★★

1924

Dangerous Money ★★★
Romola ★★★★

1925

Too Many Kisses ★★★
Faint Perfume ★★★
My Lady's Lips ★★★
The Beautiful City ★★★

1926

White Mice ★★★
Sea Horses ★★★
Desert Gold ★★★
The Runaway ★★★
Aloma of the South Seas ★★★
Beau Geste ★★★★
Tin Gods ★★★
The Great Gatsby ★★★

1927

New York ★★★
Love's Greatest Mistake ★★★
Senorita ★★★
Special Delivery ★★★
Time to Love ★★★
Paid to Love ★★★
Nevada ★★★
She's a Sheik ★★★

1928

The Last Command ★★★
Beau Sabreur ★★★
Feel My Pulse ★★★
Partners in Crime ★★★
The Dragnet ★★★★
The Vanishing Pioneer ★★★
Forgotten Faces ★★★
Interference ★★★★

1929

The Canary Murder Case ★★★★
The Four Feathers ★★★
Charming Sinners ★★★
The Greene Murder Case ★★★
Pointed Heels ★★★

1930

Behind the Make-up ★★★
Street of Chance ★★★
The Benson Murder Case ★★★
Paramount on Parade ★★★
Shadow of the Law ★★★
For the Defense ★★★★

1931

Man of the World ★★★
Ladies' Man ★★★
The Road to Singapore ★★★

1932

High Pressure ★★★
Jewel Robbery ★★★
One Way Passage ★★★★
Lawyer Man ★★★

1934

Private Detective 62 ★★★
Double Harness ★★★
The Kennel Murder Case ★★★
Fashions of 1934 ★★★
Manhattan Melodrama ★★★★
The Key ★★★
The Thin Man ★★★★
Evelyn Prentice ★★★★

1935

Star of Midnight ★★★★
Reckless ★★★
Escapade ★★★★
Rendezvous ★★★★

1936

The Great Ziegfeld ★★★★
The Ex-Mrs. Bradford ★★★★
My Man Godfrey ★★★★
Libeled Lady ★★★★
After the Thin Man ★★★★

1937

The Last of Mrs. Cheyney ★★★
The Emperors' Candlesticks ★★★
Double Wedding ★★★★

1938

The Baroness and the Butler ★★★

1939

Another Thin Man ★★★★

1940

I Love You Again ★★★

1941

Love Crazy ★★★
Shadow of the Thin Man ★★★★

1942

Crossroads ★★★

1943

The Youngest Profession (cameo)

1944

The Heavenly Body ★★★

1945

The Thin Man Goes Home ★★★

1947

Ziegfeld Follies (cameo)
The Hoodlum Saint ★★★★

1947

Life With Father ★★★★
Song of the Thin Man ★★★

1948

The Senator Was Indiscreet ★★★★
Mr. Peabody and the Mermaid ★★★★

1949

Take One False Step ★★★
Dancing in the Dark ★★★

1952

It's a Big Country★ ★ ★
The Treasure of Lost Canyon★ ★ ★

1953

The Girl Who Had Everything★ ★ ★
How to Marry a Millionaire★ ★ ★ ★

1955

Mister Roberts★ ★ ★ ★

TYRONE POWER
★ ★ ★ 2.98 STARS

Unlike most pretty-boy stars, Tyrone Power had acting ability. His roles rarely allowed him to exercise it, but in a good vehicle such as *Witness for the Prosecution*, he got underneath the surface of the character.

Power was born in 1913, in Cincinnati, Ohio. His father was a famous matinee idol who encouraged him in his acting aspirations. Power did some radio and stage work, got a bit part in *Tom Brown of Culver*, and launched his career with the film *Lloyds of London*. He starred with Loretta Young in *Love Is News* (a forced comedy) and Sonja Henie in *Thin Ice* (a thin script as well). *In Old Chicago* was an entertaining spectacle, and Power was at his best opposite Alice Faye though Alice Brady won the Oscar as his mother. The Irving Berlin score carried *Alexander's Ragtime Band*, and he had little to do in *Marie Antoinette*.

His parts did get better in the films: *Jesse James*, as the title character, and *The Rains Came*, as an Indian Prince. His performance in *The Rains Came* was better than Richard Burton's in the remake, *The Rains of Ranchipur. Rose of Washington Square* was a thinly veiled account of Fanny Brice's love for Nicky Arnstein. Power was effective as the nice young man turned criminal in Henry Hathaway's *Johnny Apollo*, and then he had his most enjoyable role of the 1940s in *The Mark of Zorro. Blood and Sand* was—and remains—the best film about bullfighting, and Power was excellent. After that, *A Yank in the R.A.F.* and *Son of Fury* were letdowns. He loved Joan Fontaine in the patriotic *This Above All* and competed with Dana Andrews for Anne Baxter in *Crash Dive*.

After three years in the service, Power returned to do *The Razor's Edge*. He had to convey an almost unbelievable amount of spirituality and goodness, but he brought it off.

Tyrone Power in *Nightmare Alley*.

The movie itself was an absorbing adaptation of Somerset's Maugham's novel with other superb portrayals (Anne Baxter, who won an Oscar, Clifton Webb, who should have, and Gene Tierney). *Nightmare Alley* was just as good but extremely grim—the story of a carnival barker who manipulated his way to the top and wound up as a freak exhibit. He deserved an Oscar nomination for his work, but poor box office undercut his Academy chances. *Captain From Castille* was more popular, but tedious, and *The Luck of the Irish* and *That Wonderful Urge* seriously threatened his popularity. *Prince of Foxes, The Black Rose, Rawhide*, and *I'll Never Forget You* also failed to stir up much excitement.

Power disliked working with Kim Novak in *The Eddie Duchin Story* ("Confusion between temperament and bad manners is unfortunate"), but the movie was a smash. The piano interludes were enjoyable and the stars were beautiful to look at. He had the finest part of his career in *Witness for the Prosecution* as the surprise murderer. Power started filming *Solomon and Sheba* but died of a heart attack in 1958. Recent biographies depict him as a troubled homosexual, but their sordid revelations seemed unrelated to the nice, clean-cut young man who gave audiences so much pleasure.

FILMOGRAPHY

1932

Tom Brown of Culver (bit)

1934

Flirtation Walk★ ★

1936

Girls' Dormitory★ ★
Ladies in Love★ ★ ★

1937

Lloyds of London★ ★ ★
Love Is News★ ★ ★
Cafe Metropole★ ★ ★
Thin Ice★ ★
Second Honeymoon★ ★

1938

In Old Chicago★ ★ ★
Alexander's Ragtime Band★ ★ ★
Marie Antoinette★ ★
Suez★ ★

1939

Jesse James★ ★ ★
Rose of Washington Square★ ★ ★
Second Fiddle★ ★ ★
The Rains Came★ ★ ★
Day-Time Wife★ ★ ★

1940

Johnny Apollo★ ★ ★ ★
Brigham Young—Frontiersman★ ★ ★
The Mark of Zorro★ ★ ★ ★

1941

Blood and Sand★ ★ ★ ★
A Yank in the R.A.F.★ ★ ★

1942

Son of Fury★ ★ ★
This Above All★ ★ ★
The Black Swan★ ★ ★

1943

Crash Dive★ ★ ★

1946

The Razor's Edge★ ★ ★ ★

1947

Nightmare Alley★ ★ ★ ★
Captain From Castile★ ★ ★

1948

The Luck of the Irish★ ★
That Wonderful Urge★ ★ ★

1949

Prince of Foxes★ ★

1950

An American Guerilla in the Philippines★★★
The Black Rose★★

1951

Rawhide
I'll Never Forget You★★★

1952

Diplomatic Courier★★★★
Pony Soldier★★★

1953

The Mississippi Gambler★★★

1954

King of the Khyber Rifles★★★

1955

The Long Gray Line★★★★
Untamed★★

1956

The Eddie Duchin Story★★★

1957

Abandon Ship!★★★★
The Rising of the Moon (cameo)
The Sun Also Rises★★★

1958

Witness for the Prosecution★★★★

ELVIS PRESLEY
★½ 1.65 STARS

Elvis Presley is still the king of rock 'n' roll. No single individual has sold as many records, nor inspired such a fanatic cult following. For a while, he was the film box-office king too, in a series of silly, tailor-made vehicles. Fans never minded his total lack of talent as an actor.

Presley was born in 1935, in Tupelo, Mississippi. He recorded first for Sun Records then switched to RCA, and immediately tied up the number one spot on record charts for a decade. Films came begging and his shrewd manager, Colonel Tom Parker, made lucrative deals with 20th Century Fox *and* MGM. *Love Me Tender* was his first picture, an uninspired western, but fans jammed theatres around the country. After that all his movies were built around him. *Loving You* was among the best of these; Presley was a rock singer discovered by Lizabeth Scott. The press (always hostile about his "dangerous appeal" in the mid-1950s) began to relent as publicity poured out emphasizing his devotion to mother and church. He had romances with Natalie Wood and Ann-Margret while continuing to deliver an assembly-line product. *Jailhouse Rock* featured a witty Leiber and Stoller score, and *King Creole* showed a hint of acting ability—the first and last time Presley would suggest a character on the screen other than himself. Still, Alan Weiss (scriptwriter of many of his films—*Blue Hawaii, Roustabout*), said, "We knew instantly we were in the presence of a phenomenon. . .he was a force, and to fail to recognize it would be the same as sticking a finger into a live socket and denying the existence of electricity."

Elvis Presley.

G.I. Blues was another hit, as were *Flaming Star, Wild in the Country* (peculiarly cast as an aspiring writer), *Blue Hawaii*, and *Kid Galahad* (better than the rest). Critics and fans both conceded that he made good chemistry with Ann-Margret in *Viva Las Vegas*. Historian Douglas McVay in The Musical Film wrote, "At least five of their numbers ("The Lady Loves Me," "What'd I Say," "The Climb," the gym sequence, and the title song) have sufficient horsepower and sex in writing, singing, dancing and shooting to make an otherwise colorfully ugly and verbally custom-built movie worth a peep."

Roustabout gave him an impressive co-star (Barbara Stanwyck), but *Tickle Me* and *Harum Scarum* were so bad that his sensational box office was endangered for the first time. In *Speedway,* he was a race car driver plagued by problems with the IRS in the form of Nancy Sinatra. It had one good song, "Your Time Hasn't Come Yet, Baby," but no script. Even the quality of the songs deteriorated in *Double Trouble* and *Clambake*. He co-starred with Mary Tyler Moore, who played a nun, in the pathetic *Change of Habit*.

After a hiatus to re-evaluate his career, Presley appeared in two documentaries (*Elvis—That's the Way It Is* and *Elvis on Tour*). His record sales picked up again with an inspirational ballad, "If I Can Dream," and continued strongly until his death in 1977. A very different Presley (power-mad, drug-addicted, with a penchant for wild sexual scenes and young girls) emerged in Albert Goldman's irresponsibly vicious biography, Elvis. One thing is certain, however; he was a prisoner of his stardom, a simple, uneducated youth who tried to reconcile the "nice" and "bad" aspects of his personality and failed.

FILMOGRAPHY

1956

Love Me Tender★★

1957

Loving You★★★
Jailhouse Rock★★★

Elvis Presley in *Loving You.*

1958

King Creole★★★

1960

G.I. Blues★★
Flaming Star★★

1961

Blue Hawaii★★
Wild in the Country★★

1962

Follow That Dream★★
Kid Galahad★★
Girls! Girls! Girls!★★

1963

It Happened at the World's Fair★★
Fun in Acapulco★

1964

Roustabout★★
Kissin' Cousins★
Viva Las Vegas★★

1965

Girl Happy★★
Tickle Me★
Harum Scarum★

1966

Spinout★
Frankie and Johnny★★
Paradise Hawaiian Style★

1967

Easy Come, Easy Go★
Double Trouble★
Clambake★

1968

Stay Away Joe★
Speedway★
Live a Little, Love a Little★

1969

Charro!★
The Trouble With Girls★
Change of Habit★

1970

Elvis: That's the Way It Is (documentary)
Elvis On Tour (documentary)

1981

This Is Elvis (documentary)

ROBERT PRESTON
★★★ 2.88 STARS

Robert Preston's explosive Music Man charm rarely surfaced in the numerous pictures he did during the 1940s. They were generally westerns or adventure epics, and more often than not, he was a weakling or a villain.

Preston (Robert Preston Meser-

Robert Preston with Julie Andrews in *Victor Victoria*.

vey) was born in 1918, in Newton Highlands, Massachusetts. After a few minor parts *(King of Alcatraz, Illegal Traffic,* and *Disbarred),* he got an important role in Cecil B. De Mille's *Union Pacific*. In this lively western, bad guy Preston was pitted against hero Joel McCrea. *Beau Geste* was another plus, and De Mille used him again in *North West Mounted Police*.

There was a western with Loretta Young, *The Lady from Cheyenne*, and a more sympathetic appearance as a detective in his first classic, *This Gun for Hire*. The movie made Alan Ladd a star, but it also pushed Preston forward. He was the cowardly husband killed by wife Joan Bennett during an African safari in *The Macomber Affair,* a fine adaptation of a Hemingway story compromised by its upbeat ending. He supported Alan Ladd again in a western, *Whispering Smith. The Lady Gambles* was a powerful look at a compulsive gambler played by Barbara Stanwyck, and Preston was believable as the husband who tried helplessly to make her stop.

A few more uninteresting vehicles, *When I Grow Up, My Outlaw Brother,* and *Cloudburst*, drove him to Broadway. His larger-than-life style was ideal for the stage, and he had a series of successes in "The Magic and the Loss," "The Tender Trap," "The Hidden River," and most of all, in "The Music Man."

He returned to the screen after an eight-year absence to do *The Dark at the Top of the Stairs,* a strong, virile performance and followed that with the film version of *The Music Man*. Other impressive portrayals followed: *All the Way Home, Child's Play, Mame, Semi-Tough,* and *S.O.B.*

He had a spectacular comeback in 1982 with *Victor Victoria*, where he played an aging drag queen who coached Julie Andrews into impersonating a female impersonator. It was a bravura performance, one that recalled all the pomp and exuberance and flashy charm that defined his best roles.

FILMOGRAPHY

1938

King of Alcatraz★★★
Illegal Traffic★★★

1939

Disbarred★★★
Union Pacific★★★
Beau Geste★★★★

1940

Typhoon★★★
North West Mounted Police★★★
Moon Over Burma★★★

1941

The Lady from Cheyenne★★
Parachute Batallion★★★
New York Town★★★
Pacific Blackout★★
The Night of January 16th★★

1942

Reap the Wild Wind★★★
This Gun for Hire★★★
Wake Island★★★
Star Spangled Rhythm (cameo)

1943

Night Plane From Chungking★★★

1947

Variety Girl (cameo)
The Macomber Affair★★★★
Wild Harvest★★★

1948

Big City★★
Blood on the Moon★★★

Robert Preston in *Whispering Smith*.

1949

Whispering Smith ★ ★ ★
Tulsa ★ ★ ★
The Lady Gambles ★ ★ ★ ★

1950

The Sundowners ★ ★ ★

1951

My Outlaw Brother ★ ★
When I Grow Up ★ ★ ★
Best of the Badmen ★ ★
Cloudburst ★ ★

1952

Face to Face ★ ★ ★

1956

The Last Frontier ★ ★

1960

The Dark at the Top of the Stairs ★ ★ ★ ★

1962

The Music Man ★ ★ ★ ★
How the West Was Won ★ ★ ★

1963

Island of Love ★ ★
All the Way Home ★ ★ ★ ★

1972

Junior Bonner ★ ★
Child's Play ★ ★ ★

1974

Mame ★ ★

1977

Semi-Tough ★ ★ ★

1981

S.O.B. ★ ★

1982

Victor Victoria ★ ★ ★ ★

VINCENT PRICE
★ ★ ★ 3.10 STARS

Vincent Price seems to love being mean. His combination of ego, oily menace, and humor have entertained horror and nonhorror fans alike for decades.

He was born in 1911, in St. Louis, Missouri. His family was wealthy, and he attended Yale as an art history major. His stage appearances ("Victoria Regina," "The Wild Duck," and "Elizabeth the Queen") led to a film contract with Universal. Early films were costume dramas (*The Private Lives of Elizabeth and Essex*, *Tower of London*, and *The House of the Seven Gables*). Although he was never bad, he was seldom outstanding.

The Song of Bernadette gave him a good role as a prosecutor skeptical of Jennifer Jones' visions. He was weak rather than villainous in *Laura*, but certain characteristics—the wheedling, the hypocrisy, the nastiness, the devious wit—suggested the kind of character he would develop in later horror vehicles. These qualities were also essential to his unctuous District Attorney in *Leave Her to Heaven*.

Vincent Price.

A full-scale step into villiany yielded disappointing results in *Dragonwyck*, but the screenplay was the culprit. Script trouble also hampered *Up in Central Park*, in which he co-starred with a waning Deanna Durbin. Nobody paid any attention to *Rogue's Regiment* or *The Bribe*, but Price had a field day as a gleefully conniving soap executive in the hilarious *Champagne for Ceasar.* He also had a great role as a hammy matinee idol who meets real-life adventure in *His Kind of Woman*. He now considers *The Baron of Arizona* one of his finest pictures though TV viewing ratings don't substantiate his opinion.

There were a few more time-fillers *(Curtain Call at Cactus Creek* and *Adventures of Captain Fabian)* before he hit his stride. *House of Wax* gave him, at last, a specific star image. It was the most successful horror film of its time, in box-office terms. He played *The Mad Magician* and then returned to Broadway for "Richard III." Just before committing himself totally to the horror genre, Price performed in *The Ten Commandments* (as a slave driver) and *While the City Sleeps.* Neither of these was as enjoyable as *The Fly* or *House on Haunted Hill*, where he plotted to murder his wife and her boyfriend. *Return of the Fly* wasn't as good as the original, but *The House of Usher*, directed by Roger Corman, offered all the chills fans could ask for.

The Pit and the Pendulum continued his winning cycle, and he gathered new fans with *The Raven*, co-starring Peter Lorre and Boris Karloff. Occasionally he switched gears as in *Beach Party* and *Dr. Goldfoot and the Bikini Machine*, where the quality of the scripts provided the only horror. Price did *The Haunted Palace*, *The Masque of the Red Death*, and *The Tomb of Ligeia* before an Elvis Presley vehicle, *The Trouble With Girls*.

He hit a plateau of sorts with *The Abominable Dr. Phibes* and its sequel, *Dr. Phibes Rises Again.* These wonderfully camp mock-horror films gave Price free rein to ham it up and he seemed to have had as much fun as audiences did. *Theatre of Blood* was also a ghoulish delight, the ultimate fantasy of unappreciated theatre people—killing off critics in a variety of hideous, bloody ways. Price made only one more horror movie *Madhouse*, but his repertoire of ghoulish and horrific films are frequently on TV for buffs to savor.

FILMOGRAPHY

1938

Service de Luxe ★ ★ ★

1939

The Private Lives of Elizabeth and Essex ★ ★ ★
Tower of London ★ ★ ★

1940

The Invisible Man Returns ★ ★ ★
Green Hell ★ ★ ★
The House of the Seven Gables ★ ★ ★ ★
Brigham Young—Frontiersman ★ ★ ★ ★

1941

Hudson's Bay ★ ★ ★

1943

The Song of Bernadette ★★★★

1944

The Eve of St. Mark ★★★
Wilson ★★★
Laura ★★★★

1945

The Keys of the Kingdom ★★★
A Royal Scandal ★★★
Leave Her to Heaven ★★★★

1946

Shock ★★★
Dragonwyck ★★

1947

The Web ★★★
Moss Rose ★★★
The Long Night ★★★

1948

Up in Central Park ★★
Abbott and Costello Meet Frankenstein (voice only)
The Three Musketeers ★★★
Rogue's Regiment ★★★

1949

The Bribe ★★★
Bagdad ★★

1950

Champagne for Caesar ★★★★
The Baron of Arizona ★★★
Curtain Call at Cactus Creek ★★★

1951

His Kind of Woman ★★★★
Adventures of Captain Fabian ★★

1952

The Las Vegas Story ★★★
Pictura (narration)

1953

House of Wax ★★★★

1954

Dangerous Mission ★★★
Casanova's Big Night (cameo)
The Mad Magician ★★★

1955

Son of Sinbad ★★

1956

Serenade ★★★
While the City Sleeps ★★★
The Vagabond King (narration)
The Ten Commandments ★★★

1957

The Story of Mankind ★★

1958

The Fly ★★★

1959

House on Haunted Hill ★★★★
The Big Circus ★★★
The Bat ★★★
Return of the Fly ★★★
The Tingler ★★★

1960

The House of Usher ★★★★

1961

The Pit and the Pendulum ★★★★
Master of the World ★★★
Naked Terror (documentary)

1962

Queen of the Nile ★★
Rage of the Buccaneers ★★
Tales of Terror ★★★★
Convicts 4 ★★★
Confessions of an Opium Eater ★★★
Tower of London ★★★★

1963

The Raven ★★★★
Diary of a Madman ★★★★
Beach Party ★★
Twice Told Tales ★★★
The Graveside Story ★★★
Taboos of the World (documentary)

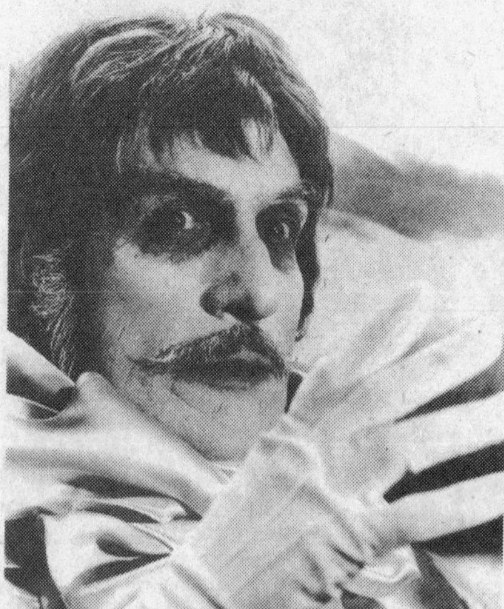

Vincent Price in *The Abominable Dr. Phibes.*

1964

The Haunted Palace ★★★
The Last Man on Earth ★★★
The Masque of the Red Death ★★★★
The Tomb of Ligeia ★★★★

1965

War-Gods of the Deep ★★★
Dr. Goldfoot and the Bikini Machine ★★

1966

Dr. Goldfoot and the Girl Bombs ★★

1967

House of 1000 Dolls ★★

1968

Witchfinder General ★★★
Spirits of the Dead (narration)

1969

More Dead than Alive ★★★
The Oblong Box ★★★
The Trouble With Girls ★★

1970

Scream and Scream Again ★★★
Cry of the Banshee ★★★

1971

The Abominable Dr. Phibes ★★★★

1972

Dr. Phibes Rises Again ★★★★

1973

Theatre of Blood ★★★★

1974

Madhouse ★★★
The Devil's Triangle (documentary)
Percy's Progress ★★★

1975

Journey Into Fear ★★★

1980

Romance in the Juglar Vein ★★★

RICHARD PRYOR
★★★ 3.07 STARS

Richard Pryor once commented, "I wanted to be John Wayne. I didn't know John Wayne hated my guts." Nobody hates his guts today. Pryor is easily the most popular, most bankable actor/comic on the scene today.

He was born in 1940, in Peoria, Illinois. Pryor made his initial mark in nightclubs and on records, and two albums won Grammys, "This Nigger's Crazy" and "Is It Something I Said?" His first picture was a vehicle for Sid Caesar, *The Busy Body,* though Pryor (along with Dom De Luise, Godfrey Cambridge, Marty Ingels, and Jan Murray) had funny moments.

Neither *You've Got to Walk It Like You Talk It or You'll Lose That Beat* or *Dynamite Chicken* established him as a star, but his part as the sympathetic Piano Man in *Lady Sings the Blues* netted him a Best

Richard Pryor with Harvey Keitel and Yaphet Kotto in *Blue Collar.*

Supporting Actor Oscar nomination. He also supplied enjoyable monologues in a musical documentary, *Wattstax. The Mack* was more serious, a grim drama about a black pimp which offered little entertainment value.

Uptown Saturday Night, with Sidney Poitier and Bill Cosby, was an improvement, but *Silver Streak* made him a box-office hit. *Silver Streak* was a thinly disguised reworking of Hitchcock's *North By Northwest.* Pryor's appearance half way through energized the frail script, especially when he gave Gene Wilder lessons on how to be black. The movie was a smash, and so was *Greased Lightning,* though critic Leonard Maltin thought the film "a waste of Pryor, both dramatically and comically."

Richard Pryor in *Car Wash.*

By this time, however, the media was singing his praises. James Wolcott wrote, "His dirty mouth monologues have a scabrous, druggy lyricism...his genius is for corrupt flamboyance." The New York Times added, "French cuffs and smooth cognac notwithstanding, there is a kind of crazy, desperate energy in this man that Cary Grant never possessed."

Car Wash packed theatres, and *Which Way Is Up?* maintained his hold on a growing public. He played a dirty old man, a minister, and an orange picker. *Blue Collar* with Harvey Keitel and Yaphet Kotto, was by far his strongest vehicle; Pryor was an auto worker discovering crooked union practices. He was the one redeeming feature of Lumet's disastrous *The Wiz,* and he nearly rescued the weakest segment in *California Suite.*

Pryor's professional life continued on its upward curve. Personally there were problems—four (some sources say six) failed marriages, and a near-fatal accident which left him with burns over 50% of his body. Doctors didn't expect him to recover but he did, going on to greater glory than ever with *Richard Pryor Live on the Sunset Strip* and *The Toy.* Of the latter Rolling Stone wrote: "Full of uplifting messages and brightly colored gadgets. But it's really just a Christmas package with nothing inside...Pryor is acting cute in shallow comedies."

Pryor has recently signed a new movie deal that will give him control of his own films. One suspects that the undeniable talent of Richard Pryor, which has seeped inevitably out of weak or minor roles, will now burst out full-force on the screen.

FILMOGRAPHY

1967

The Busy Body (bit)★★★

1968

Wild in the Streets★★★

1970

The Phynx★★★

1971

You've Got to Walk It Like You Talk It or You'll Lose That Beat★★★

1972

Lady Sings the Blues★★★★
Dynamite Chicken★★

1973

The Mack★★★
Hit!★★★
Wattstax★★★
Some Call It Loving★★★

1974

Uptown Saturday Night★★★★

1976

The Bingo Long Traveling All-Stars and Motor Kings★★★★
Car Wash★★★★
Silver Streak★★★★
Adios Amigo★★★

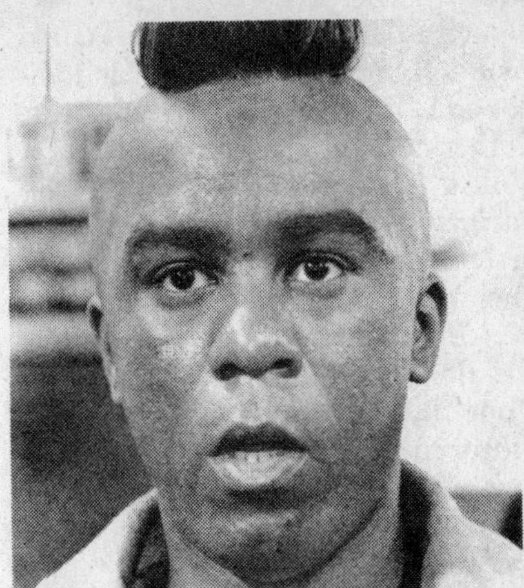

Richard Pryor in *The Bingo Long Traveling All-Stars and Motor Kings.*

1977

Greased Lightning★★★
Which Way Is Up?★★★

1978

Blue Collar★★★★
The Wiz★★★
California Suite★★

1979

The Muppet Movie (cameo)
Richard Pryor-Live in Concert★★★★

1980

Stir Crazy★★★★
Wholly Moses★★
In God We Trust★★

1981

Bustin' Loose★★★★

1982

Richard Pryor Live on the Sunset Strip★★★
The Toy★★
Some Kind of Hero★★★

1983

Superman III★★

ANTHONY QUINN
★★★ 2.79 STARS

Once Anthony Quinn became Zorba the Greek, he inserted pieces of that character into most of his subsequent roles. As of this writing, Quinn is also on the road with a musical version of Zorba, yet his pre-Zorba career is filled with much more interesting and varied performances.

Quinn was born in 1915, in Chihuahua, Mexico, of Irish-Mexican parentage. After his first picture, *Parole!,* Cecil B. De Mille gave him a part as an Indian in *The Plainsmen*. Quinn later married and divorced De Mille's daughter, Katherine, and also appeared in De Mille's *The Buccaneer* and *Union Pacific*. *Blood and Sand* was the first of several bullfighting movies (including *The Brave Bulls* and *The Magnificent Matador*), and a hit. His flair for humor surfaced with Hope and Crosby in *The Road to Morocco*, and he was highly effective in the painful *The Ox-Bow Incident*, as a man who was unjustly lynched.

In the mid 1940s, Quinn played Stanley Kowalski on a road tour of "A Streetcar Named Desire." Critics raved, and there was general applause for his conniving manager in *The Brave Bulls*. He won the first of two Best Supporting Actor Oscars for his role in *Viva Zapata!*—the other was for *Lust for Life* he had an "art" success with *La Strada*. *Wild Is the Wind* was expertly acted by Quinn and Anna Magnani, and deserved a better commercial fate than it received. *Hot Spell*, despite a contrived ending, was also underrated. He helped Lana Turner kill her husband in *Portrait in Black* and participated in two huge hits, *The Guns of Navarone* and *Lawrence of Arabia*.

Zorba the Greek continued the winning trend, but afterward there were more failures than successes (*A High Wind in Jamaica*, *The Magus*, *The Shoes of the Fisherman*, and *A Walk in the Spring Rain*). *The Greek Tycoon* was an embarrassment; Quinn played a thinly veiled Onassis to Jacqueline Bisset's Jackie Kennedy.

FILMOGRAPHY

1936

Parole! (bit)
Sworn Enemy ★★
Night Waitress ★★

1937

The Plainsman ★★
Swing High, Swing Low ★★★
Waikiki Wedding ★★
The Last Train from Madrid ★★★
Partners in Crime ★★
Daughter of Shanghai ★★

1938

The Buccaneer ★★
Dangerous to Know ★★

Anthony Quinn with Hardy Kruger in *The Secret of Santa Vittoria*.

Tip-Off Girls ★★
Hunted Men ★★
Bulldog Drummond in Africa ★★
King of Alcatraz ★★★

1939

King of Chinatown ★★
Union Pacific ★★★
Island of Lost Men ★★★
Television Spy ★★

1940

Emergency Squad ★★★
Road to Singapore (bit)
Parole Fixer ★★★
The Ghost Breakers ★★★
City for Conquest ★★★
Texas Rangers Ride Again ★★

1941

Blood and Sand ★★★★
Knockout ★★★
Thieves Fall Out ★★★
Bullets for O'Hara ★★★
They Died With Their Boots On ★★★
The Perfect Snob ★★★

1942

Larceny Inc. ★★★★
The Road to Morocco ★★★
The Black Swan ★★★

1943

The Ox-Bow Incident ★★★
Guadalcanal Diary ★★★

1944

Buffalo Bill ★★★
Roger Touhy-Gangster ★★★
Ladies of Washington ★★★
Irish Eyes Are Smiling ★★★

1945

China Sky ★★
Where Do We Go From Here? ★★★
Back to Bataan ★★★

1947

Sinbad the Sailor ★★★
The Imperfect Lady ★★★
Black Gold ★★★
Tycoon ★★★

1951

The Brave Bulls ★★★★
Mask of the Avenger ★★

1952

Viva Zapata! ★★★★
The Brigand ★★
The World in His Arms ★★★
Against All Flags ★★★

1953

City Beneath the Sea ★★★
Seminole ★★★
Ride Vaquero ★★★
East of Sumatra ★★★
Blowing Wild ★★★★

1954

Ulysses ★★★
Fatal Desire ★★★
Angels of Darkness ★★★
Attila ★★★
La Strada ★★★★
The Long Wait ★★★

1955

The Magnificent Matador ★★★
The Naked Street ★★★
Seven Cities of Gold ★★★

1956

Lust for Life ★★★★
Man From Del Rio ★★★
The Wild Party ★★★
Notre Dame De Paris ★★★

1957

The River's Edge ★★★
The Ride Back ★★★
Wild Is the Wind ★★★★

Anthony Quinn with Alan Bates in *Zorba the Greek*.

1958

The Black Orchid ★★★
Hot Spell ★★★★

1959

Warlock ★★★
Last Train from Gun Hill ★★★★

1960

Heller in Pink Tights ★★★
The Savage Innocents ★★★
Portrait in Black ★★★

1961

The Guns of Navarone ★★★★
Barabbas ★★

1962

Requiem for a Heavyweight ★ ★ ★
Lawrence of Arabia ★ ★ ★

1964

Behold a Pale Horse ★ ★
The Visit ★ ★ ★
Zorba the Greek ★ ★ ★

1965

A High Wind in Jamaica ★ ★ ★
Marco the Magnificent ★ ★

1966

Lost Command ★ ★ ★

1967

The 25th Hour ★ ★ ★
The Happening ★ ★
The Rover ★ ★ ★

1968

Guns for San Sebastian ★ ★ ★
The Shoes of the Fisherman ★ ★
The Magus ★

1969

The Secret of Santa Vittoria ★ ★ ★
A Dream of Kings ★ ★

1970

A Walk in the Spring Rain ★ ★
R.P.M. ★
Flap ★ ★

1972

Across 110th Street ★ ★ ★

1973

Deaf Smith and Johnny Ears ★ ★
The Don Is Dead ★ ★ ★

1974

The Destructors ★ ★ ★

1976

The Inheritance ★ ★ ★
High Rollers ★ ★ ★
Mohammed, Messenger of God ★ ★
Tigers Don't Cry ★ ★

1977

The Con Artists ★ ★

1978

The Greek Tycoon ★
The Children of Sanchez ★ ★ ★

1979

Caravans ★ ★ ★
The Passage ★ ★ ★
Omar Mukhtar-Lion of the Desert ★ ★

1981

High Risk ★ ★ ★

1983

Valentina ★ ★

GEORGE RAFT
★★½ 2.27 STARS

The appeal of George Raft is difficult to pinpoint today. He looks surly and sour in most of his old films, wearing one stony expression to represent all of his emotions.

Raft was born in 1895, in New York City. He was a boxer, a dancer, and a gigolo, and he maintained close affiliations with gangsters throughout his life. He was a murderer in *Dancers in the Dark*, and his appearance in *Scarface* brought stardom. Quarrels with studio executives began when he refused to do *The Story of Temple Drake* for Paramount, but he did appear in *Midnight Club, The Bowery*, and *All of Me*.

George Raft with Leo Carrillo in *It Had to Happen*.

He co-starred with Carole Lombard in the well-received *Bolero*, and then did a comedy with Rosalind Russell, *It Had to Happen*. However, there were few outstanding scripts in his filmography until he teamed with Cagney in a prison tale, *Each Dawn I Die. They Drive by Night*, with Bogart, was a pungent drama about truckers, and he did *Manpower* with Edward G. Robinson. They quarreled bitterly, but Raft surprised Robinson when the latter lay dying with a note from "your friend, George Raft."

He was no judge of vehicles, turning down *Casablanca, The Maltese Falcon, Dead End*, and *High Sierra*. One might also say that he created Bogart's legend with his bad judgment, and the bad judgment continued through *Nob Hill, Johnny Angel, Christmas Eve*, and *Race Street*. A good part, which he played well, in *Black Widow* revived Hollywood's interest, and he also had a cameo in *Around the World in 80 Days*.

He also had walk-ons in *Some Like It Hot, Casino Royale*, and an appalling musical comedy, *The Fat Spy*, with Jayne Mansfield. Looking back over Raft's dozens of films, he made more mediocre pictures than any other actor of his stature.

FILMOGRAPHY

1929

Queen of the Night Clubs ★ ★

1931

Quick Millions ★ ★
Hush Money ★ ★
Palmy Days ★ ★
Goldie ★ ★

1932

Taxi! ★ ★
Dancers in the Dark ★ ★
Scarface ★ ★ ★ ★
Night World ★ ★
Love Is a Racket ★ ★
Madame Racketeer ★ ★
Night After Night ★ ★
If I Had a Million ★ ★
Undercover Man ★ ★

1933

Pick Up ★ ★
Midnight Club ★ ★
The Bowery ★ ★
The Eagle and the Hawk ★ ★ ★

1934

Bolero ★ ★ ★
All of Me ★ ★
The Trumpet Blows ★ ★
Limehouse Blues ★ ★

1935

Rumba ★ ★ ★
Stolen Harmony ★ ★
The Glass Key ★ ★
Every Night at Eight ★ ★
She Couldn't Take It ★ ★

1936

It Had to Happen ★ ★
Yours for the Asking ★ ★

1937

Souls at Sea ★ ★ ★

1938

You and Me ★ ★ ★
Spawn of the North ★ ★ ★

George Raft in *For Those Who Think Young.*

1939

The Lady's From Kentucky ★★★
Each Dawn I Die ★★★
I Stole a Million ★★
Invisible Stripes ★★

1940

The House Across the Bay ★★★
They Drive by Night ★★★

1941

Manpower ★★★

1942

Broadway ★★

1943

Stage Door Canteen (cameo)
Background to Danger ★★

1945

Follow the Boys ★★
Nob Hill ★★
Johnny Angel ★★

1946

Whistle Stop ★★★
Mr. Ace ★★
Nocturne ★★

1947

Christmas Eve ★★
Intrigue ★★

1948

Race Street ★★

1949

Outpost in Morocco ★★
Johnny Allegro ★★
A Dangerous Profession ★★
Red Light ★★

1950

Nous irons à Paris ★★

1951

Lucky Nick Cain ★★

1952

Loan Shark ★★

1953

The Man From Cairo ★★
I'll Get You ★★

1954

Rogue Cop ★★★
Black Widow ★★★

1955

A Bullet for Joey ★★

1956

Around the World in 80 Days (cameo)

1959

Jet Over the Atlantic ★★
Some Like It Hot (cameo)

1960

Ocean's Eleven (cameo)

1962

The Ladies' Man (cameo)

1964

The Patsy (cameo)
For Those Who Think Young (cameo)

1965

The Fat Spy (cameo)

1966

The Upper Hand ★★

1967

Casino Royale (cameo)

1968

Five Golden Dragons (cameo)
Skidoo! (cameo)
Madigan's Millions (cameo)
The Silent Treatment (cameo)

1972

Hammersmith Is Out ★★

1978

Sextette (cameo)

1980

The Man With Bogart's Face (cameo)

CLAUDE RAINS
★★★½ 3.66 STARS

Claude Rains combined worldliness and urbane wit with a common touch. He always made his aristocratic parts seem very real and human.

Rains was born in 1889, in London. He did a great deal of respected stage work in "The Doctor's Dilemma" and "The Devil's Disciple" in London—and "So to Bed," "Volpone," "The Man Who Reclaimed His Head," and "The Good Earth" on Broadway. In his first screen role, *The Invisible Man*, only his voice mattered, which was more than enough. Stardom came quickly and he built a solid reputation with *The Man Who Reclaimed His Head* in his old stage part. *The Mystery of Edwin Drood* was a Dickens piece that cast him as a murderer, and he was unsympathetic as a domineering patriarch in *Anthony Adverse*.

In *They Won't Forget*, Rains played an ambitious district attorney who encouraged a lynching to further his career. He was brilliant, and the high level of performance was maintained through *Gold Is Where You Find It*, *The Adventures of Robin Hood*, and particularly *Four Daughters*. An Oscar nomination validated his work in *Mr. Smith Goes to Washington*, Capra's classic comedy of good vs. evil in politics.

After a sequel to *Four Daughters*, *Four Wives*, he tried fantasy. *Here Comes Mr. Jordan* is still the best of its genre and that includes the remake, *Heaven Can Wait*. *The Wolf Man* also ranks as one of the best of *its* kind—horror—and Rains stole the picture from Bela Lugosi and Lon Chaney, Jr. He was believably obsessed with daughter Betty Field in *Kings Row*, even though the incest theme of the book had to be scrapped to pacify censors. His part in *Now Voyager* as Bette Davis's psychiatrist was small, but *Casablanca* made him immortal. He had no trouble stealing *The Phantom of the Opera* from Nelson Eddy, and his work in *Mr. Skeffington* exposed the pretentiousness of Bette Davis's emoting.

Caesar and Cleopatra didn't capture the public. The film was too slow-moving and talky, but Rains was an excellent Caesar. *Notorious* gave him his second best role since *Casablanca*; he was a German agent who unwittingly married American spy Ingrid Bergman. Surrounded by the absurdities of *Deception*, he still managed to give audiences a good time as a self-absorbed composer.

His performance in *The Passionate Friends* also provided a center to David Lean's beautiful love story.

After that, his movies dropped in quality. He played in *Song of Surrender,* as Wanda Hendrix's husband, and in *Where Danger Lives* with the inept Faith Domergue. *The White Tower* was an improvement, a tense mountain-climbing yarn, and he had a Broadway smash, "Darkness at Noon," in 1950. His last substantial role was in *This Earth Is Mine,* as a wine tycoon who disinherited daughter Dorothy McGuire. *Lawrence of Arabia* was a success, but he had little to do. Rains was married seven times, certainly a consuming drain on his emotional resources, but he was fully and brilliantly in control of his screen life until he died in May, 1967.

Claude Rains with Sir Cedric Hardwicke in *The White Tower.*

FILMOGRAPHY

1933

The Invisible Man ★★★★

1934

Crime Without Passion ★★★★

1935

The Man Who Reclaimed His Head ★★★★
The Mystery of Edwin Drood ★★★★
The Clairvoyant ★★★★
The Last Outpost ★★★★

1936

Hearts Divided ★★★★
Anthony Adverse ★★★

1937

Stolen Holiday ★★★★
The Prince and the Pauper ★★★★
They Won't Forget ★★★★

1938

Gold is Where You Find It ★★★★
The Adventures of Robin Hood ★★★★
White Banners ★★★★
Four Daughters ★★★★

1939

They Made Me a Criminal ★★★★
Juarez ★★★★
Daughters Courageous ★★★★
Mr. Smith Goes to Washington ★★★★
Four Wives ★★★

1940

Saturday's Children ★★★★
The Sea Hawk ★★★★
The Lady With Red Hair ★★★

1941

Four Mothers ★★★
Here Comes Mr. Jordan ★★★★
The Wolf Man ★★★★

1942

Kings Row ★★★★
Moontide ★★★★
Now Voyager ★★★
Casablanca ★★★★

1943

Forever and a Day ★★★
The Phantom of the Opera ★★★★

1944

Passage to Marseilles ★★★
Mr. Skeffington ★★★★

1945

Strange Holiday ★★★★
This Love of Ours ★★★★
Caesar and Cleopatra ★★★★

1946

Notorious ★★★★
Deception ★★★★
Angel on My Shoulder ★★★★

1947

The Unsuspected ★★★★

1949

The Passionate Friends ★★★★
Rope of Sand ★★★
Song of Surrender ★★★

1950

The White Tower ★★★
Where Danger Lives ★★★

1951

Sealed Cargo ★★★

1953

The Man Who Watched The Trains Go By ★★★

1956

Lisbon ★★★

1959

This Earth Is Mine ★★★★

1960

The Lost World ★★★

1961

The Pied Piper of Hamelin ★★★
Battle of the Worlds ★★★

1962

Lawrence of Arabia ★★★

1963

Twilight of Honor ★★★★

1965

The Greatest Story Ever Told ★★★

TONY RANDALL
★ ★ ★ 2.95 STARS

Tony Randall's blend of insecurity and pompous erudition has provided some amusing cinematic moments.

Randall (Leonard Rosenberg) was born in 1920, in Tulsa, Oklahoma. His film debut in *Oh Men! Oh Women!*, a farce on psychiatry that wasted Ginger Rogers and David Niven, was unpromising. However, stardom came when he did *Will Success Spoil Rock Hunter?* Randall played an ad man who induced Jayne Mansfield to endorse his company's product. Not all of the satire worked, but Randall's befuddled manner redeemed the mediocre stretches. He played in *No Down Payment*, a serious study of suburban couples and their problems, but only Joanne Woodward and Cameron Mitchell rose above the material.

Tony Randall in *Pillow Talk*.

Randall had a big hit in *Pillow Talk*, the sex comedy that propelled Doris Day to number one at the box office, and another with *Lover Come Back*. The scripts were witty, an asset lacking in *Let's Make Love*. Co-stars Marilyn Monroe and Yves Montand had no chemistry onscreen, though plenty in real life, and Randall couldn't compensate for the deficiency. After a cameo in *Robin and the 7 Hoods*, he did another Doris Day comedy (*Send Me No Flowers*), but it wasn't as good as the earlier two. *The Alphabet Murders* made little impression, though he had funny bits in Woody Allen's disjointed *Everything You Always Wanted to Know About Sex (But Were Afraid to Ask)*.

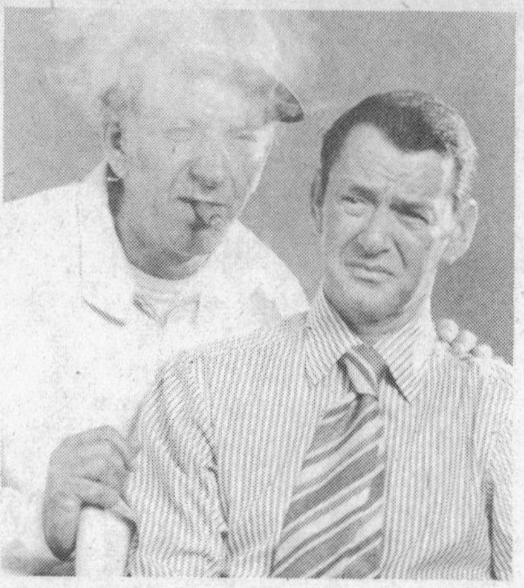

Tony Randall with Jack Klugman in "The Odd Couple."

Pauline Kael commented, "Overused and trashed, people like Tony Randall . . . are stars one minute, gone the next." TV rescued him, and "The Odd Couple" is still popular in syndication. Randall also remains a sought-after guest on Carson and Merv Griffin, as well as a star of his own series, "Love, Sydney."

FILMOGRAPHY

1957

Oh Men! Oh Women! ★ ★
Will Success Spoil Rock Hunter? ★ ★ ★
No Down Payment ★ ★ ★

1959

The Mating Game ★ ★ ★
Pillow Talk ★ ★ ★ ★

1960

Let's Make Love ★ ★
The Adventures of Huckleberry Finn ★ ★ ★

1961

Lover Come Back ★ ★ ★ ★

1962

Boy's Night Out ★ ★ ★

1963

Island of Love ★ ★

1964

The Brass Bottle ★ ★ ★
Robin and the 7 Hoods (cameo)
The Seven Faces of Dr. Lao ★ ★ ★
Send Me No Flowers ★ ★ ★

1965

Fluffy ★ ★ ★

1966

Bang! Bang! You're Dead! ★ ★ ★
The Alphabet Murders ★ ★ ★

1969

Hello Down There ★ ★ ★

1972

Everything You Always Wanted to Know About Sex (But Were Afraid to Ask) ★ ★ ★

1979

Foolin' Around ★ ★ ★
Scavenger Hunt ★ ★ ★

BASIL RATHBONE
★ ★ ★ ½ 3.40 STARS

Basil Rathbone had an interesting dual career. In the 1930s, he committed diabolical crimes as that era's greatest costumed villain. Then, in the 1940s, he *solved* diabolical crimes as film's greatest Sherlock Holmes. In either guise, he was cunning, cold, and thrilling.

He was born Phillip St. John Basil Rathbone in Johannesburg, South Africa in 1892. He got his theatrical training in England and began to act in silent films there as well. His screen career only took off, though, with the arrival of sound when he could use his polished and biting voice. He specialized in costume epics and literary adaptations, taking the role of heavy every time. He exacted an unmerciful whipping upon Freddie Bartholomew as the nefarious Mr. Murdstone in *David Copperfield*. He mistreated the peasants as the Marquis St. Evremonde in *A Tale of Two Cities*, where he snarled with cruel sarcasm, "Now wasn't that impertinent of him—to die with his rent unpaid." He drove wife Greta Garbo to infidelity as the cold Karenin in *Anna Karenina*. He was the perfect foil for Errol Flynn as Sir Guy of Gisbourne in *The Adventures of Robin Hood*.

In 1939, he first played Sherlock Holmes in *The Hound of the Baskervilles*, and forever after owned the role. Throughout the 1940s there were over a dozen Sherlock Holmes films. The films varied somewhat in quality, but Rathbone's characterization never faltered.

Basil Rathbone.

FILMOGRAPHY

1921

Innocent★★★
The Fruitful Vine★★★

1923

The Loves of Mary Queen of Scots (bit)
The School for Scandal★★★

1924

Trouping With Ellen★★★

1925

The Masked Bride★★★

1926

The Great Deception★★★

1929

The Last of Mrs. Cheyney★★★

1930

The Bishop Murder Case★★★★
A Notorious Affair★★★
The Lady of Scandal★★★
This Mad World★★★
The Flirting Widow★★★
A Lady Surrenders★★★
Sin Takes a Holiday★★★★

1932

A Woman Commands★★★

1933

One Precious Year★★★
After the Ball★★★
Loyalties★★★

1935

David Copperfield★★★★
Anna Karenina★★★★
The Last Days of Pompeii★★★
A Feather in Her Hat★★★
A Tale of Two Cities★★★★
Captain Blood★★★★
Kind Lady★★★★

1936

Private Number★★★
Romeo and Juliet★★★
The Garden of Allah★★★

1937

Confession★★★
Love from a Stranger★★★
Make a Wish★★★
Tovarich★★★★

1938

The Adventures of Marco Polo★★★
The Adventures of Robin Hood★★★★
If I Were King★★★★
Dawn Patrol★★★★

1939

Son of Frankenstein★★★★
The Hound of the Baskervilles★★★★
The Sun Never Sets★★★
The Adventures of Sherlock Holmes★★★★
Rio★★★★
Tower of London★★★★

1940

Rhythm on the River★★★
The Mark of Zorro★★★★

1941

The Mad Doctor★★★★
The Black Cat★★★★
International Lady★★★

1942

Paris Calling★★★
Fingers at the Window★★★★
Crossroads★★★
Sherlock Holmes and the Voice of Terror★★★★

1943

Sherlock Holmes and the Secret Weapon★★★★
Sherlock Holmes in Washington★★★★
Above Suspicion★★★
Sherlock Holmes Faces Death★★★★
Crazy House (cameo)

1944

Spider Woman★★★★
The Scarlet Claw★★★★
Bathing Beauty★★★
Pearl of Death★★★
Frenchman's Creek★★★

1945

The House of Fear★★★★
The Woman in Green★★★★
Pursuit to Algiers★★★

Basil Rathbone as Sherlock Holmes.

1946

Terror by Night★★★★
Heartbeat★★★
Dressed to Kill★★★★

1949

Ichabod and Mr. Toad (narration)

1954

Casanova's Big Night★★★★

1955

We're No Angels★★★

1956

The Court Jester★★★★
The Black Sleep★★★

1958

The Last Hurrah★★★

1962

Pontius Pilate★★★
The Magic Sword★★★
Tales of Terror★★★★
Two Before Zero (documentary)

1963

The Comedy of Terrors★★★★

1966

Queen of Blood★★★
The Ghost in the Invisible Bikini★★

1967

Voyage to a Prehistoric Planet★★★
Autopsy of a Ghost★★★
Hillbillys in a Haunted House★★

ALDO RAY
★★½ 2.67 STARS

When Aldo Ray was in top form in the 1950s, no one could match his characterization of the Army dogface. In *The Gentle Sergeant*, *Men in War*, and *What Did You Do in the War, Daddy?*, Ray played the brawny tough guy with the heart of gold.

He was born Aldo DaRe in 1926 in Pen Argyl, Pennsylvania. He was a frogman in World War II, and moved to California after the war. Casting agents noticed the gravel-voiced Ray while he was campaigning for sheriff in northern California. They hired Ray for *Saturday's Hero* with John Derek and Donna Reed. After eight months as a constable of a small town, he returned to Hollywood to appear with Oscar winner Judy Holliday in *The Marrying Kind*. This led to a role opposite Spencer Tracy and Katharine Hepburn in *Pat and Mike,* second billing to Humphrey Bogart in *We're No Angels*, and *God's Little Acre*. Ray's favorite of all of his war movies is *The Naked and the Dead.*

Tired of being typecast in American action-adventure and light comedy films, Ray left the United States in 1958 to pursue a career in England. But the productions he worked on never made it to the States. After having some difficulties while working with John Wayne in *The Green Berets* back in Hollywood in 1968, Ray returned to Europe and again slipped out of the limelight.

FILMOGRAPHY

1951

Saturday's Hero ★★★

1952

The Marrying Kind ★★★
Pat and Mike ★★★

1953

Let's Do It Again ★★
Miss Sadie Thompson ★★

1955

Battle Cry ★★★★
We're No Angels ★★★
Three Stripes in the Sun ★★

1956

Nightfall ★★★★
The Gentle Sergeant ★★★

1957

Men in War ★★★

1958

The Naked and the Dead ★★★★
God's Little Acre ★★★★

1959

Four Desperate Men ★★★

1960

The Day They Robbed the Bank of England ★★

1965

Sylvia ★★★
Johnny Nobody ★★★
Nightmare in the Sun ★★

1966

Dead Heat on a Merry-Go-Round ★★★
What Did You Do in the War, Daddy? ★★

1967

Riot on Sunset Strip ★★★
Welcome to Hard Times ★★★
Kill a Dragon ★★
The Violent Ones ★★★

Aldo Ray with Humphrey Bogart and Peter Ustinov in *We're No Angels.*

1968

The Power ★★★
Suicide Commando ★★★
The Green Berets ★★★

1969

Man Without Mercy ★★★
Deadlock ★★

1970

Angel Unchained ★★★

1972

And Hope to Die ★★★

1973

Tom ★★★

1974

The Dynamite Brothers ★★
The Centerfold Girls ★★

1975

Stud Brown ★★
Seven Alone ★★
The Man Who Would Not Die ★★
Gone With the West ★★
Psychic Killer ★★

1976

The Bad Bunch ★★★
Inside Out ★★★

1977

Haunts ★★

1978

Death Dimension ★★

1979

The Glove ★★

1980

Human Experiments ★★

RONALD REAGAN
★★½ 2.40 STARS

"He was a lousy actor and he'll be a lousy President," said Jane Fonda when informed that Reagan had replaced Carter in the White House. The verdict isn't in on his Presidential ability, but Reagan's old films suggest that he may have been too harshly roasted in the acting department. Most of his scripts were atrocious; still, he walked through them with professional ease though not much variety.

Born in 1911, in Tampico, Illinois, Reagan was a sportscaster before signing with Warner Brothers in 1937. *Love Is on the Air* was his first picture, and he followed it with several lacklustre vehicles. He appeared in *Swing Your Lady* with Bogart (who called it "the worst picture I ever made"), *Hollywood Hotel, Cowboy from Brooklyn,* and *Girls on Probation. Brother Rat* was much better, and Reagan gave an amiable performance. Jane Wyman, his future wife, was also in it. *Angels Wash Their Faces* was a passable drama about juvenile delinquency, and *Brother Rat and a Baby* was a mild sequel to *Brother Rat.*

Reagan's big acting chance came with *Knute Rockne-All American.* He was bogged down again in *The Santa Fe Trail*, but *Kings Row* represented the height of his career. His portrayal of a happy-go-lucky playboy whose legs were deliberately amputated by a sadistic doctor was touching, humorous, and forceful. *Kings Row* is Reagan's favorite among his movies.

He was competent as a district attorney investigating Klan activities in *Storm Warning,* and believable as

Ronald Reagan.

a GI who befriended the dying Richard Todd in *The Hasty Heart*. However, *Bedtime for Bonzo, That Hagen Girl,* and *Hellcats of the Navy* still give enemies ideal material for attack.

He concentrated on TV after *The Killers*, his one unsympathetic part, and one he considers to be a mistake. He then became Governor of California, and ultimately President of the United States. As far as actors playing Presidents go, Ronald Reagan is a far more unlikely choice than, say, Henry Fonda.

FILMOGRAPHY

1937

Love Is on the Air ★★

1938

Sergeant Murphy ★★
Swing Your Lady ★★
Hollywood Hotel ★★
Accidents Will Happen ★★
Cowboy from Brooklyn ★★
Boy Meets Girl ★★
Girls on Probation ★★
Brother Rat ★★★
Going Places ★★

1939

Secret Service of the Air ★★★
Dark Victory ★★
Code of the Secret Service ★★
Naughty but Nice ★★
Hell's Kitchen ★★
Angels Wash Their Faces ★★★
Smashing the Money Ring ★★

1940

Brother Rat and a Baby ★★★
An Angel From Texas ★★
Murder in the Air ★★
Knute Rockne-All American ★★★★
Tugboat Annie Sails Again ★★
Santa Fe Trail ★★★

1941

The Bad Man ★★
Million Dollar Baby ★★
Nine Lives Are Not Enough ★★
International Squadron ★★★

1942

Kings Row ★★★
Juke Girl ★★
Desperate Journey ★★★

1943

This is the Army ★★★

1947

The Voice of the Turtle ★★★
Stallion Road ★★
That Hagen Girl ★

1949

John Loves Mary ★★★
Night Unto Night ★★
The Girl From Jones Beach ★★★
It's a Great Feeling (cameo)

1950

The Hasty Heart ★★★
Louisa ★★★

1951

Storm Warning ★★★
Bedtime for Bonzo ★★
The Last Outpost ★★

1952

Hong Kong ★★
The Winning Team ★★★
She's Working Her Way Through College ★★★

1953

Tropic Zone ★★★
Law and Order ★★★

1954

Prisoner of War ★★★
Cattle Queen of Montana ★★

1955

Tennessee's Partner ★★

1957

Hellcats of the Navy ★★

1964

The Killers ★★

ROBERT REDFORD
★★★ 2.82 STARS

Robert Redford once said, "I do a part because I feel something for it...not because it builds my image." This integrity is reflected in his careful, thought-out performances. Even though Redford's glamorous looks are a key factor in his stardom, he never coasts on them.

Redford (Charles Robert Redford, Jr.) was born in 1937, in Santa Monica, California. His father was an accountant—but he sought creative outlets first as a painter, then an actor. A Broadway hit, "Barefoot in the Park," and TV shows, "Playhouse 90" and "Twilight Zone," led to an interesting role in a little-seen low budgeter *War Hunt*.

Inside Daisy Clover was handicapped by Natalie Wood's inability to play a Judy Garland-type star, but Redford provided a few dramatic moments as her homosexual husband. *This Property Is Condemned* reteamed him with Wood in a hard-breathing Tennessee Williams piece, and he was an escaped convict in Arthur Penn's noisily melodramatic *The Chase*. He had his first film hit in *Barefoot in the Park*, repeating his stage role, then another hit opposite Paul Newman in the amusing *Butch Cassidy and the Sundance Kid*.

Robert Redford in "Playhouse 90."

A series of dreary vehicles delayed top stardom for a while. In *Tell Them Willie Boy Is Here*, he played a sheriff chasing Indian Robert Blake, and *Downhill Racer* was a ski story without human dimension. *Little Fauss and Big Halsy* was simply a dated motorcycle yarn. His involvement in environmental causes and the outdoors presumably influenced him to do *Jeremiah Johnson*, portraying a mountain man. In *The Candidate*, he played a JFK-type Senator. The film purported to tell "the real truth," but a monotonous screenplay made the truth seem very dull. None of his early pictures with the exception of *Barefoot in the Park* (co-starring Jane Fonda) had charismatic female leads. *The Way We Were* featured Barbra Streisand, and the unlikely combination furnished unbeatable chemistry. The script was also good, an absorbing love story mixed with pertinent observations about the injustices of McCarthyism and blacklisting.

Robert Redford with David Keith and Jon Van Ness in *Brubaker.*

The public made him a number one draw after *The Sting*. He and Paul Newman were con men again, but the fun was more labored this time. Sidney Pollack directed *Three Days of the Condor,* which started out like a house on fire, but soon disintegrated into total confusion. Redford was more animated than usual, however, and so was Faye Dunaway. He and Dustin Hoffman played Woodward and Bernstein in *All the President's Men,* a tasteful version of the Watergate case. Both were impeccable. He was back with Fonda in *The Electric Horseman,* a fairly enjoyable modern western that made little demand on either star.

After the gripping prison yarn, *Brubaker,* Redford scored a different sort of coup—winning an Oscar for his superlative direction of *Ordinary People*. In fact, he elicited performances from Timothy Hutton, Mary Tyler Moore, and Donald Sutherland at least the equal of any he himself has so far contributed to the screen.

FILMOGRAPHY

1962

War Hunt ★★

1965

Situation Hopeless-But Not Serious ★★

1966

Inside Daisy Clover ★★
The Chase ★★★
This Property Is Condemned ★★

1967

Barefoot in the Park ★★★★

1969

Butch Cassidy and the Sundance Kid ★★★★
Downhill Racer ★★

1970

Tell Them Willie Boy Is Here ★★★
Little Fauss and Big Halsy ★★

1972

The Hot Rock ★★
The Candidate ★★★
Jeremiah Johnson ★★★

1973

The Way We Were ★★★★
The Sting ★★★

1974

The Great Gatsby ★★

1975

Three Days of the Condor ★★★★
The Great Waldo Pepper ★★★

1976

All the President's Men ★★★★

1977

A Bridge Too Far ★★

1979

The Electric Horseman ★★★
Brubaker ★★★

MICHAEL REDGRAVE
★★★½ 3.28 STARS

Michael Redgrave has a serious, substantial image. There are no Richard Burton-like scandals or drinking problems to counterbalance, only a long list of impressive performances on stage and screen.

Born in 1908, in Bristol, England, he began as a schoolmaster, then made his mark on the British stage. Redgrave's film career started strongly with an excellent picture, Hitchcock's *The Lady Vanishes*. He had another challenging part in *The Stars Look Down*, a superb adaptation of A.J. Cronin's novel about coal miners.

In *Kipps,* he was cast as a shopkeeper who inherited a fortune and had to choose between a rich girl and a scullery maid. It was popular and later turned into a musical, "Half a Sixpence." Redgrave later appeared in a brilliant drama about men in the R.A.F., *The Way to the Stars*. He was Oscar-nominated for the morbid and dreary *Mourning Becomes Electra,* but his highest achievement came as the betrayed schoolteacher in *The Browning Version*. Observing Redgrave's transition from self-containment to desolate tears was a breathtaking view of a performer extracting every nuance from a part. Most of his roles since have been less notable, but whatever the vehicle (*Time Without Pity, The Quiet American,* and *Shake Hands With the Devil*), his participation elevated its quality.

FILMOGRAPHY

1938

The Lady Vanishes ★★★★

1939

Climbing High ★★★
A Stolen Life ★★★
Lady in Distress ★★★
The Stars Look Down ★★★★

1941

Kipps ★★★★
Atlantic Ferry ★★★
Jeannie ★★★

Michael Redgrave in *Thunder Rock.*

1942

Thunder Rock ★★★★
The Big Blockade ★★★

1945

The Way to the Stars ★★★★
Dead of Night ★★★★

1946

The Years Between ★★★★
The Captive Heart ★★★★

1947

The Man Within ★★★
Mourning Becomes Electra ★★★
Fame Is the Spur ★★★

1948

The Secret Beyond the Door ★★★

1951

The Browning Version ★★★★
The Magic Box ★★★

1952

The Importance of Being Earnest ★★★

1954

The Green Scarf ★★★
The Sea Shall Not Have Them ★★★

1956

Confidential Report ★★★
The Night My Number Came Up ★★★
The Dam Busters ★★★
Oh, Rosalinda! ★★★

1957

Time Without Pity ★★★
The Happy Road ★★★

1958

The Quiet American ★★★★
Law and Disorder ★★★
Behind the Mask ★★★

1959

Shake Hands With the Devil ★★★
The Wreck of the Mary Deare ★★★

1961

No My Darling Daughter! ★★★
The Innocents ★★★

1962

The Loneliness of the Long Distance Runner ★★★★

1963

Uncle Vanya ★★★★

1965

Young Cassidy ★★★
The Hill ★★★★
The Heroes of Telemark ★★★

1967

The 25th Hour ★★★

1968

Assignment K ★★★

1969

Oh! What a Lovely War ★★★
Battle of Britain ★★★
Goodbye Mr. Chips ★★★

1970

Connecting Rooms ★★★
Goodbye Gemini ★★★

1971

The Go-Between ★★★★
Nicholas and Alexandra ★★★★

VANESSA REDGRAVE
★★★½ 3.35 STARS

In *Julia,* Vanessa Redgrave turned in a performance of such extraordinary power and tenderness that Academy members were forced, despite their resentment of her politics, to give her an Oscar. This is a measure of Redgrave's talent—integrity demands recognition of it, no matter what the circumstances.

She was born in 1937, in London, the daughter of Michael Redgrave and Rachel Kempson. Her mother was less known than Redgrave's father and sisters, but she was also a talented actress. Redgrave was already famous on the stage for her performances in "The Lady from the Sea" and "The Sea Gull" when she played her most successful early part in *Morgan!* The film was a weird, sometimes incomprehensible, comedy.

Vanessa Redgrave in *Julia.*

Blow-Up was also eccentric, but equally popular. *Camelot* looked promising, but Lerner and Loewe's musical was inflated into a colossal bore. Redgrave was its sole saving grace, and she fought urgently to bring life to *Isadora.* Variety called it "a major acting triumph," and she was spectacular in *The Sea Gull,* though the public ignored her achievement.

The Devils cast her as a deformed nun, and *Mary Queen of Scots* gave her the title role. Neither worked as art or entertainment. *Murder on the Orient Express* was no better, a talky, suspenseless Agatha Christie thriller, though Redgrave was effective.

It took *Julia* to showcase all aspects of her artistry: the intensity, the bravado, the sweetness, and the humor. After her controversial remark on the Oscar show about "Zionist hoodlums," work became less plentiful, and the film she finally did (*Yanks*) offered a colorless role opposite William Devane.

Controversy reached its height when she appeared in *Playing for Time,* a TV movie—written by Arthur Miller, and a true-to-life story of a Nazi victim. The cries of outrage had no effect on strong ratings, however, and Redgrave won an Emmy—another example of talent triumphing over negative publicity.

FILMOGRAPHY

1958

Behind the Mask ★★★

1966

Morgan! ★★★★
A Man for All Seasons (bit)
Blow-Up ★★★★

1967

The Sailor From Gibraltar ★★★
Red and Blue ★★★
Camelot ★★★

Vanessa Redgrave in *Blow-Up.*

1968

Tonight Let's All Make Love in London (documentary)
The Charge of the Light Brigade ★★★★
Isadora ★★★★
The Sea Gull ★★★★
A Quiet Place in the Country ★★★

1969

Oh! What a Lovely War ★★★

1970

Dropout ★★★

1971

La Vacanza ★★★
The Trojan Women ★★★★
The Devils ★★★
Mary Queen of Scots ★★★★

1974

Murder on the Orient Express ★★★

1975

Out of Season ★★★

1976

The Seven-Per-Cent Solution ★★★

1977

Julia ★★★★

1979

Agatha ★★★
Yanks ★★★
Bear Island ★★★

DONNA REED
★★½ 2.68 STARS

Most of Donna Reed's film roles were sweet and one-dimensional. She won an Oscar for her sole departure from type—as the "dance hall hostess" (prostitute) who loved Montgomery Clift in *From Here to Eternity.*

Reed (Donna Belle Mullenger) was born in 1921, in Denison, Iowa. She was a high school beauty queen, then made some films as Donna Adams: *Babes on Broadway,* and *The Getaway.* She became Donna Reed in *Shadow of the Thin Man* and *The Courtship of Andy Hardy,* but was only wallpaper until director Frank Capra chose her to star opposite James Stewart in *It's a Wonderful Life*. She was perfect and so was the film, but *Green Dolphin Street* wasted her (as Lana Turner's sister).

Director Fred Zinnemann fought to have Julie Harris in *From Here to Eternity*; producer Harry Cohn refused, foisting Reed on him. Success seemed assured when she was voted Best Supporting Actress by the Academy, but Cohn insisted on casting her in routine westerns, and she got her release from Columbia. *The Last Time I Saw Paris* was one of her best parts; she played Elizabeth Taylor's jealous older sister, and had a powerful closing confrontation scene with Van Johnson. *Ransom!* also provided a chance to emote, and she was Steve Allen's girl in *The Benny Goodman Story,* a film biography with nice music but little drama. With the erosion of her movie career, Reed turned to TV, and her "Donna Reed Show" ran for eight years. She has no fond memories of Hollywood, calling it, "A walled-in city bounded on all sides by arrogance."

FILMOGRAPHY

(billed as Donna Adams)

1941

The Getaway ★★
Babes on Broadway ★★★

(billed as Donna Reed)

Shadow of the Thin Man ★★

1942

The Bugle Sounds ★★
The Courtship of Andy Hardy ★★
Mokey ★★
Calling Dr. Gillespie ★★
Apache Trail ★★
Eyes in the Night ★★

1943

The Human Comedy ★★★
Dr. Gillespie's Criminal Case ★★
Thousands Cheer ★★★
The Man from Down Under ★★

1944

See Here Private Hargrove ★★★
Mrs. Parkington ★★★

1945

The Picture of Dorian Gray ★★★
Gentle Annie ★★
They Were Expendable ★★★

1946

Faithful in My Fashion ★★★
It's a Wonderful Life ★★★★

1947

Green Dolphin Street ★★★

1948

Beyond Glory ★★★

1949

Chicago Deadline ★★★

1951

Saturday's Hero ★★

1952

Scandal Sheet ★★★
Hangman's Knot ★★★

Donna Reed in *Scandal Sheet.*

1953

Trouble Along the Way ★★★
Raiders of the Seven Seas ★★★
From Here to Eternity ★★★★
The Caddy ★★
Gun Fury ★★★

1954

Three Hours to Kill ★★★
The Last Time I Saw Paris ★★★★
They Rode West ★★★

1955

The Far Horizons ★★

1956

Ransom! ★★★★
The Benny Goodman Story ★★
Backlash ★★
Beyond Mombasa ★★

1958

The Whole Truth ★★★

1960

Pepe (cameo)

OLIVER REED
★★½ 2.49 STARS

If a scowl meant stardom, Oliver Reed would be number one at the box office. Although he always looks angry or sullenly determined, he is simply a good actor without an abundance of charm.

Born in Wimbledon, London, in 1938, Reed was a nightclub bouncer and boxer before appearing in films. Physically he was ideal for *The Curse of the Werewolf*, and he played a motorcycle gang leader unsympathetically in a science-fiction thriller, *The Damned.* A stream of unimportant pictures *(The Pirate of Blood River, Captain Clegg, The Party's Over,* and *The Brigand of Kandahar)* kept him from reaching the top, and his performance in *The Shuttered Room* didn't rescue him from his B-picture rut.

He finally got his break in *Oliver!*, playing the vicious Bill Sikes. Directed by his uncle, Carol Reed, the movie won a Best Picture Oscar. He also clashed dramatically with Glenda Jackson in Ken Russell's superb *Women in Love,* which included Reed's nude wrestling sequence with Alan Bates. Another film directed by Russell, *The Devils,* proved much less enjoyable, but he kept busy in *The Four Musketeers, Tommy, Royal Flash,* and *The Prince and the Pauper.* Although recently he has had one bad picture after another, Reed has attacked them all with equal conviction.

Oliver Reed in *The Four Musketeers.*

FILMOGRAPHY

1960
The Angry Silence (bit)
The League of Gentlemen (bit)

1961
No Love for Johnny (bit)
The Rebel (bit)
Sword of Sherwood Forest (bit)
The Curse of the Werewolf ★★★

1962
The Pirate of Blood River ★★
Captain Clegg ★★

1963
The Damned ★★★
Paranoiac ★★
The Scarlet Blade ★★

1964
The System ★★★

1965
The Party's Over ★★
The Brigand of Kandahar ★★

1966
The Trap ★★★

1967
The Shuttered Room ★★★
The Jokers ★★★
I'll Never Forget What's 'Is Name ★★★

1968
Oliver! ★★★★

1969
The Assassination Bureau ★★★
Hannibal Brooks ★★★
Women in Love ★★★★

1970
The Lady in the Car With Glasses and a Gun ★★★
Take a Girl Like You ★★

1971
The Hunting Party ★★
The Devils ★★★★

1972
Zero Population Growth ★★
Sitting Target ★★★★

1973
Triple Echoes ★★★

1974
The Three Musketeers ★★★★

1975
The Four Musketeers ★★★★
Royal Flash ★★★
Tommy ★★★
Ten Little Indians ★★
Blood in the Streets ★★

1976
The Sellout ★★
Burnt Offerings ★★
The Great Scout and Cathouse Thursday ★★

Oliver Reed with Ian McShane in *Sitting Target.*

1977
The Prince and the Pauper ★★★
Maniac ★★

1978
Tomorrow Never Comes ★★
The Big Sleep ★★★
The Class of Miss MacMichael ★★

1979
The Mad Trapper ★★
The Brood ★★★★
Omar Mukhtar-Lion of the Desert ★★★

1981
Condorman ★★

1982
Venom ★★

1983
The Sting II ★★
Fanny Hill ★★

CHRISTOPHER REEVE
★★½ 2.50 STARS

Christopher Reeve is the perfect Superman. Square-jawed, with piercingly honest blue eyes and clean-cut features, he has a realistic look that somehow manages to capture the fantasy charm of a comic-book hero. One can be grateful that the other actors who tested for the part (Bruce Jenner, James. Caan, Robert Redford, Clint Eastwood, Charles Bronson, and Sylvester Stallone) were turned down.

Reeve was born in 1952, in New York City. His father was a professor, novelist, and translator; his mother a newspaper reporter. They encouraged his creativity, and he eventually studied under John Houseman at Juilliard (with Robin Williams and William Hurt). He admits to believing that "positive living creates luck," yet adds, "Before

Christopher Reeve with Jane Seymour in *Somewhere in Time.*

Superman, I was sponging off friends, sleeping on couches, turning into a vegetable." His talent and ambition made him compete for the role. When he got it, he pumped iron, ate four meals a day and gulped protein till reaching a muscular 242 pounds. The success of the picture brought stardom, and he continued to act on the stage in "The Fifth of July" and "A Matter of Gravity", with Katharine Hepburn.

His success led to *Superman II,* and he took a chance on a romantic fantasy in *Somewhere in Time.* Critic Vincent Canby commented, "This picture does for romance what the Hindenburg did for dirigibles." Despite rave reviews, the public did not flock to *Deathtrap.* He was superb, however, and he tried to humanize the ridiculous *Monsignor.*

Reeve does his stunts himself, a sign of his conscientiousness and concern with the authenticity of the final product. This attitude and his fine acting ability guarantee other fine characterizations in the future.

FILMOGRAPHY

1978

Superman ★★★
Gray Lady Down (bit)

1980

Somewhere in Time ★★★

1981

Superman II ★★★

1982

Monsignor ★
Deathtrap ★★★

1983

Superman III ★★

BURT REYNOLDS
★★½ 2.72 STARS

Burt Reynolds is caught in a trap between wanting artistic appreciation and doing lightweight vehicles to sustain his box-office rating. He's a highly capable actor, as his early TV movies emphasize, but until he takes risks, critical reaction will remain guarded.

Reynolds was born in 1936, in Waycross, Georgia. A knee injury destroyed his promising football career, and he pursued acting in New York playing in a City Center revival of "Mr. Roberts." His early television appearances included parts in "Riverboat," "Gunsmoke," and various "Movies of the Week." However, his early pictures (*Angel Baby, Armored Command, Fade-In, Impasse, Shark!*) led nowhere. He married and quickly divorced actress Judy Carne, and continued hamming it up in mediocre projects like *Sam Whiskey* and *Skullduggery.*

Burt Reynolds in *Navajo Joe.*

Deliverance made the difference. His aggressively macho characterization contained the elements of good-old-boy humor that later mushroomed into his entire style. The movie itself was a terrifying tale of four civilized men on a river trip. Murder and homosexual rape were some of the ingredients that gave it notoriety, and Reynolds furnished offscreen notoriety as well by doing a nude Cosmopolitan centerfold. He now regrets it, feeling that it made reviewers stop taking him seriously. There wasn't much to take seriously in *Fuzz* or *Shamus.*

The Longest Yard was terrific entertainment. It was a violent but fast-moving story dealing with a prison football team. Reynolds dominated, and he added to his reputation by appearing regularly on Johnny Carson. His approach, mainly self-deprecating, gave him an image that insured wide popularity.

W. W. and the Dixie Dancekings was pleasant but routine. *At Long Last Love* wasn't routine, it was horrible, a bad musical comedy employing Cole Porter songs. Reynolds and Cybill Shepherd didn't belong in a musical—though he tried again later with *The Best Little Whorehouse in Texas. Lucky Lady* was even worse. As critic Pauline Kael stated, "The only drama involved was the deal...an agent's picture...everybody's ripoff." Bad luck dogged him through *Gator* and *Nickelodeon.* The latter had a good subject, early moviemaking, but was sluggishly treated.

Then came *Smokey and the Bandit,* which grossed over $100 million. It was directed by former stuntman Hal Needham, and Reynolds had also been a stuntman early in his career. *Semi-Tough* was moderately successful, and though Frank Rich of Time magazine thought him miscast in *The End,* he was perfect as *Hooper.* He was reportedly angry when co-stars Jill Clayburgh and Candice Bergen received Oscar nominations for *Starting Over* and he was ignored. In truth, he was the most satisfying element of that picture.

Nobody survived *The Best Little Whorehouse in Texas,* including Dolly Parton and Dom De Luise, but Reynolds usually has the winning personality, the brazen charm, and the energy to charge up weak vehicles like this. He's likely to remain a box-office king for many years.

FILMOGRAPHY

1961

Angel Baby ★★★
Armored Command ★★★

1965

Operation CIA ★★★

Burt Reynolds with Goldie Hawn in *Best Friends.*

1967

Navajo Joe★★★

1968

Fade-In★★

1969

Sam Whiskey★★
100 Rifles★★
Impasse★★★
Shark!★★★

1970

Skullduggery★★★

1972

Fuzz★★★
Deliverance★★★★
Everything You Always Wanted to Know About Sex but Were Afraid to Ask ★★★

1973

Shamus★★★
The Man Who Loved Cat Dancing★★★
White Lightning★★★

1974

The Longest Yard★★★★

1975

W. W. and the Dixie Dancekings★★★
At Long Last Love★
Lucky Lady★
Hustle★★

1976

Silent Movie (cameo)
Gator★★★
Nickelodeon★★★

1977

Smokey and the Bandit★★★
Semi-Tough★★★

1978

The End (direction)★★
Hooper★★★★

1979

Starting Over★★★

1980

Smokey and the Bandit II★★★
Rough Cut★★★

1981

The Cannonball Run★★
Paternity★★
Sharky's Machine (direction)★★★

1982

Best Friends★★★
The Best Little Whorehouse in Texas★★

1983

Stroker Ace★★

DEBBIE REYNOLDS
★★½ 2.65 STARS

In the course of his biography, Eddie—My Life, My Loves, Eddie Fisher painted Debbie Reynolds as a cold, spotlight-stealing, penny-pinching little tyrant. But he was honest enough to add, "Debbie was a natural comedienne, a natural singer, a natural actress. This was her world, and in front of the cameras she forgot everything else."

Reynolds was born Mary Frances Reynolds in 1932, in El Paso, Texas. Her family moved to Burbank when she was eight, and she made her film debut at sixteen in *June Bride. Three Little Words* was her first noticeable bit. She played Helen Kane, the Boop Boop a Doop girl. According to Reynolds, Gene Kelly didn't want her for *Singin' in the Rain* because she was too inexperienced. MGM insisted, and she came through with a fresh, radiant peformance. In fact all the principals (Reynolds, Kelly, and Donald O'Connor) did the best work of their careers.

Afterwards, she did a couple of successful but silly musicals *I Love Melvin* and *The Affairs of Dobie Gillis. Susan Slept Here* with Dick Powell was slightly better, and *Hit the Deck* was a tuneful, old-fashioned tale of sailors on leave. The lilting Vincent Youmans score helped, but Reynolds was only one of several names (Jane Powell, Ann Miller, Tony Martin, Russ Tamblyn, and Vic Damone).

The spotlight was more firmly focused on her in *The Tender Trap,* and she had a surprisingly workable chemistry with Frank Sinatra. She was a prospective bride who caused mother Bette Davis to organize *The Catered Affair.* This performance surprised critics—Time Magazine called her "astonishingly believable." It was particularly "astonishing" since Davis overacted as a Bronx mother, and Reynolds seemed right at home in the drab surroundings.

She and Fisher were co-starred in a musical update of Ginger Rogers' *Bachelor Mother* in *Bundle of Joy.* Fisher was wooden and Reynolds couldn't save the frantic script. However, she gained a huge new following in *Tammy and the Bachelor,* keeping a straight face in the midst of rampant sentimentality. *Say One for Me* was better because it had Bing Crosby and some likable songs, and she was engagingly paired with Tony Curtis in *The Rat Race.*

When Fisher ran off with Elizabeth Taylor in 1959, Reynolds was perceived to be the victim and her box office soared. Scandal and fan magazine coverage distracted fans from the mediocre quality of *My Six Loves* and *The Second Time Around. Mary, Mary* managed to make the wit of the Broadway show seem labored, and Reynolds gave a puzzlingly arch and mechanical performance.

She was brash and energetic, however, in *The Unsinkable Molly Brown,* as a fortune hunter who

Debbie Reynolds in *The Unsinkable Molly Brown.*

pushed husband Harve Presnell to earn money and get them into society. Her triumph and an Oscar nomination didn't lead to better pictures. *Goodbye Charlie* was a vulgar piece of whimsy which Lauren Bacall had done and failed with on Broadway. *The Singing Nun* was saccharine, even by *Sound of Music* standards.

She was outstanding in *What's the Matter With Helen?* as the mother of a condemned murderer who moved in with unbalanced Shelley Winters. After that she devoted her time to the stage in "Irene," "Annie Get Your Gun," and "Woman of the Year." Her day as a screen artist may be over, but she left behind a group of spirited performances that still sparkle on TV.

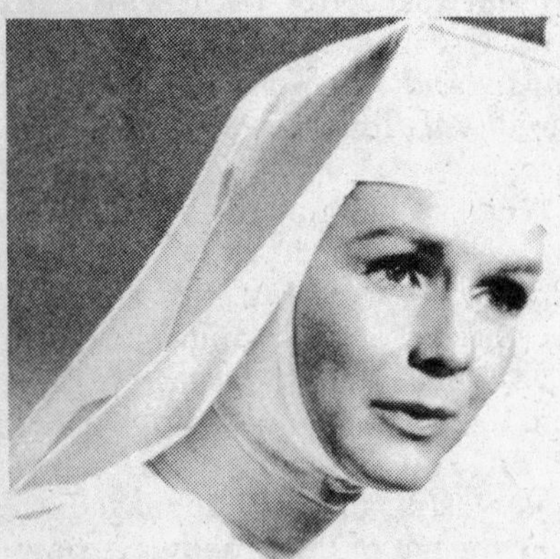

Debbie Reynolds in *The Singing Nun*.

FILMOGRAPHY

1948

June Bride (bit)

1950

The Daughter of Rosie O'Grady ★★
Three Little Words (bit)
Two Weeks With Love ★★★

1951

Mr. Imperium ★★

1952

Singin' In the Rain ★★★★
Skirts Ahoy! (cameo)

1953

I Love Melvin ★★★
The Affairs of Dobie Gillis ★★★

1954

Susan Slept Here ★★★
Give a Girl a Break ★★★
Athena ★★★

1955

Hit the Deck ★★★
The Tender Trap ★★★

1956

The Catered Affair ★★★
Meet Me in Las Vegas (cameo)
Bundle of Joy ★★

1957

Tammy and the Bachelor ★★

1958

This Happy Feeling ★★★

1959

The Mating Game ★★★
Say One for Me ★★
It Started With a Kiss ★★

1960

Pepe (cameo)
The Gazebo ★★★
The Rat Race ★★★

1961

The Pleasure of His Company ★★★
The Second Time Around ★★★

1962

How the West Was Won ★★★

1963

My Six Loves ★★
Mary Mary ★★

1964

Goodbye Charlie ★★
The Unsinkable Molly Brown ★★★

1966

The Singing Nun ★★

1967

Divorce American Style ★★

1968

How Sweet It Is ★★

1971

What's the Matter With Helen? ★★★

1973

Charlotte's Web (voice only)

1974

That's Entertainment (narration)

RALPH RICHARDSON

★★★½ 3.35 STARS

Ralph Richardson belongs to that select group of great British actors (Laurence Olivier, John Gielgud, Michael Redgrave) who can play a wide range of roles and invest even the cruelest parts (Olivia De Havilland's father in *The Heiress*, for example) with sympathy.

Born in 1902, in Cheltenham, England, Richardson played most of the great classical roles at the Old Vic—Petruchio, Henry V, Brutus. He debuted on film in *The Ghoul* and followed that with *The Return of Bulldog Drummond.* He was delightful in *The Man Who Could Work Miracles* with Roland Young, and equally accomplished in the fine screen version of A.J. Cronin's *The Citadel.* He also played in some war pictures, *The Day Will Dawn, The Silver Fleet,* and an underrated adaptation of *Anna Karenina. The Fallen Idol* was even stronger, a gripping tale of a butler who came under suspicion of murder.

In the dazzling company of Olivia De Havilland, Miriam Hopkins, and Montgomery Clift, he dominated *The Heiress.* Critics applauded his work in Olivier's *Richard III,* and he again outshone his co-stars (Dean Stockwell, Katharine Hepburn, and Jason Robards, Jr.) in *Long Day's Journey Into Night. Woman of Straw* enabled him to erase Sean Connery and Gina Lollobrigida from the screen. Richardson tried playing Wilkins Micawber in a TV version of *David Copperfield*—his one mistake. Memories of W.C. Fields in the same role were still too vivid.

He did a horror movie, *Who Slew Auntie Roo?*, but was more at home in *Lady Caroline Lamb* and the lively *O Lucky Man!* Other pictures that have gained from his participation include *Rollerball, Watership Down* (voice only), and *A Doll's House.*

FILMOGRAPHY

1933

The Ghoul ★★★
Friday the 13th ★★★

1934

The Return of Bulldog Drummond ★★★
Java Head ★★★
The King of Paris ★★★

1935

Bulldog Jack ★★★

1936

Things to Come ★★★
The Man Who Could Work Miracles ★★★★

1937

Thunder in the City ★★★

Ralph Richardson in *The Heiress.*

1938

South Riding ★★★
The Divorce of Lady X ★★★
The Citadel ★★★★

1939

Q Planes ★★★★
Four Feathers ★★★
The Lion Has Wings ★★★
On the Night of the Fire ★★★

1942

The Day Will Dawn ★★★
The Silver Fleet ★★★★

1943

The Volunteer (documentary)

1946

School for Secrets ★★★

1948

Anna Karenina ★★★★
The Fallen Idol ★★★★

1949

The Heiress ★★★★

1951

Outcast of the Islands ★★★★
Home at Seven ★★★

1952

The Sound Barrier ★★★★
The Holly and the Ivy ★★★

1955

Richard III ★★★★

1956

Smiley ★★★

1957

The Passionate Stranger ★★★

1959

Our Man in Havana ★★★★

1960

Oscar Wilde ★★★★
Exodus ★★★

1962

The 300 Spartans ★★★
Long Day's Journey Into Night ★★★★
Woman of Straw ★★★★

1965

Doctor Zhivago ★★★★

1966

Falstaff (narration)
Khartoum ★★★★
The Wrong Box ★★★

1969

Midas Run ★★★
Oh! What a Lovely War ★★★
The Bed Sitting Room ★★★
Battle of Britain ★★★

1970

The Looking Glass War ★★★

1971

Eagle in a Cage ★★★
Who Slew Auntie Roo? ★★★

1972

Tales From the Crypt ★★★
Alice's Adventures in Wonderland ★★★
Lady Caroline Lamb ★★★★

1973

A Doll's House ★★★★
O Lucky Man! ★★★★

1975

Rollerball ★★★

1978

Watership Down (voice only)

1979

Charlie Muffin ★★★

1981

Dragonslayer ★★★
Time Bandits ★★★

THELMA RITTER
★★★½ 3.68 STARS

Thelma Ritter's mother-in-law-turned-maid in *The Mating Season* is one of filmland's greatest performances. Critics rarely single it out because the movie itself was unexceptional, but for heart, humor, and sheer poignancy, the characterization has few rivals. The same was true for all of Ritter's work.

She was born in 1905, in Brooklyn, New York. After an unrewarding Broadway career, she retired but changed her mind when a part became available in *Miracle on 34th Street.* Success was assured after director Joseph Mankiewicz put her in *A Letter to Three Wives,* as a neighborhood gossip. *City Across the River,* a watered-down version of *The Amboy Dukes,* was minor fare, and so was *Father Was a Fullback.*

All About Eve, with Mankiewicz again, showed the tart, warm, down-to-earth qualities that made her unique. After *The Mating Season* ("Miss Ritter is sockeroo," commented Variety), she did a superb job as a sympathetic Miss Fixit in *The Model and the Marriage Broker.* Jeanne Crain was the model.

With a Song in My Heart gave her an opportunity to fuss over a paralyzed Susan Hayward. She played a nurse again, tending this time to James Stewart, in Hitchcock's hair-raising *Rear Window.* Even in poor pictures *(Lucy Gallant, The Proud and the Profane,* and *Pillow Talk)* she was immensely enjoyable to watch.

Thelma Ritter in *Pickup on South Street.*

She blended beautifully with Edward G. Robinson in the otherwise bland *A Hole in the Head,* and was "simply superb," according to critic Judith Crist as Burt Lancaster's controlling mother in *Birdman of Alcatraz.* Before she died in 1969, she graced several other pictures: *A New Kind of Love, Move Over Darling, For Love or Money,* and *How the West Was Won.*

FILMOGRAPHY

1947

Miracle on 34th Street ★★★★

1948

Call Northside 777 ★★★★

1949

A Letter to Three Wives ★★★★
City Across the River ★★★
Father Was a Fullback ★★★

1950

Perfect Strangers ★★★★
All About Eve ★★★★
I'll Get By ★★★

1951

The Mating Season ★★★★
As Young As You Feel ★★★
The Model and the Marriage Broker ★★★★

1952

With a Song in My Heart ★★★★

1953

Titanic ★★★★
The Farmer Takes a Wife ★★★
Pickup on South Street ★★★★

1954

Rear Window ★★★★

1955

Daddy Long Legs ★★★★
Lucy Gallant ★★★★

1956

The Proud and the Profane ★★★★

1959

A Hole in the Head ★★★★
Pillow Talk ★★★★

1961

The Misfits ★★★★
The Second Time Around ★★★

1962

Birdman of Alcatraz ★★★★
How the West Was Won ★★★★

1963

For Love or Money ★★★
A New Kind of Love ★★★
Move Over Darling ★★★★

1965

Boeing, Boeing ★★★

1967

The Incident ★★★★

1968

What's So Bad About Feeling Good? ★★★

JASON ROBARDS, JR.
★★★ 2.91 STARS

Screen charisma is usually present when an actor first shows his face on film. Occasionally, as in the case of Jason Robards, Jr., it surfaces later. Robards was dull and monotonous in his early films and then suddenly bloomed into an arresting, forceful personality.

Born in 1922, in Chicago, Illinois, his early triumphs were on the stage in the Eugene O'Neill plays "The Iceman Cometh" and "Long Day's Journey Into Night." A drab thriller with Deborah Kerr, *The Journey*, launched his movie career, and he was gloomy and uninteresting in *Tender Is the Night*. *A Thousand Clowns* released the charm that had been hidden, and he was likable as the ex-husband financially wiped out by divorce in *Divorce American Style*. *Tora! Tora! Tora!*, *Pat Garrett and Billy the Kid*, and *Mr. Sycamore* were more timekillers.

Jason Robards, Jr. in *Julia*.

Robards hit his stride with *Julia*, as Dashiell Hammett to Jane Fonda's Lillian Hellman, and in *All the President's Men* as Washington Post editor Ben Bradlee. Both portrayals won Best Supporting Actor Oscars, and Robards continued his brilliant work in *Comes a Horseman* and *Melvin and Howard*.

FILMOGRAPHY

1959

The Journey ★★

1961

By Love Possessed ★★

1962

Long Day's Journey Into Night ★★★★
Tender Is the Night ★★

1963

Act One ★★★★

1965

A Thousand Clowns ★★★

1966

A Big Hand for the Little Lady ★★★
Any Wednesday ★★★

Jason Robards, Jr. in *Melvin and Howard*.

1967

Divorce American Style ★★★★
The St. Valentine's Day Massacre ★★★
Hour of the Gun ★★★

1968

The Night They Raided Minsky's ★★★
Once Upon a Time in the West ★★★
Isadora ★★★

1970

Julius Caesar ★★★
The Ballad of Cable Hogue ★★★
Tora! Tora! Tora! ★★
Fools ★★

1971

Johnny Got His Gun ★★★
Murders in the Rue Morgue ★★

1972

The War Between Men and Women ★★★

1973

Death of a Stranger ★★★
Pat Garrett and Billy the Kid ★★★

1975

Mr. Sycamore ★★

1976

A Boy and His Dog ★★★
All the President's Men ★★★★

1977

Julia ★★★★

1978

Comes a Horseman ★★★★

1979

Cabo Blanco ★★★
Hurricane ★★
Melvin and Howard ★★★★

1980

Raise the Titanic! ★★★

1983

Something Wicked This Way Comes ★★
Max Dugan Returns ★★

CLIFF ROBERTSON
★ ★ ★ 3.09 STARS

Cliff Robertson falls somewhere between a reliable leading man and a star. He has the required good looks, charm, and acting talent, but his name was never quite enough to carry a film.

Robertson (Clifford Parker Robertson III) was born in 1925, in La Jolla, California. He served in the merchant marines and then did stage work ("Mr. Roberts" on the road) and television. A good supporting part in *Picnic,* as William Holden's wealthy friend, got him started. Later, he stole *Autumn Leaves* from Joan Crawford, playing her mentally troubled younger lover.

His portrait of a surf bum in *Gidget* was better than critics gave him credit for. The film was a hit with teenagers, but *All in a Night's Work, Underworld USA,* and *My Six Loves* missed with all ages. Robertson was personally selected by President Kennedy to portray the latter in *PT-109,* a dull, overlong war drama that failed to make him a box-office attraction. He was luckier with *Sunday in New York,* as Jane Fonda's pilot brother, and superb in *The Best Man,* possibly the finest of the "behind the scenes" political dramas.

Charly was the turning point. Robertson had played the title role, portraying a retarded man who temporarily becomes a genius, on TV. His feature film interpretation of the same part brought an Oscar. The award was well deserved, even though it was partially due to a heavy ad campaign. Unfortunately, a series of routine pictures diminished the impact of his triumph. He played in *J.W. Coop* (which he also produced and directed), *Ace Eli and Rodger of the Skies* (story by Steven Spielberg), and *Man on a Swing,* an unsatisfying thriller about a clairvoyant.

Three Days of the Condor was more prestigious, but *Obsession* was a convoluted, contrived attempt to do a Hitchcock piece. Robertson's career suffered when he accused film executive David Begelman of financial chicanery. When he came back, it was in a small role in the youth-slanted *Class,* starring Jacqueline Bisset.

Cliff Robertson in *Too Late the Hero.*

FILMOGRAPHY

1955
Picnic ★ ★ ★

1956
Autumn Leaves ★ ★ ★ ★

1957
The Girl Most Likely ★ ★

1958
The Naked and the Dead ★ ★ ★

1959
Gidget ★ ★ ★
Battle of the Coral Sea ★ ★ ★

1960
As the Sea Rages ★ ★ ★

1961
All in a Night's Work ★ ★ ★
Underworld USA ★ ★ ★
The Big Show ★ ★ ★

1962
The Interns ★ ★ ★ ★

1963
My Six Loves ★ ★ ★
PT-109 ★ ★ ★

1964
Sunday in New York ★ ★ ★ ★
The Best Man ★ ★ ★ ★
633 Squadron ★ ★ ★

1965
Love Has Many Faces ★ ★
Masquerade ★ ★ ★
Up from the Beach ★ ★ ★

1967
The Honey Pot ★ ★ ★ ★

1968
The Devil's Brigade ★ ★ ★
Charly ★ ★ ★ ★

1970
Too Late the Hero ★ ★ ★

1972
J. W. Coop (direction) ★ ★ ★
The Great Northfield Minnesota Raid ★ ★ ★

1973
Ace Eli and Rodger of the Skies ★ ★ ★

1974
Man on a Swing ★ ★

1975
Out of Season ★ ★ ★
Three Days of the Condor ★ ★ ★ ★

1976
Shoot ★ ★ ★
Midway ★ ★ ★
Obsession ★ ★ ★

1977
Fraternity Row (narration)

1979
The Pilot ★ ★ ★

1983
Class ★ ★

EDWARD G. ROBINSON
★ ★ ★ ½ 3.39 STARS

Of all the great, tough-guy actors (Cagney, Bogart, Lancaster, and Douglas), Edward G. Robinson was the least stylized, the least mannered. He also had the most shading and dimension as an actor.

Robinson (Emmanuel Goldenberg) was born in 1893, in Bucharest, Rumania. He originally thought of becoming a rabbi before he won a scholarship to the American Academy of Dramatic Arts. There was a Broadway apprenticeship of eight years in "Androcles and the Lion," "The Brothers Karamazov," and "The Man with Red Hair" before he made a screen debut in 1923's *The Bright Shawl.* His gangster image was formed early in *The Hole in the Wall* and *Night Ride,* and he had a star-making part as *Little Caesar.* He was brilliant and equally compelling in *Five Star Final*, an absorbing newspaper story.

The unsympathetic roles continued in *Two Seconds*, as a killer about to be executed, and *The Man With Two Faces. The Little Giant* paired him with Mary Astor, and he played a hood who wanted to break into society. Astor herself denigrated the picture, but it had bright moments. A good comedy *(The Whole Town's Talking)* allowed him to stretch his talents, and he was the good guy in *Bullets or Ballots*—Bogart was the bad one.

Kid Galahad was an exciting yarn about prizefighting. Although Robinson expressed his admiration for Bette Davis's portrayal in *All About Eve*, he said she came off like an "amateur" in *Kid Galahad*. He was *The Last Gangster* before he did another comedy, *A Slight Case of Murder.*

Edward G. Robinson in *Little Caesar.*

Dr. Ehrlich's Magic Bullet contained the performance Robinson regarded as his best. He felt he deserved Academy recognition for it and was disappointed when none came. The subject matter (curing syphilis) was considered daring in 1940. There were other entertaining vehicles, *Brother Orchid, Manpower* (with Dietrich and George Raft who quarreled during filming), *Unholy Partners*, and *Larceny Inc.* He had his first classic with *Double Indemnity.* He played an insurance investigator who exposed murderer Fred MacMurray with a characterization that Peter Falk borrowed for his "Colombo" series. *The Woman in the Window* almost achieved classic status, then spoiled everything with its ending (it was all a dream). This period saw many of his most memorable characterizations: as a man driven to murder in *Flesh and Fantasy*; as a Sunday painter in *Scarlet Street*; as a Nazi hunter in *The Stranger*; and as a washed-up gangster plotting a comeback in *Key Largo*.

Critics today usually downgrade *Night Has a Thousand Eyes*, but Robinson's clairvoyant was spellbinding when seen on TV. His greatest portrayal in the view of this observer was the conniving, outwardly charming banker in *House of Strangers.* At this point, the House Un-American Activities Committee persecuted him for withholding information on communist affiliations, a serious career setback. He also had to cope with a mentally ill wife and a juvenile delinquent son. His political problems eventually subsided, and he obtained a divorce losing half his legendary painting collection in the process.

Most of his later pictures *(Illegal, The Glass Web, Big Leaguer)* were second feature material. An exception was *A Hole in the Head*, with Frank Sinatra. Only Robinson survived the synthetic script.

That might serve as a fitting epitaph; Robinson's breathtaking talent could survive any script and transform it into something, if not brilliant, at least watchable. Robinson, in fact, never received an Oscar nomination in his whole career, a mind-boggling oversight. After his death, he was awarded one posthumously.

FILMOGRAPHY

1923

The Bright Shawl ★★★

1929

The Hole in the Wall ★★★

1930

Night Ride ★★★
A Lady to Love ★★★
Outside the Law ★★★
East Is West ★★★
The Widow of Chicago ★★★

Edward G. Robinson in *I Am the Law.*

1931

Little Caesar ★★★★
Smart Money ★★★
Five Star Final ★★★★

1932

The Hatchet Man ★★★
Two Seconds ★★★
Tiger Shark ★★★★
Silver Dollar ★★★★

1933

The Little Giant ★★★★
I Loved a Woman ★★★★

1934

Dark Hazard ★★★★
The Man With Two Faces ★★★★

1935

The Whole Town's Talking ★★★★
Barbary Coast ★★★

1936

Bullets or Ballots ★★★

1937

Thunder in the City ★★★★
Kid Galahad ★★★★
The Last Gangster ★★★★

1938

A Slight Case of Murder ★★★
The Amazing Dr. Clitterhouse ★★★
I Am the Law ★★★

1939

Confessions of a Nazi Spy ★★★★
Blackmail ★★★★

1940

Dr. Ehrlich's Magic Bullet ★★★★
Brother Orchid ★★★★
A Dispatch From Reuters ★★★★

1941

The Sea Wolf ★★★★
Manpower ★★★
Unholy Partners ★★★★

1942

Larceny Inc. ★★★★
Tales of Manhattan ★★★★

1943

Destroyer ★★★
Flesh and Fantasy ★★★★

1944

Tampico ★ ★ ★
Mr. Winkle Goes to War ★ ★ ★
Double Indemnity ★ ★ ★ ★
The Woman in the Window ★ ★ ★ ★

1945

Our Vines Have Tender Grapes ★ ★ ★ ★
Scarlet Street ★ ★ ★ ★
Journey Together (documentary)

1946

The Stranger ★ ★ ★ ★

1947

The Red House ★ ★ ★ ★

1948

All My Sons ★ ★ ★ ★
Key Largo ★ ★ ★ ★
Night Has a Thousand Eyes ★ ★ ★ ★

1949

House of Strangers ★ ★ ★ ★
It's a Great Feeling (cameo)

1950

My Daughter Joy ★ ★

1952

Actors and Sin ★ ★ ★

1953

Vice Squad ★ ★ ★
Big Leaguer ★ ★ ★
The Glass Web ★ ★ ★

1954

Black Tuesday ★ ★ ★

1955

Illegal ★ ★ ★ ★
The Violent Men ★ ★ ★
Tight Spot ★ ★ ★ ★
A Bullet for Joey ★ ★ ★ ★

1956

Hell on Frisco Bay ★ ★ ★
Nightmare ★ ★ ★
The Ten Commandments ★ ★ ★

1959

A Hole in the Head ★ ★ ★ ★

Edward G. Robinson in *The Biggest Bundle of Them All.*

1960

Seven Thieves ★ ★ ★
Pepe (cameo)

1962

My Geisha ★ ★
Two Weeks in Another Town ★ ★ ★ ★

1963

A Boy Ten Feet Tall ★ ★ ★
The Prize ★ ★ ★ ★

1964

Good Neighbor Sam ★ ★ ★
Robin and the 7 Hoods (cameo)
The Outrage ★ ★ ★
Cheyenne Autumn ★ ★ ★

1965

The Cincinnati Kid ★ ★ ★ ★

1967

Peking Blonde ★ ★ ★
Grand Slam ★ ★ ★
It's Your Move ★ ★ ★
Operation St. Peter's ★ ★

1968

The Biggest Bundle of Them All ★ ★
Never a Dull Moment ★ ★ ★

1969

MacKenna's Gold ★ ★ ★

1970

Song of Norway ★ ★

1973

Soylent Green ★ ★ ★
Neither By Day or Night ★ ★

GINGER ROGERS
★ ★ ★ 3.01 STARS

Fred Astaire's most famous dance partner, Ginger Rogers was a lovely and talented star in her own right. She was generally excellent throughout her long and varied career. She shone not only in musicals, but in comedy and drama as well.

Rogers was born Virginia Katherine McMath in 1911, in Independence, Missouri. After winning a Charleston contest, she had two good Broadway roles (in "Top Speed" and "Girl Crazy") before concentrating on filmmaking. Her early vehicles gave her little chance to shine—*The Tip Off, Suicide Fleet,* and *The Tenderfoot.* Though she did have a funny and clever part in *42nd Street* as Anytime Annie.

Ginger Rogers in *Lucky Partners.*

In *Flying Down to Rio,* she looked as uninteresting as the rest of the cast, including Fred Astaire, Dolores Del Rio, and Gene Raymond. However, she and Astaire danced the Carioca, and caught the attention of a dance-starved public. They were quickly reteamed for more hits: *The Gay Divorcee, Roberta, Top Hat, Follow the Fleet, Swing Time,* and *Shall We Dance?* Although choreographer Hermes Pan called their relationship one of "mutual aggression," this private animosity never came through on the screen. Years later, Astaire downplayed the friction.

Stage Door inspired a rave review from The New York Times: "Miss Hepburn and Miss Rogers, in particular, seem to be acting so far above their usual heads that, frankly, we hardly recognized them." There followed two more Astaire-Rogers musicals (*Carefree* and *The Story of Vernon & Irene Castle*) before she went her own way.

An entertaining comedy, *Bachelor Mother,* began her solo ascent, followed by *Primrose Path* and her Oscar-winning portrayal in *Kitty Foyle.* At the time, observers felt that Katharine Hepburn deserved the award, but seen today Rogers' performance holds up more effectively. *Roxie Hart* was an uneven and occasionally funny spoof of the roaring 20s. *Tender Comrade* was a preachy soap opera. She had better luck with *The Major and the Minor* where she masqueraded as a child, and with *Lady in the Dark,* a hit musical that critics were none too fond of.

I'll Be Seeing You cast her as a convict on Christmas leave; it was touching and beautifully acted, a marked contrast to the harebrained *It Had to Be You*. A reunion with Astaire occurred when Judy Garland had to withdraw from *The Barkleys of Broadway*. It was a smash, though a lesser musical than their earlier efforts.

Rogers' best vehicle after *Barkleys* was *Dreamboat*, a clever satire about silent stars with Clifton Webb. She was mannered and arch in *Black Widow*, a labored and oversized version of author Patrick Quentin's thriller. However, her performance as a police informant in *Tight Spot* was the most engaging element of that movie.

When her cinema career skidded to a halt, Rogers returned to Broadway in "Hello Dolly" and played to full houses. Her place in the hierarchy of Hollywood's legend is secure.

Ginger Rogers with Fred Astaire in *The Barkleys of Broadway.*

FILMOGRAPHY

1930

Young Man of Manhattan ★★★
Queen High ★★★
The Sap From Syracuse ★★
Follow the Leader ★★★

1931

Honor Among Lovers ★★★
The Tip Off ★★
Suicide Fleet ★★★

1932

Carnival Boat ★★★
The Tenderfoot ★★
The Thirteenth Guest ★★★
Hat Check Girl ★★★
You Said a Mouthful ★★★

1933

42nd Street ★★★
Broadway Bad ★★★
Gold Diggers of 1933 ★★★
Professional Sweetheart ★★★
A Shriek in the Night ★★
Don't Bet on Love ★★★
Sitting Pretty ★★★
Flying Down to Rio ★★★★
Chance at Heaven ★★★

1934

Rafter Romance ★★
Finishing School ★★★
20 Million Sweethearts ★★★
Change of Heart ★★★
Upper World ★★★
The Gay Divorcee ★★★★
Romance in Manhattan ★★★

1935

Roberta ★★★★
Star of Midnight ★★★
Top Hat ★★★★
In Person ★★★

1936

Swing Time ★★★★

1937

Follow the Fleet ★★★★
Shall We Dance? ★★★★
Stage Door ★★★★

1938

Having Wonderful Time ★★★
Vivacious Lady ★★★
Carefree ★★★★

1939

The Story of Vernon & Irene Castle ★★★
Bachelor Mother ★★★
Fifth Avenue Girl ★★★

1940

Primrose Path ★★★
Lucky Partners ★★★
Kitty Foyle ★★★★

1941

Tom, Dick and Harry ★★★★

1942

Roxie Hart ★★★★
Tales of Manhattan ★★★
The Major and the Minor ★★★★
Once Upon a Honeymoon ★★★

1943

Tender Comrade ★★

1944

Lady in the Dark ★★
I'll Be Seeing You ★★★

1945

Weekend at the Waldorf ★★★

1946

Heartbeat ★★★
Magnificent Doll ★★

1947

It Had to Be You ★★

1949

The Barkleys of Broadway ★★★★

1950

Perfect Strangers ★★★
Storm Warning ★★★

1951

The Groom Wore Spurs ★★

1952

We're Not Married ★★★★
Monkey Business ★★★
Dreamboat ★★★

1953

Forever Female ★★★

1954

Black Widow ★★
Twist of Fate ★★

1955

Tight Spot ★★★★

1956

The First Traveling Saleslady ★★
Teenage Rebel ★★

1957

Oh Men! Oh Women! ★★

1965

Harlow ★★★

MICKEY ROONEY
★ ★ ★ 2.93 STARS

Many stars (Cary Grant, Greta Garbo, and Charlie Chaplin) have received Special Oscars after getting the cold shoulder for years from the Academy. One of the most deserving recipients is Mickey Rooney, honored in 1983 after 57 years of film activity (he debuted in 1926). Hedda Hopper once called him the most underrated talent in show business.

Rooney (Joe Yule, Jr.) was born in 1920, in Brooklyn, New York. His parents earned their living in vaudeville, and Rooney was fully trained as dancer, mimic, and singer by the time he began motion picture work. A series of two reelers led to features, a lengthy apprenticeship in *The Beast of the City, The Lost Jungle*, and *The County Chairman*. Afterwards, he became MGM's number one box-office attraction in the Andy Hardy series: *A Family Affair, Judge Hardy's Children*, and *Love Finds Andy Hardy.*

Boys Town made critics pay attention, and a row of delightful vehicles with Judy Garland, *(Babes in Arms, Strike Up the Band*, and *Girl Crazy)* continued the momentum. He continued to draw more crowds according to box-office lists than Gable, Cooper, or Tracy, until *Summer Holiday,* an anemic musical. In *Killer McCoy,* he was an improbable prizefighter. Rooney seemed equally unlikely as Larry Hart in *Words and Music.* This "life story" of Rodgers and Hart stubbornly avoided any relation to fact. *Francis in the Haunted House* and *Platinum High School* were even more disastrous, but there was a comeback of sorts. In *Requiem for a Heavyweight,* he was excellent, but in *Breakfast at Tiffany's* he was embarrassingly miscast.

However, Rooney persevered, and by the late 1970s he was appearing in film musicals again *(Pete's Dragon),* and attracting capacity crowds to a Broadway show, "Sugar Babies."

FILMOGRAPHY

(features only)

1927

Orchids and Ermine ★ ★ ★

1932

Sin's Pay Day ★ ★ ★
The Beast of the City ★ ★
High Speed ★ ★
My Pal the King ★ ★ ★
Information Kid ★ ★ ★
Not to Be Trusted ★ ★

1933

The Big Cage ★ ★
The Life of Jimmy Dolan ★ ★ ★
Broadway to Hollywood ★ ★ ★
The Big Chance ★ ★
The World Changes ★ ★ ★
The Chief ★ ★

1934

The Lost Jungle (serial) ★ ★
Beloved ★ ★ ★
I Like It That Way ★ ★ ★
Love Birds ★ ★ ★
Manhattan Melodrama ★ ★ ★
Half a Sinner ★ ★ ★
Chained ★ ★ ★
Hide-Out ★ ★
Blind Date ★ ★
Upper World ★ ★ ★
Death on a Diamond ★ ★

1935

The County Chairman ★ ★ ★
The Healer ★ ★ ★
Reckless ★ ★ ★
A Midsummer Night's Dream ★ ★ ★ ★
Ah Wilderness! ★ ★ ★ ★

1936

Riff Raff ★ ★ ★
Little Lord Fauntleroy ★ ★ ★ ★
The Devil Is a Sissy ★ ★ ★ ★
Down the Stretch ★ ★ ★

1937

A Family Affair ★ ★ ★
Captains Courageous ★ ★ ★ ★
Slave Ship ★ ★
The Hoosier Schoolboy ★ ★ ★
Live, Love and Learn ★ ★ ★
Thoroughbreds Don't Cry ★ ★
You're Only Young Once ★ ★ ★

1938

Love Is a Headache ★ ★ ★
Hold That Kiss ★ ★ ★
Judge Hardy's Children ★ ★ ★
Lord Jeff ★ ★ ★
Love Finds Andy Hardy ★ ★ ★
Boys Town ★ ★ ★ ★
Stablemates ★ ★ ★ ★
Out West With the Hardys ★ ★ ★

1939

The Adventures of Huckleberry Finn ★ ★ ★ ★
The Hardys Ride High ★ ★ ★
Andy Hardy Gets Spring Fever ★ ★ ★
Babes in Arms ★ ★ ★ ★
Judge Hardy and Son ★ ★ ★

1940

Young Tom Edison ★ ★ ★ ★
Andy Hardy Meets Debutante ★ ★ ★
Strike Up the Band ★ ★ ★ ★

1941

Andy Hardy's Private Secretary ★ ★ ★
Men of Boys Town ★ ★ ★ ★
Life Begins for Andy Hardy ★ ★ ★

1942

Babes on Broadway ★ ★ ★
The Courtship of Andy Hardy ★ ★ ★
A Yank at Eton ★ ★ ★ ★
Andy Hardy's Double Life ★ ★ ★

1943

The Human Comedy ★ ★ ★ ★
Thousands Cheer ★ ★ ★
Girl Crazy ★ ★ ★

1944

Andy Hardy's Blonde Trouble ★ ★ ★
National Velvet ★ ★ ★ ★

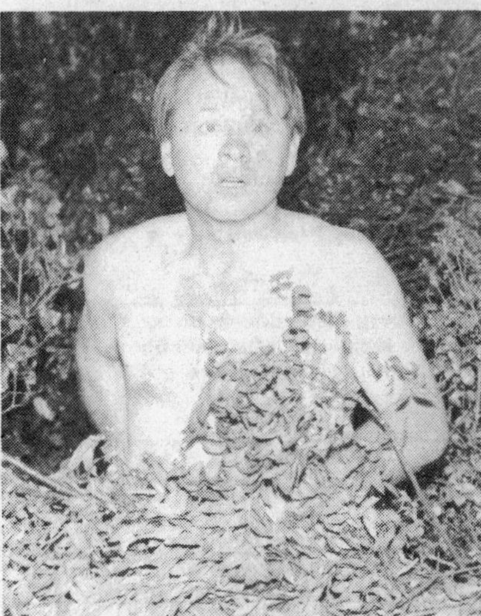

Mickey Rooney in "Wagon Train."

1947

Love Laughs at Andy Hardy ★ ★ ★
Killer McCoy ★ ★ ★

1948

Summer Holiday ★ ★ ★
Words and Music ★ ★ ★

1949

The Big Wheel ★ ★ ★

1950

The Fireball ★ ★ ★
He's a Cockeyed Wonder ★ ★ ★

1951

My Outlaw Brother ★ ★ ★
The Strip ★ ★ ★

1952

Sound Off ★ ★ ★

1953

All Ashore ★ ★ ★
Off Limits ★ ★ ★
A Slight Case of Larceny ★ ★ ★

Mickey Rooney with Leo Gordon in *Baby Face Nelson.*

1954

Drive a Crooked Road ★★★★
The Atomic Kid ★★★

1955

The Bridges at Toko-Ri ★★★
The Twinkle in God's Eye ★★★

1956

The Bold and the Brave ★★★★
Francis in the Haunted House ★★★
Magnificent Roughnecks ★★★

1957

Operation Mad Ball ★★★
Baby Face Nelson ★★★★

1958

Andy Hardy Comes Home ★★★
A Nice Little Bank That Should Be Robbed ★★★

1959

The Last Mile ★★★
The Big Operator ★★★

1960

Platinum High School ★★
The Private Lives of Adam and Eve ★★

1961

King of the Roaring 20's ★★★
Breakfast at Tiffany's ★

1962

Requiem for a Heavyweight ★★★★

1963

It's a Mad Mad Mad Mad World ★★

1964

The Secret Invasion ★★★

1965

How to Stuff a Wild Bikini ★★
24 Hours to Kill ★★★

1966

Ambush Bay ★★★
L'Arcidiavolo ★★

1968

Skidoo ★★

1969

The Extraordinary Seaman ★★★
80 Steps to Jonah ★★★
The Comic ★★★

1970

The Cockeyed Cowboys of Calico County ★★★
Hollywood Blue (documentary)

1971

B. J. Presents ★★

1972

Richard ★★★
Pulp ★★★

1974

That's Entertainment (narration)
Journey Back to Oz (voice only)
Ace of Hearts ★★★

1975

Bon Baisers de Hong Kong ★★
Rachel's Man ★★★

1977

The Domino Principle ★★
Pete's Dragon ★★

1978

The Magic of Lassie ★

1979

The Black Stallion ★★★★
An Arabian Adventure ★★
Find the Lady ★★★

1981

The Fox and the Hound (voice only)

KATHARINE ROSS
★★★ 2.84 STARS

Katharine Ross became a star quickly. Her beauty and charm made her an obvious choice for Hollywood longevity, but five years after her debut she virtually disappeared. She still makes occasional appearances but has yet to regain her former position.

Ross was born in Los Angeles, California, in 1942. She did occasional TV and made her first picture, *Shenandoah,* in 1965. She was an appealing heroine, and her appeal was sorely needed in the schmaltzy *The Singing Nun. Mr. Buddwing* was a rambling, incoherent tale of an amnesiac James Garner, but *The Graduate* made Ross famous. She was perfect as the forbidden object of Dustin Hoffman's affections, and wholesomely desirable in *Butch Cassidy and the Sundance Kid* with Redford and Newman.

Unfortunately, *Tell Them Willie Boy Is Here,* though it featured Redford again, was preachy and unpopular. She had a good chance in *The Stepford Wives,* as a candidate for cloning, but her portrayal was oddly listless and bland. She was far better in a worse film, *The Betsy,* as Laurence Olivier's mistress, but *The Swarm* nearly wrecked her career. What she needs is a first-rate script, and she'll be back on top again.

Katharine Ross in *Wrong Is Right.*

FILMOGRAPHY

1965

Shenandoah ★★★

1966

The Singing Nun ★★
Mr. Buddwing ★★

1967

Games ★★★
The Graduate ★★★★

1969

Hellfighters ★★★
Butch Cassidy and the Sundance Kid ★★★★

1970

Tell Them Willie Boy Is Here ★★★
Fools ★★★

1972

Get to Know Your Rabbit ★★
They Only Kill Their Masters ★★★

1974

Le Hasard et La Violence ★★★

1975

The Stepford Wives ★★

1976

Voyage of the Damned ★★★

1978

The Betsy ★★★
The Swarm ★★

1979

The Legacy ★★★

1980

The Final Countdown ★★★

1982

Wrong Is Right ★★★

GENA ROWLANDS
★ ★ ★ 3.15 STARS

One of Hollywood's most respected actresses, Gena Rowlands works only occasionally and then strictly in husband John Cassavetes' productions. Her performances in these have brought her critical acclaim, but not the public following her talent deserves.

Rowlands was born in Cambria, Wisconsin, in 1934. On Broadway she appeared in "The Seven Year Itch" and "Middle of the Night." She was José Ferrer's pregnant wife in her first movie, *The High Cost of Loving,* and made her scenes count in the cult favorite, *Lonely Are the Brave.* Neither struck the public fancy, nor did *A Child Is Waiting* which Cassavetes directed.

Tony Rome was a routine private-eye thriller, but she reached wide audiences in the more popular *The Spiral Road.* Her greatest personal success was *A Woman Under the Influence,* which netted an Oscar nomination. *Minnie and Moskowitz* was frantic and witless, though her gritty good humor had a fine showcase in *Gloria,* one of Cassavetes' few "commercial" entertainments.

Gena Rowlands in *Gloria.*

FILMOGRAPHY

1958

The High Cost of Loving ★ ★ ★

1962

Lonely Are the Brave ★ ★ ★ ★
The Spiral Road ★ ★ ★

1963

A Child Is Waiting ★ ★ ★

1967

Tony Rome ★ ★ ★

1968

Faces ★ ★ ★

1971

Minnie and Moskowitz ★ ★

1974

A Woman Under the Influence ★ ★ ★ ★

1976

Two-Minute Warning ★ ★ ★

1978

Opening Night ★ ★ ★
The Brink's Job ★ ★ ★

1980

Gloria ★ ★ ★ ★

1982

Tempest ★ ★ ★

JANE RUSSELL
★ ★ ½ 2.43 STARS

Jane Russell was a heavily promoted sex symbol in the 1940s. She gained notoriety as a result of her appearance in *The Outlaw.* Despite her looks, she seemed synthetic and manufactured. Only occasionally, in comedies, did glimpses of warmth and charm emerge.

She was born Ernestine Jane Geraldine Russell in 1921, in Bemidji, Minnesota. According to writer Ephraim Katz, she won a "nationwide chest hunt" conducted by Howard Hughes to star in Hughes' then-notorious *The Outlaw.* Outraged cries by censors held up the film for two years, and *Young Widow* was a dated soap opera that revealed her acting limitations.

The Paleface was a big success, however, and her teamwork with Bob Hope led to an equally enjoyable sequel, *Son of Paleface.* In between she made the best of *His Kind of Woman* and *Double Dynamite.*

There were a few more highs (the delightful *Gentlemen Prefer Blondes* with Marilyn Monroe, and *The Tall Men* with Clark Gable). However, most of Russell's movies were too mediocre for any actress to surmount: *Underwater!, Gentlemen Marry Brunettes, Hot Blood, The Revolt of Mamie Stover,* and *The Fuzzy Pink Nightgown.*

Jane Russell.

Broadway came to the rescue in the form of songwriter Stephen Sondheim with "Company," and she pleased the hard-boiled New York critics. She does little acting today but appears regularly on TV commercials.

FILMOGRAPHY

1943

The Outlaw ★ ★

1946

Young Widow ★ ★

1948

The Paleface ★ ★ ★ ★

1951

His Kind of Woman ★ ★ ★
Double Dynamite ★ ★

1952

The Las Vegas Story ★ ★
Macao ★ ★
Montana Belle ★ ★
Son of Paleface ★ ★ ★ ★
Road to Bali (cameo)

1953

Gentlemen Prefer Blondes ★ ★ ★ ★

1954

The French Line ★ ★

1955

Underwater! ★ ★
Foxfire ★ ★
The Tall Men ★ ★ ★
Gentlemen Marry Brunettes ★ ★

1956

Hot Blood ★ ★
The Revolt of Mamie Stover ★ ★

1957

The Fuzzy Pink Nightgown ★★

1964

Fate is the Hunter (cameo)

1966

Johnny Reno ★★
Waco ★★

1967

The Born Losers (cameo)

1970

Darker than Amber ★★★

ROSALIND RUSSELL
★★★ 3.04 STARS

Rosalind Russell specialized in the bright and elegant, tough and independent woman that made the sophisticated comedies of the 1940s so endearing. But she was also a powerful figure in dramas as well. Though she never won an Oscar, she was nominated four times (*My Sister Eileen, Sister Kenny, Mourning Becomes Electra,* and *Auntie Mame*).

Russell was born in 1908, in Waterbury, Connecticut. Her background was sophisticated (lawyer father and fashion editor mother) and prepared her for the worldly parts that made her famous. Stage work led to an appearance in *Evelyn Prentice,* with William Powell and Myrna Loy. She got Clark Gable as a leading man in *China Seas,* a sure sign that her career was on the rise. Then she did *Craig's Wife,* as the neurotic housewife who drives her husband away with her fanatical tidiness. It was a good performance (though not as convincing as Joan Crawford's in the 1950 remake, *Harriet Craig*).

Most of Russell's films during the late 1930s and early 1940s were excellent. *Night Must Fall* was a gripping thriller with Robert Montgomery playing the psychotic killer who threatens her life. *The Citadel* changed author A.J. Cronin's powerful ending. The wife was killed in the book, but stars rarely died in major studio productions of that era. Still, the flavor and sensitivity of the story were captured. Russell stole *The Women* from a stellar cast including Joan Crawford, Norma Shearer, Paulette Goddard, and Joan Fontaine.

His Girl Friday was *The Front Page* sexually revamped. Both she and co-star Cary Grant had a ball with the breezy, fast-moving dialogue. Her other comedies were generally enjoyable (*Hired Wife, No Time for Comedy, My Sister Eileen,* and *Design for Scandal*). She played *Sister Kenny,* the nurse who helped combat polio. It was an earnest, but plodding drama.

She was expected to win an Academy Award for *Mourning Becomes Electra.* So certain was she that she stood up at the Oscar ceremonies before the winner was announced, only to hear Loretta Young's name called for *The Farmer's Daughter.* Young was also Russell's best friend. In retrospect, the Academy made the right decision.

Russell went to Broadway and made a lasting mark in "Wonderful Town" and "Auntie Mame." When *Auntie Mame* was filmed, she repeated her role to equally favorable response. It was her last memorable film venture. *A Majority of One* cast her in the part that Gertrude Berg had played on the stage. To put it mildly, she was miscast as a Jewish matron.

Gypsy should have been ideal, but Russell was too classy, too elegant for the earthy, vulgar Mama Rose. She finally received an Oscar for her charity work (the Jean Hersholt Award) in 1972. After a long bout with arthritis and a longer one with cancer, she died in 1976. It was a cruel and painful ending for a woman who had done so much to elevate the level of screen comedy.

FILMOGRAPHY

1934

Evelyn Prentice ★★★
The President Vanishes ★★★
Forsaking All Others ★★★

1935

The Night Is Young ★★★
West Point of the Air ★★★
The Casino Murder Case ★★★

Rosalind Russell in *Auntie Mame.*

Reckless ★★★
China Seas ★★★
Rendezvous ★★★

1936

It Had to Happen ★★★
Under Two Flags ★★★
Trouble for Two ★★★
Craig's Wife ★★★★

1937

Night Must Fall ★★★
Live, Love and Learn ★★★

1938

Man-Proof ★★★
Four's a Crowd ★★★
The Citadel ★★★

1939

Fast and Loose ★★★
The Women ★★★★

1940

Hired Wife ★★★★
No Time for Comedy ★★★★
His Girl Friday ★★★★

1941

This Thing Called Love ★★★
They Met in Bombay ★★★
The Feminine Touch ★★★★
Design for Scandal ★★★★

1942

Take a Letter Darling ★★★★
My Sister Eileen ★★★★

1943

Flight for Freedom ★★★
What a Woman ★★★

1945

Roughly Speaking ★★★
She Wouldn't Say Yes ★★★

1946

Sister Kenny ★★★

1947

The Guilt of Janet Ames ★★★
Mourning Becomes Electra ★★★

1948

The Velvet Touch ★★★★

1949

Tell It to the Judge ★★★

1950

A Woman of Distinction ★★★

1953

Never Wave at a Wac ★★★★

1955

The Girl Rush ★★

1956

Picnic ★★★★

1958

Auntie Mame ★★★★

1962

A Majority of One ★
Five Finger Exercise ★
Gypsy ★★

1966

The Trouble With Angels ★★

1967

Rosie ★★
Oh Dad, Poor Dad, Mama's Hung You in the Closet and I'm Feeling So Sad ★★

1968

Where Angels Go Trouble Follows ★★

1971

Mrs. Pollifax-Spy ★★

ROBERT RYAN
★★★½ 3.28 STARS

Robert Ryan's career is conclusive evidence that stardom and versatility rarely mix. He was able to play dozens of contrasting characters brilliantly, but no one ever formed an image of a "Robert Ryan picture" as they did with a Clark Gable, Cary Grant, or James Stewart picture.

Ryan was born in 1909, in Chicago, Illinois. After a flirtation with boxing and then modeling, Ryan did a few bit parts in films like *Golden Gloves* and *Texas Rangers Ride Again* and then appeared with Randolph Scott in *Bombardier* and *Trail Street*. *Woman on the Beach* gave him a meaty role as a man goaded into murder by Joan Bennett, and *Crossfire* gave him critical recognition. He played a deadly anti-Semite. He was superb in *Act of Violence* and chillingly effective as a paranoid Howard Hughes-type multi-millionaire in *Caught*.

The Set-Up was a grimly realistic view of the fight racket which was too raw for mass appeal. His films were either excellent (*Clash by Night* and *Bad Day at Black Rock*), or poor (*House of Bamboo*), but Ryan was consistently fine in all of them. He was evil in Peter Ustinov's compelling adaptation of *Billy Budd*, a film that never received the public endorsement it merited.

Robert Ryan in *The Dirty Dozen*.

The Professionals, *The Dirty Dozen*, and *The Wild Bunch* were more in tune with audience taste—adventure tales with heavy emphasis on violence: Ryan never won an Oscar, nor did a cult following develop after his death from cancer in 1973. But his record of quiet, unflashy brilliance should eventually be reevaluated and given its due.

FILMOGRAPHY

1940

Queen of the Mob (bit)
Golden Gloves (bit)
Texas Rangers Ride Again (bit)
Northwest Mounted Police (bit)

1941

The Feminine Touch (bit)

1943

The Sky's the Limit (bit)
Behind the Rising Sun ★★★
The Iron Major ★★★
Gangway for Tomorrow ★★★
Bombardier ★★★

1944

Tender Comrade ★★★
Marine Raiders ★★★

1947

Trail Street ★★★
Woman on the Beach ★★★★
Crossfire ★★★★

1948

Berlin Express ★★★
Return of the Badmen ★★★
The Boy With Green Hair ★★★

1949

Act of Violence ★★★★
Caught ★★★★
The Set-Up ★★★★
I Married a Communist ★★★

1950

The Secret Fury ★★★
Born to Be Bad ★★★★

1951

Best of the Bad Men ★★★
Flying Leathernecks ★★★
The Racket ★★★

1952

On Dangerous Ground ★★★★
Clash by Night ★★★★
Beware My Lovely ★★★
Horizons West ★★★

1953

City Beneath the Sea ★★★
The Naked Spur ★★★
Inferno ★★★

1954

Alaska Seas ★★★
About Mrs. Leslie ★★★★
Her Twelve Men ★★★

1955

Bad Day at Black Rock ★★★★
Escape to Burma ★★★
House of Bamboo ★★★
The Tall Men ★★★★

1956

The Proud Ones ★★★
Back From Eternity ★★★

1957

Men in War ★★★

1958

God's Little Acre ★★★★

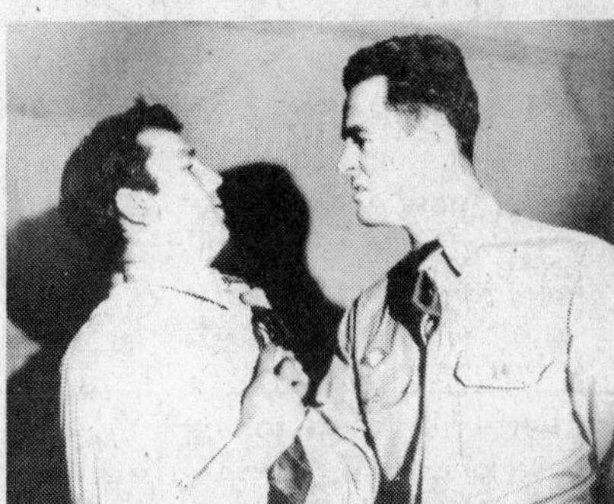

Robert Ryan with Steve Brodie in *Crossfire*.

1959

Lonelyhearts ★★★
Day of the Outlaw ★★★
Odds Against Tomorrow ★★★

1960

Ice Palace ★★★★

1961

The Canadians ★★★
King of Kings ★★★

1962

Billy Budd ★★★★
The Longest Day ★★★

1965

Battle of the Bulge ★★★
The Dirty Game ★★★

1966

The Professionals ★★★★

1967

The Busy Body ★★★
The Dirty Dozen ★★★★
Hour of the Gun ★★★

1968

Custer of the West ★★★
Escondido ★★★
Anzio ★★★

1969

The Wild Bunch ★★★★
Captain Nemo and the Underwater City ★★★

1971

The Love Machine ★★★
Lawman ★★★

1972

And Hope to Die ★★★

1973

Lolly Madonna XXX ★★★
The Iceman Cometh ★★★★
Executive Action ★★★

1974

The Outfit ★★★

EVA MARIE SAINT
★★★ 3.14 STARS

Eva Marie Saint has had few roles worthy of her abilities, but she gives every part elegance and grace. She's Faye Dunaway with warmth, and it's regrettable she couldn't have done *Chinatown* or *Network*.

Saint was born in 1924, in Newark, New Jersey. After a thorough background in radio and TV, she played Marlon Brando's girlfriend in *On the Waterfront*. An Oscar made her a hot property, and she demonstrated her sense of comedy in a lesser Bob Hope vehicle, *That Certain Feeling*. *Raintree County* was an elaborate civil war soap opera, and Saint's naturalness was a pleasant contrast to the scenery-chewing antics of Elizabeth Taylor.

She was superb in the wrenching movie version of *A Hatful of Rain* and exuded glamour in *North By Northwest*, one of Hitchcock's wittiest thrillers. Saint was touching as Warren Beatty's discarded girlfriend in the unjustly ignored *All Fall Down*. From this high, she was forced to endure the contrivances of *The Sandpiper*, playing the wife of the cheating preacher Richard Burton. *Grand Prix* and *The Stalking Moon* pointed out her acting ability but failed to cement her stardom.

FILMOGRAPHY

1954

On the Waterfront ★★★★

1956

That Certain Feeling ★★★

1957

A Hatful of Rain ★★★★
Raintree County ★★★

1959

North By Northwest ★★★★

1960

Exodus ★★★

1962

All Fall Down ★★★★

1964

36 Hours ★★★

Eva Marie Saint with Warren Beatty in *All Fall Down*.

1965

The Sandpiper ★★

1966

The Russians Are Coming, the Russians Are Coming ★★★
Grand Prix ★★★

1969

The Stalking Moon ★★★

1970

Loving ★★★

1972

Cancel My Reservation ★★

GEORGE SANDERS
★★★½ 3.29 STARS

Cynicism is generally an unappealing quality, but George Sanders made it distinctive and even likable. He brought polish to ordinary dialogue, and when he had witty lines, as in *All About Eve*, he achieved greatness.

Sanders was born in 1906, in St. Petersburg, Russia to British parents. After a period in the textile business, he tried the stage in "Conversation Piece" by Noel Coward and "Further Horizon." After performing in a number of promising early vehicles (*Strange Cargo, The Man Who Could Work Miracles, Lloyds of London*), he took on a series in The Saint. He also played in war stories (*Confessions of a Nazi Spy* with Edward G. Robinson), westerns (*Allegheny Uprising* with John Wayne), and melodramas (*Rebecca*). Sanders specialized in the nasty, supercilious villain. *Rage in Heaven* paired him with Ingrid Bergman, and he did his second series The Falcon.

Somerset Maugham's *The Moon and Sixpence* was made into an effective movie in 1942, and Sanders was believable as Gauguin. He did equally well in *The Picture of Dorian Gray* and *Hangover Square*. Most of his roles were jaded and unsympathetic. *The Ghost and Mrs. Muir* featured him as the spirit of a dead man who romanced Gene Tierney. Sanders was amusingly treacherous in De Mille's *Sam-*

son and Delilah, and he brought a note of authenticity to the overproduced and boring *Forever Amber*.

All About Eve turned the tide. As drama critic Addison De Witt, he all but stole the picture. Co-star Anne Baxter later commented that director Joseph Mankiewicz had to push and prod him into the Academy award-winning performance that finally emerged. He had the same sort of biting dialogue in *I Can Get It for You Wholesale*, a tart and entertaining look at the garment industry based on Jerome Weidman's novel.

Ivanhoe was an exciting, big-budget spectacle. After that Sanders was given an atypical part as Ethel Merman's love interest in *Call Me Madam*. He played the king of a small country with morals and integrity, for a change, and revealed a fine singing voice. He also displayed uncharacteristic warmth.

Another musical, *Jupiter's Darling*, with Howard Keel, was less successful than *Madam*, and *Never Say Goodbye* was a yawn-provoking soap opera. He was amusing as Bob Hope's rival in *That Certain Feeling*, and co-starred with wife Zsa Zsa Gabor in *Death of a Scoundrel*. Their marriage was turbulent; Gabor turned up on the set of *Eve* to induce Sanders to go shopping, and director Joseph Mankiewicz had to throw her out.

Most of the films that followed deserved to be ignored: *That Kind of Woman* with Sophia Loren, *Bluebeard's Ten Honeymoons*, and *Operation Snatch*. There was an exception with an engrossing science-fiction thriller, *Village of the Damned*, and a popular Pink Panther comedy, *A Shot in the Dark*.

Sanders committed suicide in 1972, citing boredom as the reason. The explanation was perfectly in keeping with his world-weary, enigmatic screen image.

FILMOGRAPHY

1936

Find the Lady ★★★
Strange Cargo ★★★
The Man Who Could Work Miracles ★★★
Dishonour Bright ★★★★

George Sanders in *International Settlement*.

1937

Lloyds of London ★★★★
Love Is News ★★★
Slave Ship ★★★
The Lady Escapes ★★★
Lancer Spy ★★★

1938

International Settlement ★★★
Four Men and a Prayer ★★★

1939

Mr. Moto's Last Warning ★★★
The Saint Strikes Back ★★★★
Confessions of a Nazi Spy ★★★★
The Saint in London ★★★★
The Outsider ★★★
So This Is London ★★★
Nurse Edith Cavell ★★★
Allegheny Uprising ★★★

1940

Green Hell ★★★
The Saint's Double Trouble ★★★★
Rebecca ★★★★
The House of the Seven Gables ★★★★
The Saint Takes Over ★★★★
Foreign Correspondent ★★★★
Bitter Sweet ★★★
The Son of Monte Cristo ★★★★

1941

The Saint in Palm Springs ★★★★
Rage in Heaven ★★★
Man Hunt ★★★★
The Gay Falcon ★★★
Sundown ★★★
A Date With the Falcon ★★★

1942

Son of Fury ★★★
The Falcon Takes Over ★★★
Her Cardboard Lover ★★★
Tales of Manhattan ★★★
The Falcon's Brother ★★★
The Moon and Sixpence ★★★★
The Black Swan ★★★★

1943

Quiet Please—Murder ★★★
They Came to Blow Up America ★★★
This Land Is Mine ★★★
Appointment in Berlin ★★★
Paris After Dark ★★★

1944

The Lodger ★★★★
Action in Arabia ★★★
Summer Storm ★★★★

1945

Hangover Square ★★★★
The Picture of Dorian Gray ★★★★
The Strange Affair of Uncle Harry ★★★★

1946

A Scandal in Paris ★★★
The Strange Woman ★★★

1947

The Private Affairs of Bel Ami ★★★★
The Ghost and Mrs. Muir ★★★★
Lured ★★★★
Forever Amber ★★★

1949

The Fan ★★★
Samson and Delilah ★★★★

1950

Black Jack ★★★
All About Eve ★★★★

1951

I Can Get It For You Wholesale ★★★★
The Light Touch ★★★★

1952

Ivanhoe ★★★★
Assignment—Paris ★★★

1953

Call Me Madam ★★★★
The Lonely Woman ★★★

1954

Witness to Murder ★★★
King Richard and the Crusaders ★★★

1955

Jupiter's Darling ★★★
Moonfleet ★★★
The Scarlet Coat ★★★
The King's Thief ★★★

1956

Never Say Goodbye ★★★
While the City Sleeps ★★★
That Certain Feeling ★★★★
Death of a Scoundrel ★★★

1957

The Seventh Sin ★★★

1958

The Whole Truth ★★★
From the Earth to the Moon ★★★

1959

That Kind of Woman ★★★
A Touch of Larceny ★★★
Solomon and Sheba ★★★

1960

Bluebeard's Ten Honeymoons ★★★
The Last Voyage ★★★
Cone of Silence ★★★
Village of the Damned ★★★★

1961

Five Golden Hours ★★★
Call Me Genius ★★★

1962

Operation Snatch ★★★
In Search of the Castaways ★★★

1963

Cairo ★★★
Mondo di Notte (narration)

1964

Dark Purpose ★★★
The Cracksman ★★★
A Shot in the Dark ★★★
The Golden Head ★★★

1965

The Amorous Adventures of Moll Flanders ★★★

1966

Trunk to Cairo ★★★
The Quiller Memorandum ★★★

1967

Warning Shot ★★★
Good Times ★★★
The Jungle Book (voice only)

1968

One Step to Hell ★★★

1969

The Best House in London ★★★
The Body Stealers ★★★
The Candy Man ★★★

1970

The Kremlin Letter ★★★

1972

Psychomania ★★★

SUSAN SARANDON
★★★ 3.06 STARS

"I'd much rather do character roles," Susan Sarandon once admitted. "Leading roles for women are very boring, but the supporting cast is always much more interesting." Sarandon has adhered to this attitude with generally interesting results.

She was born Susan Tomaling in New York City, in 1946, and took the name of her ex-husband, actor Chris Sarandon. Her first film, *Joe*, offered a good part as a girl who was accidentally murdered by her bigoted father. She also stood out in *The Front Page* as Jack Lemmon's fiancee.

Susan Sarandon in *Atlantic City.*

When Sidney Sheldon's bestseller *The Other Side of Midnight* was filmed, Sarandon was offered the part of the "nice" girl who incited John Beck to murder. The movie lacked the trashy excitement of the novel because, in Sarandon's words, "it was a soap-opera melodrama and they treated it like it was Chekhov."

Her abilities were finally fully tapped in *Atlantic City.* Director Louis Malle, her lover in real life, found the depth and vulnerability beneath the quirky exterior, and Sarandon along with co-star Burt Lancaster drew world-wide praise and Oscar nominations.

FILMOGRAPHY

1970

Joe ★★★

1971

Lady Liberty ★★

1974

Lovin' Molly ★★★
The Front Page ★★★

1975

The Great Waldo Pepper ★★★
The Rocky Horror Picture Show ★★★★

1976

One Summer Love ★★★

1977

The Other Side of Midnight ★★★
The Last of the Cowboys ★★

1978

Pretty Baby ★★★★

1979

King of the Gypsies ★★★
Something Short of Paradise ★★★

1980

Loving Couples ★★★
Atlantic City ★★★★

1982

Tempest ★★★

1983

The Hunger ★★★

ROY SCHEIDER
★★★ 3.06 STARS

Roy Scheider has starred in three films that were nominated for Best Picture Oscars (*The French Connection*, *Jaws*, and *All That Jazz*). He recently starred in a big summer hit, *Blue Thunder.* And yet, he is not a star. He lacks the inner fire to make viewers wonder about the performer behind the role. When he is good, he helps his films, but good films add nothing to his allure.

He was born in 1935 in Orange, New Jersey. He went from college drama to the professional stage before entering films earnestly in the early 1970s. His average guy looks and slightly tough stance has tended to type him into cop roles.

In his one flashy performance, as the maniacally ambitious director in *All That Jazz*, he borrowed his moves from director Bob Fosse (whose life was being retold). Scheider's best recent performance was in *Still of the Night* with Meryl Streep. He made a nice team with Streep, but the film was so trite that he seemed embarrassed to be in it.

Roy Scheider in *All That Jazz.*

FILMOGRAPHY

1964

The Curse of the Living Corpse ★★★

1969

Stiletto ★★

1970

Loving ★★★
Puzzle of a Downfall Child ★★

1971

Klute ★★★
The French Connection ★★★★

1972

The Outside Man ★★★

1973

The Seven-Ups ★★★
The French Conspiracy ★★★

1975

Sheila Levine Is Dead and Living in New York ★★
Jaws ★★★★

1976

Marathon Man ★★★★

1977

Sorcerer ★★★

1978

Jaws 2 ★★★

1979

Last Embrace ★★★
All That Jazz ★★★★

1982

Still of the Night ★★★

1983

Blue Thunder ★★★

GEORGE C. SCOTT
★★★½ 3.43 STARS

George C. Scott ridiculed the Oscars as "a meaningless, self-serving meat parade," but Academy members pushed a statue on him anyway for 1968's *Patton*. His portrayal, in fact, all his portrayals are too impressive to ignore.

Scott (George Campbell Scott) was born in 1927, in Wise, Virginia. He was an aspiring writer and teacher before staking his claim to stage greatness in "Richard III." His first screen parts were unsympathetic: *The Hanging Tree* and *Anatomy of a Murder* (only his second film, but he was nominated for an Oscar). Scott's personal life was turbulent. "I'm not an aggressive man," he explained, "except when I drink." He was also married (twice) to Colleen Dewhurst, his third wife. He refused his Oscar nomination for *The Hustler* and returned to New York to appear with Dewhurst in "Desire Under the Elms."

The List of Adrian Messenger, an entertaining but unsuspenseful whodunit, made little demand on his talent. *Dr. Strangelove, or How I Learned To Stop Worrying and Love the Bomb* was "quite simply one of the greatest, funniest and most shattering motion pictures ever made...It comments unsparingly and hilariously on our alienated self-righteous society." Scott's portrayal of General "Buck" Turgidson was as magnificent as the picture. After doing a TV series, "East Side, West Side", he appeared in the film *The Bible* as Abraham. Ava Gardner was also in the movie, and they became a scandal-making item offscreen.

George C. Scott in *Patton*.

Not With My Wife You Don't! and *The Flim Flam Man* were artistically beneath him. *Petulia* was a shrill, disjointed "mod" comedy that used dazzling photographic tricks to mask a thin story line. *Patton* was a large-scale saga about the famous General. Scott's power was such that he reduced the epic dimensions of the production to miniscule size, dominating totally. He again said he didn't want an Oscar, but the Academy insisted, and he still hasn't come to claim it. (His attitude may be softening—he attended the 1982 Oscar ceremonies.) He also won the New York Film Critics Award which he *did* accept.

George C. Scott in *The Prince and the Pauper*.

He was forceful as a policeman in the mutilated movie adaptation of Joseph Wambaugh's best-seller *The New Centurions* (one of several Wambaugh works destroyed by Hollywood). *The Hospital* was better; he was cast as a doctor rescued from impotence by the attractive Diana Rigg in a satire of the medical profession. However, a run of inferior pictures (*Oklahoma Crude* and *The Day of the Dolphin*) undercut his strengh at the box office.

Scott decided *he* could do better, and directed *The Savage Is Loose* with his wife Trish Van Devere. The story about a shipwrecked couple and their son who grew up and looked to Mom for sex was tasteless and suffered from heavy handling. In *The Hindenburg*, he attempted to develop a low-key, conscientious variation on the disaster genre, but it was merely disastrous.

Fortunately, *Movie Movie*, a satire of old movies, was delightful. Good vehicles, however, seem harder for him to find though he personally is mesmerizing under any condition.

FILMOGRAPHY

1959

The Hanging Tree ★★★
Anatomy of a Murder ★★★★

1961

The Hustler ★★★★

George C. Scott in *Islands in the Stream.*

1963

The List of Adrian Messenger ★★★

1964

Dr. Strangelove, or How I Learned to Stop Worrying and Love the Bomb ★★★★
The Yellow Rolls-Royce ★★★

1966

Not With My Wife You Don't! ★★★
The Bible ★★★★

1967

The Flim Flam Man ★★★

1968

Petulia ★★★★

1969

This Savage Land ★★★

1970

Patton ★★★★

1971

The Hospital ★★★★
They Might Be Giants ★★★★
Jane Eyre ★★★★
The Last Run ★★★

1972

The New Centurions ★★★★
Rage ★★★

1973

Oklahoma Crude ★★★
The Day of the Dolphin ★★★

1974

The Savage Is Loose (direction) ★★
Bank Shot ★★★

1975

The Hindenburg ★★★

1977

Islands in the Stream ★★★★
The Prince and the Pauper ★★★★

1978

Movie Movie ★★★★

1979

Hardcore ★★★★
The Changeling ★★★

1981

The Formula ★★★

1982

Taps ★★★

RANDOLPH SCOTT
★★½ 2.58 STARS

Although his career was long and distinguished enough to guarantee him a place in anyone's history of Hollywood, the "tragedy" of Randolph Scott was that he only realized his potential as a screen actor in his last few films. It was only in the remarkable series of westerns made with director Budd Boetticher in the late 1950s that the Scott persona acquired shadings, depth, and meaning.

He was born in Virginia in 1903. He entered World War I at age fourteen, and then returned to study engineering. He got into films when he accidentally met movie producer and airplane mogul Howard Hughes on a golf course. Ruggedly handsome and convincingly innocent, Scott first entered the movies as the attractive "other man" in 1930s musicals or romantic comedies. Yet, even his good performances in these years were less than fully satisfying; as opposed to Ralph Bellamy, he was too sincere to laugh at.

Perhaps sensing this, Scott switched almost exclusively to action roles, especially westerns. By the mid-1950s, he had slipped down to the lower rungs of the "B" western. This did, however, give him a chance to work with talented directors such as Andre De Toth (*Man in the Saddle, The Bounty Hunter*) and Joseph H. Lewis (*A Lawless Street*). Then, on the suggestion of John Wayne, Budd Boetticher cast Scott as the lead in *Seven Men From Now.* The combination was magical; working together seemed to bring out the best in both artists.

Scott and Boetticher went on to make six more films together, all of which are referred to as the "Ranown Cycle." In the Ranown films, Scott stands for the accumulated sum of worldly wisdom; always self-described as a former rancher, former sheriff, or former *something.* Scott arrives on the scene of the action as a man on a mission. After the Ranowns, Scott made one more film, Peckinpah's *Ride the High Country,* and then retired to extremely comfortable anonymity.

FILMOGRAPHY

1929

The Far Call ★★

1931

Women Men Marry ★★

1932

Sky Bride ★★
A Successful Calamity ★★
Hot Saturday ★★★
Wild Horse Mesa ★★

1933

Hello Everybody! ★★★
Heritage of the Desert ★★
Murders in the Zoo ★★★
Supernatural ★★★
Sunset Pass ★★★
Cocktail Hour ★★
Men of the Forest ★★★
To the Last Man ★★
Broken Dreams ★★
The Thundering Herd ★★★
The Lone Cowboy ★★★

1934

The Last Round-Up ★★
Wagon Wheels ★★★

1935

Home on the Range ★★
Roberta ★★★
Rocky Mountain Mystery ★★★
Village Tale ★★
She ★★
So Red the Rose ★★

1936

Follow the Fleet ★★
And Sudden Death ★★
The Last of the Mohicans ★★★
Go West Young Man ★★

1937

High Wide and Handsome ★★★

1938

Rebecca of Sunnybrook Farm ★★★
The Texans ★★
The Road to Reno ★★

1939

Jesse James ★★★
Susannah of the Mounties ★★
Frontier Marshall ★★★
Coast Guard ★★
20,000 Men a Year ★★

1940

Virginia City ★★
My Favorite Wife ★★
When the Daltons Rode ★★★

1941

Western Union ★★★
Belle Starr ★★

1942

Paris Calling ★★
To the Shores of Tripoli ★★★
The Spoilers ★★
Pittsburgh ★★

1943

The Desperados ★★
Bombardier ★★
Corvette K-225 ★★★
Gung Ho! ★★

1944

Follow the Boys (cameo)
Belle of the Yukon ★★

1945

China Sky ★★
Captain Kidd ★★

1946

Abilene Town ★★
Badman's Territory ★★★
Home, Sweet Homicide ★★★

1947

Trail Street ★★
Gunfighters ★★
Christmas Eve ★★

Randolph Scott in *Sugarfoot.*

1948

Albuquerque ★★
Coroner Creek ★★
Return of the Badmen ★★★

1950

The Walking Hills ★★★
Canadian Pacific ★★
The Doolins of Oklahoma ★★★
The Nevadan ★★
Colt .45 ★★★
Cariboo Trail ★★

1951

Sugarfoot ★★★
Santa Fe ★★★
Fort Worth ★★
Starlift (cameo)
Man in the Saddle ★★★★

1952

Carson City ★★★★
Hangman's Knot ★★

1953

Man Behind the Gun ★★★
The Stranger Wore a Gun ★★★
Thunder Over the Plains ★★★

1954

Riding Shotgun ★★
The Bounty Hunter ★★★★

1955

Ten Wanted Men ★★★
Rage at Dawn ★★★
Tall Man Riding ★★★
A Lawless Street ★★★

1956

Seven Men From Now ★★★★
7th Cavalry ★★★

1957

The Tall T ★★★★
Shoot-Out at Medicine Bend ★★
Decision at Sundown ★★★

1958

Buchanan Rides Alone ★★★

1959

Ride Lonesome ★★★★
Westbound ★★★

1960

Comanche Station ★★★★

1962

Ride the High Country ★★★★

JEAN SEBERG
★★½ 2.62 STARS

The tragedies of Jean Seberg's life (exploitation by minority groups, pursuit by the FBI, and suicide) are more haunting and memorable than most of her work on film. She had an intriguing all-American look, but her acting was only partially effective in European pictures and never convincing in American ones.

Born in 1938, in Marshalltown, Iowa, Seberg became a heroine in her hometown when Otto Preminger chose her to play *Saint Joan*. Critics jeered, but Preminger stubbornly put her into an equally unsuitable part, as David Niven's spoiled daughter in *Bonjour Tristesse*. Things took a mild upswing with a popular Peter Sellers comedy *The Mouse That Roared,* though her contribution was minimal. The world finally applauded when she did *Breathless*.

Jean Seberg in *Breathless*.

A series of French films, *The Five Day Lover* and *In the French Style*, supplied a specific image, and she was convincing as George Peppard's adulterous wife in *Pendulum*. *Airport* was a huge hit, but she had little to do, and *Paint Your Wagon* was a botched and bloated version of the Lerner and Loewe musical.

She garnered publicity through her marriage to novelist Romain Gary and continued to do European pictures. Her vogue was over by the time she died. Seberg's life is a study in fame, and the complex, often fatal demands it can make on an immature, unsophisticated personality.

FILMOGRAPHY

1957

Saint Joan ★

1958

Bonjour Tristesse ★★

1959

The Mouse That Roared ★★★

1960

Breathless ★★★★
Let No Man Write My Epitaph ★★★

1961

The Five Day Lover ★★★
Time Out for Love ★★★
Playtime ★★★

1963

In the French Style ★★★

1964

Backfire ★★★
Lilith ★★★

1966

Moment to Moment ★★
A Fine Madness ★★
La Ligne de Demarcation ★★★

1967

Who's Got the Black Box? ★★

1968

Birds in Peru ★★★

1969

Pendulum ★★★
Paint Your Wagon ★★

1970

Airport ★★
Macho Callahan ★★

1972

Kill! ★★

1973

The Corruption of Chris Miller ★★★
The French Conspiracy ★★★

1974

Cat and Mouse ★★★

1975

Le Grand Delire ★★★

1976

The Wild Duck ★★

GEORGE SEGAL
★★★ 2.76 STARS

In recent films, *Who is Killing the Great Chefs of Europe?*, for example, George Segal tended to mug and overact shamelessly. In his best period, during the late 1960s and early 1970s, he was a delightfully unaffected master of light comedy.

Segal was born in 1934, in New York City. He worked as a jazz musician while seeking theatre and film work, and still plays with a group in Beverly Hills. His notable stage appearances in "Antony and Cleopatra" and "The Iceman Cometh" led to his first picture, *The Young Doctors.*

He was unconvincing as a struggling artist in *Ship of Fools*, another early film. Elizabeth Ashley claimed that he refused to slap her, as the script required, for fear of being seen as unsympathetic. As a result, he destroyed the plausibility of their screen relationship.

He was likable in *No Way to Treat a Lady* as a detective, and outstanding opposite a strident Barbra Streisand in *The Owl and the Pussycat. Where's Poppa?* was a bizarre comedy with Ruth Gordon that pleased a few buffs, and *A Touch of Class* paired him hilariously with an acerbic Glenda Jackson. *Blume in Love*, though meandering, had a bittersweet appeal.

Then it was downhill—in *The Black Bird*, a strained spoof of *The Maltese Falcon*, and *The Duchess and the Dirtwater Fox. Fun With Dick and Jane* was poor though mildly successful at box offices, while *Lost and Found* and *The Last Married Couple in America* found no favor in any department. His one interesting performance during this period was in a thriller, *Rollercoaster.*

The talent is undeniably there; all Segal needs is a solid script and a director who can calm his excessive energy and spotlight his charm.

FILMOGRAPHY

1961

The Young Doctors ★★

1963

Act One ★★★

1964

The New Interns ★★★
Invitation to a Gunfight ★★★

1965

Ship of Fools ★★
King Rat ★★★

1966

Who's Afraid of Virginia Woolf? ★★★★
Lost Command ★★
The Quiller Memorandum ★★★

1967

The St. Valentine's Day Massacre ★★★

1968

Bye Bye Braverman ★★
No Way to Treat a Lady ★★
Tenderly ★★★

1969

The Southern Star ★★
The Bridge at Remagen ★★★

1970

Loving ★★★
The Owl and the Pussycat ★★★
Where's Poppa? ★★★

1971

Born to Win ★★★

George Segal in *No Way to Treat a Lady.*

1972

The Hot Rock ★★★

1973

A Touch of Class ★★★★
Blume in Love ★★★★

1974

The Terminal Man ★★
California Split ★★★

1975

Russian Roulette ★★
The Black Bird ★★★

1976

The Duchess and the Dirtwater Fox ★★

1977

Fun With Dick and Jane ★★★
Rollercoaster ★★★

1978

Who Is Killing the Great Chefs of Europe? ★★★

1979

Lost and Found ★★★
The Last Married Couple in America ★★

1981

Carbon Copy ★★

PETER SELLERS
★★★ 2.88 STARS

He was a scene stealer, a leading man, a bumbler, but above all, Peter Sellers was a master imitator. His nuances and intuitions for how a character should look and sound were uncannily correct. And with his death in July 1980, the screen lost its most versatile satiric actor.

Sellers was born in 1925 in Southsea, England, the only child of music hall entertainers. He used his vocal gift of mimicry to land his first job on BBC radio. He impersonated two comedy stars on the phone recommending Sellers to the station. He spent most of the 1950s as a member of "The Goon Show" on radio and in films. After appearing as the youngest of a gang of hoodlums led by Alec Guinness in *The Ladykillers*, Sellers then made his first major impression in *The Mouse That Roared*. He played alternately a prime minister, a duchess, and a constable.

Sellers also played three roles in Stanley Kubrick's *Dr. Strangelove, or How I Learned to Stop Worrying and Love the Bomb*. He played Merkin Muffley, the U.S. president; the German scientist Strangelove (some said patterned after Henry Kissinger, but Sellers denied it), and an R.A.F. officer. Kubrick wanted Sellers to take on even more parts because "nobody else in the world can play each of those parts like Sellers."

Peter Sellers in *The Pink Panther Strikes Again*.

Sellers, whose list of other alter egos included James Bond in *Casino Royale* and Clare Quilty in *Lolita*, said once that he had no personality of his own. He was a vacuum to be filled by a Bond or a Strangelove.

And yet with the emphasis on comedy in Sellers' 50-plus films, his personal life was less than happy. In addition to four marriages, Sellers was a workaholic who only slowed down between heart attacks.

But if his private life had its darker sides, Sellers' audiences weren't aware of them. His most popular films were the five Pink Panther movies he made with director Blake Edwards. Sellers played the bumbling Inspector Clouseau with great dignity "because I feel he thinks he is probably one of the greatest detectives in the world. He is a complete idiot, but he would *never* want anyone else to know that."

Sellers looked upon *Being There* as his best movie, and so did audiences and critics. It was his crowning achievement. In the film adaptation of Jerzy Kosinski's comic novella, Sellers played Chauncey Gardiner, a sweet illiterate whose knowledge of the world is limited to what he has learned from television. His rise to advisor to the president is the source of the film's black humor. Of Sellers' performance, Pauline Kael wrote in The New Yorker: "None of this broad irony would work with a lesser actor at its center, and the wonder of Mr. Sellers' performance is that his look of absolute emptiness does not alter, and yet it never bores us or becomes affected or excessive."

The memory of Peter Sellers' Inspector Clouseau was besmirched when the greedy filmmakers tried to make a final Pink Panther movie with unused footage from previous films, *The Trail of the Pink Panther*.

FILMOGRAPHY

1951

Penny Points to Paradise★★

1952

Down Among the Z Men★★

Peter Sellers with Capucine in *Trail of the Pink Panther*.

1954

Orders are Orders★★

1955

John and Julie★★
The Ladykillers★★★★

1957

The Smallest Show on Earth★★★
The Naked Truth★★★★

1958

Up the Creek★★★
Tom Thumb★★★

1959

Carlton-Browne of the F.O.★★★
The Mouse That Roared★★★★
I'm All Right Jack★★★★
The Battle of the Sexes★★★★

1960

Two-Way Stretch★★★★
The Millionairess★★
Never Let Go★★

1961

Mr. Topaze★★

1962

Only Two Can Play★★★★
Waltz of the Toreadors★★★
The Dock Brief★★★
The Road to Hong Kong (cameo)
Lolita★★★★

1963

The Wrong Arm of the Law★★★★
Heavens Above★★★
The Pink Panther★★★★

1964

The World of Henry Orient★★★
A Shot in the Dark★★★
Strangelove, or How I Learned to Stop Worrying and Love the Bomb★★★★

1965

What's New, Pussycat?★★★

1966

The Wrong Box★★★★
After the Fox★★★★

Peter Sellers in *Heavens Above!*

1967

Casino Royale ★ ★
Woman Times Seven ★ ★
The Bobo ★ ★

1968

The Party ★ ★
I Love You Alice B. Toklas! ★ ★ ★

1969

The Magic Christian ★ ★

1970

Hoffman ★ ★
There's a Girl in My Soup ★ ★
A Day at the Beach ★ ★

1972

Where Does it Hurt? ★ ★
Alice's Adventures in Wonderland ★ ★

1973

The Optimists ★ ★

1974

The Blockhouse ★ ★
Soft Beds Hard Battles ★ ★
The Great McGonagall ★ ★

1975

The Return of the Pink Panther ★ ★ ★

1976

Murder by Death ★ ★ ★
The Pink Panther Strikes Again ★ ★ ★

1978

Revenge of the Pink Panther ★ ★ ★

1979

The Prisoner of Zenda ★ ★ ★
Being There ★ ★ ★ ★

1980

The Fiendish Plot of Dr. Fu Manchu ★ ★

1982

Trail of the Pink Panther (outtakes)

ROBERT SHAW
★ ★ ★ 3.25 STARS

Robert Shaw died in 1978 just as he was entering the top plateau of stardom. He was a lusty, expansive performer with an unlimited acting range.

Shaw was born in 1927, in Westhoughton, England, He trained at the Royal Academy of Dramatic Art and made his first screen appearance in Michael Anderson's exciting war film, *The Dam Busters. Hell in Korea* and *Sea Fury* were routine action dramas, but *From Russia With Love* was one of the most popular James Bond thrillers. It made Shaw well known, and he drew a convincing portrait of mental illness in *The Guest*.

His Irish dreamer was touching and all-too-recognizably human in *The Luck of Ginger Coffey.* However, most of these were art films without mass appeal. *A Man for All Seasons* was both, and Shaw's portrayal of Henry VIII added greatly to its impact. He did another dialogue piece, *The Birthday Party*; Harold Pinter wrote this one as well as *The Guest*.

In *Young Winston*, a sluggish close-up of the Prime Minister, Shaw played Lord Randolph Churchill.

It took *The Sting* to make him a star. Moviegoers relished the con games played by Shaw, Robert Redford, and Paul Newman, and they sat breathless as Shaw took Roy Scheider and Richard Dreyfuss out to sea to search for a killer shark in *Jaws*. He gave both parts a kind of distinctive, humorous menace. He was also good in *Robin and Marian*, but the script was a disgraceful distortion of well-loved characters.

Swashbuckler desperately needed his light touch, and he dove below sea level again in *The Deep*. Shaw was living with his third wife in Ireland when he died of a heart attack at age fifty-one.

Robert Shaw in *Jaws.*

FILMOGRAPHY

1954

The Dam Busters ★ ★ ★

1956

Hell in Korea ★ ★ ★

1959

Sea Fury ★ ★ ★

1962

The Valiant ★ ★ ★

1963

From Russia With Love ★ ★ ★ ★
The Guest ★ ★ ★

1964

The Luck of Ginger Coffey ★ ★ ★ ★

1965

Battle of the Bulge ★ ★ ★

1966

A Man for All Seasons ★ ★ ★ ★

1968

Custer of the West ★ ★ ★
The Birthday Party ★ ★ ★

1970

Battle of Britain ★ ★ ★
The Royal Hunt of the Sun ★ ★ ★
Figures in a Landscape ★ ★ ★

1971

A Town Called Hell ★ ★ ★

1972

Young Winston ★ ★ ★

1973

A Reflection of Fear ★ ★ ★
The Hireling ★ ★ ★
The Sting ★ ★ ★ ★

1974

The Taking of Pelham 1-2-3 ★ ★ ★ ★

1975

Jaws ★ ★ ★ ★
Diamonds ★ ★ ★
End of the Game ★ ★ ★

1976

Robin and Marian ★★★
Swashbuckler ★★★

1977

The Deep ★★★
Black Sunday ★★★★

1978

Force 10 from Navarone ★★★

NORMA SHEARER
★★★ 3.04 STARS

Much of Norma Shearer's screen work appears affected and overblown to the modern eye. It's worth remembering, however, that she was one of the superstars of the 1930s, and a critic's pet as well.

Shearer (Edith Norma Shearer) was born in 1900, in Montreal, Canada. Her determined stagemother gave her piano lessons and fought to secure her extra work in films. Irving Thalberg promoted Shearer to stardom at MGM, and married her. Joan Crawford once commented that Thalberg was a cold figure and stated, "I didn't envy Norma, but I did long for a friend at court." Under his guidance, she got good roles and extensive publicity.

Some of her hits included: *The Trial of Mary Dugan*, *The Last of Mrs. Cheyney*, and particularly *A Free Soul* with Clark Gable. She and Gable were reteamed in *Strange Interlude* and *Idiot's Delight*, a part Crawford coveted and felt Shearer "simply couldn't bring off." Shearer was fine in *Riptide*, with Herbert Marshall, and saccharine in *The Barretts of Wimpole Street*.

She was a strong candidate for *Gone With the Wind*, but she finally bowed out; she also rejected *Mrs. Miniver*. This lack of script judgment (Thalberg had died in 1936 of a heart ailment) brought an unexpected ending to her screen career.

She married a ski instructor and disappeared from the news. Years afterward, she expressed regret to Geraldine Fitzgerald about her retirement and her sadness that it was "too late" to return. Shearer died in 1983.

FILMOGRAPHY

1920

The Flapper ★★★
The Restless Sex (bit)
Way Down East (bit)
The Stealers ★★★

1921

The Sign on the Door ★★★

1922

Channing of the Northwest ★★★
The Bootleggers ★★★
The Man Who Paid ★★★

1923

The Devil's Partner ★★★
A Clouded Name ★★★
The Wanters ★★★
Pleasure Mad ★★★
Lucretia Lombard ★★★
Man and Wife ★★★

Norma Shearer in *Romeo and Juliet*.

1924

Broadway after Dark ★★★
Trail of the Law ★★★
Blue Waters ★★★
The Wolf Man ★★★
Empty Hands ★★★
Broken Barriers ★★★
He Who Gets Slapped ★★★
The Snob ★★★
Married Flirts ★★★

1925

Lady of the Night ★★★
Waking Up the Town ★★★
Pretty Ladies ★★★
A Slave of Fashion ★★★
Excuse Me ★★★
The Tower of Lies ★★★
His Secretary ★★★

1926

The Devil's Circus ★★★
The Waning Sex ★★★
Upstage ★★★

1927

The Demi-Bride ★★★
After Midnight ★★★
The Student Prince ★★★

1928

The Latest from Paris ★★★
The Actress ★★★
A Lady of Chance ★★★

1929

The Trial of Mary Dugan ★★★★
The Last of Mrs. Cheyney ★★★
The Hollywood Revue of 1929 ★★★
Their Own Desire ★★★

1930

The Divorcee ★★★
Let Us Be Gay ★★★

1931

Strangers May Kiss ★★★
A Free Soul ★★★★
Private Lives ★★★★

1932

Strange Interlude ★★★★
Smilin' Through ★★★★

1934

Riptide ★★★
The Barretts of Wimpole Street ★★

1936

Romeo and Juliet ★★

1938

Marie Antoinette ★★★

1939

Idiot's Delight ★★★
The Women ★★★

1940

Escape ★★★★

1942

We Were Dancing ★★
Her Cardboard Lover ★★

MARTIN SHEEN
★★★ 3.24 STARS

If Dennis Hopper is known for seething uncontrollably, Martin Sheen specializes in a kind of bottled rage. Even when his characters burst out in violence, one senses that it is still only the tip of the iceberg.

Martin Sheen was born Ramon Estevez to Spanish and Irish parents in Dayton, Ohio on August 1, 1940. He went from high school to off-off-Broadway theater, supporting himself as a janitor, a soda-jerk, a messenger, and a car washer. In 1964, he appeared on Broadway in "The Subject Was Roses." He made an inauspicious film debut as a punk in *The Incident* in 1967, and the next year repeated his stage role in the film version of *The Subject Was Roses*.

After a small part in *Catch-22*, the lead in the low-budget *No Drums, No Bugles*, and a part in actor George C. Scott's directorial debut *Rage*, Sheen got the first part that really matched his abilities. In Terrence Malick's brilliant *Badlands*, he plays Kit, a self-centered, unbalanced garbage collector who erupts on a killing spree after his fifteen-year-old girlfriend's father disapproves of him. Malick's brilliance consists largely in removing any trace of moral justification from the film, and Sheen delivers a performance of terrifying unhinged intensity. After a few more years of small parts, he delivered another explosive performance, as Captain Willard in Francis Ford Coppola's *Apocalypse Now*. His performance, beginning with a scene of drunken frustration and rage that is apparently as real as it is acted, is by far the best thing about the film.

Sheen suffered a heart attack during the filming of *Apocalypse Now*. Sheen has only recently returned to work, and has limited himself to emotional but undemanding parts: *That Championship Season*, *Man, Woman and Child*, and *Gandhi*.

Martin Sheen.

FILMOGRAPHY

1967

The Incident★★★

1968

The Subject Was Roses★★★★

1970

Catch-22★★★

1971

No Drums, No Bugles★★★

Martin Sheen in *Man, Woman And Child.*

1972

Pickup on 101★★★
Rage★★★

1973

Badlands★★★★

1975

The Legend of Earl Durand★★★

1977

The Little Girl Who Lives Down the Lane★★★
The Cassandra Crossing★★★

1979

Apocalypse Now★★★★
Eagle's Wing★★★

1980

The Final Countdown★★★

1982

That Championship Season★★★
In the King of Prussia (documentary)
Gandhi★★★★

1983

Enigma★★★
Man, Woman and Child★★★

ANN SHERIDAN
★★★½ 3.27 STARS

Ann Sheridan made acting look easy. She was warm, capable, and unpretentious, a down-to-earth heroine with a deep voice and a healthy, unthreatening sexuality.

Sheridan (Clara Lou Sheridan) was born in 1915, in Denton, Texas. She won a beauty contest and did a film in 1934 capitalizing on her victory *(Search for Beauty)*. Her early films are best forgotten *(Red Blood of Courage, The Patient in Room* However, stardom was assured when Warner Brothers decided to promote her as the "Oomph" girl. Some good roles helped too: *Angels With Dirty Faces* (with James Cagney) and *They Made Me a Criminal* (with John Garfield). There was an Errol Flynn western (*Dodge City*) and a prison drama reuniting her with Garfield (*Castle on the Hudson*).

Kings Row gave Sheridan her best-remembered role, as the nice girl who marries Ronald Reagan after his legs have been sadistically amputated by quack doctor Charles Coburn. Two soap operas (*Nora Prentiss* and *The Unfaithful*) kept her in the limelight, and she was hilarious opposite Cary Grant in the zany *I Was a Male War Bride*.

Curiously, her most compelling portrayal appeared in an overlooked thriller, *Woman on the Run* (She was superb in the film's finale, trapped on a moving roller coaster while her husband goes to meet his death). Sheridan also appeared in a successful TV series ("Pistols and Petticoats") before she died of cancer in 1967.

FILMOGRAPHY

(billed as Clara Lou Sheridan)

1934

Search for Beauty ★★★
Bolero (bit)
Come on Marines (bit)
Kiss and Make Up ★★★
Shoot the Works ★★★
The Notorious Sophie Lang ★★★
Ladies Should Listen ★★★
Wagon Wheels ★★★
Mrs. Wiggs of the Cabbage Patch ★★★
College Rhythm ★★★
You Belong to Me ★★★
Limehouse Blues ★★★

1935

Enter Madame ★★★
Home on the Range ★★★
Rumba ★★★

(billed as Ann Sheridan)

Behold My Wife ★★★
Car 99 ★★★
Rocky Mountain Mystery ★★★
Mississippi ★★★
The Glass Key ★★★
The Crusades ★★★
Red Blood of Courage ★★★
Fighting Youth ★★★

1936

Sing Me a Love Song ★★★

Ann Sheridan.

1937

Black Legion ★★★★
The Great O'Malley ★★★★
San Quentin ★★★★
Wine, Women and Horses ★★★
The Footloose Heiress ★★★
Alcatraz Island ★★★

1938

She Loved a Fireman ★★★
The Patient in Room 18 ★★★
Mystery House ★★★
Cowboy from Brooklyn ★★★
Little Miss Thoroughbred ★★★
Letter of Introduction ★★★
Broadway Musketeers ★★★
Angels With Dirty Faces ★★★★

1939

They Made Me a Criminal ★★★★
Dodge City ★★★
Naughty but Nice ★★★
Winter Carnival ★★★

1940

Castle on the Hudson ★★★★
It All Came True ★★★
Torrid Zone ★★★
They Drive by Night ★★★★
City for Conquest ★★★★

1941

Honeymoon for Three ★★★
Navy Blues ★★★

1942

The Man Who Came to Dinner ★★★★
Kings Row ★★★★
Juke Girl ★★★
Wings for the Eagle ★★★
George Washington Slept Here ★★★★

1943

Edge of Darkness ★★★★
Thank Your Lucky Stars (cameo)

1944

Shine on Harvest Moon ★★★
The Doughgirls ★★★★

1946

One More Tomorrow ★★★

1947

Nora Prentiss ★★★★
The Unfaithful ★★★★

1948

The Treasure of the Sierra Madre (cameo)
Silver River ★★★
Good Sam ★★★★

1949

I Was a Male War Bride ★★★★

1950

Stella ★★★
Woman on the Run ★★★★

1952

Steel Town ★★★
Just Across the Street ★★★

1953

Take Me to Town ★★★
Appointment in Honduras ★★★

1956

Come Next Spring ★★★★
The Opposite Sex ★★★

1957

Woman and the Hunter ★★★

JEAN SIMMONS
★★★½ 3.40 STARS

When Joseph Mankiewicz directed Jean Simmons in *Guys and Dolls*, he called her "fantastic." Critics have been saying the same thing for years through good vehicles (*Elmer Gantry*) and bad (*Hilda Crane* and *Mr. Buddwing*).

Simmons was born in 1929, in London. She trained to be an actress from early childhood, and began doing extra work at fifteen in *Give Us the Moon* and *Mr. Emmanuel*. She was coolly beautiful and intriguing as the young Estella in David Lean's classic *Great Expectations*, and won an Oscar nomination for her work in Olivier's *Hamlet*. Simmons also had the role in *The Blue Lagoon* that Brooke Shields later played in the 1980 remake.

In 1950, she married Stewart Granger. In his autobiography, Granger wrote that Simmons was prevented from doing *Roman Holiday* by Howard Hughes. She was signed to RKO—Hughes's company—and he wouldn't release her because she rejected his advances.

The Robe, with Richard Burton, offered compensation commercially, but audiences ignored *Footsteps in the Fog*, an absorbing suspense drama with Granger. She was delectable in the otherwise heavy-handed *Guys and Dolls*. Even Sam Goldwyn, not known for giving compliments, embraced her and said, "I'm so glad we couldn't get Grace Kelly!"

Home Before Dark featured her best performance—as a mental patient—and she was magnificent playing an evangelist in *Elmer Gantry*. Her stage appearance in "A Little Night Music" was well-received, and she was nothing less than electrifying in the TV mini-series, *The Thorn Birds*. Happily for audiences, her professional activity seems to be increasing after a period of semi-retirement.

FILMOGRAPHY

1944

Give Us the Moon ★★★
Mr. Emmanuel ★★★
Kiss the Bride Goodbye ★★★
Meet Sexton Blake ★★★

1945

The Way to the Stars ★★★
Caesar and Cleopatra ★★★

1946

Great Expectations ★★★★
Hungry Hill ★★★

1947

Black Narcissus ★★★★
Uncle Silas ★★★
The Woman in the Hall ★★★

1948

Hamlet ★★★★

1949

The Blue Lagoon ★★★
Adam and Evelyn ★★★

1950

So Long At the Fair ★★★★
Cage of Gold ★★★
Trio ★★★★
The Clouded Yellow ★★★★

1952

Androcles and the Lion ★★★
Angel Face ★★★★

1953

Young Bess ★★★
Affair With a Stranger ★★★
The Robe ★★★★
The Actress ★★★★

Jean Simmons in *Black Narcissus.*

1954

She Couldn't Say No ★★★
The Egyptian ★★★
A Bullet Is Waiting ★★★
Desiree ★★★

1955

Footsteps in the Fog ★★★★
Guys and Dolls ★★★★

1956

Hilda Crane ★★★

1957

This Could Be the Night ★★★
Until They Sail ★★★

1958

The Big Country ★★★★
Home Before Dark ★★★★

1959

This Earth Is Mine ★★★★

1960

Elmer Gantry ★★★★
Spartacus ★★★★
The Grass Is Greener ★★★

1963

All the Way Home ★★★★

1965

Life at the Top ★★★

1966

Mr. Buddwing ★★★

1967

Divorce American Style ★★★★
Rough Night in Jericho ★★★

1969

The Happy Ending ★★★★

1971

Say Hello to Yesterday ★★★

1975

Mr. Sycamore ★★★

FRANK SINATRA
★★★ 2.93 STARS

Some notorious stars like Elizabeth Taylor probably owe most of their success to scandalous headlines rather than talent. Others, like Frank Sinatra, are so gifted they probably would have gotten to the top without making headlines.

Born in 1915, in Hoboken, New Jersey, Sinatra's appearance on "Major Bowes Amateur Hour" in 1935 led to more radio work. He sang with Harry James, and then Tommy Dorsey, and walked through a couple of forgotten pictures (*Las Vegas Nights, Ship Ahoy,* and *Reveille With Beverly*). A fanatically devoted bobby-soxer following established him as a hit record artist, and there were more uninteresting movies (*Higher and Higher* and *Step Lively*).

Anchors Aweigh offered a major showcase. He was endearing as Gene Kelly's sailor buddy and credits Kelly with teaching him everything he knows about musicals. Seen today, the movie is thin and overlong except for Kelly's dance with a cartoon mouse, but it was a smash in 1945.

It Happened in Brooklyn, a minor film at the time, holds up better—he and Peter Lawford competed for Kathryn Grayson. He played a priest in *The Miracle of the Bells,* and it was a miracle his career survived it. *The Kissing Bandit* sent him plummeting even further. Rescue came with *Take Me Out to the Ball Game* and *On the Town*, two delightful musicals that paired him charmingly with the lively Betty Garrett.

Then everything fell apart. Fans, voice, and record company defected simultaneously, and he had to beg Harry Cohn for the part of Maggio in *From Here to Eternity.* He got it when Eli Wallach (Cohn's first choice) accepted another offer instead. His startling portrayal of the doomed private won Him a Best Supporting Actor Oscar, and he bounced back stronger than ever on records.

Young at Heart teamed him (for the only time) with a leading lady who sang as well as he did—Doris Day. It was enjoyable, and so was *The Tender Trap*, with Debbie Reynolds. Even counting *Eternity's* Maggio, his best work was in *The Man With the Golden Arm*—a superb, sympathetic, and multi-layered characterization of a desperate junkie.

He was comedian Joe E. Lewis in a well-made but depressing biography, *The Joker is Wild*, and *Pal Joey* in a somewhat distorted movie version of the Rodgers and Hart stage hit. It was entertaining despite the alterations, and Rita Hayworth's charismatic performance helped. He was fine in *Some Came Running*, though Shirley MacLaine stole the attention and reviews.

Frank Sinatra.

For a time, Sinatra starred in movies that relied only on his image, not his acting *(Ocean's Eleven, Robin and the 7 Hoods,* and *Sergeants 3).* His last great picture was the memorable *The Manchurian Candidate*. After *Marriage On the Rocks, Tony Rome*, and *Dirty Dingus Magee*, he announced his retirement. He came back in 1974 after three years of inactivity to appear on TV and in clubs.

Sinatra inspired superlatives from columnists like Joyce Haber in the L. A. Times, and though he hasn't the vocal control of his best days, the sound is still there. He also still has that indefinable magic that has kept him magnetically alive while others (Como, Crosby) have dated.

FILMOGRAPHY

1941
Las Vegas Nights (cameo)

1942
Ship Ahoy (cameo)

1943
Reveille With Beverly (cameo)
Higher and Higher ★★

1944
Step Lively ★★

1945
Anchors Aweigh ★★★

1946
Till the Clouds Roll By (cameo)

1947
It Happened in Brooklyn ★★★

1948
The Miracle of the Bells ★★
The Kissing Bandit ★

1949
Take Me Out to the Ball Game ★★★
On the Town ★★★

1951
Double Dynamite ★★
Meet Danny Wilson ★★★

1953
From Here to Eternity ★★★★

1954
Suddenly ★★★★

1955
Young at Heart ★★★★
Not as a Stranger ★★★
Guys and Dolls ★★★
The Tender Trap ★★★
The Man With the Golden Arm ★★★★

1956
Meet Me in Las Vegas ★★
High Society ★★★★
Johnny Concho ★★★
Around the World in 80 Days (cameo)

1957
The Pride and the Passion ★★
The Joker is Wild ★★★★
Pal Joey ★★★★

Frank Sinatra with Montgomery Clift in *From Here to Eternity*.

1958
Kings Go Forth ★★★

1959
Some Came Running ★★★★
A Hole in the Head ★★★
Never So Few ★★★

1960
Can-Can ★★★
Ocean's Eleven ★★★
Pepe (cameo)

1961
The Devil at 4 O'Clock ★★★

1962
Sergeants 3 ★★★
The Road to Hong Kong (cameo)
The Manchurian Candidate ★★★★

1963
The List of Adrian Messenger (cameo)
Come Blow Your Horn ★★★
Four For Texas ★★★

1964
Robin and the 7 Hoods ★★★

1965
None But the Brave ★★★
Marriage On the Rocks ★★
Von Ryan's Express ★★★

1966
The Oscar (cameo)
Cast a Giant Shadow (cameo)
Assault on a Queen ★★

1967
The Naked Runner ★★
Tony Rome ★★

1968
The Detective ★★★★
Lady in Cement ★★★

1970
Dirty Dingus Magee ★★

1974
That's Entertainment (narration)

1980
The First Deadly Sin ★★★

EVERETT SLOANE
★★★½ 3.33 STARS

Everett Sloane has appeared in a good many of Hollywood's classics, and all of them have gained added stature by his presence.

New York-born in 1909, Sloan worked on Wall Street and then acted with Orson Welles' Mercury Theatre. He began his movie career with one of the greatest of all pictures, *Citizen Kane*, and followed it with another Welles production, *Journey Into Fear*. He was superb as Rita Hayworth's husband in *The Lady From Shanghai*.

Everett Sloane in *Patterns*.

There were other fine roles—in *The Men*, *The Enforcer*, *The Desert Fox*, and *The Blue Veil*—and a great one. In *Patterns*, he was excellent as the ruthless company head who drove Ed Begley to his death. Sloane was also outstanding as the fight promoter in *Somebody Up There Likes Me*.

He played two memorable father roles: Natalie Wood's affectionate father in *Marjorie Morningstar* and Luana Patten's obsessed father in the gripping *Home from the Hill*. *Lust for Life* was a final peak. After that, he did the best he could with *By Love Possessed* and two Jerry Lewis vehicles, *The Patsy* and *The Disorderly Orderly*.

FILMOGRAPHY

1941
Citizen Kane ★★★★

1943
Journey Into Fear ★★★★

1948
The Lady From Shanghai ★★★★

1949
Prince of Foxes ★★★

1950
The Men ★★★★

1951
The Enforcer ★★★
Sirocco ★★★
The Desert Fox ★★★
The Blue Veil ★★★

1955

The Big Knife ★ ★ ★ ★

1956

Patterns ★ ★ ★
Somebody Up There Likes Me ★ ★ ★
Lust for Life ★ ★ ★ ★

1958

Marjorie Morningstar ★ ★ ★ ★

1960

Home from the Hill ★ ★ ★

1961

By Love Possessed ★ ★ ★

1964

The Patsy ★ ★ ★
The Disorderly Orderly ★ ★

CARRIE SNODGRESS
★ ★ ★ 3.00 STARS

At the height of her career, Carrie Snodgress voluntarily quit films to concentrate on her personal relationship with rock star Neil Young. She had an appealingly ordinary face and a distinctive, throaty voice. These assets, combined with strong acting talent, had made her a sure bet for stardom. She and Young have since parted, and one hopes her comeback will recapture the success she sacrificed.

Snodgress was born in Chicago, in 1946. She had a superb role in her first picture, *Diary of a Mad Housewife*, as the married woman who has an affair with writer Frank Langella. She was nominated for an Oscar, but lost to Glenda Jackson. Her next film, *Rabbit Run*, might have discouraged her. It was a morbid study of a young athlete (James Caan) coming to grips with life after high school. After an eight year absence, Snodgress returned in *The Fury*. It was a supporting role (and she was killed off early in an orgy of violence), but the early promise was still clearly visible.

Carrie Snodgress with Richard Benjamin in *Diary of a Mad Housewife.*

FILMOGRAPHY

1970

Diary of a Mad Housewife ★ ★ ★ ★
Rabbit Run ★ ★

1978

The Fury ★ ★ ★

1981

The Attic ★ ★ ★

SISSY SPACEK
★ ★ ★ ½ 3.56 STARS

The 1970s and 1980s have produced many odd stars (Hoffman, Pacino, Streisand), but Spacek is surely the oddest—freckled, frog-voiced, and almost a cartoon. Luckily, these qualities work to her advantage on the screen, adding individuality to a dazzling talent.

Born Mary Elizabeth Spacek in 1949, in Quitman, Texas, Spacek set out originally to be a country/rock singer. Critic Rex Reed once compared her to a "crocodile fetus," and she was tagged by another writer as "a munchkin on speed." However, first cousin Rip Torn was encouraging, "She handled her career very well—better than I ever did." Even though her first film, *Prime Cut*, was a disaster, critics noticed her uniqueness.

Her second film, *Badlands*, showcased her talent more effectively. Spacek played the amoral, none-too-bright girlfriend of murderer Martin Sheen; her lack of normal emotional reaction to his crimes was more chilling than any histrionics could have been. She herself said, "I experienced the satisfaction you can get of doing something you're proud of." She also married the art director on the film, Jack Fisk, who later directed her in *Raggedy Man*.

Sissy Spacek in *Coal Miner's Daughter.*

Journalists continued to search for words to properly define Spacek's personality. After Cosmopolitan interpreted her as "a young, gritty, delightfully Texanized Audrey Hepburn," she did a classic horror film, *Carrie*, based on Stephen King's popular thriller. Her pathetic mousiness was perfect, and audiences cheered when she unleashed psychic destruction on the high school kids who had ridiculed her. Newsweek's David Ansen declared that as an actress "Spacek has perfect pitch." She won the National Society of Film Critics Best Actress award and was nominated for an Oscar.

Spacek's next film, *3 Women*, was directed by Robert Altman at his most pretentious, but it provided her with a marvelous role. Altman also produced the rambling *Welcome to L.A.*, in which Spacek played a crazy housemaid. *Heart Beat* was a somewhat disappointing drama. Spacek played Carolyn Cassady, who was married to Neal Cassady (Nick Nolte) while having an affair with beat author Jack Kerouac (John Heard). The script "had no continuity whatsoever," according to critic Leonard Maltin, but *Coal Miner's Daughter* was superb. Spacek was more brilliant than even her strongest admirers could have expected. She did the vocals herself, rather than relying on Loretta Lynn to supply them, and projected all the hope, ambition, and heartbreak of a poor country girl struggling to be a star. A richly deserved Oscar came her way, and she also was impressive as a young divorcee with two children in *Raggedy Man*.

Few actors measure up to Jack Lemmon at his best, but Spacek met the challenge and passed with flying colors in *Missing*. Another Oscar nomination confirmed her excellence. Spacek's height (5 feet), weight (barely 100 pounds) and manner of expressing herself ("Holy Moly" is a favorite) may tempt certain viewers not to take her seriously. However, a more telling personality clue comes from her own statement, "I'm very competitive with Jack [Fisk]... if he skis nine miles, so do I. It's great... it makes us both work harder." Her hard work will eventually take her to the heights of greatness.

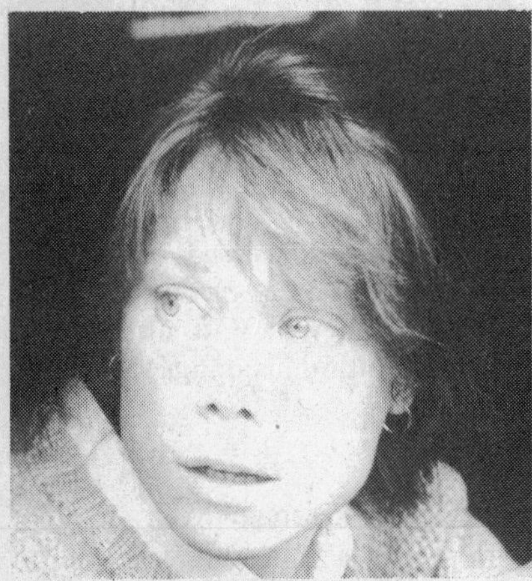

Sissy Spacek in *Missing*.

FILMOGRAPHY

1972

Prime Cut ★★

1973

Badlands ★★★★

1976

Carrie ★★★★

1977

Welcome to L.A. ★★★
3 Women ★★★★

1979

Heart Beat ★★★
Coal Miner's Daughter ★★★★

1981

Raggedy Man ★★★★

1982

Missing ★★★★

ROBERT STACK
★★★ 2.88 STARS

Robert Stack's clean-cut handsomeness was a handicap early in his career. He looked too perfect to be flesh and blood. Later, he became a powerful character actor in "The Untouchables" on TV.

Stack was born in 1919, in Los Angeles, California. After giving Deanna Durbin her first screen kiss in *First Love,* Stack had a good minor role as a potential Nazi in *The Mortal Storm.* In *A Date with Judy,* he was cast as Elizabeth Taylor's beau—a role that required little beyond a warm smile. He also made little impression in *Mr. Music, Badlands of Dakota,* or *Miss Tatlock's Millions,* but he finally had a meaty part in *The Bullfighter and the Lady.*

Most of his other films continued to be innocuous—*War Paint, Bwana Devil,* and *Sabre Jet.* Finally, he had his once-in-a-lifetime opportunity and played the alcoholic playboy who married Lauren Bacall and lost her to Rock Hudson in *Written on the Wind.* Stack was expected to win the Oscar. He was, in fact, declared a shoo-in by trade papers, but he lost to Anthony Quinn in *Lust for Life.*

Fortunately, his Elliot Ness TV character on "The Untouchables" series came along, because his feature film career never hit any startling heights again. He did several more movies (*The Tarnished Angels, The Caretakers,* and *Is Paris Burning?*), but none of them were outstanding.

He showed comic flair in the hilarious parody of disaster films, *Airplane,* and took part in Steven Spielberg's one flop, *1941.* Still youthful in his sixties, Stack deserves a shot at another powerful character part.

FILMOGRAPHY

1939

First Love ★★★

1940

When the Daltons Rode ★★★
The Mortal Storm ★★★
A Little Bit of Heaven ★★★

1941

Nice Girl? ★★★
Badlands of Dakota ★★★

1942

To Be or Not To Be ★★★
Eagle Squadron ★★★
A Date with Judy ★★★
Miss Tatlock's Millions ★★★

1949

John Paul Jones ★★★

1950

Mr. Music ★★★

1951

The Bullfighter and the Lady ★★★
My Brother, the Outlaw ★★★

1952

Bwana Devil ★★

1953

War Paint ★★
Conquest of Cochise ★★
Sabre Jet ★★★

1954

The Iron Glove ★★★
The High and the Mighty ★★★

1955

House of Bamboo ★★★
Good Morning, Miss Dove ★★★

1956

Great Day in the Morning ★★★
Written on the Wind ★★★★

1957

The Tarnished Angels ★★★★

1958

The Gift of Love ★★★

1959

Guns of Zangara ★★

Robert Stack.

1960

The Last Voyage ★ ★ ★

1962

The Alcatraz Express ★ ★ ★
The Scarface Mob ★ ★ ★

1963

The Caretakers ★ ★

1966

Is Paris Burning? ★ ★

1967

The Corrupt Ones ★ ★ ★
Action Man ★ ★

1968

The Story of a Woman ★ ★ ★

1969

Angel, Angel, Down We Go ★ ★ ★

1978

A Second Wind ★ ★ ★

1979

1941 ★ ★ ★

1980

Airplane ★ ★ ★

1982

Airplane II: The Sequel ★ ★ ★

SYLVESTER STALLONE
★ ★ ★ 2.77 STARS

For a while, Sean Connery failed consistently to shake off his James Bond image. Sylvester Stallone is confronting the same difficulty with his Rocky character. However, Stallone has so much drive, so much need to expand (as writer, producer, and director) that he's bound to burst out of the straitjacket.

Born in 1946, in New York City, his Hell's Kitchen childhood made him rebellious. He was thrown out of 14 schools, and he was a bouncer before devoting time to acting. Stallone also wanted to write, and in his first picture, *The Lords of Flatbush*, captured credit for additional dialogue. Additional or otherwise, the movie was a softheaded study about youth, though it featured many names of the future (Perry King, Stallone, Henry Winkler, and Susan Blakely). His appearance in *The Prisoner of Second Avenue* was fleeting, though he showed screen presence as Ben Gazzara's sidekick in *Capone*.

Sylvester Stallone with Mr. T. in *Rocky III.*

Sylvester Stallone in *First Blood.*

Stallone claimed he wrote *Rocky* in three days and then submitted it to producers Bob Chartoff and Irwin Winkler. The film was done on a shoestring, and Stallone got $20,000 for the screenplay. He startled the industry when it exploded at box offices around the world. He was superb as the inarticulate but sensitive Italian Stallion who "goes the distance" with world champion Carl Weathers. It was a fairytale, but an exhilarating one, and the acting by everybody (Talia Shire, Burt Young, and Burgess Meredith) was praised. Stallone was expected to win the Oscar but didn't, though the picture did.

F.I.S.T., a thinly disguised study of union leader Jimmy Hoffa, should have made an ideal vehicle for him, but the character was too ambiguous, neither villainous or heroic. He also failed to project the needed power. *Paradise Alley* was a pseudo-Rocky, too grim and drab for public acceptance.

Rocky II wasn't nearly as likable as the original. It was all manipulation with a tear-jerking finale that made *Love Story* look subtle. Still, fans roared with delight, and he decided (after trying a few more flop pictures like *Victory*) to do *Rocky III*. He claimed it was the last of the series. In any case, it was excellent. As a writer, he found a new and interesting dramatic tack. Rocky was now a champ who had grown soft and lazy, losing his title and turning to the champ he had beaten in the past (Carl Weathers) to help him regain it.

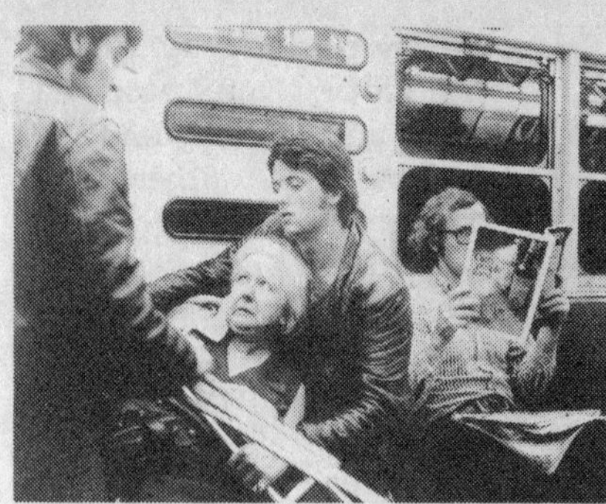

Sylvester Stallone in *Bananas.*

Stallone is somewhat limited as an actor, but he has brains and individuality. He will undoubtably be able to maintain his image through a long career.

FILMOGRAPHY

1971

Bananas (bit)

1974

The Lords of Flatbush ★ ★ ★

1975

The Prisoner of Second Avenue (bit)
Capone ★ ★ ★
Death Race 2000 ★ ★
Farewell My Lovely ★ ★ ★

1976

Cannonball ★ ★
Rocky ★ ★ ★ ★

1978

F.I.S.T. ★ ★
Paradise Alley ★ ★

1979

Rocky II (direction) ★ ★

1981

Nighthawks ★ ★ ★
Victory ★ ★ ★

1982

Rocky III (direction) ★ ★ ★ ★
First Blood ★ ★ ★

1983

Staying Alive (cameo, direction)

BARBARA STANWYCK
★★★½ 3.39 STARS

Barbara Stanwyck is revered as an actress and as a person. William Holden and Robert Preston, among others, have paid extravagant tribute to her kindness. However, she also has a reputation for feistiness, a quality that made her strong and exciting on the screen.

Born (Ruby Stevens) in 1907, in Brooklyn, New York, Stanwyck is an orphan who was raised by an older sister. Stardom came with a Broadway appearance in "Burlesque." Right from the beginning she was excellent on film, and appeared assured and professional in *Ladies of Leisure*, (directed by Frank Capra), *Ten Cents a Dance*, and *So Big*. She had a hit with *Annie Oakley*, foreshadowing the dozens of westerns she would later do on film and TV.

Her vehicles ranged from comedy in *Breakfast For Two* to soap-opera in *Always Goodbye* and *Stella Dallas*. She played opposite Robert Preston in *Union Pacific*, a good western, and both Preston and Joel McCrea raved about her. Later, she portrayed the tough but softhearted Broadway dame who loved William Holden in *Golden Boy*. Her line to Holden, "See you in 1960—maybe you'll be somebody by then," now gets laughs at film revivals. However, the movie was touching and dramatic, despite a thoroughly unbelievable ending.

The Lady Eve is generally considered to be her best comedy, and she was superb in *Remember the Night* as a shoplifter. She played with Gary Cooper's feelings in *Meet John Doe* and *Ball of Fire*, and was a classic villainess in *Double Indemnity*. No attempt was made to soften her character, and no appeals were projected to win over audiences. When she declared to Fred MacMurray in the film, "I'm rotten," she was more mesmerizing than any "lovable" heroine.

The Strange Love of Martha Ivers was almost as engrossing as *Double Indemnity*, and she conquered a Love Story-type script in *The Other Love*. She played a TB victim who disobeyed her doctor's instructions and nearly died. She did die in *Sorry, Wrong Number*, the terrifying tale of a bedridden neurotic who overheard her murder being plotted on the phone.

No actress ever conveyed the insanity of "betting fever" more convincingly than Stanwyck did in *The Lady Gambles*. Her warm humanity brought flesh and blood to the talky *East Side, West Side*, and she stood out in *Clash by Night*. This occurred despite the avalanche of publicity for Marilyn Monroe, who appeared fresh from her nude calendar scandal.

Barbara Stanwyck with Fred MacMurray in *Double Indemnity*.

Stanwyck loved to act. Hedda Hopper claimed Stanwyck lost her husband Robert Taylor by refusing to join him in Italy for *Quo Vadis*, allowing an Italian actress to supplant her. The films she stayed home to star in were hardly worth it: *Cattle Queen of Montana* with Ronald Reagan, *The Violent Men*, *The Maverick Queen*, and *These Wilder Years*. *Walk On the Wild Side* wasted everybody's talent (Jane Fonda, Laurence Harvey, and Anne Baxter), and she played second fiddle to Elvis Presley in *Roustabout*.

However, TV came through with the popular "Big Valley," which also featured Linda Evans, of "Dynasty" fame. In 1983, she totally stole her portion of a TV mini-series *The Thorn Birds*.

Barbara Stanwyck is one of the greatest actresses Hollywood ever produced. She wasn't its biggest star, but her talent matched up to all the best.

FILMOGRAPHY

1927

Broadway Nights★★★

1929

The Locked Door★★★
Mexicali Rose★★★

1930

Ladies of Leisure★★★

1931

Illicit★★★★
Ten Cents a Dance★★★★
Night Nurse★★★
The Miracle Woman★★★★

1932

Forbidden★★★★
Shopworn★★★★
So Big★★★
The Purchase Price★★★

1933

The Bitter Tea of General Yen★★★★
Ladies They Talk About★★★★
Baby Face★★★★
Ever in My Heart★★★

1934

Gambling Lady★★★★
A Lost Lady★★★★

1935

The Secret Bride★★★★
The Woman in Red★★★
Red Salute★★★
Annie Oakley★★★★

1936

A Message to Garcia★★★
The Bride Walks Out★★★
His Brother's Wife★★★
Banjo on My Knee★★★

1937

The Plough and the Stars★★★
Interns Can't Take Money★★★
This Is My Affair★★★
Stella Dallas★★★★
Breakfast For Two★★★

1938

Always Goodbye★★★★
The Mad Miss Manton★★★

1939

Union Pacific★★★★
Golden Boy★★★★

1940

Remember the Night★★★★

1941

The Lady Eve★★★★
Meet John Doe★★★★
You Belong to Me★★★

1942

Ball of Fire★★★★
The Great Man's Lady★★★
The Gay Sisters★★★

Barbara Stanwyck, Van Heflin, Lizabeth Scott in *The Strange Love of Martha Ivers.*

1943

Lady of Burlesque★★★
Flesh and Fantasy★★★

1944

Double Indemnity★★★
Hollywood Canteen★★★

1945

Christmas in Connecticut★★★

1946

My Reputation★★★
The Bride Wore Boots★★★
The Strange Love of Martha Ivers★★★★

1947

California★★★
The Two Mrs. Carrolls★★★★
The Other Love★★★
Cry Wolf★★★★

1948

B.F.'s Daughter★★★
Sorry, Wrong Number★★★★

1949

The Lady Gambles★★★★
East Side, West Side★★★★

1950

Thelma Jordan★★★★
No Man of Her Own★★★
The Furies★★★
To Please a Lady★★★

1951

The Man With a Cloak★★★

1952

Clash by Night★★★★

1953

Jeopardy★★★
Titanic★★★★
All I Desire★★★
The Moonlighter★★★
Blowing Wild★★★★

1954

Witness to Murder★★★
Executive Suite★★★★
Cattle Queen of Montana★★★

1955

The Violent Men★★★
Escape to Burma★★★

1956

There's Always Tomorrow★★★
The Maverick Queen★★★
These Wilder Years★★★

1957

Crime of Passion★★★
Trooper Hook★★★
Forty Guns★★★

1962

Walk on the Wild Side★★★

1964

Roustabout★★

1965

The Night Walker★★★

ROD STEIGER
★★★ 3.02 STARS

Sometimes a desire to meet girls can lead a person to greatness. Gene Kelly danced to make points with girls in his early days, and Rod Steiger admits he joined a dramatic group "because that's where the girls were."

Rodney Stephan Steiger was born in 1925, in Westhampton, New York. There was greasepaint in his blood since his parents were a song and dance team. After he joined the Actor's Studio, he appeared in Clifford Odets' Broadway play, "Night Music," which brought critical acclaim. Steiger also secured a screen role in the touching *Teresa* with Pier Angeli before playing the lead in *Marty* on TV. His performance was outstanding and at least the equal of Ernest Borgnine's in the film version.

In *On the Waterfront*, he was cast memorably as Marlon Brando's brother, and both actors were as good as they would ever be again. Steiger turned villainous for *The Harder They Fall*, and then had a series of average pictures: *Back From Eternity, Run of the Arrow*, and *The Unholy Wife*. In *The Mark*, he was a psychiatrist trying to help child molester Stuart Whitman. He was excellent and so was the movie, though the depressing theme discouraged audience attendance. With no box office, offers were sparse, so he did some second-rate European products, *Hands Over the City* and *Time of Indifference.*

The Pawnbroker, though still commercially weak, was artistically powerful. Steiger's repressed shopowner in Harlem brilliantly demonstrated the emotional price paid for staying isolated from human contact. An Oscar nomination led to a juicy role in David Lean's impressive *Doctor Zhivago*. Steiger was the villain who stood in the way of Julie Christie's romance with Omar Sharif. He netted the best reviews, though Christie was equally fine. He also was magnificent as a bigoted sheriff who learned to respect Sidney Poitier in *In the Heat of the Night*, a superb thriller. This time he won his Oscar, as well as a New York Film Critics Award. The movie won Best Picture.

Rod Steiger in *The Harder They Fall.*

Steiger was adventurous in choosing his roles. In *No Way to Treat a Lady,* he donned seven disguises as a mad strangler, which was macabre fun. However, *The Sergeant* failed on every level; Steiger was an army man obsessed with private John Philip Law. As usual in movies of this period (1968), homosexuality meant a kind of seething psychosis; lack of character development was also dramatically fatal. He appeared with second wife Claire Bloom in *Three Into Two Won't Go*, a study of a faltering marriage and a harbinger of personal things to come. Steiger and Bloom were divorced shortly afterward.

Steiger's talent is as strong as ever, but he hasn't had decent material in recent years. His fundamental heaviness of spirit clashed with the basic tone of *W. C. Fields and Me* just as his menacing Jud in 1955's *Oklahoma!* was too "real" for musical comedy. *F.I.S.T.* did little for anyone's career.

He did have a hit with *The Amityville Horror,* though it was poorly made, and an acting triumph as the old-fashioned Rabbi in *The Chosen.* Columnists predicted another Oscar for that performance, but the movie's lack of wide popularity hurt its Academy chances. Steiger is still relatively young and, like contemporary Paul Newman, should find a host of challenging roles to compensate for any recent clinkers.

FILMOGRAPHY

1951

Teresa★★★

1954

On the Waterfront★★★★

1955

Oklahoma!★★
The Big Knife★★★★
The Court-Martial of Billy Mitchell★★★

1956

Jubal★★★★
The Harder They Fall★★★★
Back From Eternity★★★

1957

Run of the Arrow★★★
Across the Bridge★★★
The Unholy Wife★★

1958

Cry Terror★★★★

1959

Al Capone★★★★

1960

Seven Thieves★★★

1961

The Mark★★★★

1962

The World in My Pocket★★★
13 West Street★★★
Convicts 4★★★
The Longest Day★★★

1963

Hands Over the City★★★

1964

Time of Indifference★★

1965

And There Came a Man★★★
The Pawnbroker★★★★
The Loved One★★★
Doctor Zhivago★★★★

1967

The Girl and the General★★
In the Heat of the Night★★★★

1968

The Sergeant★★
No Way to Treat a Lady★★★★

1969

Three Into Two Won't Go★★★
The Illustrated Man★★

1970

Waterloo★★

1971

Happy Birthday Wanda June★★★

1972

Duck You Sucker!★★

1973

Lucky Luciano★★★
Lolly Madonna XXX★★
The Heroes★★★

1974

The Last Days of Mussolini★★★

1975

Dirty Hands★★★
Hennessy★★★

1976

W. C. Fields and Me★★

1978

Love and Bullets★★★
F.I.S.T.★★★

1979

Sergeant Steiner★★★
The Amityville Horror★★★
Klondike Fever★★★
Cattle Annie and Little Britches★★★

1982

Lion of the Desert★★★
The Chosen★★★

JAMES STEWART
★★★½ 3.33 STARS

The hesitation, the stuttering, the aw-shucks attitude—all these characteristics would seem affected and dishonest on almost any actor. James Stewart not only wore them comfortably, he made them a believable part of many romantic roles.

Born in 1908, in Indiana, Pennsylvania, he enjoyed performing as a magician and accordionist. Though he studied engineering and architecture, his real love was acting. He and his friend Margaret Sullavan both belonged to Joshua Logan's University Players. After Sullavan got him a part in *Next Time We Love,* his career was helped by his appearance opposite Joan Crawford in *The Gorgeous Hussy.* He sang Cole Porter's "Easy to Love" in *Born to Dance,* and years later, he sang with Henry Fonda in *The Cheyenne Social Club. Of Human Hearts,* another early film, was a heavy-handed, tearful tale of a soldier encouraged by President Lincoln to write to his mother. Only Stewart's gauche sincerity could have made it plausible.

James Stewart with Margaret Sullavan.

His vehicles improved with *Vivacious Lady,* a sparkling comedy with Ginger Rogers, and *You Can't Take It With You* which won a Best Picture Oscar. *Ice Follies of 1939* temporarily derailed him. Joan Crawford, who was also in it, called it "trash." *Mr. Smith Goes to Washington* was a companion piece to Frank Capra's *Mr. Deeds Goes to Town.* Both were stories of the "little guy" who took on big city corruption. Stewart's naivete was perfect. He should have won the Oscar, but received it the following year (one of the Academy's many consolation prizes) for *The Philadelphia Story. The Shop Around the Corner* was foolproof material and he and Margaret Sullavan (thought by many to be the love of his life before he married in 1949) were ideal. *The Mortal Storm*

James Stewart with Donna Reed in *It's A Wonderful Life*.

reunited them in a superb study of a family ripped apart by Nazism.

After five years of military service, Stewart returned in 1946 to do *It's a Wonderful Life*. The film is now regarded as a classic, though it failed to draw the public on first release. He had better luck in *The Stratton Story*. Along with *Pride of the Yankees*, *The Stratton Story* was about the only baseball picture to hit the commercial bull's eye. He had an excellent partner in June Allyson in *Broken Arrow* which is still considered among the greatest westerns in Hollywood history. He and Allyson were Mr. and Mrs. in *The Glenn Miller Story*, and he was wheelchair-bound in Hitchcock's spine-tingling *Rear Window*. Another Hitchcock, *The Man Who Knew Too Much* with Doris Day, was equally exciting. The third, *Vertigo*, though more convoluted than the earlier two, enjoys a reputation with many critics as Hitchcock's masterpiece.

The success of *Bell, Book and Candle*, *Anatomy of a Murder*, and *Take Her She's Mine* sustained his popularity. However, some uninteresting ventures (*Airport'77* and *The Magic of Lassie*) did nothing to diminish his reputation. Like all great stars, he is totally unique, and though he claims,"I do variations of myself," his variations illuminated the hearts and minds of many contrasting characters.

FILMOGRAPHY

1935

The Murder Man (bit)

1936

Rose Marie (bit)
Next Time We Love★★★
Wife vs. Secretary★★★
Small Town Girl★★★
Speed★★★
The Gorgeous Hussy★★★
Born to Dance★★★
After the Thin Man★★★

1937

Seventh Heaven★★★
The Last Gangster★★★
Navy Blue and Gold★★★

1938

Of Human Hearts★★★★
Vivacious Lady★★★★
The Shopworn Angel★★★★
You Can't Take It With You★★★★

1939

Made for Each Other★★★★
Ice Follies of 1939★★
It's a Wonderful World★★★★
Mr. Smith Goes to Washington★★★★
Destry Rides Again★★★★

1940

The Shop Around the Corner★★★★
The Mortal Storm★★★★
No Time for Comedy★★★★
The Philadelphia Story★★★

1941

Come Live With Me★★★
Pot O'Gold★★★
Ziegfeld Girl★★★

James Stewart in *Harvey*.

1947

It's a Wonderful Life★★★★
Magic Town★★★

1948

Rope★★★★
On Our Merry Way★★
Call Northside 777★★★★

1949

The Stratton Story★★★★
You Gotta Stay Happy★★★

1950

Malaya★★★
Winchester 73★★★★
Broken Arrow★★★★
The Jackpot★★★
Harvey★★★★

1951

No Highway in the Sky★★★★

James Stewart with Henry Fonda in *Firecreek*.

1952

The Greatest Show on Earth★★★★
Bend of the River★★★
Carbine Williams★★★

1953

The Naked Spur★★★
Thunder Bay★★★

1954

The Glenn Miller Story★★★★
Rear Window★★★★

1955

The Far Country★★★
Strategic Air Command★★★
The Man From Laramie★★★

1956

The Man Who Knew Too Much★★★★

1957

The Spirit of St. Louis★★★
Night Passage★★★

1958

Vertigo★★★★
Bell, Book and Candle★★★

1959

Anatomy of a Murder★★★★
The FBI Story★★★

1960

The Mountain Road★★★

1961

Two Rode Together★★★★
X-15 (narration)

1962

The Man Who Shot Liberty Valance★★★★
Mr. Hobbs Takes a Vacation★★★
How the West Was Won★★★

1963

Take Her She's Mine★★★

1964

Cheyenne Autumn★★★

1965

Dear Brigitte★★★
Shenandoah★★★★

1966

The Flight of the Phoenix ★★★★
The Rare Breed ★★★

1968

Firecreek ★★★
Bandolero! ★★★

1970

The Cheyenne Social Club ★★★

1971

Fools' Parade ★★★

1974

That's Entertainment (narration)

1976

The Shootist ★★★

1977

Airport '77 ★★

1978

The Big Sleep ★★★
The Magic of Lassie ★★

MERYL STREEP
★★★ 3.11 STARS

Critic Mel Gussow of the New York Times expresed the general view when he said of Meryl Streep, "The Star of the 80s. . . a fresh, natural anti-ingenue." Of her work in *The Deer Hunter,* Gussow stated, "Streep imbues a rather ordinary woman with character. We read on her face the confusion, longings and anguish of a simple soul whose life and love are interrupted by war."

This gifted critic's darling was born in 1951, in Basking Ridge, New Jersey. She was by her own admission, a plain Jane in high school, but her talent surfaced early as a singer, then an actress (her teacher Estelle Liebling also taught Beverly Sills). Clint Atkinson, who directed Streep in a play at Vassar, remarked, "There was a volcano within her." New York audiences were equally enthusiastic; her performance in Tennessee Williams' "27 Wagons Full of Cotton" earned a Tony nomination. Joseph Papp called it "the season of Streep," and she proved him right when she won an Emmy for her superb portrait of a gentile wife married to a Jew in *Holocaust.*

Meryl Streep in *The French Lieutenant's Woman.*

Meryl Streep with Roy Scheider in *Still of the Night.*

She claims she can play so many contrasting characters because "I am a mimic. I ape gesture. The source of what I do is observation." Her role in *The Deer Hunter* was the picture's least interesting aspect, but she made herself felt in scenes with Robert De Niro and John Savage. Her real-life love, John Cazale, was also in it. He died at forty-two, leaving her devastated. She had refused to believe the seriousness of his illness.

She did *The Seduction of Joe Tynan* "on automatic pilot." Her work in this political drama written by Alan Alda was excellent. *Manhattan* showed she could do comedy, as Woody Allen's lesbian ex-wife, and there were raves and an Oscar nomination for *The French Lieutenant's Woman.* However, her meticulous portrayal lacked the mystery-woman magic that would have made the plot credible.

A different problem marred her effectiveness in *Kramer vs. Kramer.* Streep insisted on rewriting the character who was unsympathetic in the novel to soften it. In effect, the impact of the drama was diminished, and yet she still won a Best Supporting Oscar. It was almost blasphemous to criticize her, so Jack Viertel of the L. A. Herald Examiner said of a TV musical, *Alice at the Palace,* "She can sing, she can dance, and she's a capable mime. But the most remarkable thing she does tonight in *Alice at the Palace* is survive it."

Sophie's Choice brought a second Oscar, for Best Actress. Streep is talented; no one would deny it. She may even someday live up to the Oscars, Tonys, Emmys, and unending shower of superlatives that have greeted her every move.

FILMOGRAPHY

1977

Julia ★★★

1978

The Deer Hunter ★★★

1979

Manhattan ★★★★
The Seduction of Joe Tynan ★★★★
Kramer vs. Kramer ★★★

1981

The French Lieutenant's Woman ★★

1982

Sophie's Choice ★★★★
Still of the Night ★★

1983

Silkwood ★★★

BARBRA STREISAND
★★★ 2.83 STARS

Director Herbert Ross calls her "totally original, both physically and in terms of her attitudes, youth, drive, talent and native intelligence". Few except the violently anti-Streisand critic John Simon would argue. As a singer and an actress in the right films, Streisand is mesmerizing.

Born Barbara Joan Streisand in 1942, in Brooklyn, New York, she began singing in Greenwich Village,

Barbra Streisand in *Funny Girl*.

and then appeared on TV. Critic Radie Harris wondered how such an unattractive girl could seek a show business career, then listened to her sing and decided "Barbra Streisand was suddenly beautiful." She continued to prove, in Pauline Kael's words, that "talent is beauty" initially on Broadway in "I Can Get It For You Wholesale," (with co-star and ex-husband Elliott Gould), then in "Funny Girl." She wasn't certain she wanted William Wyler to direct the film version of *Funny Girl* until seeing his masterful *Wuthering Heights*. There were battles, and Wyler was pacified by a colleague, who said, "Remember, Willy, it's the first picture she's ever directed." But for all the backstage gossip, she was superb. John Kobal wrote, "In show business parlance she's a winner—her voice is a magnificent instrument, capable of giving a song a honeyed smoothness—or all the velocity and force of a demolition squad."

An Oscar (tying with Katharine Hepburn) certified her status as a superstar, though follow-up musicals were disappointing. In *Hello Dolly!*, she was miscast, and *On a Clear Day You Can See Forever* paired her unsuitably with Yves Montand. The only pleasure in either film was her singing. *The Owl and the Pussycat* was much better, a witty farce co-starring George Segal.

Funniest of all was *What's Up, Doc?*, Peter Bogdanovich's slapstick tribute to old screwball comedies. The grosses made her queen of the U.S. box office, and she gave her most brilliant performance in *The Way We Were*, as a tactless activist who alienated husband Robert Redford. The seemingly odd coupling of the two performers worked perfectly. She also matched nicely with Michael Sarrazin in *For Pete's Sake*, but the script was unbearable.

As the recipient of an Oscar, an Emmy, a Tony, *and* a Grammy, she waded in for the biggest challenge of all—a remake of Judy Garland's *A Star Is Born*. The idea for a rock version of the plot was good, but the movie didn't capture the gritty, seedy authenticity of the rock world at all. Kris Kristofferson seemed real as the burned-out hero, but Streisand herself wasn't—isn't—basically a rock performer. She's an

Barbra Streisand with Robert Redford in *The Way We Were.*

excellent *student*, a fine imitator (as her smash hits with the Bee Gees prove), but there's a polish, a Broadway veneer, that gets in the way. That shortcoming and the script were more at fault than her supposed egomania during production. Still, for all its drawbacks, the movie broke box-office records.

Streisand may be overreaching, however—she is currently working on *Yentl*, as a producer, director, writer, and star. Few Hollywood entertainers could pull it off, but if anyone can do it, Streisand can.

FILMOGRAPHY

1968

Funny Girl ★★★★

1969

Hello Dolly! ★★★

1970

On a Clear Day You Can See Forever ★★
The Owl and the Pussycat ★★★★

1972

What's Up, Doc? ★★★
Up the Sandbox ★★

1973

The Way We Were ★★★★

1974

For Pete's Sake ★★

1975

Funny Lady ★★

1976

A Star Is Born ★★

1979

The Main Event ★★★

1981

All Night Long ★★★

MARGARET SULLAVAN
★★★½ 3.50 STARS

The scope of Margaret Sullavan's ability can be measured by her last movie, *No Sad Songs For Me*, a heavy-handed soap opera. Sullavan played a dying cancer patient who nobly arranged her husband's next marriage, and she made it believable and moving without resorting to teary melodramatics.

Sullavan (Margaret Brooke) was born in 1911, in Norfolk, Virginia. She developed her craft in the theatre as one of the University Players (which also included Henry Fonda and James Stewart) in Cape Cod, and began her screen career with *Only Yesterday*, a soap-opera. She hated Hollywood, but her films were popular. *The Good Fairy, Next Time We Love*, and *The Moon's Our*

Margaret Sullavan in *The Shop Around the Corner.*

Home were all hits. She also married and divorced Henry Fonda and William Wyler.

Her portrayal in *Three Comrades* won a New York Film Critics award for Best Actress, but *The Shop Around the Corner* with James Stewart was more entertaining. *The Mortal Storm*, also with Stewart, was a powerful indictment of Nazism, and more memorable. Sullavan committed suicide in 1960. Her daughter, Brooke Hayward, later wrote *Haywire*, a brilliant, wrenching account of Sullavan's personal anguish and split personality.

FILMOGRAPHY

1933

Only Yesterday★★★

1934

Little Man What Now?★★★★

1935

The Good Fairy★★★
So Red the Rose★★★

1936

Next Time We Love★★★
The Moon's Our Home★★★

1938

Three Comrades★★★★
The Shopworn Angel★★★
The Shining Hour★★★★

1940

The Shop Around the Corner★★★★
The Mortal Storm★★★★

1941

Back Street★★★★
So Ends Our Night★★★
Appointment for Love★★★

1943

Cry Havoc★★★★

1950

No Sad Songs For Me★★★★

DONALD SUTHERLAND
★★★ 3.03 STARS

A run of poor roles and a hippie image have tended to obscure Donald Sutherland's talent. That's why his performance in *Ordinary People*, as the gently understanding, bewildered father of Timothy Hutton, came as such a surprise to Hollywood. If not for his offscreen image, he might have won the Oscar he deserved.

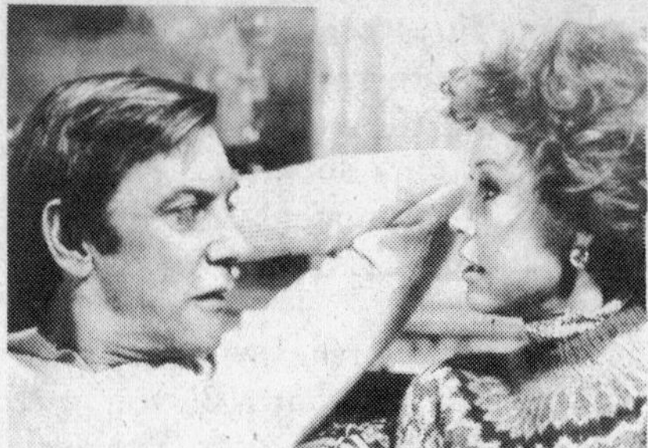

Donald Sutherland with Mary Tyler Moore in *Ordinary People*.

Born in 1934, in St. John, Canada, Sutherland was a teenage disc jockey before studying in England at the London Academy of Music and Dramatic Art. His early pictures, *Castle of the Living Dead* and *Die, Die, My Darling*, were unremarkable, but he was fine in *The Dirty Dozen* and *Kelly's Heroes*.

*M*A*S*H* made him a star, and his low-key portrait of a detective in *Klute* was a perfect contrast to Jane Fonda's high-powered call girl. They were compatible offscreen too, though a reunion in *Steelyard Blues* was hampered by script trouble, and Peter Boyle stole the picture. *Don't Look Now* paired him with another exciting female star (Julie Christie).

Most of Sutherland's movies were offbeat and represented an attempt to stretch his talent. His performances, unfortunately, were the only notable things about *Little Murders, The Day of the Locust, 1900*, and *Fellini's Casanova*. He was luckier with the remake of *Invasion of the Body Snatchers*.

After Sutherland's superb performance in *Ordinary People*, he did equally well in *Eye of the Needle* as an ice-cold killer who fell in love. So far, he seems to be one of those actors who can play different character roles and still retain enough individuality to be a star.

FILMOGRAPHY

1964

Castle of the Living Dead (bit)

1965

The Bedford Incident (bit)
Dr. Terror's House of Horrors (bit)
Die, Die, My Darling (bit)

1966

Promise Her Anything (bit)

1967

The Dirty Dozen★★★★

1968

Sebastian★★
Interlude★★★
Oedipus the King★★★
The Split★★★
Joanna★★★

1970

M*A*S*H★★★★
Start the Revolution Without Me★★★
Kelly's Heroes★★★
Alex in Wonderland★★★
Act of the Heart★★★

1971

Little Murders★★★
Klute★★★★
Johnny Got His Gun★★★

1972

F.T.A. (documentary)

1973

Steelyard Blues★★★
Lady Ice★★★
Don't Look Now★★★

1974

S*P*Y*S★★★

1975

Alien Thunder★★★
End of the Game (cameo)
The Day of the Locust★★★★

1976

1900★★★★
Fellini's Casanova★★★
The Eagle Has Landed★★★

1977

The Kentucky Fried Movie★★
Disappearance★★★

1978

Les Liens de Sang★★★
National Lampoon's Animal House★★★
Invasion of the Body Snatchers★★★
The Great Train Robbery★★★

1979

Murder by Decree★★★
Very Big Withdrawal★★★
Bear Island★★
Nothing Personal★★★
A Man, a Woman and a Bank★★★

1980

Ordinary People★★★★

1981

Gas★
Eye of the Needle★★★
Blood Relatives★★★

1983

Threshold★★★

ELIZABETH TAYLOR
★★½ 2.66 STARS

Elizabeth Taylor's acting has always drawn extreme reaction, pro or con. Richard Burton once proclaimed her "the greatest actress in cinema," and the Harvard Lampoon castigated her for a "total inability to act." Her career is a curious jumble of uneven performances, multiple marriages, and endless publicity.

London-born in 1932, Taylor's ambitious mother took her to Los Angeles. Mrs. Taylor worked relentlessly to establish her daughter as an actress, cultivating all the important columnists, including Hedda Hopper who said of the little girl, "I liked and pitied her from the start." Taylor's first major role was *Lassie Come Home*, and her next advance came opposite Mickey Rooney in the classic *National Velvet*.

Most people, including Taylor herself, dismiss her teenage work but, in fact, some of it looks more natural and unaffected than the pretentious, strident portrayals of later years. She was sweetly sincere in *Cynthia* with Mary Astor and appropriately shallow as Amy in *Little Women*.

Her beauty took care of everything in *Father of the Bride* and *Father's Little Dividend*. Then came *A Place in the Sun*, and she was outstanding as the rich girl who unwittingly induced Montgomery Clift to murder his pregnant sweetheart.

Giant ushered in her best period. She gave what many consider her best performance as Rock Hudson's independent wife. *Raintree County* encouraged her to chew up the scenery; her uncontrolled screeching was beginning to appear. She was seductive in *Cat on a Hot Tin Roof*, and undeniably powerful in *Suddenly Last Summer*, playing the girl who was nearly lobotomized.

Taylor received her first Oscar for *Butterfield 8*, and most observers felt it was a sympathy award because she had been gravely ill. Rival nominee Deborah Kerr, however, called Taylor's performance superb. There was one more moment of greatness—her blowsy, embittered Martha in *Who's Afraid of Virginia Woolf?* But after *Cleopatra*, dubbed "a monumental mouse" by critic Judith Crist, it was mostly downhill.

She had no screen chemistry with real-life lover Richard Burton, yet they starred in film after film each one worse than the last. One could see Taylor fighting to match Burton's booming classical style, and it only accentuated her pretentious diction and tendency to scream in big dramatic scenes. Taylor grew startlingly plump, what Rex Reed called "a hideous parody of her former self," and she overacted unmercifully in *Reflections in a Golden Eye*, *The Comedians*, and *The Taming of the Shrew*. *Boom!* was based on a Tennessee Williams play, but should have been retitled *Thud* after the box-office returns.

Elizabeth Taylor.

In these declining years, Taylor still had her champions. Critic Pauline Kael thought her rejected wife in *X, Y and Zee* was one of her best performances, and there were those who liked her in *The Only Game in Town*. Unfortunately, she was ridiculously miscast as a youthful Vegas dancer.

In reviewing her career, the issue of acting is irrelevant. Even her beauty is beside the point. What matters is her ability to survive the pressures of illness, divorce, suicide attempts, and excessive drinking—and start again. In a strange, convoluted way, she offers hope and inspiration to the millions who watch her and think, "if she can come back, I can too."

FILMOGRAPHY

1942

There's One Born Every Minute ★★

1943

Lassie Come Home ★★★

1944

Jane Eyre ★★★
The White Cliffs of Dover ★★★
National Velvet ★★★★

1946

Courage of Lassie ★★★

1947

Cynthia ★★★
Life With Father ★★★

1948

A Date With Judy ★★★
Julia Misbehaves ★★★

1949

Little Women ★★★

1950

Conspirator ★★
The Big Hangover ★★
Father of the Bride ★★★
Quo Vadis (cameo)

1951

Father's Little Dividend ★★★
A Place in the Sun ★★★★
Callaway Went Thataway (cameo)

1952

Love Is Better Than Ever ★★
Ivanhoe ★★★

1953

The Girl Who Had Everything ★★

1954

Rhapsody ★★
Elephant Walk ★★★
Beau Brummel ★★
The Last Time I Saw Paris ★★★★

1956

Giant ★★★★

1957

Raintree County ★★★

1958

Cat on a Hot Tin Roof ★★★★

1959

Suddenly Last Summer ★★★★

1960

Scent of Mystery (cameo)
Butterfield 8 ★★★★

Elizabeth Taylor in *Cleopatra.*

1963

Cleopatra ★
The V.I.P.S ★ ★ ★

1965

The Sandpiper ★ ★

1966

Who's Afraid of Virginia Woolf? ★ ★ ★ ★

1967

The Taming of the Shrew ★ ★
Dr. Faustus ★
Reflections in a Golden Eye ★ ★
The Comedians ★ ★

1968

Boom! ★
Secret Ceremony ★ ★ ★

1970

The Only Game in Town ★ ★

1971

Under Milk Wood ★ ★

1972

X, Y and Zee ★ ★ ★
Hammersmith Is Out ★ ★

1974

Night Watch ★ ★ ★
Ash Wednesday ★ ★ ★
That's Entertainment (narration)
The Driver's Seat ★ ★

1976

The Bluebird ★ ★

1977

A Little Night Music ★

1979

Winter Kills (cameo)

ROBERT TAYLOR
★★½ 2.69 STARS

Robert Taylor was handsome and competent but seldom exciting. Occasionally he gave a fine performance (*Waterloo Bridge*), but his ability even in a superior picture was limited.

Taylor (Spangler Arlington Brugh) was born in 1911, in Filley, Nebraska. The son of a doctor, he preferred creative pursuits (playing the cello) and acting. Ida Koverman, producer Louis B. Mayer's assistant and power behind the throne, recommended Taylor to MGM. No one remembers his early vehicles (*A Wicked Woman, Society Doctor,* and *Times Square Lady*), but he was a big hit in *Broadway Melody of 1936* with Eleanor Parker.

Magnificent Obsession launched him in the part played later by Rock Hudson. He portrayed a spoiled socialite who found moral fibre through loving Irene Dunne. Barbara Stanwyck, later his wife, shared billing in *His Brother's Wife,* and he played opposite Joan Crawford in *The Gorgeous Hussy.*

His participation in *Camille* was panned, and everyone felt he was over his head appearing with Garbo. However, the match seems equal now, since Garbo's work is a bit "theatrical" for today's taste. *A Yank at Oxford* was more enjoyable; it benefited from a charming portrayal by then-unknown Vivien Leigh. Taylor was also Leigh's leading man in the haunting *Waterloo Bridge,* although she fought to get Olivier for the part. He was excellent as the officer whose girlfriend turned to prostitution when she believed him dead. The movie delighted him personally because, "it came at a time when I didn't think I was a good actor. When I saw the picture I was surprised."

Robert Taylor with Barbara Stanwyck in *The Night Walker.*

Billy the Kid was a sturdy western though the character was romanticized. Taylor was convincing as a gang boss in *Johnny Eager,* but supporting co-star Van Heflin won the Oscar that year. *Undercurrent* presented him as a psychotic killer in uncharacteristic casting that didn't work. He also was miscast in *Quo Vadis* as the communist who married Elizabeth Taylor and was ordered by the party to do her in. *Quo Vadis* was a huge success though extended location work in Italy broke up his marriage to Stanwyck. *Ivanhoe* was also spectacular and engaging entertainment. Elizabeth Taylor was in that one too, and Taylor reportedly had a crush on her.

His acting ability was irrelevant in his last pictures except for one, *Saddle the Wind.* The film was an absorbing western in which Taylor played a "good" brother trying to stop the lawless activities of the "bad" one, John Cassavetes. *Party Girl* for incomprehensible reasons enjoys cult status. The titles tell the story of his later career: *Cattle King, A House Is Not a Home, Johnny Tiger, The Day the Hot Line Got Hot.*

If Taylor had not died in 1969, of cancer, he would have gone on working in major roles. Louis B. Mayer once said of John Wayne: "He has an endless face and he can go on forever." The same was true of Taylor.

FILMOGRAPHY

1934

Handy Andy ★ ★
There's Always Tomorrow ★ ★
A Wicked Woman ★ ★

1935

Society Doctor ★ ★
Times Square Lady ★ ★
West Point of the Air ★ ★
Murder in the Fleet ★ ★
Broadway Melody of 1936 ★ ★
Magnificent Obsession ★ ★ ★

1936

Small Town Girl ★ ★ ★
Private Number ★ ★ ★
His Brother's Wife ★ ★ ★
The Gorgeous Hussy ★ ★

1937

Camille ★ ★
Personal Property ★ ★
This Is My Affair ★ ★ ★
Broadway Melody of 1938 ★ ★

Robert Taylor with Vivien Leigh in *Waterloo Bridge*.

1938

A Yank at Oxford★★★★
Three Comrades★★★
The Crowd Roars★★★

1939

Stand Up and Fight★★★
Lucky Night★★
Lady of the Tropics★★
Remember?★★

1940

Waterloo Bridge★★★★
Escape★★★★

1941

Flight Command★★★
Billy the Kid★★★
When Ladies Meet★★★

1942

Johnny Eager★★★
Her Cardboard Lover★★

1943

Stand By for Action★★★
Bataan★★★
The Youngest Profession (cameo)

1944

Song of Russia★★
The Fighting Lady (documentary)

1946

Undercurrent★★

1947

High Wall★★★

1949

The Bribe★★★

1950

Ambush★★★
Conspirator★★
Devil's Doorway★★★

1951

Quo Vadis★★★

1952

Westward the Women★★
Ivanhoe★★★★

1953

Above and Beyond★★★
I Love Melvin (cameo)
Ride Vaquero★★★
All the Brothers Were Valiant★★★

1954

Knights of the Round Table★★★★
Valley of the Kings★★★
Rogue Cop★★★

1955

Many Rivers to Cross★★★
The Adventures of Quentin Durward★★★

1956

The Last Hunt★★★
D-Day the Sixth of June★★
The Power and the Prize★★★

1957

Tip on a Dead Jockey★★★

1958

Saddle the Wind★★★★
The Law and Jake Wade★★★
Party Girl★★★★

1959

The Hangman★★★
The House of the Seven Hawks★★★

1960

Killers of Kilimanjaro★★★

1963

Miracle of the White Stallions★★★
Cattle King★★

1964

A House Is Not a Home★

1965

The Night Walker★★★

1966

Savage Pampas★★
Johnny Tiger★★

1967

Hondo (cameo)
The Glass Sphinx★★

1968

Where Angels Go Trouble Follows★★
The Day the Hot Line Got Hot★★

SHIRLEY TEMPLE
★★½ 2.66 STARS

Graham Greene once called Shirley Temple an unhealthy sexual influence and suffered a lawsuit. More accurately, she was a charming, sometimes overly-cute moppet who mysteriously dominated box offices for a decade.

Temple was born in 1928, in Santa Monica, California. Her mother recognized her star potential and got her into some shorts and then features (*Out All Night* and *Mandalay*). A song-and-dance number "Baby, Take a Bow," from *Stand Up and Cheer,* brought attention, and she was given the lead in the first version of *Little Miss Marker* with Adolphe Menjou. Then she played in *Now and Forever* with Gary Cooper and Carole Lombard who objected to being second fiddle to the child.

Her famous "On the Good Ship Lollipop" appeared in *Bright Eyes,* a mild comedy. In *The Little Colonel,* she danced with Bill "Bojangles" Robinson. Buddy Ebsen later admitted he was terrified dancing with her in a film, that he would drop or otherwise hurt this "prize property." Unfortunately this was a feeling her other grown-up male partners also shared.

Shirley Temple.

Prize property was the correct definition—she was in the box office top 10 in 1934 (at 8th), 1935-1938 (at Number 1), and 1939 (at 5th). The films that did it were *Captain January* with Guy Kibbee, *Poor Little Rich Girl* with Alice Faye, and *Dimples* with Frank Morgan. Tears poured copiously in theatres all around the world when Temple did *Heidi,* softening the heart of Jean Hersholt. She also scored in *Rebecca of Sunnybrook Farm,* dancing with Bojangles again.

More smashes included *The Little Princess, Little Miss Broadway* (amusing opposite Jimmy Durante), and *Susannah of the Mounties. The Blue Bird* was her first box-office disappointment. She was expected to be as successful a teenager as she had been a child. However, the vehicles that began the transition would have sunk any actress. In *Kathleen*, she played a matchmaker for Herbert Marshall and Laraine Day, and she also did the melodramatic *Miss Annie Rooney.*

Her material improved when Selznick cast her in *Since You Went Away.* She wasn't particularly good, but Selznick claimed she was getting more fan mail than any other female star at the studio. *I'll Be Seeing You* was engrossing and popular, but her acting was awkward. She was more appropriately cast as a typical 1940s teenager in *Kiss and Tell,* and showed a flair for comedy in the hilarious *Bachelor and the Bobby-Soxer.* Playing opposite Cary Grant and Myrna Loy at their best helped.

Guy Madison wasn't talented enough to give her much backup in *Honeymoon,* and *That Hagen Girl* with Ronald Reagan was a low point for both performers. The problem was Temple had no dimension other than the cuddly charm that had sustained her through childhood. She tried TV and when that failed, turned to politics. There have been no attempted comebacks since then.

Temple is now married to Charles Black, a business executive she met after divorcing actor John Agar for habitual drunkenness. She still has the distinction of being the most popular child ever to appear in movies.

FILMOGRAPHY

(features only)

1932

The Red-Haired Alibi★★

1933

To the Last Man★★
Out All Night★★

1934

Carolina (bit)
Mandalay★★
Stand Up and Cheer★★★
Now I'll Tell★★
Change of Heart★★

Shirley Temple in the short film, *Glad Rags to Riches.*

Little Miss Marker★★★
Baby Take a Bow★★
Now and Forever★★★
Bright Eyes★★★★

1935

The Little Colonel★★★★
Our Little Girl★★★
Curly Top★★★★
The Littlest Rebel★★★

1936

Captain January★★★★
Poor Little Rich Girl★★★
Dimples★★
Stowaway★★★

1937

Wee Willie Winkie★★★
Heidi★★★★

1938

Rebecca of Sunnybrook Farm★★★
Little Miss Broadway★★★
Just Around the Corner★★★

1939

The Little Princess★★★
Susannah of the Mounties★★★

1940

The Blue Bird★★
Young People★★★

1941

Kathleen★★

1942

Miss Annie Rooney★

1944

Since You Went Away★★★

1945

I'll Be Seeing You★★★
Kiss and Tell★★★

1947

Honeymoon★★
Bachelor and the Bobby-Soxer★★★
That Hagen Girl★

1948

Fort Apache★★★

1949

Mr. Belvedere Goes to College★★★
Adventure in Baltimore★★
The Story of Seabiscuit★★
A Kiss for Corliss★

GENE TIERNEY
★★★ 3.03 STARS

Gene Tierney was underrated in her heyday. Her portrayal of a demented murderess in *Leave Her to Heaven* prompted Noel Coward to remark, "*That* was acting." She herself quoted a line in her autobiography spoken by one of her directors: "Gene must be a better actress than some people think. How else could she survive so many awful pictures?"

Tierney was born in 1920, in Brooklyn, New York. After scoring on Broadway in "The Male Animal," she signed with Twentieth Century Fox and did *The Return of Frank James* and *Hudson's Bay.* Other unmemorable roles followed in *Belle Starr, Rings on Her Fingers,* and *Thunder Birds,* but she was haunting in the classic *Laura.* She, however, was never satisfied with her own performance. Tierney was also exquisite in Lubitsch's *Heaven Can Wait,* and she brought power to the shallow Isabel in *The Razor's Edge.*

The Ghost and Mrs. Muir was an enjoyable comedy, and Rex Harrison played the ghost.

Personal tragedy—a retarded daughter, severe mental problems, and unhappy romances with Ali Kahn and John F. Kennedy—hampered her professional progress. Consequently, most of her pictures from the late 1940s on were less distinguished than the early ones. Still, she was effective as a kleptomaniac dominated by evil hypnotist José Ferrer in *Whirlpool.* She was also competent, if secondary to Thelma Ritter, in *The Mating Season.*

Gene Tierney.

FILMOGRAPHY

1940

The Return of Frank James★★★

1941

Hudson's Bay★★★
Tobacco Road★★★
Belle Starr★★★
Sundown★★

1942

The Shanghai Gesture★★★
Son of Fury★★
Rings on Her Fingers★★★
Thunder Birds★★★

1943

China Girl★★
Heaven Can Wait★★★★

1944

Laura★★★★

1945

A Bell for Adano★★★
Leave Her to Heaven★★★★

Gene Tierney in *A Bell for Adano.*

1946

Dragonwyck★★★
The Razor's Edge★★★★

1947

The Ghost and Mrs. Muir★★★★

1948

The Iron Curtain★★★
That Wonderful Urge★★★

1950

Whirlpool★★★
Night and the City★★★
Where the Sidewalk Ends★★★

1951

The Mating Season★★★
On the Riviera★★★
The Secret of Convict Lake★★★
Close to My Heart★★★

1952

Way of a Gaucho★★
Plymouth Adventure★★★

1953

Never Let Me Go★★★

1954

Personal Affair★★★
Black Widow★★★
The Egyptian★★

1955

The Left Hand of God★★★

1962

Advise and Consent★★★

1963

Toys in the Attic★★★

1964

The Pleasure Seekers★★★

FRANCHOT TONE
★★★ 2.93 STARS

Franchot Tone's golden talent was squandered in glossy, uninspired films. Even his wife Joan Crawford ventured, "there was never any doubt in my mind that Franchot's talent was greater than mine." In a substantial role as in *Mutiny on the Bounty,* Tone proved her right.

He was born Stanislas Pascal Franchot Tone in 1905, in Niagara Falls, New York. His father was a wealthy executive, and Tone attended Cornell University. His excellent theatre work brought a movie offer in *The Wiser Sex,* and he did several films with Crawford including: *Today We Live,* a failure, and *Dancing Lady,* a big hit.

The Lives of a Bengal Lancer was his best early vehicle, and he earned critical points opposite Bette Davis in *Dangerous.* He earned her personal admiration too, along with a statement of regret, "Alas, Miss Crawford had him!" Their turbulent marriage ended when Crawford found him with another woman.

After starring in *The Bride Wore Red,* his screen popularity began to diminish. He continued to play comedy (*Every Girl Should Be Married*) and drama (*Phantom Lady*) with skill and returned to Broadway in "A Moon for the Misbegotten." His death in 1969, of cancer, robbed both stage and screen of an exceptional performer.

Franchot Tone with Tom Conway in *Lost Honeymoon.*

FILMOGRAPHY

1932

The Wiser Sex★★★

1933

Dinner at Eight★★★
Gabriel Over the White House★★★
Today We Live★★★
Midnight Mary★★★
The Stranger's Return★★★
Stage Mother★★★
Bombshell★★
Dancing Lady★★★
Lady of the Night★★★

1934

Four Walls★★★
Gentlemen Are Born★★
Moulin Rouge★★★
The World Moves On★★★
Sadie McKee★★
Straight Is the Way★★
The Girl from Missouri★★

1935

The Lives of a Bengal Lancer★★★★
Reckless★★★
One New York Night★★★
No More Ladies★★★
Mutiny on the Bounty★★★★
Dangerous★★★★

1936

Exclusive Story★★★
The Unguarded Hour★★★
Suzy★★
The Gorgeous Hussy★★★
Love on the Run★★★
The King Steps Out★★★
Girl's Dormitory★★

1937

Quality Street★★★★
They Gave Him a Gun★★★
Between Two Women★★★
The Bride Wore Red★★

1938

Man-Proof★★★
Love Is a Headache★★★
Three Comrades★★★★
Three Loves Has Nancy★★★

1939

Fast and Furious★★★
Thunder Afloat★★★
The Girl Downstairs★★
The Gentle People★★★

1940

Trail of the Vigilantes★★

1941

Virginia★★★
Highly Irregular★★★
Nice Girl?★★
This Woman Is Mine★★★
She Knew All the Answers★★★

1942

The Wife Takes a Flyer★★★

1943

Five Graves to Cairo★★★★
Star Spangled Rhythm★★★
Pilot No. 5★★★
His Butler's Sister★★★
True to Life★★★

1944

Phantom Lady★★★
The Hour Before Dawn★★★★
Dark Waters★★★★

1945

That Night With You★★★

1946

Because of Him★★★

1947

Her Husband's Affair★★★
Two Men and a Girl★★★
Honeymoon★★★
Army Comes Across★★
Lost Honeymoon★★★

1948

I Love Trouble★★
Every Girl Should Be Married★★★

1949

Without Honor★★★
The Man on the Eiffel Tower★★★

1950

Gun Moll★★★

1951

Here Comes the Groom★★

1958

Uncle Vanya★★★

1962

Advise and Consent★★★★

1964

The Good Soup★★
Big Parade of Comedy (documentary)

1965

In Harm's Way★★★
Mickey One★★★

1968

The High Commissioner★★★

RIP TORN
★★★ 3.17 STARS

"Rock" and "Tab" are silly names even for romantic sex symbols, and "Rip" is particularly inappropriate for a serious character actor. But Rip Torn's talent has diverted attention from his frivolous name, winning the respect of critics and audiences alike.

Born Elmore Torn, in 1931, in Temple, Texas, his training included dancing under Martha Graham and lessons with Strasberg at the Actor's Studio. Torn's first film, *Baby Doll*, was a good one, and he was outstanding as a brainwashed soldier in the absorbing *Time Limit*. He held his own with Paul Newman and Ed Begley in Richard Brooks' *Sweet Bird of Youth*, but had little to do in *Critic's Choice* with Bob Hope.

Rip Torn in *Heartland*.

Torn and his wife Geraldine Page were properly zany in Coppola's neglected *You're a Big Boy Now*, but *Beach Red* and *Sol Madrid* were ordinary. Although he did a masterful impersonation of Henry Miller in *Tropic of Cancer*, his recent movies have been an odd, mixed bunch. In *Nasty Habits*, *The Man Who Fell to Earth* (with David Bowie), and *Birch Interval*, Torn's professionalism consistently added depth to his characterizations. He made an uncanny Nixon in the television adaptation of John Dean's Watergate confessional, Blind Ambition. In films, he has delivered bravura performances in the leads of small, offbeat productions like *Payday* and *Heartland*, but has yet to break through in a film of sufficient popularity to assure stardom.

Rip Torn in *A Stranger Is Watching*.

FILMOGRAPHY

1956

Baby Doll★★★

1957

A Face in the Crowd★★★
Time Limit★★★★

1959

Pork Chop Hill★★★

1961

King of Kings★★★

1962

Sweet Bird of Youth★★★★

1963

Critic's Choice★★★

1965

The Cincinnati Kid★★★

1966

One Spy Too Many★★★

1967

You're a Big Boy Now★★★★
Beach Red★★★

1968

Sol Madrid★★★
Beyond the Law★★★

1969

Coming Apart★★

1970

Tropic of Cancer★★★★

1971

Maidstone★★

1972

Slaughter★★★

1973

Payday★★★★
Crazy Joe★★★

1976

The Man Who Fell to Earth★★★
Birch Interval★★★★
Nasty Habits★★

1977

The Private Files of J. Edgar Hoover★ ★ ★

1978

Coma★ ★ ★ ★

1979

The Seduction of Joe Tynan★ ★ ★
Heartland★ ★ ★ ★

1980

One Trick Pony★ ★ ★
First Family★ ★ ★

1981

A Stranger Is Watching★ ★ ★

1982

Jinxed★ ★ ★

SPENCER TRACY
★ ★ ★ ½ 3.51 STARS

Spencer Tracy.

Spencer Tracy said modestly of his work in *Judgment at Nuremberg,* "I just sat there listening and these other fellows did the work." What that statement omits is the *importance* of "just listening" in movies. Not just listening, but reacting in absolutely natural, understated fashion, as Tracy always did.

Tracy was born in 1900, in Milwaukee, Wisconsin. He made a strong impression as a gangster in his second movie *Quick Millions* and established his reputation with *Sky Devils, Disorderly Conduct,* and *Me and My Gal.* He played in a hard-hitting prison drama, *20,000 Years in Sing Sing,* with Bette Davis, which was later remade with John Garfield as *Castle On the Hudson.*

By the time he did *A Man's Castle* with Loretta Young, his exceptional gifts as an actor were recognized by audiences and critics alike. Young was his offscreen interest as well, but Tracy's strong Catholicism made marriage impossible (he never divorced his wife Louise). These were days, according to Stanley Kramer, when "nobody—but nobody—could drink or fight or cause more trouble than Tracy." Despite his alcoholism, he continued to give precise, disciplined performances.

Fury was a notable drama about lynching. Co-star Sylvia Sidney quite correctly said, "When you consider the limitations of making a strong social statement in a Hollywood film, I think it was the best picture he (director Fritz Lang) made in this country." *San Francisco* was even more popular, an enjoyable tale of a rogue (Clark Gable) and a priest (Tracy) who remained friends through fighting, business failure, and an earthquake. Tracy won his first Oscar for *Captains Courageous* in 1937.

He was cast opposite Joan Crawford in the dreary *Mannequin.* Rock Hudson observed that there was "absolutely no chemistry between them," although Crawford's biographer Bob Thomas said they had a romance in real life. Crawford later referred to Tracy as an "unmitigated son of a bitch." That definition didn't tie in with his saintly activities in *Boys Town* (as Father Flannagan) or the follow-up, *Men of Boys Town.*

He was *Edison, the Man,* then *Dr. Jekyll and Mr. Hyde* in a role that brought him his first bad reviews. *Woman of the Year* established the Tracy/Hepburn team; they were engaging though the movie is talky and dated now. *Keeper of the Flame* was verbose political trivia. Two good Tracy/Hepburn vehicles were *Adam's Rib* and *Pat and Mike,* and he played in *Father of the Bride,* a delightful comedy without Hepburn. He didn't come across well in *The Actress* (though well done) or *Plymouth Adventure* (not well done). Tracy was magnificent in *Inherit the Wind,* outshining co-star Fredric March.

Guess Who's Coming To Dinner was a touch-and-go proposition; he was mortally ill, and Hepburn and director Stanley Kramer put up their salaries as insurance so he could appear in it. The result was a "cinematic antique," according to critic Judith Crist.

In spite of all the nonsense surrounding him, Tracy had one long monologue that made it all worthwhile, a speech that expressed love for co-star Katharine Hepburn and seemed to be expressing that love for her in real life as well.

FILMOGRAPHY

(features only)

1930

Up the River ★★★

1931

Quick Millions ★★★★
Six Cylinder Love ★★★
Goldie ★★★

1932

She Wanted a Millionaire ★★★
Sky Devils ★★
Disorderly Conduct ★★★
Young America ★★★
Society Girl ★★★
The Painted Woman ★★★
Me and My Gal ★★★

1933

20,000 Years in Sing Sing ★★★★
Face in the Sky ★★★★
Shanghai Madness ★★★
The Power and the Glory ★★★★
The Mad Game ★★★
A Man's Castle ★★★★

1934

The Show-Off ★★★★
Looking for Trouble ★★★★
Bottoms Up ★★★★
Now I'll Tell ★★★★
Marie Galante ★★★

1935

It's a Small World ★★★★
The Murder Man ★★★
Dante's Inferno ★★★★
Whipsaw ★★★★

1936

Riffraff ★★★★
Fury ★★★★
San Francisco ★★★★
Libeled Lady ★★★★

1937

They Gave Him a Gun ★★★
Captains Courageous ★★★★
Big City ★★★

1938

Mannequin ★★★
Test Pilot ★★★★
Boys Town ★★★★

1939

Stanley and Livingstone ★★★★

1940

I Take This Woman ★★★
Northwest Passage ★★★★
Edison, The Man ★★★★
Boom Town ★★★★

1941

Dr. Jekyll and Mr. Hyde ★★
Men of Boys Town ★★★

1942

Woman of the Year ★★★★
Tortilla Flat ★★★
Keeper of the Flame ★★★

1943

A Guy Named Joe ★★★

1944

The Seventh Cross ★★★★
Thirty Seconds Over Tokyo ★★★★

1945

Without Love ★★★

1947

The Sea of Grass ★★★
Cass Timberlane ★★★★

1948

State of the Union ★★★★

1949

Edward, My Son ★★★
Adam's Rib ★★★★

Spencer Tracy in *Guess Who's Coming to Dinner*.

1950

Father of the Bride ★★★★
Malaya ★★★

1951

The People Against O'Hara ★★★
Father's Little Dividend ★★★

1952

Pat and Mike ★★★★
Plymouth Adventure ★★★

1953

The Actress ★★★★

1954

Broken Lance ★★★★

1955

Bad Day at Black Rock ★★★★

1956

The Mountain ★★★★

1957

Desk Set ★★★

1958

The Old Man and the Sea ★★★★
The Last Hurrah ★★★★

1960

Inherit the Wind ★★★★

1961

The Devil at 4 O'Clock ★★★
Judgment at Nuremberg ★★★★

1963

It's a Mad Mad Mad Mad World ★★

1967

Guess Who's Coming to Dinner ★★★★

JOHN TRAVOLTA
★★½ 2.57 STARS

When John Travolta walked down the street in *Saturday Night Fever* to the tune of "Staying Alive," most viewers responded immediately to his powerful, individual presence. Later detractors claimed that this was the perfect once-in-a-lifetime blend of actor and role (like Sylvester Stallone in *Rocky*), but it's still too early to tell.

Born in 1954, in Englewood, New Jersey, Travolta quit school at sixteen and concentrated on acting. A TV series, "Welcome Back Kotter," shot him to fame; he played the hilarious Vinnie Barbarino. He also gave his best pre-*Saturday Night Fever* portrayal in a TV movie, *The Boy in the Plastic Bubble*.

Travolta had the ability to dig deep inside and project the false bravado of the typical teenage leader. A superb score by the Bee Gees also helped *Saturday Night Fever*. The music was less outstanding in *Grease*, but Travolta repeated his thug-with-a-heart-of-gold, and the movie surpassed the gigantic grosses of his first starring film.

John Travolta in *Blow Out*.

It seemed as though superstardom was inevitable, until he chose to appear with Lily Tomlin in the unbelievably tedious *Moment by Moment*. Travolta explained to Rolling Stone: "I didn't feel Lily and I had good chemistry. As people we had incredible chemistry, but onscreen it didn't work." He followed with *Blow Out*, Brian De Palma's exciting though unpopular thriller.

Urban Cowboy was also a disappointment. Travolta protested, "It did 100 million. Now, what's wrong with that? If it had been my first movie, I'd have been a big movie star." The problem was, he didn't have the same vulnerable-macho magic that was so striking in *Grease* and *Saturday Night Fever*. The script was partly at fault, but even that couldn't explain why Travolta seemed so callow and colorless next to the movie's villain, Scott Glen, or leading lady Debra Winger.

The safe thing was to do a *Saturday Night Fever* sequel, and Travolta entered into a partnership that guaranteed magazine covers with Sylvester Stallone as writer and director. The result—*Staying Alive*—was a disaster on a par with *Moment by Moment*. It was totally without plot or characterization, and the dance routines were overly busy, pretentious and poorly filmed. Worst of all, the camera feasted lovingly on Travolta, announcing to audiences that he was an idol for them to worship. His new, muscular body was impressive but his acting was coy, embarrassing, and for all the posturing, sexless.

Still, other stars have survived unfortunate vehicles and if Travolta can pick more wisely next time, he ought to climb back up to artistic respectability.

FILMOGRAPHY

1975

The Devil's Rain (bit)

1976

Carrie ★★

1977

Saturday Night Fever ★★★★

1978

Grease ★★★
Moment by Moment ★

1980

Urban Cowboy ★★★

1982

Blow Out ★★★

1983

Staying Alive ★★

CLAIRE TREVOR
★★★½ 3.28 STARS

Claire Trevor was an excellent actress who unfortunately got typecast into playing the gun moll or dance hall floozy in countless B-movies.

Trevor (Claire Wemlinger) was born in New York City, in 1909. After making her reputation in the theatre (including "Whistling in the Dark" with Edward Arnold), she was brought to Hollywood. She was immediately dropped in forgettable trivia like *Life in the Raw*, *Hold That Girl* and *Navy Wife*. Although she occasionally got some worthy co-stars (Spencer Tracy in *The Mad Game*, Humphrey Bogart in *Dead End*), she floundered in obscurity until she co-starred with John Wayne in *Stagecoach*. It remains her best known film.

She had to wade through several more mediocre films (*I Stole a Million, Allegheny Uprising, Desperadoes, Honky Tonk*) before another good opportunity would surface. It came in *Key Largo*. In the company of Humphrey Bogart, Lauren Bacall, and Edward G. Robinson, her portrait of an aging and alcoholic gangster's moll stood out. It won the Best Supporting Actress Oscar in 1949. Her films improved somewhat after that: *Borderline, The High and the Mighty, Lucy Gallant, Marjorie Morningstar, Two Weeks in Another Town,* and her performances still made them seem beneath her. She was excellent as a protective Jewish mother in *Marjorie Morningstar*, and she got a second Oscar nomination for her role in an early airplane disaster film, *The High and the Mighty*. The list of films she appeared in was a fairly dismal affair overall, but Claire Trevor herself never gave a bad performance.

FILMOGRAPHY

1933

Life in the Raw ★★★
The Last Trail ★★★
The Mad Game ★★★★
Jimmy and Sally ★★★

1934

Hold That Girl ★★★
Baby Take a Bow ★★★
Wild Gold ★★★

1935

Beauty's Daughter ★★★
Elinor Norton ★★★
Dante's Inferno ★★★
Spring Tonic ★★★
Black Sheep ★★★
My Marriage ★★★
Navy Wife ★★★

Claire Trevor in *Texas*.

1936

The Song and Dance Man ★★★
Human Cargo ★★★
To Mary With Love ★★★
Star for a Night ★★★
15 Maiden Lane ★★★
Career Woman ★★★

1937

Big Town Girl ★★★
Time Out for Romance ★★★
One Mile from Heaven ★★★
Second Honeymoon ★★★
King of Gamblers ★★★
Dead End ★★★★

1938

Walking Down Broadway ★★★
The Amazing Dr. Clitterhouse ★★★★
5 of a Kind ★★★
Valley of the Giants ★★★

1939

Stagecoach ★ ★ ★
I Stole a Million ★ ★ ★
Allegheny Uprising ★ ★ ★

1940

The Dark Command ★ ★ ★

1941

Honky Tonk ★ ★ ★ ★
Texas ★ ★ ★

1942

The Adventures of Martin Eden ★ ★ ★
Crossroads ★ ★ ★
Street of Chance ★ ★ ★

1943

Desperados ★ ★ ★
The Woman of the Town ★ ★ ★

1944

Murder My Sweet ★ ★ ★ ★

1945

Johnny Angel ★ ★ ★

1946

Crack-Up ★ ★ ★ ★
The Bachelor's Daughters ★ ★ ★

1947

Born to Kill ★ ★ ★
Bachelor Girls ★ ★ ★

1948

Raw Deal ★ ★ ★ ★
The Babe Ruth Story ★ ★ ★ ★
The Velvet Touch ★ ★ ★ ★
Key Largo ★ ★ ★ ★

1949

Lucky Stiff ★ ★ ★

1950

Borderline ★ ★ ★

1951

Best of the Badmen ★ ★ ★
Hard Fast and Beautiful ★ ★ ★ ★

1952

Hoodlum Empire ★ ★ ★
My Man and I ★ ★ ★ ★
Stop! You're Killing Me! ★ ★ ★

1953

The Stranger Wore a Gun ★ ★ ★

1954

The High and the Mighty ★ ★ ★ ★

1955

Man Without a Star ★ ★ ★
Lucy Gallant ★ ★ ★ ★

1956

The Mountain ★ ★ ★

1958

Marjorie Morningstar ★ ★ ★ ★

1962

Two Weeks in Another Town ★ ★ ★ ★

1963

The Stripper ★ ★ ★ ★

1965

How to Murder Your Wife ★ ★ ★ ★

1967

The Cape Town Affair ★ ★ ★

LANA TURNER
★ ★ ½ 2.73 STARS

Kirk Douglas thought co-star Lana Turner was "excellent" in *The Bad and the Beautiful*, and director Vincente Minnelli felt she had "a consuming talent." Not too many critics agreed, but a look at Turner's career shows that she was better than she ever got credit for.

Turner (Julia Jean Mildred Frances Turner) was born in 1920, in Wallace, Idaho. Her father was murdered when she was nine, and her mother (a beautician) moved with Turner to California. She was discovered in Schwab's Drugstore on Sunset Boulevard by Billy Wilkerson of the Hollywood Reporter. Sidney Skolsky wrote that for years every aspiring starlet sat at Schwab's counter and all they did was "get fat."

Turner debuted in *They Won't Forget*, a grim lynching drama as the killer's victim. She wore a sweater, and it led to her "sweater girl" tag. *Love Finds Andy Hardy* gave her a chance to learn ease before a camera, as did *Rich Man Poor Girl, Calling Dr. Kildare*, and *Two Girls On Broadway. Ziegfeld Girl* was a showy part, and she handled it deftly.

Stardom began with *Honky Tonk* opposite Clark Gable—a teaming that made Gable's wife, Carole Lombard, jealous. *Somewhere I'll Find You* paired them again with equally dynamic box-office results. She played opposite Robert Taylor in *Johnny Eager* and, according to her memoirs, Taylor fell madly in love with her.

Turner's reviews early in her career were warm; the critics started carping in the early 1940s. However, most of them agreed that she was

Lana Turner.

magnetic in *The Postman Always Rings Twice*, her best picture. Dressed entirely in white, she cut a smoldering, provocative figure as the wife of elderly Cecil Kellaway, lusting after John Garfield and planning Kellaway's demise. This version (in 1946) was less explicit than the later one with Jack Nicholson and Jessica Lange. In effect, it showed how much more powerful events could be if they were suggested rather than shown. She was back with Gable in the romantic and underrated *Homecoming* and played the nurse, "Snapshot," with great warmth. Turner portrayed Milady De Winter in *The Three Musketeers*, a part Angela Lansbury unsuccessfully fought to obtain for herself.

She found time throughout her career to get married (seven times) and was known as The Queen of the Nightclubs. Notoriety only helped her popularity, though fans were disappearing after *A Life of Her Own, Mr. Imperium*, and *The Merry Widow*. Minnelli worked carefully with her on *The Bad and the Beautiful* and extracted a fine performance in a part modeled after Diana Barrymore.

She surprised everyone by getting an Oscar nomination for *Peyton Place*, though personal events outdid the script for drama. Her daughter Cheryl Crane killed her gangster lover Johnny Stompanato in 1958, and a trial followed. She rebounded with the syrupy and successful *Imitation of Life* and then *Portrait in Black* (both for producer Ross Hunter).

She now appears semi-regularly on a hit TV series, "Falcon Crest," not as beautiful or as accomplished as in her heyday, but still every inch a star.

FILMOGRAPHY

1937

A Star Is Born (bit)
They Won't Forget★★★
The Great Garrick★★★

1938

The Adventures of Marco Polo★★
Four's a Crowd★★
Love Finds Andy Hardy★★
The Chaser (bit)
Rich Man Poor Girl★★
Dramatic School★★

1939

Calling Dr. Kildare★★★
These Glamour Girls★★★
Dancing Co-Ed★★★

1940

We Who Are Young★★★
Two Girls on Broadway★★★

1941

Honky Tonk★★★★
Dr. Jekyll and Mr. Hyde★★★
Ziegfeld Girl★★★★

Lana Turner in *Madame X*.

1942

Somewhere I'll Find You★★★
Johnny Eager★★★

1943

Slightly Dangerous★★
The Youngest Profession★★★
Du Barry Was a Lady (cameo)

1944

Marriage Is a Private Affair★★

1945

Keep Your Powder Dry★★★
Weekend at the Waldorf★★★

1946

The Postman Always Rings Twice★★★★

1947

Cass Timberlane★★★★
Green Dolphin Street★★★

1948

Homecoming★★★★
The Three Musketeers★★★

1950

A Life of Her Own★★

1951

Mr. Imperium★★

1952

The Merry Widow★★
The Bad and the Beautiful★★★★

1953

Latin Lovers★★

1954

Flame and the Flesh★★
Betrayed★★★

1955

The Rains of Ranchipur★★★
The Sea Chase★★★
The Prodigal★

1956

Diane★★

1957

Peyton Place★★★★

1958

The Lady Takes a Flyer★★
Another Time, Another Place★★★

1959

Imitation of Life★★★★

1960

Portrait in Black★★★

1961

By Love Possessed★★
Bachelor in Paradise★★★

1962

Who's Got the Action?★★

1965

Love Has Many Faces★★

1966

Madame X★★★

1969

The Big Cube★

1974

Persecution★★

1976

Bittersweet Love★★★

JON VOIGHT
★★★ 2.80 STARS

Jon Voight takes chances, and he seems to enjoy flexing his acting muscles. This kind of adventurousness is admirable, but it can backfire. Voight is still a question mark at the box office despite an Oscar, and contemporary Burt Reynolds who takes no risks at all is number one.

Voight was born in 1938, in Yonkers, New York. His brother, Chip Taylor, became a well-known songwriter with "Wild Thing," but Voight preferred acting. There were stage appearances in two musicals, "Camelot" on tour and "The Sound of Music" on Broadway, and he also did "Gunsmoke" and "Cimarron Strip" on television. Early screen appearances, (*Frank's Greatest Adventure* and *Out of It*), reached only limited audiences, but *Midnight Cowboy* reached everyone.

Jon Voight in *Midnight Cowboy.*

Voight's simple-minded hustler was a breathtakingly original characterization. He projected the dreams, the naivete, and male strength that first choice Michael Sarrazin could probably not have managed. He should have won an Oscar, but Dustin Hoffman was also in the movie and (as so often happens) they cancelled each other out. However, the New York critics recognized his work.

Catch-22, Mike Nichols' grim comedy based on the Joseph Heller book about military insanity, did nothing for Voight. He had better luck with *Deliverance*, a morbid and terrifying tale of urban vacationers confronting the ignorance of backwoods culture. Voight was sincere and convincing, though Burt Reynolds had the scene-stealing part.

He was *Conrack* in a version of Pat Conroy's autobiographical novel about a southerner teaching illiterate black children. The absence of Conroy's beautiful prose left a void filled in by some pleasant but leisurely anecdotes. Voight, personally, was superb. He hunted Nazis in *The Odessa File*, and then co-starred with Maximilian Schell in a passable thriller, *The End of the Game*.

Coming Home also loomed as a commercial failure, but critical approval helped. After Voight and Jane Fonda won Oscars as Best Actor and Actress, the movie took off. It was a romanticized look at Vietnam, with some sensitive sequences—Voight was a paraplegic and quite eloquent. An abrasive rock score intruded on some of the movie's best moments, and the Best Picture prize went to another Vietnam expose, *The Deer Hunter* (which reportedly infuriated Fonda).

Voight was again in demand, so he did *The Champ*, a remake of Wallace Beery's classic. His braininess and class got in the way of an honest attempt to play a not-too-bright horse trainer, and Faye Dunaway was miscast and pretentious as his ex-wife. Nevertheless, his integrity and talent will always attract certain producers. Not even bad box office can keep an actor with this much talent down.

FILMOGRAPHY

1967

Hour of the Gun★★
Frank's Greatest Adventure★

1967

Out of It★★★
Midnight Cowboy★★★★

1970

Catch-22★★★
The Revolutionary★★★

1972

Deliverance★★★★

1973

The All-American Boy★★★

1974

Conrack★★★
The Odessa File★★★

1975

The End of the Game★★★

1978

Coming Home★★★★

1979

The Champ★★

1982

Lookin' to Get Out★★

1983

Table for Five★★

ROBERT WAGNER
★★ 2.19 STARS

Robert Wagner looked a little too perfect in his youth, gleaming teeth, wide, ingratiating grin. The years melted off some of his rich-boy glitter, and he matured into a capable actor.

Wagner was born into a wealthy family in Detroit, Michigan, in 1930. He first appeared on the screen at age nineteen in *The Happy Years* and then made some action films: *The Halls of Montezuma* and *The Frogmen*. He stood out as a shellshocked soldier in *With a Song in My Heart*, but his role as a teen idol sentenced him to innocuous vehicles like *Prince Valiant*. *A Kiss Before Dying* cast him boldly against type as a conscienceless murderer who tossed Joanne Woodward off the ledge of a roof. He was spine-chillingly effective, but the momentum diminished with *Between Heaven and Hell*, *Stopover Tokyo*, and *The Hunters*.

Robert Wagner in *Banning*.

Marriage to Natalie Wood made him, more than ever, the darling of the fan magazines, so that a good performance in *The War Lover*, as Steve McQueen's buddy, was overlooked by critics. Later on, Wagner appeared to advantage in *Harper*, *The Towering Inferno*, and particularly in *Winning*. He played the racer who stole Joanne Woodward from Paul Newman. Wagner's polish and finesse can be enjoyed weekly on the highly-rated "Hart to Hart" series.

FILMOGRAPHY

1950

The Happy Years★★

1951

The Halls of Montezuma★★
The Frogmen★★
Let's Make It Legal★★

1952

With a Song in My Heart★★
What Price Glory★★
Stars and Stripes Forever★★★

1953

Titanic★★
Beneath the 12-Mile Reef★★

1954

Prince Valiant★★★
Broken Lance★★

1955

White Feather★★

1956

A Kiss Before Dying★★★
Between Heaven and Hell★★
The Mountain★★

1957

The True Story of Jesse James★★★
Stopover Tokyo★★

1958

The Hunters★★★
In Love and War★★

1960

Say One for Me★
All the Fine Young Cannibals★★

1962

Sail a Crooked Ship★
The Longest Day (cameo)
The War Lover★★★
The Condemned of Altona★★★

1964

The Pink Panther★★★

1966

Harper★★

1967

Banning★

1968

The Biggest Bundle of Them All★★
Don't Just Stand There!★★

1969

Winning★★★

1974

The Towering Inferno★★

1976

Midway (cameo)

1979

Airport '79—The Concorde★★

ROBERT WALKER
★★★ 3.16 STARS

Robert Walker's likably gangling "Corporal Hargrove" screen image was misleading; in real life, Walker was an alcoholic with suicidal tendencies. His personal instability resulted in his death at the age of thirty-two, just when he was coming into his own as an actor.

He was born in 1918, in Salt Lake City, Utah. He spent his childhood at a military Academy, which he hated, and broke into acting via radio. Walker and his wife Jennifer Jones appeared as lovers onscreen in *Since You Went Away*, a big success, but professional recognition didn't save their marriage. Jones married mentor David O'Selznick shortly afterward.

Walker had a few more hits *(See Here Private Hargrove, Thirty Seconds Over Tokyo,* and *The Clock),* and most of his films were positive, even sentimental. *Till the Clouds Roll By, What Next Corporal Hargrove?*, and *Her Highness and the Bellboy* gave no hint of his actual troubles—he was confined at Menninger's clinic for bouts of what Hedda Hopper called his "searing melancholy."

When he was offered a meaty role as Burt Lancaster's weak brother in *Vengeance Valley,* he demonstrated startling talent. His portrait of a psychotic and possibly homosexual murderer in Hitchcock's *Strangers On a Train* remains

Robert Walker in *Since You Went Away.*

one of the classic characterizations in film history. It helped compensate for his last project, a ridiculous communist melodrama *My Son John* with Helen Hayes.

FILMOGRAPHY

1939

Winter Carnival (bit)
These Glamour Girls (bit)
Dancing Co-Ed (bit)
Pioneer Days (bit)

1943

Bataan★★★
Madame Curie★★★

1944

See Here Private Hargrove★★★
Since You Went Away★★★★
Thirty Seconds Over Tokyo★★★★

1945

The Clock★★★★
Her Highness and the Bellboy★★★
What Next Corporal Hargrove?★★★

1946

Till the Clouds Roll By★★
The Sailor Takes a Wife★★★

1947

The Sea of Grass★★★
The Beginning or the End★★★
Song of Love★★

1948

One Touch of Venus★★★

1950

Please Believe Me★★★
The Skipper Surprised His Wife★★★

1951

Vengeance Valley★★★★
Strangers on a Train★★★★

1952

My Son John★★★

JOHN WAYNE
★★½ 2.45 STARS

Men and women loved John Wayne and continued to adore him until his death. Acting ability had little to do with it; his range was small. He discovered early that he had sincerity and admitted, "I've been selling it like blazes ever since."

Wayne (Marion Michael Morrison) was born in 1907, in Winterset, Iowa. He attended the University of California on a football scholarship and then met director John Ford at 20th Century Fox. He made dozens of westerns that pleased only the undiscriminating including: *Range Feud, Ride Him Cowboy, Sagebrush Trail, West of the Divide, The Lawless Frontier,* and *Westward Ho* until 1939's masterpiece, *Stagecoach*. The difference was in the acting ability of the cast (Claire Trevor, Thomas Mitchell, and John Carradine), and the depth of the characterizations.

Wayne was suddenly more than king of Saturday matinees, and he did another few westerns with the talented Trevor *(Allegheny Uprising* and *The Dark Command).* He was Republic Studios' one important star. Wayne played a seaman in *The Long Voyage Home* and co-starred with Marlene Dietrich in both *The Spoilers* and *Pittsburgh*. (He expressed his love for Dietrich in an interview shortly before his death).

He wasn't in the Box Office Top Ten yet, but his popularity increased with each picture *(The Fighting Seabees, Tall in the Saddle,* and *Tycoon).* In *Angel and the Badman* he was cast opposite Gail Russell (reportedly an offscreen interest and the reason one of his wives sued for divorce—he was married three times).

She Wore a Yellow Ribbon is generally regarded as one of Wayne's greatest films though his *acting* rarely aroused comment. However, his acting did earn him an Oscar nomination for *Sands of Iwo Jima*. He hit the Top 10 that year, where he remained through 1974—with the exception of 1958. His performance as a tough Marine officer was powerful, and he also dominated *The Quiet Man. The High and the Mighty* was 1954's version of *Airport;* it concerned a jet in trouble with passengers revealing their personal problems. He was miscast as a German in *The Sea Chase* and ludicrous in *The Conqueror* and *The Barbarian and the Geisha*.

These were only temporary setbacks in a spectacular career. Even *The Alamo* (which he directed ineptly) made money, and *How the West Was Won* was a smash. Wayne was operated on for lung cancer in 1963, but returned in 1965, to do *The Sons of Katie Elder. True Grit* captured the elusive Oscar against Richard Burton, who had been particularly anxious to win. He wound up his acting days in *The Shootist*, an even better portrayal as a terminally ill gunman.

His cancer returned in 1978 and he also underwent open heart surgery. He died in 1979. He bore his pain stoically, demonstrating the kind of impressive courage that had made him a legend on the screen.

FILMOGRAPHY

1927

The Drop Kick (bit)

1928

Hangman's House (bit)

1929

Words and Music★★
Salute (bit)

1930

Men Without Women (bit)
Rough Romance (bit)
Cheer Up and Smile (bit)
The Big Trail★★

1931

Girls Demand Excitement★★
Three Girls Lost★★
Men Are Like That★★
The Deceiver (bit)
Range Feud★★
Maker of Men★★

1932

Shadow of the Eagle (serial)★★
Texas Cyclone★★
Two-Fisted Law★★
Lady and Gent★★
The Hurricane Express (serial)★★
Ride Him Cowboy★★
The Big Stampede★★
Haunted Gold★★

1933

The Telegraph Trail★★
The Three Musketeers (serial)★★
Central Airport (bit)
Somewhere in Sonora★★
His Private Secretary★★
The Life of Jimmy Dolan (bit)
Baby Face★★
The Man From Monterey★★
Riders of Destiny★★
College Coach (bit)
Sagebrush Trail★★

1934

The Lucky Texan★★
West of the Divide★★
Blue Steel★★
The Man from Utah★★
Randy Rides Alone★★
The Star Packer★★
The Trail Beyond★★
The Lawless Frontier★★
'Neath Arizona Skies★★

John Wayne in *The Conqueror.*

1935

Texas Terror★★
Rainbow Valley★★
The Desert Trail★★
The Dawn Rider★★
Paradise Canyon★★
Westward Ho★★
The New Frontier★★
The Lawless Range★★

1936

The Oregon Trail★★
The Lawless Nineties★★
King of the Pecos★★
The Lonely Trail★★
Winds of the Wasteland★★
The Sea Spoilers★★
Conflict★★

1937

California Straight Ahead★★
I Cover the War★★
Idol of the Crowds★★
Adventure's End★★
Born to the West★★

1938

Pals of the Saddle★★
Overland Stage Raiders★★
Santa Fe Stampede★★
Red River Range★★

1939

Stagecoach★★★★
The Night Riders★★
Three Texas Steers★★
Wyoming Outlaw★★
New Frontier★★
Allegheny Uprising★★★

1940

The Dark Command★★★
Three Faces West★★★
The Long Voyage Home★★★★
Seven Sinners★★★★
Melody Ranch (stunt)

1941

A Man Betrayed★★★
Lady from Louisiana★★★
The Shepherd of the Hills★★

1942

Lady for a Night★★
Reap the Wild Wind★★★
The Spoilers★★★
In Old California★★★
Flying Tigers★★★
Reunion in France★★
Pittsburgh★★★

1943

A Lady Takes a Chance★★
In Old Oklahoma★★★

1944

The Fighting Seabees★★★
Tall in the Saddle★★

1945

Flame of the Barbary Coast★★★
Back to Bataan★★
They Were Expendable★★★★
Dakota★★

1946

Without Reservations★★

1947

Angel and the Badman★★
Tycoon★★

1948

Fort Apache★★★★
Red River★★★★
Wake of the Red Witch★★★
Three Godfathers★★★
The Fighting Kentuckian★★★
She Wore a Yellow Ribbon★★★★

John Wayne in *Rio Bravo.*

1950

Sands of Iwo Jima★★★★
Rio Grande★★★★

1951

Operation Pacific★★
The Bullfighter and the Lady★★★
Flying Leathernecks★★★

1952

The Quiet Man★★★★
Big Jim McLain★★

1953

Trouble Along the Way★★
Island in the Sky★★
Hondo★★★

1954

The High and the Mighty★★★

1955

The Sea Chase★★
Blood Alley★★★

1956

The Conqueror★
The Searchers★★★★

1957

The Winds of Eagles★★
Jet Pilot★★★
Legend of the Lost★★

1958

I Married a Woman (cameo)
The Barbarian and the Geisha★★

1959

Rio Bravo★★★★
The Horse Soldiers★★★

1960

The Alamo★★
North to Alaska★★★

1961

The Comancheros★★★

1962

The Man Who Shot Liberty Valance★★★★
Hatari!★★★
The Longest Day★★★
How the West Was Won★★★★

1963

Donovan's Reef★★★
McLintock!★★

1964

Circus World★★★

1965

The Greatest Story Ever Told★★
In Harm's Way★★★
The Sons of Katie Elder★★★

1966

Cast a Giant Shadow★★

1967

The War Wagon★★
El Dorado★★★

John Wayne with Katharine Hepburn in *Rooster Cogburn*.

1969

The Green Berets★★
Hellfighters★★
True Grit★★★★
The Undefeated★★

1970

Chisum★★
Rio Lobo★★

1971

Big Jake★★★

1972

The Cowboys★★★
Cancel My Reservation (cameo)

1973

The Train Robbers★★
Cahill-United States Marshal★★

1974

McQ★★

1975

Brannigan★★
Rooster Cogburn★★

1976

The Shootist★★★★

CLIFTON WEBB
★★★ 3.22 STARS

No one ever gained as much mileage from arch superiority as Clifton Webb. His Mr. Belvedere in *Sitting Pretty* made him an unlikely but highly amusing box-office attraction. He was also capable of strong dramatic acting.

Webb (Webb Parmallee Hollenbeck) was born in 1891, in Indianapolis, Indiana. His singing and dancing talents weren't utilized on film, but he was trained in both since earliest childhood. He even sang with the Boston Opera Company. Webb was a famous ballroom dancer in New York and then a hit on Broadway in "As You Were," "Jack and Jill," "Sunny," and many others. There were a few silent pictures (*Polly With a Past*, *The Heart of a Siren*, and *New Toys*), but Broadway claimed most of his time and attention with "The Man Who Came to Dinner" and "Blithe Spirit."

Stardom began onscreen with *Laura*. He was the witty but inwardly murderous Waldo Lydecker, and his portrayal is chiefly responsible for the movie's classic status today. *The Dark Corner* with Lucille Ball was gripping, and then he had his second immortal acting role (snobbish Elliott Templeton in *The Razor's Edge*). He turned a shallow situation—despair at not receiving an invitation to an important party—into a genuinely tragic predicament.

Clifton Webb in *Sitting Pretty*.

Sitting Pretty was 1948's funniest comedy. Webb played Mr. Belvedere, the babysitter who disrupted a small town. The dialogue was clever, and he gave it a polished edge. His participation affected everyone because the other cast members—Maureen O'Hara and Robert Young—were at the peak of their form. *Mr. Belvedere Goes to College* wasn't as good, but his snob act still provided pleasure.

He had a tailor-made part as the father of twelve in *Cheaper by the Dozen*, a true story of an efficiency expert who ran his family like a business. It was popular, more so than the sequel, *Belles On Their Toes* (because he wasn't in it). Webb "died" at the end of the first film. *Mr. Belvedere Rings the Bell* indicated that the series had run out of steam. However, *Dreamboat* was delightful, a spoof of silent movies, and he was fine as the captain of the doomed *Titanic*.

Webb went to Rome to play in *Three Coins in the Fountain*. He was the crotchety older man loved by spinster secretary Dorothy McGuire. The match was odd, but both actors had the skill and charm to put it over. In *Woman's World* he was cast as an executive searching for a new vice president (Fred MacMurray, Van Heflin, and Cornel Wilde were the candidates). His contribution was impeccable and continued to be through *The Man Who Never Was, Boy on a Dolphin, The Remarkable Mr. Pennypacker*, and *Holiday for Lovers*.

It's likely that most of his non-Belvedere work (good as it was) will be forgotten. He created only one real character, but that character was so entertaining that it will be enjoyed by film buffs for generations to come.

FILMOGRAPHY

1920

Polly With a Past ★★★

1925

New Toys ★★★
The Heart of a Siren ★★★

1944

Laura ★★★★

1946

The Dark Corner ★★★
The Razor's Edge ★★★★

1948

Sitting Pretty ★★★★

1949

Mr. Belvedere Goes to College ★★★

1950

Cheaper by the Dozen ★★★★
For Heaven's Sake ★★

1951

Mr. Belvedere Rings the Bell ★★★
Elopement ★★★

1952

Dreamboat ★★★★
Stars and Stripes Forever ★★★

1953

Titanic ★★★★
Mister Scoutmaster ★★

1954

Three Coins in the Fountain ★★★
Woman's World ★★★★

1956

The Man Who Never Was ★★★

1957

Boy on a Dolphin ★★★

1959

The Remarkable Mr. Pennypacker ★★★
Holiday for Lovers ★★★

1962

Satan Never Sleeps ★★★

JOHNNY WEISSMULLER
★★ 2.17 STARS

Today's era of the heavily promoted athlete owes much to Johnny Weissmuller. He was the first sports hero to cash in his fame at the box office. His acting range was limited, but his was the ideal marriage of image and casting. Johnny Weissmuller was the perfect Tarzan.

Weissmuller was born in Windber, Pennsylvania, in 1904. A champion swimmer, he won five gold medals at the 1924 and 1928 Olympics, and he set many U.S. and world swimming records. When Metro-Goldwyn-Mayer set about the task of doing a series of films based on Edgar Rice Burrough's character Tarzan, Weissmuller was the obvious choice to play the Lord of the Jungle. The Tarzan series proved very successful, primarily because of Weissmuller's casting. After a dozen Tarzan features had run their course, Weissmuller moved to Columbia where he starred in the Jungle Jim series. This time he played a guide and adventurer, but Weissmuller was never able to recapture the box-office draw of his Tarzan role. In 1958 the Jungle Jim series was moved to television and its termination was also the end of Weissmuller's acting career.

Johnny Weissmuller with Maureen O'Sullivan, Johnny Sheffield and Cheetah.

FILMOGRAPHY

1929

Glorifying the American Girl (cameo)

1932

Tarzan the Ape Man ★★★

1934

Tarzan and His Mate ★★★

1936

Tarzan Escapes ★★★

1939

Tarzan Finds a Son ★★★

1941

Tarzan's Secret Treasure ★★★

1942

Tarzan's New York Adventure ★★★

1943

Tarzan Triumphs ★★★
Stage Door Canteen (cameo)
Tarzan's Desert Mystery ★★★

1945

Tarzan and the Amazons ★★★

1946

Tarzan and the Leopard Women ★★★
Swamp Fire ★★

1947

Tarzan and the Huntress ★★★

1948

Tarzan and the Mermaids ★★★
Jungle Jim ★★

1949

The Lost Tribe ★★

1950

Captive Girl ★★
Mark of the Gorilla ★★
Pygmy Island ★★

1951

Jungle Manhunt ★★
Fury of the Congo ★★

1952

Jungle Jim in the Forbidden Land ★★
Voodoo Tiger ★★

1953

Savage Mutiny ★
Valley of the Headhunters ★
Killer Ape ★

1954

Jungle Man-Eaters ★
Cannibal Attack ★

1955

Jungle Moon Men ★
Devil Goddess ★

1970

The Phynx (cameo)

RAQUEL WELCH
★ ★ 2.14 STARS

Beautiful faces and hour-glass figures were the stuff that Hollywood was made of. Starlets who looked like Raquel Welch were destined for fame, no matter what their acting talent. However, Welch had the misfortune to follow in that tradition in more demanding times. To say that she was trashed by critics is an understatement. She has felt the criticism and made efforts to improve her acting skills.

She was born Raquel Tejado in Chicago, in 1940. She was raised in California. She took ballet lessons as a child and won several beauty contests at the age of fourteen. After an early failed marriage, her career began to take off when press agent Patrick Curtis promoted her as a sex goddess. A publicity tour, with posters and press conferences, created a furor and announced her arrival. She became a major international star without appearing in a film of any importance. Her image was set when she starred in a remake of *One Million Years B.C.*

After her marriage to Patrick Curtis ended in 1971, Welch made interestingly off-beat, if not critically acclaimed, movies like *Fuzz*

Raquel Welch in *Myra Breckinridge*.

(with Burt Reynolds), *Mother Jugs and Speed, The Three Musketeers,* and *The Prince and the Pauper.* She has recently won hard-earned acclaim for a TV movie, *The Legend of Walks Far Woman,* and for a brief but dazzling appearance in the Broadway play "Woman of the Year."

FILMOGRAPHY

1964

A House Is Not a Home (bit)
Roustabout (bit)

1965

A Swingin' Summer ★

1966

Shoot Loud . . . Louder . . . I Don't Understand ★
The Queens ★
Fantastic Voyage ★ ★
One Million Years B.C. ★ ★

1967

The Oldest Profession ★ ★
Fathom ★ ★
Bedazzled ★ ★ ★

1968

The Biggest Bundle of Them All ★ ★
Bandolero! ★ ★
Lady in Cement ★ ★

1969

Flareup ★ ★
100 Rifles ★ ★ ★
The Magic Christian ★ ★

1970

Myra Breckinridge ★

1971

Hannie Caulder ★ ★

1972

The Beloved ★ ★
Bluebeard ★ ★
Fuzz ★ ★
Kansas City Bomber ★ ★ ★

1973

The Last of Sheila ★ ★ ★

1974

The Three Musketeers ★ ★ ★

1975

The Four Musketeers ★ ★ ★
The Wild Party ★ ★ ★

1977

Mother Jugs and Speed ★ ★
The Prince and the Pauper ★ ★ ★

1978

L'Animal ★ ★

1979

Restless ★ ★

TUESDAY WELD
★ ★ ★ 2.91 STARS

No actress as gifted as Tuesday Weld has ever appeared in so many mediocre pictures. Even her critical triumphs were usually ignored by mass audiences. Fortunately, Weld is still young, and if she keeps working, that one great part is bound to come along.

Tuesday Weld.

Weld (Susan Ker Weld) was born in 1943, in New York City. Her childhood brought professional success (as a model and an actress) and personal turmoil (drinking and a suicide attempt). She showed talent on Broadway in "The Dark at the Top of the Stairs," but her movies, *Because They're Young, High Time, Sex Kittens Go to College,* were foolish, teen-oriented affairs. *Return to Peyton Place* was a pale shadow of the original, except for Mary Astor's performance, and she was trapped in a Presley vehicle, *Wild in the Country.*

Weld's first fine picture was *The Cincinnati Kid,* playing Steve McQueen's girlfriend. She was excellent, and her comedic flair was obvious in *Lord Love a Duck. Pretty Poison* rated high with journalists, if not moviegoers, and *A Safe Place* was rejected by all. Her role in Richard Brooks' *Looking for Mr. Goodbar* finally provided critical applause (she was Oscar-nominated) *and* a box-office success.

Tuesday Weld in *Who'll Stop the Rain?*

FILMOGRAPHY

1956

Rock Rock Rock★★

1958

Rally Round the Flag Boys! ★★★

1959

The Five Pennies★★★

1960

Because They're Young★★★
Sex Kittens Go to College★★★
High Time★★★
The Private Lives of Adam and Eve★★★

1961

Return to Peyton Place★★★
Wild in the Country★★★

1962

Bachelor Flat★★★

1963

Soldier in the Rain★★★

1965

The Cincinnati Kid★★★★
I'll Take Sweden★★

1966

Lord Love a Duck★★★

1968

Pretty Poison★★★★

1970

I Walk the Line★★★

1971

A Safe Place★

1972

Play It As It Lays★★

1977

Looking for Mr. Goodbar★★★★

1978

Who'll Stop the Rain?★★★

1979

Serial★★★

1981

Thief★★★

ORSON WELLES
★★★ 3.02 STARS

Orson Welles once said, "America treated me like a God. It was all because I was young. If you're only young enough in America you can demand the world and they'll give it to you. Now I'm over forty, so America lost interest in me." America has never quite lost interest in Welles because of the classic *Citizen Kane*. However, the diminishing excitement can be traced to later work, which never lived up to early achievements.

Welles was born in 1915, in Kenosha, Wisconsin. As a child he showed talent as poet, cartoonist, painter, and actor. His talent for organization surfaced when he managed the Woodstock Theatre Festival in Illinois. As director of the Negro People's Theatre in 1937, he helmed a black "Macbeth" and then founded the Mercury Theatre with John Houseman. A radio version of The War of the Worlds that he narrated sent people scurrying to the streets in panic. Soon afterward, he starred in, co-wrote (with Herman Mankiewicz), and directed *Citizen Kane*. It was innovative and engrossing, but the title character (a thinly disguised William Randolph Hearst) was treated less than flatteringly. Hearst fought successfully to suppress the film encouraging his hatchet woman, critic Louella Parsons, to attack Welles mercilessly in print. The box office suffered.

Orson Welles in *Citizen Kane*.

The Magnificent Ambersons also had striking qualities particularly Agnes Moorehead's performance, but the Hearst press undermined that one too. As a consequence, Welles tried straight acting as Rochester in *Jane Eyre*. He was convincing though Joan Fontaine recalled him as an egomaniac. He was superb in *Tomorrow Is Forever* as the crippled husband Claudette Colbert didn't remember when he returned from the war. *The Stranger* followed, an absorbing study of a Nazi living in a small town.

Welles cast then-wife Rita Hayworth as *The Lady From Shanghai*, dying her hair blond and altering her image. The public stayed away, and studio head Harry Cohn was apoplectic, though Hayworth claimed years later, "I knew we were making a classic."

To do projects like *Macbeth*, Welles was forced to appear in disasters like *Black Magic* and *Prince of Foxes*. His greatest role as an actor came in *The Third Man* as the grinningly evil Harry Lime, and the success of the picture brought work in *The Black Rose* and *Trent's Last Case*. His performing became increasingly mannered in *Touch of Evil* and *Man With a Shadow*, though his corpulent, conniving Big Daddy part in *The Long Hot Summer* was one of its finest ingredients. He had a long, effective speech as Clarence Darrow in the bleak *Compulsion*.

A commercial project—*The V.I.P.S.*—showed him in good if pretentious form, and he had the required stature for *A Man for All Seasons*. A critic once remarked that Welles had "more genius than talent," and perhaps that's the clue. He had vision, he marched to his own drummer, but he lacked the conventional, commercial instincts of his inferiors.

FILMOGRAPHY

1940

The Swiss Family Robinson (narration)

1941

Citizen Kane ★★★★
(direction, co-screenplay)

1942

The Magnificent Ambersons
(narration, direction)

1943

Journey Into Fear ★ ★ ★

1944

Follow the Boys (cameo)
Jane Eyre ★ ★ ★ ★

1946

The Stranger (direction) ★ ★ ★ ★
Tomorrow Is Forever ★ ★ ★ ★

1947

Duel in the Sun (narration)

1948

The Lady From Shanghai (direction) ★ ★ ★ ★
Macbeth ★ ★ ★

1949

Black Magic ★ ★
The Third Man ★ ★ ★ ★
Prince of Foxes ★ ★

1950

The Black Rose ★ ★ ★

1952

Othello ★ ★ ★

Orson Welles in *Crack in the Mirror.*

1953

The Beast ★ ★
Trent's Last Case ★ ★ ★

1954

Royal Affairs in Versailles ★ ★
Trouble in the Glen ★ ★ ★

1955

Confidential Report ★ ★ ★
Three Cases of Murder ★ ★ ★
Out of Darkness (documentary)
Napoleon ★ ★

1956

Moby Dick ★ ★ ★ ★

1957

Man With a Shadow ★ ★ ★

1958

Touch of Evil (direction) ★ ★ ★ ★
The Long Hot Summer ★ ★ ★ ★
The Roots of Heaven ★ ★ ★
The Vikings (narration)

1959

Compulsion ★ ★ ★ ★
High Journey (narration)
Ferry to Hong Kong ★ ★ ★

1960

David and Goliath ★ ★ ★
Crack in the Mirror ★ ★ ★
Battle of Austerlitz ★ ★

1961

The Tartars ★ ★
King of Kings (narration)

1962

Lafayette ★ ★ ★
Rogopag ★ ★ ★
The Trial (direction) ★ ★ ★

1963

The V.I.P.s ★ ★ ★

1964

The Finest Hours (documentary)

1965

Marco the Magnificent ★ ★ ★
A King's Story (documentary)

1966

A Man for All Seasons ★ ★ ★ ★
Is Paris Burning? ★ ★ ★
Falstaff (direction) ★ ★ ★ ★

1967

Casino Royale ★ ★ ★
The Sailor From Gibraltar ★ ★ ★
I'll Never Forget What's 'is Name ★ ★ ★

1968

Oedipus the King ★ ★ ★
Kampf um Rom ★ ★ ★

1969

The Southern Star ★ ★ ★
Tepepa ★ ★ ★
Barbed Water ★ ★ ★
Una su 13 ★ ★ ★
Michael the Brave ★ ★ ★
House of Cards ★ ★ ★

1970

Battle of Neretva ★ ★ ★
Start the Revolution Without Me (narration, cameo)
The Kremlin Letter ★ ★
Catch-22 ★ ★ ★
Waterloo ★ ★

1971

Directed by John Ford (documentary)
Sentinels of Silence (documentary)
A Safe Place ★ ★

1972

Ten Days' Wonder ★ ★ ★
Malpertuis ★ ★ ★
The Canterbury Tales ★ ★ ★
Treasure Island ★ ★ ★

1972

Get to Know Your Rabbit ★ ★ ★
Necromancy ★ ★

1975

Bugs Bunny Superstar (narration)

1976

The Challenge (documentary)
Voyage of the Damned ★ ★ ★

1979

The Late Great Planet Earth (narration)
The Muppet Movie ★ ★ ★
Tesla ★ ★ ★

1981

The Man Who Saw Tomorrow ★ ★ ★
History of the World-Part I (narration)

1982

Genocide (narration)
Butterfly (cameo)

MAE WEST
★ ★ ★ 3.17 STARS

Mae West created her own legend. And perhaps never before and never again in film history will a career be predicated on such a legend. When she made her first film, she was forty. She only made 12 films. Yet the queen of double entendres, the master of witty sexuality was an institution for more than 50 years. She is credited with changing society's attitudes toward women as sexual beings.

Mae West was born in Brooklyn in 1892. At age eighteen, West turned down Florenz Ziegfeld to headline musical-comedy revues on Broadway. By 1926, she was writing and starring in her own plays. The first, "Sex," was closed by the police in its second year, and West spent time in jail for corrupting the morals of youth. Her fourth play and biggest stage success was "Diamond Lil," in which she played a Gay

Mae West.

Nineties saloon singer. After touring in the show, she arrived in Hollywood and singlehandedly saved Paramount Pictures from bankruptcy and selling out to MGM.

Her first film, *Night After Night*, co-starred George Raft. Sauntering into Raft's nightclub, West is noticed by a hatcheck girl, who remarks, "Goodness! What beautiful diamonds!" To which West replies, tongue planted firmly in cheek, "Goodness had nothing to do with it."

Her second film, *She Done Him Wrong*, was a screen version of "Diamond Lil." West launched the career of Cary Grant by picking him out of hundreds of chorus boys to be her co-star. The film broke box-office records only to be surpassed by her next feature, *I'm No Angel*. In her heyday in the 1930s, she received $300,000 for a starring role and an additional $100,000 for a script.

West and her films are reportedly what brought about the Hays Production Code, which prohibited her type of suggestive humor. For a society that repressed its sexuality, it certainly paid dollars to view the woman of the hourglass figure. One can still picture West purring her lines, punctuating her words by moving her hand off her hip to primp her cascading blonde coiffure: "I used to be Snow White, but I drifted."

After such films as *Belle of the Nineties* and *Klondike Annie*, West wrote a script for herself and W. C. Fields, *My Little Chickadee*. It allowed Fields to interject his own brand of humor and the mock western was an instant classic and a box-office success. Unhappy with her next movie, *The Heat's On*," she didn't make another film until *Myra Breckenridge* in 1970.

In the interim, she appeared in a Las Vegas-style cabaret act with young musclemen dressed only in loincloths. In that show, she met Paul Novak, a former professional wrestler, who remained her companion until her death in 1980. She once said, "I lived like a man, in some ways—decided what I wanted and went after it. I'm not sorry."

FILMOGRAPHY

1932

Night After Night ★★★

1933

She Done Him Wrong ★★★★
I'm No Angel ★★★★

1934

Belle of the Nineties ★★★★

1935

Goin' To Town ★★★

1936

Klondike Annie ★★★
Go West Young Man ★★★

1938

Every Day's a Holiday ★★★★

1940

My Little Chickadee ★★★★

1943

The Heat's On ★★★

1970

Myra Breckinridge ★★

1978

Sextette ★

BILLY DEE WILLIAMS
★★★½ 3.40 STARS

Sidney Poitier was the first romantic black superstar whose popularity didn't hinge on ethnic parts. No one has come along to fill that void, but Billy Dee Williams seems a likely candidate.

Williams was born in 1937, in New York City. Between stage roles, he made a few now-forgotten film appearances in *The Last Angry Man* and *The Out of Towners*. His suave, polished good looks were perfect for *Lady Sings the Blues*. As Diana Ross' lover, he offered the kind of protective devotion that guaranteed mass response from female viewers.

Billy Dee Williams with Diana Ross in *Lady Sings the Blues*.

His honesty was crucial in another Diana Ross vehicle, *Mahogany*. The script was a disastrous hodgepodge, and Williams played an aspiring politician with enough sincerity to breathe life into plastic situations. *The Bingo Long Traveling All-Stars and Motor Kings* gave him a more worthwhile role; Williams was a baseball player who started his own team.

Billy Dee Williams in *The Bingo Long Traveling All-Stars and Motor Kings*.

He finally got his big break in the hugely successful *The Empire Strikes Back*. Recently seen in *Return of the Jedi*, Williams' future is limitless if talent, charisma, and charm are prerequisites.

FILMOGRAPHY

1959

The Last Angry Man (bit)

1970

The Out of Towners (bit)

1972

The Final Comedown ★★★
Lady Sings the Blues ★★★★

1973

Hit! ★★★

1974

The Take ★★★

1975

Mahogany ★★★

1976

The Bingo Long Traveling All-Stars and Motor Kings ★★★★

1977

Scott Joplin★★★★

1980

The Empire Strikes Back★★★★

1981

Nighthawks★★★

1983

Return of the Jedi★★★

SHELLEY WINTERS
★★★ 2.92 STARS

Shelley Winters denies being difficult, but co-workers on the placid Disney lot remember a goodly share of temperament during the filming of *Pete's Dragon*. As usual, she turned in a terrific performance, justifying the turbulent shennanigans behind the scenes.

Winters (Shirley Schrift) was born in 1922, in St. Louis, Missouri. She grew up in Brooklyn and modeled for a while before scoring a hit in an amateur revue, "Pins and Needles." She was (unlike her current image) thin and sexy in early vehicles *(The Gangster, Red River,* and *Living in a Big Way). A Double Life* showed the powerful talent that would singlehandedly save picture after picture in the years to come. She played a waitress murdered by Ronald Colman.

The 1949 version of *The Great Gatsby* (vastly underrated and superior to the Robert Redford film) cast Winters as Myrtle accidentally run over by Betty Field. Her energy brought humor to *South Sea Sinner,* and she was also lively and amusing in *Frenchie*.

Recognition as a serious actress came when she pressured George Stevens into giving her a leading part in *A Place in the Sun*. Montgomery Clift objected to her approach: "She telegraphs her tragedy from the minute she's on the screen," but most observers thought she was hauntingly pathetic and brilliant. In 1951, "Vivien Leigh won *my* Oscar," according to Winters, and she went back to some ordinary vehicles *(Behave Yourself, The Raging Tide,* and *Phone Call From a Stranger).*

Shelley Winters in *Tonight and Every Night.*

There were epic fights with Frank Sinatra on the set of *Meet Danny Wilson*; the feud has lasted to this day although Winters is a great admirer of his singing. More mediocrity followed in *Untamed Frontier, Tennessee Champ,* and *My Man and I*. She got into an excellent drama about big business, *Executive Suite*, and was startingly effective as the murder victim of psychotic preacher Robert Mitchum in *The Night of the Hunter.*

Theatre work claimed her in the early 1950s in "Born Yesterday," "A Streetcar Named Desire," "Wedding Breakfast," and a long-running Broadway smash, "A Hatful of Rain" with future husband Anthony Franciosa. *The Diary of Anne Frank* was miserably disappointing to anyone who had seen the memorable stage original. Millie Perkins in the title role was the main defect. Winters, however, was outstanding as one of the frightened Jews hiding in the basement, and she won an Academy Award. "I've waited fifteen years for this Oscar," she sobbed at the ceremonies. Her movies continued to vary sharply in quality from the ludicrous *The Chapman Report* to the enjoyable *Wives and Lovers. Harper* was first class too. There was a foray into horror in *The Mad Room*, a remake of *Ladies in Retirement* and a sordid gangster flick, *Bloody Mama*.

FILMOGRAPHY

1943

What a Woman! (bit)

1944

Sailor's Holiday (bit)
The Racket Man (bit)
Nine Girls (bit)
Two-Man Submarine (bit)
She's a Soldier Too (bit)
Knickerbocker Holiday★★★
Cover Girl (bit)

1945

Tonight and Every Night (bit)
A Thousand and One Nights (bit)

1947

Living in a Big Way (bit)
The Gangster (bit)

1948

Red River (bit)
A Double Life★★★★
Larceny★★★
Cry of the City★★★

1949

Take One False Step★★★
The Great Gatsby★★★★
Johnny Stool Pigeon★★★

1950

Winchester '73★★★
South Sea Sinner★★★

1951

Frenchie★★★
He Ran All the Way★★★★
Behave Yourself★★
A Place in the Sun★★★★
The Raging Tide★★★

1952

Phone Call From a Stranger★★★★
Meet Danny Wilson★★★
Untamed Frontier★★★
My Man and I★★★★

1954

Saskatchewan★★★
Executive Suite★★★
Tennessee Champ★★★
Playgirl★★★
Cash on Delivery★★★

1955

Mambo★★★
I Am a Camera★★★
The Night of the Hunter★★★★
The Big Knife★★★★
I Died a Thousand Times★★★★
The Treasure of Pancho Villa★★★

1959

The Diary of Anne Frank★★★
Odds Against Tomorrow★★★

1960

Let No Man Write My Epitaph★★★

1961

The Young Savages★★★★

1962

Lolita★★★
The Chapman Report★★★

1963

The Balcony★★★
Wives and Lovers★★★

1964

Time of Indifference★★
A House Is Not a Home★★

1965

The Greatest Story Ever Told★★
A Patch of Blue★★★★

1966

Alfie★★★★
Harper★★★

1967

Enter Laughing★★★

1968

Wild in the Streets★★★
The Scalphunters★★★

1969

Buona Sera Mrs. Campbell★★★
The Mad Room★★★

1970

Bloody Mama★★★
How Do I Love Thee?★★
Flap★★

1971

What's the Matter With Helen?★★★★
Who Slew Auntie Roo?★★

1972

The Poseidon Adventure★★
Something to Hide★★★

1973

Blume in Love★★★
Cleopatra Jones★★

1975

Poor Pretty Eddie★★
Diamonds★★
That Lucky Touch★★★
Journey Into Fear★★★

1976

Next Stop Greenwich Village★★
The Tenant★★★
La Dahlia Scarlatta★★★
Mimi Bluette★★★

1977

Un Borghese Piccolo Piccolo★★★
Tentacles★★
Pete's Dragon★★★
Gran Bollito★★★
The Three Sisters★★★

Shelley Winters in *Pete's Dragon.*

1979

The Magician of Lublin★★
City on Fire★★
King of the Gypsies★★
Redneck County Rape★★
The Visitor★★

1981

S.O.B.★★

NATALIE WOOD
★★½ 2.75 STARS

After her tragic death by drowning, novelist Thomas Thompson felt compelled to praise Natalie Wood's talent in People magazine. Thompson was certain that many of her films would be remembered and added, "I loved her and R.J. (Wagner) knew it."

He wasn't the only one. From the time of her first major role as an orphan in *Tomorrow Is Forever,* the public began a love affair with Wood that lasted until she died. One only has to look at other child stars to appreciate her. She was natural, bubbly, but never (like Margaret O'Brien) tearful and cloying. She was born Natasha Gourdin, in 1938, in San Francisco, California and acted on stage by age five. *Miracle on 34th Street* is still treasured because of her wide-eyed belief in Edmund Gwenn's Kris Kringle. Her other movies as a child were pleasant though not memorable, but her appearance enlivened them all: *Father Was A Fullback, Our Very Own, The Blue Veil,* and *Just for You.*

She fought like a tiger for the role of Judy in *Rebel Without a Cause* and her love scene opposite James Dean established her as a sensitive and gifted adult actress. An Oscar nomination followed, but poor pictures temporarily retarded her progress. *The Burning Hills* was one of them, a hackneyed western that tried unsuccessfully to build Wood and Tab Hunter into a great love team. She floundered in *The Girl He Left Behind* and *Bombers B-52,* but *Marjorie Morningstar* helped although Wood failed to impart any ethnic shadings to the Jewish Marjorie. In *Kings Go Forth,* her beauty and charm were apparent as Frank Sinatra's unattainable love, and she was convincing despite a wavering French accent. *All the Fine Young Cannibals* was a fiasco with husband Robert Wagner.

Her comeback film was *West Side Story,* a disappointing though hugely successful film transcription of the exciting Leonard Bernstein classic. No one in the cast (particularly leading man Richard Beymer) suggested the grimness and squalor of tenement life, including Wood,

Natalie Wood.

although she had a powerful closing scene. She was better—in fact, brilliant—in Kazan's heartbreaking *Splendor in the Grass.* Her hopeless love for Warren Beatty and subsequent nervous breakdown was vividly portrayed. The Academy came forth with another deserved Oscar nomination, and she was nominated a third time for *Love With the Proper Stranger.* As the pregnant salesgirl who won Steve McQueen, Wood gave perhaps her finest performance.

Her efforts to embrace new challenges sometimes backfired as in *Gypsy.* She was sweetly believable in the earlier segments but physically and temperamentally inappropriate as a buxom stripper. *Sex and the Single Girl* and *The Great Race* were frantic comedies. Nor was *Inside Daisy Clover* a success though Wood claimed it was the film she cared about most. *Bob & Carol & Ted & Alice* brought her back in glory. The script by Paul Mazursky was good except for a cop-out ending, and her co-stars (Robert Culp, Dyan Cannon, and Elliott Gould) added to the merriment.

Beyond her appeal, Wood's career is notable because she represented many things on the screen: the "typical" teenager; the ideal girlfriend of angry rebels; and the woman trying to cope in a world of changing social and sexual mores. She wasn't a great actress, but she convincingly embodies the modern woman in all stages of development. She would have gone on doing so if she had lived.

FILMOGRAPHY

1943

Happy Land ★★★

1946

Tomorrow Is Forever ★★★★
The Bride Wore Boots (bit)

1947

Miracle on 34th Street ★★★★
The Ghost and Mrs. Muir ★★★
Driftwood ★★★

1949

Scudda-Hoo, Scudda-Hay! ★★★
Chicken Every Sunday ★★★
The Green Promise ★★★
Father Was a Fullback ★★★

1950

No Sad Songs for Me ★★★
Our Very Own ★★★
Never a Dull Moment ★★★
The Jackpot ★★★

1951

Dear Brat ★★★
The Blue Veil ★★★

1952

Just for You ★★★
The Rose Bowl Story ★★★

1953

The Star ★★★

1954

The Silver Chalice ★★

1955

One Desire ★★★
Rebel Without a Cause ★★★★

1956

The Searchers ★★★
The Burning Hills ★★
A Cry in the Night ★★★
The Girl He Left Behind ★★

1957

Bombers B-52 ★★

Natalie Wood with John Payne, Maureen O'Hara and Edmund Gwenn in *Miracle on 34th Street.*

1958

Marjorie Morningstar ★★
Kings Go Forth ★★★

1960

Cash McCall ★★
All the Fine Young Cannibals ★

1961

Splendor in the Grass ★★★★
West Side Story ★★★

1962

Gypsy ★★

1963

Love With the Proper Stranger ★★★★

1964

Sex and the Single Girl ★★

1965

The Great Race ★★

1966

Inside Daisy Clover ★★
This Property Is Condemned ★★
Penelope ★★

1969

Bob & Carol & Ted & Alice ★★★

1972

The Candidate (cameo)

1976

Peeper ★★

1978

Meteor ★★

1979

The Last Married Couple in America ★★

1983

Brainstorm ★★★

JOANNE WOODWARD
★★★ 3.22 STARS

Joanne Woodward is certainly as talented as her husband Paul Newman (he himself rated her superior to him), but she hasn't achieved a fraction of his public acceptance. Woodward is superb in comedy and drama, and she has warmth and humanity. Her failure is lack of an image, but she's a character actress with star billing.

She was born in 1930, in Thomasville, Georgia, the daughter of a publisher. She developed her craft at the Actor's Studio and was hired as an understudy for Broadway's "Picnic" (Newman was understudying the male lead). A number of TV appearances led to a movie role in *Count Three and Pray,* and she was pathetically convincing as the girl Robert Wagner tossed off a roof in *A Kiss Before Dying.* Her third picture, *The Three Faces of Eve,* brought an Oscar.

The Oscar meant stardom, and she co-starred with Newman in their most enjoyable venture together, Faulkner's *The Long Hot Summer.* It had wit and suspense, and vibrated with their real-life chemistry. *Rally Round the Flag Boys!* paired them again, this time ineffectually. Woodward then had the misfortune to appear with Marlon Brando during his box-office poison period. *The Fugitive Kind* was a slow-moving pretentious film version of a Tennessee Williams Broadway flop. Rescue came with *From the Terrace;* she was Newman's social-climbing wife.

Woodward was an odd choice to play the lead in *The Stripper.* She caught the vulnerability and desperation of an over-the-hill show girl in love with a teenage boy, Richard Beymer, but her fundamental class was too evident. She also lacked the vulgar sexuality required. In *A New Kind of Love* with Newman, she gave comedic sparkle to witless lines. Her husband wasn't even able to do that—Newman, as proven by *The Secret War of Harry Frigg,* can't bring off comedy. More disappointments followed in: *A Fine Madness* with Sean Connery and *A Big Hand for the Little Lady* with Henry Fonda.

There was difficulty finding the backing for *Rachel, Rachel.* Woodward herself commented at the time that the combination of "the script and me was hardly like offering Elizabeth Taylor and Tennessee Williams." Nevertheless, it finally got on and she was superb. She played a thirty-ish spinster, and her portrait of loneliness and yearning spoke for single people everywhere. Her luck held briefly with *Winning,* although her character, a racer's wife, was slightly hard to fathom.

WUSA was a noisy political charade, and *They Might Be Giants* was an uncommercial fable of a psychiatrist. Woodward played the psychiatrist opposite George C. Scott, her patient who claimed to be Sherlock Holmes. Fortunately, after her last, unsuccessful pairing with Newman in *The Drowning Pool,* TV claimed her for a cluster of outstanding parts. She won an Emmy, as a marathon runner in *See How She Runs,* and she also played in *Sybil* and *Come Back Little Sheba.*

Joanne Woodward in *Three Faces of Eve.*

FILMOGRAPHY

1955

Count Three and Pray★★★

1956

A Kiss Before Dying★★★★

1957

The Three Faces of Eve★★★★
No Down Payment★★★★

1958

The Long Hot Summer★★★★
Rally Round the Flag Boys!★★★

1959

The Sound and the Fury★★★

1960

The Fugitive Kind★★★
From the Terrace★★★

1961

Paris Blues★★★

1963

The Stripper★★★
A New Kind of Love★★★

1965

Signpost to Murder★★★

1966

A Big Hand for the Little Lady★★★★
A Fine Madness★★★

1968

Rachel, Rachel★★★★
Winning★★★★

1970

King (documentary)
WUSA★★

1971

They Might Be Giants★★★

1972

The Effect of Gamma Rays on Man-in-the-Moon Marigolds★★★

1973

Summer Wishes, Winter Dreams★★★

1975

The Drowning Pool★★★

1978

The End★★

JANE WYMAN
★★★ 3.19 STARS

In their book, Films in America, Martin Quigley, Jr. and Richard Gertner had this to say of Jane Wyman's *Johnny Belinda* characterization: "The Wyman performance is incandescent...the innocence and beauty of the character were all written in her eloquent face. She won an Oscar and seldom has it been so justified."

Wyman (Sarah Jane Fulks) was born in 1914, in St. Joseph, Missouri. She tried, unsuccessfully, to break into films as a child actress but achieved some recognition later for her singing on radio. Her early films typed her as a blonde glamour girl in *Smart Blonde* and *Ready Willing and Able.* She met her second husband Ronald Reagan when they co-starred in the hit comedy, *Brother Rat.* There was a less popular sequel, *Brother Rat and a Baby* plus a whole slew of Bs: *Kid Nightingale, An Angel From Texas, Gambling on the High Seas,* and *The Body Disappears.*

A part as Olivia De Havilland's friend in *Princess O'Rourke* made the difference. Billy Wilder had been considering De Havilland for *The Lost Weekend* but cast Wyman instead. She was excellent, especially in the climactic confrontation scene with Ray Milland. She was even more impressive in *The Yearling* as Claude Jarman, Jr.'s strict mother. "You can't fault that one, honey, it's a classic," Wyman told Rex Reed—and she was right. She also worked feverishly to meet the demands of her *Johnny Belinda* role. "If it comes to a divorce I think I'll name *Johnny Belinda* correspondent" said Ronald Reagan in 1948. Her haunting portrait of a deaf-mute still holds up beautifully on TV.

A couple of foolish comedies, *A Kiss in the Dark* and *The Lady Takes a Sailor,* slowed her down temporarily, but she was convincing in *Stage Fright.* It wasn't a box-office hit because, in Wyman's words, "Michael Wilding mumbled all the way through...they had to re-dub his dialogue. By the time it came out that kind of movie was dead." *The Glass Menagerie* drew mixed reviews though it seems less mannered than the later TV version done with Katharine Hepburn. Wyman had a triumph in the sentimental *Blue Veil.* Her popularity held firmly through *Magnificent Obsession,* a lush soap opera that lifted Rock Hudson to top stardom. They were reteamed in *All that Heaven Allows,* also a success; Wyman was a widow, Hudson her gardener lover.

Wyman is also on record as being partial to *Miracle in the Rain:* "I don't like to bring up my own work, but what a wonderful movie!" She blamed excessive studio promotion of *Giant* for the film's box-office failure. *Pollyanna* did better, and so did another Disney picture, *Bon Voyage*. Wyman had her own TV show in the 1950s, and after a long period of semi-retirement, she returned to headline another series, "Falcon Crest."

The authority and magnetism are still as strong as ever. Critical reporters have suggested that her weekly audience hold is due to being a President's ex-wife. It's doubtful. Nobody who watched her manipulating Mel Ferrer, Lorenzo Lamas, and Robert Foxworth thought of anything but the compelling villainess they saw on the screen.

FILMOGRAPHY

1936

Gold Diggers of 1937 (bit)
My Man Godfrey (bit)
King of Burlesque (bit)

1937

Smart Blonde (bit)
Stage Struck (bit)
The King and the Chorus Girl ★★★
Ready Willing and Able (bit)
Slim (bit)
The Singing Marine (bit)
Public Wedding (bit)
Mr. Dodd Takes the Air (bit)

1938

The Spy Ring (bit)
He Couldn't Say No (bit)
Wide Open Faces (bit)
Fools for Scandal ★★
The Crowd Roars (bit)
Brother Rat ★★★

1939

Tail Spin ★★★
Private Detective ★★
The Kid From Kokomo ★★
Torchy Plays With Dynamite ★★★
Kid Nightingale ★★

1940

Brother Rat and a Baby ★★★
An Angel From Texas ★★★
Flight Angels ★★★
My Love Came Back ★★
Tugboat Annie Sails Again ★★★
Gambling on the High Seas ★★★

1941

Honeymoon for Three ★★★
Bad Men of Missouri ★★★
You're in the Army Now ★★★
The Body Disappears ★★★

1942

Larceny Inc. ★★★★
My Favorite Spy ★★★
Footlight Serenade ★★★

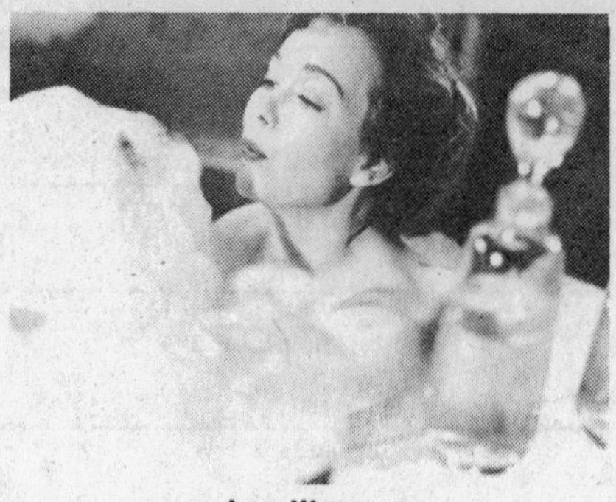

Jane Wyman.

1943

Princess O'Rourke ★★★★

1944

Make Your Own Bed ★★★
Crime by Night ★★★
The Doughgirls ★★★
Hollywood Canteen ★★★

1945

The Lost Weekend ★★★★

1946

One More Tomorrow ★★★
Night and Day ★★★

1947

The Yearling ★★★★
Cheyenne ★★★
Magic Town ★★★★

1948

Johnny Belinda ★★★★

1949

A Kiss in the Dark ★★★
It's a Great Feeling (cameo)
The Lady Takes a Sailor ★★★

1950

Stage Fright ★★★★
The Glass Menagerie ★★★★

1951

Three Guys Named Mike ★★★
Here Comes the Groom ★★★★
The Blue Veil ★★★★
Starlift ★★★

1952

The Story of Will Rogers ★★★
Just for You ★★★

1953

Let's Do it Again ★★★
So Big ★★★★

1954

Magnificent Obsession ★★★★

1955

Lucy Gallant ★★★★

1956

All that Heaven Allows ★★★★
Miracle in the Rain ★★★★

1959

Holiday for Lovers ★★★

1960

Pollyanna ★★★

1962

Bon Voyage ★★★

1969

How to Commit Marriage ★★★

LORETTA YOUNG
★★★ 3.18 STARS

Beauty and elegance were Loretta Young's trademarks on film and television. Sometimes, her wardrobe was more dramatic than her roles, but she contributed strong portrayals when given the right material.

Young (Gretchen Michaela Young) was born in 1913, in Salt Lake City, Utah. Along with her three sisters, she worked as an extra. Her first role in *Naughty but Nice* had been intended for her sister Polly Ann Young, but Polly wasn't home, so Loretta volunteered her services. Her roles improved in *The Head Man* and *The Squall*. She did four in a row with Douglas Fairbanks, Jr.—*The Careless Age, The Fast Life, The Forward Pass,* and *Loose Ankles.*

The House of Rothschild was a big success, and she co-starred with Clark Gable in *Call of the Wild.* During this period, they had an affair, and a child was rumored to have been born. Her movies were usually entertaining, though slight (*Love Is News, Second Honeymoon,* and *Three Blind Mice*).

The Story of Alexander Graham Bell angered her because she wanted to play Mrs. Bell as a deaf-mute. The studio objected, and she finally played the character as deaf only. A bitter quarrel with Columbia head Harry Cohn centering on the cost of a costume resulted in her unofficial blacklisting. She finally called and pleaded with him to relent, and he did, though he rehired her at half her usual fee.

The pictures involved (*The Doctor Takes a Wife* and *He Stayed for Breakfast*) were both comedies. *And Now Tomorrow* which followed was a listless soap opera with Alan Ladd, but she had a strong role in Orson Welles' fascinating *The Stranger.*

The Farmer's Daughter was originally acquired for Ingrid Bergman, who rejected it. Young was also initially reluctant. It turned out to be her best and most affectionately remembered performance and an upset victory at the Oscars. Her friend Rosalind Russell had already written an acceptance speech. She was also eloquent as William Holden's backwoods wife in *Rachel and the Stranger.*

After that her film career dwindled into B pictures (*Half Angel, Paula* and *Mother Is a Freshman*), so she concentrated on television and dominated the medium for eight years. She's now retired—a friend commented that she would never allow herself to be photographed unglamourously, so character parts are out of the question. It's too bad about Young's beauty; she had the talent to test herself more strenuously than she did.

FILMOGRAPHY

1927

Naughty but Nice★★★

1928

The Whip Woman (bit)
Laugh Clown Laugh★★★
The Magnificent Flirt★★★
The Head Man★★★
Scarlet Seas★★★

1929

The Squall★★★★
The Girl in the Glass Cage★★★★
The Fast Life★★★★
The Careless Age★★★★
The Show of Shows★★★
The Forward Pass★★★★

1930

The Man from Blankley's★★★
The Second Floor Mystery★★★
Loose Ankles★★★★
Road to Paradise★★★★
Kismet★★★
The Truth About Youth★★★
The Devil to Pay★★★

1931

Beau Ideal★★
The Right of Way★★★
Three Girls Lost★★★
Too Young to Marry★★★
Big Business Girl★★★
I Like Your Nerve★★★
Platinum Blonde★★★
The Ruling Voice★★★

1932

Taxi★★★★
The Hatchet Man★★★★
Play Girl★★★
Weekend Marriage★★★
Life Begins★★★
They Call it Sin★★★

1933

Employee's Entrance★★★
Grand Slam★★★
Zoo in Budapest★★★★
The Life of Jimmy Dolan★★★
Midnight Mary★★★★
Heroes for Sale★★★
The Devil's in Love★★★
She Had to Say Yes★★★
A Man's Castle★★★★

1934

The House of Rothschild★★★★
Born to Be Bad★★★
Bulldog Drummond Strikes Back★★★
Caravan★★★
The White Parade★★★

1935

Clive of India★★★
Shanghai★★★
Call of the Wild★★
The Crusades★★★

1936

The Unguarded Hour★★★
Private Number★★★
Ramona★★
Ladies in Love★★★★

1937

Love Is News★★★★
Cafe Metropole★★★
Love Under Fire★★★
Wife Doctor and Nurse★★★
Second Honeymoon★★★

1938

Four Men and a Prayer★★★
Three Blind Mice★★★
Suez★★★
Kentucky★★★

1939

The Story of Alexander Graham Bell★★★
Wife, Husband and Friend★★★
Eternally Yours★★★

1940

The Doctor Takes a Wife★★★
He Stayed for Breakfast★★★

Loretta Young with Tyrone Power.

1941

The Lady From Cheyenne★★★
The Men in Her Life★★★

1942

Bedtime Story★★★
A Night to Remember★★★

1943

China★★★

1944

Ladies Courageous★★★
And Now Tomorrow★★

1945

Along Came Jones★★★

1946

The Stranger★★★★
The Perfect Marriage★★

1947

The Farmer's Daughter★★★★
The Bishop's Wife★★★

1948

Rachel and the Stranger★★★★

1949

The Accused★★★★
Mother Is a Freshman★★★★
Come to the Stable★★★

1950

Key to the City★★★

1951

Cause for Alarm★★★★
Half Angel★★★

1952

Paula★★★
Because of You★★★

1953

It Happens Every Thursday★★★

ROBERT YOUNG
★★★ 3.13 STARS

No one is more soothing to watch than Robert Young. In recent years, he's become everyone's favorite dad ("Father Knows Best") and doctor ("Marcus Welby"). His movie parts had more variety, but the same dependable charm was always there.

Born in 1907, in Chicago, he acted at the Pasadena Playhouse and did extra work in films. *The Sin of Madelon Claudet* was a big break—he played opposite Helen Hayes in her Oscar-winning part. He was a murderer in *Unashamed* and then co-starred with Joan Crawford in *Today We Live*. In her autobiography, Portrait of Joan, Crawford commented, "The whole picture missed—I missed most of all." *The House of Rothschild* was better, and so was *Spitfire* with Katharine Hepburn. Young was perfect in an excellent Claudette Colbert comedy, *The Bride Comes Home*, and appeared to advantage in Hitchcock's *Secret Agent*.

He had his best shot at an Oscar nomination with *H. M. Pulham, Esq.* as a proper Bostonian lured temporarily from his staid existence by Hedy Lamarr. The Academy ignored this fine portrayal. He went on, giving more-than-competent performances in *Journey for Margaret* and *Slightly Dangerous*.

Claudia was Young's next big advance. He and Dorothy McGuire were one of the most ingratiating couples the screen had ever seen. They were equally effective in *The Enchanted Cottage*, a touching, fanciful tale of two homely people who saw each other as beautiful and fell in love. *Claudia and David* was a likable sequel to *Claudia*, while *Crossfire* was a disturbingly real close-up of anti-Semitism and its sometimes fatal consequences.

He had one more smash, before his popularity began to wane, in *Sitting Pretty* and was convincing in *That Forsyte Woman* as Greer Garson's impetuous and doomed lover. He and Joan Crawford were both at their best in a sparkling political comedy, *Goodbye My Fancy*, but the public stayed home.

Robert Young in *And Baby Makes Three*.

With film work less plentiful, Young turned to TV, achieving greater success than he had ever achieved on the screen. It's hard to resist a man who seems so wholesome, normal, warm, and approachable—one who appears to have all his problems under control. A misleading image (if stories of depression and alcoholism are to be believed), but a comforting one.

FILMOGRAPHY

1931

The Black Camel★★
The Sin of Madelon Claudet★★★
The Guilty Generation★★★

1932

Hell Divers★★★
The Wet Parade★★★
New Morals for Old★★★
Unashamed★★★★
Strange Interlude★★★★
The Kid from Spain★★★

1933

Men Must Fight★★
Today We Live★★
Hell Below★★★
Tugboat Annie★★★
Saturday's Millions★★
The Right to Romance★★

1934

Carolina★★★
Spitfire★★★★
The House of Rothschild★★★★
Whom the Gods Destroy★★★
Paris Interlude★★★
Death on the Diamond★★★
The Band Plays On★★★

1935

West Point of the Air★★★
Vagabond Lady★★★★
Calm Yourself★★★
Red Salute★★★
Remember Last Night?★★★
The Bride Comes Home★★★

1936

Secret Agent★★★★
It's Love Again★★★
The Three Wise Guys★★
Sworn Enemy★★★
The Bride Walks Out★★★
The Longest Night★★★
Stowaway★★★

1937

Dangerous Number★★★
I Met Him in Paris★★★★
The Emperor's Candlesticks★★
Married Before Breakfast★★★
The Bride Wore Red★★
Navy Blue and Gold★★★

1938

Paradise for Three★★★
Three Comrades★★★★
Josette★★★
The Toy Wife★★
Rich Man Poor Girl★★★
The Shining Hour★★★

1939

Honolulu★★★
Bridal Suite★★★
Maisie★★★
Miracles for Sale★★★

1940

Northwest Passage★★★
Florian★★★
The Mortal Storm★★★★
Sporting Blood★★★
Dr. Kildare's Crisis★★★

1941

Western Union★★★
The Trial of Mary Dugan★★★
Lady Be Good★★★
Married Bachelor★★★
H. M. Pulham, Esq.★★★★

1942

Joe Smith American★★★
Cairo★★★
Journey for Margaret★★★★

1943

Slightly Dangerous★★★
Sweet Rosie O'Grady★★★
Claudia★★★★

1944

The Canterville Ghost★★★★

1945

The Enchanted Cottage★★★★
Those Endearing Young Charms★★

1946

The Searching Wind★★★★
Claudia and David★★★★
Lady Luck★★★

1947

They Won't Believe Me★★★★
Crossfire★★★★

1948

Relentless★★★
Sitting Pretty★★★★

1951

Adventure in Baltimore★★
That Forsyte Woman★★★★
Bride for Sale★★★
And Baby Makes Three★★★
The Second Woman★★★★
Goodbye My Fancy★★★★

1952

The Half-Breed★★★

1954

Secret of the Incas★★★